W9-BPL-289

WORLD WAR II

A Student Encyclopedia

WORLD WAR II

A Student Encyclopedia

VOLUME II: D–K

Dr. Spencer C. Tucker
Editor

Dr. Priscilla Mary Roberts
Editor, Documents Volume

Mr. Jack Greene
Col. Cole C. Kingseed, USA Ret., Ph.D.
Dr. Malcolm Muir Jr.
Dr. Priscilla Mary Roberts
Maj. Gen. David T. Zabecki, USAR, Ph.D.
Assistant Editors

FOREWORD BY
Dr. Allan R. Millett

GCLS/MULLICA HILL BRANCH
389 WOLFERT STATION ROAD
MULLICA HILL, NJ 08062

GCLS/GLASSBORO BRANCH
2 CENTER STREET
GLASSBORO, NJ 08028

A B C ✸ C L I O

Santa Barbara, California   Denver, Colorado   Oxford, England

Copyright © 2005 by ABC-CLIO

All rights reserved. No part of this publication may be reproduced, stored in a retrieval system, or transmitted, in any form or by any means, electronic, mechanical, photocopying, recording, or otherwise, except for the inclusion of brief quotations in a review, without prior permission in writing from the publishers.

Library of Congress Cataloging-in-Publication Data

World War II : a student encyclopedia / Spencer C. Tucker, editor;
Priscilla Mary Roberts, editor, Documents volume.
        p. cm.
    Includes bibliographical references and index.
    ISBN 1-85109-857-7 (hardback : alk. paper) — ISBN 1-85109-858-5 (e-book)
1. World War, 1939–1945—Encyclopedias.   I. Title: World War Two.   II. Title: World War 2.
III. Tucker, Spencer, 1937–   IV. Roberts, Priscilla Mary.
      D740.W64   2005
      940.53'03—dc22   2004029951

10   09   08   07   06   05   10 9 8 7 6 5 4 3 2 1

This book is also available on the World Wide Web as an ebook.
Visit abc-clio.com for details.

ABC-CLIO, Inc.
130 Cremona Drive, P.O. Box 1911
Santa Barbara, California 93116–1911

This book is printed on acid-free paper ∞ .
Manufactured in the United States of America

Contents

List of Entries

List of Maps

General Maps

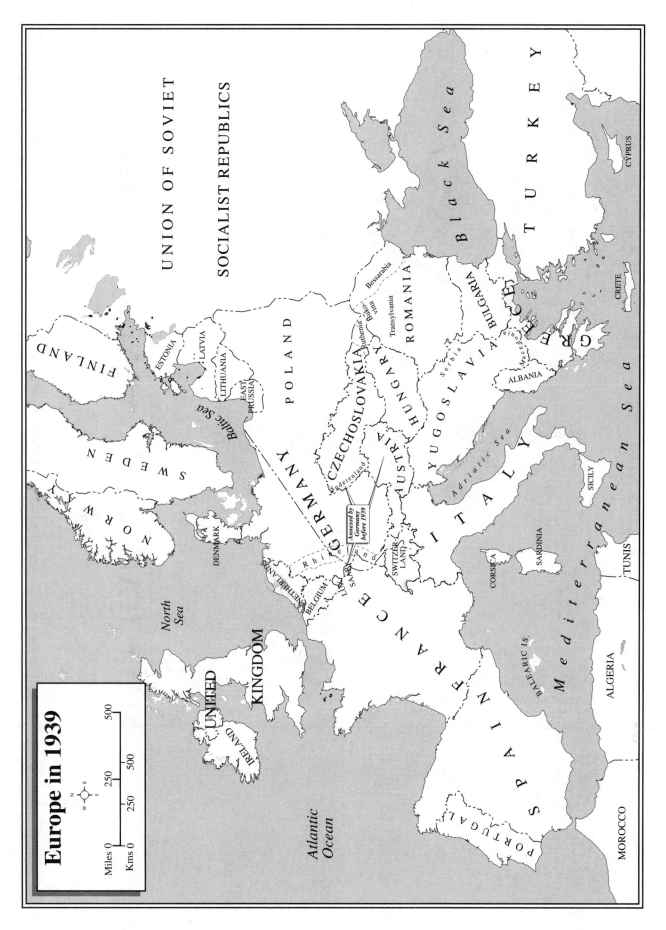

Europe in 1939

Miles 0   250   500

Kms 0   250   500

Atlantic Ocean

UNITED KINGDOM

IRELAND

NORTH Sea

NORWAY

SWEDEN

FINLAND

DENMARK

NETHERLANDS

BELGIUM

LUX.

GERMANY

Rhineland

SAAR

SWITZER-LAND

FRANCE

SPAIN

PORTUGAL

Balearic Is.

CORSICA

SARDINIA

ALGERIA

MOROCCO

TUNIS

Mediterranean Sea

ITALY

SICILY

UNION OF SOVIET SOCIALIST REPUBLICS

ESTONIA

LATVIA

LITHUANIA

EAST PRUSSIA

Baltic Sea

POLAND

CZECHOSLOVAKIA

Sudetenland

Annexed by Germany before 1939

AUSTRIA

HUNGARY

Ruthenia

Bukovina

Bessarabia

Transylvania

ROMANIA

YUGOSLAVIA

Serbia

Macedonia

BULGARIA

ALBANIA

GREECE

Adriatic Sea

Black Sea

TURKEY

CRETE

CYPRUS

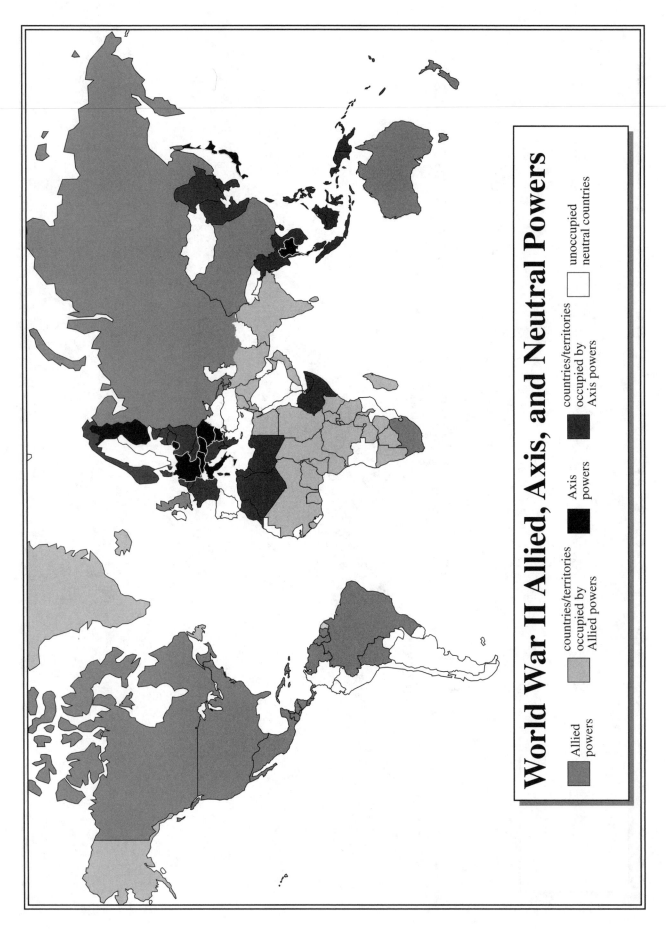

World War II Allied, Axis, and Neutral Powers

Allied powers

countries/territories occupied by Allied powers

Axis powers

countries/territories occupied by Axis powers

unoccupied neutral countries

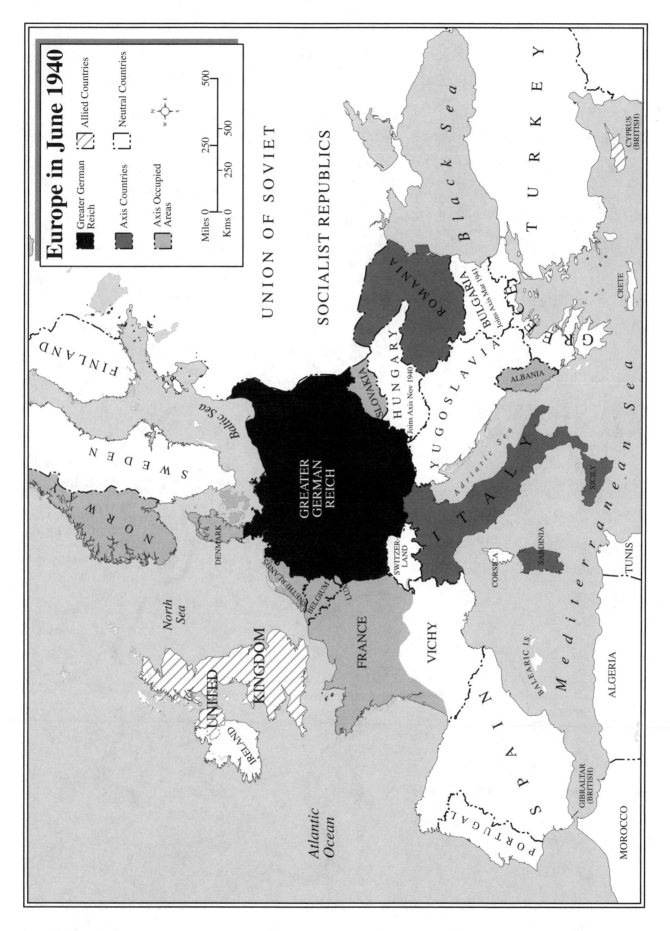

Europe in June 1940

Greater German Reich

Allied Countries

Axis Countries

Neutral Countries

Axis Occupied Areas

Miles 0 250 500
Kms 0 250 500

UNION OF SOVIET SOCIALIST REPUBLICS

FINLAND

SWEDEN

NORWAY

Baltic Sea

DENMARK

NETHERLANDS

BELGIUM

LUX.

GREATER GERMAN REICH

SLOVAKIA

HUNGARY
Joins Axis Nov 1940

ROMANIA

BULGARIA
Joins Axis Mar 1941

Black Sea

TURKEY

YUGOSLAVIA

ALBANIA

GREECE

ITALY

Adriatic Sea

SICILY

SARDINIA

CORSICA

BALEARIC IS.

Mediterranean Sea

CRETE

CYPRUS (BRITISH)

SWITZER-LAND

FRANCE

VICHY

SPAIN

PORTUGAL

GIBRALTAR (BRITISH)

MOROCCO

ALGERIA

TUNIS

North Sea

UNITED KINGDOM

IRELAND

Atlantic Ocean

Eastern Front 1941

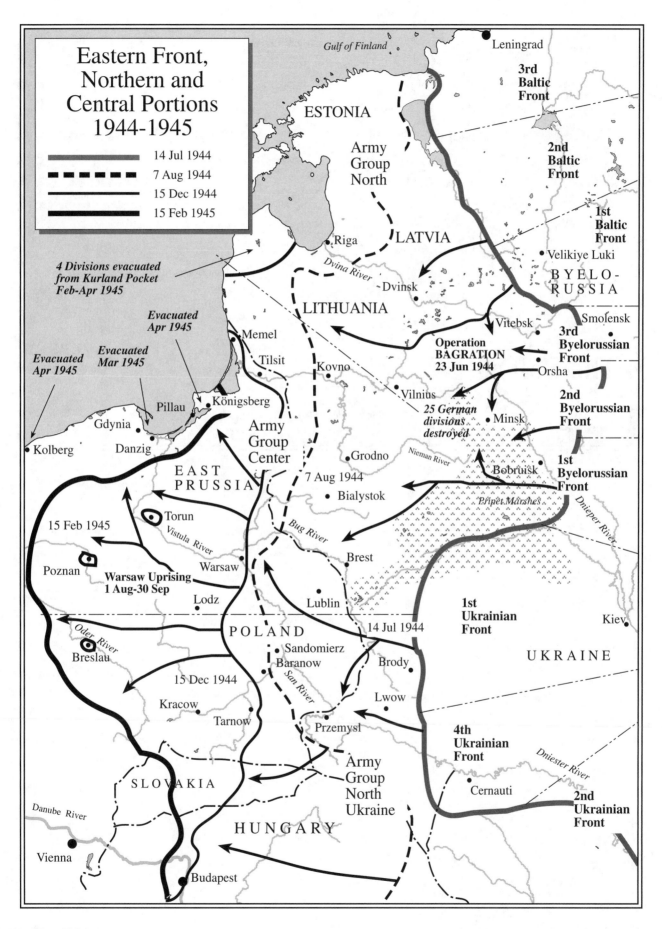

Eastern Front, Northern and Central Portions 1944-1945

- ▬▬▬ 14 Jul 1944
- ▬ ▬ ▬ 7 Aug 1944
- ───── 15 Dec 1944
- ━━━━ 15 Feb 1945

4 Divisions evacuated from Kurland Pocket Feb-Apr 1945

Evacuated Apr 1945

Evacuated Apr 1945

Evacuated Mar 1945

Gulf of Finland

Leningrad

3rd Baltic Front

ESTONIA

2nd Baltic Front

Army Group North

Riga

LATVIA

1st Baltic Front

Velikiye Luki

Dvina River

Dvinsk

BYELO-RUSSIA

LITHUANIA

Smolensk

Vitebsk

3rd Byelorussian Front

Memel

Kovno

Operation BAGRATION 23 Jun 1944

Orsha

Tilsit

Vilnius

2nd Byelorussian Front

Pillau

Königsberg

25 German divisions destroyed

Minsk

Gdynia

Danzig

Kolberg

EAST PRUSSIA

Army Group Center

Grodno

Nieman River

Bobruisk

1st Byelorussian Front

Pripet Marshes

Dnieper River

Torun

15 Feb 1945

Vistula River

7 Aug 1944

Bialystok

Bug River

Brest

Poznan

Warsaw

Warsaw Uprising 1 Aug-30 Sep

Lodz

Lublin

1st Ukrainian Front

Kiev

Oder River

Breslau

POLAND

14 Jul 1944

Sandomierz

Baranow

Brody

UKRAINE

15 Dec 1944

San River

Lwow

Kracow

Tarnow

Przemysl

Army Group North Ukraine

4th Ukrainian Front

Dniester River

SLOVAKIA

Cernauti

2nd Ukrainian Front

Danube River

HUNGARY

Vienna

Budapest

The Balkans 1944-1945

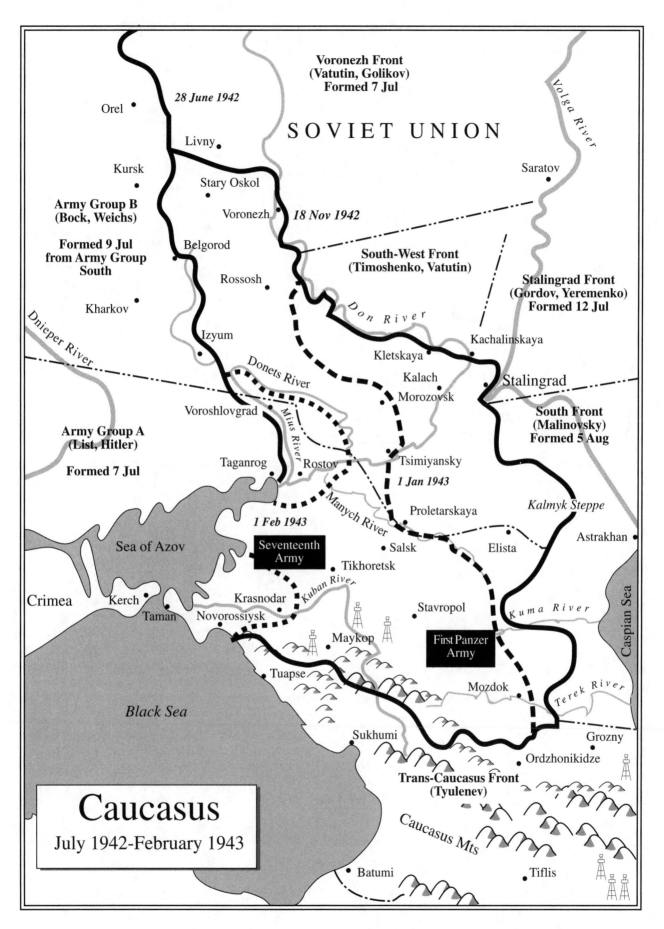

Voronezh Front
(Vatutin, Golikov)
Formed 7 Jul

28 June 1942

Orel

Livny

Kursk

Stary Oskol

Voronezh   *18 Nov 1942*

SOVIET UNION

Saratov

Volga River

Army Group B
(Bock, Weichs)

Formed 9 Jul
from Army Group
South

Belgorod

Rossosh

Kharkov

Izyum

South-West Front
(Timoshenko, Vatutin)

Don River

Stalingrad Front
(Gordov, Yeremenko)
Formed 12 Jul

Kachalinskaya

Kletskaya

Kalach

Morozovsk

Stalingrad

Donets River

Mius River

Voroshlovgrad

Army Group A
(List, Hitler)

Formed 7 Jul

Taganrog

Rostov

Tsimiyansky

1 Jan 1943

South Front
(Malinovsky)
Formed 5 Aug

Manych River

Proletarskaya

Kalmyk Steppe

Astrakhan

1 Feb 1943

Sea of Azov

Seventeenth
Army

Salsk

Elista

Crimea   Kerch

Taman

Novorossiysk

Krasnodar

Tikhoretsk

Kuban River

Stavropol

First Panzer
Army

Kuma River

Caspian Sea

Maykop

Tuapse

Mozdok

Terek River

Black Sea

Sukhumi

Grozny

Ordzhonikidze

Trans-Caucasus Front
(Tyulenev)

Caucasus Mts

Caucasus
July 1942-February 1943

Batumi

Tiflis

Dnieper River

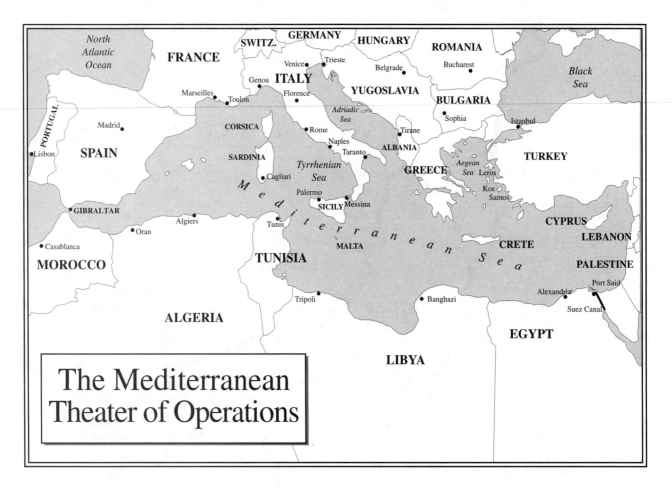

The Mediterranean Theater of Operations

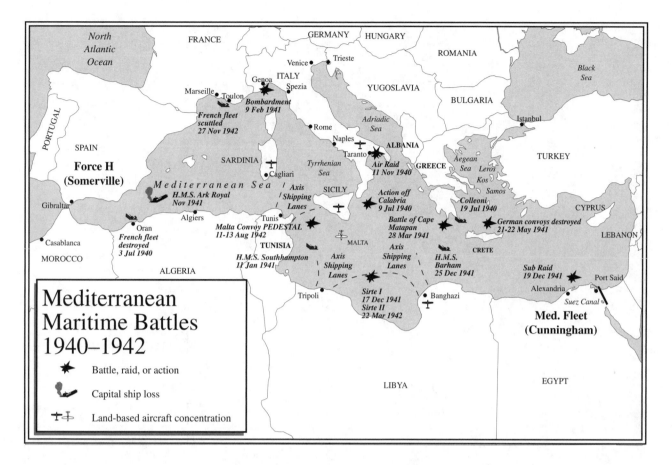

North
Atlantic
Ocean

FRANCE

GERMANY

HUNGARY

ROMANIA

Black
Sea

Venice • Trieste

Marseille • Toulon

Genoa • ITALY
Spezia

*Bombardment
9 Feb 1941*

*French fleet
scuttled
27 Nov 1942*

YUGOSLAVIA

PORTUGAL

SPAIN

**Force H
(Somerville)**

SARDINIA

Rome •

Naples •

Taranto •

*Adriatic
Sea*

ALBANIA

BULGARIA

Istanbul •

TURKEY

*Air Raid
11 Nov 1940*

GREECE

*Aegean
Sea* Leros •
Kos •

Samos •

Mediterranean Sea

Gibraltar •

*H.M.S. Ark Royal
Nov 1941*

*Axis
Shipping
Lanes*

*Tyrrhenian
Sea*

Cagliari •

SICILY

*Action off
Calabria
9 Jul 1940*

*Colleoni
19 Jul 1940*

CYPRUS

Algiers •

Oran •

*French fleet
destroyed
3 Jul 1940*

Casablanca •

MOROCCO

ALGERIA

Tunis •

*Malta Convoy PEDESTAL
11-13 Aug 1942*

TUNISIA

*H.M.S. Southhampton
11 Jan 1941*

*Battle of Cape
Matapan
28 Mar 1941*

MALTA

*Axis
Shipping
Lanes*

*Axis
Shipping
Lanes*

*German convoys destroyed
21-22 May 1941*

CRETE

*H.M.S.
Barham
25 Dec 1941*

LEBANON

*Sub Raid
19 Dec 1941*

Port Said •

Alexandria •

Suez Canal

**Med. Fleet
(Cunningham)**

Tripoli •

*Sirte I
17 Dec 1941
Sirte II
22 Mar 1942*

Banghazi •

LIBYA

EGYPT

Mediterranean
Maritime Battles
1940–1942

★ Battle, raid, or action

  Capital ship loss

✈ Land-based aircraft concentration

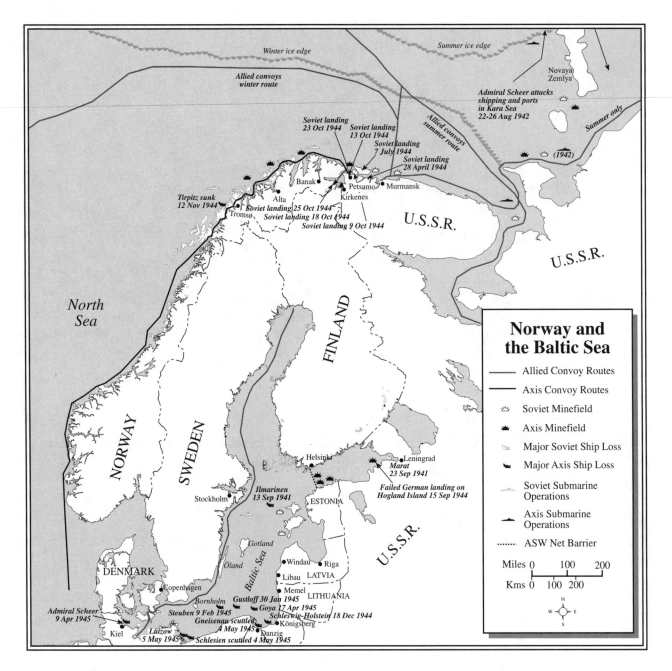

Norway and the Baltic Sea

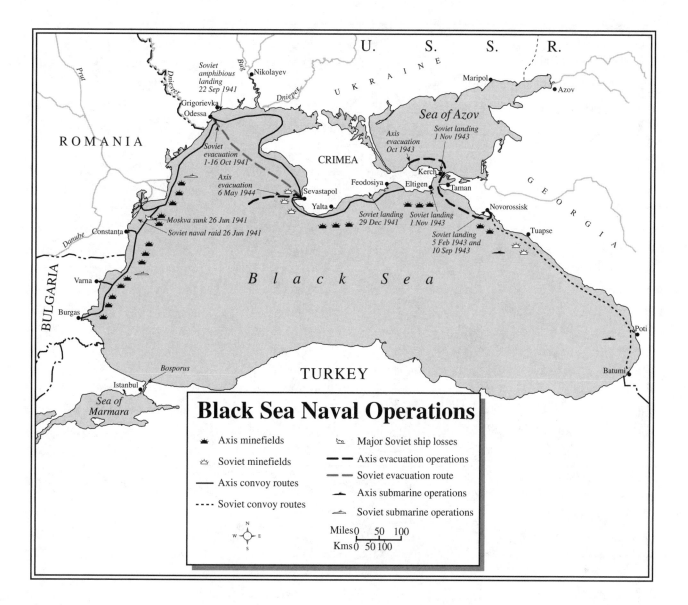

Black Sea Naval Operations

Axis minefields	Major Soviet ship losses
Soviet minefields	Axis evacuation operations
Axis convoy routes	Soviet evacuation route
Soviet convoy routes	Axis submarine operations
	Soviet submarine operations

Miles 0 50 100
Kms 0 50 100

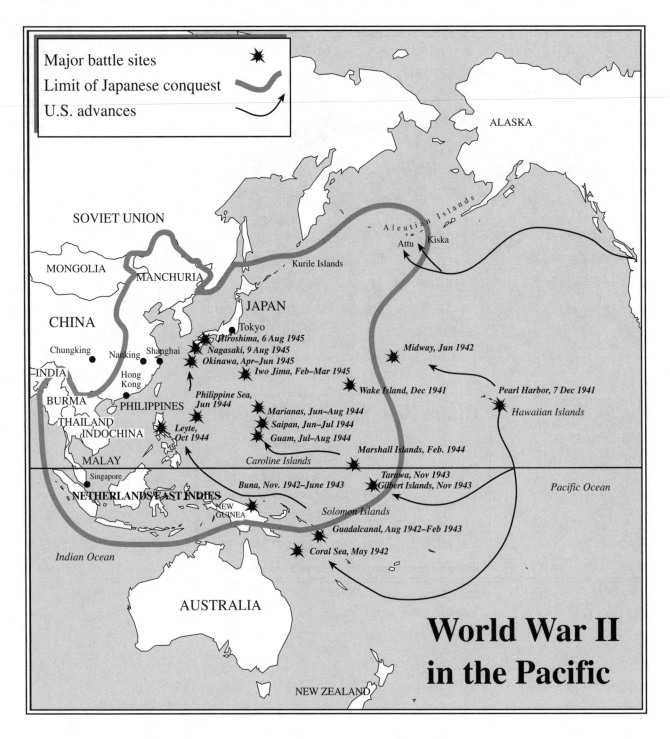

Major battle sites ✦
Limit of Japanese conquest
U.S. advances

ALASKA

SOVIET UNION

MONGOLIA

MANCHURIA

Aleutian Islands

Attu   Kiska

Kurile Islands

JAPAN

CHINA

Chungking   Nanking   Shanghai

Tokyo
Hiroshima, 6 Aug 1945
Nagasaki, 9 Aug 1945
Okinawa, Apr–Jun 1945
Iwo Jima, Feb–Mar 1945

Midway, Jun 1942

Wake Island, Dec 1941

Pearl Harbor, 7 Dec 1941

Hawaiian Islands

INDIA

Hong Kong

BURMA   PHILIPPINES

THAILAND
INDOCHINA

Philippine Sea,
Jun 1944

Leyte,
Oct 1944

Marianas, Jun–Aug 1944
Saipan, Jun–Jul 1944
Guam, Jul–Aug 1944

Marshall Islands, Feb. 1944

MALAY

Caroline Islands

Singapore

Tarawa, Nov 1943
Gilbert Islands, Nov 1943

Pacific Ocean

NETHERLANDS EAST INDIES

Buna, Nov. 1942–June 1943

NEW
GUINEA

Solomon Islands

Guadalcanal, Aug 1942–Feb 1943

Indian Ocean

Coral Sea, May 1942

AUSTRALIA

World War II
in the Pacific

NEW ZEALAND

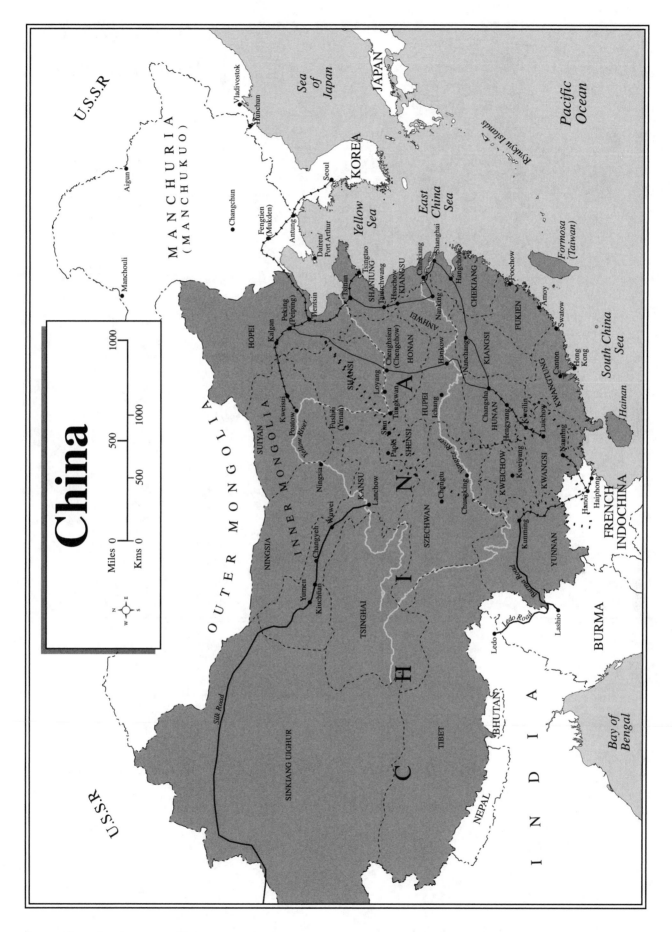

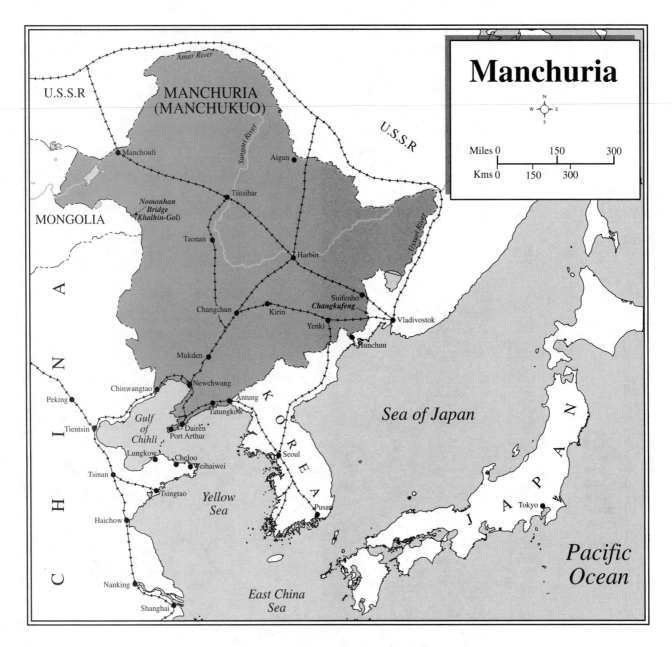

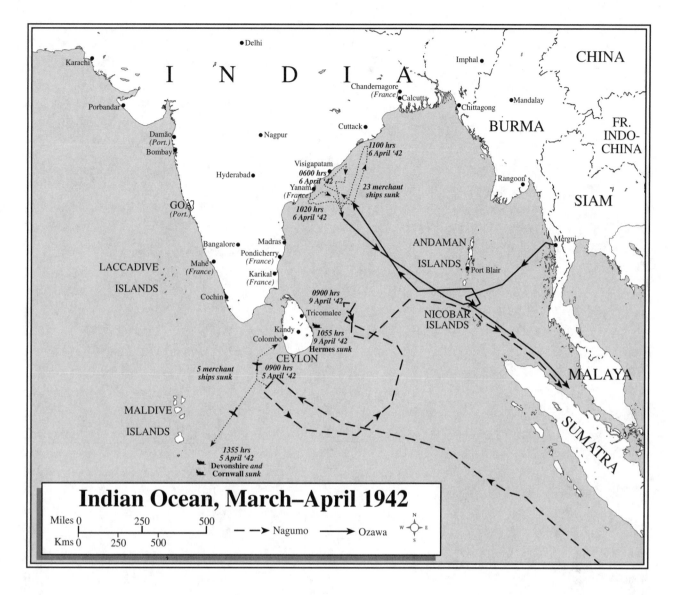

Indian Ocean, March–April 1942

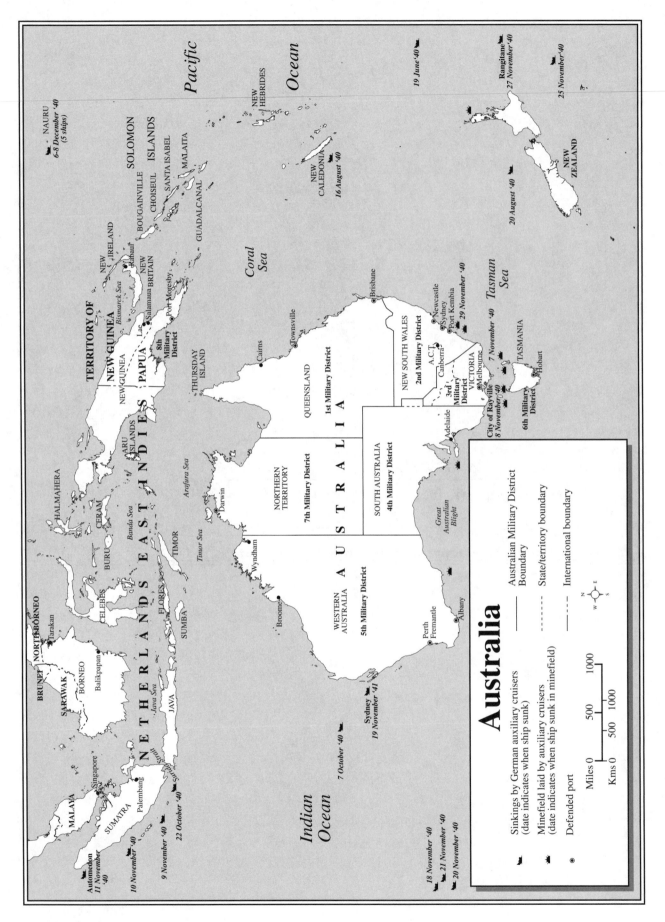

Australia

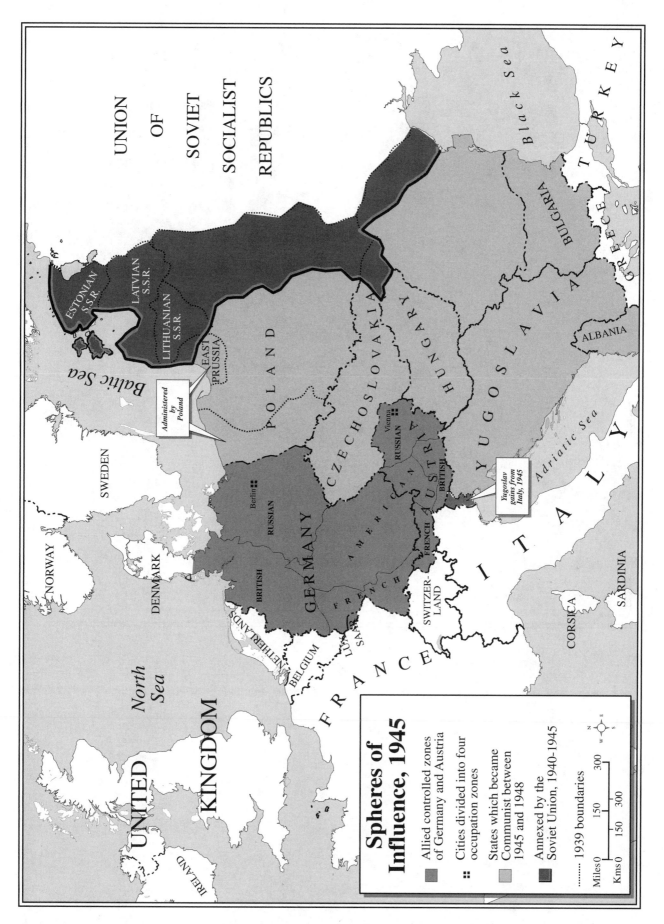

UNION OF SOVIET SOCIALIST REPUBLICS

Black Sea

TURKEY

BULGARIA

ESTONIAN S.S.R.

LATVIAN S.S.R.

LITHUANIAN S.S.R.

EAST PRUSSIA

GREECE

ALBANIA

Baltic Sea

Administered by Poland

POLAND

CZECHOSLOVAKIA

HUNGARY

YUGOSLAVIA

Adriatic Sea

SWEDEN

Vienna

RUSSIAN

AUSTRIA

BRITISH

Yugoslav gains from Italy, 1945

Berlin

GERMANY

RUSSIAN

AMERICAN

FRENCH

NORWAY

DENMARK

North Sea

BRITISH

FRENCH

SWITZER-LAND

ITALY

CORSICA

SARDINIA

NETHERLANDS

BELGIUM

LUX.

SAAR

FRANCE

UNITED KINGDOM

IRELAND

Spheres of Influence, 1945

- Allied controlled zones of Germany and Austria
- ⸬ Cities divided into four occupation zones
- States which became Communist between 1945 and 1948
- Annexed by the Soviet Union, 1940–1945
- .... 1939 boundaries

Miles 0   150   300
Kms 0   150   300

N W E S

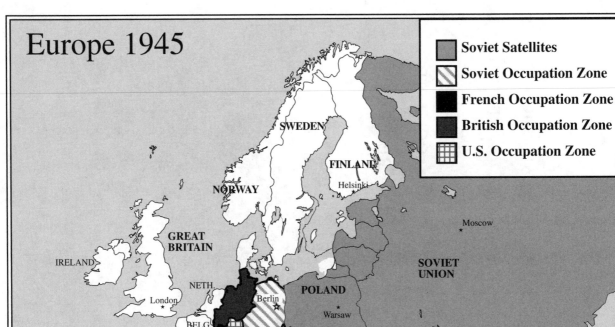

Europe 1945

Soviet Satellites
Soviet Occupation Zone
French Occupation Zone
British Occupation Zone
U.S. Occupation Zone

SWEDEN

FINLAND

Helsinki

NORWAY

Moscow

GREAT
BRITAIN

SOVIET
UNION

IRELAND

NETH.

POLAND

Berlin

London

Warsaw

BELG.

Prague

Paris

LUX.

CZECHOSLOVAKIA

FRANCE

Vienna

SWITZ.

Budapest

HUNGARY

ROMANIA

ITALY

Belgrade

Bucharest

YUGOSLAVIA

BULGARIA

PORT.

ANDORRA

Rome

ALBANIA

SPAIN

GREECE

TURKEY

Athens

MALTA

LIBYA

D

D Day
See Normandy Invasion and Campaign.

Dachau
See Concentration Camps, German.

DAK
See Afrika Korps.

Dakar, Attack on (23–25 September 1940)

Vichy-held West African port. Following the defeat of France by the Germans in June 1940, the new Vichy government assumed control of most of the French colonial empire. In late August, Free French leader General Charles de Gaulle convinced French Equatorial Africa to continue the fight against Germany under his leadership. De Gaulle next turned to French West Africa and its capital, Dakar. Located in the most westerly part of Africa, Dakar boasted an excellent deep-water port and was equidistant from Europe and Brazil. The British feared that the Germans might pressure the Vichy French to allow them to use Dakar as a base from which to launch air and naval attacks against British shipping. De Gaulle pushed for an attack—eager to expand his power base in Africa, to show himself a key Allied figure, and to encourage other Vichy-held African territories to rally to his cause. The resulting joint British–Free French plan was named Operation MENACE.

Previously, on 8 July, British aircraft flying from the carrier *Hermes* had attacked and immobilized the modern French battleship *Richelieu* at Dakar. This operation followed the British attack on the French fleet at Mers-el-Kébir in Algeria on 3–4 July and gave ample warning to the Vichy French forces that the British were willing to attack their former allies. Despite this aggressive move, both British Prime Minister Winston L. S. Churchill and de Gaulle hoped for a bloodless victory at Dakar.

Operation MENACE involved 23 warships, including the battleships *Barham* and *Resolution,* the aircraft carrier *Ark Royal,* 4 cruisers, and 11 destroyers. These warships escorted 11 transports carrying 7,900 men, 3,600 of whom were Free French. The Allies hoped that the authorities at Dakar would rally to the Free French. Failing that, the French troops would go ashore; the British troops were to be employed only in an emergency.

Operation MENACE was plagued with problems from the beginning. The Allies lacked a clear picture of the strength of the Dakar defenses, which were to include three Vichy French cruisers and three destroyers. These ships arrived at Dakar just in advance of the Allied ships.

On 23 September, the French administrator at Dakar, Pierre Boisson, refused to talk to the Free French negotiators. The negotiators went ashore, and the French coastal batteries at Dakar opened fire on the Allied ships. The Allied ships

Soldiers in the ruins of a government building after an air attack at Dakar. (Hulton-Deutsch Collection/Corbis)

See also
Churchill, Sir Winston L. S.; Darlan, Jean Louise Xavier François; de Gaulle, Charles; Mers-el-Kébir
References
Churchill, Winston L. S. *The Second World War.* Vol. 2, *Their Finest Hour.* Boston: Houghton Mifflin, 1949.
de Gaulle, Charles. *The Complete War Memoirs of Charles De Gaulle.* Vol. 1, *The Call to Honor, 1940–1942.* Trans. Jonathan Griffin. New York: Simon and Schuster, 1968.
Heckstall-Smith, Anthony. *The Fleet That Faced Both Ways.* London: A. Blond, 1963.
Kersaudy, François. *De Gaulle and Churchill.* New York: Atheneum, 1981.
Marder, Arthur. *Operation Menace: The Dakar Expedition and the Dudley North Affair.* London: Oxford University Press, 1976.
Paxton, Robert O. *Vichy France: Old Guard and New Order, 1940–1944.* New York: Columbia University Press, 1982.

returned fire. Over the next several days, the exchange of fire included both the French shore batteries and ships, especially the 15-inch guns of the immobilized *Richelieu.* The Vichy submarine *Beveziers* damaged the battleship *Resolution* with a torpedo, and several other British ships were hit by shell fire. The lack of adequate naval support combined with foggy conditions led the Allies to abandon the operation on 25 September.

The failure of Operation MENACE was a blow to British and Free French prestige and demonstrated British inexperience in combined operations. It also revealed the hatred felt by many French for the British and severely damaged the relationship between de Gaulle and Churchill. In addition, it profited the Vichy French government, which trumpeted it as a great naval victory. On 24 and 25 September, in response to the Dakar attack, Vichy bombers carried out three raids against Gibraltar—dropping some 600 tons of bombs, sinking a destroyer, and damaging the battle cruiser *Renown* and a submarine, but causing little damage to shore facilities. As a result of MENACE, Adolf Hitler saw some utility in Vichy France's assistance. He also had proof that Vichy would defend French Africa against the Free French. Admiral Jean F. Darlan then entered into talks with the Germans to allow them to use French air bases in Syria.

C. J. Horn

Daladier, Édouard (1884–1970)

French politician and premier. Born on 18 June 1884, at Carpentras (Vaucluse), Édouard Daladier was educated at the École Normale and at the Sorbonne before becoming a history teacher at the Lycée Condorcet in Paris. He served in the French army during World War I and fought at Verdun.

In 1919, Daladier was elected to the Chamber of Deputies from the Vaucluse as a Radical Socialist. He was minister of colonies in 1924 and premier from January to October 1933. Daladier formed another cabinet in January 1934 but resigned the next month over the Stavisky Scandal.

Daladier helped bring the Radicals into the leftist Popular Front coalition with the Socialists and Communists for the 1936 national elections. On the collapse of the Popular Front, he again became premier in April 1938. Under heavy pressure from British Prime Minister Neville Chamberlain and despite France's treaty obligations to Czechoslovakia, Daladier agreed at the September 1938 Munich Conference to Adolf Hitler's demands for the cession of the Sudentenland to Germany. Unlike Chamberlain, he had no illusions that the agreement had secured peace.

Daladier then did what he could to prepare France for war. On the German invasion of Poland in September 1939, he led France into war against Germany. Angered by the German-Soviet Non-aggression Pact of 23 August 1939, he reacted by outlawing the Communist Party and arresting its leaders. Daladier was criticized for France's military inaction during the so-called "Phony War" and its failure to assist Finland in Finland's war against the Soviet Union. He was forced to resign on 20 March 1940 and was replaced by Paul Reynaud. Daladier remained in the cabinet, however, as minister of war until the defeat of France in June 1940.

On 21 June 1940, Daladier and other cabinet ministers sailed from Bordeaux for North Africa in an effort to set up a

Édouard Daladier, French premier (1933, 1934, 1938–1940). (Hulton Archive/Getty Images)

government in exile, but new chief of state General Henri Pétain ordered them arrested. Daladier was among those brought to trial at Riom in 1942 by the Vichy government on charges of having caused the French defeat. The trial was suspended, but Daladier remained in custody. In 1943 he was removed as a prisoner to Germany. Released in April 1945, Daladier was one of the few leaders of the Third Republic to continue in politics during the Fourth Republic. Reelected a deputy, he served in the National Assembly from 1946 until 1958. Daladier died at Paris on 10 October 1970.

William L. Ketchersid and Spencer C. Tucker

See also
Chamberlain, Arthur Neville; France, Role in War; German-Soviet Non-aggression Pact; Munich Conference and Preliminaries; Pétain, Henri Philippe; Reynaud, Paul

References
Horne, Alistair. *To Lose a Battle: France 1940*. Boston: Little, Brown, 1969.
Rémond, René, and Janine Bourdin. *Édouard Daladier, chef de gouvernement, avril 1938–septembre 1939*. Paris: Presse de la Fondation Nationale des Science Politiques, 1977.
Reynaud, Paul. *In the Thick of the Fight*. Trans. James D. Lambert. New York: Simon and Schuster, 1955.
Werth, Alexander. *France and Munich: Before and After the Surrender*. New York: H. Fertig, 1969.

D'Aquino, Iva Ikuko Toguri

See "Tokyo Rose."

Darby, William O. (1911–1945)

U.S. Army officer credited with creation of the elite force the Rangers. Born on 9 February 1911 at Fort Smith, Arkansas, William Darby graduated from the U.S. Military Academy at West Point in 1933 and was commissioned a second lieutenant of field artillery. Over the next seven years, he held several routine assignments and was promoted to captain in October 1940. He then commanded an artillery battery of the 99th Field Artillery Regiment (1941–1942).

In June 1942, Brigadier General Lucian K. Truscott Jr. selected Darby to put together an elite force similar to the British commandos. The name "Rangers" derived from the force of the same name led by Major Robert Rogers during the French and Indian War. Promoted to temporary major,

Lieutenant Colonel William O. Darby (right) congratulated by Lieutenant General George S. Patton. Gela, Sicily, August 1943. (Photo by Bob Landry/Time Life Pictures/Getty Images)

Darby trained his men at Achnacarry, Scotland, under the guidance of British commandos. The Rangers were seen as elite troops to be employed on hit-and-run commando raids. A charismatic person, Darby believed in leadership by example from the front. Officially, Darby commanded only the 1st Ranger Battalion, but he also trained and led the 3rd and 4th Battalions. In December 1943, Darby was promoted to colonel and given command of all three battalions.

Darby's Rangers, as his force came to be known, were first employed in combat during the ill-fated August 1942 raid on Dieppe. In November 1942, six companies performed well in Operation TORCH, the Allied invasion of French North Africa then under Vichy control. The companies also participated in Operation HUSKY, the invasion of Sicily. In the invasion of Italy at Salerno, four U.S. Ranger battalions and the 41st British Commandos secured the coast at Maiori. After the destruction of the 1st and 3rd Battalions at Anzio, Darby was assigned to the Operations Division of the War Department's General Staff.

Darby returned to Italy in March 1945 and managed to secure a posting as executive officer of the 10th Mountain Division. On 30 April 1945, only a week before the end of the war in Europe, Darby was struck and killed in northern Italy by a German shell fragment. Darby was posthumously promoted to brigadier general.

Roy B. Perry III

See also
Anzio, Battle of; Dieppe Raid; Salerno Invasion; Sicily, Invasion of; TORCH, Operation; Truscott, Lucian King, Jr.

References
Darby, William O. *Darby's Rangers: We Led the Way.* Novato, CA: Presidio, 1993.
King, Michael J. *William Orlando Darby, A Military Biography.* Hamden, CT: Archon Books, 1981.

Darlan, Jean Louis Xavier François (1881–1942)

French navy admiral. Born on 7 August 1881 in Nérac (Lot-et-Garonne), France, Jean Darlan graduated from the École Navale in 1902. A specialist in naval gunnery, he served in the Far East on cruisers and then in the Mediterranean. Promoted to commander in 1912, he was then an instructor on the training cruiser *Jeanne d'Arc.* During World War I, he commanded heavy naval artillery on land. He was promoted to commander in July 1918 and took charge of the Rhine Flotilla.

Promoted to captain in August 1920, Darlan was assigned to the Far East, where he commanded cruisers. He was advanced to rear admiral in November 1929 and played an important role in the reorganization of the navy. He next commanded naval forces in Algeria and then a cruiser divi-

sion in the Mediterranean. Promoted to vice admiral in December 1932, he took charge of the Atlantic Squadron during 1934–1936. He was then chief of the French naval staff.

Darlan was promoted to admiral of the fleet in June 1939 and took command of the French Navy. Following the June 1940 defeat of France, he joined the Vichy government of Marshal Henri Philippe Pétain as navy minister. In February 1941 he also became vice premier and minister of the interior, and in August 1941 he was made minister of defense. He was also Pétain's designated successor.

Darlan was an Anglophobe, especially after Operation CATAPULT and the killing of French sailors at Mers-el-Kébir. He hoped to win concessions for France through military agreements with the Germans. His May 1941 meeting with Adolf Hitler led to an agreement with German ambassador Otto Abetz. In the so-called Paris Protocols, France granted major concessions to Germany in Africa and the Middle East, but the Germans gave little in return.

By April 1942, rival Pierre Laval forced Darlan to relinquish his cabinet posts, save that of commander of the armed forces. Darlan traveled frequently to North Africa and was in Algiers when, on 8 November, the Allies invaded in Operation TORCH. Darlan agreed to cooperate with the Allies and to order a cease-fire on 10 November in return for recognition of his authority. The deal was confirmed on 11 November

French Navy Admiral Jean Darlan. (Corbis)

with U.S. Major General Mark Clark and Ambassador Robert Murphy. President Franklin D. Roosevelt approved the agreement, although some Allied leaders denounced it as an "immoral act" that gained little.

Many people including Allied leaders wanted to see Darlan removed, and on 24 December 1942, 20-year-old French royalist Fernand Bonnier broke into Darlan's office and shot him twice with a pistol. Darlan died two hours later. Bonnier was captured, tried, and executed two days afterward. The assassination of Darlan is shrouded in mystery and has been variously attributed to the United States, Britain, the Free French, French monarchists, and even the Germans.

William P. Head and Spencer C. Tucker

See also
CATAPULT, Operation; France, Navy; Pétain, Henri Philippe; TORCH, Operation

References
Dallek, Robert. *Franklin D. Roosevelt and American Foreign Policy, 1932–1945.* New York: Oxford University Press, 1979.

Maguire, G. E. *Anglo-American Policy Towards the Free French.* New York: St. Martin's Press, 1995.

Melton, George E. *Darlan: Admiral and Statesman of France, 1881–1942.* Westport, CT: Praeger, 1998.

Verrier, Anthony. *Assassination in Algiers: Churchill, Roosevelt, De Gaulle, and the Murder of Admiral Darlan.* New York: Norton, 1990.

Aftermath of attacks by Japanese bombers during their first raid on Darwin, 10 February 1942. (Bettmann/Corbis)

Darwin, Raid on (19 February 1942)

First direct Japanese attack against Australia during the war. Into early 1942, Japanese forces moved inexorably down through the Philippines and Malay Peninsula and into the Netherlands East Indies. To secure Java and protect landings at Timor, the Japanese High Command decided to attack Darwin, a port city on Australia's north coast used by the Allies to ferry aircraft, troops, and equipment to the East Indies. Commander Fuchida Mitsuo planned the raid, centered on the four aircraft carriers of Vice Admiral Nagumo Chūichi's First Air Fleet and a covering force of two battleships and three heavy cruisers under Vice Admiral Kondō Nobutake. It was the most powerful Japanese strike force since the attack on Pearl Harbor.

In two waves on 19 February 1942, the Japanese carriers in the Timor Sea launched approximately 188 aircraft against Darwin. Fifty-four land-based bombers joined them. A U.S. Navy PBY Catalina radioed a warning of the first wave but was then shot down. News reached Darwin just as 10 U.S. Army Air Forces (USAAF) P-40s of 33rd Squadron returned following an aborted attempt to reinforce Java. Five P-40s remained airborne to face the Japanese. The remaining 5 attempted to take off just as the Japanese planes arrived at about 10:00 A.M. Japanese Zeros claimed 9 of the P-40s in the air; the survivor landed with severe damage. The second raid

occurred 2 hours later. In all, the Japanese destroyed approximately 18 Allied aircraft and demolished air base facilities. The Japanese sank 8 ships, including the U.S. destroyer *Peary*, and damaged a further 9. Wharves and jetties suffered extensive damage, and 18 Allied aircraft were destroyed. The human toll was also high: some 500–600 people were killed or wounded. The Japanese accomplished all this at a cost of only 10 aircraft. This raid succeeded in its objective of assisting the Japanese conquest of the Dutch East Indies. Japanese attacks on Darwin continued during the next several months.

Rodney Madison

See also
Australia, Air Force; Fuchida Mitsuo; Kondō Nobutake; Nagumo Chūichi; Netherlands East Indies

References
Bergerud, Eric M. *Fire in the Sky: The Air War in the South Pacific.* Boulder, CO: Westview Press, 2000.

Craven, Wesley Frank, and James Lea Cate, eds. *The Army Air Forces in World War II.* Vol. 1, *Plans and Early Operations, January 1939 to August 1942.* Washington, DC: Office of Air Force History, 1983.

Lockwood, Douglas. *Australia's Pearl Harbour.* Melbourne, Australia: Cassell, 1967.

Morison, Samuel Eliot. *History of United States Naval Operations in World War II.* Vol. 3, *The Rising Sun in the Pacific, 1931–April 1942.* Boston: Little, Brown, 1948.

Davis, Benjamin Oliver, Jr. (1912–2002)

U.S. Air Force general. Born on 18 December 1912 in Washington D.C., Benjamin Oliver Davis Jr. was the son of Benjamin O. Davis, the first U.S. African American active-duty general officer. The younger Davis attended Western Reserve University and the University of Chicago. He then secured an appointment to the U.S. Military Academy at West Point, where he endured four years of isolation because of racial discrimination. He graduated in 1936 and was commissioned a second lieutenant of infantry. In July 1941 as a captain, Davis was one of the first members of a new pilot training program for African Americans at Tuskegee, Alabama. He completed training in March 1942. Tuskegee graduates formed the basis for Lieutenant Colonel Davis's 99th Pursuit Squadron, which flew P-40s. Following four months of combat in the Mediterranean Theater, Davis returned to the United States to assume command of the 332nd Fighter Group with P-51s, which he led in Italy in January 1944. Davis flew 60 missions and won promotion to colonel in March 1944.

After the war, Davis returned to the United States to command the racially troubled 477th Composite Group at Godman Field, Kentucky. In 1949, Davis attended the Air War College, and he was then assigned to Washington, D.C., as deputy chief of operations in the Fighter Branch. In October 1954, Davis was promoted to brigadier general, the first African American U.S. Air Force officer to hold that rank. He served as vice commander, Thirteenth Air Force, and then headed Twelfth Air Force in Germany from 1957 to 1959. Promoted to major general in June 1959, Davis returned to Washington in July 1961 as director of Manpower and Organization. In April 1965, Davis was promoted to lieutenant general and became chief of staff of U.S. forces in Korea and the United Nations Command. He then became deputy commander of the U.S. Strike Command.

Davis retired in February 1970. In 1971 he became assistant director of the Department of Transportation to establish the Sky Marshals program until 1975. He then served on various corporate boards. Promoted to general on the retired list in December 1998, Davis died at Washington, D.C., on 4 July 2002.

Troy D. Morgan

See also

Davis, Benjamin Oliver, Sr.; United States, Air Force

References

Davis, Benjamin O., Jr. *Benjamin O. Davis, Jr., American*. Washington, DC: Smithsonian Institute Press, 1991.

Dryden, Charles W. *A-Train: Memoirs of a Tuskegee Airman*. Tuscaloosa: University of Alabama Press, 1997.

Lee, Ulysses. *The Employment of Negro Troops*. Washington, DC: Center for Military History, 1994.

Brigadier General Benjamin O. Davis Sr. watches a Signal Corps crew erect poles in France, 8 August 1944. (National Archives)

Davis, Benjamin Oliver, Sr. (1877–1970)

U.S. Army general and first African American general in the U.S. military. Born 1 July 1877 in Washington D.C., Benjamin O. Davis enrolled at Howard University in 1897 but left school the next year to join the Eighth U.S. Volunteer Regiment. As a lieutenant during the Spanish-American War, he saw no action, but in 1899 he enlisted as a private in the regular army. Davis was commissioned a second lieutenant in the 10th U.S. Cavalry in 1901. He was military attaché to Liberia (1909–1911), professor of military science at Wilberforce University (1906–1911, 1915–1917, 1929–1930, and 1937–1938), supply officer for the 9th Cavalry in the Philippines (1917–1920), instructor with the Ohio National Guard (1924–1928), and professor of military science at Tuskegee Institute (1921–1924 and 1931–1937).

At the beginning of World War II, Davis was one of only two African American officers in the combatant arms of the U.S. Army. The other was his son, Benjamin O. Davis Jr. In October 1940, on the recommendation of President Franklin D. Roosevelt, Davis was promoted to brigadier general. He was the first African American to obtain the rank in U.S. military history.

Davis retired from the army in 1941 but was recalled to active duty as an assistant to the Inspector General of the Army, serving in the European Theater of Operations as an adviser on race relations. At the same time, he fought to end segregation and discrimination within the armed forces. Davis remained in the Inspector General's office until his final retirement in 1948. He continued to speak for desegregation in the military, which was achieved when President Harry S Truman ordered full integration of the U.S. armed forces.

In the years following his retirement from the military, Davis served on numerous civilian boards and the Battle Monuments Commission. He died in Chicago on 26 November 1970.

Nicholas W. Barcheski

See also
Davis, Benjamin Oliver, Jr.; Roosevelt, Franklin D.; Truman, Harry S
References
Astor, Gerald. *The Right to Fight: A History of African-Americans in the Military.* Navato, CA: Presidio, 1998.
Fletcher, Marvin. *America's First Black General: Benjamin O. Davis, Sr.* Lawrence: University Press of Kansas, 1989.

De Bono, Emilio (1866–1944)

Italian marshal and government figure. Born on 16 March 1866 at Cassano d'Adda, Emilio De Bono graduated from military schools in nearby Milan and in 1883 began a long army career, which is chronicled in many diaries. A self-styled "warrior," De Bono sought challenging commands in the 1911–1912 Italo-Turkish War and during World War I. He was promoted to major general and twice decorated for valor in 1916. Friction with a superior led to an inactive posting in Albania until he was recalled to corps command in Italy. He turned back an Austrian attack at Grappa in 1918.

Restive after the war, De Bono, who had never evinced attention to or interest in politics, was tempted by the bombast of Gabriele D'Annunzio's nationalistic expedition to occupy Fiume in 1919 to join that campaign. However, ambivalent careerist instincts held him in check. Still lacking any warrior role or prospects, by 1921 De Bono settled for membership in the Fascist Party as a vehicle for self-promotion. Although his military skills were pivotal in organizing the October 1922 March on Rome, they did not advance him politically despite his appointments as chief of public security in November 1922 and commander of the Fascist militia in January 1923.

After his perceived failure to prevent the June 1924 murder of socialist leader Giacomo Matteotti by the militia, De Bono was indicted but refused to implicate his superiors. Acquitted in 1925 and rewarded with the governorship of Tripolitania, by 1928 De Bono was planning the eventual war with Ethiopia. He had some success early in that war, including a victory at Adowa, but his recalcitrant pace irked Italian

leader Benito Mussolini, who replaced him in November 1935 with his rival Pietro Badoglio. De Bono demanded and received promotion to marshal immediately thereafter.

Serving ignominiously in largely ceremonial or honorary posts for the remainder of his career, De Bono soured on Mussolini, decrying Italian-German war plans, and eventually joined in the Fascist Grand Council's July 1943 ouster of Il Duce, for which he was arrested by the German occupation 4 October 1943. Tried at Verona, the old general was sentenced to death with, among others, Mussolini's son-in-law Galeazzo Ciano, whom he joined before a firing squad on 11 January 1944.

Gordon E. Hogg

See also
Badoglio, Pietro; Ciano, Galeazzo; Mussolini, Benito
References
Cannistraro, Philip. *Historical Dictionary of Fascist Italy.* Westport, CT: Greenwood, 1982.
Corvaja, Sani. *Hitler and Mussolini: The Secret Meetings.* New York: Enigma Books, 2001.
Dizionario biografico degli Italiani. Vol. 33. Roma: Istituto della Enciclopedia Italiana, 1987.

de Gaulle, Charles (1890–1970)

French Army general, leader of Free French Forces, and the president of France. Born on 22 November 1890 in Lille, Charles de Gaulle demonstrated from an early age a keen interest in the military. He graduated from the French Military Academy of Saint-Cyr in 1913 and was commissioned a lieutenant in the army.

De Gaulle's first posting was with Colonel Henri P. Pétain's 33rd Infantry Regiment. During World War I, de Gaulle was promoted to captain, and he demonstrated a high degree of leadership and courage. Wounded twice, he was captured by the Germans at Verdun in March 1916 after being wounded a third time. Later he received the Legion of Honor for this action. Despite five escape attempts, he remained a prisoner of war until the end of the war.

After the war, de Gaulle returned to teach history at Saint-Cyr, and in 1920 he was part of the French military mission to Poland. He returned to France to study and teach at the École de Guerre. De Gaulle then served as an aide to French army commander Marshal Pétain, but the two had a falling-out, apparently because Pétain wanted de Gaulle to ghost-write his memoirs. De Gaulle also became an important proponent of the new theories of high-speed warfare centered on tanks. In his 1934 book *Vers l'armée de métier* (published in English as *The Army of the Future*), de Gaulle proposed formation of six completely mechanized and motorized divisions with their own organic artillery and air support.

General Charles de Gaulle. (Library of Congress)

Another book, *Le fil de l'epée* (*The Edge of the Sword*) revealed much about de Gaulle's concept of leadership and his belief that a true leader should follow his conscience regardless of the circumstances.

Promoted to major and then to lieutenant colonel, de Gaulle served in the Rhineland occupation forces, in the Middle East, and on the National Defense Council. Although he was advanced to colonel in 1937 and had important political friends such as future premiere Paul Reynaud, de Gaulle's views placed him very much on the outside of the military establishment.

When World War II began, de Gaulle commanded a tank brigade. His warnings about the German use of tanks in Poland fell on deaf ears in the French High Command. De Gaulle commanded the 4th French Tank Division in the 1940 Battle for France. Although the division was still in formation, he secured one of the few French successes of that campaign. Promoted to brigadier general on 1 June 1940, five days later de Gaulle was appointed undersecretary of defense in the Reynaud government. De Gaulle urged Reynaud to fight on, even in a redoubt in the Brittany Peninsula or removing the armed forces to North Africa. De Gaulle's resolve won the admiration of British Prime Minister Winston L. S. Churchill.

De Gaulle and Jean Monnet visited London and suggested to Churchill a plan for an indissoluble Anglo-French union that the French government had rejected. Returning to Bordeaux from the mission to London, de Gaulle learned that the defeatists had won and France would sue for peace. On 17 June, he departed France on a British aircraft bound for England. The next day, this youngest general in the French army appealed to his countrymen over the British Broadcasting Corporation (BBC) to continue the fight against Germany. From this point forward, de Gaulle was the most prominent figure in the French Resistance. With Churchill's support and because no prominent French politicians had escaped abroad, de Gaulle then set up a French government-in-exile in London and began organizing armed forces to fight for the liberation of his country. The Pétain government at Vichy declared de Gaulle a traitor and condemned him to death in absentia.

Initially, de Gaulle's position was at best tenuous. Most French citizens did not recognize his legitimacy, and relations with the British and Americans were at times difficult. De Gaulle insisted on being treated as head of state of a major power, whereas American leaders, especially President Franklin D. Roosevelt, and even Churchill persisted in treating him as an auxiliary and often did not consult with him at all on major decisions.

The British attack on the French fleet at Mers-el-Kébir further undermined de Gaulle's credibility. Relations with the United States were not helped by a Free French effort to secure Saint-Pierre and Miquelon off Canada. The United States recognized the Vichy government and continued to pursue a two-France policy even after the United States entered the war in December 1941.

Over time, de Gaulle solidified his position as leader of the Resistance in France. Bitter over British moves in Syria and Lebanon and not informed in advance of the U.S.-British invasion of French North Africa, de Gaulle established his headquarters in Algiers in 1943, where he beat back a British-French effort to replace him with General Henri Giraud. His agent, Jean Moulin, secured the fusion of Resistance groups within France. The French Resistance rendered invaluable service to the British and Americans in the June 1944 Normandy Invasion, and French forces actually liberated Paris that August.

De Gaulle then returned to Paris and established a provisional government there. Full U.S. diplomatic recognition came only with the creation of the new government. De Gaulle secured for France an occupation zone in Germany and a key role in postwar Europe. But with the return of peace the former political parties reappeared, and hopes for a fresh beginning faded. De Gaulle's calls for a new constitutional arrangement with a strong presidency were rejected, and he resigned in January 1946 to write his memoirs.

A revolt among European settlers and the French Army in Algeria, who feared a sellout there to the Algerian nationalists, brought de Gaulle back to power in 1958. A new constitution tailor-made for de Gaulle established the Fifth Republic. De Gaulle's preservation of democracy was his greatest service to his country, but he also brought an end to the Algerian War, and he worked out a close entente with Konrad Adenauer's Federal Republic of Germany. De Gaulle was also controversial, removing France from the North Atlantic Treaty Organization's military command, creating an independent nuclear strike force, encouraging Quebec to secede from Canada, and lecturing the United States on a wide variety of issues. He remained president until 1969, when he again resigned to write a new set of memoirs. Unarguably France's greatest twentieth-century statesman, Charles de Gaulle died at his estate of Colombey-les-Deux-Églises on 9 November 1970.

Thomas Lansford and Spencer C. Tucker

See also
Armored Warfare; Churchill, Sir Winston L. S.; Dakar; France, Battle for; France, Free French; France, Vichy; France Campaign; Giraud, Henri Honoré; Maginot Line; Mers-el-Kébir; Moulin, Jean; Normandy Invasion and Campaign; OVERLORD, Operation; Pétain, Henri Philippe; Reynaud, Paul; Roosevelt, Franklin D.; TORCH, Operation

References
Berthon, Simon. *Allies at War: The Bitter Rivalry among Churchill, Roosevelt, and de Gaulle.* New York: Carroll and Graf, 2001.
Cook, Don. *Charles de Gaulle, a Biography.* New York: G. P. Putnam's Sons, 1983.
De Gaulle, Charles. *The Complete War Memories of Charles de Gaulle.* Trans. Jonathan Griffin and Richard Howard. New York: Simon and Schuster, 1969.
Kersaudy, François. *Churchill and de Gaulle.* New York: Atheneum, 1982.
Lacouture, Jean. *De Gaulle. The Rebel, 1890–1944.* Trans. Patrick O'Brian. New York: W. W. Norton, 1990.
Ledwidge, Bernard. *De Gaulle.* New York: St. Martin's Press, 1982.

de Lattre de Tassigny, Jean Joseph-Marie Gabriel

See Lattre de Tassigny, Jean Joseph-Marie Gabriel de.

Deception

Deception is a long-established and often essential element of warfare. It consists of actions designed to deliberately mislead enemy decision-makers as to one's capabilities, intentions, and operations. Deception causes the enemy to take specific actions that will contribute to the accomplishment of the friendly mission and weaken the enemy's strategic or tactical position. All major participants carried out deception operations during World War II.

Deception supports military operations by causing adversaries to misallocate resources in time, place, quantity, or effectiveness. A deceptive operation generally appears to be real to make the enemy believe that pretended hostile activities are genuine. By inducing a false sense of danger in one area, an enemy is forced to strengthen defenses there, weakening them where the real assault is intended to occur.

Deception theorists cite these overarching principles: the decision-maker is the target, the deception must cause a specific action (simply having an enemy believe something is not sufficient), centralized control avoids self-confusion and conflict with other friendly operations, security is required so that the enemy does not discover the ruse, timeliness is key as an enemy requires time to collect and analyze the deception-supporting signs, and friendly intelligence must confirm the desired enemy actions. Finally, integrating the deception with an actual operation adds credibility and enemy uncertainty.

A cover operation is a form of deception that leads the enemy to decide genuine hostile activities are harmless. Cover induces a false sense of security by disguising the preparations for the real attack, so that when it comes the enemy will be taken by surprise. A rumor campaign suggesting to the enemy that troops embarking to invade a tropical country are in fact bound for the Arctic is a simple example of a cover operation.

At the other end of the complexity spectrum, a deceptive plan may involve months of careful preparation and the movement of thousands of troops, hundreds of aircraft, and scores of warships—all to convince an enemy that a major assault is being mounted. For example, if an enemy believes an amphibious assault is planned against beachhead A, gathering ships within striking distance of beachhead A will reinforce this perception, while the ships are also within range of the true objective at beachhead B. A cover plan may be on the same scale, designed to conceal real preparations for a massive assault.

Preparations for the Normandy Invasion were surrounded by an extensive and detailed deception operation plan. The overall deception scheme, known as BODYGUARD, consisted of 36 subordinate plans designed to convince Adolf Hitler that the Allies were going to continue with peripheral attacks until at least July 1944, beyond the actual invasion date. The key sub-operation FORTITUDE SOUTH was intended to draw attention away from NEPTUNE, the actual Normandy Invasion. Operation FORTITUDE NORTH suggested an invasion of Norway by combined American, British Commonwealth, and Soviet forces, which kept 27 German divisions in Norway and idle. Once it became obvious that France, not Scandinavia, was the objective, Operation FORTITUDE SOUTH was designed to convince the Germans that the Allied invasion of northern France would come in the Pas de Calais area. This required the creation of a fictitious 1st Army Group in the Dover region under

Lieutenant General George S. Patton, with sham radio traffic, dummy equipment, and supporting hearsay evidence.

Operationally, the deception included more actual aerial bombardment of Calais than the of actual target. Little was beyond the scope of the deception planners. On one occasion before the Normandy Invasion, for example, Lieutenant Clifton James, a British Army Pay Corps officer who bore a striking resemblance to General Bernard Montgomery, met with troops in Gibraltar and Algeria so that German intelligence would believe the real field marshal was in the Mediterranean instead of in London.

Large-scale defensive decoys were also employed during the war, particularly in Britain during the 1940 Battle of Britain and thereafter. These decoys fell under the purview of the Air Ministry's Colonel J. F. Turner under the anonymous name "Colonel Turner's Department" or CTD. Thirty-six daytime airfield decoys called "K sites," with mowed runways, wood and canvas aircraft, and dummy trenches, each a decoy for a particular Royal Air Force (RAF) station, were completed by the summer of 1940. However, a German reconnaissance plane shot down in October 1941 contained a map that identified 50 percent of the decoy sites, and they were all subsequently closed by June 1942.

In tandem with K sites, nighttime Q sites were constructed using deceptive airfield lighting that was occasionally augmented by hand-moved lights to simulate taxiing aircraft. Q sites proved much more successful. Eventually, 171 Q sites were constructed throughout Britain, with 359 of 717 Luftwaffe bomber attacks targeting these decoys by 1942. The success of the Q sites led to variations: QL sites (L for lighting) simulated the presence of marshaling yards, naval installations, armament factories, and so on. Various devices emitted sparks to resemble electric train flashes; orange lights shone down onto sand, conjuring furnace glows; doors opened and closed. QF sites (F for fire) were created in response to the knowledge that a fire in the target area often drew more bombers to it. Thus, several important factories were provided with their own deceptive decoy installation. "Oil QF," an effort to protect oil reserves by simulating a refinery fire, foundered under the combined difficulties of excessive oil consumption (up to 2,500 gal of oil per hour were needed to keep the fires going realistically) and lack of support by the oil companies, which believed the decoys would attract bombers.

After the German raid on Coventry, large urban decoys called "Starfish sites" appeared. These were the war's largest and most sophisticated decoys. Assorted fire-producing decoys were produced, soaked variously with boiling oil, paraffin, or creosote to create convincing fire effects. Depending on the fires' color and intensity, burning houses, factories, and power stations were accurately simulated. The Starfish sites were immediately successful, and by January 1943 more than 200 had been built. By June 1944, British decoy sites had drawn 730 attacks that otherwise would have killed British people or destroyed valuable infrastructure.

The Soviets routinely emphasized deception in military operations and often in political operations. The military staffs incorporated the complementary concepts of *maskirovka* (deception and camouflage) and *khitrost* (cunning and stratagem) into all planning levels. Although deception had been doctrinally accepted since the early 1920s, the shock of the rapid German advance to the outskirts of Moscow and Leningrad painfully reinforced its practical utility.

The Soviets crudely but successfully hid the creation and deployment of three small armies during their Moscow counteroffensive, although this was due more to poor German intelligence and bad weather than skillful deception operations. However, the Soviets soon learned the requirements of integrating tactical deception (such as having individual tank units adhere to radio silence) with operational deception (such as moving several units to an unexpected front, creating new corps to attack where no Soviet formations had been reported). By 1944, deception planning had evolved so that strategic capabilities were possible. For example, by conducting numerous operations toward western Ukraine, the Soviets habituated the Germans into believing that the USSR's strategic axis was through Ukraine into southern Poland and Romania. Spring 1944 saw an elaborate *maskirovka* operation that concealed the redeployment of actual forces while surreptitiously creating forces for the major offensive through Byelorussia, progressing against German Army Group North and eventually dislocating the entire front. By this point, Soviet use of secrecy, ruses, and disinformation provided the USSR with an operational advantage for the remainder of the war. Even when the Germans did detect the deception, it was usually too late to counter the Soviet moves.

Deception was not limited to the European Theater. The Japanese supported their initial strategic campaign through deception. Before the Japanese attack on Pearl Harbor, Allied military attachés and other sources were shown only antiquated aircraft and were intentionally misinformed regarding pilot proficiency at night flying and shallow-water torpedo attacks. The depicted incompetencies readily reinforced preconceptions that western attachés and intelligence analysts held regarding the Japanese.

Early Japanese parachute operations, such as the capture of Menado airfield on the Celebes on 11 January 1942, succeeded superbly, but these actions informed the Allies of Japanese paratroop procedures and allowed the Allies to develop ways to counter Japan's weaker airborne forces. The Japanese responded with deception. Thus, the Japanese 21 February airborne assault on Timor commenced with a feigned paratroop assault several miles from the actual drop zones. With the Dutch defenders reacting to the deceptive attack, the main body of paratroops easily secured and held the Allied communications lines.

The United States routinely used deception in the Pacific Theater. For example, before the United States attacked Tinian Island on 24 July 1944, two dozen warships of Carrier Task Force 58 targeted Tinian Town and nearby road junctions with naval gunfire. This misled the Japanese as to the actual amphibious sites, allowing the assault ashore with greatly reduced casualties. Such deception operations played a major role in World War II.

Robert B. Martyn

See also

Britain, Battle of; Camouflage; FORTITUDE, North and South, Operations; Menado, Battle for; MINCEMEAT, Operation; Montgomery, Sir Bernard Law; Patton, George Smith, Jr.; Pearl Harbor, Attack on

References

Cruickshank, Charles. *Deception in World War II*. New York: Oxford University Press, 1979.

Glantz, David. *Soviet Military Deception in the Second World War*. London: Cass, 1989.

Howard, Michael. *Strategic Deception in the Second World War*. New York: Norton, 1995.

U.S. Department of Defense. *US Joint Pub 3–58, Joint Doctrine for Military Deception*. 31 May 1996.

Declaration on Liberated Europe (February 1945)

Declaration issued by leaders of the United States, Great Britain, and the Soviet Union—the "Big Three"—during the February 1945 Yalta Conference. At Yalta, the bargaining position of the western Allies was weak. They had recently suffered a major embarrassment in the German Ardennes Offensive (Battle of the Bulge), and the Soviet armies were poised to drive on Berlin. Soviet leader Josef Stalin seemed to hold all the cards, at least as far as eastern and central Europe were concerned. Soviet troops occupied most of that territory, including Poland. Stalin sought to secure control of a belt of East European satellite states, both to provide security against another German invasion and to protect a severely wounded Soviet Union against the West and its influences.

British Prime Minister Winston L. S. Churchill pointed out at Yalta that the United Kingdom had gone to war to defend Poland, and U.S. President Franklin D. Roosevelt was influenced by the Atlantic Charter and the United Nations Declaration but also by a large Polish constituency at home. Roosevelt pressed Stalin to agree to applying the Atlantic Charter to the limited area of "liberated Europe." This, of course, excluded both the British Empire and the Soviet Union.

Stalin agreed to the resulting Declaration on Liberated Europe. It affirmed the right of all peoples "to choose the government under which they will live" and called for the "restoration of sovereign rights and self-government" to peoples who had been occupied by the "aggressor nations." The Big Three pledged that in the liberated nations, they would work to restore internal peace, relieve distress, form governments that were "broadly representative of all democratic elements in the population," and ensure that there would be "free elections" that were "broadly representative of all democratic elements in the population" as soon as possible. But such lofty phrases were subject to different interpretations.

No institutional arrangement was established to enforce the ideas embodied in the declaration. As it transpired, the Soviets chose to regard "democratic elements" as meaning all Communist and pro-Communist factions and "free elections" as excluding all those they regarded to be fascists. The result was Soviet control over much of eastern and central Europe—at first indirect and, with the development of the Cold War, direct. The Soviet Union did pay a price for the declaration in the court of world opinion, as Stalin's promises to respect human rights were proven utterly false

Spencer C. Tucker

See also

Atlantic Charter; Churchill, Sir Winston L. S.; Roosevelt, Franklin D.; Stalin, Josef; United Nations Declaration; Yalta Conference

References

Buhite, Russell D. *Decisions at Yalta: An Appraisal of Summit Diplomacy*. Wilmington, DE: Scholarly Resources, 1986.

Clemens, Diane Shaver. *Yalta*. New York: Oxford University Press, 1970.

Gardner, Lloyd C. *Spheres of Influence: The Great Powers Partition Europe, from Munich to Yalta*. Chicago: Ivan R. Dee, 1993.

Snell, John L. *The Meaning of Yalta: Big Three Diplomacy and the New Balance of Power*. Baton Rouge: Louisiana State University Press, 1956.

Stettinius, Edward R., Jr. *Roosevelt and the Russians: The Yalta Conference*. Walter Johnson, ed. New York: Harold Ober Associates, 1949.

Dempsey, Miles Christopher (1896–1969)

British army general. Born in New Brighton, Cheshire, on 15 December 1896, Miles Dempsey graduated from the Royal Military College at Sandhurst in 1915. He saw action on the Western Front and in Iraq in World War I. He served at Sandhurst from 1923 to 1927. Dempsey was then on the staff of the War Office from 1932 to 1934 and at Aldershot from 1934 to 1936. He was promoted to lieutenant colonel in 1938.

In 1940, Dempsey commanded the 13th Infantry Brigade (Royal Berkshires) in France as an acting brigadier general, leading it with distinction during the retreat to and evacuation from Dunkerque. Dempsey then helped train new British forces, was promoted to major general in January 1941, and

General of the British Army Miles Dempsey. (Corbis)

Dempsey kept close control of his subordinates, often placing his tactical headquarters close to theirs and keeping reserves under his own control in the early phases of a battle. He sought to avoid high casualties, arranging the maximum fire support and emphasizing the use of tactical air power. Many scholars consider Dempsey's influence in the war to be minimal, dismissing him as Montgomery's cipher. Dempsey's introverted nature and his shunning of both publicity and self-promotion aid this impression. The close working relationship between Montgomery and Dempsey obscures the authorship of operational decisions, as does their shared tendency to rely on verbal orders. They worked together for so long that they thought along similar lines and anticipated each other's reactions and decisions. During the Normandy Campaign, Dempsey is credited mainly with the decision and planning of operation GOODWOOD.

In August 1945, Dempsey succeeded General Sir William Slim as commander of the Fourteenth Army for the reoccupation of Singapore and Malaya. He followed Slim again as commander in chief of Allied Land Forces in Southeast Asia. Dempsey was promoted to full general on leaving that post and was commander in chief in the Middle East in 1946 and 1947. He then retired at his own request in July 1947 and entered the private sector. Dempsey died in Yattendon, Berkshire, on 5 June 1969.

Britton W. MacDonald

See also

Dunkerque, Evacuation of; GOODWOOD, Operation; MARKET-GARDEN, Operation; Montgomery, Sir Bernard Law; Normandy Invasion and Campaign; OVERLORD, Operation; Sicily, Invasion of; Slim, Sir William Joseph

References

De Guingand, Francis W. *Generals at War*. London: Hodder and Stoughton, 1964.

Hart, Stephen Ashley. *Montgomery and "Colossal Cracks": The 21st Army Group in Northwest Europe, 1944–1945*. Westport, CT: Praeger, 2000.

Montgomery, Bernard L. *Memoirs*. London: Collins, 1958.

received command of the 42nd Armoured Division. In December 1942, at the request of Lieutenant General Bernard Montgomery, Dempsey took command of XIII Corps of the British Eighth Army and was advanced to lieutenant general. Dempsey helped plan Operation HUSKY and the invasion of Sicily, and he then commanded his corps in the assault. Dempsey also directed the assault crossing to Italy of the 1st Canadian Infantry and 5th Canadian Armoured Divisions.

By January 1944, Dempsey had returned to Britain to command the British Second Army, and, with his staff he helped develop the OVERLORD plan for the invasion of northern France. In the fall of 1944, the Second Army participated in the breakout from the Normandy beachhead, raced through France and Belgium, liberated Brussels and Antwerp, and penetrated into Holland in Operation MARKET-GARDEN. Dempsey had opposed the Eindhoven-Arnhem route, preferring instead an offensive closer to the First Army near Aachen. King George VI knighted him for his role in MARKET-GARDEN. In March 1945, the Second Army crossed the Rhine and then pushed to the Baltic. Dempsey personally took the surrender of Hamburg on 3 May 1945.

Denmark, Role in War

The small nation of Denmark with a population of some 5 million people had since 1815 sought security in neutrality, and indeed the country was neutral during World War I. As additional insurance, it signed a nonaggression pact with Germany in the spring of 1939. Although Denmark's chief trading partner was Great Britain, which received Danish exports of dairy products, it was clear that Denmark lay within Germany's sphere of influence. Its conquest by Germany was a natural extension of Operation WESERÜBUNG, Adolf Hitler's plan to take Norway in April 1940. German occupation of Denmark was essential if Germany was to control Norway.

At the time of the German invasion, Denmark had an army of 14,000 men, 8,000 of whom had been recently drafted. The small navy had only 3,000 men and 2 coast defense warships (built in 1906 and 1918). The air force, split between the army and navy, had 50 obsolete aircraft. The German invasion, mounted before dawn on 9 April 1940, was over in only 2 hours. The government ordered a cease-fire after the occupation of Copenhagen, leaving insufficient time for the government or King Frederik IX to get abroad.

Germany initially employed a soft approach in Denmark, reaching an accord with the Danish government wherein most governmental functions remained under Danish control. Denmark provided important military bases to Germany and exported essential foodstuffs, such as dairy products and meat, to Germany. Indeed, these latter amounted to some 10 percent of German requirements. This arrangement worked well for three years, 1940–1943, with only sporadic resistance. The official Danish policy was to collaborate with Germany to the extent necessary, a policy supported by most of the population.

Danish collaboration was predicated on the assumption that the Germans would honor their pledge not to interfere in Danish internal affairs, but time and again the Germans broke the agreement, demanding certain military equipment and insisting on the removal of specific government officials. The Germans also demanded that Denmark make a greater contribution to the German war effort, and Danish authorities urged some 100,000 of Denmark's citizens to work in Germany to prevent them from being conscripted.

Following the German invasion of the Soviet Union, the Germans forced the Danish government to ban the Communist Party and accept German recruitment of a Danish Free Corps to fight on the Eastern Front. In November 1941, Germany insisted that Denmark join the Anti-Comintern Pact.

There were Danes who took up cause against Germany from the beginning. On the German conquest of Denmark, 232 Danish merchant ships were at sea with some 6,000 seamen. Most of the latter helped to crew ships in the Atlantic and Arctic convoys. Ultimately, 1,500 of these men lost their lives, and 60 percent of the fleet was lost. By 1944, Danes formed the crews of two British minesweepers. Another thousand Danish nationals served with various Allied forces fighting the Axis powers.

In 1940, a Danish Council was formed in London, which in 1942 became the Free Danish Movement. Henrik Kauffmann, Danish ambassador to the United States, disassociated himself from the Danish government and signed a treaty in 1941 granting the United States military bases in Greenland. British forces also occupied the Faeroe Islands, another Danish possession, in April 1940. In May 1940, the Allies also occupied Iceland, which declared itself independent in 1944.

In the spring of 1942, Berlin appointed Werner Best as Reich commissioner for occupied Denmark. A hard-line Ger-

Cheering Danes gather in Copenhagen around British soldiers, one of whom has climbed on the hood of a military vehicle, following the liberation of the city, May 1945. (Library of Congress)

man officer Generalleutnant (U.S. equiv. major general) Hermann Hanneken took command of German troops in Denmark and was encouraged by Hitler "to rule with an iron hand." Such actions infuriated the Danes and led to an uprising in August 1943. The changing German military fortunes, British radio broadcasts, and the Danish illegal press all helped shift public opinion away from collaboration to support for resistance. The occupying Germans did not confiscate radio sets, and many Danes listened to the British Broadcasting Corporation (BBC) daily. The August demonstration and associated strikes demanded an end to collaboration. Attempts by Danish authorities to crush the demonstrations ended in fatalities and were unsuccessful. There were also violent clashes between Danes and German soldiers in some provincial cities. Consequently, the Germans declared a state of emergency on 29 August, arrested most members of the Danish military, and in effect took over rule of the country.

In September 1943, the Gestapo arrived in Denmark and initiated a Nazi reign of terror that lasted to the end of the war. Some 6,000 Danes were sent to concentration camps, and hundreds more were executed outright. Many Danes sought refuge in Sweden. The Danish Freedom Council became the de facto clandestine government, an underground army was formed, and more than 2,000 acts of sabotage were carried out, some 30 percent of these in Copenhagen. The Danish Freedom Council divided the nation into six regions, exercising central authority through its Command Committee. By the end of the war, the Danish Resistance numbered about 40,000 people. The sabotage acts had little effect on the German war effort, although news of them had a positive psychological impact on the Danish population as proof that Denmark was no longer collaborating with Germany.

Danes of all walks of life actively resisted German efforts to round up Jews. Although Best ordered the arrest of all Jews in Denmark, more than 7,000 escaped the Nazi net; 5,500 were transported to Sweden by boat. Only 472 were caught and sent to Theresienstadt. Danes did not forget those who had been sent there; they regularly sent packages of foodstuffs and clothes, and only 52 of the Jews there perished.

The Germans surrendered Denmark on 4 May, and the Danish Resistance took control of the country the next day. On 5 May, a company of the British 13th Airborne Battalion arrived in Copenhagen by plane along with Major General R. H. Dewing, head of the Supreme Headquarters, Allied Expeditionary Forces (SHAEF) mission to Denmark. British infantry troops marched into Denmark on 7 May. The following day, troops from the British 1st Parachute Brigade took the formal surrender of all German forces. When the German commander on the island of Bornholm refused to surrender, Soviet aircraft on 7 and 8 May bombed the towns of Rønne and Neks, causing great damage but few deaths. On 9 May, Soviet ships arrived at Rønne, and the Germans there surrendered. However, Soviet troops occupied the island until April 1946. Following the war, the Danish government ordered the arrest and punishment of some 34,000 Nazi collaborators.

After the war, the Danes would have preferred establishing a league of armed neutrality with Norway and Sweden, but they reluctantly followed Norway into the North Atlantic Treaty Organization (NATO). In 1951, the Danes agreed without particular enthusiasm to having U.S. naval and air bases in Greenland. Whatever hesitancy the new Danish policy might have indicated, it was a major switch from prewar neutrality and the feeling that no amount of military preparation on their part would deter their much more powerful neighbors.

Gene Mueller and Spencer C. Tucker

See also

Anti-Comintern Pact; Denmark Campaign; Himmler, Heinrich; Hitler, Adolf

References

Haestrup, Jorgen. *Secret Alliance: A Study of the Danish Resistance Movement, 1940–45*. Trans. Alison Borch-Johansen. 3 vols. Odense, Denmark: Odense University Press, 1976–1977.

Petrow, Richard. *The Bitter Years: The Invasion and Occupation of Denmark and Norway, April 1940–May 1945*. New York: Morrow Quill Paperbacks, 1979.

Thomas, John Oram. *The Giant Killers: The Story of the Danish Resistance Movement, 1940–1945*. New York: Taplinger Publishing Co., 1976.

Denmark Campaign (9 April 1940)

Code-named Operation WESERÜBUNG SUD (WESER EXERCISE SOUTH), the German invasion of Denmark began at approximately 4:15 A.M. on 9 April 1940. It formed an integral part of the much larger German assault on Norway (Operation WESERÜBUNG) that began the same day. German units quickly overran the Danish Peninsula, abrogating a nonaggression pact signed between Germany and Denmark in May 1939.

Although Danish intelligence learned of the German plans to invade as early as 4 April, the accounts were contradictory, and in any case were not believed. Certainly, the Danes had no chance whatsoever of defeating the German invaders. The poorly trained and inadequately equipped Danish army numbered only some 14,000 men, 8,000 of whom had enlisted within 8 weeks prior to the German attack. The Danish navy consisted of just 2 small vessels and approximately 3,000 men. The navy surrendered without going on alert, allowing a German troopship to arrive at Copenhagen. The Air Force had only 50 obsolete planes and a handful of pilots, no match for the vaunted Luftwaffe.

On 9 April, German seaborne forces moved into the capital of Copenhagen and secured the city by 6:00 A.M. Meanwhile, German paratroopers conducted the first airborne operation of the war when they seized the undefended fortress of Madnesø and, shortly thereafter, the airport at Aalborg in north Jutland. At the same time, German army units raced across the Jutland Peninsula in motorized columns. Although Danish Army units briefly contested the Germans in north Schleswig, the outcome was never in doubt.

German minister to Denmark Cecil von Renthe-Fink presented an ultimatum to the Danish government, demanding surrender and threatening the destruction of Copenhagen by Luftwaffe squadrons already en route if it refused. There was absolutely no chance of victory over the Germans, and eager to avoid further loss of life, King Frederik IX and Premier Thorvald Stauning believed they had no choice but to order surrender at 7:20 A.M. The campaign for Denmark was over. Danish casualties amounted to 26 dead and 23 wounded; the Germans lost 20 dead and wounded.

The German invasion provided the excuse for the Allied occupation of Iceland, which belonged to Denmark. Allied possession of strategically located Iceland proved vital in the Battle of the Atlantic. German forces occupied Denmark until the end of the war in May 1945.

Lance Janda

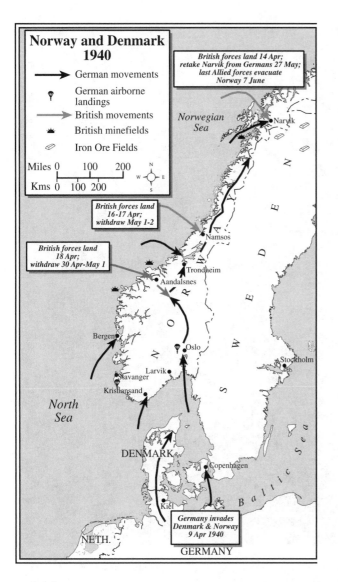

Norway and Denmark 1940

→ German movements

⚓ German airborne landings

→ British movements

⚓ British minefields

⬦ Iron Ore Fields

Miles 0   100   200

Kms 0   100   200

British forces land 14 Apr; retake Narvik from Germans 27 May; last Allied forces evacuate Norway 7 June

Norwegian Sea

Narvik

British forces land 16-17 Apr; withdraw May 1-2

Namsos

British forces land 18 Apr; withdraw 30 Apr-May 1

Trondheim

Aandalsnes

Bergen

Oslo

Stockholm

Stavanger

Larvik

Kristiansand

North Sea

DENMARK

Copenhagen

Baltic Sea

Kiel

Germany invades Denmark & Norway 9 Apr 1940

NETH.

GERMANY

See also

Airborne Forces, Axis; Denmark, Role in War; Norway, German Conquest of

References

Deighton, Len. *Blitzkrieg: From the Rise of Hitler to the Fall of Dunkirk.* New York: Alfred A. Knopf, 1980.

Heiberg, Eric. *Hitler's 'Canary Bird': The German Occupation of Denmark in 1940.* Master's thesis, Georgetown University, 1970.

Petrow, Richard. *The Bitter Years; The Invasion and Occupation of Denmark and Norway, April 1940–May 1945.* New York: William Morrow, 1974.

Depth Charges

Explosive devices designed to sink a submarine by detonating in its vicinity when triggered by water pressure, by the target's magnetic or acoustic signature, or by a variety of timers. From 1916 until 1943, well into World War II, the depth charge was the principal antisubmarine weapon of all navies,

after which more sophisticated weapons with greater range came to the fore.

In 1939, most navies used weapons similar to the British Type D Mark III (which entered service in 1916). The Mark III had a charge of approximately 200 lb and a sink rate of 6–10 ft per second and was triggered hydrostatically to explode at depths between 25 and 300 ft. Such charges had a lethal radius of 20 ft, and exploding at 40 ft, they could force a submarine to surface. Antisubmarine vessels discharged depth charges from roll-off racks and mortars (throwers) that projected them some 40 yards to the side. At the beginning of the war, the normal procedure for antisubmarine attacks was to use depth charges in patterns of five—three dropped in a line using gravity from the roll-off racks at the stern and two fired (one to each side) by throwers to produce a diamond-shaped pattern intended to bracket the target submarine.

Development during World War II concentrated on four main areas: larger charges, faster sink rates, greater fused depths, and more effective patterns. More powerful explosives such as Minol and Torpex, which were 50 percent more effective than TNT, replaced guncotton, and charges also increased in size. The U.S. and British navies introduced weapons with 600-lb explosive charges in 1941. In 1942, the Royal Navy introduced the massive Mark X weapon with a 2,000-lb charge. It was so large it was fired from 21-inch torpedo tubes retained on destroyers and escorts for this specific purpose. Sink rates rose to 22–50 ft per second, either by adding weights to conventional charges ("heavy charges") or by streamlining the cases. Modified fuses also allowed depth charges to explode deeper, doubling the maximum depth to 600 ft (at 50-ft intervals). The modified Mark X* sank faster because one buoyancy chamber was deleted and could be fused to explode down to 900 ft, while the Mark X** (which did not enter operational service) could be set to explode as deep as 1,200 ft.

Equally important were more effective dropping patterns. Modified casings resulted in more reliable and predictable underwater trajectories, newer projectors increased surface ranges to 150 yards, and mathematical analysis generated patterns having greater kill probabilities. First, the addition of another thrower on each beam allow use of a 7-charge pattern in the form of a hexagon, increasing the danger zone. Mixing standard and heavy charges created a new, highly effective 10-charge pattern that layered two diamond-shaped 5-charge patterns one above the other. The final development was a 3-layer 14-charge pattern using 4 throwers on each side and 6 charges dropped from the stern racks. Operational experience, however, demonstrated that, although the pattern was theoretically much more lethal than the 10-charge pattern, in practice the explosion of the first charges countermined the later charges and rendered them ineffective.

Sailors on the deck of the U.S. Coast Guard cutter *Spencer* watch the explosion of a depth charge that resulted in the 17 April 1943 sinking of U-175. (Still Picture Records LICON, Special Media Archives Services Division (NWCS-S), National Archives at College Park)

Therefore, the antisubmarine force reverted to the 10-charge pattern and replaced the additional throwers with stowage for extra charges.

Air-dropped depth charges played an important role during and after World War II. First designs were modifications of existing surface types, which limited their efficacy, since their weight reduced the number that could be carried and they were also subject to restrictions on dropping height and speed. The purpose-designed types that followed were lighter and less subject to dropping restrictions. Scientific analysis of attack camera records contributed mightily to the effectiveness of air-dropped depth charges. Scientists learned that charges were dropped too low and with depth fuse settings that were too deep to be effective. The ultimate fuse setting for aerial depth charges of 25 ft and new bomb sights and tactics transformed the weapons' effectiveness.

During 1944, newer weapons such as Hedgehog, Squid, and homing torpedoes surpassed depth charges in killing submarines. Nevertheless, the depth charge was still an important antisubmarine weapon until after the war's end.

Paul E. Fontenoy

See also
Antisubmarine Warfare; Hunter-Killer Groups; Sonar
References

Brown, D. K. *Nelson to Vanguard: Warship Design and Development, 1923–1945.* Annapolis, MD: Naval Institute Press, 2000.

Campbell, John. *Naval Weapons of World War II.* Annapolis, MD: Naval Institute Press, 1985.

Friedman, Norman. *Naval Institute Guide to World Naval Weapons.* Annapolis, MD: Naval Institute Press, 1994.

Hartman, Gregory K., with Scott C. Truver. *Weapons That Wait: Mine Warfare in the U.S. Navy.* Annapolis, MD: Naval Institute Press, 1991.

Destroyers

Small warships that are lightly armed and protected and capable of high speed. The destroyer originated in connection with the self-propelled torpedo, which was introduced in the late 1860s, and the consequent construction in the following decade of torpedo boats to carry the new weapon. These small, inexpensive warships offered the potential to destroy battleships, which were the most powerful and most costly vessels afloat. Most naval powers of the age, as they based their fleet strength on the battleship, endeavored to devise a defense against the torpedo boat. In 1893, Great Britain produced an answer in the *Havock,* the first modern torpedo-boat destroyer. Torpedo-boat destroyers were essentially enlarged torpedo boats that carried light guns and torpedoes. They were to hunt down and destroy enemy torpedo boats before the latter could launch their weapons against the capital ships of a battle fleet. Development in all maritime nations yielded vast improvements over the first torpedo-boat destroyers. By World War I, there were more of these warships (known by this time simply as destroyers) than of any other ship type in the world's navies.

The role of destroyers changed because of their increasing design capabilities in the years before World War I and from wartime experience. Destroyers became superior in all respects to the torpedo boats they were designed to destroy. As a result, naval powers in the prewar years largely discontinued the production of torpedo boats in favor of destroyers. The destroyer assumed the offensive role of torpedo boat while retaining the role of defending against torpedo attacks launched by enemy destroyers. World War I added extensively to the duties of these vessels. By the end of that conflict, destroyers had acted not only in the roles envisioned for their type, but also as surface combatants and bombardment ships in amphibious operations. More important than these uses, however, was their use by Great Britain, France, and later the United States as escorts for merchant convoys to defend against submarine attack. Destroyers were particularly effective in this capacity after the wartime introduction of depth charges and underwater listening devices such as hydrophones and sonar.

World War I demonstrated the importance of destroyers, and the same basic types continued during the interwar years. Great Britain had such large numbers of the craft that fresh designs were not initiated immediately after the close of the war in 1918. However, destroyer construction in Italy led France to respond, as French politicians and naval officials viewed Italy as France's principal naval competitor in the Mediterranean. In 1923, France built large vessels that began a trend toward "superdestroyers" in the world's navies. Great Britain and Japan returned to destroyer pro-

Destroyers Lost by Combatants in World War II

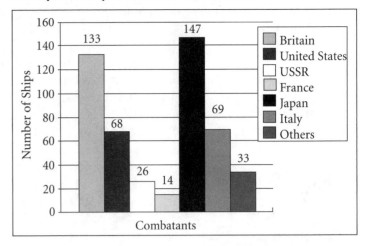

duction in the late 1920s; the United States did not initiate new construction until the early part of the next decade. Germany, although restricted by the Treaty of Versailles after World War I, began building new vessels at the same time as the United States.

This destroyer construction took place in an era of naval disarmament as the world's great powers sought to limit production as a means to prevent future wars. Unlike most other warships, few restrictions were put on the design and number of destroyers during the naval disarmament talks of the period. The 1930 London Conference limited destroyers to a maximum displacement of 1,850 tons and their guns to 5 inches or smaller, but these stipulations meant little. Until the late 1930s, the largest and most heavily armed designs met these requirements, and the limit was increasingly ignored after 1934 when the Japanese withdrew from the Washington Treaty and declared that they would not support future arms limitations discussions.

The American Somers-class is an example of destroyer design in the years immediately before the outbreak of World War II. Completed in 1937, the *Somers* measured 381' × 36' 11" and displaced 2,047 tons. She had exceptionally heavy armament: 8 × 5-inch guns, 8 × 1.1-inch guns, 2 × .5-inch weapons, and 12 × 21-inch torpedo tubes. The *Somers* had no armor protection and could steam at a maximum speed of 37 knots. Destroyers belonging to other naval powers loosely approximated the size, displacement, and armament of this vessel. France remained the exception as it continued to design destroyers that sometimes dwarfed those of other nations. The *Mogador,* launched in 1937, measured 451' 1" × 41' 7", displaced 2,884 tons, and carried no armor protection. It was armed primarily with 8 × 5.5-inch guns and 10 × 21.7-inch torpedo tubes and was capable of 39 knots. Despite the increase in the size and armament of destroyers, they were in most respects technologically the same as their World War I predecessors, although in some destroyer classes the largest guns were mounted in gun houses rather than open mounts to provide protection for crews. A further difference from the past was the incorporation of antiaircraft guns to fend off air attack.

By 1940, as during World War I, destroyers were the most numerous warships in the world's navies. Great Britain operated 247 destroyers of varying types and ages. The United States counted 149, and Japan had 116. Italy operated 90 destroyers. The other naval powers of the world also possessed large fleets: France maintained 66; the Soviet Union had 62; and Germany, through a naval policy that had violated the Treaty of Versailles, possessed 37.

> World War II proved the continued importance of destroyers and introduced a new vital duty, convoy escort.

World War II proved the continued importance of the roles destroyers had performed in the previous world conflict and introduced a new vital duty. In the Atlantic Theater, the primary task of British and Canadian destroyers was as convoy escort to guard against attack of merchant vessels by German submarines. This effort proved so important that the destroyer formed the basis for one of the first diplomatic agreements between Great Britain and the United States during the war. The 1940 Destroyers-Bases Deal transferred 50 aging World War I–era American destroyers to Great Britain in return for basing rights in the Western Hemisphere. Throughout the war, destroyers fought and helped to win the Battle of the Atlantic. Despite heavy losses in merchant vessels, ultimate Allied success in this effort allowed Great Britain to continue in the war. In addition, it enabled the transport of American troops to the European and Mediterranean Theaters after 1941.

Destroyers were also used as surface combatants, support for amphibious operations, troop transports, and resupply ships. An example in the Atlantic Theater of the first three of these roles is Germany's April 1940 invasion of Norway. Destroyers not only bombarded areas earmarked for the landing of troops, but they also attempted to fend off attacks from opposing British warships, and they transported a portion of the German ground force. The same roles existed for destroyers in the Mediterranean, where Allied vessels bombarded enemy positions during Operation TORCH, the November 1942 Allied invasion of North Africa. British vessels also acted as resupply ships for both the Allied troops in North Africa and the garrison on Malta, the principal British outpost in the Mediterranean.

These same roles were prevalent in the Pacific Theater, involving largely the forces of the United States and Japan. The Japanese used the destroyers both as surface combatants and as resupply vessels. Destroyers armed with the Long Lance torpedo were a key element of Japanese tactical operations and proved their effectiveness, especially in early night actions. The best example of a resupply effort was the famous Tokyo Express, which resupplied Japanese troops during the 1942–1943 contest for Guadalcanal. Destroyers were well suited for this resupply role as they were fast enough to make the voyage to Guadalcanal and depart still under cover of darkness. Early U.S. deficiencies in night-fighting were overcome, and American destroyers soon matched their Japanese counterparts in surface combat. In the August 1943 Battle of Vella Gulf, American destroyers sank three Japanese destroyers with no losses. The Japanese also used destroyers to protect convoys that supplied the home islands with war materiél.

In addition, use of destroyers in an antiaircraft role was widespread in the Pacific Theater. Both the Japanese and the United States sought ways to effectively defend their most important capital ships, the aircraft carriers. Destroyers partly filled the need for antiaircraft defense. This critical duty was reflected in the significant increase in the antiaircraft gun batteries of both Japanese and American destroyers during the war. The 12 Japanese Akitsuki-class vessels, launched between 1941 and 1944, mounted only 4×25-mm guns in addition to their primary armament of 8×3.9-inch guns, which could be used against surface targets or elevated and used against aircraft. By the end of the war, the complement of 25 mm guns had risen to 40–51 each for the surviving ships of the class. American destroyers showed the same shift to greater antiaircraft armament over the course of the war based on combat experience. By 1944, the 58 vessels of the Allen M. Sumner–class mounted a primary armament of 6×5-inch guns that could be used for surface combat or against aircraft and a smaller battery of 12×40-mm guns specifically devoted to antiaircraft defense.

The large number of critical roles performed by the destroyers and their consequent frequent use led to wartime construction that yielded an additional 633 destroyers among the principal naval combatants. The vast majority of these vessels were produced in the United States and Great Britain, which completed 392 and 165 ships, respectively. An example of wartime construction is the 150-ship U.S. Navy Fletcher-class. Launched between 1942 and 1944, these vessels measured 376' 5" × 39' 7", displaced 2,325 tons, and were protected by light side and deck armor. They were armed with 5×5-inch guns, 4×1.1-inch weapons, 4×20-mm guns for antiaircraft defense, and 10×21-inch torpedo tubes. They could make 38 knots.

The necessity for vessels to fulfill convoy escort roles also led to the production of a new type of destroyer that was

USS *Cassin,* one of the three destroyers sunk at Pearl Harbor, during the Japanese attack of 7 December 1941. (Hulton Archive)

cheaper and faster to build. Known as the destroyer escort, this ship was an essentially smaller, less capable destroyer with greater antisubmarine warfare capability. An example is the American TE-class escort, which measured 306' × 37' and displaced 1,432 tons. These were armed with 3 × 3-inch guns and an assortment of antisubmarine weaponry.

During the war, the belligerent powers constructed 915 destroyer escorts. The United States and Great Britain accounted for the majority of this production with 499 and 349 ships, respectively. The design of both the destroyers and destroyer escorts of the Allies and Germany and Italy benefited from the incorporation of radar, which was retrofitted to vessels produced before the war.

World War II exacted a heavy toll in terms of destroyers lost. By the end of the conflict, the belligerents had suffered a combined loss of 490 destroyers of varying types: among these, Japan lost 147; Great Britain suffered 133 sunk, largely in the Battle of the Atlantic; Italy lost 69 vessels; the United States counted 68 destroyers sunk; the Soviet Union lost 26; and France lost 14.

Eric W. Osborne

See also

Atlantic, Battle of the; Central Pacific Campaign; Convoy PQ 17; Convoys, Allied; Convoys, Axis; Depth Charges; Destroyers-Bases Deal; France, Navy; Germany, Navy; Great Britain, Navy; Guadalcanal Naval Campaign; Hunter-Killer Groups; Italy, Navy; Japan, Navy; Leyte Gulf, Battle of; Mariana Islands, Naval Campaign; Marshall Islands, Naval Campaign; Narvik, Naval Battles of; Norway, German Conquest of; Radar; *Reuben James,* Sinking of; Savo Island, Battle of; Sonar; Southeast Pacific Theater; Southwest Pacific Theater; TORCH, Operation; Torpedoes; United States, Navy; Vella Gulf, Battle of

References

Chesneau, Roger, ed. *Conway's All the World's Fighting Ships, 1922–1946.* London: Conway Maritime Press, 1980.
George, James L. *History of Warships: From Ancient Times to the Twenty-First Century.* Annapolis, MD: Naval Institute Press, 1998.
Preston, Anthony. *Destroyers.* Englewood Cliffs, NJ: Prentice-Hall, 1977.

Destroyers-Bases Deal (2 September 1940)

An agreement between U.S. President Franklin D. Roosevelt and British Prime Minister Winston L. S. Churchill in 1940 that provided Great Britain with World War I–vintage U.S. destroyers, in return giving the United States access to British bases in North America and the Caribbean.

Following the evacuation of the British Expeditionary Force from Dunkerque, Britain was virtually naked militarily, and the nation now awaited a German attack. When Churchill appealed to Roosevelt for military assistance, the U.S. reaction was immediate and extraordinary. Within days, 600 freight cars were on their way to U.S. ports filled with military equipment to be loaded aboard British merchant ships. These included half a million rifles and 900 old 75 mm field guns.

On 15 June, Churchill directly appealed to Roosevelt for 35 old U.S. destroyers. With Germany controlling both the Channel ports and Norway, Britain faced the prospect of defending against German invasion with but 68 destroyers fit for service, a stark contrast to the 433 destroyers possessed by the Royal Navy in 1918. Britain's shipping lanes were even more vulnerable to German submarines with the fall of France, and Italy's entry into the war had made the Mediterranean an area of difficult passage. As Churchill put it to Roosevelt, "We must ask therefore as a matter of life or death to be reinforced with these destroyers." Over the next days and weeks, as the number of these British warships continued to dwindle, Churchill's appeal grew to 50–60 destroyers. Roosevelt's insistence on proceeding with the aid went against the advice of Army Chief of Staff General George C. Marshall and Chief of Naval Operations Admiral Harold Stark, who believed that Britain was doomed and that such a step would strip America bare militarily before new production could materialize.

With American public opinion strongly against U.S. intervention, Roosevelt masked the transfer in a deal announced in an executive order on 3 September 1940 that was not subject to congressional approval. Britain received 50 World War I–vintage destroyers from the United States, in return granting the United States rights of 99-year leases to British bases in North America and the Caribbean Islands. The United States claimed that the agreement did not violate American neutrality because the British were providing access to naval bases and facilities deemed essential for American defense, including those in Newfoundland, Bermuda, British Guiana, Jamaica, Saint Lucia, and Trinidad. The Roosevelt administration maintained that the deal was an important step in ensuring national security and preventing the spread of the European war to the Americas.

Actually, the United States got far more than it gave. The destroyers were in wretched condition; some barely made it across the Atlantic. But the deal gave a tremendous boost to British morale at a critical juncture, and Churchill viewed this as another step by the United States toward outright participation. Privately, German leader Adolf Hitler saw this in much the same light. Anxious to unleash Japan in Asia to occupy the United States, he ordered talks opened with Japan that culminated in the Tripartite Pact of 27 September. The long war, a clash involving continents that would give advantage to nations with superior sea power, drew closer to realization. One of the destroyers, HMS *Campbeltown* (formerly the USS *Buchanan*) played a major role in the British destruction of the dry dock at Saint Nazaire, France, on 28 March 1942.

James T. Carroll and Spencer C. Tucker

See also
Churchill, Sir Winston L. S.; Dunkerque, Evacuation of; Hitler, Adolf; Marshall, George Catlett; Roosevelt, Franklin D.; Saint Nazaire, Raid on; Stark, Harold Raynsford "Betty"; Tripartite Pact

References
Lash, Joseph P. *Roosevelt and Churchill, 1939–1941: The Partnership That Saved the West.* New York: W. W. Norton, 1976.
Shogan, Robert. *Hard Bargain: How FDR Twisted Churchill's Arm, Evaded the Law, and Changed the Role of the American Presidency.* New York: Scribner, 1995.

Devers, Jacob Loucks (1887–1979)

U.S. Army general. Born on 8 September 1887 in York, Pennsylvania, Jacob Devers graduated from the U.S. Military Academy, West Point, in 1909 and was commissioned a second lieutenant of artillery. In 1912, he returned to West Point as an instructor.

During World War I, Devers was at Fort Sill, Oklahoma. In 1919, he served in the occupation of Germany and attended the French Artillery School at Treves before again teaching at West Point. Devers graduated from the General Staff College (1925) and the Army War College (1933). From 1936 to 1939 he was at West Point, where he was advanced to colonel.

After World War II began in Europe in 1939, Army Chief of Staff General George C. Marshall ordered Devers to place the Panama Canal Zone on a wartime footing. The next year, Devers was promoted to brigadier general. Following staff duty in Washington, he commanded the 9th Infantry Division at Fort Bragg, North Carolina. Supervising the rapid expansion of this base, he earned promotion to major general.

Known for his ability to train troops, Devers in July 1941 took command of the Armored Force at Fort Knox, Kentucky, and there he supervised the rapid expansion of U.S. armored forces. He soon became an enthusiastic advocate of mobile combined-arms warfare. Devers was promoted to lieutenant general in September 1942.

In May 1943, Devers took charge of U.S. Army ground forces in the European Theater of Operations (ETOUSA). He supervised the rapid U.S. buildup in Britain and hoped to lead the cross-Channel invasion. Instead, he was sent at the end of 1943 to the Mediterranean as deputy supreme Allied com-

Lieutenant General Jacob L. Devers, deputy commander in the Mediterranean Theatre, inspects a Punjab regiment 28 April 1944. (Hulton Archive)

mander there, replacing General Dwight D. Eisenhower. On 15 September 1944, Devers finally received the combat command he had long sought: the Sixth Army Group of 23 divisions, consisting of Lieutenant General Alexander Patch's Seventh Army and General Jean de Lattre de Tassigny's First French Army, which had invaded southern France in Operation DRAGOON. In March 1945, Devers was promoted to general and that same month his Sixth Army Group crossed the Rhine and drove into southern Germany and Austria, where he accepted the surrender of German forces on 6 May.

Devers commanded U.S. Army Ground Forces from 1945 to 1949 and retired in September 1949. He died in Washington, D.C., on 15 October 1979.

Brent B. Barth Jr.

See also
DRAGOON, Operation; Eisenhower, Dwight D.; Lattre de Tassigny, Jean Joseph Marie Gabriel de; Marshall, George Catlett; Patch, Alexander McCarrell, Jr.
References
Devers, Jacob L. *Report of Activities: Army Ground Forces.* Washington, DC: U.S. Army, 1946.
Perret, Geoffrey. *There's a War to Be Won: The United States Army in World War II.* New York: Random House, 1991.

Weigley, Russell F. *Eisenhower's Lieutenants: The Campaigns of France and Germany, 1944–1945.* Bloomington: Indiana University Press, 1981.
Wilt, Alan F. *The French Riviera Campaign of August 1944.* Carbondale: Southern Illinois University Press, 1981.

Dewey, Thomas Edmund (1902–1971)

U.S. politician and twice Republican Party candidate for president. Born on 24 March 1902 in Owosso, Michigan, Thomas Dewey graduated from the University of Michigan in 1923, received his law degree from Columbia University in 1925, and in 1926 was admitted to the New York bar. Dewey launched his government career five years later as chief assistant to the U.S. attorney for the southern district of New York. Dewey became U.S. attorney for the southern district of New York in 1935. Between 1935 and 1937, he garnered national attention as special prosecutor in an investigation of organized crime in New York, securing 72 convictions out of 73 prosecutions of long-established racketeers.

Dewey was district attorney of New York County in 1937 and 1938. Unsuccessful as the Republican candidate for governor of New York in 1938, Dewey won the state office for three successive terms beginning in 1942. As governor, he earned a reputation for political moderation and administrative efficiency, putting the state on a pay-as-you-go basis for capital building, reorganizing departments, and establishing the first state agency to eliminate racial and religious discrimination in employment.

The Republican nominee for U.S. president in 1944, Dewey was not able to overcome the enormous prestige of incumbent President Franklin D. Roosevelt, nor had he been expected to. Dewey refused to make an issue of the Pearl Harbor disaster of December 1941, but he charged the Democrats with inefficiencies in rearmament, an antibusiness stance, extravagance, and corruption. He also condemned Roosevelt's support of the Soviet Union. Roosevelt won the 1944 election with 25,606,585 popular votes and 432 electoral votes to Dewey's 22,321,018 popular votes and 99 electoral votes.

Dewey ran again for the presidency in 1948 against Roosevelt's successor, incumbent Harry S Truman. Although the pollsters predicted victory for Dewey, Truman won. Dewey then returned to private law practice. He died on 16 March 1971 in Bal Harbor, Florida.

John A. Komaromy

See also
Roosevelt, Franklin D.; Truman, Harry S; United States, Home Front
References
Donaldson, Gary A. *Truman Defeats Dewey.* Lexington: University Press of Kentucky, 2000.
Smith, Richard Northon. *Thomas Dewey and His Times.* New York: Simon and Schuster, 1982.

Stolberg, Mary M. *Fighting Organized Crime: Politics, Justice and the Legacy of Thomas E. Dewey.* Boston: Northeastern University Press, 1995.

Dieppe Raid (19 August 1942)

First major European amphibious operation of World War II. On 19 August 1942, a landing force of 5,000 Canadian and 1,000 British troops plus a token force of 60 U.S. Army Rangers raided the German-held French port of Dieppe on the English Channel. The raid, which was undertaken at the instigation of Chief of Combined Operations Lord Louis Mountbatten, was launched as a demonstration to the Soviet Union of Allied resolve and as a rehearsal for a subsequent major cross-Channel invasion. An assault, even a small one, could demonstrate to the people of occupied Europe that they were not forgotten and that eventual liberation was on the way.

Dieppe was selected because it was within range of fighter support from Britain and because wide beaches adjacent to the town provided good prospects for landing troops. German defenses were formidable. They included coastal artillery, an offshore minefield, nearby airfields, and the close proximity of troops who could rapidly reinforce the city's garrison.

Operation JUBILEE, as the raid was called, began before dawn on 19 August and ran into trouble early. The assault boats were discovered as they approached the landing site, and they then were fired on by five armed German trawlers. All hope for surprise was lost as the German defenders established a deadly crossfire on the beach in the predawn darkness. By 9:00 A.M. carnage reigned supreme, and the British commanders decided to withdraw the surviving troops. Allied destroyers escorted the rescue boats in under murderous German fire to extract the survivors.

By early afternoon, the rescue boats were headed back to England with the remnants of the Dieppe raiders, leaving 24 officers and 3,164 men behind who had been either killed or captured. The overall Allied personnel casualty rate was more than 40 percent, the highest of the war for any major offensive involving all three services. The Canadians suffered the worst; with 4,963 men, they made up 80 percent of the attackers, and

Allied soldiers stand guard over blindfolded German prisoners captured during the raid on Dieppe, France, in August 1942. (Library of Congress)

3,367 were casualties (907 killed). Some Canadians have called it the worst military disaster in their history. During the battle, 33 landing craft and 30 tanks were lost. Additionally, a destroyer was sunk by the Germans during the evacuation effort. The British lost 106 aircraft shot down; the Germans lost only 48.

The lessons of the failed operation, however bitter, were very important—both on the general points of how difficult it is to capture a defended port and how crucial is a preliminary bombardment to the more detailed lessons relating to equipment for beach landings. Equipment, organization, and command structure were all found sadly deficient. However, historians differ concerning the impact of these lessons on the planning and preparation for the subsequent North African landing in November 1942 and later Allied invasion of Normandy in June 1944. In any case, the Dieppe raid did bury the myth that a cross-Channel invasion would be possible in 1942, and it cast grave doubts for the success of such an operation even in 1943. It did not intimidate the Germans or cause them to transfer forces from the Eastern Front. Quite the contrary, it starkly demonstrated the pathetic state of Allied preparations to open a second front. The Dieppe raid was more than a political setback. Its most telling consequence was to dissuade Prime Minister Winston L. S. Churchill and the British chiefs of staff from any commitment to cross-Channel operations.

James H. Willbanks

See also
Amphibious Warfare; Canada, Army; Churchill, Sir Winston L. S.; Mountbatten, Louis Francis Albert Victor Nicholas; Normandy Invasion and Campaign

References
Thompson, R. W. *At Whatever Cost: The Story of the Dieppe Raid.* New York: Coward-McCann, 1957.
Villa, Brian. *Unauthorized Action: Mountbatten and the Dieppe Raid, 1940.* New York: Oxford University Press, 1990.
Whitehead, William. *Dieppe, 1942: Echoes of Disaster.* Toronto, Canada: Personal Library, 1979.

In early 1940, Dietrich received command of the Leibstandarte SS Adolf Hitler (LSSAH), which became a panzer-grenadier division in 1942. With it he took part in the invasions of France, Greece, and the Soviet Union. When the western Allies landed in Normandy in June 1944, Dietrich commanded the 1st SS Panzer Corps, and in September Hitler gave him command of the Sixth SS Panzer Army. Dietrich was awarded the Reich's highest decoration, the Diamonds to the Iron Cross, and in August 1944 he was promoted to the rank of Oberstgruppenführer. His army played an important part in the December 1944 Ardennes Offensive, but it was unable to realize Hitler's far-reaching expectations.

Dietrich then fought on the Eastern Front. His last offensive, which was in Hungary during March 1945, failed. Dietrich, to that point the prototype of the National Socialist soldier, lost Hitler's confidence because he questioned Hitler's directives and ordered the retreat of his exhausted troops.

After the war, Dietrich was found guilty of being responsible for the execution of U.S. prisoners of war (the Malmédy trial) and was sentenced to 25 years' imprisonment. Dietrich served only 10 years, but he was later arrested again and charged for murders committed in 1934. He was sentenced to only 18 months in prison. Dietrich died at Ludwigsburg on 21 April 1966.

Martin Moll

See also
Allied Military Tribunals after the War; Ardennes Offensive; France, Battle for; France Campaign; Greece Campaign; Hausser, Paul "Papa"; Himmler, Heinrich; Hitler, Adolf; Malmédy Massacre; Normandy Invasion and Campaign; Peiper, Joachim; Waffen-SS

References
Messenger, Charles. *Hitler's Gladiator: The Life and Times of Oberstgruppenführer and Panzergeneraloberst der Waffen-SS Sepp Dietrich.* London: Brassey's Defence Publishers, 1988.
Weingartner, James J. *Hitler's Guard: The Story of the Leibstandarte SS Adolf Hitler, 1933–1945.* Nashville, TN: Battery Press, 1989.

Dietrich, Josef "Sepp" (1892–1966)

German Schutzstaffel (SS) general and commander of Leibstandarte, a bodyguard unit responsible for Adolf Hitler's personal safety. Born on 28 May 1892 in Hawangen, Bavaria, Josef Dietrich volunteered for the army in 1914 and became a crewman in one of Germany's first tanks. After the war, Dietrich was active in the Freikorps before joining the National Socialist Party and the SS in 1928. He was selected as one of Hitler's bodyguards and was in charge of the buildup of the Leibstandarte. In the Blood Purge of July 1934, Dietrich led an execution squad in the elimination of the leadership of the Sturmabteilung (SA, Storm Troopers).

Dill, Sir John Greer (1881–1944)

British Army field marshal, chief of the Imperial General Staff (CIGS), and member of the Combined Chiefs of Staff (CCS). Born in Belfast, Ireland, on 25 December 1881, Dill was commissioned in the British army on graduation from the Royal Military Academy at Sandhurst in 1901. He fought in the latter stages of the 1899–1902 South African (Boer) War.

On the outbreak of World War I, Dill was a student at the Staff College of Camberley. He then held staff positions with units on the Western Front, but he also saw action and was wounded. Considered an exceptional staff officer, Dill was transferred to the operations branch, general headquarters,

Gen. Josef Dietrich, former commander of the Sixth SS Panzer Army (11); Gen. Fritz Kraemer, chief of staff to Dietrich (33); and Lt. Gen. Herman Priess, former commanding general of the I SS Panzer Corps of the Sixth Panzer Army (45) and others on trial at Dachau for the massacre of American troops at Malmédy, Belgium. (Bettman/Corbis)

and he ended the war as the head of that branch and a temporary brigadier general.

Dill served in a variety of posts after the war. In 1930 he was promoted to major general, and the next year he was appointed to head the Staff College. In 1934, he became director of operations and intelligence at the War Office. At the outset of World War II, Dill received command of I Corps but did not see action. In April 1940, he was appointed vice chief of the Imperial General Staff and succeeded Field Marshal Sir Edmund Ironside as CIGS in late May 1940. His term as CIGS was a rough one. He presided during the British military withdrawal from continental Europe and the Battle of Britain, when the United Kingdom seemed on the brink of destruction. He never got along well with Prime Minister Winston L. S. Churchill, who regarded him as too cautious. In November, the government announced that Dill would retire the next month when he reached age 60 and would be named governor-designate of Bombay, India. In recognition of his

services, he was promoted to field marshal. This was done to make room for General Alan Brooke to become CIGS. As CIGS, Brooke was Dill's staunch supporter and friend. He convinced Churchill in a meeting on 11 December 1941 that Dill should accompany the prime minister to the United States and then remain for duty with the British Joint Staff Mission.

As the Combined Chiefs of Staff were formed in January 1942, Dill became the available man to chair the British Joint Staff Mission in Washington, a new strategic organization charged with coordinating British and American strategy and logistics within the CCS. Despite his poor health, Dill soon found his way into the hearts and minds of his American colleagues, and he succeeded in a demanding assignment. He got along well with U.S. President Franklin D. Roosevelt and Army Chief of Staff General George C. Marshall. Dill became the resilient link—and the buffer—between two nations joined in a sometimes uneasy partnership at war.

Dill died in Washington on 4 November 1944 and was buried in Arlington National Cemetery, the only foreign officer ever afforded that distinction. The U.S. Congress honored him with a joint resolution in December 1944. On 1 November 1950, a magnificent equestrian statue of Dill was dedicated in Arlington Cemetery. He was awarded the American Distinguished Service Medal posthumously and had been knighted in 1937 by his own nation.

John F. Votaw

See also
Brooke, Sir Alan Francis; Churchill, Sir Winston L. S.; Combined Chiefs of Staff; Dunkerque, Evacuation of; Marshall, George Catlett; Roosevelt, Franklin D.

References
Danchev, Alex. *Very Special Relationship: Field-Marshal Sir John Dill and the Anglo-American Alliance 1941–44.* London: Brassey's, 1986.
———. *Establishing the Anglo-American Alliance: The Second World War Diaries of Brigadier Vivian Dykes.* London: Brassey's, 1990.
Danchev, Alex, and Daniel Todman, eds. *War Diaries 1939–1945: Field Marshal Lord Alanbrooke.* Berkeley and Los Angeles: University of California Press, 2001.

Displaced Persons (DPs)

The term *displaced person* (DP) was often used for refugees who at the end of the war in Europe were living outside their prewar national boundaries and needed assistance. In 1942, Great Britain and the United States solicited support from the other Allied powers for help in dealing with the expected masses of slave laborers, prisoners of war, and political prisoners in Germany and its conquered territories. These efforts culminated in November 1943 when 44 nations signed the Agreement for United Nations Relief and Rehabilitation Administration (UNRRA), the first international organization created to help to wartime refugees. As the United States would be contributing about 40 percent of UNRRA's budget, an American, former New York governor Herbert Lehman, became its first director.

UNRRA planned to provide DPs with housing, food, clothing, and other necessities until each person could be "repatriated" to his or her home nation. This did not take into account the fact that many DPs, especially Jews and ethnic Germans from eastern Europe, could not safely return home. Others, particularly Poles and Czechs, did not want to return to home nations occupied by the Soviet army. The estimated two-year time frame for UNRRA to carry out its tasks was also wildly optimistic.

UNRRA field teams for dealing with DPs were made up of multinational groups of about a dozen men and women per team. They were selected for language skills and backgrounds in administration, social work, medicine, or various mechanical abilities. In 1944, these teams began to assume administration of refugee camps that Allied military forces had established in North Africa and Italy. Teams had to rely on the Allied military for additional personnel, transportation, and assistance in enforcing the UNRRA regulations at the camps. Some local commanders were quite helpful; others were indifferent or even hostile to UNRRA. This problem lessened somewhat when the Supreme Headquarters, Allied Expeditionary Forces (SHAEF) named U.S. Major General Allen Gullion, former provost marshal general of the army and an efficient organizer, as the head of its own displaced persons branch.

By the end of the war in Europe, SHAEF and UNRRA had identified more than 10 million refugees in and around Germany. Others in Soviet-controlled areas were never accurately counted. Most DPs, primarily the former prisoners of war and slave laborers from western Europe, were repatriated before the end of 1945. But nearly 800,000 others remained and were housed in DP camps across occupied Germany.

DP camps were built from German army barracks, depots, and even some former concentration camps. In some areas, neighborhoods and entire villages became "DP towns." UNRRA organized most camps by nationality, having learned that mixed camps too often led to violence. Since DPs were permitted to move freely, over time camps took on specific national and cultural identities. This ethnic concentration was reinforced by the practice of allowing each camp to elect a governing council and maintain its own police force.

UNRRA and the military enforced occupation regulations against black marketing and the like. Throughout 1946, the DP population fluctuated; many Poles and others returned to their home countries. There were still several hundred facilities housing DPs in 1947, when the International Refugee Organization replaced UNRRA as the administrator of refugee matters. Conditions in the camps were crowded, an average of 100 sq ft or less of space allotted to families of five or more people. Food remained scarce, and daily diets in the camps seldom exceeded 2,000 calories and were often less. Packages of food from America and the International Red Cross helped somewhat. As the Cold War intensified, DP populations grew again when individuals and families fled Poland and the other eastern European nations for the west.

Finding permanent homes for these masses of men, women, and children taxed the energies of Europe and the world well into the 1950s. At first, nations such as Belgium, Australia, and Canada accepted only single men who were willing to work in mining, forestry, and other heavy-labor jobs. Great Britain, albeit with some reluctance, permitted Jewish survivors of the Holocaust into Palestine and made room at home for Polish soldiers who had fought with the United Kingdom during the war.

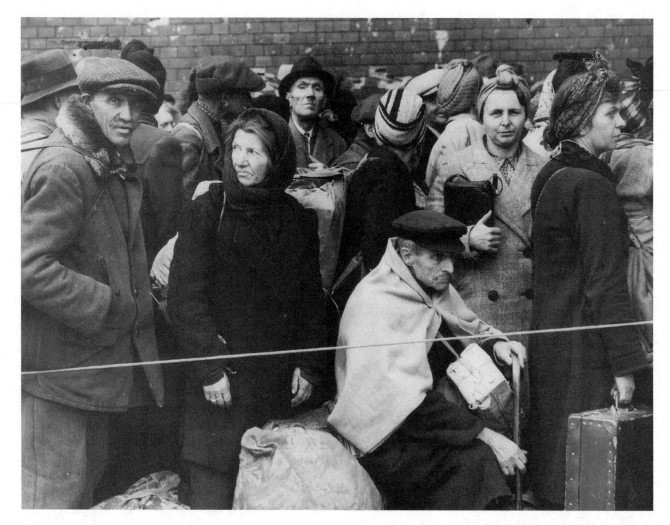

German displaced persons, carrying their few belongings as they wait in Berlin's Anhalter Station to leave the German capital in 1945. (Library of Congress)

The United States moved slowly in passing legislation to accept DP immigrants. The resulting 1948 law had long waiting periods, quotas, and other restrictions similar to those of the 1930s, but through it increasing numbers of former DPs came to the United States. Ethnic Germans obtained a plurality of American visas because they received considerable help from American church groups. Ultimately, more than 580,000 DPs settled in the United States between 1949 and 1957—more than half of the total number of DPs who went to some 113 countries by the end of the 1950s. The last DP camp closed in 1957. Those who had not found a home elsewhere, mostly the old and infirm, then became the responsibility of the government of the Federal Republic of Germany.

The DP program was an extraordinary experiment in international cooperation to salvage wrecked lives. At the camps, many refugees received the first decent treatment they had known in years. Some were able to take advantage of educational opportunities and learn new trades that increased their chances for immigration. Most of these men, women, and children eventually found new homes somewhere in the world. But it took far longer to achieve this than the originators of the program had expected, and by then new struggles had been ignited in the Middle East and in Korea that produced new refugee populations. These made it clear that the world had not seen the end of the problem of displaced persons.

Terry Shoptaugh

See also

Holocaust, The

References

Hulme, Kathryn. *The Wild Place*. Boston: Little, Brown, 1953.

Proudfoot, Malcolm J. *European Refugees, 1939–1952*. London: Faber and Faber, 1956.

Wyman, Mark. *DP: Europe's Displaced Persons, 1945–1951*. London: Associated University Press, 1989.

Dixie Mission to Yan'an (Yenan) (July 1944–March 1947)

U.S. Army Observer Group sent to Yan'an (Yenan), China, to establish a liaison with Chinese Communist forces. The Dixie Mission began in July 1944 when a nine-man U.S. Army team flew to the headquarters of Chinese Communist leader Mao Zedong (Mao Tse-tung) at Yan'an in Shaanxi (Shensi) Province in north central China. Colonel David D. Barrett, a "China hand" who had studied the language and served as a military attaché to China, headed the mission, which would continue through 1947. It included officer and enlisted personnel from all three services as well as representatives of the U.S. State Department. Barrett's mission was to collect information about Japanese and their "puppet" Chinese forces order of battle and operations. He was also to determine the extent of the Communist military effort in the war against Japan and to coordinate the search and rescue of downed Allied pilots in Communist-controlled areas.

A U.S. military mission to the Communists had first been suggested in mid-1943. Lieutenant General Joseph Stilwell's political adviser, John Paton Davies, believed strongly that U.S. advisers to Mao's headquarters could make a difference by coordinating with Chinese Communists who were fighting the Japanese. Davies drew parallels to the effort of the Allies to assist the Partisans of Tito (Josip Broz) in Yugoslavia. Fearing that American supplies and equipment would be diverted to the Communists and that U.S. leadership might develop a more favorable view of the Chinese Communist movement and operations in the territories held by them, Generalissimo Jiang Jieshi (Chiang Kai-shek) strongly opposed the mission to Yan'an. For the next year, the United States continued to pressure Jiang to allow this mission to go forward, but not until after the June 1944 visit of U.S. Vice President Henry A. Wallace could sufficient pressure be exerted on Jiang to allow the liaison mission to begin.

Communist official representative to the national government at Chongqing (Chungking) Zhou Enlai (Chou En-lai), who saw potential in a future collaboration between the United States and the Red Army in the fight against the Japanese, supported an increase in American presence and the liaison effort. By August 1944, Barrett and a team that eventually numbered more than 20 people, including State Department officials John S. Service and Raymond P. Ludden, began to meet with the most senior political and military leadership of the Communist movement and to gather information about the Japanese and their allies as well as the Chinese Communists. The mission also provided the opportunity in November for Major General Patrick J. Hurley, in his capacity as a special emissary of U.S. President Franklin D. Roosevelt, to begin an effort to get the two Chinese factions to focus their efforts on fighting the Japanese rather than each other. During the course of the mission, the Dixie group secured the rescue and return of more than 100 American pilots.

The mission served perhaps its most important function after the war as a bridge between the United States and the Chinese Communists. A mission headed by General George C. Marshall brought the two sides to the negotiating table in an effort to secure a solution to the infighting in China that had been going on for decades. The collapse of the Marshall mission in January 1947 led to the end of the observer mission.

J. G. D. Babb

See also
China, Civil War in; China, Role in War; Jiang Jieshi; Mao Zedong; Stilwell, Joseph Warren; Zhou Enlai

References
Barrett, David D. *Dixie Mission: The United States Army Observer Group in Yenan, 1944.* China Research Monograph Number Six. Berkeley: University of California Press, 1970.

Carter, Carolle J. *Mission to Yenan: American Liaison to the Chinese Communists, 1944–1947.* Lexington: University Press of Kentucky, 1997.

Romanus, Charles F., and Riley Sunderland. *Stilwell's Command Problems.* Washington, DC: U.S. Government Printing Office, 1985.

Djugashvili, Iosif Vissarionovich

See Stalin, Josef.

Dodecanese Islands

The islands of the southern Aegean Sea off the southwest coast of Anatolia were known through much of their history as the eastern or southern Sporades ("scattered"). The islands include Rhodes, Karpathos, Kassos, Haliki, Kastellorizo (Castlerosso), Alimia, Tilos, Symi (Simi), Nissyros, Kos (Cos), Pserimos, Astypalea, Kalymnos, Telendhos, Leros, Lipsi, Patmos, Arki, and Agnthonissi. Early in the twentieth century, the Young Turks revoked the historic privileges enjoyed by the islanders, who were part of the Ottoman Empire. Twelve islands (*dhodkeka nisia*) joined in a failed protest against the loss of these privileges, and the name of *Dodecanese* stuck as a term for all these islands, even though they exceeded 12 in number.

In 1912, as a consequence of the Italo-Turkish War, the Dodecanese Islands passed to Italian control. In 1941, the Germans joined their Italian allies in garrisoning the islands, which were inhabited chiefly by Greeks. The Italians had naval and air bases on Rhodes, the strategic key to the area. There was also an airfield on Kos, a seaplane base and naval batteries at Leros, and an air base on Scarpanto.

When Italy surrendered on 8 September 1943, the Dodecanese were occupied by two poorly equipped Italian divisions totaling 37,000 men; Italian morale was very low. The Germans had one division of 7,000 men, which was well equipped with tanks and artillery. The local Greek population was excited at the prospect of liberation by the Allied powers.

British Prime Minister Winston L. S. Churchill ordered that operations be conducted against the Dodecanese Islands. He believed that success there would open the way to the Dardanelles and the Balkans. He also sought to induce Turkey to join the war and to remove the stain of Britain's defeat in World War I at Gallipoli. The original plan for an invasion of the Dodecanese, prepared by the Middle East Command, was known as Operation MANDIBLES, but it was subsequently renamed Operation ACCOLADE. Churchill appealed to President Franklin D. Roosevelt and to General Dwight D. Eisenhower for aid to liberate the Dodecanese. The Americans, who were preparing a landing on the Italian peninsula at Salerno, rebuffed him. Roosevelt also suspected that the British hoped to open a new front in the Balkans. Coincidentally, the Combined Chiefs of Staff meeting in Quebec ordered most of the landing ships in the Middle East to the Indian Ocean, which starved the operation of needed assets.

When Italy surrendered on 8 September 1943, three British operatives led by Major Lord George Jellicoe parachuted onto Rhodes. They contacted Italian authorities there and urged them to take the Germans prisoner. However, Admiral Inigo Campioni, commander of Italian forces in the Aegean, hesitated. The Germans, meanwhile, acted swiftly and soon subdued the Italians.

The British nonetheless proceeded with some landings, and by October 1943—with a force of 5,000 men and a small flotilla—they secured several islands, among them Kos, Samos, Patmos, and Leros. They were not able, however, either to gain air superiority or take Rhodes, and as long as the Germans were secure at Rhodes, the British could not hold the Dodecanese.

On 3 October 1943, the Germans went on the offensive, attacking Kos. Heavy bombing of the island by Stuka aircraft reduced the British defenses, and soon the British force there surrendered. Churchill refused to consider a withdrawal, instead ordering that Leros and Samos be held at all costs. Indeed, the British reinforced Leros. On 12 November, the Germans attacked Leros with overwhelming force, taking it four days later. The British troops remaining in the Dodecanese then withdrew.

Among British units involved were the Long Range Desert Group, the Special Boat Squadron, the Raiding Forces' Levant Schooner Flotilla, the King's Own, the Royal Irish Fusiliers, and the Durham Light Infantry. The Greek navy provided 7 destroyers to assist the more numerous British vessels. In the offensive, the British lost 4 cruisers damaged and 2 submarines, 6 destroyers, and 10 small coastal vessels and minesweepers sunk. The Royal Air Force flew 3,746 sorties and lost 113 aircraft out of 288 involved. The British army lost in all about 4,800 men, while the Italians lost 5,350. German casualties totaled some 1,184 men, 35,000 tons of shipping (between late September and late November 1943), and 15 small landing craft and ferries. The operation failed as a consequence of Campioni's hesitation, German aggressiveness, noncooperation by the Americans, and the inadequacy of British resources. Holding the islands, however, stretched German resources, ultimately tying down some 60,000 Germans who might have been better employed elsewhere.

After the war, the British governed the Dodecanese until 1947. The islands were then turned over to Greece.

A. J. L. Waskey

See also

Cephallonia Island; Churchill, Sir Winston L. S.; Eisenhower, Dwight D.; Ismay, Hastings Lionel; Roosevelt, Franklin D.; Wilson, Henry Maitland

References

Churchill, Winston S. *The Second World War.* Vol. 5, *Closing the Ring.* Boston: Houghton Mifflin, 1951.

Gander, Marsland L. *The Long Road to Leros.* London: Macdonald, 1945.

Greene, Jack, and Alessandro Massignani. *The Naval War in the Mediterranean, 1940–1943.* London: Chatham, 1998.

Holland, Jeffrey. *The Aegean Mission: Allied Operations in the Dodecanese, 1943.* Westport, CT: Greenwood Press, 1988.

Molony, C. J. C., et al. *The Mediterranean and Middle East.* United Kingdom Military Series, J. R. M. Butler, ed. Vol. 5, *History of the Second World War.* London: Her Majesty's Stationery Office, 1973.

Pitt, Barrie. *Special Boat Squadron.* London: Century Publishing, 1983.

Smith, Peter, and Edwin Walker. *War in the Aegean.* London: William Kimber, 1974.

Dönitz, Karl (1891–1980)

German navy admiral who commanded the U-boats and later the full Kriegsmarine and then succeeded Adolf Hitler as head of the Third Reich. Born in Gruenau-bei-Berlin on 16 September 1891, Karl Dönitz joined the German navy in 1910. During World War I, he served on the cruiser *Breslau*, but he transferred to U-boats in 1916, commanding several submarines in the Mediterranean. In October 1918, his *U-68* attacked an Allied convoy, sinking one of the ships. His sub-

The commanding officer of the U-boats, Admiral Karl Dönitz (left), congratulating German U-boat sailors upon their return to port, May 1942. (Library of Congress)

marine was forced to the surface when it developed mechanical problems, and Dönitz was taken prisoner.

Dönitz continued in the navy after World War I. He held a variety of shore and sea assignments including command of a torpedo-boat flotilla, during which he experimented with tactics he would later develop into the *Rudeltaktik* (wolf pack) concept. German Chancellor Adolf Hitler named Dönitz commander of the fledgling German submarine force in 1935. Kapitän zue See und Kommodore (captain and commodore) Dönitz sought to build additional submarines to expand the fleet to 300 boats, a number he believed would be decisive in winning the next war. Dönitz's passionate advocacy of submarines led to friction between him and the commander of the navy, Grand Admiral Erich Raeder, who preferred to allocate scarce naval resources to a long-range program of conventional large surface ships. Their differences became moot when World War II began before either type was fully ready for decisive employment.

Promoted to Konteradmiral (U.S. equiv. rear admiral) in October 1939, Dönitz struggled to overcome the problems of insufficient numbers of U-boats and ineffective torpedoes, difficulties that nearly wrecked his operations. To combat Allied convoys, Dönitz implemented wolf pack tactics: centralized control over groups of U-boats that struck Allied convoys at night in surface attacks. In January 1943, Hitler, frustrated by the performance of his surface navy, removed Raeder and replaced him with Dönitz as head of the navy. Dönitz endeavored to continue the U-boat war, but during "Black May" in 1943, his U-boats were essentially defeated through Allied antisubmarine countermeasures including aircraft, convoys, searchlights, radar, sonar, and the ability to read Germany's encoded radio messages.

Unlike virtually all other senior German military officers, Dönitz managed to retain Hitler's confidence and favor. Dönitz's final military success was the evacuation of hundreds of thousands of Germans from the Baltic states by sea. As the Allied armies entered Germany on 15 April 1945, Hitler appointed Dönitz as commander of all forces in northern Germany. On 30 April, the day that Hitler committed suicide, Dönitz was informed that Hitler had appointed him to serve as president of the Reich and supreme commander of the armed forces. Dönitz then led the crumbling Third Reich, hoping to delay Soviet advances to allow millions of German troops and civilians to flee westward to British and U.S. lines to avoid falling into Soviet hands. Dönitz surrendered Germany unconditionally to Allied representatives on 7 May 1945.

The British arrested Dönitz on 23 May. Tried by the International War Crimes Tribunal at Nuremberg, Dönitz was found guilty of crimes against peace and violation of the rules of war and was sentenced to 10 years in Spandau Prison. He was released in 1956 and later wrote several books about his career and about submarine warfare. Unrepentant about his role in the war, Dönitz died in Aumuhle, Federal Republic of Germany, on 24 December 1980.

Steven J. Rauch

See also
Atlantic, Battle of the; Germany, Navy; International Military Tribunal: The Nuremberg Trials; Raeder, Erich; Wolf Pack
References
Doenitz, Karl. *Memoirs: Ten Years and Twenty Days.* Trans. R. H. Stevens in collaboration with David Woodward. Annapolis, MD: Naval Institute Press, 1990.
Edwards, Bernard. *Dönitz and the Wolf Packs.* London: Cassell, 1999.
Padfield, Peter. *Dönitz, the Last Führer: Portrait of a Nazi War Leader.* New York: Harper and Row, 1984.

Director of the OSS, William Joseph Donovan. (Library of Congress)

Donovan, William Joseph (1883–1959)

Head of the U.S. Office of Strategic Services (OSS). Born on 1 January 1883, in Buffalo, New York, William Donovan graduated from Columbia University with a law degree in 1907 and afterward practiced law in Buffalo. He also served as a captain in the New York National Guard. He was stationed along the Mexican border in 1916 when the guard was called up to assist in the unsuccessful effort to capture notorious Mexican bandit and revolutionary leader Pancho Villa.

After the United States entered World War I, Donovan was sent to Europe with the American Expeditionary Forces (AEF). As a major, he commanded 1st Battalion of the 69th New York Infantry Regiment in the 45th Infantry Division. Donovan took part in the September 1918 Saint Mihiel offensive. Then a lieutenant colonel, he was wounded but refused evacuation and stayed to lead his men. His actions brought him the Medal of Honor and the nickname of "Wild Bill."

After the war, Donovan returned to Buffalo to practice law. From 1924 to 1929, he was an assistant U.S. attorney general. He ran unsuccessfully for state political office and in 1929 moved to New York City. Much interested in international affairs, Donovan undertook several overseas missions for the Rockefeller Foundation and the Franklin D. Roosevelt administration. Donovan tried to convince Roosevelt and others that the United States needed an intelligence-gathering organization similar to that run by the British. His

efforts finally led to his appointment in July 1941 as head of the Office of Coordinator of Information, which after the Japanese attack on Pearl Harbor became the Office of Strategic Services (OSS). It gathered intelligence, conducted propaganda and sabotage, and assisted partisans.

After World War II, Donovan lobbied President Harry S Truman to set up a permanent intelligence organization. Truman initially rejected this step, but the coming of the Cold War led in 1947 to the formation of the Central Intelligence Agency, loosely modeled on the OSS. Donovan's hope of heading the CIA was not realized, although he briefly returned to government service as ambassador to Thailand during 1953 and 1954. Donovan died on 8 February 1959 at Walter Reed Army Medical Center, Washington, D.C.

Graham Carssow

See also
Cold War, Origins and Early Course of; Partisans; Roosevelt, Franklin D.; Truman, Harry S
References
Cave Brown, Anthony. *The Last Hero: Wild Bill Donovan.* New York: Times Books, 1982.
Dunlop, Richard. *Donovan, America's Master Spy.* Chicago: Rand McNally, 1982.
Ford, Corey. *Donovan of OSS.* Boston: Little, Brown, 1970.
Troy, Thomas F. *Wild Bill and Intrepid: Donovan, Stephenson, and the Origin of CIA.* New Haven, CT: Yale University Press, 1996.

Doolittle, James Harold "Jimmy" (1896–1993)

U.S. Army Air Forces (later Air Force) general. Born on 14 December 1896 in Alameda, California, James Doolittle grew up in Nome, Alaska. He attended Los Angeles Community College and the University of California, but he left school following the entry of the United States into World War I and enlisted as a flying cadet in the Signal Corps Reserve. He attended flight school, became a pilot, and was commissioned a second lieutenant. He then served as a flight-gunner instructor at Rockwell Field in San Diego, California. His request for assignment to France was denied because of the armistice of November 1918.

In 1920, Doolittle secured a Regular Army commission, and on 4 September 1922, he made the first transcontinental flight in less than 24 hours. He then studied at the Massachusetts Institute of Technology, where he received master's and Ph.D. degrees in aeronautical engineering. A leader in advances in both military and civilian aviation, Doolittle helped develop horizontal and directional gyroscopes and pioneered instrument flying.

Doolittle gained prominence through stunt flying, racing, and demonstrating aircraft. In 1930, he left the army to become aviation manager for Shell Oil, where he helped develop new high-octane aviation fuels that greatly benefited the United States in World War II. He won the Harmon (1930) and Bendix (1931) trophies, and in 1932 he broke the world airspeed record.

In July 1940, Doolittle returned to the army as a major. Following U.S. entry into World War II, in January 1942 he was promoted to lieutenant colonel. On 18 April 1942, Doolittle commanded the first American air strike on the Japanese mainland. The raid was a great fillip for U.S. morale, and for it he was awarded the Medal of Honor and promoted to brigadier general.

In July 1942, Doolittle took command of the Twelfth Air Force in England, which he led in Operation TORCH in North Africa. In November 1943, he was given command of the Fifteenth Air Force in the Mediterranean Theater, directing it in raids against German-held Europe. In January 1944, he assumed command of the Eighth Air Force in the European Theater, and that March he was promoted to temporary lieutenant general. On Germany's surrender in May 1945, Doolittle moved with the Eighth Air Force to Okinawa, although the Eighth arrived in the Pacific Theater too late to see much action.

In May 1946, Doolittle returned to the civilian sector as a vice president for Shell Oil, and later he became its director. He also served on the National Advisory Committee for Aeronautics, the Air Force Science Advisory Board, and the Presi-

Major General James "Jimmy" Doolittle, who led the audacious April 1942 bombing raid on Japan. (Hulton Archive)

dent's Science Advisory Committee. In June 1985 by act of Congress Doolittle was promoted to general on the retired list. He died on 27 September 1993 in Pebble Beach, California.

Sean K. Duggan

See also
Halsey, William Frederick, Jr.; Normandy Invasion and Campaign; Okinawa, Invasion of; Pearl Harbor, Attack on; Strategic Bombing; Tokyo, Bombing of (18 April 1942)

References
Doolittle, James H., with Carroll V. Glines. *I Could Never Be So Lucky Again: An Autobiography by General James H. "Jimmy" Doolittle.* Atglen, PA: Schiffer, 1991.
Glines, Carroll V. *Doolittle's Tokyo Raiders.* Salem, NH: Ayer, 1964.
Merrill, James M. *Target Tokyo: The Halsey-Doolittle Raid.* New York: Rand McNally, 1964.
Thomas, Lowell, and Edward Jablonski. *Doolittle: A Biography.* Garden City, NY: Doubleday, 1976.

Douglas, William Sholto (First Baron Douglas of Kirtleside) (1893–1969)

British air chief marshal. Born on 23 December 1893 at Headington, Oxfordshire, William Douglas was raised in London. He attended Oxford University but left to join the Royal Field Artillery at the start of World War I. Douglas soon transferred to the Royal Flying Corps, where he qualified as a fighter pilot. By the end of the war he rose to squadron commander.

In 1919, Douglas left the military to become a test pilot with the Handley Page Aircraft Company. He was dissatisfied with civilian life and returned to the Royal Air Force (RAF) in 1920 as a squadron commander. He attended the Imperial Defense College. In 1936, Douglas was named director of staff studies at the Air Ministry; he was the only fighter pilot on the senior staff. Advanced to air vice marshal, in 1938 he became assistant chief of the air staff with responsibility for training.

Douglas was a leading critic of the tactics employed by head of Fighter Command Air Chief Marshal Hugh Dowding. On 25 November 1940, Douglas succeeded Dowding as head of Fighter Command as air marshal. Among his innovations was the Big Wing concept of large formations of fighters employed in massive sweeps. He also encouraged development of night-fighting equipment and techniques. Although his new tactics enjoyed some success, critics complained that they left much of the British homeland unprotected.

In December 1942, Douglas was promoted to air chief marshal and assigned to the Middle East Air Force (MEAF) as deputy to Air Marshal Arthur Tedder. With the reorganization of Allied air forces in April 1943, Douglas assumed command of the MEAF. During the June 1944 Allied landings in Normandy, Douglas was chief of Coastal Command and commander of British Expeditionary Air Force with the mission of securing control of the English Channel.

With the return of peace, Douglas commanded the British Air Forces of Occupation and was knighted. Promoted to marshal of the RAF, in June 1946 he followed Field Marshal Bernard Montgomery as commander of British forces in Europe and military governor of the British occupation zone in Germany.

Douglas retired from active duty in 1948 and was awarded a peerage as First Baron Douglas of Kirtleside. He assumed a seat in the House of Lords and served on the boards of the two British state airlines. After completing two autobiographies, William Sholto Douglas died in Northampton on 29 October 1969.

Pamela Feltus

See also

Air Warfare; Britain, Battle of; Dowding, Sir Hugh Caswall Tremenheere; Fighter Tactics; Great Britain, Air Force; Normandy Invasion and Campaign; Tedder, Sir Arthur William

Royal Air Force Air Chief Marshal William Sholto Douglas, 24 November 1940. (Photo by Central Press/Getty Images)

References

Douglas, William Sholto, with Robert Wright. *Sholto Douglas—Combat and Command: The Story of an Airman in Two World Wars.* New York: Simon and Schuster, 1966.

Oliver, David. *RAF Fighter Command.* London: Trafalgar Square Publishers, 2000.

Richards, Denis, and Hilary St. George Saunders. *The Royal Air Force, 1939–1945.* Rev. ed. 3 vols. London: Her Majesty's Stationery Office, 1974–1975.

Douhet, Giulio (1869–1930)

Italian air force general and pioneer of strategic air doctrine. Born on 30 May 1869 in Caserta, Italy, Giulio Douhet was commissioned in the Italian Army in 1892. An early advocate of military aviation, he led Italy's first air bombardment unit during the Italo-Turkish War (1911–1912). During World War I, his unbridled criticism of Italy's General Staff led to Douhet's court-martial and dismissal. Recalled to active service after the defeat at Caporetto, which vindicated much of his comment, he took charge of the Central Aeronautical Bureau (1918). After the war he retired and in 1921 he wrote *Il dominio dell'aria (Command of the Air)*, a seminal work on airpower strategy. That same year he became a brigadier general. A strong supporter of fascism, Douhet won appointment in 1922 from Benito Mussolini as chief of Italy's aviation program.

Having witnessed Italy's costly and futile World War I campaigns on the Isonzo and the bitterness of land combat in the Alps, Douhet argued that strategic bombing attacks by heavily armed and armored "battleplanes" promised quick and decisive victories in future wars. Such a thrusting and offensive-minded approach conformed well to fascist beliefs. The fascist Douhet believed that civilian populations would panic under sustained attack; the seemingly inherent fragility of democracies proved a seductive chimera to him.

Disregarding the legality and morality of sneak attacks or the utility of graduated approaches to warfare, Douhet called for all-out preemptive air strikes to destroy an enemy's air force and bases, followed by concerted attacks on industry and civilians. A combination of high-explosive, incendiary, and poison-gas bombs, Douhet concluded, would generate psychological uproar and social chaos, fatally weakening the enemy's will to resist.

In arguing that airpower was inherently offensive and uniquely efficacious, Douhet dismissed friendly escort planes as superfluous, enemy interceptors as ineffectual, and interservice cooperation as unnecessary since battleplanes would render navies and armies obsolete. Results of the Allied Combined Bomber Offensive, however, proved Douhet wrong. He had exaggerated the destructive power and accuracy of bombing, the ability of bombers to fight their way unescorted to targets, and the fragility of democratic populations, who proved resilient under attack. Nevertheless, Douhet's call for independent air forces and offensive-minded strategic bombing proved influential, especially in Britain and the United States.

Douhet died in Rome on 15 February 1930.

William J. Astore

See also
Air Warfare; Mussolini, Benito

References

Cappelluti, Frank J. "The Life and Thought of Giulio Douhet." Doctoral dissertation, Rutgers University, 1967.

Douhet, Giulio. *The Command of the Air.* Trans. Dino Ferrari. Washington, DC: Office of Air Force History, 1983.

MacIsaac, David. "Voices from the Central Blue: The Air Power Theorists." In Peter Paret, ed., *Makers of Modern Strategy: Machiavelli to the Nuclear Age,* 624–647. Princeton, NJ: Princeton University Press, 1986.

Segrè, Claudio G. "Giulio Douhet: Strategist, Theorist, Prophet?" *Journal of Strategic Studies* 15 (September 1992), 351–366.

Dowding, Sir Hugh Caswall Tremenheere (First Baron Dowding) (1882–1970)

British air force marshal. Born 24 April 1882 in Moffat, Scotland, Hugh Dowding was educated at Winchester and the Royal Military Academy, Woolwich. Commissioned a second lieutenant of artillery in 1900, he then served in India and the Far East. He attended the Royal Staff College, Camberley (1910–1912), and learned to fly. Dowding was dubbed "Stuffy" for his seemingly aloof manner. He switched to the Flying Corps in 1914, rose to become a squadron commander in World War I, and was promoted to brigadier general.

After the war and command of No. 1 Group in south England (1922–1925), Dowding served in the Middle East. Promoted to vice air marshal in 1929 and air marshal in 1933, Dowding from 1930 to 1936 was a member of the Air Council, which was concerned with supply and research (including fighter aircraft design and planning for radar installations). He became the first chief of Fighter Command in July 1936 and worked from his Bentley Priory headquarters to integrate fighter pilots, radar, and ground control facilities. Scheduled for retirement in June 1939, Dowding stayed on when his designated successor was injured.

Air Chief Marshal Dowding's fighter aircraft were heavily outnumbered by the German Luftwaffe when active fighting began in France and the Low Countries on 10 May 1940. Dowding stoutly resisted calls by the French and Prime Minister Winston L. S. Churchill to send additional fighter squadrons to support the doomed Allied effort to halt the German invasion, knowing they would soon be needed for the defense of Britain itself. Thus when the Battle of Britain

British Air Chief Marshal Sir Hugh Dowding. (Library of Congress)

began in earnest in July 1940, he was able to maintain the narrow margin of air superiority over the British Isles that prevented implementation of the planned German invasion, Operation SEA LION.

Dowding tried to overcome a growing conflict between his two most important commanders, Keith Park at 11th Fighter Command Group in the southwest of England and Trafford Leigh-Mallory at 12th in the Midlands. Leigh-Mallory favored the Big Wing concept of using fighters to overpower the Germans, whereas Park and Dowding insisted on smaller group formations and more flexible tactics. At the same time, Luftwaffe attacks on British airfields, radar, and manufacturing centers were taking a growing toll on the thinly spread defense forces. Dowding was fortunate when Adolf Hitler turned the Luftwaffe against London (and thus away from the Royal Air Force [RAF] ground facilities) in reprisal for an RAF bombing raid on Berlin. By the end of October the battle was largely over, won by Dowding's "few" for "so many."

Dowding was now well past normal retirement age. He was relieved of command (in a poorly handled fashion, at which he felt understandably aggrieved) in November 1940 and replaced by Sholto Douglas. Dowding retired in 1942 and

was made a baron the next year. He died at Tunbridge Wells, England, on 15 February 1970.

Christopher H. Sterling

See also
Britain, Battle of; Churchill, Sir Winston L. S.; Douglas, William Sholto; Hitler, Adolf; Leigh-Mallory, Sir Trafford L.; Park, Sir Keith Rodney; Radar; SEA LION, Operation
References
Collier, Basil. *Leader of the Few: The Authorised Biography of Air Chief Marshal the Lord Dowding of Bentley Priory*. London: Jarrolds, 1957.
Wright, Robert. *The Man Who Won the Battle of Britain*. New York: Charles Scribner's, 1969.

DOWNFALL, **Operation**

U.S. plan for the invasion of Japan. On 25 May 1945, the Joint Chiefs of Staff in Washington provided a general outline of a plan to invade Japan but left the details to the two Pacific Theater commanders, General Douglas MacArthur and Admiral Chester W. Nimitz. MacArthur issued his plan, code-named DOWNFALL, three days later. It foresaw two operations. The first, to be initiated following "extensive air preparation," had the codename OLYMPIC. It consisted of a landing on southern part of the island of Kyushu by the 14 to 17 U.S. divisions already available in the Pacific Theater. The second invasion, code-named CORONET, would begin with a landing on the main island of Honshu and have as its objective the capture of Tokyo and the Yokohama areas as a base for further operations.

X day, the invasion of Kyushu, Operation OLYMPIC, was scheduled for 1 November 1945 and was to involve some 766,700 men lifted in 1,315 amphibious vessels. Sixth Army would be the principal ground element. For the invasion of southern Kyushu, MacArthur envisioned four corps of three divisions each. The follow-on force would add another two divisions. Three other divisions would be the strategic reserve. Nimitz saw aircraft carriers as the principal naval strike weapon and envisioned using 16 fleet and 6 light carriers of the U.S. Navy and 6 fleet and 4 light carriers of the British Pacific Fleet, both embarking some 1,914 aircraft. Once southern Kyushu was secured, MacArthur planned to turn it into a gigantic naval and air base for 40 air groups with approximately 2,800 aircraft.

Both OLYMPIC and CORONET faced daunting problems. The invasion of Kyushu was predicated on the assumption that the invaders would encounter only three Japanese divisions in southern Kyushu and three more in the northern part of the island. Yet ULTRA signal intercepts by early summer 1945 revealed that the Japanese were substantially reinforcing Kyushu. MacArthur dismissed out of hand intelligence estimates based on ULTRA intercepts of a higher Japanese troop strength on Kyushu. He claimed such evidence was "erroneous" and suggested that the Japanese had managed to hoodwink ULTRA. Historian Edward Drea has pointed out that MacArthur routinely dismissed ULTRA evidence that "failed to accord with his own preconceived strategic vision." The last estimate by MacArthur's intelligence chief, Lieutenant General Charles Willoughby, of Japanese troop strength on Kyushu was 195,000 men (up from an initial estimate of 137,400), whereas actual Japanese strength was 287,000.

Y day, the invasion of Honshu in Operation CORONET, was scheduled for 1 March 1946. MacArthur planned to command CORONET in person. The invading force would consist of the Eighth and Tenth Armies with a total of 14 divisions, 3 of which would be Marines. The First Army of 10 divisions from Europe would be the follow-on force. MacArthur planned to hold one airborne division of his own, presumably the 11th, in strategic reserve, augmented by a corps of three divisions deployed from Europe. In all, CORONET was projected to involve 1,036,000 personnel. As the date for the projected invasions drew closer, plans changed. For example, the Tenth Army, formed for the conquest of Okinawa, was dropped from CORONET and replaced by the First Army.

Estimates of casualties from the invasions, had they gone forward, vary considerably. Historian Ray Skates has concluded that Operation OLYMPIC alone would have taken two months and resulted in 75,000 to 100,000 U.S. casualties. This estimate, which approximates the figure presented by MacArthur based on casualties taken in the securing of Luzon in the Philippines, may have been low. Others then and since have postulated a much higher figure on the basis of the Battle of Okinawa, in which 130,000 Japanese defenders inflicted some 66,000 casualties on attacking American forces, not counting Allied naval personnel losses to kamikazes. In addition to the much higher troop strength on Kyushu than on Okinawa, Japanese authorities were assembling thousands of kamikaze aircraft and water craft and mobilizing the civilian population for a fanatical defense. It would seem logical that the Japanese would have fought even more fiercely for their home islands than they did for Okinawa. Although heavy U.S. losses would not have affected the ultimate outcome of the war, they might have brought some modification in U.S. conditions for peace.

MacArthur's revised plan of 15 August for CORONET also would have faced problems. It called for an assaulting force of 20 divisions, including 2 armored and 3 Marine. Five divisions would be in immediate reserve, with 3 others in the Philippines in strategic reserve. The total troop commitment came to 1,171,646 men. But even this revised plan faced problems. The assault would be beyond the range of most land-based aircraft, and MacArthur estimated defending forces of

7 army divisions, 160,000 naval troops, and supporting units and civilian volunteers. But the contemporary Joint Intelligence Committee estimated actual Japanese forces at perhaps double that figure, or 560,000 men.

In any case, MacArthur's plans were never tested. Operation DOWNFALL proved unnecessary, for on 15 August 1945 Emperor Hirohito announced to the Japanese people the decision to surrender.

Spencer C. Tucker

See also
Atomic Bomb, Decision to Employ; Hirohito, Emperor of Japan; Kamikaze; MacArthur, Douglas; Nimitz, Chester William

References
Allen, Thomas B., and Norman Polmar. *Code-Name* DOWNFALL: *The Secret Plan to Invade Japan and Why Truman Dropped the Bomb*. New York: Simon and Schuster, 1995.
Chappell, John D. I. Lexington: University Press of Kentucky, 1996.
Drea, Edward J. *MacArthur's Ultra: Codebreaking and the War against Japan, 1942–1945*. Lawrence: University Press of Kansas, 1992.
Frank, Richard B. *Downfall: The End of the Imperial Japanese Empire*. New York: Random House, 1999.
James, D. Clayton. *The Years of MacArthur: Triumph and Disaster, 1945–64*. Boston: Houghton Mifflin, 1985.
Skates, John Ray. *The Invasion of Japan: Alternative to the Bomb*. Columbia: University of South Carolina Press, 1994.

DPs
See Displaced Persons.

Drancy
See Concentration Camps, German.

DRAGOON, Operation (15 August 1944)

Allied amphibious operation in southern France originally intended to support and coincide with the June 1944 invasion of northern France—Operation OVERLORD—although it could not be mounted until 15 August 1944. Operation DRAGOON had its genesis under the code name ANVIL during strategic planning in 1942 as the Allies considered operations to invade continental Europe. Tied to operation SLEDGEHAMMER, the cross-Channel plan for 1942, ANVIL was to be a diversionary attack on the Mediterranean coast of France to either draw German forces there or, at a minimum, hold those

Allied troops landing in the southern French town of Saint-Tropez during Operation DRAGOON, August 1944. (AFP/Getty Images)

already there so they could not reinforce the defense against an attack on the Channel coast.

Operation DRAGOON was also entangled in European strategic discussions related to Allied planning: the direct route across the Channel pressed by the Americans, or the peripheral approach through North Africa and southern Europe urged by the British. When British Eighth Army forces were defeated in June 1942 in the Battle of Gazala in Libya and their forces at Tobruk were forced to surrender, pressure built to act against the immediate threat, and the western Allies decided on Operation GYMNAST (later renamed TORCH,) the Allied assault on North Africa. This decision canceled SLEDGE-HAMMER and delayed planning and consideration for operation ROUNDUP, the autumn 1943 cross-Channel operation with which ANVIL was still loosely associated.

Debate continued between the Americans and British over the timing and even the feasibility of a cross-Channel attack into northwest France, to which ANVIL always was linked. As operations first in Sicily and then in Italy evolved from TORCH and Operation ROUNDUP gave way to OVERLORD, debate continued as the British pressed to reinforce Italian operations at the expense of ANVIL and delay OVERLORD. Finally, at Com-

bined Chiefs of Staff discussions in the Cairo Conference in late November 1943 in preparation for the Allied Conference in Tehran, the decision was made to take Soviet views into account.

At Tehran, Soviet leader Josef Stalin came down in favor of a cross-Channel attack against Germany in northwest France. Stalin believed that ANVIL, considered a diversionary attack in southern France by the western Allies, was an integral part of the overall pincer movement against German forces. When British Prime Minister Winston L. S. Churchill suggested that operations in the eastern Mediterranean might take immediate pressure off the Soviets even if it meant delaying OVERLORD, Stalin replied that it was not worth scattering British and American forces. Before leaving Tehran, the Allies committed themselves to mounting OVERLORD with a supporting operation against southern France during May 1944. The problem then became how to conduct both OVERLORD and ANVIL with the resources available.

As planning for OVERLORD and ANVIL proceeded, it became apparent that the limiting factor would be the shortage of landing craft. Seizing the opportunity, the British again pushed for cancellation of ANVIL, not only to provide landing craft for

OVERLORD but to divert manpower to the Italian Campaign, which had bogged down. So severe was the landing-craft shortage that Supreme Commander, Allied Expeditionary Forces General Dwight D. Eisenhower found himself in favor of at least postponing ANVIL until after OVERLORD. This weakened the U.S. argument that ANVIL was necessary to divert German troops away from Normandy's beaches, but the British argument for needing additional forces in Italy evaporated with the Allied liberation of Rome. The Americans still argued they required the major Mediterranean port of Marseille to bring resources ashore for the drive against Germany.

On 10 August, the British reluctantly agreed to give ANVIL the go-ahead. Renamed because of security problems, DRAGOON (Churchill said the name was apt because he had been dragooned into agreeing to it) began five days later on 15 August 1944. Vice Admiral H. Kent Hewitt, commander of the Eighth Fleet, had charge of the landing, and four naval task forces supported the invasion. Participating ships included 5 battleships (the *Lorraine, Ramilles, Texas, Nevada,* and *Arkansas*), 24 cruisers, 7 escort carriers, and numerous smaller ships from the British, U.S., French, and Greek navies. A total of 881 ships took part, along with 1,370 landing craft. In the skies, 4,056 Allied aircraft provided support.

At dawn, contingents of three American divisions—the 3rd, 45th, and 36th—and a French armor task force came ashore on beaches between Saint-Tropez and Cannes on the French Riviera, while a combined British and American airborne task force landed to seize bridges and cut roads inland. U.S. Seventh Army commander Lieutenant General Alexander M. Patch Jr. led the Allied force. Major General Lucian Truscott Jr., VI Corps commander, was the ground force commander. Seven Free French divisions under General Jean de Lattre de Tassigny came ashore the next day and headed west to seize the ports of Toulon and Marseille.

Although DRAGOON was dwarfed by the Normandy Invasion two months earlier, the Allies nonetheless ultimately landed 250,000 American and French ground troops. German forces in southern France amounted to no more than 210,000 troops in eight and two-thirds divisions, and these were mostly second-rate formations. By the end of the first day, all three Allied divisions had secured their beachheads, and 86,000 men, 12,000 vehicles, and 46,000 tons of supplies had come ashore.

By 17 August, the Allied advance had reached 20 miles inland. Facing the possibility of substantial Germany army units being trapped in France, German leader Adolf Hitler ordered Army Group G commander General Johannes Blaskowitz to withdraw, leaving sufficient troops behind to deny the major ports to the Allies. The most serious fighting took place at the two ports of Toulon and Marseille, but within two weeks on 28 August, both fell to the French divisions of General de Tassigny's newly designated First French Army.

Operation DRAGOON cost the Allies more than 13,000 casualties (more than half of them American) but resulted in a 400-mile advance that liberated virtually all of southern France. It also hurried the introduction of Free French troops into combat and opened additional ports for supporting the drive across France into Germany. It also netted 79,000 German prisoners and sped the collapse of the Third Reich.

Arthur T. Frame

See also

Brooke, Sir Alan Francis; Cairo Conference; Churchill, Sir Winston L. S.; Falaise-Argentan Pocket; France Campaign; Gazala, Battle of; Hewitt, Henry Kent; Hitler, Adolf; Italy Campaign; Lattre de Tassigny, Jean Joseph Marie Gabriel de; Marshall, George Catlett; OVERLORD, Operation; Patch, Alexander McCarrell, Jr.; Stalin, Josef; Tehran Conference; Truscott, Lucian King, Jr.

References

Breur, William B. *Operation Dragoon: The Allied Invasion of the South of France.* Navato, CA: Presidio Press, 1987.

Harrison, Gordon A. *United States Army in World War II: The European Theater of Operations: Cross-Channel Attack.* Washington, DC: Government Printing Office, 1951.

MacDonald, Charles B. *The Mighty Endeavor: American Armed Forces in the European Theater in World War II.* New York: Oxford University Press, 1969.

Matloff, Maurice. *United States Army in World War II, The War Department: Strategic Planning for Coalition Warfare, 1943–1944.* Washington, DC: U.S. Army, Center of Military History, 1959.

Wilt, Alan F. *The French Riviera Campaign of August 1944.* Carbondale: Southern Illinois University Press, 1981.

Dresden, Air Attack on (13–15 February 1945)

Allied strategic bombing raid against the German city of Dresden. This operation, conducted 13–15 February 1945, has become the most commonly evoked image to illustrate the excesses and horror of conventional bombing of cities. The firestorm caused by Royal Air Force (RAF) Bomber Command on the night of 13 February rivaled that of the raid on Hamburg of 27 July 1943. The immediate controversy about the raid contributed to the end of Allied strategic bombing. Cold War rhetoric and sensationalist presentations in history books and movies have clouded the facts ever since.

At the Yalta Conference on 4 February 1945, the Soviets asked for Allied air attacks on communication centers to prevent the shifting of German troops to the Eastern Front. They specifically mentioned Berlin and Leipzig, but Allied planners also identified Dresden and Chemnitz as appropriate objectives to meet Soviet needs. On 8 February, Supreme Headquarters, Allied Expeditionary Forces (SHAEF) instructed RAF Bomber Command and the U.S. Strategic Air Forces to prepare an attack on Dresden because of its importance in relation to movements of military forces to the Eastern Front. Contrary to later reports,

View of the wreckage of Dresden, Germany, after it was firebombed by the Allies in 1945. The bombing, which targeted the civilian population, was one of the most devastating aerial raids in history. (Library of Congress)

concentrated accuracy of the bombing against so many wooden structures and during ideal weather conditions produced a terrible conflagration. The smoke and flames made aiming very difficult the next day for the more than 300 American B-17s attempting to drop another 700 tons of bombs on the city's marshaling yards. Obscuration of the target area was even worse for a similar attack on 15 February.

When news of the destruction of Dresden reached Britain, there was considerable public outcry over the destruction of such a beautiful city when the war seemed to be virtually won. American air leaders were worried by similar reactions in the United States, especially after careless remarks by a SHAEF briefing officer inspired such nationwide newspaper headlines as "Terror Bombing Gets Allied Approval as Step to Speed Victory." Secretary of War Henry Stimson ordered an investigation of the "unnecessary" destruction but was satisfied by the resulting report explaining the background of the operation. Public reaction in the United States was muted. The controversy contributed to the Allied decision to suspend strategic bombing in April.

The casualty figures reported by German fire and police services ranged between 25,000 and 35,000 dead. However, thousands more were missing, and there were many unidentified refugees in the city. It is probable that the death total approached the 45,000 killed in the bombing of Hamburg in July–August 1943. Some careless historians, encouraged by Soviet and East German propaganda, promulgated figures as high as 250,000. Although David Irving later recanted his claim of 135,000 dead, one can still find that number cited in many history books.

Public impressions of the excesses of Dresden were reinforced by Kurt Vonnegut's novel *Slaughterhouse Five* and the movie it inspired. More than 50 years later, when critics of U.S. air operations against Iraq or Yugoslavia needed a metaphor to condemn conventional bombing attacks on cities, almost invariably they cited Dresden in 1945.

Conrad C. Crane

See also

Aircraft, Bombers; Churchill, Sir Winston L. S.; Doolittle, James Harold "Jimmy"; Hamburg, Raids on; Strategic Bombing; Tokyo, Bombing of (9–10 March 1945)

References

Bergander, Gotz. *Dresden im Luftkrieg.* Cologne: Bohlan Verlag, 1977.

Crane, Conrad C. *Bombs, Cities, and Civilians: American Airpower Strategy in World War II.* Lawrence: University Press of Kansas, 1993.

Irving, David. *The Destruction of Dresden.* New York: Ballantine, 1965.

Smith, Melden E., Jr. "The Bombing of Dresden Reconsidered: A Study in Wartime Decision Making." Ph.D. dissertation, Boston University, 1971.

Taylor, Frederick. *Dresden: Tuesday, February 13, 1945.* New York: HarperCollins, 2004.

Dresden did contain many important industrial and transportation targets, and it was defended, although many of its guns had been sent east to fight the Soviets. The allocation of effort was also shaped by the prodding of British Prime Minister Winston L. S. Churchill, although he later tried to distance himself from the operation and the atmosphere engendered by the pursuit of Operation THUNDERCLAP. The latter was a British plan to break German morale with a massive Allied assault on the German capital, Berlin, and refugee centers. The attack on Berlin was conducted on 3 February over the protests of U.S. Eighth Air Force Commander James Doolittle. Other Americans in the U.S. Strategic Air Forces headquarters and in Washington were also uneasy over concentrating on cities such as Dresden, but that did not stop the operation.

The operation opened on the night of 13 February with two separate British raids. The first blow was delivered by 244 Lancasters dropping more than 800 tons of bombs. This attack was moderately successful. The inhabitants of the city were surprised with a second attack three hours later, this time by 529 Lancasters delivering a further 1,800 tons of bombs. The

Driscoll, Agnes Meyer (1889–1971)

U.S. cryptographer. Born in Geneseo, Illinois, on 24 July 1889, Agnes Meyer graduated from Ohio State University in 1911 with a triple bachelor's degree in mathematics, languages, and music. She taught math and music in Amarillo, Texas, at the Lowry Philips Military Academy from 1911 to 1917. She enlisted in the U.S. Navy as a chief yeoman, serving from July 1917 to September 1919. Meyer's fluency in German, French, and Japanese and her mathematical skills proved invaluable to the process of cryptography, and she was asked to remain in the Code and Signal section of the Department of Naval Communication as a civilian clerk.

From 1921 to 1922, Meyer worked at the Riverham Laboratories in Chicago in the Cipher Department and probably attended training at the "Black Chamber" at New York Laboratories. She helped to invent a cipher machine in 1922 with U.S. Navy Lieutenant William Gresham, for which she was later paid $15,000. During 1923 and 1924, Meyer acted as liaison to the navy and technical adviser to the Hebern Electrical Code Company. When that company went bankrupt, she returned to the Cryptographic Research Desk (OP-20-G) under U.S. Navy Lieutenant Lawrence Safford. Meyer married lawyer Michael Bernard Driscoll in 1924.

Driscoll, known as "Miss Aggie," was the instructor who trained many of the U.S. Navy's top cryptanalysts. She also excelled at breaking Japanese ciphers, in 1925 accomplishing the initial solution of the "Red Book" codes used for Japanese fleet maneuvers until 1930. In 1931, she used IBM machines to crack the "Blue Book," a breakthrough that revealed Japanese battleship speed in 1936 as well as the identities of two Pacific Fleet moles working for the Japanese, Harry Thompson and John Farnsworth.

In 1940, Driscoll's recognition that the Japanese code JN-25 was generated by a machine (M-1) gave the U.S. a head start in building its own decryption machine (M-3). Although briefly assigned to the Enigma codes, Driscoll concentrated on Japanese cipher traffic throughout World War II, providing crucial information in the days leading to the Battle of Midway and training most of the U.S. Navy's cryptographers.

Driscoll moved to the Armed Forces Security Agency in 1949 and to the National Security Agency in 1957, from which she retired in 1959. She died in Fairfax, Virginia, on 16 September 1971.

Margaret Sankey

See also
Signals Intelligence
References
Budiansky, Stephan. *Battle of Wits*. New York: Free Press, 2000.
Layton, Edwin. *And I Was There*. New York: William Morrow, 1985.
Lujan, Susan. "Agnes Meyer Driscoll." *Cryptologia* 15 (January 1991): 47–56.
Prados, John. *Combined Fleet Decoded*. New York: Random House, 1995.

Drum, Hugh Aloysius (1879–1951)

U.S. Army general. Born 19 September 1879 at Fort Brady, Michigan, Hugh Drum was attending Boston College at the time his father, an army captain, was killed in the 1898 Spanish-American War. Drum left school that year and joined the army. He was commissioned from the ranks and served in the Philippines.

Drum graduated from the General Staff College at Fort Leavenworth, Kansas, in 1912 and then saw service on the Mexican border. In May 1917, he joined General John J. Pershing's staff in the American Expeditionary Forces (AEF) in France, assigned to the Operations Division. In July 1918, Pershing named Drum, then a major, chief of staff of the nascent American First Army. For his outstanding performance, Drum was advanced to temporary brigadier general.

U.S. Army General Hugh A. Drum (Time Life Pictures/Getty Images)

After the war, Drum reverted back to his regular grade as major. In 1922, he was promoted to permanent brigadier general. He then commanded an infantry brigade and the 1st Infantry Division (1927–1930). Instructor general of the army in 1930 and 1931, he was promoted to major general in December 1931. Drum commanded the First Army from 1931 to 1933. He was deputy chief of staff of the army (1933–1935) and then commanded both the Hawaiian Department (1935–1937) and the Second Army (1937–1938). He next resumed command of the First Army, which was headquartered on Governor's Island, New York. He was advanced to lieutenant general in August 1939. Drum was the peacetime army's highest-ranking officer, and as such he expected to have field command of the army if the United States entered World War II. Offered the post of adviser to the Nationalist government of China, he declined (the post ultimately went to Lieutenant General Joseph Stilwell). His refusal and his criticism of his superiors, notably of Generals George C. Marshall and Lesley J. McNair, led to Drum remaining on Governor's Island and his retirement from the army in October 1943.

After his retirement, Drum headed the New York National Guard until 1948. He was also president of the Empire State Corporation, which owned and operated the Empire State Building, and he served as military adviser to Thomas E. Dewey during Dewey's 1944 presidential campaign. Drum died in New York City on 3 October 1951.

Derek J. Brown

See also
Marshall, George Catlett; McNair, Lesley James; Stilwell, Joseph Warren
References
Perret, Geoffrey. *There's A War to Be Won: The United States Army in World War II*. New York: Random House, 1991.
Pogue, Forrest C. *George C. Marshall*. Vol. 1, *Education of a General, 1880–1939*. New York: Viking Press, 1963.

DRUMBEAT, Operation (13 January–19 July 1942)

German U-boat offensive conducted off the U.S. East Coast, in the Caribbean, in the Gulf of Mexico, and off Brazil.

Commander of German U-boats Vizeadmiral (vice admiral) Karl Dönitz welcomed the entry of the United States into the war in December 1941 as an opportunity to widen the U-boat offensive in the Atlantic. In planning Operation PAUKEN-SCHLAG (DRUMBEAT), Dönitz intended to operate against the United States and into the Caribbean larger Type IX U-boats with greater operational range. He would employ shorter-range Type VII U-boats off Newfoundland and Nova Scotia, which were much closer to his U-boat bases. Dönitz requested 12 Type IX boats from the Naval War Command for the oper-

ation but was informed on 10 December that he would have only 6. Although submarine construction had accelerated, there were still too few U-boats available. Bad weather in the Baltic had also disrupted U-boat training, and the Naval War Command insisted on maintaining a large number of U-boats in the Mediterranean to assist Axis operations in North Africa. In the end, Type IX vessel *U-128* was not ready at the start of the operation, so Dönitz had less than half the force he had requested.

Operation DRUMBEAT began with only five Type IX U-boats from the Gulf of Saint Lawrence to Cape Hatteras, North Carolina. Seven Type VII U-boats went to Newfoundland and Nova Scotia. All were in place by mid-January 1942, and DRUMBEAT never involved more than a dozen German submarines at any one time. To keep the Americans off balance, a month after DRUMBEAT was launched Dönitz switched its focus to the Caribbean, where several Italian submarines joined operations.

The first victim of DRUMBEAT, the British freighter *Cyclops*, fell victim to *U-123*, a Type IX boat, on 12 January 1942. Other sinkings quickly followed. The United States was totally unprepared for the U-boat attacks. Coastal cities were ablaze with lights at night, silhouetting the merchant ships plying the coast and making them easy targets. There were also few escort vessels available, and merchant ships sailed independently in the hundreds because Chief of Naval Operations Ernest King refused to institute a convoy system, believing that an inadequately protected convoy system was worse than none. All this meant that through April 1942, German submarines sank 216 vessels aggregating 1.2 million tons in the North Atlantic, the vast majority of these in waters for which the U.S. Navy was responsible.

This so-called "second happy time" or "the American turkey shoot" for German submarines finally came to an end through a mandatory blackout of coastal U.S. cities, the instigation of convoys and antisubmarine training schools, the relocation of air assets to antisubmarine duties, and the addition of antisubmarine warships. Not only did merchant shipping losses drop off, but increasing numbers of U-boats were sunk.

On 19 July 1942, Dönitz withdrew his last two U-boats from the East Coast of the United States, relocating his submarine assets back to the mid-Atlantic and signaling an end to the campaign. American unpreparedness had come at a high price. Operation DRUMBEAT was arguably Germany's most successful submarine operation of the entire war, resulting in the sinking of some 3 million tons of shipping. Undoubtedly, Dönitz would have enjoyed even greater success had he been able to employ more U-boats at the offset of the campaign.

Berryman E. Woodruff IV and Spencer C. Tucker

See also
Atlantic, Battle of the; Dönitz, Karl; Germany, Navy; King, Ernest Joseph; NEULAND, Operation; United States, Navy

References

Blair, Clay. *Hitler's U-Boat War.* Vol. 1, *The Hunters, 1939–1942.* New York: Random House, 1996.

Gannon, Michael. *Operation Drumbeat: The Dramatic True Story of Germany's First U-Boat Attacks along the American Coast in World War II.* New York: Harper and Row, 1990.

Morison, Samuel Eliot. *History of United States Naval Operations in World War II.* Vol. 1, *The Battle of the Atlantic, 1941–1943.* Boston: Little, Brown, 1949.

Dumbarton Oaks Conference (21 August–7 October 1944)

Conference held in Washington, D.C., to decide on specifics in connection with the creation of a postwar international security organization. In the last half of 1944, as the Allies began to anticipate victory in the relatively near future, representatives of 39 nations met in the U.S. capital to devise detailed plans for creation of the United Nations, a security organization the assorted states opposing the Axis powers had committed themselves to forming. In recognition of the fact that the Soviet Union had not yet entered the Far Eastern war against Japan, the conference took places in two stages. From 21 August to 28 September 1944, Soviet delegates attended, but for the final 10 days, 28 September to 7 October, the Soviets left the gathering, yielding their place to a Chinese delegation.

The Big Three Allied powers—the United States, the Soviet Union, and Great Britain—dominated the conference as they did the wartime coalition. This was reflected in the blueprint for the new United Nations that the meeting produced. The draft proposals were heavily influenced by the view of U.S. President Franklin D. Roosevelt, which British Prime Minister Winston L. S. Churchill and Soviet Premier Josef Stalin effectively shared, that agreement among the Big Four Allied powers ("the four policemen") must be the foundation of postwar international security. In obeisance to international public opinion and to adhere to their more idealistic pronouncements about the rights of all nations and peoples to

Chinese delegation standing with other delegates at the Dumbarton Oaks Conference in Washington, D.C. (Time Life Pictures/Getty Images)

determine their own governments, the conferees nonetheless decided on a scheme that showed some respect for more idealistic visions of a world in which all powers, great and small, enjoyed equal status and protection.

After lengthy deliberations, the Dumbarton Oaks delegates agreed to create a bipartite United Nations organization modeled on the earlier League of Nations but reserving ultimate authority to the dominant Allied states. All member states were entitled to representation in the General Assembly, which would debate, discuss, and vote on issues that came before it. Executive authority rested with the 11-member Security Council, which had 5 permanent members: Great Britain, France, the United States, the Soviet Union, and China. The remaining Security Council representatives, selected from among other member states of the United Nations, served two-year terms in rotation. The 5 permanent Security Council members therefore enjoyed far greater continuity of power and could effectively dominate the new organization, and their position was enhanced by the organization's dependence on their financial contributions. Besides providing an international security mechanism to mediate and settle disputes among member states, the United Nations was also expected to promote international cooperation on economic, social, and humanitarian issues.

The Dumbarton Oaks conference left several important issues still unsettled, largely because these were so sensitive that they were deferred for personal decision by the Big Three leaders, Roosevelt, Stalin, and Churchill. Among such matters were Soviet requests for independent representation in the General Assembly for Byelorussia and the Ukraine and a Soviet suggestion that each separate permanent Security Council member should enjoy veto power over any United Nations decision. Dumbarton Oaks also neglected to establish appropriate mechanisms to administer former League of Nations mandatory territories and those areas seized from the Axis powers, an omission likewise repaired at Yalta, where the Big Three agreed to establish a trusteeship system for the purpose. Existing colonies of Allied nations fell outside this mechanism's purview unless the imperial power itself chose to hand the colonies over to United Nations administration.

From May to July 1945, the Allies held another conference at San Francisco, which drafted the actual charter of the United Nations. Although this gathering made some minor modifications granting slightly more power to small nations, the Dumbarton Oaks conference had already effectually settled the fundamental operational structure of the new international organization.

Priscilla Roberts

See also
Atlantic Charter; Churchill, Sir Winston L. S.; Hull, Cordell; Roosevelt, Franklin D.; San Francisco Conference; Stalin, Josef; United Nations, Formation of; Yalta Conference

References
Hillerbrand, Robert C. *Dumbarton Oaks: The Origins of the United Nations and Search for Postwar Security.* Chapel Hill: University of North Carolina Press, 1990.
Hoopes, Townsend. *FDR and the Creation of the United Nations.* New Haven, CT: Yale University Press, 1997.
Schild, Georg. *Bretton Woods and Dumbarton Oaks: American Economic and Political Postwar Planning in the Summer of 1944.* New York: St. Martin's Press, 1995.
Schlesinger, Stephen C. *Act of Creation: The Founding of the United Nations: A Story of Superpowers, Secret Agents, Wartime Allies and Enemies, and Their Quest for a Peaceful World.* Boulder, CO: Westview Press, 2003.

Dunkerque (Dunkirk), Evacuation of (Operation DYNAMO, 26 May–4 June 1940)

Extraction of the British Expeditionary Force (BEF) and some French forces from the English Channel port of Dunkerque, France. After the German invasion of France and the Low Countries and the rapid collapse of Allied forces, contingency planning was begun in Britain on 19 May 1940 under the supervision of Vice Admiral Bertram Ramsay, naval commander of Dover, for the possible evacuation of British forces from France. By 25 May, the Germans had already taken the French port of Boulogne, leaving only Dunkerque and Calais among the Channel ports from which an evacuation might be attempted. Calais fell the next day. Naval planners hoped they might be able to extract 40,000 members of the BEF, but in Operation DYNAMO they actually evacuated 364,628 troops, of whom 224,686 were British.

On 26 May, as the German armored thrust from the south was closing in on Dunkerque, commander of German army Group A General Karl Gerd von Rundstedt ordered it halted, believing the panzers were overextended. Hitler made this into a hard-and-fast order and kept the panzers in place until 29 May to allow the German infantry to join them. Hitler's stop order was critical, allowing the BEF to escape and Britain to continue in the war. Head of the Luftwaffe Marshal Hermann Göring, who believed the German air force had not received sufficient credit for its role in the war to date, then secured Hitler's permission to destroy the British forces on the ground with his dive-bombers. He even requested that the panzers be moved back several miles.

As it turned out, the dive-bombing was not effective; the German bombs burrowed deep into the soft sand before exploding. Meanwhile, Operation DYNAMO began. All manner of vessels, many of them manned by civilian volunteers, participated in the evacuation. Royal Air Force (RAF) fighter pilots flying from bases in southern England did what they could to protect the evacuation and disrupt the Luftwaffe, and they probably made the evacuation possible.

British prisoners at Dunkerque, France, 1940. (Still Picture Records LICON, Special Media Archives Services Division (NWCS-S), National Archives)

Among the evacuation ships, British and French destroyers rescued the most men, but they were also the chief targets for Luftwaffe attacks. By the fourth day of the evacuation, 10 destroyers had been sunk or put out of action. This led the Admiralty to take the difficult decision to remove all of its modern destroyers from the operation. The same reasoning limited the number of fighter aircraft that were available. In addition, head of Fighter Command Air Marshal Hugh Dowding refused to sacrifice valuable aircraft in a battle already lost, believing the planes would soon be required for the defense of Britain, which was certain to be the next target.

The Dunkerque evacuation was assisted by bad weather and fires from burning equipment on the beaches that inhibited Luftwaffe operations. The BEF lost more than 2,000 men during DYNAMO itself. RAF Fighter Command lost 106 aircraft and 80 pilots, and Bomber Command lost an additional 76 aircraft. Of 693 British vessels of all types that took part in the operation, one-third (226) were sunk, including 6 destroyers; 19 other destroyers were put out of action. Other nations also participated; France provided the most vessels (119), and Belgium, Norway, Poland, and the Netherlands also provided assistance. The other Allies lost 17 of their 168 vessels taking part. The BEF lost 30,000 men, including prisoners, to the Germans, and it was forced to abandon virtually all of its equipment in France. The 50,000-man French First Army had played a key role, holding the advancing Germans from the beaches and allowing the British to get away. The French contested every bit of ground, and ultimately between 30,000 and 40,000 men of their troops were forced to surrender.

The evacuation of Dunkerque was hardly a victory, but it did sweep away the half-heartedness that had marked the British war effort to that point. It also elevated the stature of Prime Minister Winston L. S. Churchill, who in a speech to Parliament on 4 June as the last British troops were being evacuated vowed that come what may, Britain would continue the fight.

David M. Grilli and Spencer C. Tucker

See also
Churchill, Sir Winston L. S.; Dowding, Sir Hugh Caswal Tremenheere; Hitler, Adolf; Ramsay, Sir Bertram Home; Rundstedt, Karl Rudolf Gerd von

References
Divine, David. *The Nine Days of Dunkirk*. New York: Norton 1959.
Gelb, Norman. *Dunkirk: The Complete Story of the First Step in the Defeat of Hitler*. New York: William Morrow, 1989.
Harman, Nicholas. *Dunkirk: The Patriotic Myth*. New York: Simon and Schuster, 1980.
Lord, Walter. *The Miracle of Dunkirk*. New York: Viking, 1982.

Dunkirk
See Dunkerque, Evacuation of.

Dutch East Indies
See Netherlands East Indies.

DYNAMO Operation
See Dunkerque, Evacuation of.

Dzugashvili, Iosif Vissarionovich
See Stalin, Josef.

E

Eaker, Ira Clarence (1896–1987)

U.S. Army Air Forces general who assumed command of the Mediterranean Allied Air Forces (MAAF) in 1944. Born on 13 April 1896 at Field Creek, Texas, into modest circumstances, Ira Eaker graduated from Southeastern State Normal School in Durant, Oklahoma, in 1917 and enlisted in the army. He completed officer training camp and was commissioned a second lieutenant in 1918. He then transferred to the Signal Corps and underwent aviation training. From 1919 to 1922, he was stationed in the Philippines.

In 1923, Eaker received permission from the army to attend law school. He studied law at Columbia University while also serving as post adjutant at Mitchell Field, Long Island, New York. In 1926, he was selected as 1 of 10 pilots to fly on a goodwill tour of South America.

Eaker took a leading role in the development of a long-range bomber for the army. In 1928, he made a record-breaking flight from Texas to the Panama Canal Zone in the new P-12. During these early years, he also became friends with Henry "Hap" Arnold and Carl A. "Tooey" Spaatz. In January 1929, Captain Eaker flew in the Fokker C-2A *Question Mark* with Major Spaatz, mission commander, Second Lieutenant Elwood Quesada, and two others to set a world endurance record. The next year, Eaker piloted the first transcontinental flight to be refueled in the air.

From 1933 to 1935, Eaker commanded the 34th Pursuit Squadron. Promoted to major in 1935, he graduated from the Air Corps Tactical School, Maxwell Field, Alabama, in 1936 and from the Command and General Staff School, Fort Leavenworth, Kansas, in 1937. As a colonel, he commanded the 20th Pursuit Group from 1940 to 1941. He was then sent to England to report on the Royal Air Force.

In February 1942, Eaker was promoted to brigadier general and sent back to England to command VIII Bomber Command of Lieutenant General Spaatz's Eighth Air Force and was soon conducting strategic bombing of German-occupied France. On 17 August 1942, he led the first mission in person, against Rouen, France. The attempt to conduct daylight precision bombing did not go as well as hoped, but Eaker's B-17s struck vital targets. Promoted to temporary major general, he took command of Eighth Air Force in December and directed attacks against Schweinfurt and Regensburg in August 1943. Publicity over high casualty rates in such raids, caused by a lack of long-range fighter protection, led to his reassignment. Promoted to temporary lieutenant general, Eaker took command of the Mediterranean Allied Air Forces, consisting of the U.S. Twelfth and Fifteenth Air Forces, in January 1944. He led MAAF with great success in a variety of missions.

At the end of the war, Eaker returned to Washington to become deputy commander of the U.S. Army Air Forces. He retired in August 1947 after helping to plan the formation of an independent air force. He was then a consultant for Douglas Aircraft, and in 1972, he became president of the U.S. Strategic Institute. Eaker remained active in the promotion of airpower through numerous books and lectures. In 1985, he was promoted to full general on the retired list by an act of Congress. Eaker died on 6 August 1987, at Andrews Air Force Base, Maryland.

Ruth J. Jun

U.S. Army Air Forces Brigadier General Ira Clarence Eaker.
(Hulton-Deutsch Collection/Corbis)

See also
Arnold, Henry Harley "Hap"; Schweinfurt and Regensburg Raids;
    Spaatz, Carl Andrew "Tooey"; Strategic Bombing
References
Copp, DeWitt S. *A Few Great Captains: The Men and Events That
    Shaped the Development of U.S. Air Power.* Garden City, NY: Dou-
    bleday, 1980.
Mets, David R. *Master of Air Power: General Carl A. Spaatz.* Novato,
    CA: Presidio, 1988.
Parton, James. *"Air Force Spoken Here": General Ira Eaker and the
    Command of the Air.* Bethesda, MD: Adler and Adler, 1986.

East Africa Campaign (January–May 1941)

British Commonwealth campaign to defeat Italian forces in East Africa. Italian East Africa was formed after the 1936 Italian conquest of Abyssinia (Ethiopia), which combined with the colonies of Eritrea and Italian Somaliland into a single entity. When Italy entered the war on 10 June 1940, the governor-general of Italian East Africa, Amedeo Umberto di Savoia, Duca d'Aosta, commanded some 350,000 troops, vastly outnumbering the 40,000 British levies from among the local population. Aosta captured British outposts on the bor-

ders of Sudan and Kenya, and in August, he occupied British Somaliland, the first British colony to fall into Axis hands.

Brigadier General William J. Slim's counterattack from Sudan on 6 November was beaten back, but Aosta was demoralized by a lack of supplies and Italian defeats in the Western Desert. He was also occupied suppressing Abyssinian rebels, known as the Patriots. At the moment of Britain's greatest weakness, he failed to take the initiative and unwisely adopted a defensive posture.

On 19 January 1941, Major General William Platt launched an offensive into Eritrea with the 4th and 5th Indian Divisions, aided by ULTRA intelligence from broken Italian army and air force codes. Platt captured Keren on 27 March after hard fighting, in what proved to be the decisive battle of the campaign. He entered Massawa on 8 April. There, the Italians scuttled one destroyer, and five others sortied into the Red Sea for an attack on Port Sudan. In the ensuing actions, the Italians had four of their destroyers sunk; the fifth was scuttled.

Meanwhile, on 11 February, Lieutenant General Alan Cunningham drove into Italian Somaliland from Kenya using the 11th and 12th African and 1st South African Divisions with startling success. After capturing Mogadishu, the capital of Italian Somaliland, on 25 February, he struck north and took Harar in Abyssinia on 26 March. A small force from Aden also captured Berbera on 16 March and quickly reoccupied British Somaliland with little opposition, to shorten the supply line, and then joined with Cunningham's force to capture Addis Ababa on 6 April. In just eight weeks, Cunningham's troops had advanced over 1,700 miles and defeated the majority of Aosta's troops, at a cost of 501 casualties.

Even more spectacular were the achievements of Lieutenant Colonel Orde Wingate, who commanded a group of 1,600 Patriots that he christened "Gideon Force." Through a combination of brilliant guerrilla tactics, great daring, and sheer bluff, he defeated the Italian army at Debra Markos on 6 April and returned Emperor Haile Selassie to his capital, Addis Ababa, on 5 May. British troops pressed Aosta's forces into a diminishing mountainous retreat at Amba Alagi until he finally surrendered on 16 May, ending Italian resistance in that theater, apart from two isolated pockets that were rounded up in November 1941.

The campaign in East Africa was important because, for the first time, a country occupied by the Axis had been liberated, another 230,000 Italian and colonial troops were captured, and British forces were released for vital operations in the Western Desert. It was also the first campaign in which ULTRA and the code-breakers at Bletchley Park played a decisive role, providing an invaluable lesson on the effective contribution that intelligence could make to the successful outcome of an operation. Success in East Africa also had an important strategic consequence, since U.S. President Franklin D. Roosevelt was able to declare, on 11 April, that the Red Sea and the Gulf of Aden were no longer war zones.

U.S. ships were thus able to deliver supplies directly to Suez, relieving the burden on British shipping.

Paul H. Collier

See also

Bletchley Park; Cunningham, Sir Alan Gordon; Roosevelt, Franklin D.; Selassie, Haile, Emperor of Ethiopia; Signals Intelligence; Slim, Sir William Joseph; Somalia; Wavell, Sir Archibald Percival; Wingate, Orde Charles

References

Glover, Michael. *Improvised War: The Abyssinian Campaign of 1940–1941.* London: Leo Cooper, 1987.

Mockler, Anthony. *Haile Selassie's War: The Italian-Ethiopian Campaign, 1935–1941.* London: Grafton, 1987.

Eastern Front

On 22 June 1941, German forces invaded the Soviet Union in Operation BARBAROSSA. The two states then became locked in a death struggle raging on a front of more than 1,800 miles, involving millions of men and thousands of tanks, artillery pieces, and aircraft and resulting in the deaths of many millions of combatants and civilians.

In the fall of 1940, following the Luftwaffe's failure to drive the Royal Air Force from the skies over Britain, Adolf Hitler ordered plans drawn up for an invasion of the Soviet Union. He postulated a quick, three-month-long campaign. "You have only to kick in the door," he told Field Marshal Karl Gerd von Rundstedt, "and the whole rotten structure will come tumbling down." Defeat the Soviet Union, he reasoned, and Britain would have to sue for peace.

Overconfidence marked German planning. The Germans had little accurate intelligence on the Soviet Union, including few adequate maps. They also had little concern for the impact on the fighting of winter weather and little understanding of the influence of the great distances and how these would render blitzkrieg, at least as it was practiced in Poland in 1939 and against France and the Low Countries in 1940, wholly impractical.

German resources were certainly inadequate for the task that lay ahead, and in the Soviet Union, Hitler's strategic overreach at last caught up with him. On 22 June 1941, the German army deployed 205 divisions, but 60 of these were in garrison or fighting elsewhere: 38 in France, 12 in Norway, 1 in Denmark, 7 in the Balkans, and 2 in North Africa. This left just 145 divisions available for operations in the east. The Germans invaded the Soviet Union with 102 infantry divisions, 14 motorized divisions, 1 cavalry division, and 19 armored divisions. In addition, they deployed 9 divisions to maintain lines of communication as the invasion progressed. There was virtually no strategic reserve. Finland, Romania, and Hungary supplied perhaps 705,000 men in 37 divisions.

The disparity in military hardware was even more striking. The Luftwaffe, still waging operations against Britain and also supporting the Afrika Korps (Africa Corps) in North Africa, was forced to keep 1,150 combat aircraft in these theaters, leaving only 2,770 combat aircraft available for use against the Soviet Union. By contrast, the Soviets had 18,570 aircraft, 8,154 of which were initially in the west. The bulk of these were tactical aircraft. Germany had some 6,000 tanks, the Soviets 23,140 (10,394 in the west), and even in 1941, the Soviets possessed some of the best tanks of the war. Their T-34 was the top tank in the world in 1941.

> "You only have to kick in the door and the whole rotten structure will come tumbling down."
> —Adolf Hitler

The German invasion plan called for three axes of advance. Field Marshal Gerd von Rundstedt's Army Group South of four armies (one Romanian) and one panzer group would drive on Kiev and the Dnieper in order to destroy Soviet armies between the Pripet Marshes and the Black Sea. Field Marshal Fedor von Bock's Army Group Center of two armies and two panzer groups was to strike east, taking Smolensk and Moscow. Field Marshal Wilhelm Ritter von Leeb's Army Group North of two armies and one panzer group would thrust north, capture Leningrad, and pin the Soviet forces there against the Baltic Sea. Finland would act in concert with the Germans, reentering the war to reoccupy the Karelian isthmus and threatening Leningrad from the north. Farther north, German Colonel General Nikolaus von Falkenhorst's Norway Army would carry out an offensive against Murmansk in order to sever its supply route to Leningrad.

Hitler had intended to invade in May, but circumstances caused him to put off the attack until late June. In the spring of 1941, German forces invaded Yugoslavia, went to the rescue of Italian troops in Greece, and drove British forces from Crete. In the process, Hitler secured his southern flank against the possibility of Allied air strikes during the German invasion of the Soviet Union. Historians have argued about the impact of this on delaying the invasion of the Soviet Union. In any case, rainy weather and appalling road conditions in the western USSR imposed delay. The tanks required firm, dry ground.

The invasion began at 3:00 A.M. on 22 June 1941, the longest day of the year, with only two hours of total darkness. The Germans and their allies moved into the Soviet Union along a 2,000-mile front and achieved complete surprise. The bulk of the Red Army's western forces were in forward positions, where they were cut off and surrounded. On the first day alone, 1,200 Soviet aircraft were destroyed, most of them

German soldier on a motorcycle in the snow on the Eastern Front. He is wearing his gas mask to protect his face from the bitter cold. (Library of Congress)

on the ground. Within two days, 2,000 Soviet aircraft had been lost. Within five days, the Germans had captured or destroyed 2,500 Soviet tanks. And within three weeks, the Soviets had lost 3,500 tanks, 6,000 aircraft, and 2 million men, including a significant percentage of the officer corps.

Army Group North broke through frontier defenses, wheeled left to trap and destroy many Soviet divisions against the Baltic, and appeared to have an open route to Leningrad. Meanwhile, Army Group Center, with the bulk of German tanks, attacked north of the Pripet Marshes, completed two huge encirclements, and destroyed vast amounts of Soviet war matériel while taking hundreds of thousands of prisoners. But unexpectedly strong Soviet defenses slowed the advance of Army Group South to Kiev, the Crimea, and the Caucasus.

This development revealed a great problem in German invasion planning. The chief of the General Staff, Colonel General Franz Halder, and many senior generals wanted to concentrate German resources in the center for a drive on Moscow, with supporting movements to the north and south. A thrust there would mean a shorter front, and its advocates believed that Moscow was so important that Soviet dictator Josef Stalin would commit many troops to its defense and thus make it easier for the German army to locate and destroy the remaining Soviet military formations before the onset of winter. But Hitler was fixated on taking Leningrad and, more important, the vast resources of the Ukraine. The compromise solution was to make a decision after the pause in August to refit and rest.

German military intelligence, meanwhile, underestimated Soviet military strength. In December 1940, it had estimated 150 Soviet divisions in the western USSR; by June 1941, that estimate had grown to 175; and now, in late summer, German intelligence concluded the Soviets still had 250 divisions, despite huge losses in the fighting. Moreover, Soviet soldiers did not give up when surrounded. Nazi racism and German violence made them realize that capture meant death, and so, many Soviet troops fought to the last bullet and attempted to break free rather than surrender. And the vast distances and onset of a severe winter posed tremendous logistical challenges for German army planners because their army had only a small mechanized/motorized force and largely relied on human and animal muscle power. While leaders at home prepared for the Soviet collapse, troops on the front lines gained a grudging respect for their Soviet adversaries.

In August, the Germans paused, and Hitler ordered the tank units of Army Group Center to help with the attack on Leningrad and to complete the encirclement of Soviet forces defending Kiev. Finally, in October, Army Group Center began Operation TYPHOON, the attack on Moscow. By November, it had come close to success, but few tanks were still operational. There was little fuel, and the men lacked winter clothing in one of the coldest Soviet winters of the twentieth century.

During the fall campaigning, Stalin prepared to defend Moscow. While troops defended a series of lines on the way to the capital, Moscow's citizens were organized to construct antitank ditches and concentric defenses. Secure in the information that Japan would not take advantage of Soviet weakness and intended to move into South Asia, the Red Army brought divisions from Asia and, having studied German tactics, prepared a counterblow against Army Group Center. On 5 December 1941, the Soviet attack began, stunning the tired, cold, and hungry German troops. Some German generals wanted to retreat all the way to the preinvasion borders, but Hitler insisted the troops remain in place, and his resoluteness and the limited capacity of Soviet logistics helped stem the Soviet winter offensive. Then came the spring thaw and a temporary lull in the fighting.

The relative force ratio had changed in a year of fighting. A summer, fall, and winter had weakened the German army to the point that it no longer had the striking power it possessed a year before. Meanwhile, the Red Army, encouraged by its winter victories, was preparing to take the offensive in 1942.

Hitler believed the Soviet state could not afford another year of manpower losses like those in 1941. He believed that if German forces could drive a wedge between the Dnieper and Don Rivers, using the Volga River as a shoulder, they could interrupt Soviet supplies moving up that great and broad transit way and fight their way to Soviet oil resources in the Caucasus region and the Caspian Sea. The German army's High Command estimated it would need 80 new divisions to replace losses and to provide the striking power for a summer offensive, but Germany could only supply 55 divisions. Hitler promised 80 divisions and obtained troop contributions from reluctant Romanian, Hungarian, and Italian allies, but it was unclear how these troops would perform in the desperate fighting conditions of the Eastern Front. To meet the requirements for mechanized equipment, the German army refitted Czech tanks taken in 1938 and French tanks seized in 1940. Consequently, the German supply system had to carry spare parts for literally hundreds of truck models and tens of tank models, greatly complicating logistics. The Soviets had no such problems. Finally, the panzer units had to move fast enough to fight around defenders and once again surround and capture huge numbers of Soviet troops. Otherwise, the Germans would have to travel as much as 1,200 miles from the offensive's jumping-off point to reach the most productive oil-producing area around Baku.

The Soviets struck first. The Red Army launched an attack in the southern front that coincidentally exposed its flank to Germans massed for the drive to the southeast. Stalin initially refused to end the attack, and losses were heavy. The German summer offensive that finally began in late June 1942 never captured the vast numbers of Soviet soldiers as in 1941.

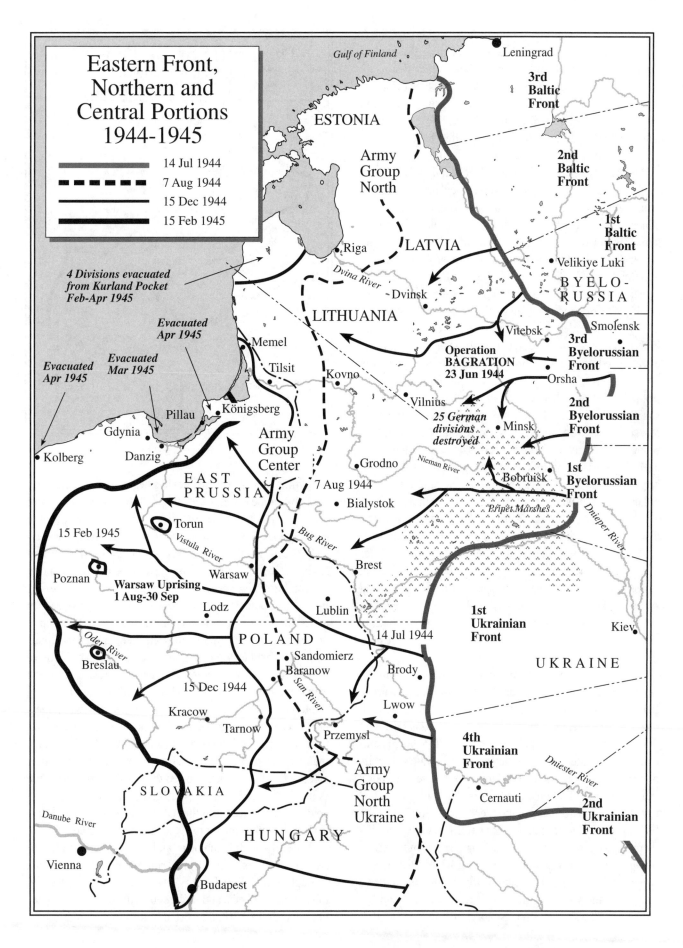

Eastern Front, Northern and Central Portions 1944-1945

- ▬▬▬ 14 Jul 1944
- ▬ ▬ ▬ 7 Aug 1944
- ——— 15 Dec 1944
- ▬▬▬ 15 Feb 1945

Leningrad

3rd Baltic Front

2nd Baltic Front

1st Baltic Front

Gulf of Finland

ESTONIA

Army Group North

LATVIA

Riga

Dvina River

Dvinsk

Velikiye Luki

BYELO-RUSSIA

Smolensk

LITHUANIA

Vitebsk

Operation BAGRATION 23 Jun 1944

3rd Byelorussian Front

4 Divisions evacuated from Kurland Pocket Feb-Apr 1945

Evacuated Apr 1945

Evacuated Apr 1945

Evacuated Mar 1945

Memel

Tilsit

Kovno

Vilnius

Orsha

25 German divisions destroyed

Minsk

2nd Byelorussian Front

Pillau

Königsberg

Gdynia

Kolberg

Danzig

EAST PRUSSIA

Army Group Center

Grodno

Nieman River

Bobruisk

Pripet Marshes

1st Byelorussian Front

Dnieper River

15 Feb 1945

Torun

Vistula River

7 Aug 1944

Bialystok

Poznan

Warsaw Uprising 1 Aug-30 Sep

Warsaw

Bug River

Brest

Breslau

Oder River

Lodz

POLAND

Lublin

1st Ukrainian Front

Kiev

Sandomierz

Baranow

14 Jul 1944

Brody

UKRAINE

15 Dec 1944

San River

Lwow

Kracow

Tarnow

Przemysl

4th Ukrainian Front

Danube River

SLOVAKIA

Army Group North Ukraine

Cernauti

Dniester River

2nd Ukrainian Front

Vienna

HUNGARY

Budapest

Moreover, Hitler kept reassigning units and thereby violating the principles of mass and economy of force. He sent key elements of the Eighteenth Army on the Crimean Peninsula north to Leningrad; he routed and rerouted the Fourth Panzer Army; and by September, when it was clear that Germany could not achieve its overarching goal of seizing the Soviet oil fields, he ordered the Sixth Army to batter its way against three defending armies into Stalingrad.

The desperate battle for control of Stalingrad, a major industrial city on the Volga, captured the world's imagination. Stalin was as determined to hold his namesake city as Hitler was to take it. The fighting was a block-by-block, house-by-house, and room-by-room affair, with the Soviets sometimes defending from across the river. As Lieutenant General Vasily I. Chuikov's Sixty-Second Army held, the Soviets prepared a massive counterstroke, building up armies of troops and many tanks and artillery pieces against the weakly defended flanks held by Romanian and Hungarian troops. On 19 November, in Operation URANUS, the Soviets attacked and quickly broke through. Within days, the Soviet pincers met at Kalach, and more than 300,000 German troops were trapped. The German commander, Field Marshal Friedrich Paulus, did not attempt to break out, and Field Marshal Erich von Manstein failed to break through and relieve Sixth Army. With only three divisions, Manstein managed to get within 35 miles of the trapped Sixth Army but could move no farther. German troops held on until the end of January, when 90,000 survivors marched off into captivity. The long battle did at least provide time for the Germans to extricate forces that had penetrated deep into the Caucasus.

The Soviets then followed this great victory with a winter offensive, but eventually, their goals outran their logistical capacity, and there was the typical pause forced by the spring thaw in 1943. As summer approached, Hitler approved a plan to pinch off a huge bulge in German lines north of Kharkov near Kursk, destroy Soviet armies trapped there, and restore the balance on the Eastern Front.

The Germans postponed the attack on the Kursk salient, Operation CITADEL, again and again into May, June, and eventually early July. Hitler wanted more of the new models of heavy German tanks, especially the Tiger, but as Germany delayed, the Soviets acted, bringing up reinforcements and constructing extensive, deep defenses, including wide belts of minefields, that were up to 60 miles deep. They also positioned reserve armies on the shoulders of the bulge and additional tanks and artillery behind them. Finally, on 5 July, the long-awaited attack began. Although German units made little progress in the north, the attacking force from the south bludgeoned its way forward. But on 10 July, British and American forces invaded Sicily, clearly threatening to drive Italy from the war. This invasion forced Hitler to end the offensive at Kursk—the greatest tank battle in history.

Within a few weeks, the Soviets began their late summer offensive in the south, which they followed up with a winter offensive that drove German forces out of the eastern Ukraine and trapped German troops on the Crimea. As the spring mud in 1944 brought the usual pause in operations, the German lines stretched from near Leningrad in the north, and along the southern edge of Army Group Center, the lines curved inward. The Soviets achieved a great tactical surprise, as they fooled the Germans into expecting a summer attack against positions in the Ukraine. The Soviets then repositioned their tanks and artillery and prepared for a massive offensive against Army Group Center in Operation BAGRATION, which would coincide with the Allied invasion of France. On 20 July 1944, the Soviets struck, and within weeks, they had largely destroyed Army Group Center. The Soviets followed this up with attacks to end the siege of Leningrad and to expel German troops from all Soviet territory. Pausing in the center before Warsaw—which allowed the Germans to destroy the Polish underground army that had joined the fighting—Soviet forces moved into the Balkans, as Romania and Bulgaria desperately sought to avoid Soviet vengeance.

The end was drawing near, and the Soviets continued to advance. One axis aimed at Berlin while the other struck through Hungary. By January 1945, the Soviets had secured most of East Prussia, and in the south, they were at the gates of Budapest. In April, they brought up supplies and reserve troops for the final drive into Germany proper. The Germans conducted a desperate defense of Berlin, using old men and young boys, and the Soviets took huge casualties as Marshal Georgii Zhukov and Colonel General Ivan Konev fought for the honor of liberating the city. In late April, Soviet and American troops met at Torgau on the Elbe, and several days later, Soviet forces occupied Berlin while Hitler committed suicide in his underground bunker. Finally, on 7 May 1945, Germany signed a surrender document that went into effect on all fronts the next day. The Eastern Front had absorbed the lion's share of German military resources from 1941 onward, and the Soviet ability to stave off defeat and then achieve victory there was critical to the war's outcome.

Charles M. Dobbs and Spencer C. Tucker

See also

BARBAROSSA, Operation; Bock, Fedor von; Chuikov, Vasily Ivanovich; Eisenhower, Dwight D.; Halder, Franz; Hitler, Adolf; Kursk, Battle of; Leeb, Wilhelm Franz Josef Ritter von; Manstein, Fritz Erich von; Moscow, Battle of; Paulus, Friedrich; Rundstedt, Karl Rudolf Gerd von; Stalin, Josef; Stalingrad, Battle of; Zhukov, Georgii Konstantinovich

References

Carell, Paul. *Hitler Moves East.* Boston: Little, Brown, 1964.
———. *Scorched Earth.* Boston: Little, Brown, 1970.
Clark, Alan. *Barbarossa: The Russian-German Conflict, 1941–45.* New York: William Morrow, 1965.
Glantz, David M. *When Titans Clashed: How the Red Army Stopped Hitler.* Lawrence: University Press of Kansas, 1995.
Hoyt, Edwin P. *Stalin's War: Tragedy and Triumph, 1941–1945.* New York: Cooper Square Press, 2003.
Werth, Alexander. *Russia at War, 1941–1945.* New York: E. P. Dutton, 1964.
Ziemke, Earl Frederick. *Stalingrad to Berlin: The German Defeat in the East.* New York: Dorset Press, 1986.

Eastern Solomons, Battle of the (22–25 August 1942)

Naval battle fought off Guadalcanal. Henderson Field, captured by the Marines following their surprise landing on Guadalcanal on 7 August, was the only U.S. air base in the Solomon Island chain. The Japanese were determined to retake the field, and they subjected the Marines to ground attacks and to frequent night bombardment from destroyers offshore. Japanese Admiral Yamamoto Isoroku devised Operation KA, a plan to land reinforcements on Guadalcanal and at the same time eliminate the defending U.S. carriers. As in the Battle of Midway, however, Japanese forces failed to concentrate on a single objective.

On 19 August, the Japanese launched a major ground attack against Henderson Field but failed to take it. The next day, Rear Admiral Raizo Tanaka dispatched to Guadalcanal a convoy from Rabaul with 1,500 reinforcements, escorted by the light cruiser *Jintsu* and six destroyers. To provide air cover for the landing, Yamamoto ordered Admiral Kondō Nobutake to steam from Truk with a task force centered on the fleet carriers *Shokaku* and *Zuikaku* and the light cruiser *Ryujo.* Also on 20 August, the Marines at Henderson Field received 31 aircraft from the escort carrier *Long Island.*

Although the Japanese had changed their codes after Midway, their radio traffic indicated something was in the offing, and on 21 August, Admiral Chester Nimitz, commander in chief of U.S. forces in the Pacific (CINCPAC), ordered Vice Admiral Frank Fletcher, commanding the *Wasp, Saratoga,* and *Enterprise* task forces, to contest the Japanese. On 22 August, U.S. patrol bomber (PBY) Catalina aircraft spotted Japanese submarines, prompting an air strike from the *Saratoga,* which failed to locate the Japanese fleet. The following day, Nimitz received faulty intelligence indicating that the Japanese attack force remained at Truk, and Fletcher released the *Wasp* to refuel.

On 24 August, a PBY spotted the Japanese light carrier *Ryujo,* and Scout Bomber Douglas (SBD) dive-bombers from the *Enterprise* reported 15 Zeros and six Kate torpedo planes from the carrier headed toward Guadalcanal. The *Saratoga* then launched a strike on the *Ryujo.* The American SBDs located the carrier and scored three hits, setting her on fire. During the attack, a PBY located the main Japanese task force, centered on the *Shokaku* and *Zuikaku* under Vice Admiral Nagumo Chūichi. Fletcher then ordered the planes attacking the *Ryujo* to strike instead the larger Japanese carriers, but this message never reached the attacking aircraft, which went on to sink the *Ryujo.* They also badly damaged the Japanese heavy cruiser *Tone,* a specially modified aircraft cruiser armed with 8×8-inch guns and carrying eight seaplanes.

Meanwhile, U.S. radar revealed the incoming strike of aircraft from the *Shokaku* and *Zuikaku,* heading toward the American carriers. The *Enterprise* and *Saratoga* were operating independently, and the Japanese first located the *Enterprise,* which launched its F-4 Wildcat fighters in defense. Soon, 30 Japanese Val dive-bombers began attacks on the *Enterprise.* Their bombs pierced her flight deck in three places, seriously damaging her. Fires soon raged below deck, and the crew of the *Enterprise* fought valiantly to save their ship. The *Saratoga* escaped, in part thanks to highly effective antiaircraft fire provided by the battleship *North Carolina.*

On 25 August, Tanaka's convoy bound for Guadalcanal came under attack by U.S. B-17 bombers from Espiritu Santo and aircraft from Henderson Field. U.S. dive-bombers scored two hits on one of the transports, which later sank. For the first time in the campaign, the B-17s also scored a hit on a Japanese escorting destroyer and sank it. The convoy, far from its objective and vulnerable, now returned to Rabaul.

The Battle of the Eastern Solomons was a U.S. victory, securing, for the time being, the American position on Guadalcanal. The Japanese lost 1 light carrier, 1 light cruiser, and 1 transport

Explosion resulting from a Japanese bomb striking the flight deck of the U.S. Navy aircraft carrier *Enterprise* during the battle of the Eastern Solomons on 24 August 1942. The photographer was killed while taking this picture. (National Archives)

along with 75 aircraft, and the United States lost 25 planes. The *Enterprise* returned to Pearl Harbor and was repaired within a month. Fletcher was slightly wounded, and Nimitz selected Vice Admiral William Halsey to replace him. One of the great "what-ifs" of the Pacific war involves Yamamoto's failure to employ the giant battleship *Yamato* off Guadalcanal. She was available, and her guns might have made a difference in the fight for Henderson Field, but Yamamoto was unwilling to risk such a powerful national symbol.

Robert W. Serig

See also
Fletcher, Frank Jack; Halsey, William Frederick, Jr.; Kondō Nobutake; Midway, Battle of; Tanaka, Raizo; Yamamoto Isoroku

References
Frank, Richard B. *Guadalcanal: The Definitive Account of the Landmark Battle.* New York: Random House, 1990.
Griffith, Samuel B. *The Battle for Guadalcanal.* Philadelphia: Lippincott, 1963.

Hammel, Eric. *Guadalcanal: The Carrier Battles.* New York: Crown Publishers, 1987.
Merillat, Herbert C. *Guadalcanal Remembered.* New York: Dodd, Mead, 1982.

Eben Emael (10–11 May 1940)

Belgian frontier fort and site of a German special operation to seize the Belgian frontier defenses at the opening of Germany's campaign in the west on 10 May 1940. FALL GELB (Operation YELLOW) involved three army groups poised to split the British, Belgian, and French forces and gain the Channel coastline for continuing operations against Great Britain.

Eben Emael was a reinforced, concrete-and-steel bunker system located on the Albert Canal at its junction with the Meuse River north of Liège, Belgium, and about 3 miles south of Maastricht in the Netherlands. The fort's plateau top was wedge-shaped, 1,100 yards long on its north-south axis, and 800 yards wide across the southern baseline. The entrance was at the southwest corner at casemate number 3. The fort guarded the bridges over the canal and the routes to the interior of the Low Countries and France beyond. At the time of the attack on 10 May, about 700 soldiers manned the fortress bunkers, which were designed for a detachment of 1,200. Belgian regular army officer Major Jean Fritz Lucien Jottrand had command. The garrison of Fort Eben Emael had been alerted to activity across the German border shortly after midnight on 9–10 May, but it took several hours to put things in order. Alerts were common, and the troops were quartered in villages near the fort.

The Germans, already skilled in assault tactics from their World War I experiences, had developed special teams to reduce fortifications. The secret operation against the fort, code-named GRANITE, had Adolf Hitler's personal interest. Captain S. A. Koch, an officer in Major General Kurt Student's airborne forces, was chosen to lead the attack. Artillery preparations cratered the ground around the fort to provide cover for the advancing German troops, and they suppressed the fire of the fort's guns.

The glider attack was to occur at the same time as other events on the ground, but flight problems required the Ju-52 tow planes to penetrate Dutch airspace to get to the required release altitude. The Dutch were alerted and began antiaircraft fire.

On the early morning of 10 May, 10 DFS-230 gliders, each carrying a squad of seven or eight men, landed silently on top of the fort. Lieutenant Rudolf Witzig's command glider had prematurely disconnected and landed in a field near Köln (Cologne). Sergeant Helmut Wenzel took charge, until Witzig's arrival at 6:30 A.M.

The assault force used shaped-charge explosives to penetrate the casemates and cupolas. Throughout the afternoon and night of 10 May, the Germans and Belgians fought inside the dank passageways of the fort. Rubber assault boats and the employment of flamethrowers helped the attack group to cross the canal and close on the fort. While the engineers of the assault detachment kept the bunker garrison occupied, Captain Koch's other airborne forces attacked the bridges over the Albert Canal. The next day, a German division arrived to complete the capture of the remaining bridges and forts. Lieutenant Witzig's assault force suffered only 26 casualties in its successful mission. Major Jottrand and his captured Belgian soldiers, after resisting for just over one day, were marched off to a prison camp in Germany to sit out the war. Vital bridges at Veldwezelt and Vroenhoven were also secured, and the German Sixth Army was able to advance. Its tanks took Liège the next day.

John F. Votaw

See also
Airborne Forces, Axis; Belgium, Army; Belgium Campaign; Engineer Operations; Flamethrowers; Parachute Infantry; Student, Kurt
References
Gudmundsson, Bruce I. *Stormtroop Tactics: Innovation in the German Army, 1914–1918.* Westport, CT: Praeger, 1989.
Mrazek, James E. *The Fall of Eben Emael.* Novato, CA: Presidio, 1970.

Eden, Sir Robert Anthony (First Earl of Avon) (1897–1977)

British politician and foreign secretary who served as a cabinet minister during World War II. Born in Windlestone, England, on 12 June 1897, Eden served in France during World War I, rising to brigade-major, and then took a degree in Oriental languages at Cambridge. He entered Parliament in 1924 and became Stanley Baldwin's foreign secretary at age 38 in December 1935. A staunch supporter of the League of Nations, Eden resigned in February 1938 in disagreement

Sir Anthony Eden, British foreign secretary (1935–1938, 1940–1945, 1951–1955) and Prime Minister (1955–1957). (Hulton Archive/Getty Images)

over Neville Chamberlain's appeasement of Benito Mussolini's policies.

With the outbreak of war, Eden returned to Chamberlain's cabinet as Dominions secretary (3 September 1939) and helped to develop the Empire Air Training Scheme that trained thousands of pilots and aircrew in Canada and Africa. When Winston L. S. Churchill became prime minister, he named Eden war minister (10 May 1940); shortly thereafter came the disastrous British Expeditionary Force (BEF) and its Dunkerque evacuation, as well as British setbacks in the Middle East.

Eden again became foreign secretary (on 23 December 1940) and attended virtually all the Allied wartime conferences. Patient and urbane, he was a superior diplomat who effectively represented British interests to the other Allies— especially the often difficult Charles de Gaulle, whose Free French cause Eden often defended. Churchill appointed Eden leader of the House of Commons in November 1942, a role he played well but at a cost to his health. Churchill also named Eden, by now part of his inner circle, as his designated successor in the event of his own death. Eden worked hard on the formation of the United Nations, and he left office only when the Labour Party won the British elections (27 July 1945). However, he retained his own seat in the House of Commons

Eden served a third time as foreign secretary in Churchill's second government (1951–1955) but never fully recovered from abdominal surgery in 1953. He was knighted in 1954, and on Churchill's retirement, he served as prime minister (6 April 1955–9 January 1957), resigning after the mishandled Suez Crisis. He was made the earl of Avon in 1961 and died on 14 January 1977, in Alvediston, England.

Christopher H. Sterling

See also
Chamberlain, Arthur Neville; Churchill, Sir Winston L. S.; de Gaulle, Charles; Dunkerque, Evacuation of; Hitler, Adolf; United Nations, Formation of

References
Aster, Sidney. *Anthony Eden.* New York: St. Martin's Press, 1976.
Barker, Elizabeth. *Churchill and Eden at War.* New York: St. Martin's Press, 1978.
Carlton, David. *Anthony Eden: A Biography.* London: Allen Lane, 1981.
Dutton, David. *Anthony Eden: A Life and Reputation.* New York: St. Martin's Press, 1997.
Eden, Anthony. *Full Circle: The Memoirs of Sir Anthony Eden.* London: Cassell, 1960.
———. *Facing the Dictators: The Memoirs of Sir Anthony Eden.* Boston: Houghton Mifflin, 1962.
———. *The Reckoning: The Memoirs of Sir Anthony Eden.* Boston: Houghton Mifflin, 1965.
James, Robert Rhodes. *Anthony Eden: A Biography.* New York: McGraw-Hill, 1986.
Thorpe, D. R. *Eden: The Life and Times of Anthony Eden, First Earl of Avon, 1897–1977.* London: Chatto and Windus, 2003.

Egypt

Strategically located in northeast Africa, Egypt was vital to the British effort in World War II to protect the Suez Canal and lines of communication to Middle East oil fields. In 1939, Egypt had a population of about 16 million people.

The British had taken control of Egypt in 1882 to secure the Suez Canal. Supposedly, they had intervened to "restore order," but the British stayed. London ended its protectorate in 1922 and granted Egypt independence as a constitutional monarchy with adult male suffrage, but it did not relinquish authority in key areas. Great Britain retained control over defense, imperial communications (the Suez Canal), protection of foreign interests and minorities, and the Sudan. In August 1936, the same year King Farouk came to the throne, Britain signed a treaty with Egypt whereby it retained the right to defend the Suez Canal until the Egyptian army could do so. The Egyptian government also agreed that, in the event of war, it would grant full use of Egyptian facilities to the British.

Throughout World War II, Port Said and Alexandria remained major British bases for operations in the eastern Mediterranean. As headquarters of the Middle East Supply Center, the Egyptian capital of Cairo was the transit point for half a million British and Commonwealth troops. Cairo was also the headquarters of the Middle East Command, and the city remained a haven for agents and spies. Egyptian nationalists were active, with many Egyptians, including Farouk and Prime Minister Ali Mahir, hoping for an Axis military victory in the war and full independence for Egypt.

Although Farouk was the constitutional monarch, British Ambassador Miles Lampson exercised real power. At the beginning of the war, the British insisted on the imposition of martial law and strict censorship and the arrest of German nationals. The Egyptian government ended diplomatic relations with Germany, but Egypt did not declare war against Germany or, later, Italy. Only reluctantly did Ali Mahir allow the confiscation of Italian property in Egypt. He also refused permission for border guards to fire on Italian troops. In June 1940, the British insisted that Farouk replace Ali Mahir. His replacement was Hasan Sabri, a moderate.

On 17 September 1940, Italian forces invaded Egypt. Despite a pledge that it would declare war if this happened, the Egyptian government merely declared a state of nonbelligerency. In November 1940, Prime Minister Sabri died and was replaced by Husayn Sirry, who headed a coalition government. Axis air attacks on Cairo in June 1941 killed some 600 people, but Egyptian sentiment remained heavily anti-British. That winter, conditions in Egypt worsened with severe shortages of many goods, including food. Bread riots occurred in Cairo in January 1942. With General Erwin Rom-

A column of Axis prisoners captured in Libya nearing the massive walls of the Citadel of Cairo, showing the Mohamed Ali Mosque (above) and the Mosque of Sultan Hassan. (Library of Congress)

mel's forces closing on Cairo, nationalist demonstrations in the capital occurred in favor of an Axis victory, and Sirry resigned in early February. The British then insisted that Farouk appoint as prime minister Mustafa Nahas, the pro-British head of the Wafd nationalist party. When Farouk hesitated, British armored cars and troops surrounded the palace, and Lampson demanded his abdication. Farouk then acquiesced, and Nahas formed a government.

Throughout 1942, pro-Axis sentiment remained strong, even among the elites and the Egyptian army. Following the November 1942 Battle of El Alamein, both the Axis threat to Egypt and British authority subsided. Despite Farouk's repeated efforts to remove him from office, Nahas remained as prime minister until October 1944, when the British allowed Farouk to replace him with Saadist leader Ahmad Mahir. The new prime minister secured Egyptian declarations of war against Germany and Japan, but he was assassinated shortly thereafter, in February 1945. The declarations of war were formally proclaimed on 26 February 1945, allowing Egypt to become a founding member of the United Nations.

As elsewhere in Africa and the Middle East, World War II heightened nationalism and anticolonialism. Following Farouk's abdication in 1952, the last British troops departed the country in 1954. Egypt did not gain its full sovereignty, however, until 1956 and the Suez debacle.

Robert W. Duvall, Jack Vahram
Kalpakian, and Spencer C. Tucker

See also

El Alamein, Battle of; Rommel, Erwin Johannes Eugen; United Nations, Formation of

References

Butt, Gerald. *The Lion in the Sand: The British in the Middle East.* London: Bloomsbury, 1995.

Cooper, Artemis. *Cairo in the War, 1939–1945.* London: H. Hamilton, 1989.

Vatikiotis, E. J. *The Modern History of Egypt.* London: Weidenfeld and Nicolson, 1980.

Eichelberger, Robert Lawrence (1886–1961)

U.S. Army general and commander of the Eighth Army in the Pacific Theater. Born 9 March 1886 in Urbana, Ohio, Robert Eichelberger attended Ohio State University for two years before attending the U.S. Military Academy, where he graduated in 1909. He served in a variety of assignments before becoming assistant chief of staff of the Siberian Expeditionary Force (1918–1919), where he was promoted to temporary lieutenant colonel.

Eichelberger served in the Philippines and in China and then on the War Department General Staff (1921–1924). He graduated from the Command and General Staff School (1926) and the Army War College (1930). Eichelberger then served at West Point (1931–1935), where he was promoted to lieutenant colonel (1934). He became secretary to the General Staff (1935–1938), and after being made colonel (1938), he commanded the 30th Infantry Regiment. Promoted to brigadier general, he was appointed superintendent of West Point (1940).

In March 1942, Eichelberger became a temporary major general and took command of the 77th Infantry Division. He commanded XI Corps and then I Corps, in Australia. He led I Corps in New Guinea in September 1942. Promoted to temporary lieutenant general the next month, he directed the successful assault of Buna-Gona (November 1942– January 1943) and then operations in New Guinea and New Britain (January 1943–July 1944).

Eichelberger took command of Eighth Army in September 1944 and led it to Leyte Island in the Philippines that December. He directed operations on Luzon (January–April 1945), including the liberation of Manila, and his forces also liberated the southern Philippine Islands, including Mindanao. He was entrusted with command of all Philippine operations in July. His Eighth Army carried out 14 major and 24 smaller landings.

U.S. Army Brigadier General Robert Eichelberger. (Library of Congress)

Between 1945 and 1948, Eichelberger commanded Eighth Army in Japan. He returned to the United States in September 1948 and retired from the army. Two years later, he published a book entitled *Our Jungle Road to Tokyo*. During the Korean War, he was briefly a special adviser in the Far East. He was promoted to full general in July 1954 and died in Asheville, North Carolina, on 26 September 1961.

Alexander D. Samms

See also

New Britain Island; New Guinea Campaign; Philippines, U.S. Recapture of

References

Eichelberger, Emma G., and Robert L. Eichelberger. *Dear Miss Em: General Eichelberger's War in the Pacific, 1942–45.* Ed. Jay Luvaas. Westport, CT: Greenwood Press, 1972.

Eichelberger, Robert L. *Our Jungle Road to Tokyo.* New York: Viking, 1950.

Shortal, John F. *Forged by Fire: General Robert L. Eichelberger and the Pacific War.* Columbia: University of South Carolina Press, 1987.

Eichmann, Karl Adolf (1906–1962)

German Schutzstaffel (SS) lieutenant colonel and key figure in the destruction of European Jewry during World War II. Born on 19 March 1906 in Solingen in the Rhineland, Germany, Karl Adolf Eichmann moved with his family to Linz, Austria, in 1914.

He left the Linz Higher Institute for Electro-Technical Studies after two years and became a salesman. In 1932, he joined the Austrian National Socialist movement, but he fled to Germany in 1934 when it was outlawed. Sent to Berlin, he joined the SS Sicherheitsdienst (Security Service, SD) and was assigned to its Jewish Office. There, he became the Nazi expert on Jewish affairs and handled negotiations concerning the emigration of German Jews to Palestine, which he visited briefly in 1937. Following the Anschluss (union) with Austria and absorption of Bohemia and Moravia, he headed the Office for Jewish Emigration.

With the beginning of World War II, Eichmann transferred to the Gestapo and created the Reich Central Emigration Office to handle the relocation of European Jews to Poland. That office was then combined with the Jewish Affairs Office to form Department IV-A-4B, known as the Dienststelle Eichmann (Eichmann Authority). He helped organize the Wannsee Conference of January 1942 that developed the mechanics of the "final solution" and was put in charge of the transportation of Jews to the death camps of Poland. Eichmann later told an associate that he would "die happily with the certainty of having killed almost six million Jews."

After the war, Eichmann lived in various places under aliases until he escaped to Argentina, where he lived and worked near Buenos Aires in obscurity under the name Ricardo Klement. On 11 May 1960, Israeli Secret Services captured him and smuggled him from the country illegally to stand trial in Israel. Eichmann claimed he was only following orders

Adolf Eichmann, on trial in Jerusalem, during trial cross-examination, standing in booth in front of microphones between two officers in courtroom. (Library of Congress)

and in any case could be accused only "of aiding and abetting" the annihilation of the Jews, not killing them. Found guilty by an Israeli court on 15 December 1961, he was sentenced to death. Unrepentant, he was hanged at Ramleh Prison on 31 May 1962. His body was then cremated and the ashes scattered.

Douglas B. Warner

See also
Holocaust, The; Wannsee Conference

References
Arendt, Hannah. *Eichmann in Jerusalem: A Report on the Banality of Evil.* New York: Viking, 1963.
Donovan, John. *Eichmann: Man of Slaughter.* New York: Avon Book Division, Hearst, 1960.
Malkin, Peter Z., and Harry Stein. *Eichmann in My Hands.* New York: Warner, 1990.
Reynolds, Quentin. *Minister of Death: The Adolf Eichmann Story.* New York: Viking, 1960.

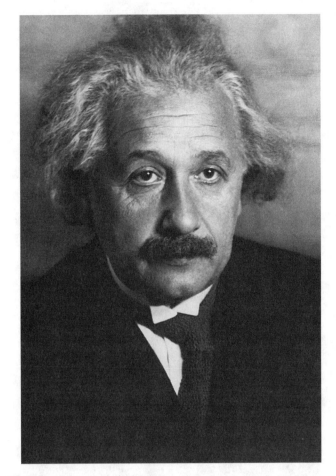

Albert Einstein. (Corbis)

Einstein, Albert (1879–1955)

Physicist, Nobel laureate, and pacifist who urged the United States to begin research into the feasibility of constructing atomic bombs. Born in Ulm, Germany, on 14 March 1879, Albert Einstein renounced German citizenship in 1896 and became a Swiss citizen in 1901. While working as a patent clerk, he developed his special theory of relativity and the famous equation $E = mc^2$ that demonstrated the equivalency of mass and energy. With the rise of Nazism and Jewish persecution, he left Berlin in 1933 for the Institute of Advanced Study in Princeton, New Jersey.

In 1939, leading physicists, including Hungarian émigrés Leo Szilard and Eugene P. Wigner as well as Italian expatriate Enrico Fermi, concluded that Germany was working on an atomic bomb. Szilard approached Einstein with a letter for President Franklin D. Roosevelt, urging that the U.S. government begin an atomic bomb project of its own to deter Adolf Hitler (assuming German efforts succeeded).

Einstein was apotheosized as perhaps the world's greatest physicist since Isaac Newton, and his signature on this letter carried considerable weight and authority. Dated 2 August 1939, it warned that it was now likely that scientists would establish and sustain a chain reaction in uranium, which could lead to the construction of "extremely powerful bombs of a new type." Einstein urged the president to form a partnership among government officials, industry specialists, and scientists to conduct feasibility studies; he also recommended securing supplies of uranium ore.

Alexander Sachs, economist and presidential confidant, delivered the letter on 11 October 1939. Sufficiently alarmed by Sachs's précis of its contents, Roosevelt appointed the Uranium Committee to begin preliminary studies, which became the basis for the MANHATTAN Project organized in 1942 to build atomic bombs.

Einstein's letter served as the catalyst for the MANHATTAN Project, but Einstein himself was excluded from the project. His pacifism, Zionism, and a supposedly lackadaisical attitude regarding military secrecy made him suspect to army intelligence. After the war, he campaigned unsuccessfully for a "world government" consisting of the United States, Great Britain, and the Soviet Union that would restrict further development and construction of atomic weapons. Einstein died in Princeton, New Jersey, on 18 April 1955.

William J. Astore

See also
Atomic Bomb, Decision to Employ; Fermi, Enrico; Groves, Leslie Richard; MANHATTAN Project; Oppenheimer, Julius Robert

References
Einstein, Albert. *Ideas and Opinions.* New York: Bonanza Books, 1954.
Fölsing, Albrecht. *Albert Einstein: A Biography.* Trans. Ewald Osers. New York: Viking, 1997.
Pais, Abraham. *"Subtle Is the Lord . . .": The Science and the Life of Albert Einstein.* Oxford: Oxford University Press, 1982.
Rhodes, Richard. *The Making of the Atomic Bomb.* New York: Simon and Schuster, 1986.

Eisenhower, Dwight D. (1890–1969)

U.S. Army general and supreme commander, Allied Expeditionary Forces, European Theater of Operations (ETO). Born in Denison, Texas, on 14 October 1890, Dwight David "Ike" Eisenhower grew up in Abilene, Kansas. Graduating from the U.S. Military Academy in 1915 as a member of the "class the stars fell on," he was commissioned a second lieutenant of infantry. His first posting after West Point was Fort Sam Houston, Texas.

Eisenhower commanded the fledgling tank corps training center at Camp Colt outside Gettysburg, Pennsylvania, during World War I. Following service in Panama, he graduated first in his class at the Command and General Staff School, Fort Leavenworth, Kansas, in 1926. He also graduated from the Army War College in 1928. During the interwar period, Eisenhower served under a number of the army's finest officers, including Generals Fox Conner, John J. Pershing, and Douglas A. MacArthur. Following his return from the Philippines in 1939, he served successively as chief of staff of the 3rd Infantry Division, IX Corps, and Third Army, where he was promoted to temporary brigadier general in October 1941 and captured Army Chief of Staff General George C. Marshall's attention for his contributions to Third Army's "victory" in the Texas-Louisiana war maneuvers of 1941.

Summoned to the War Department in the aftermath of the Japanese attack on Pearl Harbor, Eisenhower headed the War Plans Division and then the Operations Division of the General Staff before being promoted to major general in April 1942. Marshall then appointed Eisenhower commanding general of the European Theater of Operations, in June 1942. Promotion to lieutenant general followed in July 1942. His appointment was met with great skepticism from senior British military officers because of his lack of command experience.

Dwight D. Eisenhower talking to American paratroopers in England prior to the Normandy Invasion. (Library of Congress)

Eisenhower commanded Allied forces in Operation TORCH in November 1942 (the invasion of northwest Africa) and in Operation HUSKY in July 1943 (the invasion of Sicily). In the interim, he was promoted to full general in February 1943. The efficient operation of his headquarters—Allied Forces Headquarters—became a model of Allied harmony and led to increased responsibilities in the Mediterranean Theater of Operations. In September 1943, his forces invaded the Italian mainland. Eisenhower's generalship during this phase of the war has long been subject to controversy, but his adept management of diverse personalities and his emphasis on Allied harmony led to his appointment as supreme commander, Allied Expeditionary Forces for the invasion of northwest Europe.

As commander of Operation OVERLORD, the Normandy Invasion on 6 June 1944, Eisenhower headed the largest Allied force in history. Following the expansion of the lodgment area, he took direct command of the land battle on 1 September 1944. As the Allied forces advanced along a broad front toward the German border, he frequently encountered opposition from senior Allied generals over command arrangements and logistical support. He displayed increasing brilliance as a coalition commander, but his operational decisions remained controversial. His support of British Field Marshal Bernard L. Montgomery's abortive Operation MARKET-GARDEN is evidence of his unflinching emphasis on Allied harmony in the campaign in northwest Europe. In mid-December 1944, Eisenhower was promoted to General of the Army as his forces stood poised to strike into the heartland of Germany.

When Adolf Hitler launched the Ardennes counteroffensive on 16 December 1944, it was Eisenhower, among senior Allied commanders, who first recognized the scope and intensity of Germany's attack. Marshaling forces to stem the German advance, he defeated Hitler's last offensive in the west. By March 1945, his armies had crossed the Rhine River and encircled the Ruhr industrial area of Germany. As Soviet armies stood on the outskirts of Berlin, Eisenhower decided to seek the destruction of Germany's armed forces throughout southern Germany and not to launch a direct attack toward the German capital. On 7 May 1945, the mission of the Allied Expeditionary Forces was fulfilled as he accepted the unconditional surrender of Germany's armed forces.

Following the war, Eisenhower succeeded General Marshall as army chief of staff. In February 1948, he retired from the military and assumed the presidency of Columbia University, before being recalled to active field duty by President Harry S Truman in 1950 to become supreme Allied commander, Europe in the newly formed North Atlantic Treaty Organization (NATO). In 1952, Eisenhower resigned from active military service and accepted the Republican Party's nomination for president. Elected by a wide majority in 1952

and again in 1956, he stressed nuclear over conventional forces, supported expanded U.S. military commitments overseas, and warned of the dangers of a military-industrial complex. He left office in 1961 as one of this nation's most popular chief executives, his two administrations marked by unheralded peace and prosperity. In 1961, Eisenhower retired to his farm in Gettysburg, Pennsylvania. He died in Washington, D.C., on 28 March 1969.

Cole C. Kingseed

See also
Ardennes Offensive; Bradley, Omar Nelson; Cairo Conference; Falaise-Argentan Pocket; Hitler, Adolf; Italy Campaign; MacArthur, Douglas; Marshall, George Catlett; Montgomery, Sir Bernard Law; Normandy Invasion and Campaign; North Africa Campaign; OVERLORD, Operation; Patton, George Smith, Jr.; Rhine Crossings; Sicily, Invasion of; TORCH, Operation; Western European Theater of Operations

References
Ambrose, Stephen E. *Eisenhower: Soldier, General of the Army, President-Elect.* New York: Simon and Schuster, 1983.
Chandler, Alfred D., et al., eds. *The Papers of Dwight David Eisenhower: The War Years.* Vols. 1–4. Baltimore, MD: Johns Hopkins University Press, 1970.
D'Este, Carlo. *Eisenhower: A Soldier's Life.* New York: Henry Holt, 2002.
Eisenhower, David. *Eisenhower at War, 1943–1945.* New York: Random House, 1986.
Eisenhower, Dwight D. *Crusade in Europe.* New York: Doubleday, 1948.

El Alamein, Battle of (23 October– 4 November 1942)

Major Allied victory against German and Italian forces in Egypt. By the fall of 1942, there were signs that the war in North Africa was turning in favor of the British. Axis forces under Field Marshal Erwin Rommel had failed to break through the British lines at Ruwiesat Ridge in July and Alam Halfa Ridge in September. British Eighth Army commander Lieutenant General Bernard Montgomery gradually built up his strength to strike an offensive blow. Although Prime Minister Winston L. S. Churchill repeatedly pressed for an earlier attack, Montgomery set the operation, code-named LIGHTFOOT, to begin on the night of 23–24 October, under a full moon. General Sir Alan Brooke, chief of the Imperial General Staff, and General Harold Alexander, British commander in chief in North Africa, managed to placate Churchill.

By late October, Montgomery's Eighth Army numbered 195,000 men and had 1,029 tanks (including 300 U.S.-built M-4 Sherman mediums), 2,311 artillery pieces, and some 750 aircraft. Ranged against them were 104,000 Axis troops (50,000 Germans and 54,000 Italians), 489 tanks, 1,219 guns, and 675 aircraft. The Germans had, however, faced worse odds and won in North Africa. Rommel's defense was based on some

General Erwin Rommel in the desert at El Alamein, with his troops. (Library of Congress)

450,000 mines laid from the sea to the Qattara Depression, including corridors designed to funnel attackers into traps, although the Afrika Korps (Africa Corps) commander had no confidence he could hold against a determined British attack.

Montgomery planned to feint an attack to the south while Lieutenant General Sir Oliver Leese's XXX Corps delivered the major blow in the north against the strength of the Axis positions. Indeed, the elaborate British deception efforts convinced Axis intelligence that the main blow would occur in the south.

Montgomery planned to use armor to blast his way through the German positions and then carry out an envelopment of Axis forces. However, his own armor commanders, particularly General Herbert Lumsden of X Corps, thought that this was a misuse of tanks. Montgomery adapted his plan so that the armor would cover an initial infantry attack and then seize defensive ground. The infantry would "crumble" the German line, and when panzers moved forward to assist, the British armor would strike.

The attack began at 9:40 P.M. on 23 October 1942, almost totally surprising the Germans (Rommel was in Germany at the time, recuperating from an illness). British air attacks and artillery fire from 1,000 guns disrupted Axis communications and rained down on a 6-mile-wide front in the Axis lines near the Mediterranean coast. Then, XXX Corps began its attack in the north, while Lieutenant General Sir Brian Horrocks's XXX Corps began the southern attack near the Qattara Depression to fix German forces there.

XXX Corps opened two corridors through the Axis minefields, and Lumsden's X Armoured Corps then moved through them. Italian forces holding this sector fought well, however, and 15th Panzer Division's counterattack almost halted the British advance. Montgomery found that reports of progress had been overly optimistic. The commanders of his armored divisions feared that crossing the key Miteiriya Ridge would expose their tanks to the deadly fire of German 88 mm anti-tank guns, and they had not moved. Meanwhile, the Germans were extending and reinforcing their minefields. An angry Montgomery now halted the southern thrust and concentrated his resources in the north. He also stated that he would relieve commanders who failed to advance. Progress resulted, and by late afternoon on 24 October, the 1st Armoured Division reported one of its brigades on and around Kidney Hill, part of Miteiriya Ridge. Once again, however, reports were overly optimistic, and the 7th Armoured Division bogged down entirely at Himeirat. Meanwhile, General der Panzertruppen (U.S. equiv. lieutenant general) Georg Stumme, Rommel's temporary replacement as German commander, died of a heart attack while visiting the front earlier that day.

Montgomery was awakened at 2:00 A.M. on 25 October with the bad news and quickly saw his whole plan was threatened. With British forces holding only part of Kidney Hill to the north and making no progress at Hineimat in the south, the Germans would have little reason to launch counterattacks, and thus, the British armor would have no chance to destroy the panzers. Montgomery's infantry, although more successful than the armor, was also taking heavy casualties, and only his Australian division had replacements. Montgomery began to revise his plan again—the first of several changes made over the next few days. Ultimate success came, in part, from his flexibility during the battle.

The first effort was on the British far right at midnight on 25 October, but although the Australian infantry did very well, the 1st Armoured Division again failed to move beyond Kidney Hill. This time, the problems were map reading and failure to coordinate with the artillery. Thus far, Rommel, who had returned earlier on 25 October, continued to hold his ground,

which was what Montgomery wanted. Then, because of casualties, Montgomery shifted the offensive burden to Lumsden's X Corps, which was to move west and northwest from Kidney Hill. Not completely trusting Lumsden, Montgomery stayed in close touch with the operation and found that his corps commander was not keeping his artillery commander informed of plans and operations. Not wishing to risk his armor by leaving it unsupported, Montgomery again changed plans.

His new approach was to create an armored reserve to use for a decisive thrust, although the infantry would have to do the initial fighting with even less shield available than previously. At least Montgomery knew from ULTRA intercepts that, even though Rommel was thinking about breaking off, fuel shortages would not allow the Axis side to seek a battle of movement. Meanwhile, Churchill was more worried about winning a victory over the Afrika Korps before the Allied landings in western North Africa (Operation TORCH). The Vichy French were more likely to stand aside or even cooperate in these attacks if Axis forces in eastern North Africa were on the run. Churchill was thus not pleased to learn that armored units were being withdrawn from the Battle of Alamein.

As the fighting evolved, the target shifted from the northern coast road, where German troops were being brought in,

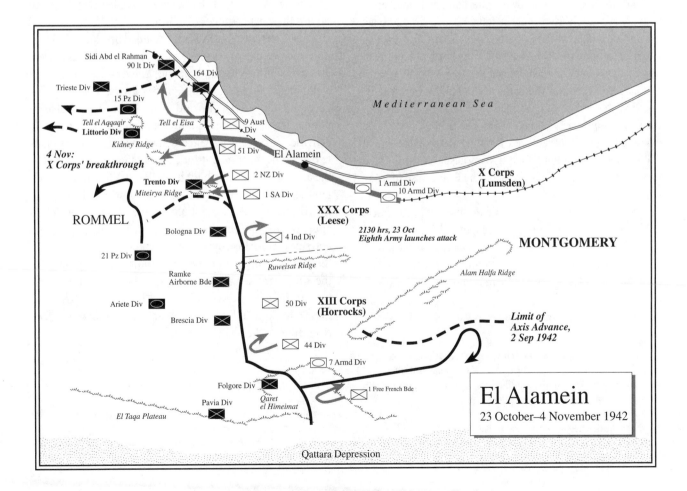

to the Miteiriya Ridge area, where the attack would hit mostly Italian units. Again, the start was delayed when the armor commanders failed to coordinate plans. The basic idea now called for two regiments of armored cars to drive behind the Axis defenders and envelop them. Early on 2 November, the attack began. And again, the infantry did well, quickly gaining 4,000 yards, but the armor failed to advance. Although slow to react because he was convinced the main attack would come farther north, Rommel organized a full-scale counterattack. This move played into the hands of the British, for their armor and antitank weapons could now take defensive positions and destroy the panzers. By the evening of 2 November, Rommel had only 35 German and 20 Italian tanks capable of combat.

Montgomery, however, had two armored divisions in reserve and spent 2 November gathering infantry reserves. He used this reserve force to break out to the southwest. By the evening of 2 November, Rommel was planning to fall back—news made available to Montgomery via ULTRA intercepts. When Adolf Hitler learned of Rommel's plan, however, he ordered the Afrika Korps to fight to the death. Rommel later claimed that this order resulted in the destruction of his army, but since it reached him more than half a day after his withdrawal started, it had little effect on the outcome. In any case, British attacks continued, and Allied air bombardment added a new destructive element. By the afternoon of 4 November, the victory was clearly won. The Italian XX Corps had been destroyed, and the Afrika Korps on its left had been shattered. On the afternoon of 4 November, Rommel ordered a retreat. Several days later, the Allies landed in western North Africa.

Casualty figures for the Battle of El Alamein vary widely. The British claimed to have inflicted 50,000 casualties, but the actual number is probably closer to 2,300 killed, 5,500 wounded, and 27,900 captured. Rommel had also lost almost all his tanks and artillery. Eighth Army casualties amounted to 4,600 killed and 9,300 wounded. The British also lost 432 tanks destroyed or disabled.

Despite the battle's outcome, historians have been critical of Montgomery for attacking the strength of the Axis line, and his subsequent claim that everything had gone according to plan is simply not true. Nonetheless, although Africa was not cleared of Axis forces for another six months, the end was plainly in sight.

Fred R. van Hartesveldt and Spencer C. Tucker

See also
Alam Halfa, Battle of; Churchill, Sir Winston L. S.; Horrocks, Sir Brian Gwynne; Leese, Sir Oliver William Hargreaves; Montgomery, Sir Bernard Law; North Africa Campaign; Rommel, Erwin Johannes Eugen; TORCH, Operation

References
Carver, Michael. *El Alamein.* London: Batsford, 1962.
Greene, Jack, and Alessandro Massignani. *Rommel's North Africa Campaign, September 1940–November 1942.* Conshocken, PA: Combined Publishing, 1999.
Guingand, Francis de. *Operation Victory.* London: Hodder and Stoughton, 1946.
Hamilton, Nigel. *Monty: The Battles of Field Marshal Bernard Montgomery.* New York: Random House, 1994.
Rommel, Erwin. *The Rommel Papers.* Ed. B. H. Liddell Hart. London: Collins, 1953.
Winterbotham, F. W. *The Ultra Secret.* New York: Harper and Row, 1974.

Electronic Intelligence

The collection and analysis of electromagnetic emissions that provide insight into an enemy's technological capabilities. The broader category of signals intelligence (SIGINT) includes both communications intelligence (COMINT) and electronic intelligence (ELINT). COMINT encompasses the monitoring of radio and telephone traffic, the decryption of coded messages, and the analysis of the contents of those messages. ELINT is the collection and analysis of electromagnetic emissions, such as telemetry and radar signals, with the expectation that the successful analysis of ELINT will provide information about enemy technology and lead to the development of effective countermeasures.

During World War II, signals intelligence played an important role in strategic decision making. Its best-known successes were in COMINT and included breaking the Japanese and German codes in MAGIC and ULTRA. The Axis powers also had some success in breaking Allied codes, most especially those regarding the Atlantic convoys. Signals intelligence activities during World War II were not limited to intercepting and reading communications, however. ELINT activities during the war included monitoring radar signals to determine the transmitting power, range, and accuracy of the air defense systems built by both the Allies and the Axis powers. In the Atlantic and Pacific Oceans, Great Britain and the United States used sophisticated radio receivers to approximate the positions of submarines, merchantmen, and surface warships by means of triangulation (interpreting the strength and point of origin of radio transmissions). As the war progressed, ELINT techniques became more sophisticated. Because of the role played by both COMINT and ELINT in the conflict, World War II has sometimes been referred to as the SIGINT war.

Shannon A. Brown

See also
Signals Intelligence
References
Budiansky, Stephen. *Battle of Wits: The Complete Story of Codebreaking in World War II.* New York: Simon and Schuster, 2000.
Kahn, David. *The Codebreakers: The Comprehensive History of Secret Communication from Ancient Times to the Internet.* New York: Scribner's, 1999.

Laqueur, Walter. *World of Secrets: The Uses and Limits of Intelligence.* New York: Basic Books, 1985.

Prados, John. *Combined Fleet Decoded: The Secret History of American Intelligence and the Japanese Navy during World War II.* New York: Random House, 1995.

Emilia Plater Independent Women's Battalion (1943–1945)

First Polish cohesive, all-female combat unit, consisting of volunteers forcibly resettled in the Soviet Union and ironically named after a leader of an insurrection in 1830 directed against Russia.

Initially attached to the lst Tadeusz Kościuszko Division, the battalion swore the oath of allegiance on 15 July 1943. It became directly subordinated to the I Polish Corps in August 1943 and to the First Polish Army in July 1944. Unlike women's auxiliary units in the West, the battalion lacked special military regulations. Its command personnel were men, and its political officers were women.

In August 1943, the battalion included five companies (two infantry and one each of fusiliers, machine guns, and handheld antitank grenade launchers) and six platoons (mortar, reconnaissance, signals, medical, engineer, and logistics). In late 1943, one transport platoon was added. Because the battalion also provided basic training to women subsequently assigned elsewhere, its strength fluctuated.

Women subsequently trained at the Infantry Officers' School in Ryazań, and they commanded companies and platoons of the new Polish army because of the drastic shortage of male Polish officers (of whom about 15,000 had been killed at Soviet prisoner-of-war camps in 1940). Among these women was Second Lieutenant Emilia Gierczak, platoon commander of the 10th Infantry Regiment. She distinguished herself in the fighting on the Pomeranian Rampart, while leading an assault group in Kołobrzeg (Kolberg).

About 70 women in the battalion died in the war. In May 1945, its strength of roughly 500 women was only a small percentage of the total of women serving in two Polish armies formed in the Soviet Union, with estimates ranging from 8,500 to 14,000.

Kazimiera J. Cottam

See also

Katyń Forest Massacre; Poland, Army; Poland, Role in War; Women in World War II

References

Cottam, K. Jean. "Veterans of Polish Women's Combat Battalion Hold a Reunion." *Minerva* no. 4 (Winter 1986): 1–7.

Drzewicka, S. *Szłyśmy z nad Oki* (We Came from Oka River shores). 2nd ed. Warsaw: MON, 1985.

Pawłowski, Edward. "Platerówki." *Wojsko Ludowe* no. 6 (June 1985): 93–95.

Empress Augusta Bay, Battle of (2 November 1943)

Naval battle between U.S. and Japanese naval forces during the Bougainville Campaign. On 1 November 1943, Major General A. H. Turnage's 3rd Marine Division, which had been reinforced, landed at Empress Augusta Bay, about halfway up the west coast of Bougainville Island in the northern Solomon Islands. The landing was part of Operation CARTWHEEL, which was designed to neutralize the major Japanese air and naval base at Rabaul on New Britain Island to the north.

In addition to air attacks from Rabaul, which were thwarted by Allied fighter aircraft, the Japanese dispatched a scratch naval task force to attack the Torokina beachhead on Bougainville. Commanded by Rear Admiral Omori Sentaro, the force consisted of the heavy cruisers *Myoko* and *Haguro*,

Wounded in the initial invasion at Empress Augusta Bay, Bougainville, this American is hoisted aboard a Coast Guard–manned transport off shore, November 1943. (Still Picture Records LICON, Special Media Archives Services Division (NWCS-S), National Archives at College Park)

two light cruisers, six destroyers, and five destroyer transports carrying 1,000 troops who were to be landed on Bougainville. Rear Admiral Ijuin Matsuji commanded the left flank screen with the light cruiser *Sendai* and three destroyers, and Rear Admiral Osugi Morikazu had the right with the light cruiser *Agano* and three destroyers.

The transports turned back late in the evening of 1 November after Omori concluded that the task force had been sighted by American planes. Omori, however, continued to Bougainville with his other ships in the expectation that he could destroy the Allied transports and cargo vessels in a night battle. Unknown to him, the transports had been quickly unloaded and had left Empress Augusta Bay earlier that day.

Learning of Omori's task force from U.S. Army reconnaissance aircraft, Rear Admiral A. Stanton Merrill, whose Task Force 39 had been providing bombardment support for the Bougainville landing force, moved to intercept the Japanese about 20 miles north of Empress Augusta Bay. Task Force 39 was centered on Merrill's Cruiser Division 12, consisting of the light cruisers *Montpelier* (the flag), *Cleveland, Columbia,* and *Denver.* Captain Arleigh Burke's Destroyer Division 45 made up the van, and Commander B. L. Austin's Destroyer Division 46 comprised the rear. Merrill hoped to engage the Japanese ships at long range to avoid a torpedo attack while making use of his radar-controlled, 6-inch guns.

The two task forces encountered each other at 2:27 A.M. on 2 November and fought a complicated battle that was really three engagements in one: Merrill's cruisers against Omori's cruisers and individual battles waged respectively by the two destroyer divisions. Although the Japanese were superior in gunfire and torpedoes and although Omori thought he had inflicted serious losses on the Americans, he broke off the battle after an hour, at 3:27.

Merrill's cruisers sank the Japanese light cruiser *Sendai,* and Destroyer Division 46 sank the Japanese destroyer *Hatsukaze,* which already had been badly damaged in a collision with the cruiser *Myoko,* Omori's flagship. Task Force 39's losses were limited to damage to two ships; the destroyer *Foote* had her stern blown off by a torpedo. Merrill abandoned pursuit of the Japanese ships at dawn to await the inevitable Japanese air response from Rabaul. It came at about 8:00 A.M. in the form of 100 Japanese aircraft, which were met by a smaller number of Allied fighters. The Japanese inflicted only minor damage, with the cruiser *Montpelier* taking two bomb hits on her starboard catapult. Omori was subsequently relieved of command for failing to carry out his orders.

The Battle of Empress Augusta Bay did not end the Japanese naval threat to the Allied lodgment on Bougainville. However, the prompt U.S. Navy reaction prevented Japanese disruption of the landing, and along with massive air raids against Rabaul over the next days and the naval battle of Cape St. George on 25 November, it helped ensure the success of the Bougainville Campaign.

John Kennedy Ohl

See also

Bougainville Campaign; Cape St. George, Battle of; Rabaul; Solomon Islands, Naval Campaign; Southeast Pacific Theater

References

Gailey, Harry A. *Bougainville: The Forgotten Campaign, 1943–1945.* Lexington: University Press of Kentucky, 1991.

Morison, Samuel Eliot. *History of United States Naval Operations in World War II.* Vol. 6, *Breaking the Bismarcks Barrier, 22 July 1942–1 May 1944.* Boston: Little, Brown, 1950.

Prados, John. *Combined Fleet Decoded: The Secret History of American Intelligence and the Japanese Navy in World War II.* New York: Random House, 1995.

England

See Great Britain.

Enigma Machine

At the 1923 International Postal Congress, Arthur Scherbius, a German, demonstrated his invention of a commercial encoding machine, known as the Enigma device. Enigma resembled a typewriter in appearance with a series of rotors or wheels, the settings of which could be changed. Early versions of the device enabled the operator to encode a plaintext in any of 150 million possible ways.

As with all major military powers, the Germans sought to develop a secure means of military communications and assumed that messages encoded by Enigma were unbreakable. By 1928, the German military was using the Enigma, and Japan and Italy also bought the machine and used it. Other countries, such as the United States, purchased the Enigma machine but did not attempt to unlock its secrets.

The Poles, concerned about a resurgent Germany as a threat to their own security, formed a special cryptography group at the University of Poznan in 1928. They also purchased the commercial model of Enigma, and by 1935, they had broken into the German radio codes, information they largely shared with the British and French in 1938. Late that year, however, the Germans added a sixth rotor, which helped to convince the Poles that the Germans were about to make an aggressive military move. The Poles modified their own machines to keep up with the German advances, and they continued to break into the German codes, but the defeat of their country came too quickly for Enigma to be of use to them.

An Enigma cipher machine, used by the German military in World War II. (Hulton Archive)

After Poland's defeat, the Polish code-breakers and their machines were spirited away to France and England. At Bletchley Park outside of Buckingham, the British assembled a mixed group of experts to continue the work begun by the Poles. Over time, Bletchley Park developed additional devices that could sort through the possible variations of an encoded text, although the Enigma's changeable settings meant that most messages could not be read in "real time." Nonetheless, Enigma proved invaluable in the Allied military effort and undoubtedly shortened the war. Information on ULTRA intercepts was not made public until 1974, when Group Captain F. W. Winterbotham published *The Ultra Secret.* Its revelations forced the rewriting of most earlier histories of the war.

Spencer C. Tucker

See also

Bletchley Park; Counterintelligence Operations; Electronic Intelligence; Signals Intelligence

References

Lewin, Ronald. *Ultra Goes to War.* New York: McGraw-Hill, 1978.

Winterbotham, F. W. *The Ultra Secret.* New York: Harper and Row, 1974.

Eniwetok, Capture of (17–22 February 1944)

Eniwetok Atoll lies on the northwestern edge of the Rilik Chain in the Marshall Islands, some 2,000 miles west of Pearl Harbor. Thirty small islands comprise this coral atoll, mostly on the western edge of a circular lagoon. The three major islands are Eniwetok in the south, Parry in the southeast, and Engebi in the north. Following the capture of islands in the Gilbert chain in November 1943, Vice Admiral Raymond A. Spruance took command of operations against the Marshalls.

Because of the rapid success in securing Kwajalein Atoll in the Marshalls, American planners decided to proceed with Operation CATCHPOLE to take Eniwetok. The assault force of just under 8,000 men centered on the 22nd Marine Regiment and soldiers of the army's 27th Division and attached troops. Brigadier General T. E. Watson had overall command, with Rear Admiral Harry W. Hill commanding the landing group. Unlike assaults in the Gilberts, adequate numbers of LVTs (landing vehicles, tracked) were available, and this operation saw the first extensive use of the DUKW amphibious trucks. Initially, fewer than 60 naval personnel defended Eniwetok Atoll, but on 4 January, Major General Bishida Yoshimi's 1st Amphibious Brigade, a veteran fighting unit, arrived, bringing total Japanese strength on the atoll to nearly 3,500 men.

The Eniwetok Expeditionary Group sortied from Kwajalein Lagoon on 15 February, covering the 326 miles to Eniwetok by two different routes. Engebi was the main U.S. objective because it had the atoll's only airfield. Including soldiers of the 27th Division and attached units, there were just under 8,000 men in the assault force. The invasion began at 8:44 A.M. on 17 February 1944, with the 1st and 2nd Battalions of the 22nd Marine Regiment landing on the southeastern beach. The attackers were supported by medium tanks of the 2nd Separate Tank Company. Initial Japanese resistance was light, and the only organized resistance occurred near Skunk Point. By 2:50 P.M., the island was declared secured, although mopping up continued into 18 February.

Operations against Parry and Eniwetok Islands would be more difficult. At 7:19 A.M. on 19 February, U.S. naval gunfire pounded Eniwetok Island, which was defended by 808 Japanese troops. The fire expended was minimal compared with that on the other islands, and few Japanese positions were damaged. At 9:17 A.M., the 1st and 3rd Battalions of the army's 106th Infantry Regiment landed. Things went badly from the start. The terrain prevented many of the LVTs from moving inland, and the Japanese covered the beach with automatic weapon and mortar fire.

These Marines, dirty and weary from two days and two nights of fighting, were typical of the victors of Eniwetok Atoll. (Still Picture Records LICON, Special Media Archives Services Division (NWCS-S), National Archives at College Park)

At midday on 19 February, the Japanese launched a spirited counterattack with 300 to 400 men. The 106th was able to defeat the counterattack but at heavy cost. Shortly after 12:00 P.M., the 3rd Battalion, 106th Infantry was committed, but it failed to influence the course of the battle. An hour later, the 3rd Battalion, 22nd Marines was ordered ashore and directed to support the army's left flank. That night, the American units completed the capture of the western edge of the island and consolidated a defensive line near the beach.

The battle to secure the eastern side of Eniwetok was similar to the western battles. The 3rd Battalion, 106th Infantry landed on Yellow Beach 1 beginning at 9:17 A.M. on 19 February. Many of the Japanese beach defenses had been destroyed by naval gunfire, but once they were inland, the attackers discovered and were delayed by bunkers, pillboxes, and spider holes. Supported by carrier aircraft, the attacking troops secured the island on 21 February.

Parry Island was defended by 1,347 Japanese. Fortunately for the attackers, prisoner interviews and intelligence material captured on Engebi and Eniwetok revealed the Japanese defensive positions and provided U.S. planners a framework for a detailed preinvasion bombardment. Beginning at 10:00

P.M. on 20 February and continuing until the landing two days later, the battleships *Tennessee, Pennsylvania,* and *Colorado,* assisted by two heavy cruisers, pounded the island. Aircraft from three escort carriers also joined the assault.

Beginning at 9:08 A.M. on 22 February, the 1st and 2nd Battalions of the 22nd Marines landed abreast and were met by Japanese machine-gun and mortar fire at the water's edge. At 10:00 A.M., the Japanese opened up with 77 mm field guns, which were quickly silenced by naval gunfire. Meanwhile, the 3rd Battalion, 22nd Marines went ashore. The Marines fought to the ocean side of the island and then formed two lines. Each line battled to the opposite end of the island. By 7:30 P.M. that day, Parry was declared secure.

The battles to capture Eniwetok Atoll were the last major battles of the Eastern Mandates Campaign. Although planners expected this effort to be easy, stiff Japanese resistance from well-prepared positions slowed the progress of the U.S. forces. American casualties were 195 killed and missing and 521 wounded. Of the total Japanese force of some 3,431 men, only 64 prisoners were taken. No American ships were lost during the operation, although there was some damage from friendly fire. No Japanese surface ships contested the landing, but four submarines were sunk, along with a number of small supply ships and patrol craft.

Troy D. Morgan and Spencer C. Tucker

See also

Kwajalein, Battle for; Marshall Islands, Naval Campaign; Spruance, Raymond Ames

References

Crowl, Philip A., and Edmund G. Love. *The United States Army in World War II: The War in the Pacific—Seizure of the Gilberts and Marshalls.* Washington, DC: U.S. Government Printing Office, 1955.

Heinl, Robert D., Jr., and John A. Crown. *The Marshalls: Increasing the Tempo.* Washington, DC: Historical Branch, U.S. Marine Corps, 1954.

Morison, Samuel E. *History of United States Naval Operations in World War II.* Vol. 7, *Aleutians, Gilberts, and Marshalls.* Boston: Little, Brown, 1951.

Sham, Henry I., Bernard C. Nalty, and Edwin T. Turnbladh. *History of Marine Corps Operations in World War II.* Vol. 3, *Central Pacific Drive.* Washington, DC: U.S. Government Printing Office, 1966.

Estonia

The Baltic state of Estonia received its independence as a consequence of World War I. The smallest and most northerly of the three Baltic states, Estonia feared both Germany, because of dispossessed German landowners, and Russia. On 2 February 1920, however, the Russian Soviet Federated Socialist Republic recognized Estonia as an independent country. The Estonian government in Tallinn subsequently negotiated nonaggression pacts with the Soviet Union in June 1932 and Germany in June 1939. In 1939, the country was ruled by the nationalist Peasant Party, headed by K. Päts. Estonia was a member of the League of Nations.

Another nonaggression pact, this one between Germany and the Soviet Union in August 1939, proved to be Estonia's downfall. Arrangements under this pact consigned the country to Soviet influence. After the German invasion of Poland in September, the Soviet Union increasingly encroached on Estonian sovereignty. On 28 September, Estonian officials reluctantly signed a mutual assistance pact with the Soviet Union, which allowed the Soviets to station troops and to establish naval and air bases on Estonian soil. By 17 June 1940, Estonia was occupied by Soviet troops, and the process of Sovietization began.

Soviet officials then managed, through coercion and violence, to secure the election of favorable candidates to the legislature, which then voted to make Estonia a Soviet republic.

On 6 August 1940, the Estonian Soviet Socialist Republic was formally admitted to the Soviet Union. The Estonian government also nationalized industry and large banks and collectivized land. It also imposed censorship and restructured the schools. The Soviet regime dealt brutally with any opposition, executing more than 2,000 Estonians and deporting 19,000 others to isolated areas of the Soviet Union.

Adolf Hitler's decision to invade the Soviet Union brought the German occupation of Estonia. German troops were on Estonian soil by 5 July 1941, and they controlled the majority of the country by August. Stiff resistance by Soviet troops in northern Estonia devastated the region.

German efforts to recruit an Estonian Schutzstaffel (SS) division had only limited success, as did attempts to convince Estonians to volunteer for labor in Germany. German racial policies also impacted Estonia: the vast majority of the country's small Jewish population was murdered. Estonians suffered as the Germans requisitioned much of their food and livestock. In addition, the German occupation forces maintained the strict government control over industry and land that had originally been imposed by the Soviets.

The westward advances of the Soviet army in February 1944 again turned Estonia into a battleground, and tens of thousands of Estonians fled to western Europe. During the war, the country lost approximately 20 percent of its prewar population of some 1,136,000 people. After the war, Soviet officials deported around 31,000 others, suspected of opposition to Communist rule. This loss of population was made up by an influx of more than 500,000 Soviet citizens. Estonia did not regain its independence until August 1991.

Laura J. Hilton

See also

BARBAROSSA, Operation; Eastern Front; German-Soviet Nonaggression Pact

References

Misiunas, Romauld, and Rein Taagepera. *The Baltic States: Years of Dependence.* Berkeley: University of California Press, 1983.

Raun, Toivo. *Estonia and the Estonians.* Stanford, CA: Stanford University Press, 1987.

Von Rauch, Georg. *The Baltic States: The Years of Independence.* Berkeley: University of California Press, 1974.

EUREKA

See Tehran Conference.

F

Falaise-Argentan Pocket (August 1944)

Military opportunity in France in which Allied forces failed to trap a significant portion of retreating German forces. In July 1944, U.S. Operation COBRA broke the monthlong stalemate in Normandy and shattered the German defensive lines, creating a war of movement. Third Army commander Lieutenant General George S. Patton Jr. envisaged a drive on the Seine River and the liberation of Paris, but a politically less dramatic and strategically more important opportunity soon developed: trapping German forces west of the Seine. If this could be accomplished, the Allied advance east to Germany would be greatly eased and the war shortened.

On 7 August, German forces counterattacked with elements of four panzer divisions at the express order of Adolf Hitler and over the opposition of Field Marshal Günther Hans von Kluge, commander of Army Group B and commander in chief west. Kluge was convinced the attack was doomed from the start. It would drive German forces into the heart of the planned Allied envelopment. Unfortunately for the Allies, it did slow the Canadian push to Falaise.

At this point, however, Allied planning began to break down. Patton suggested a deeper envelopment that would net all the Germans west of the Seine. However, his superior, Lieutenant General Omar N. Bradley, commander of 12th Army Group, rejected this and insisted on a shorter hook. On 10 August, Patton then turned units north from Le Mans, and by 12 August he had taken Alençon. The speed of Patton's movements surprised all concerned. The opportunity to close the Falaise pocket seemed in the offing.

Excluding forces in the Brittany peninsula, there were then some 350,000 German troops west of the Seine. About half were caught in the Falaise pocket, their only route of escape the 15-mile-wide Falaise gap. If American forces could close this, the envelopment would be complete.

At this point, with success apparently in hand, the cautious Bradley ordered Patton to hold at Argentan. Officially, this was to avoid a chance head-on meeting between the two converging Allied armies. but Bradley was clearly concerned about Patton's willingness to leave his flanks open. Patton regarded the risk as both limited and worth taking. Continued slow movement by British and Canadian forces from the north left the pocket open. Allied ineptness, more than German courage and skill, was the primary reason the trap was not closed in time.

Primary responsibility for this failure rests with Bradley, 21st Army Group commander General Bernard L. Montgomery, and Supreme Commander, Allied Expeditionary Forces General Dwight D. Eisenhower. Bradley wanted to take no chances, and Eisenhower preferred to let his subordinates work out strategic and tactical decisions on their own. Eisenhower failed to step in and bring the three competing generals—Montgomery, Bradley, and Patton—to consensus or to order a common plan. Montgomery failed to push his subordinate commanders hard enough, but there were also logistical problems. Other Allied military leaders, including commander of the British Second Army Lieutenant General Sir Miles Dempsey, Canadian First Army commander Lieutenant General Henry Crerar, and Free French 2nd Armored Division commander Major General Jacques Leclerc con-

U.S. soldiers pose in front of a wrecked German tank in Chambois, France, the last German stronghold in the Falaise gap area. 20 August 1944. (National Archives)

tributed to the disjointed nature of the Allied operation. A subsequent proposal by Patton to turn from his drive to the east and make a deeper envelopment was slow to reach Bradley, who ultimately rejected it.

In the Falaise pocket, the Germans lost approximately 200 tanks, 300 heavy guns, 700 artillery pieces, 5,000 vehicles, and a great many carts and horses. But the personnel losses were considerably less than hoped for—no more than 10,000 Germans killed and 50,000 captured. Some 115,000 well-trained German troops escaped the pocket. In all, 240,000 German soldiers crossed the Seine in the last week of August and established a solid defensive line protecting the western approaches to Germany. In September, the Allied Operation MARKET-GARDEN, a combined-arms assault to cross the lower Rhine River into Germany, was stymied by German units that had escaped from Normandy.

Fred R. van Hartesveldt and Spencer C. Tucker

See also

Bradley, Omar Nelson; COBRA, Operation; Eisenhower, Dwight D.; France, Free French; France Campaign (1944); Kluge, Günther Adolf Ferdinand von; Leclerc, Philippe de Hautecloque; MARKET-GARDEN, Operation; Montgomery; Sir Bernard Law; Patton, George Smith, Jr.

References

Blumenson, Martin. *The Battle of the Generals: The Untold Story of the Falaise Pocket: The Campaign That Should Have Won World War II.* New York: William Morrow, 1993.

Hamilton, Nigel. *Monty: The Battles of Field Marshal Bernard Montgomery.* New York: Random House, 1994.

Keegan, John. *Six Armies in Normandy: From D-Day to the Liberation of Paris.* London: Jonathan Cape, 1982.

Lucas, James, and James Barker. *The Killing Ground: The Battle of the Falaise Gap, August 1944.* London: Batsford, 1978.

Whitaker, W. Denis. *Victory at Falaise: The Soldiers' Story.* Toronto, Canada: HarperCollins, 2000.

Operation COBRA and the Falaise–Argentan Pocket
25 July–20 August 1944

Fermi, Enrico (1901–1954)

Italian physicist considered by many to be the "father of the atomic bomb." Born in Rome on 29 September 1901, Enrico Fermi entered the University of Pisa in 1918 and earned his doctorate there in 1922. He developed mathematical models that led to significant advances in understanding the potential for the atom, and he published papers that placed Italy in the center of theoretical and experimental physics. Fermi held professorships at the University of Florence and the University of Rome. One of the first physicists to expound the importance of nuclear physics and quantum theory, Fermi was awarded the Nobel Prize in physics in 1938 for his

Enrico Fermi seated at control panel of a particle accelerator, the "world's most powerful atom smasher." (Library of Congress)

groundbreaking work on neutrons and for identifying a new radioactive element.

After being awarded the Nobel Prize, Fermi left Italy because of his growing concern over the relationship between Fascist Italy and Nazi Germany and to ensure that his wife Laura, a Jew, would not be affected by growing anti-Semitism in Europe. Fermi accepted a professorship at Columbia University in New York City, where he continued to make significant scientific contributions.

In 1942, Fermi moved to the University of Chicago. Here he worked with a group of physicists in the Metallurgical Laboratory and was one of the main architects of the MANHATTAN Project to develop an atomic bomb. Fluent in German, Fermi was aware of the advances made by German physicists in the area of nuclear physics. On 2 December 1942, Fermi's group at the University of Chicago carried out the world's first controlled nuclear chain reaction, providing the experimental groundwork for developing a nuclear weapon. In 1944, Fermi and his team moved to New Mexico, where on 16 July 1945

the first atomic device was detonated at Alamogordo. Fermi is considered by many to be the "father of the atomic bomb." Fermi died in Chicago on 28 November 1954.

James T. Carroll

See also
MANHATTAN Project; Nuclear Weapons
References
Rhodes, Richard. *The Making of the Atomic Bomb.* New York: Simon and Schuster, 1986.
Segre, Emelio. *Enrico Fermi, Physicist.* Chicago: University of Chicago Press, 1995.

Festung Europa

"Fortress Europe," the generic term for the fortifications ringing German-occupied Europe, especially the massive defenses erected on the Atlantic coast from Norway to Spain, the so-called Atlantic Wall. Designed to guard against the possibility of an Allied amphibious invasion, these static defenses stretched from Norwegian outposts on the Arctic Ocean all the way to the more integrated beach and harbor defenses along the Bay of Biscay. In modern military terms, this series of engineering works was an exercise in "force multiplication" in that, by constructing strong defensive works, the Germans expected to be able to use inferior military units to man them, freeing up more capable troops for open warfare elsewhere.

The Germans built the defenses largely by forced and conscripted labor. Under the control and direction of Fritz Todt, German minister of armaments and munitions (and Albert Speer, Todt's successor after February 1942), hundreds of thousands of workers labored to build the fortified positions. The work began slowly, however, only gaining momentum after the tides of war had definitively shifted against the Germans. The plans originated at the direction of Adolf Hitler himself, who ordered the construction of some 15,000 defensive positions to be defended by 300,000 men.

Although Hitler's construction objective was never reached, the numbers were nonetheless impressive. By the time of the Allied invasion of Normandy in June 1944, the Germans had placed 6.5 million mines, erected 500,000 beach obstacles, and expended 1.2 million tons of steel to reinforce 13.3 million tons of concrete in the thousands of positions that were completed.

When Field Marshal Erwin Rommel was appointed to command the likely invasion area, he decried the state of the defenses as he found them. Doubling and tripling the workload, Rommel greatly strengthened the defenses. Nevertheless, his professional opinion was that these works would never be sufficient to keep the Allies off the beaches. He believed that if the Allies came ashore and could establish a lodgment, there would be no way to defeat them. Recognizing the threat not only of amphibious assault but also of parachute and gliderborne attacks, Rommel seeded the open fields and meadows behind the beaches that the Allies might use as landing zones with stout iron bars linked with barbed wire. These obstacles became known as "Rommel's asparagus." In the end, the static defenses erected by the Germans proved no more effective than the French Maginot Line had been four years earlier.

Robert Bateman

See also
Amphibious Warfare; Maginot Line; Normandy Invasion and Campaign; Speer, Albert; Todt Organization
References
Harrison, Gordon A. *United States Army in World War II: The European Theater of Operations: Cross-Channel Attack.* Washington, DC: Center of Military History, 1951.
Kaufman, J. E., and R. M. Jurga. *Fortress Europe.* Conshohocken, PA: Combined Publishing, 1999.
Liddell Hart, Basil H., ed. *The Rommel Papers.* New York: Harcourt Brace, 1953.

Fighter Tactics

Methods and procedures for employing fighter aircraft against enemy aircraft. The sky offers extremes of visibility and no natural cover save clouds. The victor in any fight is usually the one who sees his opponent first. Seeing enemy aircraft is generally difficult; visibility from the cockpit of a typical World War II fighter varied from very bad to good, and there was always a blind area to the rear and below. Early war aircraft such as the Messerschmitt Bf-109E had particularly poor cockpit visibility; later aircraft, such as the Typhoon and P-51D, had bubble canopies that afforded better visibility, but their pilots could still be surprised from behind and below.

Assuming that the cockpit framing and bulletproof windscreen didn't get in the way, individual fighter-sized aircraft could usually be seen perhaps two miles away, four-engine bombers from three or four. A formation or group of aircraft could sometimes be seen six or seven miles away. Visual detection range could be doubled if enemy aircraft were maneuvering. However, aircraft could not be seen by anyone looking directly at or close to the sun, and clouds could provide concealment.

To mount a coordinated attack on a target, it was necessary for a group of fighters to fly in formation. The number of aircraft in the formation and their positions had a relatively large influence on the aircrafts' effectiveness and survivability.

Before World War II, the basic formation used by many air forces (including the British Royal Air Force [RAF]) was a V or "vic" of three aircraft flying very close together, about a wingspan apart. A squadron was typically composed of four vics. This was fine for air displays and flying in cloud, but its severe disadvantage was that every pilot except the formation leader was concentrating on maintaining formation, leaving little time to look for enemy aircraft. Considering that about 80 percent of all pilots who were shot down never saw their attackers, the folly of using this type of formation can be readily understood. Several instances are recorded of a single enemy plane shooting down two or three aircraft without the rest of the formation noticing anything amiss.

The Luftwaffe had learned from combat experience in the Spanish Civil War, and at the urging of Werner Mölders, a leading German fighter pilot in Spain, it adopted a widely spaced *Rotte* (pair) as the basic tactical unit, the two aircraft flying a few hundred yards apart. Each pilot was then free to search for enemy aircraft without worrying about avoiding collision and could easily check the other's blind area, making a surprise attack less likely. When the formation leader attacked a target, the wingman's duty was to guard his leader's tail. The basic unit of maneuver was two pairs arranged side by side like the four fingers of a hand, with the leaders of the pairs at positions two and three. When the RAF and most other air forces eventually adopted this formation during 1941 and 1942, it was usually known as the Finger Four.

The U.S. Navy adopted a variation of this in which the pairs flew farther apart (about one turn radius). When either of the pairs was attacked, the two pairs turned toward each other, providing one pair with a head-on shot at the other pair's attacker. This tactic was known as the Thach Weave after its originator, Lieutenant Commander John S. "Jimmy" Thach. A variant was used by the Soviet air force later in the war. The Soviet air force also learned lessons from the Spanish Civil War, but many of the officers who might have been able to make a systematic change were removed in Josef Stalin's purges.

The nature of fighter-versus-fighter combat is such that the greatest chance of success is to be obtained by gaining a position advantage on an opponent, making a single unobserved attack, and then breaking off. This is essentially the technique used by German ace Erich Hartmann on the Soviet Front. There are numerous recorded instances of this technique working for a single attacker against a large formation of aircraft. The fact is that a single aircraft is much more difficult to spot than a formation, and a formation is more difficult to control than a single aircraft.

A position advantage is really any position that allows an aircraft to launch an attack, the precise nature of which will vary depending on the characteristics of the fighter and target aircraft. When attacking single-seaters, this was somewhere in the rear hemisphere of the target, preferably positioned so that the target would have to look into the sun to see the attacker and usually positioned higher so that the fighter could dive on the target with a speed advantage. The fighter would then open fire in the dive or would dive below the target and shoot in a shallow climb. This variation was favored by German ace Adolf Galland. Many aces were good shots; some went very close to their targets—a few yards, in some cases—to be sure of a kill.

The art of air-to-air gunnery is to ensure that the projectiles and target arrive at the same point in space simultaneously. To accomplish this, the pilot must aim some distance in front of the target; this is called the *deflection angle*. This applies only unless the shooter is immediately behind the target or attacking head-on. Some pilots were able to instinctively apply the correct amount of deflection, but most could not. The British introduced the Gyro Gun Sight in 1944, which dramatically increased the number of hits scored by the average squadron pilot.

Having delivered the attack, the pilot could then either break off combat or convert his speed advantage into an altitude advantage and reattack if necessary. This tactic could be particularly effective if the fighter had good dive acceleration and zoom-climb capabilities (e.g., Messerschmitt Bf-109, P-51 Mustang).

The usual counter to a fighter attack was a very hard ("break") turn toward the attacking aircraft to present a difficult firing solution. After the attacker had fired, several possible courses of action were open to the defender—assuming, of course, that the attacker had failed to do significant damage on his first pass. If the attacker was forced to overshoot, a roll reversal back toward the attacker could yield a firing solution for the defender, but this would probably be fatal if the attacker had a wingman. This maneuver could degenerate into what in current terminology is called a "scissors"; in it, each aircraft repeatedly turns hard toward the other to try to force an overshoot. The advantage in this case would usually be with the aircraft that had the lower wing loading, although pilot skill played a part.

Alternatively, if the attacker continued turning in an effort to get a firing solution and was flying a significantly more maneuverable aircraft (e.g., Spitfire IX versus Messerschmitt Bf-109G or Mitsubishi Zero versus Curtiss P-40), the defender's best option was to break off the engagement. The preferred method of doing this varied with the aircraft's relative capabilities. If the attacker did not have a significant top speed or dive advantage, a favored technique was to half-roll and enter a full-throttle vertical dive (the "split-s" or *Abshwung*). This could lose as much as 10,000 ft of altitude, and if the attacker did not also immediately dive, the defender would usually be able to get sufficient separation and speed to break off the engagement. Finally, if the defender had a maneuverability or performance advantage, he could elect to stay and fight it out by turning hard to get onto his opponent's tail. If his aircraft had a significantly lighter wing loading, three or four circles were usually enough to gain a firing position.

If a formation of disadvantaged aircraft were attacked by enemy aircraft, a viable tactic was to form a defensive circle or "Lufbery," named for a famous American World War I fighter pilot. In this tactic, the defenders flew in a circle so that each aircraft covered the one in front. An attacker would then have to fly through the field of fire of the following aircraft to attack any aircraft in the formation. The defensive circle could be a double-edged sword; during the Battle of Britain, Spitfires were able to get inside defensive circles of Messerschmitt Bf-110s flying in the opposite direction and were able to engage each aircraft in turn without exposure to significant enemy fire. In June 1942, German ace Hans Joachim Marseille managed to shoot down six South African P-40 Tomahawks over Libya by making repeated diving and zoom-climb passes inside a defensive circle and shooting at very high deflection angles.

If the target aircraft had a second crew member, the priority was to approach in such a way that the target was not aware of the presence of the fighter. In the case of a two-seater, this usually meant attacking from below and behind out of the field of fire of defensive weapons. If an unobserved approach was impossible (e.g., for a well-armed four-engine bomber), the choices came down to either approaching from a direction that had poor defensive coverage (e.g., from the beam if the target only had nose and tail weapons) or approaching in such a way as to present a difficult target for defensive weapons (e.g., with a large speed advantage from the rear quarter). If the attacking pilots could shoot accurately, however, the frontal attack was a better and possibly safer option. Bombers usually had fewer and less-effective weapons firing forward, the attackers were exposed to defensive fire for a much shorter period of time, and the bomber's defensive armor was designed to protect from attacks originating from below and behind the bomber rather than from the front.

If the target had defensive armament and was flying in formation, the other aircraft in the formation would be able to contribute defensive fire, and attacking became significantly more hazardous. The effect of defensive fire could be reduced by making multiple simultaneous attacks or by selecting a target on the edge of the formation. Some antibomber weapons (e.g., the German Wgr-21 rocket) were designed to break up formations and allow individual targets to be picked off.

Late in the war, German jet fighters were used against bombers, and the amount of excess speed generated in a dive made sighting extremely difficult. To cope with this, a roller-coaster–type attack was developed whereby the attacking jets approached from the rear of the formation, dived through the fighter screen at speed to a position 1,500 ft below and behind the bombers, and then pulled up into a steep climb to bleed off most of the excess speed before selecting a target and opening fire.

The tactics employed by radar-guided night fighters were concerned more with accurate interception techniques and visual acquisition before firing than with violent maneuvering, although there were exceptions. The tactics were dominated by the target-acquisition performance of onboard radar; the British AI Mk IV had an effective range of 3–4 miles at 15,000 ft, degrading to half a mile at 3,000 ft. The minimum usable radar range was usually about 1,000 yards and the maximum visual acquisition range was usually about 1,400 yards, although this varied depending on moon and cloud conditions.

Most home-defense night fighters relied heavily on ground controllers, although both sides had electronic devices that allowed a fighter to home onto a target from many miles away. The Germans had a Flensburg receiver that homed onto the Monica tail-warning radar and Naxos that detected H2S bombing radar; the British had Serrate, which homed onto German airborne radar transmissions and Perfectos that triggered German aircraft IFF (Identification Friend or Foe) equipment.

Ground control and radar operators usually aimed to approach the target from astern and from slightly below so that the target was silhouetted against the night sky, maximizing the chance of visual acquisition. Very low targets were, however, usually approached from above to maximize radar detection range. German night fighters fitted with *Schräge Musik* (upward-firing cannon) could attack from almost directly below the target and were very effective against RAF bombers until the tactic became known.

Andy Blackburn

See also
Aircraft, Bombers; Aircraft, Fighters; Britain, Battle of; Hartman, Erich Alfred; Identification Friend or Foe (IFF); Kondor Legion; Radar

References
Franks, Norman. *Aircraft versus Aircraft*. London: Grub Street, 1998.
Price, Alfred. *World War II Fighter Conflict*. London: Macdonald and Janes, 1975.
Spick, Mike. *Luftwaffe Fighter Aces: The Jagdflieger and Their Combat Tactics and Techniques*. Mechanicsburg, PA: Stackpole, 1996.
———. *Allied Fighter Aces of World War II*. Mechanicsburg, PA: Stackpole, 1997.

Film and the War

By the beginning of World War II, the governments of the nations involved certainly had grasped the proven persuasive power of film as well as its potential for motivating or manipulating their populations. Whether employed in narrow focus for military training and indoctrination or more widely as documentaries, newsreels, spectacles, dramas, and comedies produced for mass consumption, the medium played a journeyman role during the war years in promoting and sustaining sentiments of national unity and patriotism.

Men and women in military service on all sides of the conflict received intensive practical training, and as a matter of course they also participated in activities designed to increase morale, unit cohesion, and unity of purpose. For many, this preparation included viewing hours of films both instructional and inspirational. In the United States, for example, training films ran the gamut from featurettes or "shorts" on personal hygiene, literacy promotion, and knowing the enemy to detailed elucidations of artillery, aircraft, or naval component operation and maintenance—even a 1942 U.S. Army series on horsemanship for cavalry recruits. The Disney Studios weighed in between 1942 and 1945 with dozens of animated and live-action educational shorts remembered with varying degrees of fondness by many World War II veterans.

In the years leading to war, film studios in the United States (which led world production) began addressing the larger political environment beyond its borders. Although most of the nation tended toward isolationism, Hollywood, with its influential Jewish contingent, reflected a concern with the growing

Nazi and Fascist threat in Europe. Charles Chaplin portrayed a buffoonish Adolf Hitler–like character in his *The Great Dictator* (1940), and the horrors of life in Nazi Germany were revealed in Sherman Scott's *Beasts of Berlin* (1939), which harked back to a sensationalist World War I–era film, *The Kaiser, Beast of Berlin*. Hollywood also produced heroic nationalist films, such as *Sergeant York* (1941), a movie by Howard Hawks about Alvin York, a U.S. Army icon of World War I. Hollywood's anti-Germany/pro-Britain stance is most clearly seen in Henry King's *A Yank in the RAF* (1941), starring Tyrone Power as an American who joins the Royal Air Force. After the United States entered the war, the administration of President Franklin D. Roosevelt mobilized Hollywood with creation of the Office of War Information (OWI) in 1942. Directors and movie stars alike assisted the war effort in a wide variety of ways, from production of training films to starring roles in an increasing number of war epics. Director Frank Capra, famous for his screwball comedies, created an important seven-part documentary series intended for both military and civilian audiences, *Why We Fight* (1942–1944). Hollywood stars were also prominently active in bond rallies, United Service Organizations (USO) tours, and Red Cross events. Actress Carole Lombard, returning from a bond-promoting tour, died in an airplane crash near Las Vegas in 1942.

The studios steadily turned out films that portrayed the heroic efforts of the American armed services, including John Farrow's *Wake Island* (1942), Ray Enright's *Gung Ho!* (1943), Lloyd Bacon's *Action in the North Atlantic* (1943), Tay Garnett's *Bataan* (1943), Lewis Seiler's *Guadalcanal Diary* (1943), Delmar Daves' *Destination Tokyo* (1943), Zoltan Korda's *Sahara* (1943), John Stahl's *Immortal Sergeant* (1943), and Mervyn Le Roy's *Thirty Seconds over Tokyo* (1944). The studios also raised American audiences' spirits with patriotic comedies and musicals including Michael Curtiz's *Yankee Doodle Dandy* (1942), Charles Vidor's *Cover Girl* (1944), Bruce Humberstone's *Pin Up Girl* (1944), and George Sidney's *Anchors Aweigh* (1945).

While Disney labored to produce training films, it also released a popular cartoon in 1943 called *Der Fuehrer's Face* or *Donald Duck in Nutzi Land*. Warner Brothers, on the other hand, routinely spiced theater fare from 1939 through 1945 with a cavalcade of propaganda cartoons featuring Bugs Bunny and Daffy Duck. More complex, studied treatment of the war's personal impact was offered in American films such as Curtiz's *Casablanca* (1943) and Alfred Hitchcock's *Lifeboat* (1944). As the war ground on toward its end, grimmer depictions of real combat emerged from Hollywood, among them John Ford's *They Were Expendable* (1945), William A. Wellman's *The Story of GI Joe* (1945), Edward Dmytryk's *Back to Bataan* (1945), and Lewis Milestone's *A Walk in the Sun* (1946).

In Great Britain, the film industry responded to the war in a fashion mirroring its influential American counterpart.

Before 1937, mainstream British cinema addressed little in the way of international politics or foreign policy, but with the onset of war in 1939—and under heavy government censorship via the Ministry of Information—Britain began one of the most aggressive propaganda film efforts of any warring power. Newsreels abounded, and dramatized documentaries such as *Target for Tonight* (1941), *Coastal Command* (1942), *Fires Were Started* (1943), and *Western Approaches* (1944) had widespread and enthusiastic audiences. Feature films such as Penrose Tennyson's *Convoy* (1941), Anthony Asquith's *Freedom Radio* (1941) and *The Demi-Paradise* (1943), Bernard Miles' *Tawny Pipit* (1944), David Lean's *This Happy Breed* (1944), Michael Powell and Emeric Pressburger's controversial *The Life and Death of Colonel Blimp* (1943) and the morality tale *A Canterbury Tale* (1944), and Asquith's RAF tribute *The Way to the Stars* (1945) personified the resolute British determination to see the war through to victory. Heroic acts of British warriors—not always in World War II—were portrayed in numerous movies, including Powell's *The Lion Has Wings* (1939), Harold French's *The Day Will Dawn* (1942), Charles Friend's *The Foreman Went to France* (1942), Powell's *One of Our Aircraft Is Missing* (1942), Noel Coward's *In Which We Serve* (1942), Frank Launder and Sidney Gilliat's *Millions Like Us* (1943), Sergei Nolbandov's *Undercover* (1943), Carol Reed's *The Way Ahead* (1944), and Sir Laurence Olivier's *Henry V* (1944), famously scored by composer Sir William Walton.

The Soviet film industry, in the firm grip of Stalinist censors by the mid-1930s, produced a string of propaganda works preceding the war that glorified traditional Russian and Soviet heroes such as Peter the Great, the young Civil War commander Vasilii Chapaev, and socialist-realist author Maxim Gorky, balanced evenly by a stream of purely escapist fare. Director Sergei Eisenstein anticipated the coming war with Germany in his epic *Alexander Nevsky* (1938) and obliquely depicted Josef Stalin's dictatorship in his sprawling, two-part *Ivan the Terrible* (1944–1946); both films were brilliantly scored by composer Sergei Prokofiev. Fridrikh Ermler directed perhaps the most emblematic Soviet narrative of the Great Patriotic War, *She Defends the Motherland* (1943), which, along with Mark Donskoi's *The Rainbow* (1944), celebrated Soviet women partisans. Ukrainian Mark Dovzhenko confined his output to *Battle for Our Soviet Ukraine* (1943) and *Victory in Right-Bank Ukraine* (1945). Eminent director Vsevolod Pudovkin portrayed Catherine the Great's military champion in *Suvorov* (1940), addressed the war with *In the Name of the Motherland* (1943), and labored on the eponymous film biography of the tragic nineteenth-century Russian hero of Sevastopol, *Admiral Nakhimov*, which was released in 1946. Unlike in other major Allied and Axis film industries, wartime Soviet production focused primarily on the war at hand, departing from that

James Cagney (front) performing in Yankee Doodle Dandy. (Undated movie still, Bettmann/Corbis)

agenda only to present historical dramas or filmed versions of opera.

French cinema, the most cosmopolitan in Europe just before the war, divided its art between lighthearted fare like Sacha Guitry's *The Story of a Cheat* (1936) and Marcel Pagnol's *The Baker's Wife* (1938) and a darker stratum of melodramas typified by Anatole Litvak's *Mayerling* (1936) and Abel Gance's *Paradise Lost* (1939) and poetic realist films such as Jean Renoir's *The Human Beast* (1938) and Marcel Carne's *Daybreak* (1939). With the German occupation of France in 1940, directors and actors who did not emigrate (many went to the United States) were able to find work in the Vichy-governed free zone or with the German-controlled industry in Paris. Production by the latter rapidly outstripped that of the cash-strapped south. During this period, Pagnol and Gance filmed the trenchant *Well-Digger's Daughter* and *The Blind Venus* (both 1940). Filmmakers were safest, however, producing escapist comedies, musicals, and period dramas such as Carne's *Children of Paradise* (1943–1945), which nonetheless managed to boost the

independent-French spirit. Postliberation film production at first concentrated on documentaries and features detailing the heroic French Resistance. Within several years, however, the war theme became submerged for a time as postwar French film reestablished its place in world cinema.

Italy, like France, endured wartime division, but one of both territory *and* time, marked by the September 1943 armistice and the subsequent military occupation by Germany of its former Axis ally. Since 1926, the Fascist Party had enjoyed a monopoly on the production of documentaries and newsreels, but it displayed ambivalence in using feature films as convenient propaganda vehicles. Only about 5 percent of the more than 700 films produced in Italy between 1930 and 1943 overtly championed Italian accomplishments or adventures in World War I (Goffredo Alessandrini's *Lucio Serra, Pilot* in 1938); in the naval dominion of the Mediterranean Theater (Roberto Rosselini's *The White Ship* of 1941); in the Spanish Civil War (Augusto Genina's 1939 epic *The Seige of Alcazar*); and in the conquest of Africa, glorified in Carmine

Gallone's Roman costume epic *Scipio the African* (1937). The huge body of film not directly concerned with nationalist jingoism was characterized in 1943 by director Luchino Visconti as "a cinema of corpses." Visconti's own *Obsession* (1943) pointed the way out of the Italian morass of Hollywood-inspired "white telephone" features (which, set in opulent surroundings where elegant characters often conversed vacuously on such appliances, obliquely satirized the privileged classes in 1930s Italy) and empty costume dramas toward the postwar achievement of Visconti and his fellow neorealists, whose films offered simple depictions of lower-class life.

As the Nazis consolidated their power during the 1930s, film became the medium of choice for promoting their government's point of view to the German people. By 1937, the National Socialist Party exercised total control over the German film industry, and five years later no private film production companies remained in Germany. Joseph Goebbels took charge of monitoring the film industry, advising executives as to what constituted a "good" film and banning outright several dozen films he believed ran counter to Third Reich values. Of the more than 1,000 films made in Germany under the aegis of the Nazi regime, however, fewer than 15 percent constituted pure propaganda. These were powerfully conceived, such as Leni Riefenstahl's masterful prewar *Triumph of the Will* (1935) and *Olympia* (1938). The ubiquitous newsreels, depicted as Goebbels saw fit, were designed to promote the Nazi Party as Germany headed toward war. Fritz Hippler's overtly anti-Semitic pseudodocumentary *The Wandering Jew* (1940) trumpeted the party's persistent shibboleths; Veit Harlan's *Jew Suss* (1940) couched its message in a costume drama. The numerous dramas and comedies produced for wartime entertainment were not without their political or ideological content: the Prussian spirit was lionized in Wolfgang Liebeneier's *Bismarck* (1940) and Harlan's *The Great King* (1942), the plight of Mary Queen of Scots at the hands of the English was set to music in Carl Froelich's *The Heart of a Queen* (1940), and the nobility of the Afrikaner resisting British dominion in South Africa was celebrated in Hans Steinhoff's *Uncle Kruger* (1941). Eduard von Borsody's *Request Concert* (1940) presented a cavalcade of German musical figures in support of the war effort. As the tide of war turned against the Third Reich, audiences were entertained by outrageous fantasy in Josef von Baky's *Munchausen* (1943). Harlan struggled to film his apocalyptic *Kolberg* during late 1943 and 1944; by the time of its premiere in January 1945, many German theaters had fallen to Allied bombs.

Japan's conquest of China spawned scores of films in the 1930s that lionized the military. As the army grew in power, it acted to control the medium through official means: by 1936 the film industry operated under the Media Section of the Japanese Imperial Army. Strict laws enacted in 1939 governed the production of national policy films designed to portray the dedication and bravery of Japanese warriors and their supporters on the home front, among them Tomotaka Tasaka's *Mud and Soldiers* (1939), Naruse Mikio's *The Whole Family Works* (1939), Ozu Yasujiro's *Brothers and Sisters of the Toda Family* (1941), Tetsu Taguchi's *Generals, Staff, and Soldiers* (1942), and Yamamoto Kajiro's *The War at Sea from Hawaii to Malaya* (1942). Kurosawa Akira's debut *Sanshiro Sugata* (1943) was followed by his industrial paean *The Most Beautiful* in 1944. Period epics such as Uchida Tomu's *History* (1940) and Kinugasa Teinosuke's *The Battle of Kawanakajima* (1941) bolstered reverence for Japanese tradition, and Uchida's *Earth* (1939) portrayed simple farmers. Kurosawa's *They Who Tread on the Tiger's Tail* (1945) endured criticism from both Japanese and U.S.-occupation censors and was not officially released until 1954. The ravages of sustaining the war had taken a grievous toll: from its pinnacle in the 1930s, Japanese film production had dropped from a yearly output of about 500 releases to a mere 26 by the end of 1945.

Since the war's end in 1945, filmmakers in countries touched directly or indirectly by World War II have examined and reexamined its details and have tried to express its lasting political or personal effects throughout the world. Immediately after the war, films such as William Wyler's *The Best Years of Our Lives* (1946) and Fred Zinnemann's *The Men* (1950) depicted the trauma of servicemen returning to civilian life in the United States. Heroism and bravery characterized William Wellman's *Battleground* (1949), Allan Dwan's *Sands of Iwo Jima* (1949), and Henry King's *Twelve o'Clock High* (1949). More complex in tone were Zinneman's *From Here to Eternity* (1953) and David Lean's *Bridge on the River Kwai* (1957). The 1960s and 1970s brought several epic historical dramas to the screen, including *The Longest Day* (Andrew Marton, Ken Annakin, and Bernhard Wicki, 1962), Otto Preminger's *In Harm's Way* (1965), Annakin's *The Battle of the Bulge* (1965), Franklin Schaffner's *Patton* (1970), and the Japanese-American collaboration *Tora! Tora! Tora!* (Masuda Toshio, Fukasaku Kinji, Ray Kellogg, and Richard Fleischer, 1970). American and British audiences also responded favorably to cinematic war stories such as J. Lee-Thompson's *The Guns of Navarone* (1961), John Sturges' *The Great Escape* (1963), Robert Aldrich's *The Dirty Dozen* (1967), Guy Hamilton's *Battle of Britain* (1969), Brian G. Hutton's *Where Eagles Dare* (1969), Mike Nichols' irreverent *Catch-22* (1970), and Richard Attenborough's *A Bridge Too Far* (1977). As the twenty-first century approached, the horrors of combat in World War II, which has been called "the good war," were startlingly revisited to great realistic effect, notably in Terrence Malick's *The Thin Red Line* (1998) and Steven Spielberg's *Saving Private Ryan* (1999). Overblown and historically inaccurate blockbusters such as Michael Bay's *Pearl Harbor* (2001) have contributed little to the cinematic record of the war.

The Soviet Union's nearly Pyrrhic victory in World War II left an indelible mark on the USSR. Such was the collective trauma of coping with more than 20 million deaths in battle and in the ravaged cities that memorializing the Great Patriotic war soon displaced the great October Revolution as the national touchstone—becoming, in effect, the secular state religion. Film would become indispensable in the solemnization of the immense national loss, but in the immediate postwar period Soviet studios were hamstrung by a general ideological retrenchment that oppressively slowed film production. Emerging from this situation was a film expressing the apotheosis of the Stalinist cult of personality blended with the glory of the recent victory over Germany, Mikhail Chiaureli's two-part *The Fall of Berlin* (1949–1950). In the years after Josef Stalin's death in 1953, a cultural thaw gradually yielded more expressive and complex war films such as Mikhail Kalatozov's *The Cranes Are Flying* (1957), Grigorii Chukhrai's *Ballad of a Soldier* (1959), Andrei Tarkovsky's *Ivan's Childhood* (1962), and Alexander Askoldov's allegory of the October Revolution, *The Commissar* (1967). The stagnant Leonid Brezhnev years of the late 1960s to the early 1980s produced a string of mostly forgettable rote panegyrics to the war's memory, but standing out due to its massive scale, length (five parts), and sheer volume was Iurii Ozerov's epic *Liberation* (1972). This was balanced soberly in 1985 by Elem Klimov's tragic and unrelenting *Come and See*. With the artistic freedom afforded them beginning in the late 1980s by Mikhail Gorbachev's perestroika and glasnost, Soviet directors indulged in social and cultural criticism as never before. Yet the war still loomed in Ozerov's *Stalingrad* (1989) and Mikhail Ptashuk's *August 1944* (2000).

France and Italy evinced complex and ambivalent political and artistic landscapes as a result of their war experiences. The war's compromised memory was expressed in haunting films from French director Alain Resnais such as *Hiroshima Mon Amour* (1959) and *Muriel* (1963) and by Italian directors Roberto Rosselini's *Open City* (1945), Carlo Borghesio's satirical *How I Lost the War* (1947), and Rosselini's grim *Paisa* (1946) and nihilistic *Germany, Year Zero* (1948). The urban and economic ruins of postwar Italy informed classics like Vittorio de Sica's *Shoeshine* (1946), *The Bicycle Thief* (1947), and *Umberto D.* (1952). The Fascists and the war receded from mainstream cinematic view until renewed interest was revealed in such varied films as Bernardo Bertolucci's *The Conformist* and *The Spider's Strategem* of 1970, de Sica's *Garden of the Finzi-Continis* (1971), Federico Fellini's nostalgic *Amarcord* (1973), Ettore Scola's *A Special Day* (1977), Paolo and Vittorio Taviani's *The Night of the Shooting Stars* (1982), and Gabriele Salvatores' *Mediterraneo* (1991). Acknowledgment of the German occupation and the Vichy era emerged in the work of French directors, including Claude Chabrol's *Line of Demarcation* (1966), Marcel Ophuls' *The Sorrow and the Pity* (1969), Louis Malle's *Lacombe Lucien*

(1974), François Truffaut's *The Last Metro* (1980), Malle's *Au Revoir les Enfants* (1987), Ophuls' *Hotel Terminus* (1987), and Chabrol's *The Story of Women* (1988) and *Eye of Vichy* (1993).

Germany and Japan shared in their utter defeat and subsequent occupation by the Allies, and their film industries came under strict censorship. In Japan, copies of more than 200 films on topics forbidden by the Americans were rounded up and burned in 1946; similar German films not already expropriated by the Soviets were likewise confiscated. In East Germany, the base of the film industry, Wolfgang Staudte depicted the postwar situation in *The Murderers Are Among Us* (1946), while Slatan Dudow offered tribute to the new socialist order in *Our Daily Bread* (1949) and Gerhard Klein offered a study of love divided by politics in *Berlin Romance* (1956). West Germans were held to a strict regimen of Allied reeducation, under which depressing melodramas like Josef von Baky's *The Sky Above Us* (1947) found approval, but U.S. imports like *Gone with the Wind* were banned. In West Germany in 1951, Peter Lorre directed *The Lost Man*, Robert Siodmak exposed the Gestapo in *The Devil Strikes at Midnight* (1957), and Bernhard Wicki questioned the war in *The Bridge* (1959). Ichikawa Kon directed moving Japanese war stories in *The Burmese Harp* (1956) and *Fires on the Plains* (1959), Kumai Kei explored Japanese treatment of American prisoners of war in *The Sea and Poison* (1986), and Japan's nuclear trauma was expressed in Imamura Shohei's *Black Rain* (1989). Perhaps the most outstanding film ever produced about submarine warfare was the German film *Das Boot* (1982), directed by Wolfgang Petersen.

Andrzej Wajda of Poland directed significant films about the war: *Generation* (1955), *Kanal* (1957), and *Ashes and Diamonds* (1958). Polish film also addressed the aftermath of Auschwitz in Andrzej Munk's *The Passenger* (1963), and Janusz Zaorski's *Mother of Kings* (1976) examined Poland's history from the period of World War II to Stalinist times. The effects of the war on India were explored in Satyajit Ray's *Distant Thunder* (1973). In presenting the theme of a controversial romance between a Thai woman and a Japanese officer in wartime Thailand, director Euthana Mukdasanit's *Sunset at Chaopraya* (1996) moved almost full circle in echoing the similar tension of Japanese director Fushimizu Osamu's notorious propaganda film of 1940, *China Nights*.

Whether triumphant, tragic, sentimental, dispassionate, or cynical in tone, these postwar films bear witness to the persistence of World War II in collective human memory and the questions the war continues to provoke.

Gordon E. Hogg and T. Jason Soderstrum

See also
Goebbels, Paul Joseph; Hitler, Adolf; Propaganda
References
Chambers, John Whiteclay, II, and David Culbert, eds. *World War II, Film and History*. New York: Oxford University Press, 1996.

Chapman, James. *The British at War: Cinema, State, and Propaganda, 1939–1945.* London and New York: I. B. Tauris, 1998.

Doherty, Thomas. *Projections of War: Hollywood, American Culture, and World War II.* New York: Columbia University Press, 1993.

Ehrlich, Evelyn. *Cinema of Paradox: French Filmmaking under the German Occupation.* New York: Columbia University Press, 1985.

Gillespie, David. *Russian Cinema.* New York: Longman, 2003.

Landy, Marcia. *Fascism in Film: The Italian Commercial Cinema, 1931–1943.* Princeton, NJ: Princeton University Press, 1986.

Murphy, Robert. *British Cinema and the Second World War.* London: Continuum, 2000.

Nowell-Smith, Geoffrey, ed. *The Oxford History of World Cinema.* Oxford and New York: Oxford University Press, 1996.

Rentschler, Eric. *The Ministry of Illusion: Nazi Cinema and Its Afterlife.* Cambridge, MA: Harvard University Press, 1996.

Richie, Donald. *Japanese Cinema.* Oxford and New York: Oxford University Press, 1990.

Finland, Air Force

In the 1930s, two controversies hindered Finnish aircraft acquisition. The first was the issue of whether fighters or bombers should have priority (the need for fighters seeming paramount). The second was the country from which to purchase aircraft. The head of the Defense Council, Carl Mannerheim, favored Germany, and the air force commander, Colonel Jarl Lundquist (later a lieutenant general), favored Britain. Mannerheim stressed the danger of air attacks on Finnish cities when arguing for more funds for the air force, but he gave priority to air support for ground forces when war came.

In September 1939, the Finnish Air Force (FAF) had only 36 modern interceptors (Dutch Fokker D-XXIs) and 21 bombers (14 Bristol Blenheims and 7 Junkers K430s). Lundquist deployed his limited fighter assets forward to protect the army and defend as much Finnish air space as possible. Following the Soviet invasion of Finland in November 1939, Finnish bombers attacked airfields and supported ground forces. In late December 1939, the FAF was able to purchase additional Fokker fighters, but its best aircraft came in the form of Morane-Saulnier MS-406s purchased from France. The Finns purchased additional Blenheims, U.S. Brewster F2A Buffalos (the Finns enjoyed considerable success with this much-maligned aircraft), Italian Fiat G-50s, and additional MS 406s. Most arrived too late for the war.

During this Finnish-Soviet War of 1939–1940, also called the Winter War, the FAF supposedly accounted for approximately 200 Soviet aircraft, and more than 300 others were destroyed by antiaircraft fire or on the ground. Finnish losses during the war amounted to 62 aircraft.

In 1941, when Finland again went to war with the Soviet Union (the Finnish-Soviet War of 1941–1944, also called the Continuation War), Finland's air force had increased substantially. It possessed 144 modern fighters (a mixture of U.S., British, French, Dutch, and Italian planes); 44 British and ex-Soviet bombers; and 63 mostly British and German reconnaissance planes. Once the Continuation War began, Finnish access to aircraft from other nations except Germany was cut off. The Finns did have their own aircraft industry, which produced limited numbers of aircraft including the VL Myrsky II fighter.

Finnish Air Force strategy stressed aggressiveness; isolated fighters usually attacked no matter the number of Soviet aircraft. The FAF employed a blue swastika marking (no relation to the Nazi version) for national identification. The Luftwaffe and FAF cooperated in this conflict, although neither could prevent Soviet air raids into Finnish territory nor completely screen the Finnish army from air attacks.

Britton W. MacDonald

See also

Aircraft, Bombers; Aircraft, Fighters; Finland, Defeat of; Finnish-Soviet War (Continuation War); Finnish-Soviet War (Winter War); Germany, Air Force; Mannerheim, Carl G. E. von

References

Kirby, D. G. *Finland in the Twentieth Century.* Minneapolis: University of Minnesota Press, 1979.

Tillotson, H. M. *Finland at Peace and War, 1918–1993.* Wilby, UK: Michael Russell, 1993.

Trotter, William R. *A Frozen Hell: The Russo-Finnish War of 1939–40.* Chapel Hill, NC: Algonquin Books, 1991.

Finland, Army and Navy

In September 1939, Finland had a small military establishment. Finland's war mobilization plan dated from May 1934 and divided the country into nine military regions. Depending on its size and population density, each region had two or three districts. Each district furnished one infantry regiment of three battalions and a field artillery battalion of 12 guns. The more populous districts provided additional support troops or regiments. On full mobilization, Finland could call up some 337,000 men. Carl Gustav Mannerheim, commander of the Finnish armed forces, designed the plan. Despite his best efforts, the military services were constantly underfunded, underequipped, and plagued by a government that insisted on relying on domestic sources that often did not exist.

When the first Finnish-Soviet War (the Winter War) began in 1939, the Finns concentrated their forces in key areas along the Soviet border, much of it impassable wilderness. The army fought hard and well, uninhibited by any rigid military doctrine or tactical theory. It used initiative and guile in exploiting terrain to its advantage—making fierce, sudden attacks according to *motti* tactics (motti is the Finnish word for a pile of logs held together by stakes ready to be chopped into firewood) to ambush and destroy road-bound Soviet

Finnish infantry troops in action in World War II. (Hulton-Deutsch Collection/CORBIS)

columns. Finnish military thought had stressed encirclement tactics since the 1930s. The Motti tactics were highly successful, involving mobile Finnish ski troops trained to fight in winter conditions who took advantage of their familiarity with the terrain. By February 1940, however, in consequence of Soviet air supremacy, the Finns could hold their lines only by withdrawing during the day and counterattacking at night. Finally, the Finnish army was ground down by vastly superior Soviet numbers and firepower. During the Winter War, the Finnish military sustained 22,425 killed, 1,424 missing, and 43,557 wounded.

On the conclusion of peace, Mannerheim immediately began making plans to rebuild the military. His new mobilization plan provided for 16 divisions with a total strength of 475,000 troops, or 13 percent of the entire population. Because of the limited Finnish economic base, any future war would have to be concluded speedily. Mannerheim also increased the amount of artillery in the army, forming a tank battalion equipped with tanks captured from the Soviets and acquired from Britain plus a heavy-tank platoon and seven independent-tank platoons.

The second Finnish-Soviet War (1941–1944), known as the Continuation War, began in late June 1941. In this war, the Finns took back their 1939 borders and a slight amount of additional territory. The Soviets fought stubbornly, and the Finns suffered unexpectedly high casualties. After reaching those borders in late September, the Finns advanced into Soviet territory to shorten their three front lines on the Karelian isthmus, but they refused to take part in operations against Leningrad as the Germans wished. A lull in the fighting allowed 20 percent of the troops to be demobilized and returned to industry and agricultural pursuits in the early months of 1942. When the tide of war on the Eastern Front turned decisively against Germany, the Soviets renewed their attacks against the Finns in June 1944, and with vastly superior resources they soon overwhelmed the Finnish positions. Fighting was concluded by a cease-fire in September 1944. During the Continuation War, the Finns suffered approximately 65,000 dead against the Soviets and a further 2,000 against the German forces following the end of fighting with the Soviets.

The Finnish navy was quite small, and its activities were largely limited to minelaying. At the start of the Winter War, Finland had 5 submarines, 2 armored coastal vessels, 4 gunboats, and 10 motor torpedo boats. Operations in the Gulf of Finland halted in the winter when it froze. The Finnish navy cooperated with German naval units during the Continuation

War to confine the Soviet Baltic Fleet to the eastern end of the Gulf, and it mined the Soviet coast. Throughout the Continuation War, Finnish naval strategy was defensive, designed to prevent the Soviets from interfering with trans-Baltic shipping or intervening in the land battles.

Britton W. MacDonald

See also

BARBAROSSA, Operation; Finland, Air Force; Finland, Role in War; Finnish-Soviet War (Continuation War); Finnish-Soviet War (Winter War); Mannerheim, Carl Gustav Emil von

References

Erfurth, Waldemar. *The Last Finnish War.* Washington, DC: University Publications of America, 1979.

Kirby, D. G. *Finland in the Twentieth Century.* Minneapolis: University of Minnesota Press, 1979.

Mannerheim, Carl. *The Memoirs of Marshal Mannerheim.* London: Cassell, 1953.

Tillotson, H. M. *Finland at Peace and War, 1918–1993.* Wilby, UK: Michael Russell, 1993.

Trotter, William R. *A Frozen Hell: The Russo-Finnish War of 1939–40.* Chapel Hill, NC: Algonquin Books, 1991.

Finland, Role in War

Finland numbered some 3.6 million people in September 1939. The country had secured its independence from Russia in 1917, but the Finns had to fight to maintain it. Concerned about the growth of German military power, in the late 1930s Soviet dictator Josef Stalin applied pressure on Finland for territory in the Karelian Isthmus and for the naval base of Hango on the Gulf of Finland to provide protection for Leningrad, the Soviet Union's second-largest city. In return, Stalin was prepared to yield more territory than he sought, but it was far to the north. The Finnish leadership, believing the Soviets were bluffing, rejected the demands. The Soviet Union invaded Finland in November 1939, and the first Soviet-Finnish War (known as the Winter War) lasted until March 1940. The governments of both Great Britain and France discussed the possibility of military intervention, in large part to cut Germany off from Swedish iron ore, but both Norway and Sweden denied transit rights to the Allies. Commander of Finnish armed forces Marshal Carl Mannerheim led a spirited Finnish defense. However, the Finns were overwhelmed by sheer weight of Russian numbers and military hardware. On 12 March 1940, the Finns signed the Treaty of Moscow. By the terms of the treaty, which went into effect at noon the next day, Finland lost one-tenth of its territory, including the entire Karelian Isthmus. The country then had to absorb 400,000 refugees, as virtually all the Finns moved out of the surrendered territory rather than live under Soviet rule.

New Soviet pressure angered the Finns, who signed a secret transit agreement with Germany in August 1940 allowing German troops to pass through Finland to northern Norway. Discussions began between the German and Finnish staffs regarding Operation BARBAROSSA, the German invasion of the Soviet Union, but the Germans never told the Finns details of the plan until the invasion was about to commence. The Germans began arms shipments to Finland in 1941, particularly artillery and antitank weapons. By June 1941, the Finnish government of President Risto Ryti committed to the plan but resisted a formal alliance with Germany, maintaining that the Finns were merely fighting a defensive war against Soviet aggression and were a cobelligerent. Indeed, the Finns managed to evade every request for such an alliance throughout the war.

Finland never defined war aims for this second Soviet-Finnish War, the Continuation War. Halting offensive military operations 50 to 90 miles beyond the 1939 borders (the additional territory taken for defensive reasons) was the clearest statement of its aims. Carl Mannerheim, commander of Finnish armed forces, hoped that by limiting its advance into Soviet territory, Finland might retain its friendship with the United States and Great Britain. The Finnish government endeavored to convey the impression that Finland had been drawn into the conflict, although this was hard to accomplish with German troops in Finland before the commencement of BARBAROSSA, with naval cooperation between Finland and Germany, and with the German air force flying in Finnish air space and refueling at Finnish airfields. Britain warned Finland at the end of September to advance only to the 1939 frontiers and declared war on Finland on 6 December 1941, the same day Finland halted its advance into Soviet territory.

The front with the Soviet Union was stable from May 1942 until June 1944, when the Soviets launched a powerful offensive with vastly superior manpower and firepower. The Ribbentrop-Ryti agreement between the German foreign minister, Joachim von Ribbentrop, and Ryti was signed in late June 1944, promising that Finland would not seek a separate peace in exchange for weapons. Finland had earlier in the year rejected peace terms from the Soviet Union because of their harshness and because Finland hoped that an Allied invasion of Germany would cause the Red Army to race to Berlin. By July, the Red Army was doing exactly that; President Ryti resigned, and Mannerheim assumed office. Mannerheim repudiated Ryti's agreement and negotiated a cease-fire with the Soviet Union. As part of the cease-fire, concluded on 19 September 1944, Finland had to expel or intern all German troops on its soil. This went peacefully until the Germans tried to seize Suursaari Island, which led to bitter fighting there and in Lapland in northern Finland. Although the campaign was virtually over at the end of November 1944 (the date established by the cease-fire agreement for Finnish demobilization), the last German troops did not depart Finland until April 1945.

A Finnish ski patrol looking for Russian troops on the Petsamo front, in northern Finland during the Finnish-Soviet War (Winter War) of 1939–1940. (Library of Congress)

The cease-fire and later armistice with the Soviet Union reaffirmed the 1940 borders, accepted Soviet reparations demands for raw materials and machinery, and limited the Finnish military in numbers and types of weapons. Finland lost in the nearly 92,000 dead (including 2,700 civilians) during World War II. The Soviet Union did not occupy Finland, and Finland's political institutions were left intact—the only eastern enemy of the Soviet Union so treated.

Britton W. MacDonald

See also

BARBAROSSA, Operation; Finland, Air Force; Finland, Army and Navy; Finnish-Soviet War (Continuation War); Finnish-Soviet War (Winter War); Mannerheim, Carl Gustav Emil von; Stalin, Josef

References

Erfurth, Waldemar. *The Last Finnish War.* Washington, DC: University Publications of America, 1979.

Kirby, D. G. *Finland in the Twentieth Century.* Minneapolis: University of Minnesota Press, 1979.

Mannerheim, Carl. *The Memoirs of Marshal Mannerheim.* London: Cassell, 1953.

Tillotson, H. M. *Finland at Peace and War, 1918–1993.* Wilby, UK: Michael Russell, 1993.

Warner, Oliver. *Marshal Mannerheim and the Finns.* London: Weidenfield and Nicolson, 1967.

Finnish-Soviet War (30 November 1939–12 March 1940) (Winter War)

Regional conflict between Finland and the Soviet Union. In late 1939, Soviet leader Josef Stalin was concerned with the sharp increase in German power following the conquest of Poland, and he sought to acquire additional territory to protect portions of the Soviet Union from possible German attack through Finland. He was especially anxious to protect approaches to Leningrad, which was only 20 miles from the Finnish border on the Karelian Isthmus. These security concerns prompted Stalin to demand that Finland cede much of the isthmus, destroy all fortifications there, and cede certain islands in the gulf, as well as to grant the Soviet Union land for a naval base to the west on the Hango Peninsula. Stalin was prepared to grant more territory than he demanded—

Troops Involved in Finnish-Soviet War, 1939–1940

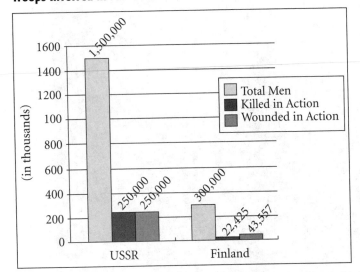

2,134 square miles in return for 1,066—although the Soviet territory Stalin offered was in the less desirable north in East Karelia above Lake Ladoga.

With a population of only 3.6 million people (the Soviet population was 193 million in 1941), Finland hardly seemed in position to reject Stalin's demands. Although the Finns were open to some compromise regarding territory above Leningrad, they were upset about demands for the destruction of their fortifications and a for naval base on the Hango Peninsula. Tough negotiations continued for two months without result. Finnish leaders believed that Stalin was bluffing, but after a contrived border incident on 26 November, Stalin ordered the invasion, which began on 30 November 1939. It was not one of Stalin's finer military exploits. Despite overwhelming superiority in manpower, resources, and equipment, it took the Red Army nearly four months to crush its tiny opponent.

About the only advantages for Finland were the harsh climate, soldiers' familiarity with the area, superior leadership and training, and high morale (the Finns were fighting for their homeland). The abundant forests provided good cover and concealment amid sparse settlements and poor trails. Only the Karelian Isthmus had developed towns and farming areas with roads. This environment worked against mechanized operations and gave the advantage to mobile forces equipped with skis. Marshal Carl Gustav Mannerheim, commander of the Finnish forces, possessed keen insight regarding the strengths and weaknesses of the Red Army, and Finnish commissioned and noncommissioned officers were well trained and exhibited considerable initiative.

In all, the Finns fielded about 300,000 men. They had only 422 artillery pieces, 32 tanks, and a few aircraft. Many independent battalions and separate companies were dispersed throughout the country. The Finns lacked equipment of all

sorts, and what they had was a mixed variety provided from different countries. The soldiers were well acclimated and wore white camouflage uniforms to facilitate swift movement. The Finns also did what they could to strengthen their natural defensive line on the Karelian Isthmus by constructing obstacles, trenches, and bunkers.

For the initial invasion, Stalin employed only 20 Soviet divisions against 16 Finnish divisions, and he must bear responsibility for the initial Soviet military failure in Finland. Fresh from the Red Army's relatively bloodless triumph in Poland, Stalin personally intervened to reject the plan advanced by his chief of staff, Marshal Boris M. Shaposhnikov, which entailed a careful buildup and use of the best Soviet troops, even those from the Far East. Many of the Soviet units were poorly trained and improvised formations. Worse, the Soviet troops were unprepared for winter fighting. Stalin rebuked Shaposhnikov for overestimating the Finns and underestimating the Red Army. The new plan, worked out on Stalin's orders and confirmed by him, led to the fiasco of the early Soviet defeats, leaving Shaposhnikov to remedy the situation.

The Soviet military was in wretched shape; recent purges had decimated the officer corps and left in command unqualified men who were reluctant to take the initiative. The soldiers were poorly trained in winter fighting and breaching fortified lines. The standard Soviet rifle division was well manned and equipped, but the heavy material was not suited to such a primitive operational environment. The Soviets did have an advantage in heavy artillery, but very little coordination had been developed between the arms, so attacks were not synchronized for effectiveness. A severe lack of communications equipment added to the problems of coordination and tactical flexibility. Among the rank and file, morale was poor. These factors mitigated overwhelming Soviet advantages in manpower and quantities of equipment.

In December 1939, the Finns halted the main Russian thrust across the Karelian Isthmus at the so-called Mannerheim Line. The Finns gained an early advantage when they obtained the Soviet tactical codes through the corps level. Thus they could monitor Soviet radio communications and decrypt Soviet units' locations. This intelligence became a force multiplier and helped the Finns to detect, outmaneuver, and defeat far larger Soviet formations. The Finns would cut off the enemy line of communications, separate the road-bound columns into pockets called *mottis* (motti is the Finnish word for a pile of logs held together by stakes ready to be chopped into firewood), and then destroy them piecemeal. By moving quickly, firing from concealed positions, and rapidly eliminating Soviet patrols, the Finns produced fear that reduced the ability of Soviet forces to react. The Finns also showed great ability in improvisation (as with the gasoline bomb in a bottle hurled at Russian tanks and dubbed "Molotov cocktail"), by their effec-

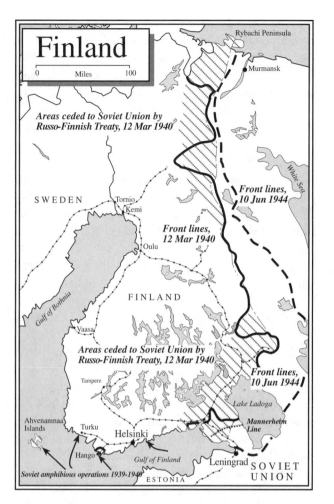

concessions well in excess of those sought before the war. The Finns were forced to yield some 25,000 square miles of territory, including the Karelian Isthmus. The war also displaced some 400,000 Finns, for virtually all left the territory ceded to the Soviet Union.

Although Soviet terms were regarded as harsh by the Finns and by Finland's many international supporters, they were mild compared with those the Soviet Union imposed on the other three Baltic countries. In the case of Finland, Stalin may have been deterred by strong anti-Soviet sentiment that the invasion had aroused throughout the world. Indeed, 11,500 volunteers went to Finland to fight against the Soviets. Britain and France actually considered military intervention against the Soviet Union, including bombing strikes against the Caucasian oil fields and an "uninvited landing" in Norway as a preliminary step to sending troops to Finland. Seen in retrospect, such a step would have been disastrous to the Allied war effort. Stalin may also have been restrained by his desire to keep open the option of a possible alliance with the west against Hitler and to minimize the many disadvantages resulting from the Soviet aggression. One consequence for the Soviet Union of its invasion, expulsion from the League of Nations, was not a major blow.

Ultimately, the Soviets threw 1.5 million men (almost half their army in Europe), 3,000 aircraft, and nearly as many tanks against Finland. The Soviets suffered 230,000 to 270,000 dead—many the result of the cold and because of poor Soviet medical services—and a comparable number of wounded. They also lost 1,800 tanks and 634 aircraft. The Finns sustained far fewer casualties (22,425 killed and 43,557 wounded), and 62 of the 162 planes of their largely antiquated air force were lost.

> The Soviets threw 1.5 million men, 3,000 aircraft, and nearly as many tanks against Finland.

One of the war's most important effects was the damage to Soviet military prestige. Many observers believed that the Soviet Union was incapable of waging a large-scale war. This was a conclusion Hitler was too quick to draw. Another consequence was the Soviet decision to adopt the Finnish automatic sidearm. After the German invasion of the Soviet Union in June 1941, Finland waged war against the Soviet Union as a cobelligerent of Germany, a decision that led to it unfairly being branded as an Axis power and to its second defeat in 1944.

Steven J. Rauch and Spencer C. Tucker

See also

Finland, Role in War; Mannerheim, Carl Gustav Emil; Shaposhnikov, Boris Mikhailovich; Stalin, Josef; Timoshenko, Semen Konstantinovich

tive use of ski troops, and by fitting largely antiquated biplane aircraft with skis so that they could operate in snow.

After decisive tactical defeats destroyed several of their divisions at Tolvajarvi and Suomussalmi, the Soviets brought in new divisions and spent almost a month training intensively in tactics to develop better coordination among infantry, tanks, and artillery. In addition, they focused on better close-air support and the development of mobile reserves to exploit breakthroughs. At the small-unit level, special assault groups were organized to destroy Finnish bunkers efficiently.

Not until February 1940 did Soviet forces mount an effective assault on the Mannerheim Line. They doubled their strength against the Mannerheim Line with the Northwest Front, commanded by Marshal Semyon K. Timoshenko, and concentrated more than 35 divisions, which included heavy artillery and new-model tanks, against the weakened Finns. Sheer weight of numbers enabled the Soviets to break through the Finnish line at Summa on 11 February, and by 8 March they captured part of the key Finnish defensive anchor at Viipuri (Vyborg).

Stalin then dictated a peace settlement. Stalin did not annex Finland, or even Helsinki, but he exacted territorial

References

Condon, Richard. *The Winter War.* New York: Ballantine Books, 1972.

Trotter, William R. *A Frozen Hell: The Russo-Finnish Winter War of 1939–1940.* Chapel Hill, NC: Algonquin, 1991.

Upton, A. F. *Finland in Crisis, 1940–1941.* Ithaca, NY: Cornell University Press, 1964.

Warner, Oliver. *Marshal Mannerheim and the Finns.* London: Weidenfield and Nicolson, 1967.

Finnish-Soviet War (25 June 1941– 4 September 1944) (Continuation War)

Renewal of warfare between Finland and the Soviet Union, also called the Continuation War. The fighting occurred mainly northwest and northeast of the Soviet city of Leningrad.

Finland's rejection of Soviet demands for territory and bases to protect access to Leningrad—including the cession of Viipuri (Vyborg), Finland's second-largest city, and the surrounding Karelian Isthmus—led to the first Finnish-Soviet War, known as the Winter War. The war began in November 1939, and although the Finns fought well, the odds against them were hopeless. In March 1940, Finland was obliged to sue for peace, in which it had to cede even more territory that the Soviets had originally demanded.

Fearing additional Soviet demands and resenting Soviet interference in its policies, Finland aligned itself with Germany. In fall 1940, chief of the Finnish General Staff Lieutenant General Erik Heinrichs held talks in Berlin with German leaders, who requested Finnish assistance during Operation BARBAROSSA, the planned German invasion of the Soviet Union (chiefly of Leningrad and Murmansk). The Finnish government welcomed this as an opportunity to recover territory lost to the Soviet Union in the Winter War. As planning progressed, the Germans and Finns agreed that German forces would secure the nickel-rich Petsamo region and attack Murmansk in the far north, while the Finns would be responsible for operations in the southeast toward Leningrad and Soviet Karelia, centered around Petrozavodsk. General Carl Mannerheim (he was raised to field marshal in 1942) commanded the Finnish forces, as he had in the Winter War of 1939–1940. Mannerheim had 16 divisions: 11 along the frontiers, 1 opposite the Russian base at Hanko, and 4 in reserve.

On 22 June 1941, the Germans launched their massive invasion of the Soviet Union. Finland had already secretly mobilized its forces and declared war on 25 June, but as a cobelligerent of Germany rather than as an ally. The German drive in the far north from Petsamo eastward fell short of both Murmansk and the large Soviet naval base at Polyarny. German forces also had little luck driving east from the northern city of Rovaniemi, failing to cut the Soviet rail line running from Murmansk south along the White Sea coast. In the south, however, the Finns made much better progress. Preoccupied with the massive German onslaught, Red Army forces north of Leningrad were outnumbered.

General Mannerheim divided his forces into two armies: one drove down the Karelian Isthmus between the Gulf of Finland and Lake Ladoga, and the other marched southeast between Lake Ladoga and Lake Onega toward the Svir River to take Petrozavodsk, capital of Karelia. On 29 June, the Finnish Karelian Army (II, IV, VI, and VII Corps) attacked to the west and east of Lake Ladoga, crossing the Russo-Finnish border of 1940, recapturing Finnish Karelia, and driving on toward Leningrad. Aided by German contingents, Army Group Mannerheim attacked Soviet Karelia. Farther north, combined Finnish and German forces recaptured lost Finnish territory around Salla while the German mountain troops, coming from Norway, reached as far as the Litsa River on their drive toward Murmansk.

The Finns had originally planned to unite their troops with German Army Group North around Leningrad. On 1 September, the Finns reached the old Russo-Finnish border. Despite heavy fighting, the Soviets were able to withdraw, but by late August the Finns had recovered all territory lost to the Soviet Union in the Winter War. The Finnish attacks stalled north of Lake Ladoga in September.

Although the Finns were not eager to take non-Finnish land, they did advance somewhat beyond the pre– November 1939 borders for defensive purposes. Much to Germany's displeasure, however, they refused to cooperate with German troops against the city of Leningrad. Finnish and German commanders disliked each other, and the German air force failed to provide as much air cover as had been promised. German troops did not perform well in the northern part of the front. In the dense forests and swamps that marked the terrain in the north, tanks, heavy artillery, and aircraft were often ineffective. Finnish casualties were not light, and Finland had a small population and insufficient resources for a long war. Given these points, the Finns only undertook those operations that suited them, and that did not include Leningrad. The Finns were nonetheless disappointed that the German army was unable to secure a rapid defeat of the Soviet Union.

After capturing Petrozavodsk and Medweschjegorsk on the western and northern shore of Lake Onega, in December the Finns established a defensive position somewhat inside Soviet territory and about 20 miles from Leningrad. Had the Finns advanced farther, Leningrad would probably have fallen to the Germans, with uncertain consequences for the fighting on the Eastern Front. The Finnish Front remained largely static from early 1942. Despite some Soviet counterattacks toward Petsamo, the battle lines changed very little in the months to follow.

At this point, in August 1942, Moscow offered the Finns extensive territorial concessions in return for a separate peace, but the Finns, confident of an ultimate German victory, refused. In September 1941, London and Washington made it clear to Helsinki that any Finnish effort to advance beyond its prewar frontiers would mean war. Indeed, Britain declared war on Finland in December 1941.

As the war continued into 1942 and then 1943, the Finns lost enthusiasm for the struggle, especially when German military fortunes changed. In January 1944, a Soviet offensive south of Leningrad broke the blockade of that city. With the tide fast turning against Germany, the Finns asked the Soviets for peace terms, but the response was so harsh that Finland rejected it. Not only would Finland have to surrender all its territorial gains, but it would have to pay a large indemnity.

Soviet leader Josef Stalin then decided to drive Finland from the war. The Soviets assembled some 45 divisions with about half a million men, more than 800 tanks, and some 2,000 aircraft. Using these assets, in June 1944 the Soviets began an advance into Finland on both flanks of Lake Ladoga on the relatively narrow Karelian and Leningrad Fronts. While the Finns were well entrenched along three defensive lines, they could not withstand the Soviet onslaught. Viipuri fell on 20 June after less stubborn resistance than during the Winter War. Heavy fighting also occurred in eastern Karelia. Although they failed to achieve a breakthrough, Soviet forces caused the Finns to retreat and took the Murmansk Railway.

After the fall of Viipuri, the Finnish government requested German assistance. The Germans furnished dive-bombers, artillery, and then some troops, but it demanded in return that Finland ally itself firmly with Germany and promise not to conclude a separate peace. President Risto Ryti, who had been forced to provide a letter to that effect to German Foreign Minister Joachim von Ribbentrop (which bound him, but not his country, to such a policy), resigned on 1 August in favor of Marshal Mannerheim.

On 25 August, Helsinki asked for terms. Moscow agreed to a cease-fire to take effect on 4 September, but Soviet forces actually fought on for another day after that. One of the cease-fire terms was that the Finns should break diplomatic relations with Berlin and order all German troops from Finnish soil by 15 September. German leader Adolf Hitler refused the Finnish request for an orderly departure of his forces and ordered German troops in northern Finland to resist expulsion and, if forced to retreat, to lay waste to the countryside. The German troops followed this order to the letter. Because there were 200,000 Germans in Finland, the damage to Lapland, where they were located, was considerable. During October, the Russian Fourteenth Army threw back German forces at Liza, supported by a large amphibious landing near Petsamo, and by the end of the month the Germans had withdrawn completely into Norway.

The war ended for Finland on 15 October 1944. The Continuation War cost Finland some 200,000 casualties (55,000 dead)—a catastrophic figure for a nation of fewer than 4 million people. Finland also had to absorb 200,000 refugees. Finland agreed to withdraw its forces back to the 1940 frontiers, placed its military on a peacetime footing within two and one-half months, granted a 50-year lease of the Porkkala District, allowed the Soviets access to ports and airfields in southern Finland, and provided the Soviet Union use of the Finnish merchant navy while the war continued in Europe. Finland also paid reparations of US$300 million in gold over a six-year period. Stalin did refrain from absorbing the entire country, but in the coming decades Western-oriented democratic Finland was obliged to follow policies that would not alienate the Soviet Union.

Michael Share and Spencer C. Tucker

See also

Finland, Air Force; Finland, Army and Navy; Finland, Role in War; Finnish-Soviet War (Winter War); Hitler, Adolf; Leningrad, Siege of; Mannerheim, Carl Gustav Emil von; Northeast Europe Theater; Ribbentrop, Ulrich Friedrich Willy Joachim von; Stalin, Josef

References

Lundin, C. Leonard. *Finland in the Second World War.* Bloomington: Indiana University Press, 1957.

Vehviläinen, Olli. *Finland in the Second World War.* New York: Palgrave, 2002.

Wuorinen, J. H. *Finland and World War II, 1939–1944.* New York: Ronald Press, 1948.

Flamethrowers

Modern flamethrowers were first used by the German army in World War I. A flamethrower is a pressure-operated device that shoots a stream of inflammable liquid. The liquid is ignited as it leaves a nozzle, which can be placed at the end of a hand-held tube or mounted on a tube projecting from an armored fighting vehicle. A flamethrower consists of four elements: the fuel container, a mechanism to force the fuel from the container, a projecting tube and nozzle, and an igniting system that will set the stream of fuel on fire. Ignition systems are based on powder cartridge, electric coil, and electric spark designs.

Flamethrowers can be used in both antimatériel and antipersonnel roles. Typically, they are used in complex terrain with short standoff distances, such as in trench, city, and jungle fighting. They are used against hard targets such as bunkers, pillboxes, and mobile and dug-in tanks. German forces also used flamethrowers as defensive mines. Although these weapons possess combat advantages, the advantages are balanced by disadvantages including short burn times, the fact that the user immediately becomes a priority target, and the vulnerability of their fuel cylinders, which can explode if struck by a bullet or shrapnel.

Men of the 7th Division using flamethrowers to drive Japanese from a block house during fighting on Kwajalein Island, 4 February 1944. (National Archives)

U.S. military forces used the 70 lb M-1 model fielded in 1942 and also used the M1-A1 model. The M-1 could generate a 10 sec stream of fire, carried 4 gal of fuel, and was man-portable. It had a range of 82 ft. The improved M1-A1 model had a range of 131 ft.

In addition to using flamethrowers in infantry assault forces and ad hoc mechanized forces, the U.S. Army created the 713th Flame Throwing Tank Battalion in November 1944. It consisted of 54 M-4 Sherman tanks. Each Sherman was retrofitted with a Ronson flamethrower gun and had a 300 gal fuel capacity and a flamethrowing range of 75–100 yards. The unit saw action during the invasion of Okinawa and was used to kill more than 4,500 Japanese soldiers.

> The U.S. M1-A1 flamethrower was man-portable and had a range of 131 feet.

British man-portable flamethrowers were based on the 1940 No. 1 Mk-II "Marsden" and 1942 No. 2. Mk-II "Lifebuoy" models. The Marsden was an 85 lb unit with a 98 ft range. The Lifebuoy (also called the "ack-pak" unit) was a 64 lb doughnut-shaped device with a 131 ft range. The British also fielded a flamethrower tank built on the tank chassis of a Churchill tank. Known as the Crocodile, it carried 10 minutes' worth of fuel and could tow a trailer holding fuel for an additional 30 minutes. The tactical disadvantage of the trailer was that, if hit by enemy fire, it could explode like a massive bomb, killing the tank crew. Crocodile tanks were organized in three battalions of the 79th Armored Division and operated in platoons attached to other military units.

French flamethrowers were incidental to the war, given France's early defeat. They were based on the World War I man-portable Schilt model. Early Soviet models were variants of German designs, but the Soviets introduced improved flamethrowers in 1943 with the 50 lb ROKS-2 and 75 lb ROKS-3 man-portable models. They had effective ranges of 115 ft and 230 ft, respectively. A triple-tank man-portable model known as the LPO-50 also existed. The Russians used numerous armored fighting vehicle-mounted flamethrowers during the war. Typically, they were retrofitted to the turrets and chassis of older tanks.

German forces used a wide variety of flamethrowers. Man-portable systems were the Model 35, Model 40, Model 41, and Model 42. They ranged in weight from 35 to 79 lb and projected a stream of fire about 25–35 yards. A lighter and highly accurate para-flamethrower used by Schutzstaffel (SS, bodyguard) troops and a "field gun" trailer flamethrower with a weight of 900 lb also emerged.

The Germans placed flamethrowers on the Sd Kfz 251 3 ton half-track, the Panzerjäger 38 chassis, and the Pz. Kpfw. II and III tank series. Typical fuel capacity was 150 to 200 gal with flame-throwing ranges out to 65 yards. The static flamethrower (Abwehrflamenwerfer 42) was used as a defensive mine and was fired by electrical squibs. It shot a flame 5 yards wide by 3 yards high out to 30 yards.

Italian flamethrowers were the Lanciaflamme models 35 and 40, introduced in 1935 and 1940, respectively. *Guastori* (Italian combat engineers) employed them in fighting in Ethiopia, North Africa, and the Soviet Union. The Italian flamethrowers lacked the range of German flamethrowers, but these manpacks were simple in design and effective. A larger version built for the small Italian L3 tank pulled a fuel wagon.

Japanese flamethrowers were based on the Type 93 and Type 100 man-portable models. The Type 93 had a weight of 55 lb and a range of 25–30 yards. It could shoot a stream of fire lasting 10–12 sec and relied on a revolving 10-cylinder blank cartridge ignition system. The Type 100 was a shorter and lighter variant of the Type 93, with a removable, rather than a fixed, nozzle outlet tip. Flamethrowers were not normally mounted in Japanese armored fighting vehicles.

Robert J. Bunker

See also

Okinawa, Invasion of; Tanks, All Powers

References

Barnes, Gladeon M. *Weapons of World War II.* New York: D. Van Nostrand, 1947.

Mountcastle, John Wyndham. *Flame On! U.S. Incendiary Weapons, 1918–1945.* Shippensburg, PA: White Mane Publishing, 1999.

U.S. War Department. *Handbook on Japanese Military Forces.* Baton Rouge: Louisiana State Press, 1995 (reprint of 1944 handbook).

———. *Handbook on German Military Forces.* Baton Rouge: Louisiana State Press, 1995 (reprint of 1945 handbook).

Fletcher, Frank Jack (1885–1973)

U.S. Navy admiral. Born in Marshalltown, Iowa, on 29 April 1885, the son of Rear Admiral Thomas Jack Fletcher, Frank

Fletcher graduated from the U.S. Naval Academy in 1906. Commissioned an ensign in 1908, Fletcher commanded the destroyer *Dale* in the Asiatic Torpedo Flotilla in 1910. Fletcher saw action in the 1914 U.S. intervention at Veracruz, Mexico. For his bravery in moving more than 350 refugees to safety, he earned the Medal of Honor. Lieutenant Fletcher then served in the Atlantic Fleet. Following U.S. entry into World War I in 1917, he won promotion to lieutenant commander and commanded the destroyer *Benham* on convoy escort and patrol operations. Fletcher's postwar commands included submarine tenders, destroyers, and a submarine base in the Philippines, where he helped suppress an insurrection in 1924.

Fletcher attended both the U.S. Naval War College (1929–1930) and U.S. Army War College (1930–1931). From 1933 to 1936, he served as aide to the secretary of the navy. From 1936 to 1938, Fletcher commanded the battleship *New Mexico* and then served in the navy's Bureau of Personnel. Following his promotion to rear admiral, Fletcher commanded Cruiser Division 3 in the Atlantic Fleet.

On 15 December 1941, Fletcher took command of the Wake Island relief force centered on the carrier *Saratoga,* but he moved cautiously, and the island fell on 23 December before he could arrive. In January 1942, Fletcher received command of Task Force 17, which was centered on the carrier *Yorktown.* He participated in carrier raids on the Marshall and Gilbert Islands and joined Task Force 11 in attacks on Japanese shipping in the Solomon Islands. Fletcher commanded U.S. forces in the May 1942 Battle of the Coral Sea. Following his return to Pearl Harbor for hasty repairs to the *Yorktown,* Fletcher raced back with her to join the U.S. force near Midway, where he helped orchestrate the dramatic U.S. victory on 3–6 June 1942, in which four Japanese carriers were lost in exchange for the *Yorktown.*

Fletcher then commanded the three-carrier task force supporting 1st Marine Division assaults on Tulagi and Guadalcanal (Operation WATCHTOWER). Unwilling to risk his carriers, Fletcher took the controversial decision to withdraw them before the transports had completed unloading supplies to the Marines, forcing the transports to depart as well. He then committed his forces against the Japanese counterattack toward Guadalcanal, resulting in the Battle of the Eastern Solomons. Fletcher was wounded when his flagship, the carrier *Saratoga,* was torpedoed, and he returned to the United States.

After his recovery, Fletcher commanded the 13th Naval District and the Northwestern Sea Frontier. Fletcher's reputation for caution led Chief of Naval Operations Admiral Ernest J. King in 1943 to assign him to command the North Pacific area. Following Japan's surrender in August 1945, Fletcher oversaw the occupation of northern Honshu and Hokkaido.

U.S. Navy Vice Admiral Frank Jack Fletcher. (Corbis)

In 1945, Fletcher joined the navy's General Board, which advised the secretary of the navy; he served as its chairman from May 1946 until May 1947, when he was promoted to full admiral and retired. Fletcher died at Bethesda, Maryland, on 25 April 1973.

Stephen Patrick Ward

See also
Aircraft Carriers; Aviation, Naval; Coral Sea, Battle of the; Eastern Solomons, Battle of the; Guadalcanal Naval Campaign; Midway, Battle of; Wake Island, Battle for

References
Hammel, Erich. *Carrier Clash: The Invasion of Guadalcanal and the Battle of the Eastern Solomons, August 1942.* Pacifica, CA: Pacifica Press, 1997.

Morison, Samuel E. *History of United States Naval Operations in World War II.* Vol. 3, *The Rising Sun in the Pacific, 1931–April 1942;* Vol. 4, *Coral Sea, Midway and Submarine Actions, May 1942–August 1942.* Boston: Little, Brown, 1948, 1949.

Regan, Stephen. *In Bitter Tempest: The Biography of Frank Jack Fletcher.* Ames: Iowa State Press, 1994.

Flossenberg (or Flossenburg)
See Concentration Camps, German.

Flying Tigers (American Volunteer Group, AVG)
Group of American volunteer pilots officially named the American Volunteer Group (AVG) who flew for China in the early months of 1942. The Flying Tigers were commanded by Claire Lee Chennault, who, after retiring from the U.S. Army Air Corps as a captain in 1937, went to China as an aviation adviser to Nationalist leader Jiang Jieshi (Chiang Kai-shek). Chennault also served as a colonel in the Chinese Air Force. Following several frustrating years of trying to build up a Chinese air force while China was fighting one war against Japan

A Chinese soldier guards a line of American P-40 fighter planes, painted with the shark-face emblem of the Flying Tigers, at a flying field in China, circa 1942. (National Archives)

and a civil war against the Communist forces of Mao Zedong (Mao Tse-tung), Chennault finally developed a plan to form a volunteer group of American pilots and ground crews to be recruited directly from the U.S. Army and U.S. Navy.

Chennault overcame great hurdles to implement his plan, but China had powerful friends within the U.S. government, including Secretary of the Navy Frank Knox. On 15 April 1941, President Franklin D. Roosevelt issued an unpublished executive order authorizing reserve officers and enlisted men to resign from the U.S. military for the purpose of joining the AVG. In another deal, the British government agreed to waive its rights to a production run of 100 almost obsolete P-40B fighters in exchange for guaranteed priority on another order of a later model. The tiger-shark jaws that AVG pilots painted on the noses of their P-40s contributed to their nickname, which was bestowed on them by *Time* magazine in its 27 December 1941 issue.

Members of the AVG signed a one-year contract with the Central Aircraft Manufacturing Company, a U.S. firm that had the contract with the Chinese government to provide pilots, planes, and crews. Pilots' salaries ranged from $250 to $750 per month. Not part of the written contract was an agreement that pilots were also to receive $500 for each Japanese plane shot down.

The first contingent of AVG pilots departed for China by ship in July 1941. The next month, they commenced training at the British air base in Toungoo, Burma. Training focused on air-combat theories, then somewhat unconventional, that Chennault had developed during his years in the U.S. Army Air Corps and tested in China after 1937. Chennault's tactics were built on the two-plane element and a careful analysis of the relative strengths and weaknesses of the opposing aircraft. Chennault stressed, for example, that his pilots should never try to turn with the more maneuverable Japanese aircraft. Instead, they should take advantage of the P-40's heavier weight to attack from above and then dive to break contact with the enemy. Chennault insisted that his pilots learn their enemy's fighter tactics better than the Japanese pilots knew the tactics themselves.

When the entire contingent arrived in Asia, the AVG was organized into three squadrons: the 1st ("Adam and Eves"), the 2nd ("Panda Bears"), and the 3rd ("Hell's Angels"). The AVG first went into combat over Yunnan Province in China on 20 December 1941, almost two weeks after the Japanese attacked Pearl Harbor. The AVG then had 82 pilots and 79 operational P-40s.

As soon as the United States entered World War II, plans were immediately developed to bring the AVG personnel back into the U.S. military. Chennault himself returned to active duty in the U.S. Army Air Forces (USAAF) on 7 April 1942 as a colonel. The AVG was to be reintegrated by 4 July 1942 to become the 23rd Fighter Group, which would be commanded by Colonel Robert L. Scott, who was newly arrived from India. The 23rd would be part of the larger China Air Task Force (CATF), which would be commanded by Chennault as a brigadier general and subordinate to the U.S. Tenth Air Force in India. The CATF later grew to become the Fourteenth Air Force, commanded by Chennault as a major general.

The pilots and ground crew of the AVG were offered assignments in the USAAF and were strongly encouraged to accept them or face the draft board back home. Many, however, objected to the strong-arm tactics. In the end, only 5 AVG pilots agreed to rejoin the U.S. military and fly for the CATF. Another 19 stayed in China and continued to fly for China National Airways. To help Chennault with the transition, however, 20 pilots and 24 ground crew agreed to serve two weeks beyond 4 July. Two of those volunteer pilots were killed during that period. Other AVG pilots who did not stay in China later made significant contributions in other theaters of war. They included James Howard, who flew with the 354th Fighter Group in Europe, and Gregory Boyington, who flew with the Marines in the Pacific. Both subsequently earned the Medal of Honor.

Although some military experts predicted at the time that the AVG would not last three weeks, it achieved one of the more impressive records in air warfare. In less than seven months in combat, the unit destroyed 299 Japanese aircraft and probably destroyed another 153. The AVG lost only 12 P-40s and 4 pilots killed in air-to-air combat. It lost another 6 pilots to ground fire: 3 were captured and 3 were killed on the ground by enemy bombs. Another 10 pilots died in flying accidents.

Despite the fact that most members of the AVG came from the U.S. military (and many returned to the military to serve in World War II), they were branded as mercenaries for many years following the war. In 1991, a U.S. Air Force panel concluded that all members of the AVG had been fighting for the United States at the time and were eligible for veterans' benefits on the basis of that service. On 8 December 1996, the air force further recognized the AVG by awarding the Distinguished Flying Cross to the pilots and the Bronze Star Medal to the ground crews.

David T. Zabecki

See also

Jiang Jieshi; Knox, William Franklin; Mao Zedong; Roosevelt, Franklin D.; Sino-Japanese War

References

Byrd, Martha. *Chennault: Giving Wings to the Tiger.* Tuscaloosa: University of Alabama Press, 1987.

Ford, Daniel. *Flying Tigers: Claire Chennault and the American Volunteer Group.* Washington, DC: Smithsonian Institution Press, 1995.

Greenlaw, Olga. *The Lady and the Tigers: Remembering the Flying Tigers of World War II.* Daniel Ford, ed. San Jose, CA: Writers Club Press, 2002.

Scott, Robert Lee. *God Is My Co-Pilot.* New York: Charles Scribner's Sons, 1943.

Formosa

See Taiwan.

Forrestal, James Vincent (1892–1949)

U.S. secretary of the navy and later secretary of defense. Born in Beacon, New York, on 15 February 1892, James Forrestal entered Dartmouth College in 1911. The next year he transferred to Princeton, but he left school without graduating in 1914. Two years later, Forrestal secured a position with the investment-banking corporation of William A. Read and Company (later known as Dillon Read Company). When the United States entered World War I in April 1917, Forrestal enlisted in the navy. Soon afterward, he transferred to the aviation branch; he trained in Canada with the Royal Flying Corps but never saw combat. At the end of the war, he left the navy as a lieutenant and returned to Dillon Read Company, becoming its vice president in 1926 and its president in 1938.

In 1940, Forrestal resigned his position to join the Franklin D. Roosevelt administration as undersecretary of the navy. His primary role was in procurement, which was vital in preparing the U.S. Navy for World War II. He worked closely with his army counterpart, Undersecretary of War Robert P. Patterson, to streamline contracting and purchasing policies. Forrestal oversaw the rapid expansion of the navy in the early years of the war, including not only number of ships but also facilities and training. On the sudden death of Secretary of the Navy William F. Knox, Forrestal succeeded to the post in May 1944 and continued in the position until 1947.

In September 1947, Forrestal became the first secretary of defense. In this capacity he is sometimes referred to as the "godfather of the national-security state." Forrestal was a staunch proponent of efforts to halt what he saw as Soviet

James V. Forrestal, ca. 1942. (Library of Congress)

expansionist policies, and he lobbied hard for George Kennan's Containment Doctrine and the North Atlantic Treaty Organization (NATO). He also supported the concept of a balanced military establishment.

The immense strain of his position weighed on Forrestal and led to irrational behavior. In January 1949, President Harry S Truman informed Forrestal that he was replacing him as defense secretary with Louis Johnson. On 1 March 1949, Forrestal resigned his post. Admitted to Bethesda Naval Hospital, Maryland, for psychiatric care, on 22 May 1949 Forrestal leaped to his death from the sixteenth floor of that facility.

Todd M. Wynn

See also
Cold War, Origins and Early Course of; Knox, William Franklin; Roosevelt, Franklin D.; Truman, Harry S; United States, Navy

References
Albion, Robert Greenhalgh, and Robert Howe Connery, with Jennie Barnes Pope. *Forrestal and the Navy.* New York: Columbia University Press, 1962.
Forrestal James. *The Forrestal Diaries.* Walter Millis, ed., with E. S. Duffield. New York: Viking Press, 1951.
Hoopes, Townsend, and Douglas Brinkley. *Driven Patriot: The Life and Times of James Forrestal.* New York: Knopf, 1992.
Rogow, Arnold A. James Forrestal: A Study of Personality, Politics, and Policy. New York: Macmillan, 1963.

FORTITUDE, North and South, Operations (1944)

Deception operations in support of Operation OVERLORD, the Allied invasion of Normandy in June 1944. Operation OVERLORD was a vast operation, impossible to conceal, that involved more than 150,000 troops and 5,000 ships. Operation FORTITUDE was the elaborate deception plan designed to mislead the German defenders as to the timing and location of the Allied invasion.

Operation FORTITUDE had two components: FORTITUDE NORTH and FORTITUDE SOUTH. Operation FORTITUDE NORTH was designed to convince the Germans that the Allies planned to invade Norway in cooperation with a Soviet offensive designed to drive Finland from the war. Operation FORTITUDE NORTH was an attempt to deceive the Germans into thinking the Norwegian invasion would take place prior to an invasion in France. The intent was to cause the Germans to shift divisions from France to Norway or to have these forces in transit so they could not take part in the battle. To achieve this, the British in Scotland employed dummy vehicles, inflatable tanks and aircraft, fake radio transmissions, and dummy subordinate headquarters simulating the Fourth Army Group in "preparations" for an invasion of Norway. German reconnaissance aircraft were allowed to fly over the "assembly points" and report this information to Berlin. Operation FORTITUDE NORTH worked, as the Germans actually reinforced Norway.

As the time for OVERLORD approached, the second component of the deception plan, FORTITUDE SOUTH, became critical. Knowing that the Allied buildup in southern England could not be kept hidden, the British and Americans planned to persuade the Germans that the chief Allied assault would fall in the Pas de Calais (across the English Channel from Dover) rather than in Normandy (the actual landing area). The Pas de Calais was the most obvious choice for a major amphibious operation. It was the closest point on the French coast to England and would minimize the length of Allied supply lines as well as offer an extensive road network that could be exploited in follow-on attacks through the Low Countries toward Germany once the beaches were taken.

The first step was to leak plans of the sham invasion of Calais. This was done, as during FORTITUDE NORTH, through the British secret services, which planted stories and documents with double agents. Incredibly, the British seem to have identified or turned (recruited as a double agent) every German agent in Britain during the war. Double agents were particularly useful for providing small bits of information, which the

Germans could then piece together. The British also arranged to leak sham information through neutral diplomats with Axis sympathies.

To build the desired perception on the part of German intelligence, a fictitious First U.S. Army Group (FUSAG) was portrayed directly across from Calais in Kent and Sussex. Lieutenant General George S. Patton, whose reputation as a hard-driving army leader was very well known by the Germans, was repeatedly identified as FUSAG's commander. This fictitious force was composed of the U.S. Fourteenth Army and Fourth British Army. With the exception of three real British divisions included in the fictitious British army, all of these formations were bogus. The ghost divisions had elaborate stories woven around them to make their existence more believable. The Allies even created shoulder patches for the nonexistent FUSAG and its subordinate divisions. The Allies also had real soldiers wear the ghost division patches in case enemy agents were in a position to report their existence.

Special Allied signal units were used to transmit false radio transmissions from FUSAG and to simulate division, corps, and other army-level communications; these were transmitted in easily breakable ciphers so the Germans could decode the messages. In addition, false references to the fake headquarters were mentioned in bona fide messages.

As in FORTITUDE NORTH, dummy tanks and airplanes built of inflatable rubber were placed in realistic looking "camps" where German aerial reconnaissance was bound to see them. The deception was made even more believable by FUSAG troop movements in southeast England. Some were elaborate hoaxes, but in most cases they corresponded to actual preinvasion movements by real British and Canadian divisions. Even though the "real" movements were being made to support the Normandy invasion, they were close enough to the FUSAG area to convince German aerial photo interpreters that they were seeing the imminent invasion of Calais.

A fleet of landing craft deemed unseaworthy but still useable bobbed in British ports across from Calais. Instructions for acts of sabotage were radioed to the French Resistance in the Calais area. In addition, to reinforce the notion that FUSAG would debark on the short route to Calais, the Allied air forces in their program of bombardment prior to OVERLORD dropped three times the tonnage east of the Seine as they did to the west.

In all these activities, Allied intelligence, knowing what picture it wanted the Germans to see, had carefully taken apart FUSAG and sent bits and pieces about it where they knew the German intelligence services would pick them up. The Allies relied on the Germans to put the pieces of the puzzle together for themselves.

Soon it became apparent that the deception was bearing fruit. ULTRA signals intercepts of German classified message traffic made reference to FUSAG. This was the proof the FOR-TITUDE operators needed. They could not expect to fool the Germans forever, but they hoped to minimize German anticipation of a Normandy landing until it was actually under way—and thereafter to keep alive anxiety that the "real" invasion would follow in the Pas de Calais at a later stage.

German intelligence arrived at the desired conclusion. German army maps captured following the Normandy invasion indicated the presence of FUSAG in southeast England. Division areas and corps headquarters corresponded almost exactly with the areas indicated by the Allied deception plan. However, Adolf Hitler was only partly deluded. On 4 and 20 March and 6 April, he alluded to the likelihood of a Normandy landing in messages to his senior commanders. Still, apart from allocating Panzer Lehr and 116th Panzer Divisions to Normandy in the early spring, he made no decisive alteration of German defensive dispositions. Indeed, until he allowed divisions to cross the Seine into Normandy from the Pas de Calais at the very end of July, he himself remained prisoner to the delusion of a second "main" invasion in the Calais area throughout the critical weeks following the initial landings at Normandy.

James H. Willbanks

See also

Deception; Eisenhower, Dwight D.; Hitler, Adolf; Normandy Invasion and Campaign; OVERLORD, Operation; Patton, George Smith, Jr.; Signals Intelligence

References

Brown, Anthony Cave. *Bodyguard of Lies.* New York: Harper and Row, 1975.

Cruickshank, Charles. *Deception in World War II.* New York: Oxford University Press, 1980.

Hesketh, Roger. *Fortitude: The D-Day Deception Campaign.* London: St. Ermin's, 1999.

Kneece, Jack. *Ghost Army of World War II.* Gretna, LA: Pelican Publishing, 2001.

Latimer, Jon. *Deception in War.* Woodstock and New York: Overlook Press, 2001.

Fortress Europe

See Festung Europa.

Fourcade, Marie-Madeleine Bridou (1909–1989)

French Resistance leader. Born in Marseille on 8 November 1909, Marie-Madeleine Bridou married in 1929, had two children, and was divorced by the time World War II began. She sent her children to safety in Switzerland shortly after she became involved in the Resistance movement in June 1940.

Marie-Madeleine Fourcade, who was the head of the French resistance unit Alliance called Noah's Ark during World War II, shown here in 1979. (AFP/Getty Images)

Fourcade was recruited for the French Resistance by Georges Loustaunau-Lacau, the leader of the Navarre network, which was primarily involved in gathering information for the British. When he was arrested in May 1941, she assumed command under the code name POZ 55. Fourcade was the only woman to run a major resistance network in France during the war. The Navarre network became known as the Alliance. The Germans knew it as Noah's Ark, for its members were assigned animal names. Fourcade's code name was Hedgehog. The Alliance reported German troop movements and monitored submarine activities and German military operations within France. It also published propaganda tracts and journals. Members of the network also helped identify launch facilities for V-1 buzz bombs and V-2 rockets. Under Fourcade's guidance and supported by British money and equipment, the network grew to more than 3,000 members. Arrested by the Gestapo twice, Fourcade escaped each time. The first time she was caught because a wireless operator sent by the British turned out to be a double agent working for the Germans.

In 1941 and 1942, Fourcade's network helped to conceal British airmen who had been shot down and then to smuggle them out to Spain and safety. In July 1943 after 30 months of leading the Navarre network, Fourcade was evacuated by the British along with some of the downed airmen. She continued to run the network from a house in Chelsea until July 1944, when she returned to France. Of more than 3,000 members in her network, 438 were caught and executed.

After the war, Fourcade was active in organizing the Union for the New Republic, the political party of Charles de Gaulle. She also championed recognition for former Resistance members. Fourcade died at Paris on 20 July 1989.

Laura J. Hilton

See also
France, Vichy; Resistance
References
Ehrlich, Blake. *Resistance: France, 1940–1945.* Boston: Little, Brown, 1965.
Fourcade, Marie-Madeleine. *Noah's Ark: The Secret Underground.* New York: Zebra Books, 1973.
Sweets, John. *Politics of Resistance in France, 1940–1944.* Dekalb: Northern Illinois University Press, 1976.

France, Air Force

Recriminations over the poor performance of the French air force (Armée de l'Air) in 1940 began even before the armistice with the Germans, and they were a key element in the notorious Riom Trial held by the Vichy authorities in 1942 to prosecute the alleged saboteurs of France's war effort. Postwar historiography was scarcely less politically charged, and it is only with the passage of more than half a century that the history of France's wartime air force may be examined with some necessary detachment. Whatever the cause, the air service's accomplishments in the 1940 Battle for France were extremely disappointing, and its contribution to the national catastrophe was significant. Why this should have been so, when France in 1940 boasted an experienced cadre of fighter and bomber pilots and many aircraft comparable in quality to the best fielded by the German Luftwaffe and British Royal Air Force, will probably always remain something of a mystery. It can be better understood, however, by looking at the air service's convoluted and often tempestuous development between World War I and World War II.

In many respects, France led the world in aviation technology in the 1920s and 1930s. Its aircraft manufacturers produced many combat machines, and half of the world's airspeed records were set in French-built planes. But the country did not create an independent air service until 1928, and the motivation for its creation was more political than strategic. From its inception, the Armée de l'Air was a pawn in the long-standing intrigue between the Third Republic's political class and its generals, many of whom had never reconciled themselves to civilian authority. The air force was intended as a counterweight to the war ministry, and this atmosphere of interservice rivalry was exacerbated by the country's most influential prewar air minister, Popular Front appointee Pierre Cot, who served from 1933 to 1940. For all his undoubted administrative skill, Cot's overbearing style only deepened military suspicions that the Armée de l'Air was "the armed service of the Left," with all the ideological contamination that implied.

As with many of their contemporaries, the French air chiefs between the wars were intrigued by the strategic bombing theories of Giulio Douhet and other air-power advocates. Not only was an independent strategic role a fashionable concept in aviation circles, but it also entrenched the Armée de l'Air's autonomy from the war ministry. Cot was an enthusiast, but in trying to simultaneously placate both the strategic bombing advocates and army commanders who urged him to create a tactical support arm for the ground forces, he proposed the ill-fated BCR solution: a multi-role fighter-bomber aircraft that was necessarily mediocre in all its capacities and a waste of much time and money. After Cot's replacement by Guy La Chambre in 1938, the strategic bombing plan was theoretically sidelined, but its influential proponents within the air service felt betrayed by the government and began a policy of tacit noncooperation with both state and army. Despite official doctrine, little or no progress was made on genuine collaboration between the ground and air forces prior to the outbreak of World War II.

In principle, neither supply nor quality of aircraft was a key problem. By May 1940, the Armée de l'Air possessed no fewer than 4,360 machines, of which approximately 2,900 were modern combat aircraft, with 67 fully equipped fighter squadrons, 66 bomber squadrons, and 30 observation squadrons (escadrilles). Some 619 new aircraft were arriving from French factories each month, as well as regular shipments of Curtiss 75A (export version of the Curtiss P-36 Hawk) fighters from the United States. The chief problem lay in lack of pilots, technical support, and trained ground crews, rather than lack of aircraft.

The best of France's own fighters, in particular the brand-new Dewoitine 520 (which went into service a few days after the German assault in the west), were on a par with their chief adversary, the Messerschmitt BF-109E. But scarcely one-quarter of this force was deployed on the crucial northeastern front. Explanations for this critical waste of resources have frequently focused on accusations of personal incompetence or even treachery, but the real culprit appears to have been France's inadequate supply of pilots. The aviation training program had not kept pace with the expansion in combat machines, so that even by calling up middle-aged reservists, the service's wartime commander General Joseph Vuillemin was unable to crew nearly the number of planes that were available. Far too many excellent aircraft remained uselessly crated up in storage while the air battle over France intensified.

Nor were the aircraft committed to France's defense well used. In February 1940, Vuillemin had relented to a demand that his frontline units be subordinated in command to General Alphonse Georges' individual army groups, maintaining for Vuillemin's personal direction only the strategic bomber reserve. Neither the airmen nor their peers in the land forces were properly trained in close-support techniques, and the resulting air/ground "cooperation" proved tragically inept: aircraft and pilots were wasted in piecemeal assaults on the German spearheads that lacked any coherent choreography with the army's counterattacks. Individual skill and bravery could not overcome such clumsy organization, and the withdrawal of the best squadrons to North Africa, which started five days before the armistice, indicates how profoundly the air force had lost confidence in its own ability to resist.

In the Vichy settlement, the army took its revenge on the Armée de l'Air, stripping it of its ministerial independence and reducing it once more to being a branch of the regular ground forces. The surviving 19 metropolitan squadrons were equipped with obsolescent machines; the superior escadrilles were posted mostly to Algeria and Morocco, where in time they would be absorbed into de Gaulle's forces after the 1942 Operation TORCH Allied landings in North Africa.

Despite its undoubted weaknesses, the air force's contribution to the Allied war effort should not go unrecognized. The 600–1,000 German aircraft it destroyed in May and June 1940 were sorely missed by the Luftwaffe during the ensuing Battle of Britain. But perhaps Cot's postwar eulogy concludes the story best: "The French did not lose the air battle; bad organization did not even let them fight it."

Alan Allport

See also
Aircraft, Bombers; Aircraft, Fighters; Aircraft, Production of; Aviation, Ground-Attack; Fighter Tactics; France, Army; France, Battle for; France, Role in War; Georges, Alphonse Joseph

References
Cain, Anthony Christopher. *The Forgotten Air Force*. Washington, DC: Smithsonian Institution, 2002.
Kirkland, Faris, "The French Air Force in 1940: Was It Defeated by the Luftwaffe or by Politics?" *Air University Review* 36 (September-October 1985): 101–118.
May, Ernest. *Strange Victory: Hitler's Conquest of France*. New York: Hill and Wang, 2000.

France, Army

The "strange defeat" of the French army in the May–June 1940 Battle for France invites some of the most intriguing counterfactual assumptions of World War II. Was France's enervated and demoralized military fated to suffer catastrophe against the German Ardennes offensive—or could sounder deployment, more energetic leadership, and a little more luck in the field have forestalled the sudden German victory? When did the slow decay within the antebellum army become truly critical? To address such questions, one must acknowledge the dual importance of contingency and determinism in matters of war. Certainly, the success of German leader Adolf Hitler's May 1940 PLAN YELLOW (FALL GELB), the assault on France and the Low Countries, relied to some extent on specific errors of judgment by the French and British political-military leadership that greater forethought might well have prevented. However, the collapse of the Third Republic was symptomatic of deep and profound flaws within its army's prewar preparations, flaws that would have inevitably compromised France's defense no matter how spirited or ingenious its commanders had proved to be in 1940.

The dilemma for France's military planners in the 20 years after the 1918 armistice was how to provide effective national security from a resurgent Germany when France faced a now permanently weakened manpower base and diminishing prospects of allied support. The horrific casualties of World War I began their demographic payoff in the mid-1930s as the "hollow classes" of conscripts fell 140,000 people short of target each year. At the same time, political considerations demanded the reduction of the traditional three-year draft into the army regiments to a single year, and although the draft was increased to two years in 1935, the new law was not uniformly enforced. One option was to consider a smaller but better-equipped and better-trained army of career professional soldiers. Such was the case sketched by young Major Charles de Gaulle in his provocative 1934 work *Vers l'armée du métier* (*The Army of the Future*), in which he proposed the creation of six heavily armored divisions that would form an elite cadre for future offensive operations. Quite apart from cost, the civilian ministers recoiled at the thought of this potential Praetorian guard; relations between the army and the Republican political class were still bad enough in the 1930s for the possibility of a military coup to be taken seriously.

The army, then, would remain a mass conscripted force. France's deficiency in manpower would be made up instead by defensive works, applying the lessons of Verdun—however incompletely understood—to the Maginot Line, a series of sophisticated frontier fortifications along the Franco-German border named for Minister of War André Maginot. The line was designed to canalize any German attack to the north, and it accomplished this in 1940. Comfortably ensconced behind this apparently impregnable fortress wall, the field army's task would be to stand in reserve and repel intrusions between the main Maginot forts while thrusting into Belgium to engage any German assault north of the Ardennes. With a heavy concentration on defense and a battlefield this time mercifully removed from France's industrial heartland, the hope was to oppose and halt a westward attack despite the significant numerical advantage the Germans would enjoy.

At the outbreak of war, the Armée Metropolitaine mobilized 94 frontline and reserve divisions for the defense of France, with 215 infantry regiments all told—less than two-thirds the number mustered in August 1914. These divisions were organized into nine field armies and four army groups, with supreme command vested in General Maurice Gamelin, chief of staff of national defense. Gamelin's authority was, however, compromised by the unclear chain of responsibility between him and General Alphonse Georges, his commander on the crucial northeast front. Personal antagonism between the two men did nothing to dispel this ambiguity. Georges' 1st and 2nd Army Groups of three armies apiece were disposed along the Franco-Belgian border along with the newly arrived British Expeditionary Force (BEF), while the 3rd Army Group under General Antoine Besson kept watch in Alsace-Lorraine. General René Henri Olry's Army of the Alps commanded the mountainous frontier against Italy. As it turned out, it accomplished this task magnificently after Italy's clumsy offensive in June 1940, the only redeeming chapter in France's agony that year. Scattered units of General Henri Honoré Giraud's Seventh Army guarded the French coasts.

A quartet of bureaus administered this great force: 1st (personnel and organization), 2nd (intelligence), 3rd (operations), and 4th (transport and services). Their staffs were located with neither Gamelin nor Georges, a characteristic multiplicity of headquarters that abetted the natural confusion caused by the commander in chief's refusal to take wireless communications seriously. The delays in transmitting and receiving messages to and from the respective commands—messages usually dispatched by motorcycle courier—would have been tardy by World War I standards; they were inexcusable in a war of portable radios and high-speed maneuver.

A typical *division d'infanterie* (infantry division) out of the 63 at Gamelin's disposal would consist of 17,500 men: 9 battalions of infantry (870 men each), 2 regiments of artillery—many of them equipped with the famous but now obsolete 75 mm World War I field gun—and individual companies of antitank, reconnaissance, pioneer, engineer, signals, transport, medical, and supply troops. *Divisions légères mécaniques* (DLMs, light mechanized divisions), created in the scramble after the BEF evacuation at Dunkerque, had only 6 battalions and a single artillery regiment each. About half of this total force were reserve divisions, divided into type A and type B according to age. There were also several miscellaneous reserve units judged unfit for combat duty that performed light communications and security duties behind the line.

As part of war minister (from 1936 to 1938) Édouard Daladier's massive rearmament program from 1936 onward, a small number of modern armored divisions (*divisions cuirassées de réserve* [DCRs]) were planned, which would each boast 4 battalions of more than 150 heavy and light tanks. The most powerful of France's armored vehicles, such

General Lattre de Tassigny, commander in chief of the French armies in France, inspecting the Allied Sherman tanks that liberated the French city of Colmar, 11 February 1945. (Hulton Archive)

as the 30-ton Char B1 bis with 75 mm and 47 mm armament, could comfortably outgun any German tanks of the period and were generally better armored, although they tended to lack speed, range, and radio equipment. Supply shortages and ministerial penny-pinching meant that the first two DCRs were not, however, created until January 1940, and only then at half strength. A third division appeared in March, while the fourth, commanded by Colonel Charles de Gaulle, did not make its entrance until the battle for France was well under way.

Partly compensating for this shortfall were the three DLMs, former cavalry divisions that had been totally upgraded with Somua and Hotchkiss medium tanks as well as motorized dragoon and reconnaissance elements. Three *divisions légères de cavalerie* were a less successful variant on this. They were hybrid formations consisting of 1 mounted brigade and 2 battalions of motorized dragoons each. Those vehicles operated by the *chars de combat,* the army's tank arm, that were not delegated to one of the armored or mechanized divisions—more than half of France's tanks—were

instead scattered across the various army groups in small packets for infantry support, sometimes at battalion level but more often to companies or platoons.

As well as its metropolitan army, France could also call on its two imperial forces: the Armée d'Afrique, raised in Algeria, Tunisia and Morocco; and the Troupes Coloniales, who guarded France's sub-Saharan territories, Madagascar, and Indochina. Each force was a combination of European French–only *Zouave* and African *tirailleur* infantry regiments. The Tirailleurs Sénégalais of the Troupes Coloniales were especially prized for their fearsome reputation. The Armée d'Afrique also included *spahis*—irregular mounted troops and the 12-regiment-strong French Foreign Legion. Many colonial units were shipped to France at mobilization, so that by May 1940 there were 21 regiments of Algerian and Tunisian Tirailleurs at the front line and several brigades of African cavalry.

Following the armistice with Germany, the rump Vichy regime was allowed only 100,000 men for metropolitan defense (presumably in conscious mimicry of the allowance given the Reichswehr in the Treaty of Versailles following World War I). This Armée de l'Armistice was organized into 8 divisions, which because of the army's modest size were quite well provided with personal infantry weapons but which lacked all motorized transportation and heavy equipment. By contrast, the Germans were sufficiently impressed by the vigorous defense of Dakar by Free French Forces in late 1940 that they allowed the two imperial armies to expand. The Armée d'Afrique grew first to 127,000 and later to 225,000 men strong and was allowed the use of tanks, heavy guns, and other modern weaponry. Unfortunately for their German sponsors, however, neither of Vichy's colonial armies was willing to use its windfall of hardware when it encountered more substantial opposition, such as the Anglo-American TORCH landings in November 1942. It was these landings that precipitated the winding up of the Vichy independent government and the final dissolution of the vestiges of the Third Republic's army. France's military future then lay elsewhere.

Alan Allport

See also

Dakar, Attack on; de Gaulle, Charles; Dunkerque, Evacuation of; France, Air Force; France, Battle for; France, Free French; France, Role in War; France, Vichy; Gamelin, Maurice G.; Georges, Alphonse Joseph; Hitler, Adolf; Lattre de Tassigny, Jean Joseph Marie Gabriel de; Maginot Line; Saar, French Invasion of; Sedan, Battle of; TORCH, Operation

References

Chapman, Guy. *Why France Fell: The Defeat of the French Army in 1940.* New York: Holt, Rinehart and Wilson, 1969.

Horne, Alistair. *To Lose a Battle: France, 1940.* Boston: Little, Brown, 1969.

Kiesling, Eugenia. *Arming against Hitler: France and the Limits of Military Planning.* Lawrence: Kansas University Press, 1996.

May, Ernest. *Strange Victory: Hitler's Conquest of France.* New York: Hill and Wang, 2000.

Sumner, Ian, and François Vauvillier. *The French Army, 1939–1945.* London: Osprey, 1998.

France, Battle for (10 May–11 July 1940)

Germany's sudden strike west in May 1940 through neutral Holland and Belgium caught the Allies by surprise, leading to military defeat and the collapse of the French government. Despite Germany's successful April 1940 invasions of Norway and Denmark, France remained committed to the defensive posture it had assumed on mobilization. The French and the British Expeditionary Force (BEF), grown to nearly 400,000 men, could not occupy their intended defensive positions in neutral Belgium until events forced that nation into the war. When the blow came, the Allied failure to prepare a realistic defense strategy, France's weak government, Germany's blitzkrieg tactics, and the lingering influence of the Phony War ("Sitzkrieg") period combined to produce a rapid German victory.

The Germans did not have numerical or technological superiority over their opponents. Against Adolf Hitler's 136 divisions (2.5 million men), the French, British, Belgians, and Dutch could field 135 divisions (more than 2 million men). The Allies and neutral powers also had more tanks (perhaps 3,600, compared with 2,500 for the Germans). The Allies were sadly deficient, however, in numbers of antiaircraft guns and aircraft. Against 1,444 German bombers, the Allies could send up only 830 fighters. These would have to cope with 1,264 German fighter aircraft, more than 1,000 of which were Bf-109s. Overall, the German air fleets deployed in the west numbered 3,226 combat aircraft, whereas the British and French had half that number.

Well aware of this parity, the German General Staff were reluctant to undertake any assault in the late fall of 1939, instead producing the Phony War, when both sides were largely idle. Hitler's insistence on striking into France forced the issue, producing a series of changing operational plans that eventually invalidated the assumptions underlying the French defensive strategy. That strategy, and France's ability to execute it, suffered substantial defects by May 1940. The prolonged period of inactivity along the front since the fall of Poland had seriously eroded both Allied military morale and confidence in France's military and civilian leadership. Defeatism and internal political struggles divided Premier Paul Reynaud's government. The French High Command deliberately overestimated German strength in its pronouncements to provide an excuse in the event of disaster, and bureaucratic inertia and stubbornness hampered efforts by Colonel Charles de Gaulle and others to concentrate France's greater number of tanks into armored units capable of opposing Germany's panzer divisions. The first three French tank divisions did not assemble until January 1940, and they lacked radios. Most of France's tanks were parceled out in small packets along the front to act in support of infantry.

Allied strategy predicted that any German assault would bypass the fortified Maginot Line by moving through the neutral Low Countries and then pivoting north of Liège to fall upon the Channel ports and move against France from the north. But following the January 1940 compromise of the original German plan, which would have met Allied strength, Generals Fritz Erich von Manstein and Heinz Guderian convinced Hitler to abandon this approach in favor of concentrating the bulk of the resources on a more southern axis. Under the new plan, while other units extended the line to the sea, the main German force would drive through the Ardennes forest south of Liège to strike the French army as it moved to defend Belgium.

General Feodor von Bock's Army Group B, charged with invading Belgium and Holland, was downgraded from 37

Soldiers of the British Expeditionary Force on the beach at Dunkerque fire at German aircraft, which are bombing the ships sent to evacuate them, June 1940. (Fox Photos/Getty Images)

divisions in the original plan to only 28 in the Manstein plan, and 3 rather than 8 armor divisions. General Gerd von Rundstedt's Army Group A, which was to move through the Ardennes, was upgraded from 17 to 44 divisions, including 7 rather than a single armor division. Thus, at the point of the breakthrough, the Germans would outnumber the French 44 divisions to 9.

By early May, the signs of an impending attack were obvious to those who wished to see, but its direction, speed, and success caught the Allies by surprise. French intelligence services, usually among the world's best, completely misread German intentions and strengths. Manstein's plan capitalized on the French tendency to anticipate a repetition of the World War I offensive inspired by the Schlieffen Plan. Therefore, the operation began on 10 May with an attack into Holland by von Bock's Army Group B. Although some positions held for two or three days, German blitzkrieg tactics drove the bulk of the Dutch army back in short order. The French Seventh Army raced across Belgium to the rescue, arriving on 12 May only to join the retreat.

The great fortress of Eben Emael anchored Belgium's defenses on the south. A German glider assault took the allegedly impregnable position in just 28 hours, opening the path for German tanks. Similar airborne assaults carried bridgeheads and lesser defensive positions, overwhelming Belgian defenses. There, too, help arrived on 12 May. British and French forces executing the planned strategy managed to slow the German advance through Belgium by 14 May, but the concurrent German strike through the Ardennes obliterated that planned strategy. Quickly overrunning Luxembourg, von Rundstedt's Army Group A advanced through the Ardennes to reach the main French line along the Meuse River on 12 May. French army commander General Maurice Gamelin's belated efforts to stem the tide with reinforcements came too late to prevent German forces from crossing the Meuse. The Germans took Sedan and punched a 50-mile-wide gap in France's defenses. By 16 May, they were on the Aisne River in open country.

The BEF and many French armor forces were already committed to battle in the north. Gamelin now ordered up reserves and formed a new army under General Robert Auguste Touchon, the Sixth, to try to seal the gap. General Henri Giraud took over command of the Ninth Army, but his forces were badly mauled by the Germans on 17 May, and Giraud himself was captured. From 17 to 19 May, Colonel Charles de Gaulle scored the only French successes of the bat-

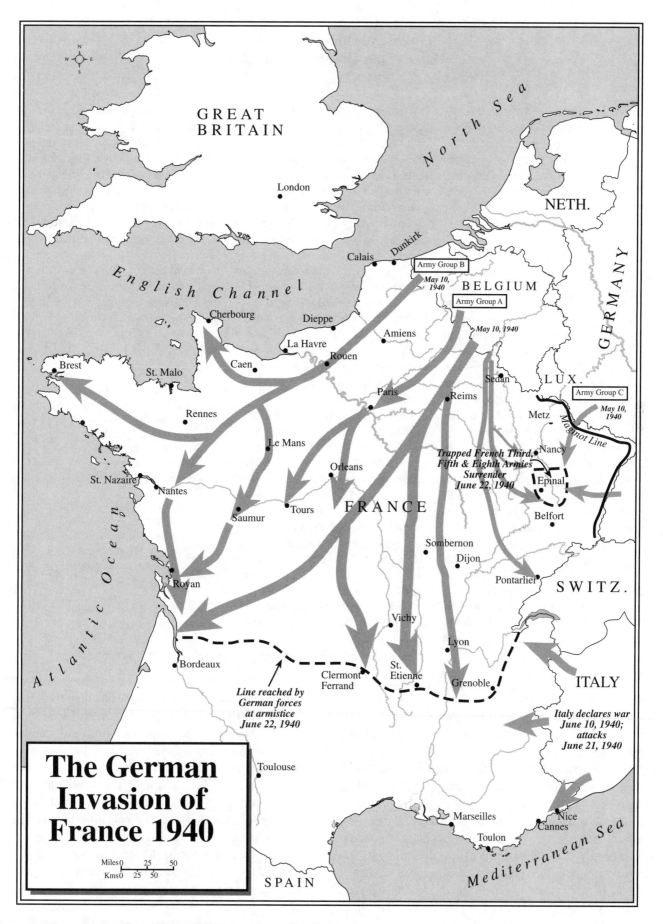

GREAT
BRITAIN

London

NETH.

North Sea

GERMANY

English Channel

Calais
Dunkirk

Army Group B
May 10,
1940

BELGIUM

Army Group A

May 10, 1940

LUX.

Army Group C
May 10,
1940

Cherbourg
Dieppe
La Havre
Rouen
Amiens
Sedan
Metz
Maginot Line

St. Malo
Caen

Paris
Reims
Nancy

Brest
Rennes

Le Mans
Orleans

Trapped French Third,
Fifth & Eighth Armies
Surrender
June 22, 1940

Epinal

FRANCE

Belfort

St. Nazaire
Nantes
Saumur
Tours

Sombernon
Dijon

Atlantic Ocean

Royan

Pontarlier

SWITZ.

Vichy

Lyon

Bordeaux

Line reached by
German forces
at armistice
June 22, 1940

Clermont
Ferrand

St.
Etienne

Grenoble

ITALY

Italy declares war
June 10, 1940;
attacks
June 21, 1940

Toulouse

**The German
Invasion of
France 1940**

Marseilles
Toulon

Nice
Cannes

Mediterranean Sea

Miles 0   25   50
Kms 0 25 50

SPAIN

HISTORIOGRAPHICAL CONTROVERSY
Hitler's Stop Order (24 May 1940)

German leader Adolf Hitler's *Haltebefehl* (halt or stop order) of 24 May 1940 was one of the most controversial decisions in connection with the fighting in Europe and Hitler's first major military mistake. This decision allowed the British Expeditionary Force (BEF) to carry out its epic evacuation from the French port of Dunkerque and continue the war.

The German plan for the French Campaign, SICHELSCHNITT (CUT OF THE SICKLE), designed to cut off the best British and French armies after they advanced into Belgium, worked to perfection, and the BEF withdrew to the French Channel port of Dunkerque. Reichsmarschall (Reich Marshal) Hermann Göring, commander of the German air force, was worried that the Luftwaffe, which had performed brilliantly in the campaign, would nonetheless not receive the credit it deserved. On the afternoon of 23 May, Göring telephoned Hitler and declared that, if Hitler would order the army to stand back and provide room, credit for the destruction of the BEF would go to the German air arm (the creation of National Socialism) rather than the army of the Prussian aristocrats.

Göring's arguments fell on fertile ground. Hitler was worried about his armor, convinced that Flanders was not suitable tank country. Also, he had to preserve his tanks to take Paris and was reluctant to see his armor formations shattered in an effort to defeat nine desperate British divisions with their backs to the sea. Göring's arguments seemed to make good sense. In any case, a pause in the panzer operations would allow infantry to close on the evacuation beaches in support.

On 24 May 1940, Hitler flew to Charleville to consult with General Gerd von Rundstedt, commander of Army Group A. There Rundstedt explained that he had stopped the panzers on 23 May to allow the remainder to catch up. He favored having the infantry continue on east of Arras while the tanks held fast on the Aa Canal Line, where they could simply defeat the BEF as it was driven back by German Army Group B from the other side of the pocket.

Hitler immediately approved Rundstedt's decision, emphasizing the importance of maintaining the panzers for the coming offensive against French forces regrouping to the south. Any further advance by the tanks would make it more difficult for the Luftwaffe's Ju-87 Stuka dive-bombers. That afternoon, a new order went out—more explicit than that issued by Rundstedt the day before—ordering the tanks to go no farther than the Lens-Béthaume-Aire-Saint Omer-Gravelines line.

German panzer commanders at the front could not believe the order, which Hitler issued in ignorance of the actual situation. Several generals, including commander in chief of the army General Walther von Brauschitsch, tried without success to persuade Hitler to change his mind. By 26 May, even Rundstedt had doubts about the order, which was finally lifted that afternoon. Necessary preparations for the panzers and their crews to recommence the offensive, however, meant that the advance was not resumed until the predawn hours of 27 May, when the Dunkerque evacuation was already under way.

Thomas J. Weiler and Spencer C. Tucker

See also
Brauchitsch, Heinrich Alfred Hermann Walther von; Dunkerque, Evacuation of; France, Battle for; Göring, Hermann Wilhelm; Hitler, Adolf; Rundstedt, Karl Rudolf Gerd von; SICHELSCHNITT, Operation.

References
Liddell Hart, Basil H. *The German Generals Talk.* New York: William Morrow, 1948.
Lord, Walter. *The Miracle of Dunkirk.* New York: Viking Press, 1982.
Manstein, Erich von. *Lost Victories.* Ed. and trans. Anthony G. Powell. Chicago: Henry Regnery, 1958.
Overy, Richard. *Why the Allies Won.* New York: Norton, 1996.

---

tle when he flung his 4th Armored Division in three successive thrusts against the southern flank of the German advance from Laon. Aided by air power, the Germans blunted the Allied attacks and swept on.

The speed of the German advance caught even von Rundstedt by surprise, as his armor commanders subverted instructions to slow down, slipped around areas of heavy resistance, and reached the English Channel by 21 May. Germany's spectacular success broke General Gamelin's ability to respond. French communications were abysmal, and there was no strategic reserve. Convinced of France's inevitable defeat, Gamelin ceased to exercise effective command. Premier Reynaud dismissed him on 19 May and replaced him with General Maxime Weygand, but the situation was already too far gone for Weygand to stave off disaster. The BEF was trapped in the north, and cooperation between it and the French First Army broke down. Forced to choose between supporting an increasingly unlikely French breakout (which both Weygand and British Prime Minister Winston L. S. Churchill ordered) or maintaining his line of retreat to the sea, on 24 May BEF commander General Sir John Gort ordered the BEF to withdraw to the north and the port of Dunkerque.

This proved to be one of the important decisions of the war, for it saved the BEF to fight another day. Hitler now committed his first major military mistake of the war, which allowed the BEF to escape. On 26 May, Rundstedt, worried about the speed of the advance, halted the panzer divisions when they were within striking range of the last Channel ports open to the British. Hitler then converted this temporary halt into a firm order. He wanted to allow time for the infantry to come up and was convinced by Luftwaffe commander General Hermann Göring that the Luftwaffe could destroy the British on the beaches, preventing their escape. Not until 29 May did Hitler release the tanks again, and by that time the BEF was in place, protected in large part by the French First Army. In the week-long Operation DYNAMO, the British evacuated some 365,000 men from France, of whom nearly 225,000 were British.

Reynaud's new cabinet proved to be unable to deal with the deteriorating situation. The French government increasingly disintegrated into rival factions and descended into defeatism. Although much of the army was still intact, it was bereft of leadership or sound strategy and psychologically defeated. Although Churchill proposed a union of Britain and France to keep the latter in the war, he refused, under pressure from the RAF, to commit the remainder of his fighter aircraft to the battle for France. It appeared to Paris that Britain was withdrawing from the war, leaving France to fight alone.

By 5 June, the Germans had repositioned the bulk of their forces in preparation for the final conquest of France. France opposed the onslaught with a greatly weakened military and an already defeated government. On 8 June, von Bock's Army Group B reached the Seine. One of his generals, Erwin Rommel, pushed on to Rouen before turning back up the coast, encircling the remaining British and French units along the seashore. East of Paris, French forces held out, perhaps in response to Weygand's futile and foolish 8 June order to hold without thought of retreat. But on 12 June, Rundstedt's forces broke through the French line at Châlons. Before his tanks stretched open ground and the retreating French army. That same day, the French government abandoned Paris for Bordeaux in the southwest. On 13 June, the government declared Paris an open city to spare it the fate of Warsaw and Rotterdam, and the next day German troops took peaceful possession of the capital.

For a full week, the French government struggled to find a solution while its demoralized forces fought an unorganized withdrawal without any clear strategy. The cabinet rejected alternatives ranging from a retreat to North Africa and the still-secure resources of the colonies to the outright union of France and Britain. The premier summoned Marshal Henri Philippe Pétain, hoping he could restore morale and reinvigorate resistance. Unfortunately, the aged hero believed the war was lost and added his voice to the defeatists opposing Reynaud. On 10 June, Italy entered the war on Germany's side, although Italian forces did not attack France in the southeast until 20 June.

Late on the evening of 16 June, with the Germans having taken Verdun and beginning to cut off the Maginot Line from the rear, Reynaud resigned. With his departure, any hope of France remaining in the war disappeared. Pétain succeeded him as premier, proclaiming in a radio address to the French people the next day that the country had lost the war and "the fighting must stop." Many army commanders interpreted this as an order, and the German advance continued largely without resistance. Brigadier General de Gaulle and a few other Frenchmen escaped to Britain.

France and Germany signed a cease-fire on 22 June 1940, but operations continued at Hitler's insistence until the Italians agreed to the armistice on 25 June. Signed at Compiègne—at the same site and in the same railway carriage that had witnessed the signing of the armistice with Germany in 1918—the 1940 armistice allowed Germany to occupy northern France and the Atlantic coastal regions to the Spanish border, with France to pay for the German costs of administration. French prisoners of war remained under German control. The French fleet, much of which had escaped to North Africa, would remain under French control but was to be demobilized. The French government, having fled Paris, continued to rule the unoccupied zone from Vichy under the leadership of Pétain.

Jeffery A. Charlston

See also

Bereker, John Standish Surtees Pendergast (Lord Gort); Blitzkrieg; Bock, Feodor von; Churchill, Sir Winston L. S.; de Gaulle, Charles; Dunkerque, Evacuation of; Gamelin, Maurice Gustave; Giraud, Henri Honoré; Göring, Hermann Wilhelm; Guderian, Heinz; Hitler, Adolf; Laon, Battle of; Manstein, Fritz Erich von; Norway, German Conquest of; Pétain, Henri Philippe; Reynaud, Paul; Rommel, Erwin Johannes Eugen; Rundstedt, Karl Rudolf Gerd von; Weygand, Maxime

References

Barber, Noel. *The Week France Fell.* New York: Stein and Day, 1976.

Benoist-Méchin, Jacques. *Sixty Days That Shook the West: The Fall of France 1940.* New York: G. P. Putnam's Sons, 1963.

Chapman, Guy. *Why France Fell: The Defeat of the French Army in 1940.* New York: Holt, Reinhardt and Winston, 1968.

Horne, Alistair. *To Lose a Battle: France 1940.* Boston: Little, Brown, 1969.

Reynaud, Paul. *In the Thick of the Fight 1930–1945.* Trans. James D. Lambert. New York: Simon and Schuster, 1951.

Shirer, William L. *The Collapse of the Third Republic: An Inquiry into the Fall of France in 1940.* New York: Simon and Schuster, 1969.

France, Free French

On 18 June 1940, French army Brigadier General Charles de Gaulle—until the previous day undersecretary of war in the Paul Reynaud government—appeared before the microphones of the British Broadcasting Corporation in London and broadcast an appeal for Frenchmen to rally to him and continue the fight, saying that "France has lost a battle, but France has not lost the war."

General Charles de Gaulle inspecting members of the newly formed Free French command unit at Wellington Barracks, ca 1942. (Hulton Archive)

Of nearly 100,000 French troops in England at that time—most of whom had been evacuated from the area around Dunkerque—only 1,300 volunteered to stay in England and join de Gaulle; the remainder returned to France. Of the volunteers, 900 were Foreign Legionnaires of the 13th Demi-Brigade who had recently been evacuated from Norway. Undeterred by the limited response, de Gaulle recruited forces and established the "Fighting French" (Free French Forces). On 2 August, a court-martial initiated by Marshal Henri Philippe Pétain's Vichy French government sentenced de Gaulle to death in absentia for treason. On 7 August, de Gaulle signed an agreement with the British government regulating the French forces and placing them under the "general directives of the British High Command."

Over the next year, de Gaulle's small force steadily increased in number. In August 1940, sufficient troops to form four battalions joined from Equatorial Africa (Chad, Cameroon, Middle Congo, and Gabon). Hoping to enlist units in West Africa, de Gaulle mounted a 1,445-man expedition with British naval support against Dakar in West Africa, but the city remained loyal to Vichy France and the operation failed.

Other Free French Forces served abroad. Volunteers from Syria were formed into the 1st Marine (Naval) Infantry, which was attached to the British 7th Armoured Division. These troops assisted in the capture of Tobruk, Libya, in January 1941. In December 1940, Colonel Raoul-Charles Magrin-Vernerey (a.k.a. Monclar) formed the Brigade d'Orient of 1,200 men from several units of infantry (including the 13th Demi-Brigade) and a horse cavalry squadron. The brigade fought in Eritrea from January to May 1941, the cavalry unit making the last French cavalry charge in history (against Italian cavalry).

On 25 May 1941, Major General Paul Louis Legentilhomme formed the 5,400-man 1st Free French Light Division from several units of French Legionnaires, Africans, and Arabs. On 8 June, operating with British Commonwealth forces, the division invaded Syria, meeting bitter resistance from Vichy forces there. The campaign ended on 11 July. Of the 38,000 Vichy troops in Syria, 5,331 (including 1,000 Legionnaires) joined the Free French; the remainder were allowed to return to France. On 20 August 1941, the Light Division was disbanded; with additional reinforcements, it became several independent brigade groups, some of which remained in Syria for garrison duties.

The 1st French Brigade, commanded by Brigadier General Marie Pierre Koenig, was formed in December 1941. It consisted of the 13th Demi-Brigade and several naval infantry battalions. These *Fusiliers-Marins* provided a bit of color, as the sailors retained their red pom-pom naval caps and the chief petty officers wore their peaked caps. Assigned to the British XIII Corps, the 1st Brigade was posted to the "box" at Bir Hacheim at the left end of the Gazala Line in Libya.

Attacked by the Italian Ariete Division and elements of the German 90th Light Division on 27 May 1941, the 1st Brigade held, despite continuous combat and constant Luftwaffe attack. On 11 June it was ordered to withdraw, breaking through to British lines. Bir Hacheim was the defining battle for the Free French. Prior to it, British support had been lukewarm. However, after the brigade withstood German Afrika Korps assaults longer than any of the Commonwealth "boxes" on the Gazala Line, there were no longer any doubts that the Free French would fight and fight well.

By the time of the Battle of El Alamein in October 1942, Free French units were fighting with the British 7th Armoured Division, 50th Infantry Division, and the Long-Range Desert Group. The 1st Free French Division was formed 1 February 1943 for the campaign in Tunisia under Koenig, who was now a major general. After a brief resistance to the Allied landings on 8 November 1942, eight divisions of the French North and West African Armies went over to the Allied side. The XIX Algerian Corps under Major General Alphonse Pierre Juin fought alongside the British First Army in Tunisia, although Juin refused to take orders from the British commander. Additional political problems arose when some elements of the Free French forces refused to associate with the North African ex-Vichy troops.

On 4 August 1943, a new French army came into being, consisting of eight infantry divisions, four armored divisions, four regiment-sized groups of French North African troops, six commando battalions, and one parachute regiment. Under the terms of an inter-Allied agreement, the United States assumed responsibility for rearming, reequipping, training, and supplying the French forces. Language problems and the emphasis on fielding the greatest number of combat units possible at the expense of support units were the most prominent obstacles encountered. Other problems arose over weapons (the French never received the excellent U.S. M1 Garand rifle) and supplies (the French never received tanker jackets and, more seriously, initially received a smaller ration scale than American troops). Eventually most problems were resolved.

A French Expeditionary Corps of five divisions was formed on 18 May 1943. Commanded by Major General Juin and sent to Italy in late 1943 and early 1944, it was instrumental in winning the Fourth Battle of Cassino, outflanking the German position by moving through the mountains as Juin suggested. A reinforced Free French division liberated the Mediterranean islands of Corsica and Elba in September 1943 and June 1944, respectively.

On 15 August 1944, what became the French First Army under Major General Jean Marie Gabriel de Lattre de Tassigny landed in southern France as part of the U.S. Sixth Army in Operation DRAGOON. Its eight divisions and 200,000 men fought their way up the Rhône Valley, arriving on the right flank of U.S. Lieutenant General George S. Patton's Third Army. The French First Army advanced into southwest Germany, and by the end of the war it had reached the Tyrol in western Austria. In addition, Major General Philippe Leclerc's Free French 2nd Armored Division served with the U.S. First Army, liberated Paris, and joined the French First Army in February 1945. By the end of the war, the rebuilt French air force consisted of 25 fighter, bomber, and reconnaissance squadrons equipped with American and British aircraft. The Free French navy, which initially consisted of only three ships, had grown by war's end to a total of 240 warships.

At a cost of 23,500 killed and 95,500 wounded, the Free French Forces demonstrated a will to fight that impressed their Allied counterparts. Although it was significant, the Free French contribution to the Allied victory in Europe is not generally recognized.

Dana Lombardy and T. P. Schweider

See also

Cassino/Rapido River, Battles of; Dakar, Attack on; de Gaulle, Charles; de Lattre de Tassigny, Jean M. G.; DRAGOON, Operation; El Alamein, Battle of; Gazala-Bir Hacheim Line, Battle of; Juin, Alphonse P.; Koenig, Pierre; Leclerc, Philippe; Legentilhomme, Paul L.; Normandy Invasion; OVERLORD, Operation (Planning); Paris, Liberation of; Patton, George S., Jr.; Pétain, Henri Phillipe; Reynaud, Paul; Tobruk, First Battle of; TORCH, Operation; Tunisia Campaign

References

de Gaulle, Charles. *The Complete War Memoirs of Charles DeGaulle.* Trans. Jonathan Griffin and Richard Howard. New York: Simon and Schuster, 1969.

Lattre de Tassigny, Jean Marie Gabriel de. *The History of the French First Army.* London: George Allen and Unwin, 1952.

Rossignoli, Guido. *The Allied Forces in Italy, 1943–45.* New York: Random House, 2000.

Vigneras, Marcel. *The United States Army in World War II: Special Studies: Rearming the French.* Washington, DC: U.S. Government Printing Office, 1957.

France, Navy

In 1939 France possessed a powerful battle fleet. The navy had been largely rebuilt beginning in the 1920s and was generally regarded as the world's fourth most powerful maritime force. Georges Leygues, a National Assembly French deputy who had served as minister of marine, was a chief architect. Admiral Jean Darlan, the personification of a political admiral,

Part of the French navy's fleet at sea, the cruisers *Diadem, Cleopatra,* and *Dido,* 1941. (Hulton Archive)

commanded it. The navy was undoubtedly the most pro-American and anti-British of the three French services during World War II.

In the pre–World War II era, French naval planning was guided by the formula that the navy should be equal in strength to the combined German and Italian navies. In addition, while the bulk of the French fleet was stationed in the Mediterranean, the navy was to be capable of operating elsewhere in the world, primarily in the Atlantic. Between 1925 and 1937, the French laid down new warships at the rate of 32,426 tons a year. With the approach of war, this increased to 41,000 tons annually, severely straining France's shipyard capacity.

The French fleet was centered on the battleship. France's two oldest battleships were seized by the British in July 1940 during Operation CATAPULT, but they were of so little worth that they would not see further naval action. Its next three older—but slow—battleships of the Bretagne-class had been reconstructed in the interwar period. The *Bretagne* was sunk at Mers-el-Kébir during CATAPULT, and the *Provence* was damaged there and later scuttled at Toulon. The *Lorraine* joined the Free French fleet in 1943.

In the 1930s, the French built two fast battleships, the *Dunkerque* and the *Strasbourg*. Displacing 35,500 tons fully loaded, they were rated at 29 knots and were armed with 8 × 13-inch guns in the distinctive French quadruple turrets. Under construction the French had two of the best battleships in Europe in armor design, the *Jean Bart* and the *Richelieu*. Both were armed with 8 × 15-inch guns in two quadruple turrets. Both would see action as Vichy and Free French warships and would survive the war. France also had one elderly aircraft carrier, the *Bearn*, that would remain idle in the West Indies most of the war. Two aircraft carriers were under construction but were never completed.

France maintained a cruiser force centered on 7 heavy ships. With the exception of the *Algérie*, they were probably the worst armored heavy cruisers of any major navy. It also possessed 12 modern light cruisers, of which 6 were Gloire-class ships: fast, well armed, and well armored. France also developed a unique destroyer force. It had built 32 large destroyers of a type designated as *contre-torpilleurs*. Fast, long-ranged, and almost light cruisers in concept, the best known were the 6 ships of the Le Fantasque–class. Capable of maintaining 37 knots at full load, they were for the whole of their careers the fastest flotilla craft afloat (*Le Terrible* made 45 knots in her trials). Displacing 2,800 tons (3,400 tons fully loaded), they were armed with 5 × 5.5-inch guns. These "superdestroyers" were designed to operate in squadrons of 3 each. France also had 26 destroyers designed for fleet operations (*torpilleurs d'escadre*) and 12 light destroyers, the latter being 610-ton torpedo-boats similar to the Italian Spica-class vessels. A total of 23 destroyers of all types were under construction in 1940, but none would be completed.

With the exception of the legendary monster submarine *Surcouf,* France's submarines consisted of three types. France had 38 first-class submarines of 900 to 1,800 tons displacement, 32 second-class submarines of approximately 600 tons displacement each, and 6 minelaying submarines. Rounding out the fleet were numerous sloops, patrol boats, and other small craft; many trawlers and similar small vessels were requisitioned during the war for coastal work.

France did not have sonar until after the outbreak of the war, and during the Vichy era there was only very limited introduction of radar. Free French naval units were dependent for advanced equipment on the British and the United States, chiefly the latter. Meanwhile, the greatest gift by Vichy France to the Axis war effort may have been Darlan's presentation to the German navy of the "Metox" device for detection of radar.

During the war, the French Navy had no role during the Polish Campaign, but it did participate in the Norwegian Campaign. The latter included a destroyer raid into the Skagerrak, an arm of the North Sea between Norway and Denmark. The navy also conducted convoy and antisubmarine operations as well as operations in the Atlantic against German raiders. French naval units also participated in the Dunkerque evacuation, losing several destroyers to German aircraft. With the fall of France, the majority of the ships passed to Vichy government control. After the British attack at Mers-el-Kébir, most of the now-truncated fleet was relocated at Toulon, where virtually all were lost in a mass scuttling on 27 November 1942. Seventy-seven ships went down: 3 battleships (the *Strasbourg,* the *Dunkerque,* and the old *Provence*), 7 cruisers, 32 destroyers, 16 submarines, and 19 other craft. A few destroyers and smaller ships were raised and towed to Italy, but the Axis powers gained little from them. Five submarines escaped; 1 was badly damaged by bombing and had to be scuttled, another was interned in Spain, and 3 arrived in Algeria.

Some Vichy warships participated in actions against the Allies, primarily off Syria, Madagascar, and Dakar and during Operation TORCH. The French warships also conducted convoy operations to France. The successful Vichy defense of Dakar on 23–24 September 1940 was an important factor in Adolf Hitler's decision to continue backing the Vichy regime in 1940–1941.

Charles de Gaulle placed the few mostly smaller warships of the Free French under Vice Admiral Émile Muselier. As late at January 1943, this modest force had only 5,314 men, but it would expand as the war progressed to include several small British- and U.S.-built warships. They would operate in all oceans, participate in operations against the Vichy territories, and later take part in Operation OVERLORD and in Pacific Ocean battles with Japan.

Major wartime losses for French ships were 4 battleships, 4 heavy cruisers, 6 light cruisers, and 58 destroyers and large torpedo boats. Unfortunately for France, its navy was little able to influence events at the beginning of the war, and the defeat of France in June 1940 came too soon for the navy to contribute in a meaningful way.

Jack Greene

See also
Dakar, Attack on; Darlan, Jean Louis Xavier François; de Gaulle, Charles; France, Vichy; Mers-el-Kébir; OVERLORD, Operation; Toulon

References
Couhat, Jean Labayle. *French Warships of World War II.* London: Ian Allen, 1971.
Goda, Norman J. W. *Tomorrow the World: Hitler, Northwest Africa, and the Path toward America.* College Station: Texas A&M University Press, 1998.
Hood, Ronald Chalmers, III. *Royal Republicans: The French Naval Dynasties between the World Wars.* Baton Rouge: Louisiana State University Press, 1985.
Jenkins, E. H. *A History of the French Navy: From Its Beginnings to the Present Day.* Annapolis, MD: Naval Institute Press, 1973.
Melton, George E. *Darlan: Admiral and Statesman of France, 1881–1942.* Westport, CT: Praeger, 1998.
Meyer, Jean, and Martine Acerra. *Histoire de la Marine Française des Origines à nos Jours.* Rennes, France: Éditions Ouest-France, 1994.
Salerno, Reynolds Mathews. *Vital Crossroads: Mediterranean Origins of the Second World War, 1935–1940.* Ithaca, NY: Cornell University Press, 2002.

France, Role in War

On 3 September 1939, for the second time in a generation, France found itself at war with Germany. In sharp contrast to August 1914, this time the mood in the Third Republic was one of somber resignation. Although France was among the victors in World War I, it had been devastated by the war, with 1,385,300 dead and 4,329,200 wounded (690,000 permanently disabled). One-quarter of all French males of military age lay dead. Much of the fighting had been on French soil, and large stretches of northeastern France had been scarred by the fighting. Buildings and railroads would have to be rebuilt and farms put back in cultivation. The costs were staggering, and finances remained a major problem for French governments of the 1920s. Political instability caused by frequent changes of cabinet and the lack of a strong executive were other major problems.

Denied the genuine national security in terms of protection from Germany that it had sought in the Paris Peace Conference following World War I, France played a Cassandra role in the 1920s and 1930s, warning of the German threat and finding little support in this from Great Britain and the United States, its World War I allies. When the German government defaulted on reparations, in 1923 French troops occupied the Ruhr. Although this action forced the German government to live up its treaty obligations and French troops then departed, the financial cost of the operation was high, and it brought condemnation of France from Britain and the United States. It also brought the Left to power in France in 1924.

The Ruhr occupation was the last such independent French action before World War II. Thereafter, France followed Britain's lead regarding Germany in return for a guarantee of Britain's support in the event of a German invasion. Successive British governments, however, refused to commit themselves to collective security arrangements regarding eastern Europe that might have prevented war. Meanwhile, German leader Adolf Hitler tore up the Treaty of Versailles and the Locarno Pacts, the latter of which Germany had voluntarily signed. In 1936, Hitler sent German troops into the Rhineland. The French army was then regarded as the world's most powerful military force, and France might have acted unilaterally and halted this step, which could have meant the end of Hitler. When the British refused to support military intervention, though, French leaders took this as an excuse to do nothing.

In September 1938, France and Britain permitted Hitler to seize the Sudetenland from Czechoslovakia, a French military ally. In March 1939, Hitler secured the whole of Czechoslovakia, prompting Britain, in the worst possible circumstances, to extend a guarantee to Poland—Germany's next target and already a French ally—that Britain would defend it against attack. Following the German invasion of Poland on 1 September 1939, the French government joined Great Britain in declaring war two days later.

The Popular Front that had come to power in France in 1936 had launched a major disarmament program, but on the eve of war France had begun to rearm. It made substantial outlays in arms expenditures and sharp increases in weapons, especially tanks, of which the French army had more than the German army. Time was vital if France (and Britain) were to catch up with German rearmament. The most glaring French military weaknesses, even by May 1940, were in modern aircraft and in antiaircraft guns.

Both London and Paris were confident of military victory, but both governments and their military establishments embarked on the war in leisurely fashion. While the French called up reservists and retrieved artillery from storage, the German army rolled over Poland. The French army carried out only a halfhearted offensive in the Rhineland. Had the offensive been on a larger scale and more forcefully prosecuted, it would have carried to the Rhine. Britain was even slower to mobilize and dispatch the British Expeditionary Force (BEF) to the Continent. France and Britain expected to blockade Germany and use their control of the seas to secure the means to match the Germans in terms of their military establishment, especially in numbers and quality of aircraft. The seven months of inactivity after the German conquest of Poland—known as the *Sitzkrieg* or Phony War—seemed to suggest that time was on the side of the Allies.

Meanwhile, there was sharp dissension on the French home front. From 1935 to 1939, the French Communist Party had been in the forefront of the antifascist crusade and urged rearmament. The German-Soviet Non-aggression Pact of August 1939, however, converted the French Communists overnight into advocates of neutrality. The government of Premier Édouard Daladier then unwisely moved against the French Communist Party, outlawing it and interning many of its leaders, including those in the National Assembly. Communist agitation against the war continued, however, helping to produce doubt and defeatism, particularly among industrial workers conscripted into the army. This led to the myth that a fifth column had been responsible for the French military defeat in 1940. Dissatisfaction over the lack of aggressive military activity also led to a cabinet crisis and change of premier in March 1940; Paul Reynaud replaced Daladier. The new premier projected energy and optimism, but politics forced Reynaud to keep Daladier as minister of war, and the continuing rivalry between the two men handicapped the war effort.

The Phony War ended on 9 April 1940 when German forces invaded Denmark and Norway. The French joined the British in sending troops to Norway, but these troops could not halt the German conquest and were withdrawn on the opening of the Battle for France. Then, on 10 May 1940, German forces invaded the Low Countries and France. The French Maginot Line, built at great cost beginning in 1929, served its intended purpose of channeling the German invasion to the north through Belgium. However, several elements led to disaster: the failure of France and Britain to work out detailed plans with Belgium (which had declared its neutrality and was fearful that cooperation with the Allies would be the excuse for a German invasion), serious flaws in the Allied command structure, inept French senior military leadership, the inability of the Allies to understand the changed tempo of battlefield conditions that represented the German blitzkrieg, and the misuse of superior armor assets.

British and French military deficiencies, especially in the air, were soon all too evident. Too late, the French attempted major command changes. Only a month after the start of the campaign, on 10 June 1940, the French government abandoned Paris for Bordeaux. To spare the city destruction by the German Luftwaffe, the government declared Paris an open city; four days later German troops moved in. On 16 June at Bordeaux, Reynaud suggested that the government and its armed forces move to French territory in North Africa and continue the fight from there. His vice premier, 84-year-old Marshal Henri Phillipe Pétain, opposed this step, as did the new commander of the French army, 73-year-old General Maxime Weygand. Both men considered the war lost and sought to end fighting that they believed could only lead to additional lives lost for no gain. When a majority of the cabinet voted to ask the Germans for terms, Reynaud resigned on 16 June.

Ironically, Reynaud had brought Pétain, hero of the World War I Battle of Verdun, into the government on 18 May to stiffen French resolve following initial Allied setbacks in the campaign for France. On 16 June, Pétain became premier and immediately opened negotiations with Germany to end the fighting. The Germans delayed to improve conditions, but the French government signed an armistice with Germany on 22 June and with Italy on 24 June. Fighting ceased on the battlefields of France on 25 June. The campaign had lasted but six weeks. Never before in its military history had France been as broken militarily and psychologically.

The armistice of 25 June 1940 divided France into occupied and unoccupied zones. A pass was necessary for French citizens who desired to move between the two. German forces occupied three-fifths of the country, including northern and western France and the entire Atlantic coast. France had to pay "administrative costs" to the Germans at the absurdly high sum of 20 million reichsmarks a day, calculated at a greatly inflated rate of exchange of 20 francs per reichsmark. This amounted to some 60 percent of French national income. Save for a few units to maintain order, all French military formations were disarmed and demobilized. Ships of the French navy were to assemble in designated ports and be demobilized. The armistice also called for all German prisoners of war to be immediately released, whereas Germany would retain until the end of the war the 1.5 million French prisoners it had captured. France was also forced to surrender German refugees on French territory.

A new French government was then established at Vichy in central France under Pétain to administer the remaining two-fifths of metropolitan France, which included the Mediterranean coast. Vichy France was left with control of its colonies, although Japan sent in troops and established de facto authority over French Indochina during 1940 and 1941. France then played a schizophrenic role until the end of the war. Most French, convinced that for the indefinite future Germany would rule Europe and disgusted with the infighting and weak leadership that had characterized the Third Republic, rallied to the Vichy regime and its calls for a conservative revolution. Meanwhile, young Brigadier General Charles de Gaulle, the only figure of some consequence to escape abroad following the defeat, sought to rally the French to the then-dim hope of eventual victory. He called on French people in Britain or those who could reach there, as well as the French Empire, to join him in continuing the fight. De Gaulle's Free French, soon recognized by the British government, slowly grew in numbers and support as the war wore on and as Germany failed to defeat Britain and suffered rebuff in its invasion of the Soviet Union. The Resistance was an amalgamation of several diverse groups that finally coalesced in May 1943 as the Conseil National de la Résistance (CNR, National Resistance Council), headed by Jean Moulin. Its military arm was the Forces Françaises de l'Interieur (FFI, French Forces of the Interior).

Although some French men and women were active in the Resistance, most of the population simply tried to endure the German occupation. Many actively collaborated with the German occupiers for financial gain, and a few fervently supported the Nazi policies opposing Communism and persecuting the Jews. The Vichy government organized a force known as the Milice to combat growing numbers of FFI.

British Prime Minister Winston L. S. Churchill's government recognized de Gaulle's government as the legitimate representative of France, but Churchill also created strong Anglophobia in France by his decision to move to secure the French fleet, most notably at Mers-el-Kébir, where fighting occurred with considerable loss of French life. This affair still rankles the French today, as the French government had promised that it would not let the Germans seize the fleet and ultimately scuttled its main fleet to honor that pledge, even after the events of Mers-el-Kébir.

U.S. President Franklin D. Roosevelt strongly distrusted de Gaulle, and the United States maintained diplomatic relations with Vichy until the Allied invasion of North Africa—Operation TORCH—in November 1942. French resistance to the Allied landings and devious dealings by Vichy representatives ended Allied attempts to negotiate with Pétain's government.

De Gaulle's Free French Forces greatly expanded after the Allied invasion of North Africa. Rearmed and reequipped by the United States, a French Expeditionary Corps of five divisions was sent to Italy in late 1943, and it made a major con-

> France had to pay 20 million reichsmarks a day to Germany during the occupation, about 60% of the French national income.

tribution to the Allied military efforts there. What became the French First Army landed in southern France in August 1944 as part of Operation DRAGOON. Its 10 divisions fought through France into Germany and Austria. Meanwhile, Allied forces had come ashore in Normandy, and the French Resistance played a key role in isolating the beachheads and preventing German resupply. Everywhere, French men and women assisted the Allied armies. Paris was liberated on 25 August, the 2nd French Armored Division leading the Allied units into the city to join with those fighting the Germans and saving the city's honor.

De Gaulle soon established his government in Paris, and French troops continued with the liberation of French territory. Following the war, nearly 40,000 French citizens were imprisoned for collaboration, including Marshal Pétain and his vice premier, Pierre Laval. Both men were sentenced to death, although de Gaulle commuted Pétain's sentence to life imprisonment in recognition of his World War I service. At least 10,000 people were executed for collaborating with the Nazis. Collaboration was and still is a highly sensitive topic in postwar France.

The high hopes and idealism of the Resistance were soon dashed. Although an overwhelming 96 percent of Frenchmen voting in an October 1945 referendum rejected the constitutional structure of the Third Republic, sharp political divisions ensured that the Fourth Republic that followed it was virtually a carbon copy of the Third. Not until 1958, when the Fourth Republic was overthrown and de Gaulle returned to power, would France have a constitution that ensured a strong executive. Despite de Gaulle's wartime promises of a new relationship with the colonies, the government in Paris pursued a short-sighted policy of trying to hold on to its major colonies, believing that only with its empire could France still be counted as a great power. Such grandiose and outdated notions led to disastrous wars in Indochina and later in Algeria, ultimately toppling the Fourth Republic.

Dana Lombardy, T. P. Schweider, and Spencer C. Tucker

See also
Churchill, Winston L. S.; Daladier, Édouard; de Gaulle, Charles; DRAGOON, Operation; France, Battle for; France, Free French; France, Vichy; France Campaign; German-Soviet Non-aggression Pact; Moulin, Jean; Normandy Invasion and Campaign; Pétain, Henri Philippe; Resistance; Reynaud, Paul; Roosevelt, Franklin D.; Saar, French Invasion of; TORCH, Operation

References
Blake, Ehrlich. *Resistance: France 1940–1945*. Boston: Little, Brown, 1965.
Burrin, Philippe. *France under the Germans: Cooperation and Compromise*. Trans. Janet Lloyd. New York: New Press, 1996.
Dank, Milton. *The French against the French*. New York: J. B. Lippincott, 1974.
Horne, Alistair. *To Lose a Battle: France 1940*. Boston: Little, Brown, 1969.
Marrus, Michael R., and Robert O. Paxton. *Vichy France and the Jews*. New York: Basic Books, 1981.
May, Ernest R. *Strange Victory: Hitler's Conquest of France*. New York: Hill and Wang, 2000.
Ousby, Ian. *Occupation: The Ordeal of France, 1940–1944*. New York: St. Martin's Press, 1997.
Paxton, Robert O. *Vichy France: Old Guard and New Order, 1940–1944*. New York: Alfred A. Knopf, 1972.
Shirer, William L. *The Collapse of the Third Republic: An Inquiry into the Fall of France in 1940*. New York: Simon and Schuster, 1969.
Warner, Geoffrey. *Pierre Laval and the Eclipse of France, 1931–1945*. New York: Macmillan, 1968.

France, Vichy

The government organized in the area of France not occupied by the Germans. The armistice of 25 June 1940 divided France into occupied and unoccupied zones. Germany occupied three-fifths of the country, including northern and western France and the entire Atlantic coast. A new government under 84-year-old Marshal Henri Phillipe Pétain, the last premier of the Third Republic, administered the remaining two-fifths of metropolitan France, including most of the Mediterranean coastline. French citizens needed a pass to cross from one zone to the other. The French government was left with its colonies (although Japan established de facto control over French Indochina during 1940–1941).

Beginning on 9 July, the French National Assembly convened in the resort town of Vichy about 250 miles south of Paris to consider Pétain's plans for the future of France. Meanwhile, several dozen politicians who had left metropolitan France to try to set up a new government in North Africa and continue the fight were arrested and returned to France, where they were charged with plotting against the security of the state.

In July 1940, Pétain enjoyed overwhelming popular support. The vast majority of the French assumed the war was lost and that Britain would soon also be defeated. They were disillusioned with the leaders of the Third Republic, and the defeat produced strong support for new leadership and authoritarian government. Vice Premier Pierre Laval assumed the key role in the cabinet to draft and carry through Pétain's program. In a completely legal procedure, on 10 July 1940 the French National Assembly in a vote of 567 to 80 (most of the latter were Socialists) terminated the Third Republic and handed over full authority to Marshal Pétain to recast the state and promulgate a new constitution to be ratified by the nation.

The task of creating a new constitution was never completed, but a series of decrees issued by Pétain dissolved the parliament and eliminated the office of president. Pétain assumed the functions of "chief of the French State." Further decrees set up a court at Riom to try those "responsible for the war" and prescribed loyalty oaths for government officials and the military. The National Revolution, as Pétain

French Marshal and Vichy leader Philippe Pétain (left) and Nazi leader Adolf Hitler (right) shake hands at Montoire, while interpreter Colonel Schmidt watches. (Hulton Archive)

described his regime to the French people in a broadcast on 8 July, never in fact established its political institutions, although in 1941 the government convened a National Council of nominated notables to serve as an advisory body only.

The conservative Vichy regime claimed to be sweeping away the old corruption and factionalism that had marked its predecessor Third Republic, to replace it with a new morality under the slogan "Work, Family, and Fatherland," which now replaced the "Liberty, Equality, Fraternity" of the old republic. Vichy was, in fact, marked by factions, cliques, and considerable infighting and was notable for its constantly changing parade of officeholders.

Vice Premier Pierre Laval, the marshal's designated successor, favored active collaboration with the Germans. The key figure in the government in the early months of the new regime, Laval arranged a meeting between Pétain and Adolf Hitler on 24 October 1940 at Montoire, France. Hitler sought

French participation in the war against Britain; Pétain wanted a final peace treaty and an end to the German occupation. Neither side made the necessary concessions, and the meeting ended unsatisfactorily, but many French were appalled by the marshal's meeting with Hitler and his announcement that he accepted, in principle, collaboration with Germany.

In December 1940 Pétain abruptly dismissed Laval, who had for some time been the object of intrigues by the advisers around the marshal. Following the brief tenure of Pierre Flandin, in February 1941 Pétain appointed as his chief minister Admiral Jean Louis Xavier François Darlan, commander of the French navy but a man with a passion for politics and intrigue. Darlan lasted 14 months but was unsuccessful in his effort to turn France into Germany's favorite ally. Summing up the difference between Laval and Darlan, one German officer later said, "When we asked Laval for a chicken, he gave us an egg; and when we asked Darlan for an egg, he gave us a chicken." Darlan, who hated the British—especially following the Royal Navy's attack on the French fleet at Mers-el-Kébir—followed a policy of everything short of war against Britain. He even sought to negotiate an arrangement with the Germans that would have given them a base at Dakar and French-convoyed supplies to assist the Axis effort in North Africa. He accorded the Germans and Italians basing rights in Syria that brought British military intervention and fighting by Frenchmen against Frenchmen.

In April 1942, Darlan departed and Laval returned to power. This time the situation was different. The outcome of the war was now in doubt, and Laval pursued a double game in which he tried to dissemble and delay on German demands and to preserve some French autonomy. Initially, the majority of the French population passively accommodated the German occupation. However, as the war wore on, Britain survived, and Germany suffered reversals in the Soviet Union, support for Vichy began to ebb away. This was abetted by the system of forced labor in Germany (the *service du travail obligatoire*), in which some 700,000 Frenchmen and women were relocated to work in the Reich. Laval also cooperated with the Germans to a degree in rounding up Jews, who were then transported to the death camps. Of some 76,000 French Jews deported, only about 2,500 survived the war.

A small but vicious war developed within France pitting growing numbers of members of the French Resistance against the Germans and their Vichy allies. Laval established a special police force, the Milice, to arrest and punish "terrorists," thus freeing up the Gestapo for work elsewhere. About 8,000 Frenchmen also joined the German armed forces—most notably a legion of anti-Bolshevik volunteers that fought on the Eastern Front and became the 33rd Waffen-SS (Schutzstaffel, bodyguard unit) Charlemagne Grenadier Division.

The British government had no formal diplomatic relations with Vichy, as it officially supported the Free French movement headed by General Charles de Gaulle. However, it kept contact with Vichy through the Canadian embassy. The U.S. government maintained diplomatic ties with Vichy and entertained the vain hope that France could be persuaded to reenter the war against Germany.

Vichy's weak resistance to Operation TORCH, the Allied landings in North Africa beginning on 8 November 1942, resulted in the German occupation of the unoccupied zone and the disbanding of the French army and air force. On 27 November 1942, the French navy scuttled its ships in Toulon harbor to prevent the Germans from capturing them, rebuffing an order by Darlan (then in Algiers) on 11 November that the ships should sail to North Africa if they were in danger of capture by the Germans. Admiral Jean Abrail, who had command at Toulon, decided that the fleet's loyalty was to the

Pétain government, and 77 ships—roughly half the tonnage of the French navy—went to the bottom.

Pétain remained in office after the Germans occupied the rest of France following TORCH, but any pretense of independence was gone. The marshal failed to place himself at the head of the remaining armistice French forces or to attempt to escape to Algiers. Removed to Sigmaringen, Germany, in the summer of 1944, the Vichy government no longer had any relevance. Postwar, some 10,000 French were executed for collaboration with the Germans, including Laval. Pétain, stripped of his rank, was condemned to death, but de Gaulle commuted the sentence to life in prison. Despite de Gaulle's efforts to cast France during the war as a nation of resisters, the four-year-long Vichy regime left a legacy of shame and controversy that still haunts France today.

Dana Lombardy, T. P. Schweider, and Spencer C. Tucker

See also

Darlan, Jean Louis Xavier François; de Gaulle, Charles; France, Free French; France, Role in War; Laval, Pierre; Mers-el-Kébir; Pétain, Henri Philippe; Reynaud, Paul; TORCH, Operation; Toulon

References

Aron, Robert. *The Vichy Regime, 1940–44*. Trans. Humphrey Hare. London: Putnam, 1958.

Blake, Ehrlich. *Resistance: France 1940–1945*. Boston: Little, Brown, 1965.

Burrin, Philippe. *France under the Germans: Cooperation and Compromise*. Trans. Janet Lloyd. New York: New Press, 1996.

Dank, Milton. *The French against the French*. New York: J. B. Lippincott, 1974.

Marrus, Michael R., and Robert O. Paxton. *Vichy France and the Jews*. New York: Basic Books, 1981.

Ousby, Ian. *Occupation: The Ordeal of France, 1940–1944*. New York: St. Martin's Press, 1997.

Paxton, Robert O. *Vichy France: Old Guard and New Order, 1940–1944*. New York: Alfred A. Knopf, 1972.

Warner, Geoffrey. *Pierre Laval and the Eclipse of France, 1931–1945*. New York: Macmillan, 1968.

France Campaign (1944)

Allied campaign to liberate France. The campaign to drive the Germans out of western Europe began with the 6 June 1944 Allied landing in Normandy, the largest amphibious operation in history. U.S. General Dwight D. Eisenhower had overall command; General Bernard L. Montgomery commanded the landing force of 21st Army Group, which consisted of Lieutenant General Miles Dempsey's British Second Army and Lieutenant General Omar N. Bradley's American First Army.

Even with stiff resistance by German defenders, especially the 352nd Division at Omaha Beach, Allied forces expanded the beachhead from 5 to 20 miles inland and joined all five beaches into a single continuous front by 12 June. French Resistance forces supported the Allied effort by providing

Men of the U.S. Army 28th Infantry Division march down the Champs Elysées, Paris, in the "Victory" Parade of 29 August 1944. (National Archives)

intelligence, sabotaging bridges and railways, and conducting harassment operations. Dempsey's Second Army began the drive toward Caen but met heavy resistance from German forces, including two panzer divisions. Meanwhile, Bradley's First Army moved up the Cotentin peninsula toward the important port city of Cherbourg. Units of the U.S. VII Corps assaulted Fort du Roule and, guided by the French Resistance, scaled the cliffs. By 27 June Cherbourg was secure, but the Germans had heavily damaged the port facilities, which were unusable for more than a month.

By the beginning of July, Allied progress in Normandy had been slowed by the hedgerows of the *bocage* country, strong German positions at Caen, and the logistical challenges of supplying the Allied forces over the beaches. Enjoying the advantage of overwhelming air superiority, the eight corps of 21st Army Group pushed south, seizing Caen on 10 July and Saint-Lô on 18 July. The capture of these two important cities

set the stage for the Allied breakout west into the Brittany peninsula and east toward Paris.

The slow pace of their advance in France concerned Allied commanders who feared that fighting would bog down, resulting in trench warfare resembling that of World War I. Bradley believed the weak link in the German army defenses was General Paul Hausser's Seventh Army south of Saint-Lô. Bradley's breakout plan, code-named Operation COBRA, was temporarily put on hold so vital supplies could be sent to support the British Second Army's Operation GOODWOOD, an attempt to penetrate German lines outside of Caen. Although GOODWOOD did not achieve a breakout, it assisted COBRA by holding two German panzer divisions in place and preventing their redeployment to the Saint-Lô area.

Heavy saturation bombing along a four-mile-wide corridor preceded COBRA, as elements of Major General J. Lawton Collins's VII Corps attacked west of Saint-Lô on 25 July.

Concurrently, Major General Troy H. Middleton's VIII Corps, located west of VII Corps, struck toward Countances. Within two days, VII Corps had pushed the German defenders back 10 miles, and on 28 July elements of the 4th Armored Division secured Countances. Sensing that the breakthrough was decisive, Bradley ordered Collins to continue the drive south toward the strategic city of Avranches. By the end of July, it too was in Allied hands, and the German Seventh Army was in a precarious position with its left flank exposed.

The capture of Avranches opened the Brittany peninsula to the Allies. Meanwhile, Lieutenant General George S. Patton's U.S. Third Army became operational on 1 August as part of an overall restructuring of the Allied command. Montgomery's 21st Army Group was now composed of the British Second Army and Lieutenant General Henry D. G. Crerar's Canadian First Army. Bradley assumed command of the new 12th Army Group composed of the American First and Third Armies. Patton's Third Army gained the greatest success, and Patton was certainly the outstanding general of the campaign for France. The Third Army displayed instant efficiency and turned Operation COBRA, a local breakthrough, into a theater-wide breakout. The Third Army immediately exploited the opening at Avranches: Patton sent his VIII Corps to clear the Brittany peninsula, the XX and XII Corps south to the Loire River, and the XV Corps east toward Le Mans. These objectives were secured by 13 August.

While the Third Army moved against limited opposition, the German Seventh Army hastily reorganized to launch a counterattack toward Avranches, hoping to cut off the Third Army. Not only did this spoiling attack fail, but also it put the Seventh Army in a position in which it might be surrounded by the Allies. To accomplish this, Montgomery, who was still overall ground commander, ordered the Canadian II Corps to attack south as Patton's XV Corps drove north. The objective for both corps was the town of Argentan. Major General Wade Haislip's XV Corps reached Argentan on 13 August, but the Canadian II Corps progressed slowly and was more than 20 miles from the objective. Patton pleaded with Bradley to allow XV Corps to press northward, but the 12th Army Group commander refused, fearing that XV Corps might itself be cut off or that excessive casualties from friendly fire might result from XV Corps moving into a zone reserved for the Canadian II Corps.

Even though the gap between the towns of Falaise and Argentan was not closed until 19 August, the area was turned into a killing ground by constant Allied air attack, artillery bombardment, and direct ground fire from armored and infantry units. Although the German Seventh Army was savaged in these attacks, a great many German soldiers escaped. Failure to close the gap was one of the major mistakes of the war. Had the gap been sealed and the Seventh Army annihilated, the western Allies would have faced far less resistance as they pushed east toward Germany, and the war might have

ended in 1944. Operations following COBRA were so successful that most German forces in northwest France had to retreat to the Seine River. Paris was liberated on 25 August.

German garrisons doggedly held out in the northern port cities of Saint-Malo, Brest, Lorient, and Saint-Nazaire. Combat commands from the 4th and 6th Armored Divisions were insufficient to secure these heavily fortified ports quickly. Repeated assaults supported by air attacks and naval bombardments failed to dislodge the defenders. Saint-Malo was not taken until 2 September, and Brest fell on 19 September. In both cases, the Germans had demolished their port facilities. On the basis of these experiences, Supreme Headquarters, Allied Expeditionary Forces (SHAEF) canceled planned assaults on Lorient and Saint-Nazaire, and German garrisons there held out until the end of the war.

The western Allies addressed concern about the exposed southern flank of their armies, the need to secure a large functioning port, and interest in cutting off what German forces remained in southern France in Operation DRAGOON, the invasion of southern France. British Prime Minister Winston L. S. Churchill strongly opposed the plan because the COBRA operation had proven to be such a huge success, but Eisenhower prevailed, and DRAGOON commenced on 15 August. Lieutenant General Alexander Patch's American Seventh Army landed in southern France just east of Toulon. Major General Lucian Truscott's VI Corps spearheaded the landing, and by 17 August had established a 20-mile-deep beachhead. The French II Corps followed with the task of driving west to secure Toulon and Marseille, which it accomplished by 28 August. VI Corps moved rapidly west and then north up the east side of the Rhône River—except for an armored group, Task Force Butler, that moved east of the Rhône River valley in an effort to envelop German forces gathering at Montelimar. By this time the German Nineteenth Army, led by general of infantry Friedrich Wiese, was pulling out of southern France. However, Truscott's corps inflicted severe material damage on retreating Germans, capturing 57,000 of them and liberating Montelimar by 28 August.

By 3 September, the Seventh Army had driven north almost 250 miles up the Rhône River. The 1st Airborne Task Force was used to seal the Swiss border; the French I Corps took up a position to the right of Truscott's VI Corps, and the French II Corps flanked the left. On 14 September, Patch's Seventh Army linked up with Patton's Third Army, sealing the open southern flank. On 15 September, the 6th Army Group was formed, with Lieutenant General Jacob Devers commanding. It was composed of the American Seventh Army and General Jean de Lattre de Tassigny's French First Army. Besides securing the Allied southern flank, DRAGOON greatly aided the logistical situation by making available the large port at Marseille. Finally, southern France was cleared of German forces.

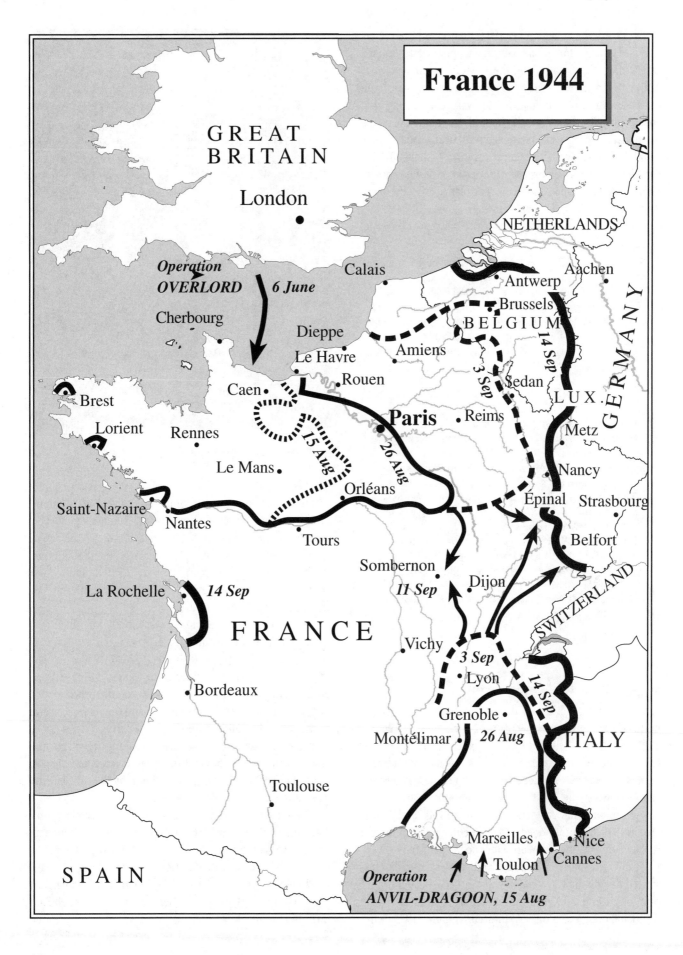

France 1944

By the middle of September 1944, France had been liberated and German forces had withdrawn into the Netherlands and to the West Wall along the western German border. Although it had been severely bloodied, the German army in the west was not annihilated but was reorganizing and entrenching itself for a long fight. Unfortunately, the Allied drive east was so fast that lines of communication and supply could not keep up with the tactical advance. With insufficient supplies to advance all his army groups at once, Eisenhower now decided to support Montgomery's plan to cross the lower Rhine into Germany, Operation MARKET-GARDEN.

Robert W. Duvall

See also

Bradley, Omar Nelson; COBRA, Operation; Collins, Joseph Lawton; Crerar, Henry Duncan Graham; Dempsey, Miles Christopher; Devers, Jacob Loucks; DRAGOON, Operation; Eisenhower, Dwight D.; Falaise-Argentan Pocket; GOODWOOD, Operation; Lattre de Tassigny, Jean Joseph Marie Gabriel de; MARKET-GARDEN, Operation; Middleton, Troy Houston; Montgomery, Sir Bernard Law; Normandy Invasion and Campaign; Patch, Alexander McCarrell, Jr.; Patton, George Smith, Jr.

References

Ambrose, Stephen. *Citizen Soldiers.* New York: Simon and Schuster, 1997.

Blumenson, Martin. *United States Army in World War II: The European Theater of Operations: Breakout and Pursuit.* Washington, DC: Center of Military History, 1961.

Breuer, William B. *Operation Dragoon: The Allied Invasion of the South of France.* Novato, CA: Presidio Press, 1987.

Guderian, Heinz G. *From Normandy to the Ruhr: With the 116th Panzer Division in WWII.* Keith E. Bonn, ed.; Mary Harris, trans. Bedford, PA: Aberjona Press, 2001.

Mitcham, Samuel W., Jr. *Retreat to the Reich: The German Defeat in France, 1944.* Westport, CT: Praeger, 2000.

Wilt, Alan F. *The French Riviera Campaign of August 1944.* Carbondale: Southern Illinois University Press, 1981.

Zaloga, Steven J. *Operation Cobra 1944: Breakout from Normandy.* Oxford, UK: Osprey Publishing, 2001.

Franco, Francisco (1892–1975)

Spanish army general and dictator of Spain. Born into a middle-class family in El Ferrol in Galicia on 4 December 1892, Francisco Paulino Hermenegildo Teódulo Franco-Bahamonde did not enter the navy, as was family tradition, because budget cuts had led to the closing of the Naval Academy following the 1898 Spanish-American War. Franco entered the Infantry Academy at Toledo in 1907 and graduated in 1910. Commissioned a second lieutenant, he refused a comfortable posting in El Ferrol for one in Spanish Morocco.

Franco's leadership, courage, and ruthlessness, demonstrated during the Riff Rebellion in Morocco, brought rapid promotion, and in 1920 he became deputy commander of the Spanish Foreign Legion in Morocco. In June 1923, King

Spanish dictator Francisco Franco. (Library of Congress)

Alfonso XIII personally promoted him to lieutenant colonel and gave him command of the Spanish foreign legion. That same year, the young colonel married María del Carmen de Polo, a member of one of Spain's most influential families; the king served as best man by proxy. In 1926, Franco was promoted to brigadier general, the youngest soldier to hold that rank in any European army.

An archconservative, Franco was closely identified with General Miguel Primo de Rivera, who governed Spain in the name of Alfonso XIII from 1923 to 1930 and who appointed Franco commander of the General Military Academy of Zaragoza (Saragossa). In 1931, on the proclamation of a republic, the Left came to power and transferred Franco to the Balearic Islands, where he served from 1931 to 1934. He returned to Spain to play a role in crushing a revolt by miners in Asturias in 1935. Later that year, he accepted the post of chief of staff of the army offered him by the conservative government.

The leftist Popular Front won the hotly contested national elections of February 1936, and the new government sent Franco to command the Canary Islands garrison. As expected, the conservative Nationalists defied the mandate, and Franco was in the forefront of the revolt that began in July 1936. The untimely deaths of Generals José y Sacanell Sanjurjo and Emilio Mola Vidal left Franco as the military leader.

Thanks to German assistance, Franco was able to airlift units of the Foreign Legion from Morocco to Spain, and he launched a drive on Madrid. In September 1936, Franco became chief of the Nationalist government, and in April 1937 he assumed leadership of the Falange Party. Franco was de facto head of Spain on the fall of Madrid in March 1939, marking the end of the Civil War. Franco then carried out a ruthless purge of the opposition. Throughout his long years in power, he remained undeviatingly true to his mission of preserving traditional Spain.

When World War II erupted, Franco openly sided with Adolf Hitler and Benito Mussolini. The Caudillo (leader), as he became known, met with Hitler at Hendaye, France, on 23 October 1940. He pledged his loyalty to Hitler but then refused to bring Spain into the war because he believed his cause was better served in "nonbelligerency" (not neutrality), a stance that infuriated Hitler. Franco did send troops—the 18,000-man well-equipped Blue Division—to fight in the Soviet Union. Throughout the war, Franco provided the Germans with observation posts in Spanish Morocco for use in monitoring Allied ship movements, and he allowed German submarines to be serviced in Spanish ports. After the Allied landings in North Africa, Franco shifted to a strictly neutral stance. But when the war was over, Spain became a primary refuge for leading Nazis and quislings (Nazi collaborators).

After the war, the Allies punished Franco's wartime conduct with quarantine treatment. Spain was kept out of the United Nations and condemned for its nature and for its close association with the Axis states. However, with the coming of the Cold War, the United States came to regard Franco's Spain as a bulwark against communism. In the revisionist version, Franco became the shining knight who had saved Europe from atheist communism. The United States established air and naval bases in Spain, and U.S. aid propped up the Franco regime, a position remembered with bitterness by many Spanish democrats.

Franco declared Spain a monarchy in 1947 but remained Caudillo until his death in 1975. Franco relaxed his authoritarian regime somewhat in the 1950s, but unrest in the 1960s led to renewed repression. Having selected Prince Juan Carlos de Bourbon, grandson of Alfonso XIII, as his heir, Franco died in Madrid on 20 November 1975. The new king presided over the transition to democracy in Spain.

Roger L. Rice and Spencer C. Tucker

See also

Spain, Role in War; Stalin, Josef

References

Beevor, Anthony. *The Spanish Civil War*. New York: Peter Bedrick Books, 1983.

Bowen, Wayne H. *Spaniards and Nazi Germany: Collaboration in the New Order*. Columbia: University of Missouri Press, 2000.

Hills, George. *Franco: The Man and His Nation*. New York: Macmillan, 1967.

Preston, Paul. *Franco: A Biography*. New York: Basic Books, 1994.

Whealey, Robert H. *Hitler and Spain: The Nazi Role in the Spanish Civil War, 1936–1939*. Lexington: University Press of Kentucky, 1989.

Fraser, Bruce Austin (First Baron Fraser of North Cape) (1888–1981)

British navy admiral. Born into a military family (his father was an army general) on 5 February 1888, Bruce Fraser was educated at Bradfield College and the fleet training school of HMS *Excellent*. His early service was in battleships and destroyers, and he became known as a gunnery officer, holding that post on cruiser *Minerva* in the Mediterranean during World War I.

In the following years, Fraser served as gunnery officer for the Mediterranean Fleet. From 1929 to 1932, he commanded the cruiser *Effingham* and then served as director of naval ordnance, playing an important role in helping to design the King George V–class battleships. Following command of aircraft carrier *Glorious* in 1936 and 1937, Fraser was promoted to rear admiral in 1938 and became chief of staff of the Mediterranean Fleet. In March 1939, Fraser was appointed controller of the navy and made third sea lord. Early in World War II, Fraser was responsible for the development of a new class of corvettes. In May 1940, Fraser was promoted to vice admiral, and a year later he was knighted. Fraser was appointed second in command of the Home Fleet in June 1942, and in May 1943 he assumed its overall command.

In that capacity, Fraser oversaw the adoption of new antisubmarine tactics against German U-boats and increased cooperation with U.S. naval forces during the height of the Battle of the Atlantic. In December 1943, Fraser personally commanded British Task Force 2, which engaged and sank the German battleship *Scharnhorst* during her sortie against an Allied Arctic convoy.

The Allied successes in the Atlantic and the resultant reduction of the German U-boat and surface raider threat led British Prime Minister Winston L. S. Churchill to assign Fraser to command the Pacific Fleet in late 1944. Fraser led the return of British naval units to the Pacific with a force built around aircraft carriers. For the remainder of the war, Fraser maintained excellent relations with American commanders and led British forces in support of U.S. amphibious and naval operations. Fraser was the British representative at the formal Japanese surrender aboard the battleship *Missouri* in Tokyo Bay on 2 September 1945.

Rewarded with the title of First Baron Fraser of North Cape, in 1948 Fraser was promoted to admiral of the fleet and appointed first sea lord and chief of naval staff. He held this post until his retirement in 1951. Fraser died in London on 12 February 1981.

Thomas Lansford

See also

Antisubmarine Warfare; Atlantic, Battle of the; Churchill, Sir Winston L. S.; Great Britain, Navy; North Cape, Battle of

References

Evans, Mark Llewellyn. *Great World War II Battles in the Arctic.* Westport, CT: Greenwood Press, 1999.

Humble, Richard. *Fraser of North Cape: The Life of Admiral of the Fleet Lord Fraser, 1888–1981.* Boston: Routledge Kegan Paul, 1983.

Roskill, Stephen W. *Churchill and the Admirals.* New York: William Morrow, 1978.

———. *White Ensign: The British Navy at War, 1939–1945.* Annapolis, MD: Naval Institute Press, 1991.

Major General Lloyd R. Fredendall. (Library of Congress)

Fredendall, Lloyd Ralston (1883–1963)

U.S. Army general. Born in Wyoming on 15 January 1883, Lloyd Fredendall attended West Point in 1902 and 1903, but he dropped out because of poor grades. He next attended the Massachusetts Institute of Technology. In 1907, he obtained a direct commission as a lieutenant of infantry, and he served in the Philippines and Hawaii. Following U.S. entry into World War I, Fredendall commanded a training center in France.

Fredendall was an instructor at the Infantry School from 1920 to 1922. He graduated from the Command and General Staff School in 1923 and the Army War College in 1925. Following a tour as professor of military science and tactics at the University of Minnesota, Fredendall commanded the 57th Infantry Regiment in the Philippines from 1936 to 1938. From August 1938 to December 1939, he served in the office of the chief of infantry.

Promoted to brigadier general in December 1939, Fredendall served with the 5th Infantry Division. In October 1940, Fredendall won promotion to major general. He then commanded the 4th Division from October 1940 to July 1941. Known as an effective troop trainer, he took charge of II Corps in August 1941 and XI Corps on its activation in June 1942. Again heading II Corps that October, Fredendall commanded the U.S. landing at Oran, Algeria, on 8 November 1942. Reportedly, he did not leave his command ship until the fighting was over. By early 1943, elements of his corps held the exposed right flank of a combined British, French, and U.S. force facing eastward into Tunisia. Short of troops, Fredendall foolishly ignored the advice of Major General Orlando Ward, commander of his 1st Armored Division, with whom he was barely on speaking terms; Fredendall scattered widely the combat elements of Ward's division. Fredendall himself remained some 70 miles behind the front at his fortresslike command post. On 19 February, German columns under Major General Hans von Arnim and Field Marshal Erwin Rommel initiated an offensive against Fredendall's forces that resulted in the Battle of Kasserine Pass. This first major clash for the Americans with German troops resulted in a major U.S. defeat. Fredendall apparently suffered a temporary breakdown during the battle. The Allied forces rallied, however; the Germans were unable to exploit their victory and soon withdrew.

This defeat, combined with Fredendall's abrasive manner and his habitual absence from the front, cost him the confidence of subordinates and superiors alike. On 6 March, General Dwight D. Eisenhower replaced Fredendall with Major General George S. Patton Jr. Sensitive to public opinion, the War Department decided not to disgrace Fredendall. Instead, he was recalled to the United States, promoted to temporary lieutenant general in June 1943, and assigned first as deputy commanding general and then commanding general of the Second Army from March 1943 until his retirement in March 1946. Fredendall died in La Jolla, California, on 4 October 1963.

Richard G. Stone

See also

Arnim, Hans Jürgen Dieter von; Eisenhower, Dwight D.; Kasserine Pass, Battle of; Patton, George Smith, Jr.; Rommel, Erwin Johannes Eugen; TORCH, Operation

References

Blumenson, Martin. *Kasserine Pass.* Boston: Houghton Mifflin, 1967.

Bradley, Omar N. *A Soldier's Story.* New York: Henry Holt, 1961.

Howe, George F. *United States Army in World War II: The Mediter-*

ranean Theater of Operations: Northwest Africa: Seizing the Initiative in the West. Washington, DC: Office of the Chief of Military History, Department of the Army, 1957.

Truscott, Lucian K., Jr. *Command Missions: A Personal Story.* New York: Dutton, 1954.

Free French

See France, Free French.

Frenay, Henri (1905–1988)

French army officer and Resistance leader. Born in Lyons on 19 November 1905, Henry Frenay graduated from the French Military Academy of Saint Cyr. A captain in 1940, he fought and was captured by the Germans in the Battle of the Vosges. He escaped on 27 June 1940 and made his way to Marseilles, where he became a Vichy garrison officer. Regarded as an expert on the Third Reich because of his studies at the Centre d' Études Germaniques at Strasbourg, Frenay was attached to the military intelligence division. He soon came to realize that the Vichy regime, headed by Marshal Henri Philippe Pétain, was intent on collaboration with the Germans. By early 1941, Frenay had become involved in the Resistance, creating the Mouvement de Libération Nationale, which produced three clandestine newspapers.

In November 1941, Frenay's publications merged with another, published by François de Menthon, to become Combat, the largest Resistance group in France. Frenay, code-named "Charvet," also pioneered most of the techniques used within the French Resistance. Frenay, a staunch anti-communist who had little time for any prewar French political grouping, was initially suspicious of the directing role which London-based Free French leader Charles de Gaulle claimed within the Resistance. Although Frenay eventually accepted de Gaulle's authority, his relationship with Jean Moulin, de Gaulle's representative in France, was strained. He distrusted Moulin's achievement in creating a fusion of the French Resistance groups, the National Council of the Resistance, although he eventually joined it.

In June 1943, the German military arrested most of the top French political and military Resistance leadership, including Moulin. Frenay fled to Algiers on 19 June to request additional support from the newly created French National Liberation Council. Concerned for his safety, Free French representatives persuaded him to remain, and in November 1943 Frenay became Free French minister of prisoners, deportees, and refugees, a position he retained for a further year after returning to Paris with de Gaulle in 1944.

In 1945 he went into business, representing the French film industry until 1958 and holding various directorships. Frenay was a legendary figure in France, and his memoir, *The Night Will End,* not published until 30 years after the war, was a best-seller in France. Frenay died at Porto Vecchio, Corsica, on 6 August 1988.

Priscilla Roberts

See also
de Gaulle, Charles; France, Free French; France, Vichy; Moulin, Jean; Pétain, Henri Phillippe; Resistance during War

References
Frenay, Henri. *The Night Will End: Memoirs of a Revolutionary.* New York: McGraw Hill, 1976.

Kedward, H. R. *Resistance in Vichy France: A Study of Ideas and Motivations in the Southern Zone, 1940–1942.* Oxford: Clarendon Press, 1978.

———. *In Search of the Maquis: Rural Resistance in Southern France, 1942–1944.* Oxford: Clarendon Press, 1993.

Michel, Henri. *The Shadow War: European Resistance 1939–1945.* New York: Harper, 1972.

Ousby, Ian. *Occupation: The Ordeal of France 1940–1944.* New York: St. Martin's Press, 1998.

French Indochina

On the outbreak of World War II in Europe in September 1939, France ruled Indochina. Strictly speaking, only Cochin China (southern Vietnam) was an outright colony; Annam (central Vietnam), Tonkin (northern Vietnam), Laos, and Cambodia were officially protectorates. For all practical purposes, however, France completely controlled all five entities that constituted French Indochina. In 1939, Indochina was France's richest overseas possession, producing rice, rubber, and other important raw materials.

When war broke out in Europe, Governor General Georges Catroux, who came to favor a more liberal policy toward nationalism in the French colonies, ordered a general mobilization throughout Indochina and outlawed the Indochinese Communist Party (ICP), arresting several thousand suspected communists. The Sixth Plenum of the Party Central Committee, secretly meeting outside Saigon, proclaimed a new anti-imperialist National United Front to struggle for independence.

Following the defeat of France in Europe in June 1940, French Indochina came under pressure from Japan and Thailand. Although France had 50,000 troops in Indochina, 38,000 of these were poorly trained indigenous troops of questionably loyalty. Japan had been at war with China since 1937 and was anxious to secure bases from which to strike the Burma Road and cut off assistance to China's Nationalist government. Tokyo now brought heavy pressure on Catroux to close the Sino-Vietnam border and halt shipment of supplies to

Japanese troops advancing through the port of Haiphong in Indochina, 24 November 1940. (Bettman/Corbis)

China. Catroux tried to stall for time, but he had no bargaining strength and was forced to accede to Japanese demands.

Catroux's protest of Vichy France's armistice with Germany and his independence in dealing with the Japanese led the Vichy government to replace him with Vice Admiral Jean Decoux, French commander of naval forces in the Far East. On 24 September 1940, Decoux was forced to grant Japan three air bases in Tonkin and the right to station 6,000 troops there. Then, in July 1941, similarly pressed by the Japanese, France yielded bases and concessions in southern Indochina. This placed Japanese long-range bombers within striking range of Malaya, the Netherlands East Indies, and the Philippines. These brought economic pressure on Japan by Britain, the Netherlands, and the United States that resulted in the Japanese decision to attack Pearl Harbor. Soon the Japanese had 35,000 men in Indochina, and although Japan left the French administration intact, it was clear to the Vietnamese that Japan was calling the shots. The Japanese occupation dealt an irreparable blow to the French position in Indochina.

Bangkok also sought to take advantage of French weakness to secure several provinces it claimed in Laos and Cambodia. From November 1940 to January 1941, Thailand and France fought a war on land and sea that France largely won. Tokyo, then influential in Bangkok, interceded to impose a settlement. In May 1941, France agreed to turn over to Thailand three Cambodian and two Laotian provinces on the right bank of the Mekong River—some 42,000 square miles of territory. This settlement did not last, however. In September 1945, when the French returned in force to Indochina, they demanded and secured from Thailand the seized provinces, forcing Thailand to recognize the Mekong River as the boundary separating Thailand from Laos and Cambodia.

The French had to address Vietnamese nationalism. In 1940, French authorities crushed abortive rebellions led by local communists in the area bordering China and in Cochin China. Then, in February 1941, Ho Chi Minh, a member of the executive committee of the Communist International (Comintern), returned to northern Vietnam after 13 months' imprisonment in south China, bearing with him financial support from Chinese authorities in return for his pledge to cooperate against the Japanese. Ho now presided over the Eighth Plenum of the ICP at Pac Bo. Here on 19 May, the Communists established another front organization—Viet Nam Doc Lap Dong Minh Hoi (League for Independence of Vietnam, or Viet Minh)—to fight both the Japanese and French. Although their tactics led Viet Minh leaders to conceal their communist goals and focus on national liberation to secure the widest possible support, the organization was in fact led and dominated by the ICP. Former schoolteacher Vo Nguyen Giap became the Viet Minh's military leader.

The Chinese Nationalist government grudgingly provided limited support for the Viet Minh, as did the United States through the Office of Strategic Services (OSS, the forerunner of the Central Intelligence Agency). The OSS gave the Viet Minh some light weapons, medical supplies, communications equipment, and training in return for Viet Minh aid in saving downed U.S. pilots and cooperation against the Japanese. By 1945, the Viet Minh had secured control over northern Tonkin.

Until nearly the end of World War II, the French authorities and army still were in place in Indochina; the Japanese were exercising indirect control. That changed in March 1945. The French authorities, anxious to liberate themselves, began active plotting to that end. The Japanese learned of the French plans, and on 9 March 1945, they arrested all the French officials and military personnel they could find. By announcing on 11 March the independence of Vietnam under previously French-controlled Emperor Bao Dai of Annam, Tokyo also exacerbated the postwar situation. This was the situation when Japan surrendered.

Ho Chi Minh then stepped into the vacuum. At the end of the war, starvation gripped much of Vietnam, and as many as 2 million Vietnamese died, chiefly in the north. The Viet Minh made great strides with the people by seizing rice stocks held by the Japanese and distributing them to the people. Then, on 16 August, Ho proclaimed the independence of Vietnam, and three days later the Viet Minh took power in Hanoi, capital of Tonkin. On 2 September, Ho announced establishment of the Democratic Republic of Vietnam.

Decisions taken during the Potsdam Conference in July 1945 had the Nationalist Chinese receiving the Japanese surrender in northern Vietnam and the British doing the same in the south. Ho appealed to the United States and the Soviet Union for assistance, but he received no response and was forced to negotiate first with the Chinese to secure their withdrawal and then with the French. Meanwhile, the British in the south let the French out of prison. A Viet Minh uprising there was soon crushed, and French control was reestablished in the south and then in Laos and Cambodia. The north was another matter, however. On 6 March 1946, French representative Jean Sainteny negotiated the Ho-Sainteny Agreement, in which France recognized Ho's Democratic Republic of Vietnam within the French Union and promise a plebiscite in the south to see whether the south also wanted to join. The agreement also allowed the return of some French troops to the north. The failure of the French to implement the provisions of this agreement led directly to the First Indochina War, which began in November 1946.

Claude R. Sasso and Spencer C. Tucker

See also
France, Vichy; Ho Chi Minh; Office of Strategic Services; Potsdam Conference; Thierry d'Argenlieu, Georges Louis Marie

References
Duncanson, Dennis J. *Government and Revolution in Vietnam.* New York: Oxford University Press, 1968.

Duiker, William J. *The Communist Road to Power in Vietnam.* Boulder, CO: Westview Press, 1989.

———. *Ho Chi Minh.* New York: Hyperion, 2000.

Patti, Archimedes L. A. *Why Viet Nam: Prelude to America's Albatross.* Berkeley, CA: University of California Press, 1980.

Tucker, Spencer C. *Vietnam.* Lexington: University Press of Kentucky, 1999.

Freyberg, Bernard Cyril (1889–1963)

New Zealand army general. Born in Surrey, England, on 21 March 1889, Bernard Freyberg moved with his family in 1891 to New Zealand. In 1911, Freyberg qualified as a dentist, a profession he rarely practiced. A few years later, he served as a volunteer on Pancho Villa's side in the revolutionary upheaval in Mexico. By August 1914, Freyberg was in London, where he met Winston L. S. Churchill, then first lord of the Admiralty. Through Churchill, Freyberg obtained a commission as a temporary lieutenant in the Royal Navy Volunteer Reserve. In World War I, Freyberg commanded a company in the Hood Battalion of the Royal Naval Division during the disastrous Gallipoli Campaign. In November 1916, Freyberg led the battalion in the last major attack of the Somme Campaign. Although wounded four separate times, Freyberg refused to relinquish command. For his actions, he was awarded the Victoria Cross. Wounded at least six times in World War I, Freyberg also received the Distinguished Service Order (DSO) with two bars.

Following World War I, Freyberg remained in the British military, transferring to the army. In 1937, a heart condition resulted in his medical discharge as a major general. When World War II began in September 1939, Freyberg was recalled and given a training command. But that position was too tame a job for Freyberg, who offered his services to New Zealand. With Churchill's support, Freyberg was appointed commander of the New Zealand Expeditionary Force.

Freyberg commanded Commonwealth forces on Crete in 1941, conducting the fighting withdrawal from the north to the south coast and then the evacuation. Freyberg then commanded the New Zealand Division in North Africa, where he often clashed with General Sir Claude Auchinleck, commander in chief of British Commonwealth forces in the Middle East. After a short mission to Syria, Freyberg and his New Zealanders returned to face German General Erwin Rommel at Minqar Qaim, Alam Halfa, and El Alamein. During the pursuit across Africa following Alamein, Freyberg's New Zealanders—reinforced with armor to corps size—swung wide to the left of the Mareth Line to hit the Germans at the Tebaga gap. Throughout most of these actions, Freyberg was up front in his mobile tactical headquarters, a Stuart tank with a dummy wooden gun.

In 1942, Freyberg was promoted to lieutenant general, which was almost unprecedented for an Allied divisional commander. Freyberg continued to lead the New Zealand Division through Sicily and the landings on the Italian mainland. In January 1944, the New Zealand Division came under the U.S. Fifth Army. Freyberg received control of two additional British divisions and a U.S. armored regiment to become the commander of the New Zealand Corps—while simultaneously retaining command of his own division. His mission was to break through at Cassino, which led to one of the most controversial Allied actions of the war, the bombing of the medieval monastery. Cassino and Crete were regarded as Freyberg's two major "failures" in World War II, but it is doubtful that any other general could have done better in either case. Freyberg probably saw more direct combat than any other Allied senior commander. Churchill once called him "the salamander of the British Empire." During the war, Freyberg won almost unprecedented third and fourth DSOs.

During and after the war, Freyberg received his share of honors. He was knighted in 1942 and raised to the peerage in 1951 as 1st Baron Freyberg. His identification with his New Zealanders was so strong that he was appointed governor general of New Zealand in 1945. In 1950, his term in office was extended another two years at the request of the government in Wellington. In 1952, Freyberg became the lieutenant governor of Windsor Castle. He died at Windsor on 4 July 1963.

David T. Zabecki

See also
Alam Halfa, Battle of; Auchinleck, Sir Claude John Eyre; Cassino/Rapido River, Battles of; Churchill, Sir Winston L. S.; Crete, Battle of; El Alamein, Battle of; Italy Campaign; New Zealand, Role in War; Rommel, Erwin Johannes Eugen; Sicily, Invasion of

References
Baker, John. *The New Zealand People at War*. Wellington: Historical Publications Branch, Department of Internal Affairs, 1965.

Hapgood, David, and David Richardson. *Monte Cassino*. New York: Congdon and Weed, 1984.
MacDonald, Callum. *The Lost Battle: Crete, 1941*. New York: Free Press, 1993.

Frick, Wilhelm (1877–1946)

German minister of the interior. Born on 12 March 1877 in Alsenz, Wilhelm Frick studied law from 1896 to 1901 at Göttingen, Munich, Beylin, and Heidelberg (where he received his doctorate). From 1904 to 1924, Frick worked in the Munich police department, heading the political police section after 1919. An early adherent of Adolf Hitler, Frick participated in the 1923 Munich Beer Hall Putsch, Hitler's abortive effort to seize power in Munich, and was arrested, tried, and sentenced to 15 months' imprisonment. He was able to avoid a prison term when the newly renamed National Socialist Freedom Party picked him as one of its representatives to the Reichstag in 1924. He served in the Reichstag from that point forward.

On 23 January 1930, Frick became the first National Socialist minister in a provincial government, responsible for education and the Ministry of the Interior in Thuringia. Under his administration, the Thuringian police force was purged of officers who supported the Weimar Republic; Nazi candidates for office were illegally favored; the antiwar film *All Quiet on the Western Front* was banned, as was jazz music; and rabidly militaristic, anti-Semitic propaganda was allowed to flourish unchecked. On Frick's instruction, special German freedom prayers were instituted in Thuringian schools, glorifying the German *Volk* and German national honor and military power while denouncing "traitors." Frick used his influence as interior minister to grant Hitler German citizenship by implementing a provision of the law that extended citizenship to anyone named to an official post in Germany. Frick managed to have Hitler named a councilor for the state of Braunschweig.

When the Nazis came to power in Germany in January 1933, Frick was appointed minister of the interior, a key position that he held until August 1943. In this post, he was directly responsible for many measures taken against Jews, Communists, Social Democrats, dissident churchmen, and other opponents of the regime. Frick also had charge of drafting and then administering the laws that gradually eliminated the Jews from the German economy and public life, culminating in the Nuremberg race laws that reduced Jews to second-class status in the Reich. It was Frick who framed the extraordinary law that declared all Hitler's actions during the Blood Purge of the Sturmabteilung (SA, storm troops) in June 1934 to be legal and statesmanlike. Although nominally Hein-

Persico, Joseph E. *Nuremberg: Infamy on Trial.* New York: Viking Penguin, 1994.

Wilhelm Frick, German politician and participant in Hitler's Munich putsch. (Hulton Archive)

rich Himmler's superior, Frick singularly failed to impose any legal limitations on the power of the Gestapo and the Schutzstaffel (SS, bodyguard units) nor seriously interfered with their encroachment on his area of jurisdiction.

On 24 August 1943, Frick was appointed Reichsprotektor (administrative head) of Bohemia and Moravia, a position he held until the end of the war, although real authority was concentrated in the hands of his subordinate Karl-Hermann Frank. At the Nuremberg trial, Frick was charged with and found guilty of crimes against peace, war crimes, and crimes against humanity committed in concentration camps in the Protectorate (Bohemia and Moravia). The dedicated Nazi bureaucrat and loyal implementer of Hitler's ruthless aims was hanged at Nuremberg on 16 October 1946.

Joseph C. Greaney

See also
Himmler, Heinrich; Hitler, Adolf; Holocaust, The
References
Fischer, Klaus. *Nazi Germany: A New History.* New York: Continuum Publishing Co., 1995.

Frogmen

Popular term for members of underwater demolition teams (UDTs), which played an important role in World War II. Italy was at the forefront in training combat swimmers; the Italian 10th Light Flotilla was composed mostly of sailors who manned small surface and underwater craft with explosive warheads. Their mission was to sink Allied warships and merchant shipping, a role in which they enjoyed some success.

The United States also devoted attention to such activity, training and deploying frogmen in demolition and commando tactics. The first unofficial U.S. frogmen were organized in September 1942 as a detachment of sailors who received a week of training in underwater demolition tactics before being sent to North Africa as part of Operation TORCH. They destroyed nets blocking the entrance to the Sebou River in Morocco, allowing U.S. assault ships to enter the river and offload rangers to assault Vichy-held Port Lyautey Field.

This success led Chief of Naval Operations Admiral Ernest J. King to issue orders on 6 May 1943 for the formation of UDTs. The first Naval Combat Demolition Unit consisted of 13 volunteers who trained at the Naval Amphibious Unit at Solomon Island, Maryland. They were instructed in the destruction of underwater obstacles and use of explosive charges to make channels through sandbars.

These newly designated frogmen took part in the invasion of Sicily in July 1943. They destroyed roadblocks near the coast, used bangalore torpedoes to remove barbed wire along the beach, salvaged stranded boats, and cleared channels through sandbars. On completion of their mission, most of the frogmen were sent back to the United States to work as instructors following further training at the Naval Amphibious Training Base at Fort Pierce, Florida. In the European Theater, frogmen also participated in the invasion of Normandy, where they were tasked with the destruction of steel girders and heavy timbers on Omaha and Utah Beaches, clearing the way for the landing craft. Frogmen also played a key role in the Pacific Theater, participating in the many amphibious operations. The British also used frogmen in the war. In the United States, frogmen were the forerunners of the U.S. Navy SEAL (*s*ea, *a*ir, *l*and) elite special-operations commando teams.

Gregory C. Wheal

See also
Italy, Navy; King, Ernest Joseph; Normandy Invasion and Campaign; Sicily, Invasion of; Submarines, Midget; TORCH, Operation

References

Best, Herbert. *The Webfoot Warrior.* New York: John Day Company, 1962.

Fane, Francis D. *The Naked Warrior.* New York: Appleton-Century-Croft, 1956.

Gleeson, James. *The Frogmen.* London: Evans Brothers Limited, 1950.

Greene, Jack, and Alessandro Massignani. *The Black Prince and the Sea Devils.* Philadelphia, PA: Da Capo, 2004.

Kelly, Orr. *Brave Men, Dark Waters: The Untold Story of the Navy SEALs.* New York: Pocket Books, 1993.

Fuchida Mitsuo (1902–1976)

Japanese navy officer and aviator. Born at Nagao in Nara Prefecture on 3 December 1902, Fuchida Mitsuo graduated from the Naval Academy in 1924 and completed flight training in 1927. While he was posted to the Yokosuka Kokutai (Air Corps), he developed the coordinated dive-bombing techniques intended to saturate target defenses that subsequently became standard Japanese tactics.

In 1939, Fuchida became the bomber group leader of 1st Carrier Division aboard the aircraft carrier *Akagi*. He was a major participant in planning for the Pearl Harbor attack and was selected as overall strike commander for the 330-plane force from Vice Admiral Nagumo Chūichi's First Air Fleet that surprised the U.S. Pacific Fleet on 7 December 1941. Fuchida actively participated in the attacks on Rabaul and Port Darwin and the devastating raid by the First Air Fleet into the eastern Indian Ocean during the spring of 1942. Fuchida was incapacitated by appendicitis during the Midway operation. When the *Akagi* was attacked and sunk by U.S. Navy dive-bombers he was severely wounded, barely managing to survive.

Following his recovery, Fuchida was posted to the staff of Yokosuka Kokutai and undertook a series of planning assignments before transferring to operational posts in the Mariana Islands and the Philippines. He returned to Japan with the rank of captain to participate in planning for the final defense of the home islands. Fuchida narrowly escaped death at Hiroshima; he left the city the day before the atom bomb was

Mitsuo Fuchida as he was when he led the Japanese air strike on Pearl Harbor (right) and in 1973 (left). (Photo by Keystone/Getty Images)

dropped. He attended the surrender ceremony aboard the U.S. battleship *Missouri* on 2 September 1945.

After the war, Fuchida took up farming and converted to Christianity with such fervor that he became a globe-circling evangelist. He emigrated to the United States in 1966 and became a citizen. Fuchida died while visiting Osaka on 30 May 1976.

Paul E. Fontenoy

See also
Aviation, Naval; Coral Sea, Battle of the; Darwin, Raid on; Genda Minoru; Indian Ocean, Japanese Naval Operations in; Japan, Air Forces; Japan, Navy; Midway, Battle of; Nagumo Chūichi

References
Evans, David C., and Mark R. Peattie. *Kaigun: Strategy, Tactics, and Technology in the Imperial Japanese Navy, 1887–1941.* Annapolis, MD: Naval Institute Press, 1997.

Fuchida Mitsuo and Okumya Masatake. *Midway: The Battle That Doomed Japan. The Japanese Navy's Story.* Annapolis, MD: Naval Institute Press, 1955.

Peattie, Mark R. *Sunburst: The Rise of Japanese Naval Air Power, 1909–1941.* Annapolis, MD: Naval Institute Press, 2001.

Prange, Gordon W., with Donald Goldstein and Katherine V. Dillon. *At Dawn We Slept: The Untold Story of Pearl Harbor.* New York: McGraw-Hill, 1981.

Stillwell, Paul, ed. *Air Raid: Pearl Harbor!* Annapolis, MD: Naval Institute Press, 1981.

G

Gamelin, Maurice Gustave (1872–1958)

French army general. Born in Paris on 20 September 1872, Maurice Gamelin was commissioned in the army in 1893 on graduation from the French military academy of Saint Cyr. His rise in the army was closely linked to French commanding general Joseph Joffre. Gamelin was serving as Joffre's operations officer at the beginning of the war and remained with him until the latter's dismissal in 1916. During the rest of the war, Gamelin served with distinction as a brigade commander (1916) and then a division commander (1918). After the war, Gamelin commanded French forces in the Middle East, where he helped pacify the Druze in Lebanon. He became chief of the General Staff in 1931 and commander in chief designate in 1935, replacing Maxime Weygand.

Gamelin benefited from the patronage of Radical Party politician Édouard Daladier, who was three times premier in the 1930s. The two men, both veterans of the Battle of Verdun, agreed on the need to modernize French forces. As chief of staff, Gamelin supported mechanization and investments in air power. Against his wishes, the French government proceeded with the construction of the Maginot Line, leaving little money for the reforms he championed. As with his mentor Joffre, Gamelin isolated himself and had little contact with his men, refusing even to have a telephone installed at his headquarters at Vincennes.

Gamelin urged France to fund emergency modernization measures in 1938, but French politicians, including Daladier, disagreed. In the first months of World War II, Gamelin advocated waiting for the British to rearm fully before assuming the offensive. He assumed (correctly) that Germany would not attack the Maginot Line. He also assumed (incorrectly) that the Germans would not attempt to cross the Ardennes Forest, believing they would attack through Belgium as they had done in 1914.

Gamelin bears primary responsibility for the disastrous Dyle plan, which called for Allied forces to move into Belgium to meet an anticipated German invasion. The plan underestimated the strength of the Maginot Line, devoting half of French effectives there. It also left 100 miles of the Ardennes virtually unguarded. Gamelin learned nothing from the September 1939 Polish campaign and thus failed fully to appreciate the speed and strength of the German army. The Dyle plan placed French troops in an untenable position in Belgium and northeastern France. Worse, the Germans anticipated its broad outlines and planned to defeat it by moving through the Ardennes and then north and west toward the Channel ports.

On 21 March 1940, Paul Reynaud replaced Daladier as premier. Daladier remained in the government, first as defense minister and then as foreign minister, but his patronage could not save Gamelin. On 10 May, the day of the German invasion, Reynaud was involved in discussions designed to remove Gamelin, in whom he had little confidence. Reynaud finally replaced him on 19 May with General Maxime Weygand, the man Gamelin had succeeded in 1935. Following the defeat of France, the Vichy government arrested Gamelin and brought him to trial at Riom, where he refused to defend himself. Deported to Germany in 1943, Gamelin was released by the Allies at the end of the war.

After the war, Gamelin wrote his three-volume memoir, *Servir*. He died at Paris on 18 April 1958.

Michael S. Neiberg

General Maurice Gustav Gamelin (1935), French general and chief of staff of the army, 1935–1940. (Hulton Archive)

See also

Daladier, Édouard; France, Army; France, Battle for; Maginot Line; Reynaud, Paul; Weygand, Maxime

References

Alexander, Martin S. *The Republic in Danger: General Maurice Gamelin and the Politics of French Defense, 1933–1940.* Cambridge, UK: Cambridge University Press, 1993.

Gamelin, Maurice G. *Servir.* 3 vols. Paris: Plon, 1946–1947.

Horne, Alistair. *To Lose a Battle: France, 1940.* London: Macmillan, 1965.

May, Ernest. *Strange Victory: Hitler's Conquest of France.* New York: Hill and Wang, 2000.

Shirer, William. *The Collapse of the Third Republic.* New York: Simon and Schuster, 1969.

Gandhi, Mohandas Karamchand (1869–1948)

Indian nationalist and spiritual leader, known as Mahatma or "great soul." Gandhi, a spare, short man with bowed shoulders and thick spectacles, was more than any other single individual responsible for bringing an end to the British Empire. Born 2 October 1869 in Porbandar, Kathiawar, India, Mohandas Gandhi went to England at age 19 to study law at University College, London. On being admitted to the bar, he returned to practice in India, where he had only modest professional success.

In 1893, Gandhi left India to practice law in South Africa. Here he encountered strong racial prejudice against the Indian population that had settled in Natal. The mild-mannered, passive Gandhi became an activist, protesting unjust laws through a nonviolent campaign of civil disobedience and noncooperation with the authorities. Gandhi eschewed his social position and lived a life of poverty and self-denial. During both the Boer War (1899–1902) and the Natal revolt of 1908, Gandhi organized and served with Red Cross units.

Gandhi returned to India in July 1914. He supported the British recruitment of Indian soldiers for World War I, but in 1919, with the passage of antisedition laws (the Rowlatt Acts), he began a protest against British rule. He called off the campaign, however, when violence flared. By 1921, Gandhi was the acknowledged leader of the Indian National Congress, which he transformed from a party of the upper class into a mass movement. Meanwhile, Gandhi was jailed numerous times. In 1930, he launched a campaign against the hated salt tax, and he also campaigned against prejudices toward the lowest social caste, the "untouchables." His program of passive resistance was a brilliant move because although the British had ample power to crush any armed rebellion, they were never able to devise an answer to nonviolent resistance. British rule in India and elsewhere rested primarily on the consent of the governed.

Gandhi dressed in a simple loincloth (dhoti) and worked at his spinning wheel daily, stressing his devotion to a life of simplicity. Although Gandhi condemned Hitler and fascism as well as the persecution of the Jews, he hated war more, and he naively advised nonviolent protest as the best course of action even in the event of a Japanese invasion of India. He broke with more pragmatic National Congress leaders over the degree to which India should support the Allied effort in World War II. But after a March 1942 British mission headed by Stafford Cripps failed to agree on a program that would secure Indian independence in return for support against the Japanese, most congress leaders supported Gandhi.

On 8 August 1942, the Indian National Congress passed a resolution calling on Britain to "quit India," which prompted British authorities to arrest Gandhi and other National Congress party leaders. Following considerable violence in which some 2,500 people were killed and wounded and considerable property was damaged, the British managed to restore order. Gandhi, in poor health, was held under house arrest near Poona for two years, but, with doctors reporting him to be near death, the authorities released him on 6 May 1944. He had spent a total of 2,089 days in Indian prisons and another 249 in prisons in South Africa.

Indian nationalist leader Mohandas Karamchand Gandhi, popularly known as Mahatma Gandhi, whose policy of peaceful demonstration led India from British rule to independence after World War II. (Hulton Archive)

Gandhi recovered and took a leading role in negotiations with Clement Attlee's Labour Party in Britain at the end of World War II. Attlee appointed Lord Louis Mountbatten to carry out the unwelcome task of ending British rule. The intransigence of Moslem leader Mohammad Ali Jinnah over the creation of a Moslem state led to the partition of India, despite Gandhi's great opposition. India and Pakistan were proclaimed independent states on 14 August 1947.

Independence brought near anarchy in both India and Pakistan. The problems of partition were staggering, and millions of people were uprooted and forced to move from one state to another. Religious hatred mingled with sheer greed, and perhaps a quarter of a million people died in the violence. In volatile Calcutta, Gandhi kept the peace, but only by offering his own person as a hostage and by beginning a fast unto death. Gandhi's reward for telling Hindus and Moslems that they had to learn to live together as brothers was his assassination by a young Hindu fanatic in Calcutta on 30 January 1948. Fortunately, Gandhi's death marked the end of the insensate communal killings.

A prolific writer, Gandhi influenced many others through his teachings of nonviolence. He inspired many activists, including Martin Luther King Jr., leader of the civil rights movement in the United States.

Spencer C. Tucker

See also
Attlee, Clement Richard; India; Mountbatten, Louis Francis Albert Victor Nicholas
References
Brown, Judith M. *Gandhi, Pioneer of Hope.* New Haven, CT: Yale University Press, 1989.
Collins, Larry, and Dominique LaPierre. *Freedom at Midnight.* New York: Simon and Schuster, 1975.
Fischer, Louis. *Life of Mahatma Gandhi.* New York: Harper and Brothers, 1950.
Gandhi, M. K. *An Autobiography: The Story of My Experiments with Truth.* Trans. Mahadev Desai. Boston: Beacon Press, 1949.

Garand, John Cantius (1883–1967)

Inventor of the U.S. Garand rifle. John Garand was born on 1 January 1883 on the family farm near Saint Remi, Quebec, Canada. His mother died in 1891, and he moved with his father to Connecticut in 1894. Garand dropped out of school to work in a steel mill. By 1897 he had filed for his first patent for a new type of jack screw. Garand became a machinist at the mill in 1901. Helping his father at a shooting gallery in Norwich, Connecticut, led to his interest in firearms. A few years later, Garand moved to Providence, Rhode Island, where he worked for the Federal Screw Corporation. He took up motorcycling and designed his own engine. Firearms, however, became his passion.

Garand then moved to New York City, where he worked in a micrometer plant and continued his education via correspondence courses. He also kept up his interest in rifles and marksmanship. In 1917, Garand learned that the U.S. Army was searching for a reliable machine gun, and he designed such a weapon and sent the plans for it to the U.S. Bureau of Standards. By 1919, Garand was the consulting engineer for the army's arsenal in Springfield, Massachusetts. He became a U.S. citizen in 1920.

> M.K. Gandhi spent more than 2,300 days of his life in prison to protest British policies.

In the 1920s, the Ordnance Department wanted to develop a semiautomatic rifle to replace the superb but difficult-to-master 1903 Springfield bolt-action rifle used by the U.S. Army in World War I. In 1923, Garand submitted his design for Bureau of Standards testing, and over the next 11 years he

John C. Garand, inventor of the Garand rifle, pointing out some of the features of the rifle to Major General Charles M. Wesson during his visit to the Springfield Arsenal. At right is Brigadier General Gilbert H. Stewart, commanding officer of the arsenal. (Library of Congress)

refined and improved the design until it met army standards for field testing. In 1936, the U.S. Army adopted Garand's weapon, describing it as "Rifle, Semi-Automatic, M1." The United States became the only country in World War II to have a semiautomatic rifle as a standard infantry weapon. The Garand, 43.6 inches long and weighing 9 lb 8 oz (unloaded), was a gas-operated, clip-fed, air-cooled, semiautomatic shoulder weapon that fired .30 ammunition from an 8-round clip. It had an effective range of 440 yards and a maximum range of 3,200 yards. A total of 4,040,000 M1s were produced, and it was the standard U.S. infantry firearm from 1936 to 1957.

The M1 had many advantages, including its accuracy, superior rate of firepower, and user-friendly sights. The Garand fired 40 rounds a minute in the hands of the average rifleman. It had 40 percent less recoil than the Springfield it replaced and only 72 parts. The Garand could be entirely broken down using only one tool, a .30-caliber round.

Although Garand never received what many believe to be his financial due for the development of the M1, he was awarded the Government Medal of Merit in 1944. He retired as chief ordnance engineer in 1953 and died in Springfield, Massachusetts on 16 February 1967.

Scott R. DiMarco and Gordon E. Hogg

See also
Rifles
References
Bruce, Robert. *The M1 Does My Talking!* Sandston, Va: Robert Bruce Photography, 1992.
Fangboner, Donald P. "John Garand: Inventor of the U.S. Semi-Automatic Rifle Caliber .30 M1." Master's thesis, Oneonta College, State University of New York, 1982.
Hatcher, Julian S. *The Book of the Garand.* Washington, DC: Infantry Journal Press, 1948.

Gaulle, Charles de

See de Gaulle, Charles.

Gavin, James Maurice (1907–1990)

U.S. Army general, airborne pioneer, author, and statesman. Born on 22 March 1907 at Brooklyn, New York, James Gavin was abandoned by his biological mother and subsequently adopted. At age 16, he enlisted in the army and eventually earned an appointment to the U.S. Military Academy. Graduating in 1929, he was commissioned in the infantry.

Gavin attended the Infantry School at Fort Benning, Georgia, served in the Philippines, and then was an instructor at West Point. He transferred to duty with parachute troops and, promoted to colonel in July 1942, rose to command the 505th Parachute Infantry Regiment, which eventually became part of the 82nd Airborne Division. In 1943, Gavin's 505th jumped into Sicily, where Gavin personally led a portion of his regiment during a fight on Biazza Ridge and stopped elements of the Hermann Göring Panzer Division from breaking through to the invasion beaches. After Sicily, Gavin led the 505th in another combat jump into Salerno on 14 September 1943. Promoted to brigadier general in October, he was appointed assistant division commander.

Gavin left Italy for Britain in November 1943. There he headed the airborne planning effort for Operation OVERLORD,

the invasion of France. He then rejoined the 82nd Airborne Division and made his third combat jump—into Normandy on 6 June 1944 as commander of Task Force A.

In August 1944, Gavin assumed command of the 82nd and led it on its fourth combat jump in September into Nijmegen, Holland, during Operation MARKET-GARDEN. He continued in command of the division for the remainder of the war, fighting through the Battle of the Bulge (Ardennes) and the subsequent drive into Germany. Gavin was only an observer in Operation VARSITY, the March 1945 airborne assault by the British 6th Airborne Division and U.S. 17th Airborne Division to secure British Field Marshal Sir Bernard Montgomery's bridgehead across the Rhine. However, by the end of the war, Gavin had made more combat jumps than any other general in history. At the end of the war, Gavin accepted the surrender of an entire German army.

Gavin continued to command the 82nd Airborne Division until March 1948. He was then, in succession, chief of staff of Fifth Army; chief of staff, Allied Forces South; commander of VII Corps; and deputy chief of staff of the U.S. Army. Promoted to lieutenant general in March 1955, Gavin was in line for promotion to general when he retired in 1958 because of differences with the defense policies of the Dwight D. Eisenhower administration—specifically what he regarded as its overreliance on nuclear forces. Gavin returned to public life during the John F. Kennedy administration, serving as ambassador to France in 1960 and 1961. He died at Baltimore, Maryland, on 23 February 1990.

Guy A. Lofaro

See also
Airborne Forces, Allied; Ardennes, Battle of; MARKET-GARDEN, Operation; Normandy Invasion and Campaign; OVERLORD, Operation; Salerno Invasion; Sicily, Invasion of

References
Blair, Clay. *Ridgway's Paratroopers: The American Airborne in World War II.* New York: Simon and Schuster, 1985.
Booth, T. Michael, and Duncan Spencer. *Paratrooper: The Life of Gen. James M. Gavin.* New York: Simon and Schuster, 1994.
Gavin, James M. *Airborne Warfare.* Washington, DC: Infantry Journal Press, 1947.
———. *On to Berlin: Battles of an Airborne Commander.* New York: Viking, 1978.

U.S. Army Major General James Gavin, February 1945. (Photo by MPI/Getty Images)

Gazala, Battle of (26 May–13 June 1942)

Key North African battle between Axis and Allied forces. The Battle of Gazala of 26 May–13 June 1942 sprang from Operation VENEZIA. In the operation, Adolf Hitler sought to tie down as many Allied troops as possible in North Africa while German forces fought the decisive battle in the Soviet Union. Hitler also wanted to capture Allied forward airfields so that Axis forces might render Malta harmless. Axis forces for VENEZIA, formed into Panzerarmee Afrika or Armata Corazzata Africa, consisted of two Italian infantry corps, one Italian armor corps, and the German Afrika Korps. The Afrika Korps had recently received reinforcements and new equipment.

Italy had sent some of its best units and equipment to North Africa. It had retrained its units and altered some of their structures to replicate German tactics. An Italian infantry division now numbered only 7,000 men, but it had a heavier artillery component. Although its tanks were still of limited value, Italy sent some self-propelled artillery armed with 75 mm guns, and some Italian divisions boasted both 90 mm and German 88 mm antitank guns.

German Afrika Korps commander General Erwin Rommel, nominally under General Ettore Bastico, head of Comando Superiore Forze Armate Africa Settentrionale (high command armed forces in North Africa), planned to attack the Allied forces entrenched with the protection of heavy minefields along the Gazala Line. He hoped to outflank the line from the south and then drive on and capture Tobruk, all within 10 days. Rommel could call on 332 German and 228 Italian tanks. Rommel also had the advantage in the air.

Lieutenant General Neil Ritchie commanded the British Eighth Army. Ritchie had an armored corps of two divisions and an infantry corps built around three divisions. Another division was in reserve, attached to army headquarters. All were numerically larger then the Axis divisions. The Eighth Army had recently received 242 U.S.-built Grant tanks as well as improved 6-pounder antitank guns. Ritchie could call on 839 Allied tanks, with a further 145 moving up. Both sides added tanks during the battle. Each side also had a small amphibious element, but neither was deployed in that capacity during the battle.

Ritchie had hoped to mount an attack to relieve Axis pressure on Malta, but Rommel struck first. On 26 May, while Axis infantry held the line, Axis motorized units poured around the southern Allied flank. Achieving some small successes, they stalled at the Free French fort of Bir Hacheim. Positioning themselves in the Allied rear, the Axis motorized units then took up defensive positions while also operating against Bir Hacheim, which fell on 11 June after a heroic French defense. Meanwhile, Eighth Army tanks mounted a series of assaults against Axis armor in the so-called Cauldron, but the British were repulsed with heavy losses from Axis antitank artillery guns.

The Axis forces having opened a supply line and the Eighth Army reeling from heavy tank losses, Rommel resumed the offensive on 12 June. At Knightsbridge, he ambushed British armor, destroying 120 tanks and forcing a general Allied retreat. In less than three weeks, the Axis offensive had forced the Allies to withdraw into Egypt. This paved the way for a third assault on the port of Tobruk. Ritchie was relieved of command, and General Claude Auchinleck took command of the withdrawal.

Jack Greene

See also
Afrika Korps; Auchinleck, Sir John Claude Eyre; Bastico, Ettore; France, Free French; Hitler, Adolf; Ritchie, Sir Neil Methuen; Rommel, Erwin Johannes Eugen; Tobruk, Third Battle of
References
Greene, Jack, and Alessandro Massignani. *Rommel's North Africa Campaign.* Conshohocken, PA: Combined Publishing, 1994.
Montanari, Mario. *Le Operazioni in Africa Settentrionale.* Vol. 3, *El Alamein.* Rome: Ufficio Storico, 1989.
Playfair, I. S. O., et al. *The Mediterranean and Middle East.* Vol. 3. London: Her Majesty's Stationery Office, 1960.

Geiger, Roy Stanley (1885–1947)

U.S. Marine Corps general, the first Marine ever to command an army in combat. Born on 25 January 1885 in Middleburg, Florida, Roy Geiger earned a law degree from Stetson University in DeLand, Florida, but he only briefly practiced law. He enlisted in the Marine Corps in November 1907 and received a commission in 1909. He first served with Marine detachments aboard battleships and then saw constabulary duty ashore in Panama, Nicaragua, the Philippines, and China. In Nicaragua, Geiger helped capture the fortified hills of Coyotepe and Barranca.

In 1916, as a captain, Geiger became the fifth Marine Corps aviator. Following U.S. entry in World War I, as a major he commanded Bomber Squadron A of the 1st Marine Aviation Force in France. After the war, Geiger's career centered on Marine aviation and advanced schooling. He served with Marine air units, and from 1931 to 1935 he headed Marine Corps aviation, playing a major role in its development. Geiger won promotion to colonel in 1935. He graduated from the U.S. Army Command and General Staff School (1925), the Army War College (1929), and the Naval War College (1941). Promoted to brigadier general in 1941, Geiger took command of the 1st Marine Aircraft Wing, Fleet Marine Force that September.

From September 1942, Geiger led the 1st Marine Aircraft Wing at Henderson Field on Guadalcanal. He returned to the United States in May 1943 to direct Marine Corps aviation. Promoted to major general, in November 1943 he assumed command of the I Marine Amphibious Corps on Bougainville in the Solomon Islands, which he led—following its redesignation as III Amphibious Corps—in fighting on Guam, Peleliu, and Okinawa. Following the death of Lieutenant General Simon Bolivar Buckner in the struggle for Okinawa, Geiger briefly (18–23 June) commanded the Tenth Army on Okinawa, the first Marine officer to command a numbered field army. Promoted to lieutenant general in June 1945, the next month Geiger became commanding general of the Fleet Marine Force in the Pacific. He returned to Headquarters Marine Corps in November 1946 and died on 23 January 1947 at Bethesda, Maryland. By act of Congress in July 1947, Geiger received posthumous promotion to full general.

Brandon H. Turner

See also
Bougainville Campaign; Buckner, Simon Bolivar, Jr.; Guadalcanal, Land Battle for; Guam, Battle for; Okinawa, Invasion of; Solomon Islands, Naval Campaign

References
Henderson, R. P. "Roy S. Geiger, The First Air-Ground General," *Marine Corps Gazette*, 79, no. 4 (April 1995): 78–80.
Hough, Frank O., Verle Ludwig, et al. *History of U.S. Marine Corps Operations in World War II*. 5 vols. Nashville, TN: Battery Press, 1993.
Willock, Roger. *Unaccustomed to Fear: A Biography of the Late General R. S. Geiger*. Quantico, VA: Marine Corps Association, 1983.

Genda Minoru (1904–1989)

Japanese navy officer and aviator. Born in Hiroshima on 16 August 1904, Genda Minoru graduated from the Japanese Naval Academy in 1924. Following sea service, he took flight training at Kasumigaura in 1928 and 1929, graduating at the head of his class. He served with the Yokosuka Kokutai (air corps) and aboard the carriers *Akagi* and *Ryujo* before becoming a fighter flight instructor at Yokosuka in 1934, where he gained national fame as leader of the Genda Circus, an aerobatics team. While at Yokosuka and subsequently at the Naval Staff College in 1937, Genda developed and expounded his concepts of massed air attacks under fighter umbrellas and the central role of naval aviation in future warfare. Following combat service in China and command of the Yokosuka Kokutai, he became assistant naval attaché in London from 1938 to 1940.

When Genda returned to Japan in 1940, he joined the staff of the 1st Carrier Division. On its formation in April 1941, he became chief air officer of First Air Fleet, which concentrated all of Japan's carriers into a single force to maximize their combat effectiveness, much as he had advocated since the mid-1930s. In February 1941, Genda drafted a very aggressive plan for an air assault on Hawaii, expanding on Admiral Yamamoto Isoroku's initial tentative suggestion for a preemptive strike to neutralize the U.S. Pacific Fleet. Genda played a leading role in designing the tactical plan for the Pearl Harbor attack. Although Genda's demands for concentration of force and surprise were heeded, his emphasis on destroying the U.S. carriers and following up with an inva-

sion to eliminate Hawaii as an American forward base formed no part of Yamamoto's eventual plan.

During the Pacific war, Genda served in carriers in the Pearl Harbor attack, in the Indian Ocean, in the Battle of Midway, and in the Solomon Islands. He was on the staff of the Eleventh Air Fleet at Rabaul until his promotion to captain in late 1944, when he became senior aviation officer in the Naval General Staff. In 1945, Genda was charged with the air defense of the Japanese home islands as commander of Kokutai 343, a large formation equipped with the best navy interceptor aircraft flown by the most experienced available crews. He served in this capacity until Japan's surrender.

Following World War II, Genda was first in private business; he then headed the Japanese Air Self-Defense Forces from 1955 to 1962, retiring as a full general. He was elected to the upper house of the Japanese Diet in 1962, serving there until 1982. Genda died in Tokyo on 15 August 1989.

Paul E. Fontenoy

See also
Aviation, Naval; Coral Sea, Battle of the; Darwin, Raid on; Fuchida Mitsuo; Indian Ocean, Japanese Naval Operations in; Japan, Air Force; Japan, Navy; Midway, Battle of; Nagumo Chūichi

References
Evans, David C., and Mark R. Peattie. *Kaigun: Strategy, Tactics, and Technology in the Imperial Japanese Navy, 1887–1941*. Annapolis, MD: Naval Institute Press, 1997.
Peattie, Mark R. *Sunburst: The Rise of Japanese Naval Air Power, 1909–1941*. Annapolis, MD: Naval Institute Press, 2001.
Prange, Gordon W., with Donald Goldstein and Katherine V. Dillon. *At Dawn We Slept: The Untold Story of Pearl Harbor*. New York: McGraw-Hill, 1981.
Stillwell, Paul, ed. *Air Raid: Pearl Harbor!* Annapolis, MD: Naval Institute Press, 1981.

George VI, King of England (1895–1952)

King of Great Britain and Northern Ireland and constitutional head of the British Empire. Born on 14 December 1895 at Sandringham, England, the second son of King George V and Queen Mary, George was by nature unpretentious and modest. He also suffered from a severe stammer. No intellectual, he was educated by private tutors. Following family tradition, he entered the navy at age 13 and attended the Royal Navy College of Dartmouth. George saw action in the 1916 Battle of Jutland, and in 1918 he joined the Royal Flying Corps and became a wing commander.

George married Lady Elizabeth Angela Marguerite Bowes-Lyon in 1923. They had two daughters, the future Queen Elizabeth II and Princess Margaret. As Duke of York, George

His Majesty King George VI of Great Britain. (Library of Congress)

helped set up summer camps to get young men out of industrial slums in the cities and into the countryside. George succeeded to the throne on 12 December 1936 following the abdication of his brother, King Edward VIII. He made numerous state visits in 1938 and 1939, including to the United States, which cemented valuable friendships. He was the first British monarch to visit the United States.

Despite the fact that military personnel swore allegiance to him and that military orders were issued in his name, George VI had no real powers as king. His role in World War II was to provide an example to the nation. In frequent radio broadcasts, George VI encouraged his people to remain calm, firm in resolve, and united behind the war effort. His popularity soared because he refused to leave London, despite the fact that Buckingham Palace was hit by German bombs. He also toured the bombed areas. George VI had an excellent relationship with Prime Minister Winston L. S. Churchill.

George VI established medals for citizens who exhibited wartime bravery, and his frequent wartime visits to factories and hospitals and to the troops boosted morale. He also strongly supported monarchs in exile in Britain. At the end of the war, the popular bond with the monarchy had never

been as strong in modern times. George VI lived to see dramatic changes in Britain's world position at the end of the war and the breakup of the British Empire, especially the independence of India in 1947. He died at Sandringham, England, on 6 February 1952 and was succeeded by his daughter, Queen Elizabeth II.

Annette Richardson

See also
Great Britain, Home Front
References
Bradford, Sarah. *King George VI*. London: Weidenfeld and Nicolson, 1989.
Donaldson, Frances Lonsdale. *King George VI and Queen Elizabeth*. London: Weidenfeld and Nicholson, 1977.
James, Robert Rhodes. *A Spirit Undaunted: The Political Role of George VI*. Boston: Little, Brown, 1998.
Judd, Denis. *King George VI*. London: Michael Joseph, 1982.

Georges, Alphonse Joseph (1875–1951)

French army general. Born on 19 August 1875 at Montluçon, Alphonse Georges graduated third in his class in 1897 from the French military academy of Saint Cyr and was posted to Algeria. During World War I, he was seriously wounded in 1914 while commanding a battalion. Following his recovery, he was posted to the army General Staff. He ended the war as chief of operations for Marshal Ferdinand Foch. After the war, he served as chief of staff to Marshal Henri Philippe Pétain during the Riffian Wars in Morocco. He was a division commander in Algeria from 1928 to 1932 and was then assigned to the Supreme War Council in Paris. Georges was wounded during the assassinations of King Alexander of Yugoslavia and French foreign minister Louis Barthou at Marseille in 1934. This aggravated the wound he had received in 1914.

Georges's physical condition may have played a critical role in his deteriorating abilities during the late 1930s. He expected to be named chief of staff of the French Army in 1935, but the French premier, Édouard Daladier, suspected him of right-wing tendencies. Georges was also closely linked to Paul Reynaud, Daladier's political rival. Daladier thus named General Maurice Gamelin to the position instead and named Georges as Gamelin's assistant.

The troubled professional and personal relations between Gamelin and Georges severely weakened French preparations for war during the last half of the 1930s. Georges assumed responsibility for northeast France, placing him in direct command of the units most likely to meet a German invasion. In 1940, these units included two French army groups and the British Expeditionary Force (BEF). Fully confident of the abilities of his force, Georges was stunned by its subsequent poor performance.

French General Alphonse Georges. (Photo by March of Time/Time Life Pictures/Getty Images)

Georges also bears partial responsibility for the decision to implement the Dyle plan, which placed substantial Allied units on the road to Belgium rather than in the Ardennes, the main axis of German attack. As the military situation collapsed, so did any semblance of professionalism between Georges and Gamelin. On 17 May 1940, both men were relieved of command in favor of General Maxime Weygand. Georges refused to play any role in the subsequent Vichy government, but he also had no real role in the French Resistance because he did not enjoy the confidence of Charles de Gaulle. He briefly served as minister without portfolio in the French Committee of National Liberation in 1943. Georges died in Paris on 24 April 1951.

Michael S. Neiberg

See also
Daladier, Édouard; de Gaulle, Charles; France, Army; France, Battle for; Gamelin, Maurice Gustave; Pétain, Henri Philippe; Reynaud, Paul; Weygand, Maxime
References
Horne, Alistair. *To Lose a Battle: France 1940.* Boston: Little, Brown, 1969.
May, Ernest. *Strange Victory: Hitler's Defeat of France.* New York: Hill and Wang, 2000.

German-Soviet Non-aggression Pact (23 August 1939)

Treaty between Germany and the Soviet Union (often called the Nazi-Soviet Non-aggression Pact) that facilitated Germany's 1 September 1939 invasion of Poland and its war effort before 1941. German Chancellor Adolf Hitler, having maintained that the Sudetenland of Czechoslovakia was his last territorial demand and having been granted that area in the 1938 Munich Agreement, absorbed the remainder of the country in March 1939. On 31 March, in an effort to prevent further German territorial expansion aimed at Poland, Great Britain and France jointly issued a guarantee to declare war on Germany should it invade Poland. In effect, this pledge placed Britain and France in Poland, securing for Soviet dictator Josef Stalin about as much as he could have gotten in negotiations with the two western powers.

The British and French governments now attempted to negotiate with the Soviet Union to bring it into the alliance against German expansion. Although France could attack western Germany in the event of an invasion of Poland, the British and French would be hard-pressed to get forces to Poland in time to help that nation stave off a German invasion. Negotiations of the British and French with the Soviet Union for an alliance that would preserve Poland proceeded at a leisurely pace throughout the spring and summer of 1939.

These talks yielded little, as Stalin did not trust the western powers. He also insisted on the right of Soviet forces to move into Poland and the Baltic states in the event of a German thrust east, something refused by these countries, which feared the Soviets more than the Germans. The Soviets assumed that the western powers wanted them to bear the brunt of the attack. The western powers, for their part, were unwilling to yield territory to the Soviet Union the way they had to Hitler.

Stalin was also concerned about the possibility of having to fight a two-front war against both Germany and Japan. There had already been serious fighting between Soviet and Japanese forces in the Far East in 1938 and 1939. Concern over the Japanese threat may have been a major factor in Stalin's thinking regarding an alliance with Germany. An agreement with Germany, Stalin believed, would not only gain space in the form of territorial concessions but also win the time necessary to rebuild the Soviet armed forces after the costly purges of their senior leadership.

While they were negotiating more or less openly with the British and French, the Soviets were also secretly negotiating with Germany. The western powers discounted this possibility, believing that the Soviet and German political systems were diametrically opposed and that the two powers were permanent enemies.

Although Berlin rejected Stalin's initial efforts, Hitler became convinced that Stalin was serious when in May 1939 the Soviet dictator dismissed Foreign Minister Maxim Litvinov, a champion of collective security and a Jew. The pragmatist and nationalist Vyacheslav Molotov replaced Litvinov. At the end of May, the German government indicated its willingness for a "certain degree of contact" with Moscow, beginning the process that would culminate in the German-Soviet pact.

On 21 August 1939, after a series of German communications, Stalin telegraphed Berlin and asked that Foreign Minister Joachim von Ribbentrop come to Moscow. Ribbentrop arrived on 23 August and met personally with Stalin. The pact was signed that same night, stunning the world. The pact had three major provisions, two of them secret and not revealed until the Nuremberg Tribunal after World War II had ended. The open provision consisted of a 10-year nonaggression pact between the Soviet Union and Germany.

The first of the two secret sections divided the Baltic states and Poland between the Soviet Union and Germany. The Soviet sphere of influence was to include eastern Poland, Bessarabia (a province of Romania), Estonia, Latvia, and Finland. The Germans secured western Poland and Lithuania. A month after the pact was signed, Hitler traded Lithuania to the Soviet Union in exchange for further German concessions in Poland. The second secret clause stipulated that the Soviet Union would provide Germany with massive amounts of raw materials and act as its purchasing agent abroad for items it could not itself furnish. In return, Germany agreed to provide finished goods and weapons technology from Germany. This was particularly helpful to Germany, nullifying the effects of the British naval blockade of Germany.

After signing the pact, Stalin drew Ribbentrop aside and told him that the Soviet Union would live up to its provisions and never betray Germany. Stalin understood the danger of the alliance, yet he continued to trust his ally until the German invasion of the Soviet Union, Operation BARBAROSSA, in June 1941. With the signing of the pact, Hitler freed himself of the threat of Soviet military intervention and a two-front war. He was now free to launch his invasion of Poland. On 1 September 1939, German forces crossed the border. Two days later, Great Britain and France honored their pledge to Poland and declared war on Germany. The Soviet Union denied the secret provisions of the pact until 1990.

Eric W. Osborne

See also

BARBAROSSA, Operation; Hitler, Adolf; Litvinov, Maxim; Molotov, Vyacheslav Mikhailovich; Munich Conference and Preliminaries; Origins of the War; Ribbentrop, Ulrich Friedrich Willy Joachim von; Stalin, Josef

References

Bloch, Michael. *Ribbentrop: A Biography.* New York: Crown Publishers, 1992.

Fourestier, Jeffrey de. "The Hitler-Stalin Pact: Discussion of the Non-Aggression Treaty and the Secret Protocols." Master's thesis, McGill University, 1992.

Read, Anthony, and David Fisher. *The Deadly Embrace: Hitler, Stalin, and the Nazi-Soviet Pact, 1939–1941.* New York: W. W. Norton, 1988.

Roberts, Geoffrey. *The Unholy Alliance: Stalin's Pact with Hitler.* Bloomington: Indiana University Press, 1989.

Germany, Air Force

The German air force, the Luftwaffe, existed officially for barely a decade, but during that time it was the pride of Nazi Germany. Before the war, the Luftwaffe was useful in coercing concessions from other countries. It was the world's most powerful air force in 1939, and once World War II began, it became an essential element of the blitzkrieg—the "lightning war." The Luftwaffe was, however, basically a tactical force, and it came apart under the strain of the German invasion of the Soviet Union.

The Versailles Treaty after World War I denied Germany an air force. Nonetheless, the Germans continued experimenting with aviation, and the military developed air doctrine and training programs, monitored technological developments, and built an industrial infrastructure for civilian aviation. At the same time, the German military established clandestine air facilities in the Soviet Union to build and test aircraft and train personnel. When Adolf Hitler came to power in January 1933, he pushed development of aviation and in 1935 openly began building an air force. The western Allies were reluctant to use force to halt this development, which was a direct violation of German treaty obligations.

Unlike the army and navy, the Luftwaffe was purely a Nazi creation and became the primary focus of Hitler's rearmament program. Hitler selected Hermann Göring, a World War I ace pilot, as minister of aviation and commander in chief of the Luftwaffe. Hitler was also much impressed with theories, notably those of Italian Guilio Douhet, that future wars could be won by air forces alone.

In 1936, Hitler sent the Kondor Legion, essentially a Luftwaffe outfit, to fight in the Spanish Civil War. Here the Germans gained invaluable experience in testing aircraft, tactical concepts, and experimenting with strategic bombing (as at Guernica). Hitler's boasts about German air power, although many of them were empty, helped face down the French and British in his March 1936 remilitarization of the Rhineland and in the 1938 crisis over Czechoslovakia.

As with so many other agencies in the Reich, the Luftwaffe suffered from organizational weaknesses and overlap at the

A formation of Luftwaffe Junkers Ju-87D Stuka dive-bombers in the air. (Hulton Archive)

top. Göring, one of Hitler's inner circle from the early days, was Hitler's designated successor, and Hitler allowed him to run the Luftwaffe without any real interference. The Reich Air Ministry consisted of the office of state secretary for air Erhard Milch; it supervised aviation matters apart from operations. Milch was also inspector general of the Luftwaffe. In addition there was Luftwaffe chief of staff Hans Jeschonnek. Until his suicide in 1943, Jeschonnek headed the air force's organization, operations, intelligence, training, quartermaster, and signal branches. Milch and Jeschonnek did not get along. Jeschonnek only had access to Göring on operational matters and had no control over personnel, which Göring made his own province. Ernst Udet, chief of the Technical Office and World War I ace, proved an incompetent administrator. Udet reported to Milch, who took over Udet's office after Udet's 1941 suicide. Too late, in May 1944, the administrative structure was streamlined with the creation of the Oberkommando der Luftwaffe (Air Force high command, OKL). Also in 1944, Albert Speer's Armaments Ministry gained control of all German aircraft production, and Milch's ministry was abolished.

The Luftwaffe, the newest of the military services, was the least professional and suffered the most from promotions not based on merit. Göring surrounded himself with advisers whose principal qualifications were that they were Nazis, as opposed to experienced aviation military officers. Many times they either offered poor advice or, not wishing to anger him, agreed with whatever ideas he developed. Increasingly, Göring, who held numerous offices in the Reich, largely abandoned his command of the Luftwaffe, intervening only in fits and starts and often with disastrous results, as during the 1940 Battle of Britain. During the war, the Luftwaffe was also the agency least conscious of communications security.

The Luftwaffe controlled all air services but had little interest in naval aviation. Airborne troops were Luftwaffe personnel, and the air force also had charge of antiaircraft artillery. Eventually the Luftwaffe even fielded 22 ground divisions, including the Hermann Göring Armored Division. The Luftwaffe itself was organized into Luftflotten (air fleets), constituted so as to perform a variety of roles and consisting of a wide variety of aircraft types. At the beginning of the war,

Germany had four Luftflotten, and during the course of the conflict three more were added. The next operational division was the Fleigerkorps (flier corps), and below that was the Fleigerdivision (flier division). These last two each contained several Geschwader (squadrons) that were designated as to types (including fighters, bombers, night fighters, training, and so on). Each division controlled three to four Gruppen (groups) comprising three or four Staffein (squadrons). In September 1939, the Luftwaffe had 302 Staffein.

At that point, Germany's chief advantage was in the air, for at the start of hostilities the Luftwaffe was certainly the world's most powerful air force. In September 1939, Göring commanded more than 3,600 frontline aircraft. The death in 1936 of strategic bomber proponent General Walther Wever, however, had brought a shift in emphasis to tactical air power. This remained the case throughout the war. Although Germany developed four-engine bomber prototypes, these were never placed in production. It could be argued, however, that a tactical air force was the best use of Germany's limited resources.

> Before the end of the war, the Germans introduced the Messerschmitt Me-262, the world's first operational jet aircraft.

The German air force was essentially built to support ground operations. It suited ideally the new blitzkrieg tactics, and the Junkers Ju-87 Stuka dive-bomber was a highly accurate form of "flying artillery." Impressed by U.S. Marine Corps experiments with precision dive-bombing, the Germans embraced this technique; indeed, all German bombers had to be capable of dive-bombing. This entailed considerable aircraft structural change with attendant production delays and a decrease in bomb-carrying capacity. The flying weight of the Junkers Ju-88 twin-engine bomber went from 6 to 12 tons, sharply reducing both its speed and its bomb-carrying capacity. Nonetheless, the Germans developed some exceptional aircraft. In addition to the Stuka, they had a superb air-superiority fighter in the Messerschmitt Bf-109, certainly one of the best all-around aircraft of the war. And before the end of the war, the Germans had introduced the Messerschmitt Me-262, the world's first operational jet aircraft. But Hitler also wasted considerable resources on the development of terror or "vengeance" weaponry, the V-1 and V-2.

The Luftwaffe played key roles in the German victories over Poland in 1939 and over France and the Low Countries in 1940. Its limitations first became evident during the Battle of Britain, when Göring attempted to wage a strategic bombing campaign with a tactical air force. Germany's defeat in this battle was its first setback of the war. The Luftwaffe was also impressive in the fighting against the Soviet Union, at least until the Battle of Stalingrad. But in the fighting on the Eastern Front, the superb combined-arms instrument that had been the German military to that point began to come unhinged. By the fall of 1941, Germany was overextended, and the Luftwaffe's small airlift capacity of Junkers Ju-52 trimotor transports was unable to fulfill all the missions required of it. Although Germany increased its aircraft production during the war, as the conflict continued, and under relentless Allied bombing, it suffered from lack of aviation fuel. This was the key factor in the defeat of the Luftwaffe, rather than inferior or too few aircraft.

By 1944, the Luftwaffe was feeling the effects of the Allied bomber offensive. In the first half of the year, pilot losses were averaging 20 percent a month, and the scarcity of fuel forced the routine grounding of aircraft not only for operations but also for training. In a period when replacement aircrews were desperately needed, flight time for trainees had been reduced to less than half that for their Allied counterparts. This in turn led to increasing numbers of accidents. By the time of the June 1944 Normandy invasion, the much-vaunted Luftwaffe had been largely silenced.

Pamela Feltus and Spencer C. Tucker

See also
Airborne Forces, Axis; Aircraft, Bombers; Aircraft, Fighters; Aircraft, Gliders; Aircraft, Transport; Antiaircraft Artillery and Employment; Armaments Production; Aviation, Ground-Attack; "Big Week" Air Battle; "Blitz," The; Blitzkrieg; Britain, Battle of; Crete, Battle of; Crete, Naval Operations off; Douhet, Giulio; Fighter Tactics; France, Battle for; Glider; Göring, Hermann Wilhelm; Guernica, Kondor Legion, Attack on; Hamburg, Raids on; Hitler, Adolf; Jeschonnek, Hans; Jet and Rocket Aircraft; Kesselring, Albert; Kondor Legion; Malta; Messerschmitt, Wilhelm Emil; Milch, Erhard; Parachute Infantry; Poland Campaign, 1939; Richthofen, Wolfram von; Rotterdam, Destruction of; Speer, Albert; Stalingrad, Battle of; Strategic Bombing; Student, Kurt; Udet, Ernst; V-1 Buzz Bomb; V-2 Rocket; Wilhemshaven

References
Cooper, Mathew. *The German Air Force, 1922–1945: Anatomy of a Failure.* London: Jane's, 1981.

Corum, James S. *The Luftwaffe: Creating the Operational Air War, 1918–1940.* Lawrence: University Press of Kansas, 1997.

Faber, Harold, ed. *Luftwaffe: A History.* New York: Times Book Co., 1978.

Hallion, Richard. *Strike from the Sky: The History of Battlefield Air Attack, 1911–1945.* Washington, DC: Smithsonian Institution Press, 1989.

Mason, Herbert Malloy. *The Rise of the Luftwaffe.* New York: Ballantine, 1973.

Germany, Army

At the tactical level of warfare, the German army—the Reichsheer—of World War II may well have been the best ground force in the history of warfare to that time. On the strategic level, the Germans had major blind spots that go a long way toward explaining why they lost two world wars despite having the best army in the field. At the middle level of warfare—that of operations—historians continue to argue about the German army. One school holds that the German doctrine of blitzkrieg was the most sophisticated example of the operational art to that time. The other school argues that what passed for operational art in the German army was little more than tactics on a grand scale.

The Reichsheer of World War II (the Wehrmacht was the entire German military, not just the army) grew out of the 100,000-man Reichswehr that was allowed to Germany following World War I under the terms of the Treaty of Versailles. On 1 October 1934, Adolf Hitler ordered the threefold secret expansion of the Reichswehr. Conscription was reintroduced in March 1935, establishing a further increased objective base strength of 38 divisions and approximately 600,000 troops. By 1939, the two main components of the German army were the field army (Feldheer) and the replacement army (Ersatzheer). The field army had more than 2 million soldiers and was organized into 120 divisions—99 infantry, 9 panzer, 6 motorized, 1 cavalry, 3 mountain, and 2 parachute. The replacement army consisted of a force of approximately 100,000 men in training or transit. From 1942 on, the numbers of replacements became progressively insufficient to keep frontline units up to authorized strength levels.

The infantry division was the primary tactical element of the German army. In 1940, the standard German infantry division had 17,200 troops, 942 motor vehicles, and 5,375 horses. By 1944, there were 226 infantry divisions, but their size had shrunk to 12,352 troops, 615 motor vehicles, and 4,656 horses. Despite its reputation as the master of mechanized and mobile warfare, the German army relied heavily on horses right up until the end of the war. Almost all field artillery in the infantry divisions was horse-drawn. The German divisions were organized according to a triangular structure, with (1) three infantry regiments of three battalions of three companies each; (2) a divisional artillery command with a field artillery regiment of three battalions of three batteries each, a heavy artillery battalion, and an observation battalion; (3) reconnaissance, engineer, signals, and antitank battalions; and (4) the divisional (supply) trains. Each division also generally had an antiaircraft battalion attached to it from the Luftwaffe.

The Germans did, however, field various forms of motorized or mechanized units. By 1941, they had a total of 10 motorized infantry divisions and light infantry divisions. Later in the war, these units were redesignated as panzergrenadier divisions. Germany ultimately fielded 22 of these units. They were organized along the general lines of the infantry divisions, but they had more motor vehicles and an organic tank regiment. In 1940, the standard motorized/light division had 14,000 troops, 3,370 motor vehicles, 158 tanks, and more than 1,500 horses. The 1944 panzergrenadier division had 13,833 soldiers, 2,637 motor vehicles, 48 tanks, and more than 1,400 horses.

The Germans had several specialized divisions. Mountain divisions were essentially smaller and lighter versions of the infantry division. Germany had 3 mountain divisions in 1940 and 13 in 1944. Fortress divisions and security divisions were divisions in name only; they could not be seriously equated with other divisions in the army's order of battle. The fortress divisions were little more than stationary garrisons, seldom larger than a regiment in strength. The security divisions were used to secure rear-area lines of communication and to conduct antipartisan operations on the Eastern Front. In a last act of desperation late in the war, Germany created Volksgrenadier (people's grenadier divisions) for defense of the Reich itself. Heavily manned by old men and young boys with almost no military training, these units were armed with a high proportion of automatic and antitank weapons. Because of the weapons' high firepower and the fact that the units were defending their home ground, these units sometimes gave a surprisingly good account of themselves.

The Germans began the war with one (horse) cavalry division, which fought in the Poland Campaign in 1939. By 1944, Germany actually had four such divisions, all operating on the Eastern Front. Late in the war, Germany fielded its single artillery division, which was based on the Soviet model. The Red Army, which had hundreds of thousands of artillery pieces, fielded almost 100 artillery divisions. But for the Germans, who were chronically short on artillery throughout the war, fielding an artillery division was an almost pointless exercise. The Germans did not have sufficient artillery to equip their infantry and panzer divisions, let alone form more artillery divisions.

Organizationally, all German parachute divisions were part of the Luftwaffe, but operationally they fought under army command. The Germans had 2 parachute divisions in 1940 and 11 in 1944. After the near-disaster on Crete, German parachute divisions never again jumped in combat. They spent the remainder of the war fighting as light infantry, but their traditional paratrooper élan remained, and they were fierce opponents, especially in Italy. The German air force also fielded land divisions that operated under army command. The formation of these air force field units was another desperate measure. As attrition ground down the Luftwaffe's aircraft, especially on the Eastern Front, excess personnel were hastily grouped into these field divisions. Often, the new ground soldiers had little or no infantry training. Germany had 19 such divisions in 1944.

The panzer division was the mailed striking fist of the German army. The first three panzer divisions were raised as

German soldiers in Russia, 1941. (National Archives)

completely new units in the fall of 1935, but they were not fully operational until September 1937. Thereafter, new panzer divisions were created by converting infantry or other divisions. There were 9 panzer divisions by 1939 and 26 by 1944. From 1941, the panzer divisions were in action almost constantly and continually subject to being ground down by attrition. A panzer division in 1940 had some 14,000 troops, 1,800 motor vehicles, and 337 horses. The standard panzer division had 324 tanks, and a variation known as a light panzer division had 219 tanks. By 1944, the typical panzer division had 13,700 troops, but the number of motor vehicles had decreased to 48, whereas the number of horses had increased to almost 1,700. On paper, at least, a 1944 panzer division had 150 tanks; in the last year of the war, however, many panzer divisions could only field a handful of tanks.

The Waffen-Schutzstaffel (Waffen-SS) was separate from the army and even from the Wehrmacht. However, it was essentially the Nazi Party's army, and it fielded combat divisions that fought under army command and control, much like the Luftwaffe's field and parachute divisions. By 1944, there were 7 SS panzer divisions and 11 panzergrenadier divisions. The organization of the Waffen-SS divisions was similar to the organization of their Wehrmacht counterparts, but because of their unquestioning loyalty to Hitler they were often better equipped.

The echelon of command above the division was the corps, which consisted of two or more divisions and additional corps support troops and artillery. The two basic types of corps were the army corps, consisting primarily of infantry divisions, and the panzer corps, consisting primarily of panzer divisions. The XCI Armeecorps was the highest-numbered corps. The next-higher echelon of command was the field army, comprising two or more corps. Field armies normally were designated by numbers, but in a few instances they were designated by a name. Field armies also had their own pools of combat assets such as artillery and separate heavy tank battalions. The German army's largest operational unit was the army group (Heeresgruppe), which controlled several field armies or corps directly. The army group also was responsible for providing support to all units in its area, as well as for the rear-area lines of communication and logistical services. Army groups were designated by their locations, by their commander's name, or by a letter.

The Germans had several elite units designated only by their name. Grossdeutschland (greater Germany)—also called "the bodyguard of the German people"—was first formed in 1938 as a ceremonial battalion. By 1939, it had expanded to the size of a regiment, and by 1942 it was an oversized division. At the end of the war, Panzerarmee Grossdeutschland commanded five divisions under two corps. The Panzer Lehr Division, which was the most powerful German armored division in Western Europe at the time of the Allied landings in Normandy, was formed in the winter of 1943–1944 with instructors and troops from the German armored school. The Infantrie-Lehr Regiment was an elite unit formed from instructors and infantry-school troops. In 1944, Hitler personally ordered the Infantrie-Lehr to Anzio to block the Allied landings there.

Command and control in the German army suffered from a confused structure at the very top, which only compounded the German weaknesses at the strategic and operational levels. Three different high-command headquarters were seldom in agreement and often in competition. The Oberkommando das Heeres (army high command, OKH), the Oberkommando der Wehrmacht (armed forces high command, OKW), and the supreme commander (Hitler) and his staff often issued conflicting orders to the same units. In theory, OKH ran the war in the Soviet Union, and the OKW ran the war everywhere else. Hitler's Führerhauptquartier (Führer headquarters) issued all the key strategic orders.

Despite the popular stereotypes, reinforced by countless Hollywood movies and television programs, the common German soldier of World War II was anything but stupid and unimaginative, and his officers and noncommissioned officers (NCOs) were neither machinelike nor inflexible autocrats. Rather, the German army encouraged initiative among its subordinate leaders and stressed flexibility and creativity to a degree far greater than any other army prior to 1945. This was the key to its tactical excellence. German combat orders, rather than dictating detailed and rigid timelines and specific instructions on how to accomplish missions, tended to be short and as broad as possible. The principle under which the German command system operated was called *Auftragstaktik,* which can only very loosely be translated into English as "mission orders." For Auftragstaktik to work, a subordinate leader had to understand the intent of his higher commander at least two echelons up. That meant that the subordinate had the right to ask his superior why something was being done, and the superior was obligated to explain. Such a practice was virtually unheard of in almost all the other armies of World War II.

Despite superb organization and tactical tools at the lower levels, the confused high-command structure and Germany's incoherent strategy doomed the German army over the long run. Hitler did a great deal personally to subvert solid military command and control. He distrusted his generals, and for the most part they distrusted him. During the early years of the war, 1939 and 1940, Hitler was the beneficiary of outrageously good luck and inept opponents. This only served to reinforce his belief in what he thought was his divinely inspired military genius. When the commander in chief of the German army, General Walther von Brauchitsch, retired for medical reasons in late 1941, Hitler—the former World War I lance corporal—assumed direct command of the army. By

that time, however, Hitler had led Germany once again into its worst strategic nightmare, a two-front war.

The German army also suffered from several internal and external handicaps that were beyond its ability to control. Germany was chronically short of virtually every vital resource necessary for modern warfare. A panzer division in 1940 still had more than 300 horses, and four years later that number had risen to 1,700. Roughly only 10 percent of the army was ever motorized. In 1940, OKH planners estimated that it would require at least 210 divisions to execute the invasions of France and the Low Countries while simultaneously garrisoning Poland and Norway. At the time, they were 20 divisions short. The chronic shortages of manpower and motorized transport only worsened as the war progressed. The situation did not improve even after German industry was mobilized in 1944. By then, of course, it was far too late.

David T. Zabecki

See also

Anzio, Battle of; Artillery Doctrine; Blitzkrieg; Brauchitsch, Heinrich Alfred Hermann Walther von; Crete, Battle of; Hitler, Adolf; Infantry Tactics; Normandy Invasion and Campaign; Waffen-SS

References

Citino, Robert M. *The Path to Blitzkrieg: Doctrine and Training in the German Army, 1920–1939.* Boulder, CO: Lynne Rienner, 1999.

Corum, James. *The Roots of Blitzkrieg: Hans von Seeckt and German Military Reform.* Lawrence: University Press of Kansas, 1992.

Creveld, Martin van. *Fighting Power: German and U.S. Army Performance, 1939–1945.* Westport, CT: Greenwood Press, 1982.

Helber, Helmut, and David M. Glantz, eds. *Hitler and His Generals: Military Conferences, 1942–1943.* Trans. Roland Winter, Krista Smith, and Mary Beth Friedrich. New York: Enigma, 2003.

Her Majesty's Stationery Office. *German Order of Battle 1944.* Reprinted 1994.

Keegan, John. *Six Armies in Normandy: From D-Day to the Liberation of Paris, June 6th–August 25th, 1944.* New York: Viking Press, 1982.

Rosinski, Herbert. *The German Army.* New York: Praeger, 1966.

U.S. War Department. *TM-E 30–451 Handbook on German Military Forces.* Baton Rouge: Louisiana State University Press, 1990.

Wallach, Jeduha L. *The Dogma of the Battle of Annihilation: The Theories of Clausewitz and Schlieffen and Their Impact on the German Conduct of Two World Wars.* Westport, CT: Greenwood Press, 1986.

Zabecki, David T., and Bruce Condell, eds. *On the German Art of War: Truppenführung.* Boulder, CO: Lynne Rienner, 2001.

Germany, Collapse of (March–May 1945)

Adolf Hitler's failed Ardennes Offensive (Battle of the Bulge) during December 1944–January 1945, far from stalling the western Allies as Hitler had hoped, actually hastened the German military collapse. By 1 March 1945, Allied Supreme Commander in the west General Dwight D. Eisenhower had assembled sufficient forces for a full frontal assault. By April, it would be the largest coalition army ever assembled in war. Several hundred miles to the east, Soviet leader Josef Stalin massed three fronts (army groups) for the final drive on Berlin. The Soviets were consolidating their positions for a final assault and ensuring that their Baltic flank was not exposed. Supporting these huge Allied armies were their air forces, which now had complete control of the skies. Large numbers of British and U.S. aircraft continued the strategic bombing campaign against the German heartland. During the period 1–21 March, more than 10,000 American and British bombers dropped in excess of 31,000 tons of bombs on the Ruhr area alone.

Undaunted by the overwhelming odds against him, German leader Adolf Hitler clung to the hope of victory. Conducting operations from the troglodyte atmosphere of his Berlin bunker and surrounded primarily by sycophants, the Führer relied on his so-called V (for "vengeance") weapons—the V-1 buzz bomb and V-2 rocket—as well as new jet aircraft. He also hoped for some miracle, such as Allied dissension, to turn the tide. The only military realist in headquarters was army chief of staff General Heinz Guderian. His clashes with Hitler, however, led to his departure at the end of March.

The onslaught from the west began with a drive to the Rhine River. From north to south, Field Marshal Bernard Montgomery commanded the 21st Army Group. It consisted of General Henry Crerar's Canadian First Army, Lieutenant General Miles Dempsey's British Second Army, and Lieutenant General William H. Simpson's U.S. Ninth Army, temporarily assigned to Montgomery's command from that of Lieutenant General Omar N. Bradley's 12th Army Group. In the center was Bradley's 12th Army Group, the largest American field force ever commanded by a U.S. general. Bradley's army group comprised the U.S. First Army under Lieutenant General Courtney Hodges; Lieutenant General George S. Patton's U.S. Third Army; and Major General Leonard Gerow's U.S. Fifteenth Army, whose forces were engaged in occupation duty and the elimination of bypassed pockets of German resistance. In the south was the 6th Army Group of Lieutenant General Jacob Devers, which consisted of Lieutenant General Alexander Patch's U.S. Seventh Army and General Jean de Lattre de Tassigny's French First Army. The 6th Army Group eliminated the Colmar pocket and advanced toward the Rhine between the Belgian and Swiss borders.

Elements of Hodges's First Army discovered the railroad bridge at Remagen intact, and they pushed forces across it to establish a bridgehead on the eastern side of the Rhine. German troops were everywhere withdrawing toward the Rhine. In typical fashion, Hitler replaced his commander in the west, Field Marshal Gerd von Rundstedt, with Field Marshal Albert Kesselring. The western Allies then launched Operation UNDERTONE, an assault on the Saar-Palatinate region, wherein the U.S. Third and Seventh Armies broke through the German Siegfried Line and destroyed Schutzstaffel Oberstgruppenführer Paul Hausser's German First Army. On 22–23 March, Montgomery launched Operation PLUNDER, a large-scale attack on the lower Rhine. Meanwhile, Patton's troops crossed the Rhine at Oppenheim on 22 March. All along the front, Allied forces moved relentlessly eastward. In April, the XVIII Airborne Corps encircled Field Marshal Walther Model's Army Group B, resulting in the surrender of 300,000 German troops. German cities capitulated rapidly; many streets were lined with white flags. On 20 April, Nuremberg fell to Patch's U.S. Third Army.

On 31 March on the Eastern Front, three Soviet fronts (army groups) opened the Berlin Campaign to take the German capital. They were Marshal Ivan Konev's 2nd Ukrainian Front, Marshal Georgii Zhukov's 1st Belorussian Front, and Marshal Konstantin Rokossovski's 2nd Belorussian Front. Konev's troops, supported by massive artillery barrages, cut across the Neisse River, destroying the German Fourth Panzer Army. Zhukov faced stiff German resistance and sustained heavy casualties, although his forces wore down the defenders. By this time, the German armies were only shadows of their former selves and included many young untrained levies. Steadily the Soviets drove Army Group Vistula back near Berlin. Hitler, meanwhile, insisted on a scorched-earth policy; he also called on German citizens to act as "werewolves," and he dared to hope that the miracle of the House of Brandenburg of the Seven Years' War—in which the coalition against Prussian King Frederick II came undone on the death of Russian Tsarina Elizabeth—might be repeated. He even seized on the death of U.S. President Franklin D. Roosevelt on 12 April 1945 as an omen that Germany would yet survive. As propaganda minister Josef Goebbels exhorted the people of Berlin to defend their city, Hitler called up Volkstrum troops (the largely untrained older civilian militia) and the Hitler Youth to defend his dying Third Reich.

At the same time, millions of German refugees were fleeing west to avoid falling into the hands of the Soviets, The German navy evacuated hundreds of thousands of Germans from the Baltics. Many others made their way west on foot. Ultimately, perhaps 16 million Germans were displaced from their homelands in Poland, Czechoslovakia, and elsewhere. More than 2 million may have been killed in the exodus that followed. Those who escaped or were forced to leave added yet another burden on already strained German social services.

On Hitler's birthday, 20 April 1945, Zhukov's troops pierced through three German defensive lines defending Berlin. On 22 April, Soviet troops were fighting in the city itself, and three days later they had surrounded Berlin. That same day, 25 April, elements of Bradley's 12th Army Group

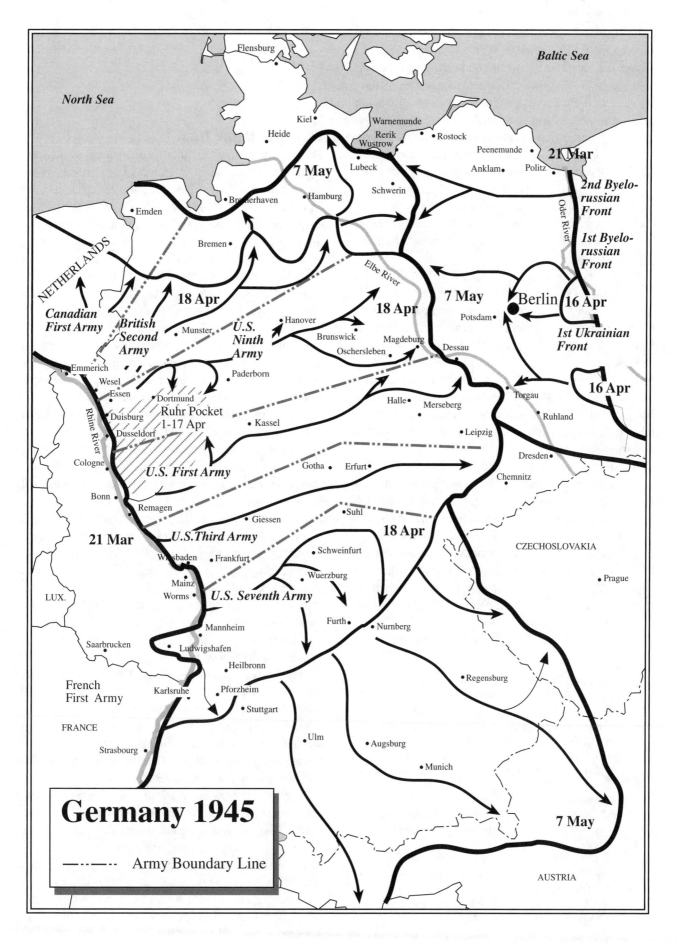

Germany 1945

—·—·— Army Boundary Line

linked up with Soviet troops of Konev's 1st Ukrainian Front at Torgau on the Elbe River.

The last significant German counterattack of the war occurred on 25–26 April when General der Waffen-SS Felix Steiner's Eleventh Army struck at Soviet forces driving on Berlin near Oranienburg, to no avail. Almost 500,000 Soviet troops were now battling for Berlin. Hitler, defiant to the last, refused to leave his capital and committed suicide on 30 April. To the end, he refused to accept responsibility and blamed others for Germany's defeat. Hitler's designated successor as chief of state, Grossadmiral Karl Dönitz, then took over what remained of German forces. Meanwhile, the Allies had overrun northern Italy. Remaining German forces there surrendered on 2 May.

In the west, Lieutenant General Walton Walker's XX Corps of Patton's Third Army reached the Austrian border opposite Braunau. Then, on 2 May, Lieutenant General Helmuth Weidling, commander of Berlin, surrendered the German capital to Soviet Colonel General Vassili Chuikov. On 3 May, elements of Montgomery's 21st Army Group linked up with Rokossovsky's 2nd Byelorussian Front at Wismar. Marshal Rodion Malinovsky's 2nd Ukrainian Front moved from Hungary into Austria and Czechoslovakia and prepared to link up with Patton's Third Army, which was advancing down the Danube near Linz.

Remaining German forces under Dönitz still controlled Norway, Denmark, western Holland, and portions of Germany, Yugoslavia, Austria, and Czechoslovakia. Although Dönitz realized defeat was certain, he briefly stalled for time to rescue additional German refugees fleeing westward. On 7 May, Dönitz surrendered all German forces unconditionally to the victorious Allies; a formal ceremony was held the next day. The guns fell silent. Germany lay prostrate and in ruins, its social services a shambles and its cities great wastelands of twisted girders and rubble.

Gene Mueller and Spencer C. Tucker

See also

Ardennes Offensive; Berlin, Land Battle for; Devers, Jacob Loucks; Dönitz, Karl; Eisenhower, Dwight D.; Gerow, Leonard Townsend; Guderian, Heinz; Hausser, Paul "Papa"; Hitler, Adolf; Hodges, Courtney Hicks; Jet and Rocket Aircraft; Jodl, Alfred; Keitel, Wilhelm; Kesselring, Albert; Konev, Ivan Stepanovich; Lattre de Tassigny, Jean Joseph Marie Gabriel de; Malinovsky, Rodion Yakovlevich; Model, Walther; Montgomery, Sir Bernard Law; Patch, Alexander McCarrell, Jr.; Patton, George Smith; Remagen Bridge; Rokossovsky, Konstantin Konstantinovich; Rundstedt, Karl Rudolf Gerd von; Simpson, William Hood; Stalin, Josef; Walker, Walton Harris; Zhukov, Georgii Konstantinovich

References

Beevor, Antony. *The Fall of Berlin, 1945.* New York: Viking, 2002.

Clark, Alan. *Barbarossa: The Russian-German Conflict, 1941–45.* New York: William Morrow, 1965.

Erickson, John. *The Road to Berlin: Stalin's War with Germany.* New Haven, CT: Yale University Press, 1983.

Weigley, Russell F. *Eisenhower's Lieutenants: The Campaign of France and Germany, 1944–1945.* Bloomington: Indiana University Press, 1981.

Germany, Home Front

The popular assumption that Nazi Germany was a well-organized war machine is patently false. It is true, however, that no time was likely to be as favorable as September 1939 for German leader Adolf Hitler to join in war with the western powers. Britain and France were only then rearming, and Germany had a population of 80 million people, a strong industrial base, and the world's most powerful army and air force. The economy was unbalanced, with imports running well in excess of exports, but Hitler planned to redress this imbalance by seizing in war all that the Reich required.

The National Socialist state controlled the media, with propaganda minister Joseph Goebbels adroitly manipulating the press, radio, film, and party rallies. Informers on every block and the Gestapo (secret state police) kept a close watch on activities, but most Germans accepted the Führer's policies. Sullen resignation over the start of the war in September 1939 turned to euphoria after Germany's victories over France and the Low Countries. In the winter of 1941, when the military situation began to deteriorate on the Russian plains, Germans settled into a sort of stoic determination that lasted until near the end. Most Germans were aware of the price their nation was exacting from the rest of Europe, and they could thus believe the Allies would repay them in kind. However, to ensure the loyalty of the Reich's citizens, Hitler ordered that judges ignore established law and procedure and dispense only "National Socialist justice." Hitler expressly approved the Gestapo's use of torture. The complete subversion of the German legal system to Nazi rule came with the appointment in August 1942 of Roland Freisler as president of the Volksgerichthof (people's court).

Once he had secured power in 1933, Hitler sought to harness the German economy for war preparation. He well understood that his desire for new lands in the east (lebensraum) had to be realized through a series of swift and decisive military victories. The German economy could not sustain a long drawn-out war. Thus the blitzkrieg (lightning war) was born of economic necessity.

In 1936, Hitler instituted a Four-Year Plan for the economy under Reichsmarschall (Reich Marshal) Herman Göring. The idea was designed to centralize the economy. However, as with everything else in the Third Reich, the rivalry of higher-ranking officials, encouraged by Hitler, meant that the economy remained a battlefield for various competing interests, even within the armed forces themselves. Despite these inefficiencies, Germany rebuilt its mili-

General view of the German city of Nuremberg, following the cessation of organized resistance. In the distance, the twin-spired Lorenz Church; on the right and surrounded with rubble is a statue of Kaiser Wilhelm I, 1945. (Roberts Commission, National Archives)

tary. Spending on the armed forces, however, was consuming 50 percent of the budget, or approximately 60 billion reichsmarks, per year. Hjalmar Schacht, head of the Reichsbank, pointed out that this level of expenditure could not be sustained.

Besides military growth, another goal of the Four-Year Plan was German economic autarky in such key areas as the petrochemical industry and reduction of imports of other raw materials necessary for war production, including rubber and minerals. From 1936 to 1938, the Four-Year Plan concentrated on production of raw materials; after 1938, attention was focused on production of finished goods such as tanks, aircraft, and artillery pieces for immediate war use. Between 1936 and 1942, the Four-Year Plan represented 50 percent (13.25 billion reichsmarks) of total German industrial investment.

Memories of World War I, when the British naval blockade starved Germany of raw materials and foodstuffs, underpinned German planning. The August 1939 German-Soviet Non-aggression Pact, however, removed much of the impact of the blockade during World War II, as did the addition of

Romania—with its important oil fields of Ploesti—to the Axis alliance after the war began.

Despite emphasis on military production, the Nazi hierarchy feared the impact on home-front morale of shortages of consumer goods. Production of consumer goods from 1936 to 1939, when Germany was straining to increase its armaments, actually went up by 25 percent. This continued during the war; Germans enjoyed both "guns and butter" and a relatively high standard of living until 1944. After the successful military campaigns of 1939 and 1940, Hitler recommended a reduction in arms production in order not to affect civilian morale. The government pacified the population with incentives such as bonuses for night shifts and overtime pay on holidays. Despite an official decree to freeze salaries, average wages from September 1939 to March 1941 rose by 10.4 percent.

Even in 1942, consumer expenditures were maintained at about the 1937 level, and few new economic restrictions were imposed. Raw materials were in short supply, but these were deliberately depleted in the expectation of a quick victory over the Soviet Union. This optimistic outlook changed with the German reverses in the winter of 1941–1942. In February 1942, when Fritz Todt, minister of armaments and production, died in a plane crash, Hitler named Albert Speer as Todt's replacement.

An organizing genius with a keen interest in efficiency rather than ideology, Speer created a centralized machinery of control in the Central Planning Board. By 1943, Speer had nearly complete control of the national economy and was able substantially to boost production. He also enacted industrial policies to standardize production by limiting the number of different types of armaments produced and promoting factory assembly-line methods. In fact, German war production was at its height in 1944, despite Allied bombing, and production of consumer goods dropped only slightly. In March 1944, German aircraft plants went on double shifts and a seven-day workweek. Thus Germany attained its highest levels of aircraft, tanks, and munitions production in late 1944 while bearing the full brunt of Allied bombing. But by then it was too late. When the Allies shifted their bombing emphasis to lines of communication and petroleum production, the transportation system collapsed and there was no fuel to operate the tanks and new jet aircraft.

Speer might have accomplished more had he not been handicapped by jealous rivals, such as the multi-hatted Hermann Göring and Reichsführer-Schutzstaffel (leader for the Reich, RFSS) Heinrich Himmler. Himmler was a major hindrance. Constantly scheming to enhance the power of the SS within the Reich, he actually undermined the economy. The SS grew to be a state within a state, and Hitler even approved Himmler's proposal to build an SS-owned industrial concern to make it independent of the state budget.

Major factors in Speer's success, of course, were the substantial territory and resources Germany had acquired by 1942. Germany could exploit the resources of this new empire—skilled labor, industry, and metallurgical resources from France and Belgium; foodstuffs and other resources from Denmark, Norway, and the Balkans. There were also substantial resources in the vast stretches of the Soviet Union occupied by the German army from June 1941 onward, although many of these resources were simply those Germany had depended on in the past.

Spain was a friendly neutral country, and Sweden, Portugal, and Switzerland continued to trade with the Reich and conduct its business. In addition, ruthless German economic exactions helped finance the war. German-occupied Western Europe provided substantial raw materials and money to fuel the German war machine. Of the total German war expenditure of 657 billion reichsmarks, the German people paid only 184.7 billion. France alone paid "administrative costs" to Germany at the absurdly high sum of 20 million reichsmarks a day, calculated at the greatly inflated rate of exchange of 20 francs per reichsmark and amounting to some 60 percent of French national income.

The National Socialist regime failed to use two readily available sources of labor, however. The Nazis had done all in their power to reverse the emancipation of women during the Weimar Republic. Restricting women to the "three Ks" of *Kinder, Kirche,* and *Küche* (children, church, and kitchen) meant that during the Great Depression jobs were secured only for men. This system carried forward into the war with serious implications for the war economy. Speer claimed that mobilizing the 5 million women capable of war service would have released 3 million German males for military service. Such a step might have altered the results of battles and campaigns, although it probably would not have affected the overall outcome of the war.

As early as 1942, Speer recommended that women be recruited for industry, but Hitler rejected this advice. Not until 1943 were women between 17 and 45 years of age required to register for compulsory work. Later, the upper age limit for women was raised to 50, and the age span for men was set at 16 to 65. By 1944, German women actually outnumbered men in the civilian labor force at 51.6 percent.

Another available source of skilled labor that had served the Fatherland well during World War I was the Jews. Numbering about 600,000 when Hitler came to power, many German Jews soon escaped abroad. Virtually all who remained and were identified perished in the "final solution." The systematic extermination of European Jewry also took its toll on the war effort, as considerable manpower was absorbed simply in rounding up and transporting European Jews to the death camps.

The Third Reich sought to compensate for labor shortages by using foreign workers. In March 1942, Fritz Sauckel became general Reich director for labor, or minister of labor. In 1942, there were 3.8 million fewer people employed in the German economy than in 1939. The Germans tried to attract foreign skilled workers with financial incentives. When this approach failed, the occupiers simply rounded up those they thought necessary and shipped them to Germany to work in appalling conditions. By the end of 1942, the total number of people working in the German arms industry had risen by 1.3 million. By September 1944, there were 7.5 million foreign and 28.4 million German workers, and at the end of the war there were upward of 10 million foreign workers in the Reich. Such labor was hardly efficient. Speer noted that in October 1943, some 30,000 prisoners working in armaments production produced over a seven-month period only 40,000 carbines, whereas 14,000 U.S. workers turned out 1,050,000 carbines in the same amount of time. Until 1944, most German factories only ran a single shift per day, and only 10 percent of employees were working a second or third shift.

Only at the very end of the war, when it was clear even to the German leadership that the war was lost, did the regime risk disrupting the German home front. By then, of course, German cities were being devastated by Allied strategic bombing. The suffering of his people did not seem to disturb Hitler. He held that Germans had proven "unworthy" of him and thus deserved to perish with him.

Neville Panthaki and Spencer C. Tucker

See also
German-Soviet Non-aggression Pact; Germany, Collapse of; Göring, Hermann Wilhelm; Himmler, Heinrich; Sauckel, Fritz; Speer, Albert; Strategic Bombing; Todt Organization; Women in World War II

References
Burleigh, Michael. *The Third Reich: A New History.* New York: Hill and Wang, 2000.

Grunberger, Richard. *The 12-Year Reich: A Social History of Nazi Germany, 1933–45.* New York: Holt, Rinehart and Winston, 1971.

Kershaw, I. *The Nazi Dictatorship: Problems and Perspectives of Interpretation.* Baltimore, MD: E. Arnold, 1985.

Koonz, Claudia. *Mothers in the Fatherland: Women, the Family and Nazi Politics.* New York: St. Martin's, 1987.

Shirer, William L. *The Rise and Fall of the Third Reich: A History of Nazi Germany.* New York: Simon and Schuster, 1960.

Speer, Albert. *Inside the Third Reich: Memoirs.* New York: Macmillan, 1970.

Stern, J. P. *Hitler: The Führer and the People.* Berkeley: University of California Press, 1979.

Germany, Navy

Under Adolf Hitler, Germany embarked on a program to rebuild its navy on a global scale. The German navy (Kriegsmarine) began this major effort after the signing of the Anglo-German Naval Treaty in June 1935. The goal was creation of a balanced fleet that would serve as the core of a future bluewater navy dominated by battleships. This Z Plan envisioned a powerful fleet that would one day challenge Britain and the United States for world naval mastery.

In 1938, Hitler's aggressive foreign policy forced the navy to consider the possibility of a future naval war against Great Britain. The navy's commander, Grand Admiral Erich Raeder, designed a strategy to attack the British sea-lanes. His proposal to build ships more suited to a commerce war, including additional U-boats, was rejected by Hitler, who was intent on building a battleship-dominated navy that would serve as an instrument of political and military force commensurate with a world power. Shortages of resources contributed to delays in naval construction, and Raeder's blind confidence in the Führer's diplomatic successes and promises that war would not come before 1942 or 1943 found the navy unprepared for war in September 1939.

At the beginning of the war, the German navy consisted of 79,000 men, 2 battleships, 3 pocket battleships (small, fast, strongly constructed battleships), 1 heavy cruiser, 6 light cruisers, and 33 destroyers and torpedo boats. Fewer than half of the 57 U-boats available were suitable for Atlantic

operations. In spite of Raeder's initial pessimism that the navy could only "die gallantly," thereby creating the foundations for a future fleet, he intended to carry out an aggressive naval strategy that would attack British sea communications on a global basis using his concept of diversion and concentration in operational areas of his own choosing and timing. Raeder persistently argued with Hitler that only total economic warfare against England could have a decisive impact.

Hitler's restrictions on naval operations, particularly on the U-boats, frustrated Raeder's attempts to seize the initiative and achieve early successes. In late 1939, concerned that the British were planning to invade Norway, Raeder instigated planning for the successful German occupation of Norway and Denmark (Operation WESERÜBUNG). This April 1940 operation was for the navy its "feat of arms"—justifying its contribution to the war effort and future existence. Although the navy did secure important port facilities for surface raiders and U-boats in Norway as well as the shipping route for iron ore from Sweden, it also suffered substantial losses in the operation in the form of 3 cruisers and 10 destroyers. In June, with the defeat of France, the navy acquired additional ports on the Atlantic and Bay of Biscay for surface ships and submarines. But the navy also now had to protect an extended coastline from occupied France to Scandinavia. From 1940 to 1943, Germany also sent to sea 9 armed auxiliary cruisers.

Raeder's intent to prove the worth of the surface fleet, in particular the battleships, led him to demand of his commanders that they take risks yet avoid unnecessary combat that could lead to losses. Two fleet commanders lost their jobs when they failed to exhibit the necessary aggressiveness. The scuttling of the pocket battleship *Graf Spee* in December 1939 and Hitler's displeasure over this loss further reinforced the inherent contradictions in Raeder's orders to strike boldly but avoid damage to the navy's own ships. With new battleships *Bismarck* and *Tirpitz* joining the fleet, Raeder envisioned a new phase of the Atlantic surface battle, with task forces that would engage Allied convoys protected by capital ships. In an effort to prove the value of the battleships, Raeder pressed the *Bismarck* into service before the other battleships were available for action. Her loss in May 1941 represented the end of the surface war in the Atlantic and Hitler's increasing interference in the use of Germany's remaining capital ships.

Unable to achieve the conditions for a cross-Channel invasion (Operation SEA LION) in September 1940, Raeder tried to divert Hitler from his plans to attack the Soviet Union. Raeder advocated an alternative strategy in the Mediterranean to defeat Britain first, especially given the growing cooperation between that nation and the United States. After the Japanese attack on Pearl Harbor, Raeder saw an opportunity to link up with the Japanese in the Indian Ocean and use the French African colonies and the Atlantic islands of Portugal and Spain to expand the bases for a long-term war against the

Anglo-American naval forces in the Atlantic. These plans never materialized, as the war against the Soviet Union faltered and Germany was forced to come to the aid of Italy and secure its southern flank in the Balkans.

Nervous about British threats to Norway and Allied support to the Soviets in the north, Hitler ordered that the two battleships in Brest—the *Gneisenau* and *Scharnhorst*—and the heavy cruiser *Prinz Eugen* be either moved to Norway or scrapped. The "Channel dash" in February 1942 was a tactical success but a strategic defeat for the navy. With the fleet relegated to Norway as a "fleet-in-being," the U-boat arm, under the command of Admiral Karl Dönitz, continued its role as the navy's primary weapon. The lack of Luftwaffe support, though, continued to seriously hamper all operations. The navy never resolved the issue of whether the U-boat war was a "tonnage" war or a commerce war in which U-boats attacked targets that had the greatest potential for a decisive impact. Dönitz continued to argue that all resources should go to the U-boat war and disagreed with the diversion of U-boats to other theaters such as the Mediterranean or to the defense of Norway.

In late December 1942, the failure of the *Hipper* and *Lützow* to close with a weakly defended convoy in the Barents Sea (Operation RAINBOW) led an angry Hitler to attack Raeder and the surface fleet. Raeder resigned, and Dönitz succeeded him. Although Dönitz was determined to prosecute the submarine war ruthlessly, as with the surface fleet, the defeat of the U-boats in May 1943 resulted from Allied technology and successes in code-breaking that reflected the shortcomings in the naval leadership and military structure of the Third Reich. As the military situation of Germany deteriorated, the navy provided support to the army, particularly in the Baltic, where it conducted a massive and highly successful evacuation effort of troops and civilians.

In sharp contrast to the navy's collapse after World War I, the German navy during World War II enforced strict discipline until the end. In April 1945, Hitler named a loyal Dönitz as his heir and successor.

Keith W. Bird

See also
Atlantic, Battle of the; *Bismarck,* Sortie and Sinking of; Channel Dash; Convoy PQ 17; Dönitz, Karl; DRUMBEAT, Operation; Hitler, Adolf; Narvik, Naval Battles of; North Cape, Battle of; Plata, Río de la, Battle of; Prien, Günther; Raeder, Erich; SEA LION, Operation; Signals Intelligence; WESERÜBUNG, Operation; Z Plan

References
Bird, Keith W. *German Naval History: A Guide to the Literature.* New York: Garland, 1985.
Blair, Clay. *Hitler's U-Boat War.* 2 vols. New York: Random House, 1996, 1998.
Howarth, Stephen, and Derek Law, eds. *The Battle of the Atlantic, 1939–1945.* London and Annapolis, MD: Greenhill Books and Naval Institute Press, 1994.
Militärgeschtliches Forschungsamt. *Das Deutsche Reich und der Zweite Weltkrieg* (Germany and the Second World War). Trans. Dean S. McMurrey, Edwald Osers, and Louise Wilmott. 7 vols. Oxford, UK: Clarendon Press, 1990–2001.
Salewski, Michael. *Die Deutsche Seekriegsleitung 1935–1945.* 3 vols. Munich, West Germany: Bernard and Graefe, 1970–1975.

Germany, Surrender of (8 May 1945)

German leader Adolf Hitler resolutely refused appeals from his subordinates for an end to the war. Claiming that the German people were unworthy of him, Hitler asserted that they must suffer the consequences. On 30 April 1945, with much of Germany in ruins and with Berlin under siege, Hitler committed suicide. His handpicked successor, Admiral Karl Dönitz, assumed the office of president of the Reich. Dönitz established a new government at Flensburg in the German province of Schleswig-Holstein.

This administration, dedicated to preserving the Third Reich, was compelled by the sharply deteriorating military situation to surrender German forces to the Allied powers. Dönitz's chief consideration at the beginning of May was to negotiate an armistice with only the western Allied powers in order for German forces in the east to conduct a fighting withdrawal that would save them from Soviet captivity. This goal, however, was frustrated by the insistence of the western Allies that Germany surrender unconditionally to all of the Allied powers.

Dönitz tried to stave off absolute capitulation through the piecemeal surrender of portions of the Third Reich and occupied Europe. On 3 May, Admiral Hans-Georg von Friedeberg surrendered German forces in Denmark, Holland, and northern Germany to British Field Marshal Sir Bernard Montgomery. Dönitz was able to avoid complete surrender for several additional days after Friedeberg's action, which allowed 3 million German troops to escape the Soviets. Unable to postpone action any longer, however, on 7 May 1945 Colonel General Alfred Jodl signed a surrender document at Supreme Commander, Allied Expeditionary Forces General Dwight D. Eisenhower's headquarters in Rheims, France. Lieutenant General Walter Bedell Smith and Major General Ivan Sousloparov represented the western Allies and the Soviet Union, respectively. Also in attendance was Major General François Sevez of the French army. The agreement specified the unconditional surrender of all German land, sea, and air forces to the Supreme Commander, Allied Expeditionary Forces and also to the Soviet High Command.

The terms of the German surrender stipulated that all German military forces would cease fighting at 11:01 P.M. central European time on 8 May 1945. The final terms of the agreement stated that the surrender could be superseded by any similar

German officers sign unconditional surrender in Rheims, France. (National Archives)

legislation passed by the United Nations, and it promised swift retaliation were any German forces to resume combat operations. This document signaled the end of fighting, but the actual surrender of German troops in German-occupied regions stretched until a capitulation on 11 May at Helgoland, an island located in the North Sea off the coast of Germany.

At the insistence of Soviet Premier Josef Stalin, a second, formal surrender instrument containing largely the same stipulations was signed in Berlin just after midnight on 9 May, despite the fact that the cease-fire had already gone into effect. Acting on behalf of the German High Command were Admiral Hans-Georg von Friedeburg, Field Marshal Wilhelm Keitel, and Colonel General Hans Jürgen Stumpff. Marshal Georgii Zhukov and Air Marshal Sir Arthur W. Tedder represented the Soviet Union and the western Allies, respectively. Also in attendance were French General Jean de Lattre de Tassigny and U.S. Army Air Forces General Carl Spaatz.

Although the agreement signed at Rheims signaled the end of Germany's participation in World War II, it did not terminate the Third Reich. The Allies retained Dönitz's government initially to deal with the immediate postwar problems of food distribution to German citizens and refugees. On 23 May 1945, however, Dönitz and his cabinet were removed and arrested by the Allies. The new rulers of Germany, as of 5 June, were the Allied powers. They soon implemented plans for postwar Germany determined during wartime diplomatic conferences.

Eric W. Osborne

See also

Berlin, Land Battle for; Dönitz, Karl; Eisenhower, Dwight D.; Hitler, Adolf; Jodl, Alfred; Keitel, Wilhelm; Lattre de Tassigny, Jean Joseph Marie Gabriel de; Montgomery, Sir Bernard Law; Smith, Walter Bedell; Spaatz, Carl Andrew "Tooey"; Tedder, Sir Arthur William; Tehran Conference; Unconditional Surrender; Yalta Conference; Zhukov, Georgii Konstantinovich

References

Germany Surrenders, 1945. Washington, DC: National Archives and Records Administration, 1989.

Williamson, D. G. *The Third Reich*. London: Pearson Education, 2002.

Gerow, Leonard Townsend (1888–1972)

U.S. Army general. Born in Petersburg, Virginia, on 13 July 1888, Leonard Gerow graduated from the Virginia Military Institute in 1911 and was commissioned a second lieutenant of infantry. Gerow took part in the 1914 occupation of Veracruz,

Lieutenant General Leonard T. Gerow. (Library of Congress)

in campaigns through northern France and the Rhineland. In January 1945, Gerow was promoted to lieutenant general and took command of the new Fifteenth Army, which secured the western French coast, taking the ports of Saint-Nazaire and Lorient. The area was also a staging ground for training and equipping units to join the 12th Army Group, which carried the battle into Germany itself.

From October 1945 to January 1948, Gerow was commandant of the Command and General Staff College. He then commanded the Second Army at Fort Meade, Maryland, retiring in July 1950. He died at Petersburg, Virginia, on 12 October 1972.

Priscilla Roberts

See also
Eisenhower, Dwight D.; France Campaign; Normandy Invasion and
    Campaign
References
Ewing, Joseph. *29, Let's Go: A History of the 29th Infantry Division in
    World War II.* Washington, DC: Infantry Journal Press, 1948.
Roy, Claude. *Eight Days That Freed Paris.* London: Pilot Press, 1945.
Weigley, Russell F. *Eisenhower's Lieutenants: The Campaigns of
    France and Germany, 1944–1945.* Bloomington: Indiana Univer-
    sity Press, 1981.

Mexico. Following U.S. entry into World War I, Gerow served in France from April 1918 with the Signal Corps, fighting in the Second Battle of the Marne and the St. Mihiel and Meuse-Argonne Offensives.

Following the war, Gerow won promotion to permanent major in June 1920. Between the wars he commanded the Signal Corps (1919–1921) and alternated staff assignments in Washington; tours in Shanghai and the Philippines; and training courses at Fort Benning, Georgia; and Fort Leavenworth, Kansas, where he excelled. From 1935 onward, Gerow served in the War Department's War Plans Division. Promoted to brigadier general in October 1940, he became chief of the War Plans Division in December 1940. From December 1941, he served simultaneously as assistant chief of staff.

In February 1942, Gerow was promoted to major general and took command of the 29th Infantry Division, which began advanced training in Britain the following October. Gerow was a leading member of the talented group of top American officers that General Dwight D. Eisenhower gathered around himself when he was supreme commander in Europe. In July 1943, Gerow took command of V Corps of what became Lieutenant General Omar N. Bradley's First Army, which experienced heavy fighting in the Normandy Invasion of June and July 1944. On 25 August 1944, Gerow was the first Allied general to enter Paris. He then led V Corps

Ghormley, Robert Lee (1883–1958)

U.S. Navy admiral. Born in Portland, Oregon, on 15 October 1883, Robert Lee Ghormley graduated from the University of Idaho in 1902 and from the U.S. Naval Academy in 1906. Ghormley's first assignments were in cruisers. During World War I, he served as aide to the commander of the Battleship Force, Atlantic Fleet. He was then assistant director of the Overseas Division, Naval Overseas Transportation Service.

Between the wars, Ghormley held a variety of staff positions. In 1935 and 1936, Captain Ghormley commanded the battleship *Nevada*. He then directed the War Plans Office and, in 1939, became assistant to the chief of naval operations. In August 1940, now a rear admiral, Ghormley was sent to London as a naval observer and to recommend possible U.S. naval aid to Britain.

In June 1942, newly promoted to vice admiral, Ghormley was named commander to the South Pacific Area and Force. He assumed his new command as plans for the invasion of the U.S. Guadalcanal were in progress. Believing his forces to be unready, he requested a postponement in the operation, which was denied. He then seems to have distanced himself from the operation, while tensions between his subordinate commanders were left unresolved. After the Allied defeat in the Battle of Savo Island, Ghormley feared that the entire Guadalcanal operation would fail. As a result, he continued to maintain strong garrisons on other islands in the event of future Japanese

U.S. Vice Admiral Robert L Ghormley. (Photo by Keystone/Getty Images)

advances, rather than using those forces to assist in winning the protracted struggle on Guadalcanal. Ghormley suffered from a severely abscessed tooth at the time, which may have interfered with his decision making. In October 1942, following the Battle of Cape Esperance, Admiral Chester W. Nimitz, commander of the Pacific Fleet, replaced Ghormley with Vice Admiral William F. Halsey Jr., who infused an offensive spirit into the campaign that Ghormley seemed incapable of maintaining.

In 1943, Ghormley commanded the Hawaiian Sea Frontier, and in 1944 he took charge of the 14th Naval District, Hawaii. At the end of the war, Ghormley assumed command of U.S. Naval Forces in Germany (Task Force 124), which was charged among other things with demobilizing the German navy. Ghormley retired from the navy as a vice admiral in August 1946, and he died at Bethesda, Maryland, on 21 June 1958.

Edward F. Finch

See also

Cape Esperance, Battle of; Eastern Solomons, Battle of the; Guadalcanal Naval Campaign; Halsey, William Frederick, Jr.; Nimitz, Chester William; Santa Cruz Islands, Battle of the; Savo Island, Battle of

References

Frank, Richard B. *Guadalcanal*. New York: Random House, 1990.

Miller, Eric. *Guadalcanal: The Carrier Battles*. New York: Crown, 1987.
———. *Guadalcanal: Decision at Sea*. New York: Crown, 1988.
Morison, Samuel Eliot. *History of the United States Naval Operations in World War II*. Vol. 5, *The Struggle for Guadalcanal*. Boston: Little, Brown, 1949.

GI Bill (22 June 1944)

U.S. social welfare program for those serving in World War II. Officially known as the Serviceman's Readjustment Act of 1944, the GI Bill remains one of the most popular and effective government programs in American history. Although federal law protected the right of veterans to return to their prewar jobs, many wanted and expected more than a return to their 1941 positions. The GI Bill was born partly out of a desire to reward the men of America's military for their service. President Franklin D. Roosevelt had originally envisioned a much larger program that included job retraining, but he agreed to a slightly less ambitious plan advanced by an alliance of Democrats and progressive Republicans.

Signed on 22 June 1944, the GI Bill paid for college tuition and vocational training and provided students with housing and medical benefits. Other aspects of the bill made available low-interest loans guaranteed by the federal government for mortgages and starting businesses. Unemployed veterans received cash payments. Supporters sought to use the program to empower veterans through education and training, thus making them less dependent on corporations, unions, or—in the long run—the federal government. The bill had the support of veterans' groups such as the American Legion, which helped to draft the legislation, and the Veterans of Foreign Wars. The Hearst newspapers also lent their support.

The GI Bill had motives beyond showing the nation's gratitude to returning veterans. Remembering the plight of World War I veterans and the ignoble episode of the 1932 Bonus Army—when some 20,000 World War I veterans, impoverished by the Great Depression, converged on Washington in 1932 in the hope of collecting their adjusted compensation bonuses immediately rather than in 1945 as legislated—the bill aimed to ease veterans into the workplace slowly. Many economists and politicians feared that if 12 million veterans descended on the job market at the same time, the United States might return to economic depression. By placing some veterans in schools and supporting the desires of others to start small businesses, the GI Bill sought to lessen these pressures.

The GI Bill had a long and lasting influence on American society. More than 1 million veterans attended colleges and universities using the bill's benefits, and more than 8 million veterans used one or more of its programs. The bill

Books and supplies, as well as tuition and other fees, up to a total of $500 per year, were furnished to each veteran under the GI Bill. (UPI/Bettman/Corbis)

underwrote more than 3.5 million mortgages, and in 1947 it funded almost 40 percent of all housing starts in the United States. The GI Bill thus helped to fuel the postwar economic boom by stimulating the construction industry and all of its subsidiary industries. It also provided enormous cash infusions into American colleges and universities. Since World War II, the U.S. government has enacted various legislation offering GI Bill–type benefits to veterans of the Korean and Vietnam Wars, as well as to some members of the peacetime military.

Michael S. Neiberg

See also
Roosevelt, Franklin D.; United States, Home Front
References
Bennett, Michael. *When Dreams Came True: The GI Bill and the Making of Modern America.* Dulles, VA: Brassey's, 1996.
Olson, Keith. *The G.I. Bill, Veterans, and the Colleges.* Lexington: University Press of Kentucky, 1974.
Ross, Davis. *Preparing for Ulysses: Politics and Veterans during World War II.* New York: Columbia University Press, 1969.

Gilbert Islands Campaign (November 1943)

U.S. amphibious campaign in the Central Pacific and an important advance toward the Japanese home islands. The 16 atolls that constitute the Gilbert Islands lie astride the equator. The Americans invaded the Gilbert Islands in late November 1943; approximately 200 ships and more than 30,000 troops seized the atolls of Makin, Tarawa, and Abemama in Operation GALVANIC. Fifth Fleet commander Vice Admiral Raymond A. Spruance had overall command of the operation, and Rear Admiral Charles A. Pownall commanded Task Force 50.

Following preparatory air strikes against Rabaul, the 11 fleet carriers in Task Force 50, which were divided into 4 different carrier groups, neutralized Japanese bases in the Marshall Islands and pounded Makin and Tarawa in preparation for landings there. At the latter two atolls, 7 battleships and

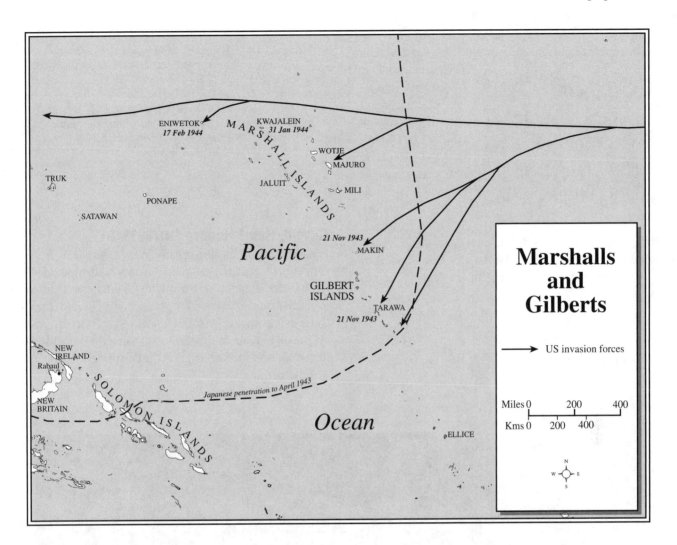

accompanying cruisers bombarded the shore for more than an hour the morning of the invasion. On 20 November, Rear Admiral Richmond K. Turner's Task Force 54 landed elements of the army's 27th Division on Butaritari Island; 2nd Marine Division troops landed on on Betio Island.

At Butaritari, 4 battalions from the 27th Division assaulted Beach Yellow in the lagoon and Beach Red on the western face of the island. Although the reef line forced the men in the lagoon to wade the last 300 yards to shore, initial resistance was light since only 300 Japanese combat troops defended the island. The attack became bogged down by enemy snipers and small counterattacks, however, and it took three days to secure the island. The army suffered 64 killed and 150 wounded.

Resistance was heavier on Betio, a small but well-fortified island defended by 4,000 Japanese troops. Initially, three Marine battalions landed on Beach Red along the wide lagoon side of the island. These troops ran into heavy fire, and, as low tide prevented heavy equipment from crossing the reef line, the attack stalled in the face of determined Japanese resistance. Two additional battalions landed as reinforcements

later that day, and a sixth battalion landed the following morning. All suffered heavy casualties in the process. The situation improved late on the second day when destroyers and aircraft supported the landing of a seventh battalion at the narrow western end of Betio. Using tanks, grenades, TNT blocks, and flamethrowers, the Marines secured most of the island by 22 November. Two Japanese counterattacks were repulsed that evening, and the entire atoll was cleared six days later. The United States lost 980 Marines and 29 sailors killed; 2,106 troops were wounded. Only 17 Japanese survived the battle; they were taken prisoner along with 129 Korean laborers.

Although the Japanese surface navy did not intervene, Japan's air and submarine units did strike the American invasion force. At dusk on 20 November, 16 twin-engine "Betty" bombers attacked a carrier group off Tarawa and torpedoed the light carrier *Independence*. The explosion killed 17 sailors and wounded 43, and it forced the carrier to retire for repairs. At least three similar raids followed over the next week, although none scored hits because American air cover— including the first use of night-combat air patrols—broke up the attacks. More deadly were Japanese submarines, one of which torpedoed and sank the escort carrier *Liscombe Bay* on 24 November, killing 642 sailors. Overall, the Gilbert landings cost the lives of roughly 1,800 Americans and 5,000 Japanese, including the crews of 4 lost Japanese navy submarines. The Gilbert Islands Campaign provided important lessons in amphibious operations, and it paved the way for the next U.S. amphibious operation, which was conducted against the Marshall Islands in January and February 1944.

> The Gilbert landings cost the lives of roughly 1,800 Americans and 5,000 Japanese.

Timothy L. Francis

See also

Central Pacific Campaign; Marshall Islands, Naval Campaign; Spruance, Raymond Ames; Tarawa, Battle of; Turner, Richmond Kelly

References

Crawford, Danny J. *The 2nd Marine Division and Its Regiments.* Washington, DC: History and Museums Division, Headquarters, U.S. Marine Corps, 2001.

Cressman, Robert J. *The Official Chronology of the U.S. Navy in World War II.* Annapolis, MD: Naval Institute Press, 2000.

Morison, Samuel E. *History of United States Naval Operations in World War II.* Vol. 7, *Aleutians, Gilberts and Marshalls, June 1942–April 1944.* Boston: Little, Brown, 1951.

Giraud, Henri Honoré (1879–1949)

French army general. Born in Paris on 18 January 1879, Henri Giraud graduated from the French Military Academy of Saint-Cyr in 1900. During World War I, he fought on the Western Front. As a captain he was taken prisoner by the Germans near Guise in late August 1914, but he escaped that October and returned to France in February 1915. Giraud distinguished himself in later fighting, rising at the end of the war to command a battalion.

165th Infantry assault wave attacking Butaritari, Yellow Beach Two, find it slow going in the coral bottom waters. Japanese machine gun fire from the right flank makes it more difficult for them, Makin Atoll, Gilbert Islands, 20 November 1943. (National Archives)

Giraud was in Turkey from 1918 to 1922 and in Morocco from 1922 to 1934. He played an important role in the Riffian Wars in Morocco, and his forces captured Moroccan nationalist leader Abd-el-Krim in 1926. Giraud was promoted to colonel in 1927, to brigadier general in 1930, to major general in 1934, and to lieutenant general in 1936. He commanded the Sixth Military Region at Metz, France, from 1936 to 1939. On the French military mobilization for World War II on 2 September 1939, he took command of Seventh Army as a full general. Giraud had little comprehension of the new theories of high-speed warfare with tanks operating en masse.

When the Germans invaded France and the Low Countries in May 1940, Giraud led the Seventh Army into Belgium in accordance with the Allied plan. On 15 May, he assumed command of the collapsing Ninth Army. The Germans captured Giraud on 18 May at Wassigny and imprisoned him at Königstein in Saxony. Giraud escaped on 17 April 1942 and crossed Germany to Switzerland and then to Vichy France—embarrassing Vichy officials, who had been attempting to improve relations with the German occupiers. At a meeting on 2 May 1942 attended by Admiral Jean François Darlan and Pierre Laval, Giraud refused to accept German Ambassador Otto Abetz's invitation to return to prison.

In November 1942, Giraud was spirited out of France and transported by the British submarine *Seraph* to North Africa. (The Anglophobic Giraud had insisted on an American boat, but none was available, and so he was tricked into believing the *Seraph* was a U.S. submarine). U.S. and British officials, hoping that Giraud might replace Charles de Gaulle as leader of Free French Forces, made him commander of French forces in North Africa in December 1942. On 30 May 1943, de Gaulle arrived in Algiers, and on 3 June agreement was reached whereby Giraud became co-president with de Gaulle of the French Committee of National Liberation. De Gaulle was easily able to elbow the politically inept Giraud aside, and the arrangement only lasted until 9 November 1943, when Giraud resigned.

As commander in chief of French armed forces until 4 April 1944, Giraud continued to play an important role in rebuilding the French military forces before being forced to retire. In June 1946, Giraud won election to the French National Assembly from Moselle, and he continued to serve as vice president of the Supreme War Council until 1948. Giraud died at Dijon on 11 March 1949.

John MacFarlane

See also
Casablanca Conference; Darlan, Jean Louis Xavier François; de Gaulle, Charles; France, Free French; France, Vichy; Laval, Pierre; Roosevelt, Franklin D.; TORCH, Operation;

References
de Charbonnières, Guy de Girard. *Le duel Giraud–de Gaulle*. Paris: Plon, 1984.

Giraud, Henri. *Mes évasions*. Paris: Julliard, 1946.
———. *Un seul but, la victoire*. Paris: Julliard, 1949.
Kaspi, André. *La mission de Jean Monnet à Alger*. Paris: Publications de la Sorbonne, 1971.

Glide Bombs

Precursor to today's cruise missiles developed by the Germans. The Germans developed two types of weapons systems, the first of which was the free-fall FX-1200 bomb. Designed by Max Kramer of the Ruhrstahl AG, it weighed 3,460 lb with a warhead of 771 lb. The FX-1200 had small 5 ft 3-inch wings to enable it to glide, and it was radio-controlled by means of an electrical tail unit. Glide bombs were carried by such German aircraft as the Dornier Do-217, Heinkel He-117, and Junkers Ju-88 and Ju-290.

On 9 September 1943, after Italy had announced an armistice with the Allies, the Germans used FX-1200 glide bombs to sink the Italian battleship *Roma;* half of her crew was lost. The Germans also severely damaged the battleship *Italia*. The FX-1200 could be dropped from an altitude of 18,500–22,700 ft and a distance of up to 3 mi from the target.

The second glide bomb was the Hs-293, designed by Herbert Wagner of the Henschel Company. The Hs-293 was a rocket-assisted, guided, winged bomb, initially designed for use against ships. It was fitted with a Walter 109–507B rocket motor of 1,323 lb thrust, giving it a speed of about 360 mph. The Hs-293 was 13 ft 4 inches long with a wingspan of 10 ft 7 inches. It weighed about 2,140 lb, of which about 165 lb was in the rocket and 1,124 lb was in the warhead—a substantial ratio of warhead to delivery system. The Hs-293 employed a Dortmund/Duisburg wire-guided system for control, and it had a useful range of almost 10 nautical miles.

Modifications to the Hs-293 included the Hs-294 (16 ft 5 inches long with a wingspan of 14 ft 2 inches), Hs-295, Hs-296, Hs-297, Hs-298, and Hs-344. The Hs-298, a smaller version of the Hs-293, was designed to be launched from night fighters against Allied bombers. It had a two-stage rocket motor and could operate at heights up to 20,000 ft. Its warhead weighed about 150 lb. The Hs-344 was another lightweight version designed for use by fighters against other aircraft. These versions were largely just tested.

The Germans first used the Hs-293 on 24 August 1943 in the Bay of Biscay. During Allied Operation PERCUSSION, an antisubmarine air and surface attack on German U-boats, the Canadian 5th Support Group came under air attack from 14 Dornier Do-217 bombers of the 2nd Squadron of Kampfgeschwader 100 and 7 Junkers Ju-88Cs of another unit. The attackers employed Hs-293s to damage the sloop *Landguard* in 4 near hits and the sloop *Bideford* in 1 near hit. On 28 August, 18

Do-217s attacked the relieving 1st Support Group and sank the British sloop *Egret* and heavily damaged the Canadian destroyer *Athabaskan*.

Kapfgeschwader 100 mounted further attacks with the Hs-293 in the Mediterranean in September 1943. During the U.S. landing at Salerno on 11 September, Kapfgeschwader 100's Do-17s attacked and heavily damaged the cruiser *Savannah* and narrowly missed the cruiser *Philadelphia*. On 13 September, the British cruiser *Uganda* was hit and heavily damaged. The *Philadelphia* and British destroyers *Loyal* and *Nubian* were both damaged. The hospital ship *Newfoundland* was sunk, probably by an Hs-293. On 16 September, the British battleship *Warspite* sustained heavy damage from 2 Hs-293 hits. Among other Allied warships that were struck and sunk were the British destroyer *Intrepid* and the Greek destroyer *Vasillissa Olga* on 26 September, the Italian destroyer *Euro* on 1 October, and the British destroyer escort *Dulverton* on 13 November 1943.

During the landing at Anzio, Do-217s and Ju-88s again attacked Allied ships with Hs-293 glide bombs. On 23 January 1944, these glide bombs sank the British destroyer *Janus* and damaged the destroyer *Jervis*. On 29 January, Hs-293s sank the British cruiser *Spartan,* and on 25 February they sent to the bottom the British destroyer *Inglefield.*

The glide bomb was well conceived and well tested. Some 2,300 were used in combat, but production was limited by the many other demands on the German armaments industry at the time. The Germans claimed that the glide bombs sank or damaged 400,000 tons of Allied shipping, but this was an exaggeration. The Germans also sent plans for their rocket motors by submarine to the Japanese, who used them to develop their Oka manned rocket bomb.

Late in the war, the United States tested several types of air-to-surface missiles, including the Fletcher XBG-1, Fletcher XBG-2, Cornelius XBG-3, Pratt-Reed LBE, Piper LBP, and Taylorcraft LBT. The term "glomb" was used as shorthand for "glide bomb." The Eighth Air Force used the GB-1 series of glide bombs beginning on 28 March 1944. Some 1,000 were launched, but they lacked accuracy. Later versions incorporated television guidance, but only one version (Project Batty, a GB-4) was used in combat. Instead, bombs without wings but with a guidance system were used. One was the Azon (for "azimuth only"); another was the Razon (azimuth and range guidance). Azons were used successfully in combat. A later version, the Tarzon, was used effectively during the Korean War.

The most advanced winged missile of World War II was the Bat, a glide bomb with a 1,000 lb bomb and semiactive radar homing. Employing PBY-42s Privateer aircraft, the U.S. Navy used the Bat with great success against Japanese shipping. The Bat had a 10 ft wingspan, was a little longer than 11 ft, weighed 1,880 lb, and achieved 300 mph in the glide.

Range depended on the release height; a Bat sank a Japanese destroyer at 20 mi distance from the drop aircraft.

David Westwood, Walter Boyne, Jürgen Rohwer, and Spencer C. Tucker

See also
V-1 Buzz Bomb; V-2 Rocket
References
Jane's Fighting Aircraft of World War II. London: Jane's Publishing Co., 1946.
Kens, Karlkeinz, and Heinz J. Nowarra. *Die deutschen Flugzeuge 1933–1945*. Munich: J. Flehmanns Verlag, 1968.
Rohwer, Jürgen, and G. Hummelchen. *Chronology of the War at Sea, 1939–1945*. London: Greenhill, 1992.

Gliders

See Aircraft, Gliders.

Goebbels, Paul Joseph (1897–1945)

Key German official and minister of propaganda. Born on 29 October 1897 at Rheydt in the Rhineland, Joseph Goebbels was physically small with a clubfoot. He grew up in a deeply religious Catholic setting, but on graduation from the University of Heidelberg with a doctorate in literature in 1921, he renounced his faith.

Unsuccessful in his desired literary career, Goebbels temporarily worked in a bank. In 1924, he formed a close association with Adolf Hitler. After spreading Nazi propaganda as the editor of the *Voelkische Freiheit* (people's freedom) at Elberfeld, "the Little Doctor," as he came to be called, moved up in the Nazi Party hierarchy. Hitler recognized his abilities and appointed him Gauleiter (leader) of Berlin in November 1926, charging him with rebuilding the party organization there. From 1927 to 1935, Goebbels edited the weekly newspaper *Der Angriff* (*The Attack*), which eventually became a daily and a financial success. Goebbels displayed considerable organizational skill and ability as a motivational speaker. He also ordered the Sturmabteilungen (Storm Troops, SA) to use physical force in the streets against the leftist opposition. In 1928, Goebbels won election to the Reichstag, and in 1929 he took charge of Nazi Party propaganda, playing an important role in building Nazi political strength throughout Germany.

Goebbels successfully used American advertising tools, psychology, and modern propaganda techniques to spread the message of Nazism. He made Horst Wessel, a thug who was killed in a barroom brawl, into a Nazi martyr, and he pushed the use of the Nazi salute and of "Heil Hitler"

German Nazi propagandist and politician Paul Joseph Goebbels. (Hulton Archive)

as a mandatory greeting. He also advanced new slogans and myths, including the *Führermythos,* that Hitler was the one savior of the German nation. He engaged in gross anti-Semitism.

Hitler rewarded Goebbels in March 1933 by appointing him to the cabinet as minister of propaganda. Goebbels exercised complete control over mass communication—the press, films, theater, radio, and sports—organizing all of it to work for the Nazi cause and later the war effort. He lived up to his own slogan, "Propaganda has nothing to do with truth." Throughout the war, Goebbels worked to buoy the confidence of the German people. He trumpeted the claim of a "final victory" and in a speech in February 1943 invoked "total war." Appointed plenipotentiary for total war in July 1944, Goebbels called on the German people for more and more sacrifices, imposing longer working hours and reducing benefits. He also proclaimed the advent of German "miracle weapons" that would win the war.

At war's end, Goebbels and his family joined Hitler in the *Führerbunker* in Berlin. On 1 May 1945, a day after Hitler's suicide, Goebbels and his wife Magda also committed suicide after first having poisoned their six small children.

Goebbels's diaries are an important source of information about the National Socialist regime.

A. J. L. Waskey

See also
Germany, Home Front; Hitler, Adolf; Propaganda; Unconditional Surrender
References
Goebbels, Joseph. *The Goebbels Diaries, 1942–1943.* Edited and trans. Louis P. Lochner. Garden City, NY: Doubleday, 1948.
———. *Final Entries, 1945: The Diaries of Joseph Goebbels.* Edited by Hugh Trevor Roper. Translated by Richard Barry. New York: Putnam, 1978.
———. *The Goebbels Diaries, 1939–1941.* Ed. and trans. Fred Taylor. New York: G. P. Putnam's Sons, 1983.
Heiber, Helmut. *Goebbels.* New York: DaCapo Press, 1983.
Herzstein, Robert E. *The War That Hitler Won: Goebbels and the Nazi Media Campaign.* New York: Paragon House Publishers, 1987.
Reuth, Ralf Georg. *Goebbels.* New York: Harcourt Brace, 1993.
Roberts, Jeremy. *Joseph Goebbels: Nazi Propaganda Minister.* New York: Rosen Publishing Group, 2000.

Goerdeler, Carl Friedrich (1884–1945)

German political figure and Nazi opposition leader. Born in Schneidemuhl, Pomerania, on 31 July 1884, Carl Goerdeler studied law and entered the civil service. An officer in World War I, he became deputy mayor of Königsberg in 1922 and lord mayor of Leipzig in 1930. In 1932, German Chancellor Heinrich Brüning appointed Goerdeler as commissioner of prices, a post he held until July 1935.

Adolf Hitler came to power in Germany in January 1933. At first, the traditionalist Goerdeler supported the new government, especially its centralization of authority. Goerdeler also believed that Hitler might solve Germany's pressing economic problems. However, it soon became apparent that the new government insisted on total submission. In protest, Goerdeler resigned as mayor of Leipzig in 1937. Goerdeler was troubled not only by the regime's domestic policies but also by its aggressive foreign policy, which he feared would lead to a general European war. He became one of the first to publicly speak out against the Nazi government and soon emerged as one of the leaders of the German Resistance movement against Hitler.

Once war began in September 1939, Goerdeler became a leading member of a conspiracy to overthrow Hitler. He wrote documents spelling out the goals of the Resistance and what should take place politically following Hitler's removal from office. Throughout, Goerdeler maintained a close relationship with General Ludwig Beck, leader of the army officers who opposed Hitler. Although Goerdeler vigorously urged Hitler's removal from office, he initially opposed an assassination that might make Hitler a martyr. Goerdeler argued that the Führer should be arrested and his guilt exposed in a public trial. Others in the Resistance, however, believed assassinating Hitler was the certain course of action. By early July 1944, Goerdeler reluctantly agreed. According to plans developed by the Resistance groups, Goerdeler was to become the chancellor in a post-Hitler Germany.

On the failure of the 20 July 1944 bomb plot against Hitler, Goerdeler went into hiding. Arrested on 12 August, Goerdeler endured interrogation and was then sentenced to death. He wrote several essays and letters while in prison, and he was executed at Plötzensee Prison, Berlin, on 2 February 1945.

Gene Mueller

See also
Beck, Ludwig; July Bomb Plot; Resistance; Stauffenberg, Claus Philip Schenk

References
Hamerow, Theodore. *On the Road to Wolf's Lair: German Resistance to Hitler*. Cambridge, MA: Harvard University Press, 1997.
Reich, Innes. *Carl Friedrich Goerdeler: Ein Oberbürgermeister gene den NS-Staat*. Köln, Germany: Böhlau, 1997.
Ritter, Gerhard. *The German Resistance: Carl Goerdeler's Struggle against Tyranny*. Freeport, NY: Books for Libraries Press, 1970.

GOODWOOD, Operation (18–20 July 1944)

British Second Army attack in an attempt to break out of the Normandy beachhead near Caen, France. Operation GOODWOOD was originally suggested as an operation supporting Lieutenant General Omar Bradley's Operation COBRA, the breakout of his American 12th Army Group from Saint-Lô. British General Bernard Montgomery later saw GOODWOOD as a opportunity for his 21st Army Group to achieve a breakthrough or even perhaps a double breakout by both U.S. and British forces. Operation GOODWOOD involved three corps: three armored divisions of the British VIII Corps in the east provided the main effort to gain the rolling plain southeast of Caen rising toward Falaise, the Canadian II Corps was to secure the southern half of Caen, and the British XII Corps would conduct diversionary attacks on the right several days before the 18 July 1944 kickoff.

The concept for GOODWOOD, developed by commander of the British Second Army Lieutenant General Miles Dempsey, was to use massed airpower and artillery followed by an armor breakthrough of the German defensive crust. Prior to the ground attack, 1,700 heavy bombers from the Royal Air Force (RAF) Bomber Command and the U.S. Eighth Air Force, plus nearly 400 medium bombers and fighter-bombers of the U.S. Ninth Air Force, dropped 7,700 tons of bombs on the German defenses. Only fighter-bombers attacked in the zone of the main effort to prevent the massive cratering that had slowed British armor in its earlier attacks to seize Caen.

The air and ground bombardment began at 5:30 A.M. on 18 July, and the ground attack by the three armored divisions of VIII Corps occurred on schedule at 7:30 A.M. The effects of the bombardment and tactical surprise allowed the ground elements to advance more than 3 miles in slightly over an hour. In only about 3 hours, VIII Corps was nearing a clean breakthrough when it encountered the final German defensive line of antitank and flak guns. In an oversight, this defensive line had not been targeted for air bombardment and it, combined with dogged German defense, ground the advance to a halt. Limited local attacks continued on 19 and 20 July, but a heavy thunderstorm on 20 July turned the landscape into a quagmire, and GOODWOOD came to an end.

During the four-day operation, the Canadian II Corps captured the rest of Caen and part of the plain to the southeast, and the British VIII Corps secured nearly 35 square miles of terrain. However, the operation cost VIII Corps more than 4,000 casualties and the loss of 500 tanks—36 percent of all British armor on the Continent at that time. Although General Montgomery declared that the purposes of GOODWOOD had been achieved, the results were more disappointing. Some in the higher levels of Allied command, even on the British side, hinted that it might be time for Montgomery's removal. The failures of GOODWOOD focused Allied hopes for a breakout in Normandy on Operation COBRA.

Arthur T. Frame

See also
Bradley, Omar Nelson; Carpet Bombing; COBRA, Operation; Dempsey, Miles Christopher; Montgomery, Sir Bernard Law

References
Blumenson, Martin. *United States Army in World War II: European Theater of Operations: Breakout and Pursuit*. Washington, DC: U.S. Army, Center of Military History, 1984.
Callahan, Raymond. "Two Armies in Normandy: Weighing British and Canadian Military Performance." In Theodore A. Wilson, ed., *D-Day 1944*. Lawrence: University Press of Kansas, 1994.
Keegan, John. *Six Armies in Normandy: From D-Day to the Liberation of Paris*. New York: Penguin Books, 1984.
Wilt, Alan. "The Air Campaign," In Theodore A. Wilson, ed., *D-Day 1944*. Lawrence: University Press of Kansas, 1994.

Göring, Hermann Wilhelm (1893–1946)

German air force marshal and head of the Luftwaffe. Born on 12 January 1893 in Rosenheim, Bavaria, Hermann Göring was educated in military school in Karlsruhe. He then entered officers' training school at Gross Lichterfelde, and on graduation in 1912 he was commissioned in the infantry. He served in the German army and fought in World War I with the infantry until 1915, when he joined the air service. Göring succeeded Baron Manfred von Richthofen on the latter's death as commander of the Richthofen Squadron in July

German Reichsmarshall Hermann Göring. (Library of Congress)

1918. Credited with 22 aerial victories in World War I, Göring was awarded the coveted Pour le Mérite.

After the war, Göring moved to Scandinavia, where he took up show flying and married a Swedish baroness. He returned to Germany in 1921 and became a close associate of Adolf Hitler. In 1922, Hitler gave Göring charge of the Sturmabteilungen (SA, Storm Troopers), which grew dramatically in strength. Seriously wounded in the 1923 Beer Hall Putsch, Göring fled Germany but returned in 1927. In 1928, Göring was elected to the Reichstag, and in 1932 he was its president. Göring had easy access to influential individuals in industry, banking, and the military, and he acted as liaison between them and Hitler, playing a key role in the Nazi accession to power.

After Hitler became German chancellor in January 1933, Göring secured even more power and influence. Among his many offices were minister without portfolio, minister of the interior for the state of Prussia, and minister of the air force (Luftwaffe). Göring soon began rebuilding the Luftwaffe, and he was instrumental in all major policy decisions affecting its composition and training. In April 1933 out of the Prussian political police Göring established the Geheime Staatspolizei (Gestapo, political police), a force designed to crush all resistance to Nazism. In 1936, he was appointed to oversee the Four-Year Plan, which gave him virtual control over the economy. As far as the Luftwaffe was concerned, Göring supported the notion of a tactical air force at the expense of strategic bombing, arguably the correct decision given the heavy military demands on Germany's industrial base. In 1939, Hitler appointed Göring Reichsmarshall (Reich Marshal) and designated him as his heir. Göring was also instrumental in the development of concentration camps, and he worked with Reinhard Heydrich, chief of Reich security, in formulating an *Endlösung* or "final solution" to the "Jewish question." Göring also amassed a large fortune and, especially during World War II, indulged his passion for collecting fine art.

Göring's Luftwaffe was influential in the early Nazi victories in Poland in 1939 and France in 1940. His interventions in the Battle of Britain in 1940, however, negatively affected the German effort and led to a loss of his influence with Hitler. Göring opposed Operation BARBAROSSA, Hitler's invasion of the Soviet Union, favoring a Mediterranean strategy instead. He was blamed, probably falsely, for having suggested that the Luftwaffe, with only a limited transport capacity, could supply the Sixth Army at Stalingrad. Popular opinion also turned against him as Allied air raids on the Reich became increasingly effective. Increasingly marginalized, Göring spent more time at his estate of Karinhall, where he indulged his interests in hunting and art collecting. Although Hitler had designated Göring as his successor, the latter's impatience at the end of the war—painted by Martin Bormann, head of the Party Chancery, and others as an attempt by Göring to wrest power from Hitler—led the Führer to order that Göring be stripped of his posts and arrested. Göring surrendered to elements of the U.S. 9th Infantry Division on 9 May 1945 and was tried at the International Military Tribunal at Nuremberg. Unrepentant, he was found guilty and sentenced to death. Göring committed suicide by swallowing poison on 15 October 1946 only hours before his planned execution.

Wendy A. Maier

See also

Aircraft, Bombers; Aircraft, Fighters; BARBAROSSA, Operation; France, Battle for; Germany, Air Force; Germany, Home Front; Heydrich, Reinhard Tristan Eugen; Hitler, Adolf; Holocaust, The; International Military Tribunal: The Nuremberg Trials; Poland Campaign; Stalingrad, Battle of

References

Davidson, Eugene. *The Trial of the Germans: An Account of the Twenty-Two Defendants Before the International Military Tribunal at Nuremberg.* New York: Macmillan, 1966.

Fest, Joachim. *The Face of the Third Reich: Portraits of Nazi Leadership.* New York: Ace Books, 1970.

Göring, Emmy. *My Life with Göring.* London: David Bruce and Watson, 1972.

Mosley, Leonard. *The Reich Marshal: A Biography of Hermann Goering.* Garden City, NY: Doubleday, 1974.

Swearingen, Ben. *The Mystery of Hermann Göring's Suicide.* New York: Dell, 1985.

Gort, Lord John

See Vereker, John Standish Surtees Pendergast (Sixth Viscount Gort).

Gott, William Henry Ewart "Strafer" (1897–1942)

British army general. Born on 13 August 1897 in Leeds, England, William Gott was educated at Harrow and Sandhurst. Commissioned into the King's Royal Rifle Corps (KRRC) in February 1915, Gott fought in France during World War I, where he was wounded, awarded the Military Cross (MC), and taken prisoner. Gott continued in the army after the war, serving in the 13th London Regiment. He was promoted to major in January 1934 and saw service in India. Advanced to lieutenant colonel in 1938, Gott commanded a battalion of the KRRC.

In 1940, Gott was promoted to brigadier general and appointed as a staff officer to Major General Percy Hobart's Mobile Force in Egypt, which he was rapidly developing into an armored division. As commander of the Support Group of the 7th Armoured Division, Gott took part in Operation COMPASS in December 1940, and in May 1941 he led the composite armored strike force for Operation BREVITY, the first Allied attempt to relieve Tobruk. Gott was then promoted to major general and given command of the 7th Armoured Division, which he led with great daring during Operation CRUSADER.

As with most other British officers, Gott—himself an infantry officer—initially failed to comprehend the concept of mobile mechanized warfare. However, on the basis of his experience fighting the Germans, who coordinated antitank guns, artillery, and infantry with their tanks, Gott suggested using 25-pounder field artillery to support British tanks. He was primarily responsible for the belated British policy of breaking down the traditional and rigid divisional organization into combined all-arms brigade groups, which became standard throughout the British army.

Gott built a reputation as a brilliant and energetic armored commander, and he was widely recognized as knowing more about the desert than any other senior British officer. Standing 6 feet 2 inches and built like a heavyweight boxer, Gott had an imposing presence and was one of the most inspiring commanders in the Middle East. Gott had an unrivaled knowledge of the exigencies and possibilities of desert warfare and a reputation for a lightning-quick grasp of a situation and a faculty for making rapid decisions. A legend in the desert fighting, Gott was known as a "British Rommel," tirelessly roaming the battlefield to rally and drive on the shaken troops.

Promoted to lieutenant general in 1942—one of the youngest officers of that rank in the British army—Gott took command of XIII Corps and led it through the defeats at Gazala and Mersa Matrûh. Nevertheless, his reputation was not tarnished during the British withdrawal to El Alamein. In August 1942, British Prime Minister Winston L. S. Churchill selected Gott to replace Auchinleck as commander of the Eighth Army. Although Gott protested that he was tired out and depressed by fatigue and defeat and would like nothing more than three months' leave in England to recuperate, he agreed to take on the new post. On 7 August 1942, he flew to Cairo to take up his appointment. His aircraft was intercepted by a lone German fighter and shot down. Although his plane managed to land safely, Gott had been shot and killed. Following his death, Churchill immediately appointed his second choice, Lieutenant General Bernard Montgomery, as commander of the Eighth Army. Gott's death, therefore, had a great impact on succeeding events in the desert and subsequently in Europe.

Paul H. Collier

See also
Alam Halfa, Battle of; Auchinleck, Sir Claude John Eyre; Churchill, Sir Winston L. S.; COMPASS, Operation; CRUSADER, Operation; El Alamein, Battle of; Gazala, Battle of; Mersa Matrûh, Battle of; Montgomery, Sir Bernard Law; North Africa Campaign; Ruweisat Ridge, Battles of; Tobruk, Third Battle of
References
Moorehead, Alan. *Desert War: The North African Campaign, 1940–1943.* London: Cassell, 2001.
Pitt, Barrie. *The Crucible of War.* 2 vols. London: Jonathan Cape, 1980–1982.
Vernon, Dick. *Strafer Gott: 1897–1942.* Winchester, UK: Regiment Headquarters, Royal Green Jackets, 1984.

Graziani, Rodolfo (Marchese di Neghelli) (1882–1955)

Italian army marshal. Born at Filettino near Rome on 11 August 1882, Rodolfo Graziani joined the Italian Army and served in Libya in 1914 before being posted to the Italian Front during World War I. There he commanded a brigade, was wounded twice, and won promotion to major. A colonel at the end of World War I, Graziani earned a reputation as Italy's most successful colonial general. Distinguishing himself in Tripolitania in the 1920s, for which he was promoted to brigadier general in 1923, he was dispatched to Cyrenaica, where he conducted a brutal but effective pacification campaign against the Senussi in 1930–1932. Promoted to major ary 1941, and Graziani returned to Italy in semidisgrace and resigned from the army.

Because Graziani was the only general of note to remain loyal to the fascist regime after its collapse in 1943, that September Mussolini appointed him defense minister and chief of staff of the rump Italian Social Republic. Graziani spent the remainder of the war attempting unsuccessfully to rebuild the army in an atmosphere of intensifying civil warfare and German domination. In 1950, Graziani was sentenced to 19 years in prison for war crimes, but he was released after only a few months. He then headed the neofascist Italian Socialist Movement. Graziani died in Rome on 11 January 1955.

John M. Jennings

See also
Balbo, Italo; Italy, Army; Mussolini, Benito; North Africa Campaign
References
Ciano, Galeazzo. *The Ciano Diaries, 1939–1943: The Complete, Unabridged Diaries of Count Galeazzo Ciano, Italian Minister for Foreign Affairs.* New York: Doubleday and Company, 1946.
Deakin, Frederick W. *The Brutal Friendship: Mussolini, Hitler, and the Fall of Italian Fascism.* New York: Harper and Row, 1962.
Mack Smith, Denis. *Mussolini's Roman Empire.* New York: Viking Press, 1976.

Italian army Marshal Rodolfo Graziani. (Library of Congress)

general in 1930 and to lieutenant general in 1932, Graziani commanded a corps and then was appointed governor of Somalia in 1935. Graziani participated in the attack on Ethiopia in 1936 and destroyed the remnants of the Ethiopian army in February 1937. His successes earned him promotion to marshal and viceroy of Ethiopia on the departure of Marshal Pietro Badoglio. However, Graziani's savage rule provoked a widespread insurgency. He was severely wounded in an assassination attempt on 29 February 1937, and the Italian army crushed the uprising only with great difficulty. The Italians employed poison gas and were guilty of other atrocities.

Graziani left Ethiopia in January 1938 and was made honorary governor of Italian East Africa. In October 1939, Italian dictator Benito Mussolini appointed Graziani army chief of staff. Mussolini sent Graziani to Libya to replace Italo Balbo, who was killed in an airplane crash on 28 June 1940.

Although the 250,000 Italian forces in North Africa vastly outnumbered the scanty British troops there, Graziani refused to launch an offensive into Egypt, citing serious deficiencies in supplies and equipment. Infuriated by Graziani's timidity, Mussolini ordered him to attack. The subsequent tentative Italian offensive sparked a devastating British counteroffensive that drove the Italians from Cyrenaica in Febru-

Great Britain, Air Force

The future of the Royal Air Force (RAF) appeared bleak at the end of World War I. With extensive personnel and aircraft drawdowns, the RAF's existence as an independent service remained in doubt until the appointment of General Sir Hugh Trenchard as chief of the Air Staff in January 1919. As dogged as he was visionary, Trenchard proved the viability of the third service, and by the mid-1920s he secured the RAF's future. In search of a mission, the RAF turned to imperial policing, especially in Somaliland, Aden, Palestine, India, and Iraq, where it proved highly successful.

Still, growth in force size was slow due to economic difficulties and an ever-shrinking defense budget. Of the 52 squadrons approved in 1923, only 42 had been established by 1934. In 1935, the transition to monoplane designs began, a process resulting in the most successful British fighter aircraft of the early war years—the Hawker Hurricane designed by Sydney Camm, which entered service in 1937; and the Supermarine Spitfire, designed by R. J. Mitchell, which appeared in 1938. In 1936, future manpower needs were addressed with the establishment of an RAF Volunteer Reserve. By January 1939, the total RAF establishment consisted of 135 squadrons.

Despite advancements in fighter types as defense against strategic bombers, the prevailing attitude throughout European air services reflected the airpower theories of such visionaries as Brigadier General Billy Mitchell in the United States and Guilio Douhet in Italy, both of whom argued the primacy of the bomber. To overcome the loss of strategic mobility, a difficulty that was suffered by the armies of the Western Front in World War I, Britain embraced the concept of strategic bombing. This concept was based on the theory that long-range bombing would inevitably undercut an opponent's will and civilian morale, as well as cripple his economic ability to wage war.

The beginning of World War II in September 1939 found the RAF considerably better prepared than it had been only four years earlier. The Bomber Command order of battle included 54 squadrons equipped with Bristol Blenheims, Vickers Wellingtons, Armstrong Whitleys, and Handley Page Hampdens. The critical weakness lay in the match between air strategy and the instruments of war available in 1939. The RAF had no heavy bomber capable of delivering the crippling physical and economic blows necessary for strategic bombing success. Not until the Handley Page Halifax heavy bomber entered service in late 1940 did Bomber Command possess a heavy bomber that could carry the air war deep into enemy territory.

Fighter Command entered the war considerably better prepared in terms of equipment capability. The 35 home-based fighter squadrons with first-line Hurricanes and Spitfires were enhanced by a series of coastal radar stations known as Chain Home. Though relatively primitive, the radar network soon proved robust and difficult for the German Luftwaffe to destroy. Thus with a total of 1,466 aircraft, of which roughly 1,000 were first-line, the RAF faced Reichsmarshall Hermann Göring's Luftwaffe.

The first months of the war can best be characterized as a sparring match characterized by mainly frustrated attempts by the RAF to attack German navy warships. In France, Air Chief Marshal Sir Hugh Dowding, commander in chief of Fighter Command, insisted on sending only squadrons for the Advanced Air Striking Force (AASF) that were equipped with older, less robust aircraft such as the Gloster Gladiator. He feared losing first-rate aircraft and stripping home defense of fighting capability. Despite Dowding's conservatism, the RAF lost nearly 1,000 aircraft in the Battle of France, half of them fighters.

The Luftwaffe had high hopes of quickly dispatching the undermanned and outgunned RAF when as a precursor to invasion it launched Operation SEA LION, Germany's main air offensive against Britain, on 8 August 1940. However, Dowding's prewar innovations soon showed their worth. Fighter Command employed the group/area command-and-control system, in which each group was subdivided into sectors encompassing forward and primary airfields. Initially, groups 11 and 12 covered the country; they were later further divided into four groups. Within each sector and group, an operations room controlled activities; the whole enterprise was coordinated at Fighter Command Headquarters. Connected by telephone to the Chain Home system and the Observer Corps, the command-and-control system allowed for a reaction to a raid in a matter of minutes with an appropriate number of aircraft being vectored to target. The system allowed Fighter Command to husband resources, identify incoming raids, scramble appropriate units, vector aircraft to target, and essentially ambush incoming German raids. This combination of the Chain Home system, coordinated sector control, and superior air frames—all due in large measure to the prewar efforts of Dowding—proved to be the decisive factors that led the United Kingdom to win the Battle of Britain.

In the first phase of the Battle of Britain, the Germans sought to draw the RAF into the air and destroy its fighting strength by attrition. By late August, that strategy had failed, and the Germans turned to destroying British airfields south of the Thames. This far more dangerous threat to RAF viability took a great toll of RAF men and machines by early September. Dowding estimated that three more weeks of such assaults would destroy Fighter Command's ability to mount any viable defense. Then, on the night of 24 August, German bombers were dispatched to strike an oil storage depot near London. Their navigation was faulty, and they dropped their bombs on London. Churchill immediately ordered the bombing of Berlin on the night of 25 August. One hundred and three British aircraft took off that night for Germany, 89 of them for Berlin. Only 29 bombers actually reached Berlin because of clouds and poor navigation equipment. The raid was certainly not a success, but it led Adolf Hitler to order a concentration on London. The Luftwaffe's primary target became the destruction of London rather than the vastly more important RAF airfields and production facilities. The shift to bombing London on 7 September allowed Fighter Command to repair airfields and facilities. For the next several months, British cities suffered through an almost nightly bombing campaign dubbed the Blitz, a failed strategy to attack civilian morale. Although the Chain Home radar network did not operate especially well at night, improved radar and night fighters, including the Beaufighter, proved capable of challenging German night bombing, and German losses mounted. In early autumn 1940, Hitler canceled SEA LION, and by May 1941 the air assault abated. Of the more than 3,000 pilots who flew in the RAF in the Battle of Britain as Winston Churchill's "few," some 500 died in combat.

In the initial stages of the war, the RAF had been loath to attack German industrial targets, despite the doctrine of strategic bombing. During the battles for France and Britain, Bomber Command had been reduced to attacking German shipping and invasion force transport. Some successful raids against Luftwaffe airfields occurred with good results. The turning point for the strategic air campaign occurred on the night of 23 September 1940, when 84 bombers attacked

Firebombs being loaded into a Royal Air Force Short Stirling bomber before an attack on industrial Germany. (Library of Congress)

Berlin. Although bomb damage and RAF losses were minimal, the RAF had commenced the practice of night bombing first industrial (especially oil) and infrastructure and later civilian targets. In 1942 the Avro Lancaster heavy bomber arrived in numbers. Having a range of more than 1,600 miles and capable of carrying 22,000 lb of bombs, the Lancaster was Britain's mainstay heavy bomber of World War II, and it enabled Bomber Command to carry the air war deep into Germany. The Lancaster Mark II, which appeared in 1943, had a range of 2,250 miles and could carry 14,000 lb of bombs. However, night navigation and target identification proved highly problematic. With no visual reference aids at night, bomber crews relied on Pathfinders. First fielded in August 1942, Pathfinder aircraft flew ahead of the formations, identified targets, and dropped color-coded marker flares. As the war progressed, electronic navigation improved, including the relatively primitive radio set known as "Gee," followed by the more-sophisticated blind-bombing device called "Trinity." The latter was a precursor of the advanced "Oboe" system, which employed a ground-distance-measuring station. The H2S system provided a radar display indicating prominent geographic features such as rivers, coastline, and urban structures, thus providing the hitherto missing navigational landmarks.

Night-bombing accuracy always suffered compared with the daylight assaults carried out by the B-17s and B-24s of the U.S. Army Air Forces (USAAF) Eighth Air Force beginning in 1943. To counter the night bombing, the Luftwaffe developed efficient night fighters and relied on massed antiaircraft artillery. When the Blitz ended, Bomber Command increased the intensity of night strategic bombing. In a night raid on Hamburg on 8 May 1941, 300 bombers dropped several new 4,000 lb bombs.

On 22 February 1942, Air Chief Marshal Sir Arthur Harris took charge of Bomber Command. An energetic and enthusiastic advocate of terror bombing, Harris resolved to bludgeon Germany into submission. Night bombing of industrial targets increased immediately. To underscore the new attitude (and the advantage of the Lancasters with improved electronic navigation and targeting gear), Harris ordered the first thousand-bomber raid, which struck the German city of Köln (Cologne) on 30 May 1942. Simultaneously, the newly fielded and capable De Havilland Mosquito quickly established itself as an extraordinary melding of mission capabilities, including reconnaissance, bomber, fighter-bomber, and night fighter. Under Harris, British strategic night bombing increased in intensity, capability, and destructive force for the next three years.

Italy's entry into the war on 10 June 1940 found the RAF in the Middle East and Mediterranean dispersed over 4 million square miles of mainly desolate and hostile terrain. Its 300 first-line aircraft were organized into 29 operational squadrons. Most of the aircraft represented previous generations of fighters. Whereas this was suitable for imperial policing against tribesmen and ill-organized rebels, the Italian and later German air forces presented a difficult problem. The Italians could send up to 1,200 additional aircraft from Sicily and Italy to augment the 500 already in Africa. With imperial strategic interests threatened, notably the tenuous India/Far East supply line through the Suez Canal, Britain embarked on rapid air and troop reinforcement. Because few aircraft could make the journey completely by air, a scheme developed for shipping aircraft by sea to the Gold Coast; the planes then made a difficult flight across Africa to Egypt. Gradually, the Desert Air Force established air superiority in North Africa and aided Field Marshal Archibald Wavell's advance through Libya. Additionally, Malta, a linchpin of British Mediterranean power, was heavily reinforced; the island and its RAF garrison withstood furious, concerted Axis air assaults.

With the injection into North Africa in February 1941 of German ground forces supported by the Luftwaffe, the air advantage temporarily swung back to the Axis. As more Hurricanes, Spitfires, and American-made Curtiss Kittyhawks arrived, the Desert Air Force slowly overwhelmed the Axis air forces. By the time of the Battle of El Alamein at the end of October 1942, RAF aircraft outnumbered Axis aircraft by 1,200 to 690. Because it had more aircraft and was reinforced by top-of-the-line fighters and because many of its pilots were veterans of the Battle of Britain, the RAF gained air superiority and contributed heavily to the eventual Allied North African victory.

The war effort of the RAF Coastal Command is often overlooked, yet it played a tremendous part in subduing the submarine threat and keeping the sea lifeline open. In the early months, before Germany could mount a credible U-boat threat, the RAF concentrated maritime defense efforts against enemy commerce raiders. With only 19 home-based squadrons operating outdated aircraft, Coastal Command could do little more than close-in coastal patrol. As equipment and numbers improved, particularly with the arrival of the Short Sunderland and the American B-24 Liberator, Coastal Command's reach extended to practically the entire world. By late 1940, Coastal Command aircraft had begun minelaying operations and raids on the coast of France and in the North Sea.

By 1941, the German submarine threat intensified, and Coastal Command took up the challenges of shipping protection in the approaches and submarine hunting. The most dangerous area lay in a reconnaissance gap halfway across the Atlantic that land-based aircraft could not reach. In this area,

U-boats inflicted great casualties until the wide-scale employment of the Liberator, which operated from bases in Scotland, Iceland, and Canada and closed the gap in aerial coverage. Additionally, a new airborne radar, the ASV, improved air-dropped depth charges, and the organization of antisubmarine warfare (ASW) forces into hunter-killer groups of combined air and ship units all contributed to the growing effectiveness of ASW air operations. By late 1943, the Battle of the Atlantic had been won, and Coastal Command had played a major role in that victory. Of German U-boat losses in the Atlantic, 55 percent are believed to have been the result of air attack (although many of these losses were to aircraft flown from escort carriers). A further 19 percent of U-boat losses were the result of combined aircraft-warship actions.

In short, the RAF grew from a relatively small force wedded to strategic bombing and imperial policing in the early 1930s to a highly capable multimission force by the end of the war. Aircraft design advanced measurably with attendant gains in effectiveness and lethality. By 1943, the RAF deployed thousands of aircraft to every theater of operations and simply wore down the enemy through superior technology and weight of numbers. Advances in technology—particularly bomber navigation, targeting, and ASW radar—far outstripped Axis technological development, giving Britain's RAF not only a decisive quantitative advantage, but also a qualitative advantage by 1943.

In many respects, the RAF had established itself by 1945 as a coequal partner with the Royal Navy in defense of the British Empire and home islands. Certainly, the RAF consumed a huge portion of Britain's war economy, and its role and sacrifice in the war cannot be discounted. Fighter Command saved the nation in 1940, and Coastal Command challenged and eventually helped nullify the U-boat maritime trade threat. Although the effectiveness and morality of the strategic bombing offensive may be debated, its destruction of key German industrial targets, notably those of oil production and transportation, contributed significantly to the eventual Allied victory.

From an initial manning of 175,692 personnel (RAF and Women's Auxiliary Air Force [WAAF]) on 1 September 1939, the RAF reached a peak of 1,079,835 personnel of all ranks, branches, and nationalities (including Allied personnel serving in the RAF and Imperial/Dominion forces) by 1 May 1945. Of that number, 193,313 served as aircrew. The RAF had 9,200 aircraft of all types in all theaters in an operational status as of 1 May 1945. The cost was high. Relative to all other British services and branches, the RAF suffered the greatest personnel losses. From 1939 to 1945, the RAF lost 70,253 personnel killed or missing. Bomber Command flew 372,650 sorties, losing 8,617 aircraft and 47,268 men killed in combat or taken prisoner and a further 8,305 killed in training accidents. Deaths from other causes cost Bomber Command ground crews and WAAFs a further 1,570 deaths. Fighter Command lost 3,690 aircrew killed in action and 1,215 seriously wounded.

Stanley D. M. Carpenter

See also
Aircraft, Bombers; Aircraft, Fighters; Aircraft, Production of; Atlantic, Battle of the; Blitz, The: Britain, Battle of; Churchill, Sir Winston L. S.; Convoys, Allied; Depth Charges; Douhet, Giulio; Dowding, Sir Hugh Caswall Tremenheere; Dresden, Air Attack on; El Alamein, Battle of; Egypt; Fighter Tactics; Göring, Hermann Wilhelm; Harris, Sir Arthur Travis; Hunter-Killer Groups; Köln, Raid on; Malta; North Africa Campaign; Pathfinders; Radar; SEA LION, Operation; Strategic Bombing; Wavell, Sir Archibald Percival

References
Dean, Sir Maurice. *The Royal Air Force and Two World Wars.* London: Cassell, 1979.

Goulter, Christina J. M. *A Forgotten Offensive: Royal Air Force Coastal Command's Anti-Shipping Campaign, 1940–1945.* London: Frank Cass, 1995.

Hough, Richard, and Denis Richards. *The Battle of Britain: The Greatest Air Battle of World War II.* New York: W. W. Norton, 1989.

Mason, Francis K. *The British Fighter Since 1912.* Annapolis, MD: Naval Institute Press, 1992.

Rawlings, John D. R. *The History of the Royal Air Force.* New York: Crescent Books, 1984.

Robertson, Scot. *The Development of RAF Strategic Bombing Doctrine, 1919–1939.* Westport, CT: Praeger, 1995.

Saunders, Hilary St. George. *Per Audua: The Rise of British Air Power, 1911–1939.* London: Oxford University Press, 1945.

Terraine, John. *The Right of the Line: The Royal Air Force in the European War, 1939–1945.* Ware, Hertfordshire, UK: Wordsworth Editions Limited, 1997.

Great Britain, Army

For many of the British army's commanding officers who had served as infantry subalterns during World War I 20 years earlier, the events of September and October 1939 must have conjured up a powerful sense of déjà vu. Then, as in 1914, a small expeditionary force of two corps assembled to take up position on the left of the French line in Flanders, awaiting the inevitable German advance across the Belgian plain. Decades-old plans for entrenchment and the tactics of a static war of attrition were dusted off and reissued. However familiar the first months of World War II may have been to these veterans of Arras and Ypres, however, their army's war was to take a dramatically unexpected turn less than a year later when the British Expeditionary Force (BEF) was ignominiously ejected from the European mainland after just a few weeks of sharp, mobile combat. They were not to return for another four years. Of the seven army-strength formations raised by Britain during the period 1939–1945, only one, the 2nd, was to fight in northwest Europe again. The bulk of Britain's land operations were conducted far from its old World War I trench lines—in the Western Desert of North Africa, Sicily and Italy, the Balkan peninsula, Norway, Malaysia, Burma, and the northeast frontier of India. Such a fast-paced global struggle required a very different kind of army from that of World War I, with much greater technical specialization and more attention paid to the thorny problems of supply, communications, and control.

Although many key aspects of army life, such as the centuries-old regimental system, were carried forward mostly unaltered into World War II, the British army of 1939–1945 was to a large degree a hurriedly reinvented institution. This ad hoc metamorphosis was a necessary reaction to the new conditions of warfare, for which the interwar years had inadequately prepared the army's leaders and structures. After the demobilization that followed the 1918 armistice, the British army had quickly returned to its traditional role as a small imperial security force made up of long-service regulars, the part-time home reserve of the Territorial Army (TA), and a variegated auxiliary of colonial troops overseas. The problems of policing such trouble spots of the Empire as Palestine and India were far removed from the new theories of mechanized breakthrough warfare being discussed by forward-thinking military strategists in Europe, and the army languished in its attachment to the bayonet and the quick-firing rifleman—important for crowd control in overseas colonies, but less useful on the modern battlefield.

There were, in spite of this, significant attempts to bring the army up to date. Captain B. H. Liddell Hart's revised infantry manual stressed the "expanding torrent" tactics of mobility and exploitation, and Colonel J. F. C. Fuller called for fresh thinking on tank warfare. The Experimental Mechanized Force established briefly in the late 1920s was the world's first prototype for the armored division. But a combination of Treasury parsimony and knee-jerk opposition from the "Colonel Blimps" who dominated the army's upper echelons prevented any profound reform until the eve of war, when—prompted by the dynamic but ill-fated Minister of War Leslie Hore-Belisha—the government finally accepted the need for rearmament funding and a peacetime conscription bill. The doubling in size of the Territorial Army in March 1939 and passage of the National Service Act a month later provided for hundreds of thousands of new recruits, but in the short term these developments only added to the administrative confusion of a force hurriedly trying to reequip for a new continental commitment in alliance with France.

At the outbreak of war, the army's manpower stood at 897,000, the regulars and TAs having merged by government decree. Five regular infantry divisions were available in the United Kingdom for transportation to France. Two infantry divisions were deployed in Palestine suppressing the Arab revolt; the Western Desert Force (WDF) in Egypt had a fledgling armored division (another was forming in the UK, and would eventually join the BEF); and the remainder of the Empire was garrisoned either by individual battalions of regulars, units from the 300,000-strong Indian army, or indigenous militia like the King's African Rifles (KAR) in Kenya and Uganda. From these modest beginnings, the government of Prime Minister Neville Chamberlain proposed to recruit an army of 55 divisions (32 British, the remainder Indian and Dominion) for what it suggested would be at least a three-year war. There was as yet little clear plan as to where these divisions would be employed, or when.

Political control of the armed forces was exercised during hostilities through the War Cabinet, a subset of the full cabinet that liaised with the Chiefs of Staff Committee (COS) representing the uniformed heads of the army, Royal Navy, and Royal Air Force (RAF). The chief of the Imperial General Staff (CIGS) was the army's representative on the COS and, after the appointment of General Sir Alan Brooke in 1941, its permanent chairman. The CIGS had a vice-chief responsible for operations, plans, intelligence, and training and a deputy chief in charge of general organization. With the adjutant general (personnel), quartermaster general (logistics), and master general of ordnance, these men collectively made up the Army Council, which was chaired by the secretary of state for war. The War Office retained nominal ministerial responsibility for the army. However, Winston L. S. Churchill, appointed Prime Minister and Minister of Defence in May 1940, preferred to deal with the uniformed chiefs directly, and so Whitehall was relegated to a purely administrative function.

Operational control in the United Kingdom was vested in General Headquarters (GHQ) Home Forces, and the country was divided into a series of command districts: South Eastern, Southern, Western, Northern, Scottish, Eastern, London, and Northern Ireland. Various overseas GHQs were established in the Middle East, East Africa, Persia, and Iraq and in other theaters according to the vagaries of war; the commander in chief of the Indian army held sway across the Indian subcontinent. In 1939 and 1940, there was an unsuccessful attempt to create a viable Anglo-French Supreme War Council, but as the multinational character of the war developed with the entry of the United States in December 1941, command of British forces was increasingly delegated to pan-Allied authorities such as the Combined Chiefs of Staff at the strategic level and Supreme Headquarters, Allied Expeditionary Forces (SHAEF) and South-East Asia Command (SEAC) at the operational level.

The spiritual core of the army remained the 5 guard and 64 line infantry regiments that performed a unique administrative, but nontactical, function. Following the pattern established in World War I, the army expanded not by creating new regiments but by adding battalions to existing regiments, some of which traced their origins to the seventeenth century. The heart of the regiment was an organizational depot located at the home barracks, while its component field battalions served scattered across the world in various brigade formations. It was uncommon for two or more of the same regiment's battalions to serve closely together at the front.

Regimental tradition was a powerful reinforcement of esprit de corps, particularly as most regiments had a regional recruitment base. But as the war progressed and manpower became scarcer, the territorial associations of each regiment were weakened, with a corresponding loss of group identity. The remainder of the army was similarly divided into administrative units with regimental or corps-level designations but no tactical roles. The Royal Armoured Corps was a composite of the old cavalry regiments, now mechanized, and the Royal Tank Regiment. The Royal Corps of Signals handled communications for the entire army down to individual battalion levels, where company signalers took over. Some of the services, such as the Royal Artillery and the Royal Engineers, had traditions and battle honors every bit as distinguished as those of the infantry; others, such as the Reconnaissance Corps, were newly created and short-lived. The most important noncombat services were the Royal Army Service Corps, which carried supplies to troops in the field; the Royal Army Ordnance Corps (RAOC), responsible for the procurement and maintenance of equipment; and the Royal Army Medical Corps, which handled the sick and wounded.

The greater emphasis in World War II on technical and logistical matters caused a much larger proportion of manpower to be allocated to the "tail" (as opposed to the "teeth") of the army than was the case during World War I. Some support formations became so unwieldy that they gave birth to spin-off services of their own, such as the Royal Electrical and Mechanical Engineers, which was formed from the RAOC in 1942. Other notable services handled pay, military policing, spiritual affairs (the Royal Army Chaplains), intelligence, catering, physical training, and education—the last being accused by many conservative officers of foisting socialist ideology onto the rankers, precipitating the Labour Party's 1945 election victory! Eventually a General Service Corps was created to process incoming recruits and provide basic training and ultimate service allocation. The all-women's Auxiliary Territorial Service played an increasingly critical role in support of the regulars, as did the Queen Alexandra's Imperial Military Nursing Service and the First Aid Nursing Yeomanry on the medical front.

Tactically, each late-war British army was divided into four corps, each with two infantry divisions and one armored division. An infantry division of 18,000 men consisted of three brigades of three battalions apiece, an independent machine-gun battalion, three Royal Artillery (RA) field regiments, and an antitank and antiaircraft regiment, plus the usual supporting attachments of signalers, engineers, and so on. Tank brigades were often temporarily attached to infantry divisions on an as-needed basis. The full-strength infantry battalion had four rifle companies of three platoons apiece, a headquarters company, and a support company. The structure of armored divisions changed markedly throughout the war as experiments to find the best mixture of tanks to other services evolved. In 1939, there were two armored brigades per division, each of three regiments, with a motorized infantry battalion, field artillery regiment, and accompanying support units. By D day, this had changed to a single armored brigade of three tank regiments (78 tanks per regiment) plus a fully mechanized infantry battalion in armored personnel carriers, a motorized infantry brigade in trucks, an armored reconnaissance regiment, one or two RA field regiments, and a plethora of antitank, antiaircraft, and other support formations, for a total of 343 armored vehicles at full strength.

Two forces existing out of the standard army structure, special services and the Home Guard, deserve mention. The special services or "Commando" brigades were created after the Battle of France as Britain's only way of directly striking back at the Germans on the European continent. Although their hit-and-run tactics were of limited utility in the absence of an Allied second front, they played an important propaganda role in the testing years before Operation OVERLORD and later became a useful auxiliary to the conventional armies fighting in France and the Low Countries. Certain theaters of war spawned their own commando-like units, such as the Special Air Service (SAS) in the Western Desert and Orde Wingate's Chindits in Burma. The Parachute Regiment, which by the end of the war was two divisions strong, was originally a part of special services. The Home Guard, formed by a call for underage and over-age volunteers after Dunkerque, was originally intended as a last-ditch militia in the event of a German invasion of the British Isles. As the threat of attack receded, the Home Guard's function adapted to take over security and antiaircraft duties in the home islands from the regular army and to act as a training service for those about to be conscripted. At its peak in 1943, there were 1.7 million Home Guardsmen in 1,100 battalions.

By the end of the war, more than 3.5 million men and women had served in the regular forces, with the peak of 2.9 million reached in 1945. Eleven armored, 34 infantry, and 2 airborne divisions had been created. Other Imperial forces had expanded at an even greater rate: the Indian army was over 2.5 million men strong by V-J Day. Despite its early muddles and campaign disasters, the army had matured to become one of the world's preeminent fighting forces and a signal contributor to the ultimate Allied victory. It had accomplished this with casualties of 264,443 killed, 41,327 missing, and 277,077 wounded.

Alan Allport

See also
Airborne Forces, Allied; Alexander, Harold Rupert Leofric George; Armored Warfare; Brooke, Sir Alan Francis; Chindits; Churchill, Sir Winston L. S.; Combined Chiefs of Staff; Commandos/Rangers; Dill, Sir John Greer; Ironside, Sir William Edmund; Montgomery, Sir Bernard Law; OVERLORD, Operation; Slim, Sir William Joseph; Vereker, John Standish Surtees Pendergast (Gort, Lord); Wavell, Sir Archibald Percival; Wingate, Orde Charles

References
Brayley, Martin, and Mike Chappell. *The British Army, 1939–1945.* London: Osprey, 2001.
Chandler, David, ed. *The Oxford Illustrated History of the British Army.* Oxford, UK: Oxford University Press, 1994.
Crang, Jeremy. *The British Army and the People's War, 1939–1945.* Manchester, UK: Manchester University Press, 2000.
Fraser, David. *And We Shall Shock Them: The British Army in the Second World War.* London: Hodder and Stoughton, 1983.
French, David. *Raising Churchill's Army: The British Army and the War against Germany, 1919–1945.* Oxford, UK: Oxford University Press, 2000.
Graham, Dominick. *Against Odds: Reflections on the Experiences of the British Army, 1914–45.* New York: St. Martin's Press, 1999.
Place, Timothy. *Military Training in the British Army, 1940–1944: From Dunkirk to D-Day.* London: Frank Cass, 2000.

Great Britain, Auxiliary Territorial Service (ATS)

Women's unit of the British army that provided ancillary and support services. The ancestry of the Auxiliary Territorial Service (ATS) can be traced to the World War I Women's Army Auxiliary Corps (WAAC), a quasi-military female support unit created in January 1917 with the aim of freeing more men for fighting. Its 57,000 members served in clerical positions and as telephone operators, cooks, and waitresses, but its women "officers" were not granted military commissions or titles. It disbanded in 1921.

In September 1938, as European war seemed ever more likely, the British government decided to establish a women's auxiliary army to be attached to the existing territorial army. The new ATS incorporated the venerable First Aid Nursing Yeomanry (FANY), formed by Lord Horatio Herbert Kitchener in 1907, whose members constituted most of the ATS Transport Section. ATS recruits received two-thirds of the pay of men. Initially, numbers were small, and most new enlistees served as cooks or storekeepers or in clerical positions. In spring 1940, 300 volunteered to accompany the British Expeditionary Force (BEF) to France, and ATS telephonists were among the last British service personnel evacuated from Dunkerque, France.

With the April 1941 introduction of national civilian or military service for all childless and single British women aged between 18 and 30, ATS numbers rose dramatically, reaching 65,000 within six months. Only women between the ages of 17 and 43 were eligible to enlist, a provision waived for female WAAC veterans of the previous war. In July 1941, ATS enlistees were granted full military status, although no woman could be compelled to serve in situations where she might be subject to physical attack nor to operate a weapon without her prior consent. The range of ATS duties also expanded enormously. Among other duties, women functioned as mechanics, drivers, stevedores, orderlies, dental clerks, masseuses, photographers, munitions inspectors, and military police. They administered postal services and operated antiaircraft batteries, guns, and radar installations. Women were banned from active combat duty, but their ancillary functions were often physically hazardous, especially when they took part in overseas campaigns in Egypt, North Africa, Italy, France, and Asia. A total of 198,000 women joined the ATS, of whom 335 were killed on duty. Another 302 were wounded, 94 went missing in action, and 22 became prisoners of war, a rate proportionately higher than that in either the women's naval or aviation auxiliary services. In part, these figures reflected the fact that appreciable numbers of ATS women were recruited as agents for the dangerous Special Operations Executive (SOE), which mounted covert operations in occupied Europe and elsewhere.

Although the ATS continued in existence after 1945, its numbers fell precipitously as all British armed forces experienced substantial postwar demobilization. In 1949, the ATS was disbanded and its remaining members were absorbed in the new Women's Royal Army Corps, which in 1992 finally amalgamated completely with the British army.

Priscilla Roberts

See also
Great Britain, Army; Great Britain, Women's Auxiliary Air Force; Great Britain, Women's Royal Naval Service; Special Operations Executive; Women in World War II

References
Birdwell, S. *The Womens' Royal Army Corps.* London: Leo Cooper, 1977.
Cowper, J. M., comp. *The Auxiliary Territorial Service.* London: War Office, 1949.
Dady, Margaret. *A Woman's War: Life in the ATS.* Lewes, UK: Book Guild, 1986.
Gooding, Joan B. *They Gave Us Khaki Bloomers.* London: Avon, 1996.
Roy, Terry. *Women in Khaki: The Story of the British Woman Soldier.* London: Columbus, 1988.

Great Britain, Home Front

Prime Minister Neville Chamberlain headed a coalition government on the outbreak of war. When Britain declared war on Germany on 3 September 1939, the public mood was one of resignation rather than the enthusiasm that had greeted entry into World War I. Indeed, during the period September 1939–May 1940, the so-called Phony War, there was a rather nonchalant attitude toward the war.

The United Kingdom of England, Wales, Scotland, and Northern Ireland numbered nearly 48 million people. The nation had been battling the worldwide economic depression and, although the government had belatedly begun rearmament, much of the economy remained stagnant, and unemployment was high. Britain sustained few casualties in the early fighting, although the war was brought home by the mass evacuation of children from the cities, especially London, and imposition of a blackout at night. On the whole, however, domestic life was not much disturbed.

Although Parliament passed an Emergency Powers Act in September 1939 granting the government control of the economy, Chamberlain sought a more limited effort than was essential to bring victory. Aerial attack was a great concern, and the government endeavored to relocate families, especially those in London, to rural areas of the country. But Britain was slow to mobilize its assets for the war, especially its land forces. In the spring of 1940, Britain was still producing civilian automobiles, and unemployment was at 1 million people. Not until the German invasion of France and the Low Countries in May 1940 did the government and the people discover the true seriousness of the situation.

The Allied debacle in Norway precipitated a political crisis. Despite the fact that the Conservatives held a large majority in Parliament, Prime Minister Chamberlain was forced from office on 10 May 1940, the same day the German Army invaded France and the Low Countries. Former First Lord of the Admiralty Winston L. S. Churchill became prime minister. Completely committed to total victory, Churchill was one of history's great war leaders. Perhaps more at home in the nineteenth century, as far as spheres of influence and his attitude toward colonialism were concerned, Churchill was both eloquent and effective in rallying the British people behind the war effort. Flashing his famous "V for victory" sign, he later took it on himself to visit the bombed-out areas of London (unlike German leader Adolf Hitler, who never mingled with the German people). To the rest of the world, Churchill was the embodiment of British pluck and resolve.

Despite the efforts of his service chiefs to keep him at arm's length, Churchill insisted on a hands-on approach to the war, often intervening in military matters. The one sin for Churchill was inaction, but his decisions often had deleterious effects. Churchill also took a lively interest in scientific developments, in code-breaking, and in a wide range of schemes and gadgets that might be employed against the Axis powers.

Early on, Churchill developed a close relationship with President Franklin D. Roosevelt of the United States, but the British leader's vision of the world, in which Britain was a major imperial power, was fading. Churchill's influence over strategy also waned in the course of the war as the military strength of the United States grew dramatically vis-à-vis that of Great Britain.

With the German invasion of the west in May 1940, all the "phoniness" of the war disappeared. The government rapidly

Firemen at work in bomb-damaged street in London, after a German air attack in 1941. (New Times Paris Bureau Collection, National Archives)

expanded the Emergency War Powers Act of the year before, giving it "complete control over persons and property." The nation survived the debacle of the German conquest of Western Europe and the subsequent Battle of Britain, thanks to the English Channel, the Royal Navy, and the Royal Air Force (RAF). Citizens were proud of their defiant stand against Germany—what Churchill referred to as the nation's "finest hour." Despite depredations by Axis submarines, Britain continued to access world resources, and the next year both the Soviet Union and United States entered the war on its side, ensuring an eventual Allied victory.

With the nation at last committed to total war, economist John Maynard Keynes supervised a survey of British resources. Completed in 1941, it greatly aided the government in assuming the direction of the entire economy. The government introduced strict price controls and rationing and mobilized its civilian population fully for the war effort. The National Service (Armed Forces) Act of 2 December 1941 authorized conscription of all males ages 18 to 50 for the mil-

itary, industry, or other national service. In June 1944, some 22 percent of adults were in the military and another 33 percent were in civilian war work. Women played a key role; by 1944 they comprised 37.9 percent of the civilian labor force.

The British government enjoyed great success increasing its production of armaments. In 1940, for example, Britain produced more aircraft than Germany (15,049 to 10,249). Labour Party member Ernest Bevin was a highly effective minister of labor. There was little unrest among British workers, especially as burdens were seen to be shared, and the standard of living was not seriously depressed.

About half of national resources went into the war effort, as exports dropped off and imports, especially of food, rose. The government sharply raised taxes to avoid as much borrowing as possible. The basic tax rate was 50 percent, whereas excess business profits were taxed at 100 percent. Some called this tax policy "war socialism." Without Lend-Lease from the United States and assistance from Commonwealth nations, however, it would have been very difficult for Britain to survive.

Britain suffered far less material damage than most other warring states. It sustained in the war 244,723 military and 60,595 civilian deaths. But Britain's massive wartime effort, the expenditure of capital at home, the recall of overseas investment, the disruption of trade, and deficit spending all hastened a national economic decline already in progress. The hardships of war that imparted a sense of a shared national effort also heightened interest in reform at the end of the war. As early as 1942, the Beveridge Report called for establishment after the war of a minimum income level, medical insurance, and cradle-to-grave security for all citizens. Even during the war, Parliament extended to the entire population the right to a secondary school education. Popular interest in wide-ranging reform was not understood by Churchill, who focused almost exclusively on the war, but this mood led the Labour Party leadership to demand elections after the defeat of Germany. Held in July 1945 while the war against Japan was still in progress, the elections produced a surprising Labour upset; the party won 393 of the 640 seats in the House of Commons. In a nearly seamless transition, Labour leader and Deputy Prime Minister Clement Attlee replaced Churchill in the midst of the Potsdam Conference.

Although the United Kingdom experienced the exhilaration of victory, the country was hard hit economically and socially. Indeed, to finance long overdue social legislation, the Labour government was forced to cut in many other areas. The government also began a program of retrenchment abroad, and this meant giving full independence to much of the British Empire—India being the most dramatic example. The Labour government also soon determined that Britain could no longer continue as the world's policeman, and by 1947 it had largely passed that burden to the United States.

Spencer C. Tucker

See also
Attlee, Clement Richard; Chamberlain, Arthur Neville; Churchill, Sir Winston L. S.; Lend-Lease; Potsdam Conference; Roosevelt, Franklin D.

References
Addison, Paul. *The Road to 1945: British Politics and the Second World War.* London: Pimlico, 1994.
Calder, Angus. *The People's War: Britain, 1939–1945.* New York: Pantheon Books, 1969.
Churchill, Winston S. *The Second World War.* 6 vols. Boston: Houghton Mifflin, 1948–1953.
Hylton, Stuart. *Their Darkest Hour: The Hidden History of the Home Front, 1939–1945.* Stroud, UK: Sutton, 2001.
Lee, J. M. *The Churchill Coalition, 1940–1945.* Hamden, CT: Archon Books, 1980.
Lewis, Peter. *A People's War.* London: Thames Methuen, 1986.
Mackay, Robert. *Civilian Morale in Britain during the Second World War.* Manchester, UK: Manchester University Press, 2002.
Marwick, A. *The Home Front: The British and the Second World War.* London: Thames and Hudson, 1976.
Smith, H., ed. *War and Social Change: British Society in the Second World War.* Manchester, UK: Manchester University Press, 1986.

Great Britain, Navy

The somewhat disappointing performance of the Royal Navy during World War I led to considerable improvements in many tactical and operational areas by 1939. Despite the treaty limitations of the interwar years, the Royal Navy had reemerged as the world's dominant naval force by 1939. (The U.S. Navy did not embark on a massive rebuilding program until the Two Ocean Navy Act of 1940, and it became the larger naval and maritime force only by 1944.) Significant improvements in tactical and operational doctrine occurred in the 1920s and 1930s, especially in surface action and night-fighting techniques. In contrast to the lack of offensive-mindedness with concomitant reluctance to risk assets that characterized the Royal Navy in World War I, the Royal Navy of 1939 was imbued with a reinvigorated offensive spirit.

Weaknesses did hamper operations, notably the poor state of naval aviation, particularly when compared with naval aviation in the United States and Japan. Of the seven aircraft carriers in service at the start of 1939, only the *Ark Royal* (laid down in 1935) could be considered a modern carrier. Four of the other six had been modified earlier from battleship or battle cruiser hulls. The five new fleet carriers under construction would not begin operational service until well into 1940.

Despite the lessons of antisubmarine warfare (ASW) learned by 1918 and the need to protect merchant shipping and convoys, the Royal Navy had relatively poor commerce protection capabilities in 1939. Warship design had primarily emphasized coastal protection and submarine hunting, resulting in the short-range corvette ship type, which first came into service in 1939, and small escort destroyers. Although these ships had long-endurance capabilities, they proved unsuitable for open-ocean convoy escort primarily because of their size. Open-ocean convoy protection had been neglected, especially in training programs, and larger destroyers capable of trans-Atlantic convoy protection were in short supply. Despite the drawbacks, Britain managed to improve ASW capability and assets fairly quickly in response to the German U-boat threat. Although the smaller corvettes proved minimally effective for long-range mid-ocean operations, their successor—the larger, more seaworthy frigate, particularly the *River*-class dating from the 1940 building program—proved especially effective for convoy escort after 1942.

The initial German threat came from a three-part German offensive against commerce (*Handelskreig*) based on submarines, mines, and surface raiders. The Royal Navy quickly and effectively addressed each threat, although significant casualties did occur. Germany began the war with not many more submarines than it had at the start of World War I—just 51 operational U-boats, about half of them coastal vessels. The organization of British convoys in the Western Approaches, combined with the Straits of Dover mine barrage, resulted in nine U-boats sunk by the end of 1939.

Although some vessels were lost to German mines, the navy reduced this menace with new technology, including degaussing against magnetic mines. Surface raiders threatened British commerce, particularly in the remote waters of the Indian Ocean and South Atlantic. Although Germans raiders such as the *Atlantis* and pocket battleship *Graf Spee* provided some tense moments early in the war, by late 1941 most surface raiders had been hunted down and sunk.

In April 1940, Germany attacked Norway, primarily to secure its northern flank and the vital iron ore trade with Sweden. The British navy opposed the German landings, but a daring run of 10 German destroyers into Narvik subdued the Norwegian defenses. The combination of the entire German surface fleet with German land-based air power quickly resulted in the occupation of Norway. Reacting to the German moves, a Royal Navy force of destroyers attacked the Germans at Narvik, but it suffered heavy losses. A follow-on attack three days later by a large force based around the battleship *Warspite* devastated the Germans, which severely hampered future enemy surface operations. Ultimately, though, the Royal Navy could not prevent German victory, especially in the face of effective enemy airpower. Additionally, the German fast battleships *Scharnhorst* and *Gneisenau* sank the fleet carrier *Glorious*.

The fall of France and loss of French ports heralded a realignment of Royal Navy forces, because prior to World War I, Britain had relied on France for the bulk of Mediterranean sea power. With the appearance of a hostile Vichy government, though, the navy established Force H based at Gibraltar under Vice Admiral Sir James Somerville and charged with controlling the western Mediterranean. Force H carried out a distasteful duty in the bombardment of the French Fleet at Mers-el-Kébir in July 1940. Force H also played a central role in the destruction of the German battleship *Bismarck* in May 1941, as well as in hunting down and destroying the Atlantic commerce raiders. But the loss of France allowed Germany to base long-range U-boats in Bay of Biscay ports such as Brest and Lorient. The toll on British and Imperial shipping dramatically increased by autumn 1940 as Adolf Hitler declared (on 17 August 1940) a total blockade of the British Isles.

By autumn 1941, the tide in the commerce war had turned in favor of Britain. Escort ships provided by the United States (50 World War I–era destroyers) and the increasing number of Royal Canadian Navy destroyers, improved detection equipment including radar; high-frequency direction-finding sets and Antisubmarine Detection Investigation Committee (ASDIC or sonar), implementation of a cohesive and effective enemy submarine tracking system based on radio intercepts and code-breaking, and better cooperation with RAF Coastal Command all contributed to the reduction of the German submarine threat and effectiveness. Additionally, Germany's loss of the *Bismarck* and the relatively ineffective German effort to use heavy surface units to interdict the convoys to the northern Soviet Union across the Arctic above Norway all helped to lessen the threat to British maritime commerce by the middle of 1943. The Soviet convoys began receiving more robust escort following the destruction of the ill-fated PQ17 convoy in summer 1942. This enhanced escort included greater destroyer strength and escort carriers. The destruction of the battleship *Scharnhorst* off the Norwegian North Cape in December 1943 by a British battleship and cruiser force essentially ended the German surface threat to British and Allied maritime shipping.

Finally, despite a high number of U-boats operating in the Atlantic by March 1943 (up to 70 at any given time), the increasing skill of Allied submarine hunters and the closing of the "Black Hole" area south of Greenland, where air cover had not been previously available, meant a diminishing submarine threat and higher losses in U-boats. Escort carriers provided air cover while long-range maritime patrol aircraft (primarily modified B-24 Liberator bombers) made U-boat operations less effective. Additionally, hunter-killer escort groups attached to vulnerable convoys mauled the Germans.

In the Mediterranean, Italy's entry into the war in May 1940 required reinforcement of the theater naval forces under Admiral Sir Andrew Cunningham. With some modernized older battleships and the new carrier *Illustrious*, Cunningham defeated the Italians in fleet engagements at Calabria in July 1940 and Cape Matapan in March 1941 and raided the Italian anchorage at Taranto in November 1941 with naval aircraft. Cunningham stressed the improvement of antiaircraft protection, which paid off as the naval war in the Mediterranean increasingly devolved into attacks on shipping and naval vessels by Axis aircraft.

Faced with substantial damage to their supply convoys by British destroyers and submarines, the Germans dispatched U-boats to the Mediterranean in October 1941, resulting in the sinking of the battleship *Barham* and the carrier *Ark Royal*. At the fleet anchorage in Alexandria, the battleships *Queen Elizabeth* and *Valiant* were sunk at their moorings by Italian *Maiale* human torpedoes.

Faced with the loss of capital ships and the threat of enemy aircraft and submarine attack, British resources in the Mediterranean were stretched dangerously thin. Malta, the linchpin of Britain's efforts to hold the Mediterranean, came under horrendous air attack. Convoys to resupply and reinforce the island suffered substantial casualties, among them the aircraft carrier *Eagle*.

The British aircraft carrier Ark Royal, seen from an accompanying destroyer, ca. 1940. (Hulton Archive)

The entry of the United States into the war in December 1941 had a profound impact on the Mediterranean Theater. Operation TORCH, the Allied landings in North Africa in November 1942, resulted in the eventual destruction of Axis forces in North Africa. Reinforced and reconstituted, the Mediterranean Fleet conducted an ambitious and destructive assault on Italian shipping throughout 1942 and 1943 that crippled enemy resupply efforts. Cunningham admonished his sailors and airmen to "sink, burn and destroy: let nothing pass." By the end of 1942, Britain had again established maritime supremacy in the Mediterranean, despite substantial losses.

In the Pacific Theater, Japan entered the war against Britain concurrent with the assault on the United States. Quickly overrunning Hong Kong, the Japanese army forced the capitulation of Singapore, Britain's "Gibraltar of the Pacific." Faced with the loss of basing facilities, the Royal Navy withdrew from Southeast Asian waters, particularly after the loss of the battleship *Prince of Wales* and battle cruiser *Repulse* to air attack in December 1941 (Force Z under Admiral Sir Tom Phillips). The admiral's disregard of the air threat coupled with woefully inadequate antiaircraft protection (the navy had only two modern destroyers) greatly aided the land-based Japanese aviators, who easily sank both capital ships.

Following the crippling of the U.S. Pacific Fleet at Pearl Harbor, Japan's main striking force—Vice Admiral Nagumo Chūichi's First Air Fleet—wreaked havoc on the remnants of British sea power in the Indian Ocean in spring 1942. In carrier-based air attacks against British surface units, the veteran Japanese naval aviators sank detached portions of Admiral Sir James Somerville's forces based in Ceylon, including two cruisers and the carrier *Hermes*. However, Somerville avoided a general action and preserved his force as the Japanese withdrew to support their thrust into New Guinea and the Solomon Islands. Naval action in the Pacific Theater after May 1942 involved mainly U.S. and Australian naval units, but, with the defeat of Germany in May 1945, the Royal Navy again engaged Japan with substantial forces.

Under Admiral Sir Bruce Fraser, the Pacific Fleet of four carriers (later joined by two additional decks) and two battleships with substantial escort destroyers and cruisers arrived in the Pacific in March 1945, where they joined the Americans in the assault on the Japanese home islands and Okinawa. Equipped with the U.S. Hellcat and Corsair fighters, Royal Naval aviators did great destruction to the Japanese. American aircraft proved greatly superior to earlier British Seafire (modified from the Spitfire), Martlet, Fulmar, and Sea Hurricane models. The heavily armored British carrier decks proved worthwhile as a defense against Japanese suicide kamikaze aircraft (the lightly armored American carriers suffered more extensive damage).

From strategic and operational viewpoints, the Royal Navy performed exceptionally well in the war. Although losses were heavy (1,525 warships of all types, including 224 major surface units of which 5 were battleships or battle cruisers and 5 were fleet carriers; and 50,000 personnel dead), the aggressiveness and risk-taking nature of senior and individual ship commanding officers overcame the tenacious and highly competent Axis opponents. In the Atlantic, the Axis commerce warfare offensive failed to starve the country into submission or impede the arrival of overwhelming U.S. forces and personnel. In the Mediterranean, the Royal Navy kept British and Imperial ground and air forces supplied and reinforced while simultaneously strangling the Axis supply lines to North Africa. In the Pacific, despite initial defeats by the Japanese, British sea power returned late in the conflict and helped the U.S. Navy carry the fight to the Japanese home islands. As it had not done in the previous war, the navy at all levels showed exceptional ability to adapt rapidly to technological and methodical innovations and advances in doctrine, organization, and training. To man the new ships of more than 900 major combatants and the supporting shore establishment (training, research, logistics, support, and administration), by war's end Royal Naval personnel had increased from the prewar 129,000 to 863,500, which included 72,000 women in the Women's Royal Naval Service (WRNS). In short, the navy vindicated itself following the disappointments of World War I. British sea power both kept Britain in the fight until the United States arrived in force and subsequently provided the domination needed to attack the Axis powers at all vulnerable points with little interference.

Stanley D. M. Carpenter

See also

Aircraft, Fighters; Antisubmarine Warfare; Atlantic, Battle of the; Aviation, Naval; *Bismarck,* Sortie and Sinking of; Calabria, Battle of; Cape Matapan, Battle of; CATAPULT, Operation; Commerce Raiders, German Surface; Convoy PQ 17; Convoys, Allied; Crete, Naval Operations off; Cunningham, Sir Andrew Browne; Depth Charges; Destroyers-Bases Deal; Dönitz, Karl; Fraser, Bruce Austin; Hunter-Killer Groups; Indian Ocean, Japanese Naval Operations in; Kamikaze; Malta; Mers-el-Kébir; Mines, Sea; Minesweeping and Minelaying; Narvik, Naval Battles of; Naval Warfare; North Africa Campaign; North Cape, Battle of; Norway, German Conquest of; Phillips, Sir Tom Vaughan; *Prince of Wales* and *Repulse; Royal Oak,* Sinking of; Singapore, Battle for; Somerville, Sir James Fownes; Sonar; Southwest Pacific Theater; Taranto, Attack on; TORCH, Operation; Two Ocean Navy Program

References

Barnett, Correlli. *Engage the Enemy More Closely: The Royal Navy in the Second World War.* New York: W. W. Norton, 1991.

Gray, Edwyn. *Operation Pacific: The Royal Navy's War against Japan, 1941–1945.* London: Cooper, 1990.

Jackson, Robert. *The Royal Navy in World War II.* Annapolis, MD: Naval Institute Press, 1997.

Roskill, Stephen W. *The War at Sea, 1939–1945.* 4 vols. London: Her Majesty's Stationery Office, 1954–61.

———. *White Ensign: The British Navy at War, 1939–1945.* Annapolis, MD: Naval Institute Press, 1960.

Titterton, G. A. *The Royal Navy and the Mediterranean.* Vol. 1. London: Whitehall History in association with Frank Cass, 2002.

Great Britain, Women's Auxiliary Air Force (WAAF)

Women's arm of the Royal Air Force that provided support services. In September 1939, the Women's Auxiliary Air Force (WAAF), an auxiliary branch of the Royal Air Force (RAF) with a mission to provide support services tailored to RAF needs, was established. Its precedent was the Women's Royal Air Force (WRAF), which came into existence on 1 April 1918 during World War I and was disbanded exactly two years later.

On 10 April 1941, the WAAF was formally incorporated as an official part of the armed services of the British crown. Theoretically, only women aged between 18 and 43 could serve in the WAAF, but some members, especially those with World War I service credentials, were older, and one young woman who managed to join at the age of 14 was allowed to remain. A total of 171,200 women served in the WAAF, 187 of whom were killed in service. Another 420 were wounded, and 4 went missing while on duty.

Although British women aged between 18 and 30 were subject to conscription for war work from 1941 onward, they were permitted to choose agriculture, industrial work, or the armed services. Even in the women's auxiliary units of the armed forces, moreover, no woman could be compelled to serve in a situation in which she might have to wield a weapon. As with their female naval counterparts, members of the WAAF had a particularly glamorous reputation, which their relatively smart uniforms and association with the much-admired pilots enhanced.

Although supposedly restricted to noncombat roles, WAAFs often had important responsibilities, especially when functioning either as radar plotters to track incoming hostile airplanes and warn of forthcoming air raids or as radar controllers directing formations of British fighters and bombers. Many young women relished the independence and freedom such employment conferred on them. WAAFs also served in a wide variety of clerical and other support roles—as drivers and mechanics, for example—freeing up

WAAF personnel work on the advanced rigging maintenance of a Lysander aircraft. (Hulton Archive)

men for active duty. A small minority of women became pilots, although to do so they had to join the Air Transport Auxiliary (ATA) and become civilians. They were restricted to ferrying and delivering airplanes and could not undertake combat duties. Thousands of WAAFs served overseas in the Egyptian and North African Campaigns and in Europe, controlling air operations as Allied forces advanced. Some WAAFs were also recruited for dangerous clandestine work in the Special Operations Executive, which mounted covert operations in countries occupied by Axis powers. Others took part in ULTRA code-breaking operations at Bletchley Park. The British Dominions, Canada, New Zealand, and Australia all established similar women's auxiliary air forces.

In recognition of WAAF wartime contributions, the service remained in existence after World War II, although by 1950 only 517 of the wartime recruits remained in the service. In 1948, however, 14 WAAFs who were ex-ATA members became flying officers. In February 1949, the WAAF reverted to its old name and once again became the WRAF, and in 1994 it finally merged completely with the RAF.

Priscilla Roberts

See also

Bletchley Park; Great Britain, Air Force; Great Britain, Auxiliary Territorial Service; Great Britain, Women's Royal Naval Service; Special Operations Executive; Women in World War II

References

Escott, Beryl E. *Our Wartime Days: The WAAF in World War II.* Stroud, UK: Sutton, 1996.

Hall, Archie, ed. *We, Also, Were There: A Collection of Recollections of Wartime Women of Bomber Command.* Braunton, UK: Merlin, 1985.

Small, A. N., ed. *Spit, Polish and Tears.* Edinburgh, UK: Pentland Press, 1995.

Stone, Tessa. "The Integration of Women into a Military Service: The Women's Auxiliary Air Force in the Second World War." Ph.D. dissertation, University of Cambridge, 1998.

Great Britain, Women's Land Army (WLA)

The Women's Land Army (WLA) was a British wartime program to provide female laborers to help overcome labor shortages in agriculture. As war clouds began to gather in the 1930s, British government officials realized that if war should break out, the country would require numerous additional workers. For agricultural work, officials made plans to find more laborers from a variety of sources including older and younger workers, seasonal labor from nearby towns, and, as the war progressed, prisoners of war. The most widely publicized effort was the Women's Land Army.

In April 1938, the government asked Lady Gertrude Denman, the dynamic head of the Women's Institutes, to lead the new organization. Using a Women's Land Army formed in World War I as a guide, Lady Denman, her coworkers, and local authorities were able to launch a national recruiting campaign in the spring and summer of 1939. By the time the call came in September, more than 1,000 volunteers had signed up, and soon afterward WLA recruits began arriving at British farmsteads.

The "land girls," as they were called, had to be at least age 17 to join. They were primarily from cities, where they had been employed as barmaids, hairdressers, store clerks, and in other similar positions. They underwent four weeks of training and then were sent to individual farms or lived under supervision in hostels. They were given uniforms consisting of a green sweater; brown, knee-length trousers; high black boots; a light brown overcoat; and a brown felt hat. They usually worked 11-hour days and were to have half a day per week and Sundays off, but often that was impossible because of the nature of their jobs. They did all kinds of work, from weeding and threshing to cleaning ditches and milking cows. Some eventually became tractor drivers. They were paid the equivalent of about $3.50 per week, half of it for room and board.

Farmers at first were reluctant to hire WLA workers. By the spring of 1940, however, the labor market had become tighter, and farmers became more receptive to the idea. By the end of the year, 6,000 women were working in rural areas. The number reached a peak of 87,000 in July 1943, and total of 250,000 had enrolled by war's end.

Shirley Joseph has written movingly about her life as a land girl. She recalled being interviewed and asked, among other things, whether she realized that cows had to be milked every day. She was then trained and sent out to work. Her first job was at Warborough farm in Oxfordshire, where she worked from 6:15 A.M. to 5:00 P.M., and her most important task was to assist with morning and late-afternoon milking. On Wednesdays, she received a half day off and often used the time to hitchhike to her home nearby. She lived part of the time in a cottage with no electricity and no running water. Later she worked out of three different hostels, and although she was allowed to do some milking, her main jobs were threshing and hoeing crops, which she described as dirty, hard work. She remembered hard bunks, queuing for meals,

Jocelyn Elliott of the Women's Land Army holding up silage she is feeding to cattle, March 1941. (Photo by Central Press/Getty Images)

the total lack of privacy, boyfriends (some of them American GIs), and long hours of work. Her experiences were probably typical of those who served.

The Women's Land Army gained increasing acceptance from the public, partly because it was well organized. Lady Denman and other WLA leaders gave talks over the radio about the Land Army's service, kept local supervisors informed, and even published a magazine, *The Land Girl,* that was distributed to the workers. Denman was also able to enlist influential patrons. Queen Mary, for example, was a major supporter, and she employed land girls at one of the royal family's country estates. Although the Women's Land Army may not have played as large a role in solving the agricultural labor problem as its backers have claimed, it did help, and it was a worthwhile experiment.

Alan F. Wilt

See also
Women in World War II
References
Joseph, Shirley. *If Their Mothers Only Knew: An Unofficial Account of Life in the Women's Land Army.* London: Faber, 1946.
Sackville-West, Victoria. *The Women's Land Army.* London: Michael Joseph, 1944.
Tyrer, Nicola. *They Fought in the Fields: The Women's Land Army: The Struggle of a Forgotten Victory.* London: Sinclair and Stevenson, 1996.

Great Britain, Women's Royal Naval Service (WRNS)

Women's arm of the British Royal Navy, reconstituted in 1939. The Women's Royal Naval Service was first created in 1917, during World War I. Before the organization was disbanded on 1 October 1919, 6,000 British women had undertaken naval support duties, during the course of which 23 died.

In 1938, on the approach of another war, planning began to reestablish the WRNS. The organization was reconstituted in April 1939 under the direction of Vera Laughton Mathews. Enlistment was initially voluntary, but under the April 1941 Registration of Employment Order, all single and childless British women aged between 19 and 30 and not yet engaged in work "essential to the war effort" became subject to conscription and were offered the choice of factory work, service in one of the auxiliary service units, or enrollment in the Women's Land Army.

As with the other female auxiliary services, especially the Women's Auxiliary Air Force, the WRNS (its members were called Wrens) constituted something of a prestigious and elite service. In the course of the war, 74,620 women enlisted in the WRNS, of whom 102 were killed and 22 wounded. Government regulations prevented female civilian volunteers and military personnel to serve without their consent in hazardous circumstances in which they were liable to come under physical attack—manning antiaircraft guns, for example—nor could they be compelled to operate weapons. Even in the auxiliary armed forces, women were restricted to noncombat roles, and the primary function of WRNS members was perceived as releasing male naval personnel from shore jobs. As the war progressed, however, the WRNS and other female auxiliary military units undertook an increasingly wide range of duties—more than 200 jobs by 1944. Many served in clerical positions or as wireless telegraphists, electricians, fitters, radio mechanics, photographers, technicians, cooks, stewards, gardeners, dispatch riders, or stokers; others helped to plan and organize naval operations. Thousands served overseas, often in hazardous conditions. A small minority qualified as naval pilots, although, as with those in the quasi-civilian Air Transport Service, they were normally barred from combat duties and restricted to ferrying planes.

Thousands of women also enlisted in associated naval units including the Fleet Air Arm, Coastal Forces, Combined Operations, and the Royal Marines. In all, 303 British women died during World War II while on active duty in the various naval services. Canada, Australia, and New Zealand established similar women's naval auxiliary services. British women's naval contributions were highly respected, and the WRNS became a permanent service arm in February 1949. In 1993, the WRNS disappeared as a separate unit when it became fully integrated into the British navy.

Priscilla Roberts

See also
Great Britain, Auxiliary Territorial Service; Great Britain, Navy; Great Britain, Women's Auxiliary Air Force; Women in World War II
References
Fletcher, M. H. *The WRNS: A History of the Women's Royal Naval Service.* Annapolis, MD: Naval Institute Press, 1989.
Mathews, Dame Vera Laughton. *Blue Tapestry: An Account of the Women's Royal Naval Service.* London: Hollis and Carter, 1948.
Pushman, Muriel Gane. *We All Wore Blue.* London: Robson, 1989.
Thomas, Lesley, and Chris Howard Bailey. *WRNS in Camera: The Women's Royal Naval Service in the Second World War.* Sutton, UK: Stroud, 2002.
Wilson, Rosemary Curtis. *C/o GPO London: With the Women's Royal Naval Service Overseas.* London: Hutchinson, 1949.

Greece, Air Force

In 1940, Greece's Air Ministry administered the Royal Greek Air Force (*Vassiliki Aeroporia*). The navy controlled the naval cooperation squadrons, and the army controlled fighters, bombers, and ground-support squadrons. The Greek air force's modern aircraft were grouped into four fighter squadrons and three bomber squadrons. At the start of the war with Italy in October 1940, Greece deployed 216 first- and second-line aircraft of all types, including liaison. Greece also had about 60 obsolete aircraft dating back to World War I. At the beginning of its invasion of Greece, Italy operated 187 modern aircraft from Albania, and it could also draw on hundreds of aircraft operating from Italy. The Greek air force was composed of a mélange of Czech, Polish, German, French, and later British machines. Greece had no reserves and was totally dependent on the British for resupply. Securing replacement parts was a nightmare, and the lack of parts meant that many aircraft became inoperable.

During 1940 and 1941, the Greek air force aggressively operated with some success in support of army operations on the Albanian Front. However, as the army advanced into mountainous Albania, flying distances became longer and more problematic, whereas Italian aircraft were able to operate closer to their own bases. By the time Germany invaded Greece in April 1941, the Greek air force was down to 41 operational aircraft. Following the Axis victory at the end of April, the Greek government in exile maintained an air force of two fighter squadrons and one bomber squadron in the Mediterranean under British control.

Jack Greene

See also

Aircraft, Bombers; Aircraft, Fighters; Greece, Army; Greece, Navy; Greece Campaign (28 October 1940–March 1941); Greece Campaign (1941)

References

Arena, Nino. *La Regia Aeronautica, 1939–1943.* Vols. 1–4. Rome: Uffico Storico, 1982–1986.

Shores, Christopher, et al. *Air War for Yugoslavia, Greece and Crete, 1940–41.* Carrollton, TX: Squadron Signal Publications, 1987.

Greece, Army

In October 1940, at the time of the Italian invasion, the Greek army, commanded by General Alexandros Papagos, numbered some 430,000 men in 18 divisions. By April 1941, when the Germans invaded Greece, army strength was some 540,000 men. Each division numbered at full strength approximately 18,500 men, formed in three regiments of three battalions each. Most of these were of World War I type and were lightly armed mountain divisions. The army had almost no tanks, although in the course of the fighting the Greeks captured some Italian L3 "tankettes" and formed a weak motorized division. The Greeks also had little in the way of antiaircraft artillery, and much of the army's equipment was also antiquated. Although the Greeks had few mortars, they possessed more machine guns and more effective heavy artillery than did the Italians. Greek supply services were poor, leading to much hardship among the troops in the mountains and during the winter.

In October 1940, when the Italian army invaded from Albania, the Greek army had four first-line divisions on the Albanian frontier. The Greek army fought well against the Italians; in its counterattack, it expelled the Italian army from Greece and penetrated into Albania. The Greeks were overwhelmed when the German army entered the fighting in April 1941, however. During the 1940–1941 campaign, the Greek army sustained 13,408 killed and 42,485 wounded. Some 9,000 soldiers were evacuated to Crete, and others escaped through Turkey to Egypt. Ultimately, the Greeks formed the 18,500-man Royal Hellenic Army, which fought under British command in the Middle East. It consisted of three infantry brigades, an armored-car regiment, an artillery regiment, and the Greek Sacred Regiment composed entirely of officers.

Greek gun crew at work during the campaign in Albania in 1940. (Library of Congress)

One brigade of the Royal Hellenic Army fought in the Battle of El Alamein, but most of the force saw little action, the consequence of political infighting. A mutiny in 1944 led to the internment of much of the army, although part of it was used in nonoperational duties. A newly formed unit, the 2,500-man Third Mountain Brigade, did fight with distinction in the Italian Campaign, where it was known as the Rimini Brigade.

Spencer C. Tucker

See also

Greece, Air Force; Greece, Navy; Greece, Role in War; Greece Campaign (28 October 1940–March 1941); Papagos, Alexandros

References

Bitzes, John G. *Greece in World War II to April 1941.* Manhattan, KS: Sunflower Press, 1989.

Dear, I. C. B., and M. R. D. Foot. *The Oxford Companion to World War II.* New York: Oxford University Press, 1995.

Higham, Robin, and T. Veremis, eds. *The Metaxas Dictatorship: Aspects of Greece, 1936–1940.* Athens: Hellenic Foundation for Defense and Foreign Policy, 1993.

Montanari, Mario. *L'Esercito Italiano nella campagna di Grecia.* 2d ed. Rome: Ufficio Storico, 1991.

Spyopoulos, Evangelos. *The Greek Military (1909–1947) and the Greek Mutiny in the Middle East (1941–1944).* New York: Columbia University Press, 1993.

Greece, Navy

In late 1939 the Royal Hellenic Navy (RHN) was a relatively small force of obsolescent warships, some of which dated to before World War I. The navy consisted of the armored cruiser *Giorgios Averoff* (built in Italy in 1910), six destroyers, six submarines, one minelayer, several torpedo boats, and an assortment of auxiliary vessels. No warships were under construction, although the RHN planned to take delivery of two additional (British-built) destroyers. In addition to generally obsolete equipment, the RHN suffered from the national political schism of the 1930s that brought purges of the officer corps.

In mid-1940, Italy began a period of harassment that included air attacks on Greek ships at sea and the sinking on 15 August 1940 of the anchored minelayer *Helle* by the Italian submarine *Delfino*. Once Italy declared war on Greece on 28 October 1940, the RHN was active in supporting the army and in conducting destroyer sweeps in the Ionian Sea. The RHN experienced severe losses from air attacks following the April 1941 German invasion of Greece. The surviving Greek ships, their bases seized by Germans troops, withdrew first to Crete and then to Egypt, where they were integrated into the British Royal Navy.

The Royal Navy had operational control of the Greek ships, and the RHN was responsible for their administration. The Greek ships were in need of refit and modernization, and they received from the British Navy modern fire-control systems and antiaircraft and antisubmarine armaments. The British also transferred to the RHN a variety of destroyers, corvettes, submarines, and smaller craft, including minesweepers.

RHN ships then served throughout the eastern Mediterranean. Beginning in 1942, the RHN experienced nearly continual political unrest concerning the composition of the Greek government in exile. This culminated in the April 1944 mutiny of virtually the entire RHN at Alexandria and Port Said. Although the mutiny was crushed, the Greek ships were out of action for about four months while units were purged of mutineers.

After the German retreat from the Balkans, in October 1944 the RHN returned to Greek waters. It spent the remainder of the war reestablishing itself in its home territory, opening ports, engaging communist groups that resisted the return of the government from Egypt, and containing German garrisons on the larger islands of the Aegean Sea.

Mark C. Jones

See also

Greece, Air Force; Greece, Army; Greece, Role in War; Mediterranean Theater; Metaxas, Ioannis

References

Jones, Mark C. "Misunderstood and Forgotten: The Greek Naval Mutiny of April 1944." *Journal of Modern Greek Studies* 20, no. 2 (2001): 367–397.

Païzis-Paradellis, Constantin. *Hellenic Warships, 1829–2001.* Athens: Society for the Study of Greek History, 2002.

Papastratis, Procopis. "A Fighting Navy in Exile: The Greek Fleet in the Mediterranean and Beyond." In Jack Sweetman, ed., *New Interpretations in Naval History: Tenth Naval History Symposium,* 363–373. Annapolis, MD: Naval Institute Press, 1991.

Greece, Role in War

The nation of Greece, with a population of some 7.3 million people in 1940, was drawn into World War II by Italy's invasion from Albania. Greek dictator General Ioannis Metaxas had sought to maintain his nation's neutrality, but that policy ended when an Italian invasion began a Balkan campaign that drew in Britain as well as Germany and other Axis powers. The result of these developments was Axis control of the Balkans until the last months of the war. Greece suffered horribly in the war and continued to suffer in the years immediately afterward in a costly civil war from 1946 to 1949.

In October 1940, without informing his ally Adolf Hitler in advance, Italian dictator Benito Mussolini launched an invasion from Albania. Having both superior numbers and greater military hardware, Mussolini confidently expected to complete the conquest before winter set in. The Greeks, however, resisted valiantly. They not only held the Italians but went on the offensive and drove them back, while the British bombed Albania and neutralized the Italian navy. Mussolini's invasion of Greece turned into a disaster from which neither he nor his regime recovered. Determined to shore up his southern flank before he began an invasion of the Soviet Union, Hitler stepped in. Metaxas died at the end of January 1941, and in April the Führer sent the German army against both Greece and Yugoslavia, quickly overwhelming both. Neither the courage and will of the Greeks nor British army reinforcements sufficed to withstand the Luftwaffe and the panzers.

The Axis occupation of Greece involved German, Italian, and Bulgarian troops and lasted three years. It was a dark period in the history of a nation that had undergone much suffering since Roman times. The Germans set up a puppet government and insisted that the Greeks pay the full cost of the occupation, which resulted in catastrophic inflation. The Germans also requisitioned resources and supplies, with no concern for the fate of a population that, even in the best of times, was obliged to import most of its food. Famine and disease decimated Greece and killed perhaps 100,000 people in the winter of 1941–1942 alone. The suffering was such that British Prime Minister Winston L. S. Churchill agreed— under pressure from the Greek government in exile and the United States—to partially lift the blockade so the International Red Cross might bring in food supplies. Greeks living in Western Thrace and Eastern Macedonia also had to undergo forced Bulgarianization. The flourishing Jewish community in Salonika was devastated in the Holocaust; fewer than 10,000 of an estimated 70,000 Greek Jews survived the war. The Greek underground fought back with sabotage and ambush and tied down 120,000 Axis troops. In reprisal, the Germans and Italians burned whole villages and executed large numbers of Greek hostages for every Axis soldier slain.

Greek King George II and his ministers went into exile in Egypt with the retreating British forces in 1941. Almost immediately, Greek resistance groups formed. Of the various resistance movements that had appeared during the German occupation, the largest was the National Liberation Front (EAM), with the National People's Liberation Army as its military wing. Relations were poor between it and the National Republican Greek League. Indeed, actual fighting broke out between the two groups in the winter of 1943–1944, although a truce was arranged in February 1944. As in Yugoslavia, the communist-dominated EAM apparently enjoyed wider support than the nationalist underground. When the Germans pulled out of Greece, EAM held the vast majority of the country. Greek society was fractured into three factions: the monarchists, republicans, and communists.

At approximately the same time, in October 1944 Churchill journeyed to Moscow to meet with Soviet leader Josef Stalin. Churchill struck a bargain with Stalin concerning predominance in various Balkan states, under the terms of which Britain was to have 90 percent predominance in Greece. The Greek communists, who had carried the brunt of resistance

against the Axis and now controlled the majority of territory, understandably resented this imperial arrangement struck in Moscow and were unwilling to submit to it.

When the Nazis withdrew, George Papandreou, a left-of-center statesman, headed a government of national unity. Fearing the communist underground, however, he requested British troops, who began arriving early in October 1944. When the British called on the guerrilla forces to disarm and disband, EAM quit the cabinet, called a general strike, and held protest demonstrations. In this serious situation, Churchill took the impetuous decision to fly with foreign secretary Anthony Eden to Athens on Christmas Day 1944. Though the government and EAM reached accord early in 1945, it quickly broke down. EAM members took to the hills with their weapons.

In the first Greek elections, held in 1946, the Royalist People's Party was victorious, and a royalist ministry took office. A September 1946 plebiscite resulted in a majority vote for the king's return. King George II, who was unpopular in Greece, died the following April and was succeeded by his son Paul, who reigned until 1964.

By the end of 1946, communist rebels were ready to attempt a comeback, assisted by the communist governments of Yugoslavia, Bulgaria, and Albania. (Ironically, Tito's support for the civil war in defiance of Stalin was one reason Yugoslavia was subsequently expelled from the international communist movement). The communists came close to winning in Greece, but Greece was saved as a Western bastion because the British were determined that the nation—with its strategic control of the eastern Mediterranean—not become communist. But in February 1947, deep in its own economic problems, Britain informed a shocked Washington that it could no longer bear the burden of supporting Greece. U.S. President Harry S Truman agreed to take over the responsibility, and in March 1947, he announced the Truman Doctrine of aid to free nations threatened by internal or external aggression. This policy received the enthusiastic support of the U.S. Congress and an appropriation of $400 million for both Greece and Turkey. Ultimately, the United States contributed about $750 million for the final three years of guerrilla warfare.

Gradually, General Alexander Papagos, Greek commander in chief, dismissed incompetent officers and created a military force sufficient to turn the military tide. Another important factor was that Marshal Tito (Josip Broz) needed to concentrate on resisting Soviet pressures, cutting off many of the supplies for the rebel cause. By the end of 1949, the communists had been defeated and Greece saved for the West. The cost of the civil war to Greece was as great as the cost from the tormented years of World War II and the Nazi occupation. As with so many civil wars, the struggle had been waged without quarter on either side. Thousands of hostages had been taken and simply disappeared. A million Greeks had been uprooted and displaced by the fighting. Casualties may have been as high as half a million people—all of them Greeks killed by Greeks. After the war, the purges and reprisals continued for some time. Unfortunately for Greece, further upheaval fanned by other nations and dictatorship lay ahead before true democracy could be achieved.

Spencer C. Tucker

See also

Balkans Theater; Churchill, Sir Winston L. S.; Cold War, Origins and Early Course of; Eden, Sir Robert Anthony; Greece, Air Force; Greece, Army; Greece, Navy; Greece Campaign (28 October 1940–March 1941); Greece Campaign (April 1941); Metaxas, Iaonnis; Papagos, Aleksandros; Truman, Harry S

References

Clogg, Richard. *A Short History of Modern Greece.* Cambridge, UK: Cambridge University Press, 1979.

Hondros, John L. *Occupation and Resistance: The Greek Agony.* New York: Pella Publishing, 1983.

Mazower, M. *Inside Hitler's Greece: The Experience of Occupation, 1941–1944.* New Haven, CT: Yale University Press, 1993.

Woodhouse, C. M. *The Struggle for Greece, 1941–1949.* London: Hart-Davis, MacGibbon, 1976.

Greece Campaign (28 October 1940–March 1941)

In April 1939, Italian dictator Benito Mussolini ordered the Italian army to invade Albania to secure control of the Adriatic Sea. On taking over Albania, Italy began a major engineering project there to improve roads to the Greek border. This was accompanied by assurances from Rome to Athens that Italy would not attack Greece. Simultaneously, on 13 April, Britain and France extended guarantees to both Greece and Romania to preserve their integrity.

In spite of assurances to the Greek government, Italy was indeed planning an invasion. Code-named CASE G, the plan for an attack on Greece received major impetus from foreign minister (and Mussolini's son-in-law) Galeazzo Ciano, who was much involved in Albanian affairs and sponsored this operation to expand his influence over Greece as well. Mussolini also resented Adolf Hitler's decision to send German troops to Romania to protect the Ploesti oil fields, a move destroying Italian influence in Romania. Mussolini was determined to redress the Balkan balance.

On 15 October 1940, Mussolini met in Rome with his military leaders, including chief of General Staff Marshal Pietro Badoglio and deputy chief of the army staff General Mario Roatta, to discuss the attack on Greece. Also present was General Sebastiano Visconti-Prasca, commander of the Eleventh Army in Albania and author of the invasion plan, a much

shrunk CASE G. Although questions were raised during the meeting, none of those present seriously opposed the decision to begin the invasion in a few days. At this time, Mussolini wrote to Hitler seeking advice and informing him of his intentions; but by delaying sending this letter, Mussolini hoped to surprise his ally, just as Hitler had surprised him with his timing of the invasion of France. Hitler, who had accurate information about Italian intentions, made no effort to restrain his ally.

Before dawn on 28 October 1940, the Italian ambassador in Athens presented an ultimatum to Greek prime minister and dictator General Ioannis Metaxas, accusing Greece of allowing British ships to use Italy's territorial waters and demanding free passage of Italian troops on Greek soil. Athens rejected the ultimatum, and at 5:30 A.M. that same day, Italy began its invasion.

For the invasion, the Italians had deployed in Albania six infantry divisions (two regiments each, reinforced with a lightly armed Blackshirt Legion, with a total of 12,500 to 14,500 men in each division). These were the Siena, Ferrara, Piemonte, Parma, Venezia, and Arezzo Divisions. In addition, the Italians had the Centauro Armored Division and the Julia Alpine Division. In all, the army deployed some 150,000 men—giving them only a slight numerical superiority over the Greek army before mobilization, instead of the 2:1 advantage that Visconti-Prasca claimed.

The weather was poor, with torrential fall rains. The main body of the Italian troops, consisting of the Ferrara, Centauro, and Siena Divisions, advanced near the Adriatic coast where the terrain was more favorable, trying to push across the Kalamas River and reach Janina. The Julia Division attacked toward Metsovon Pass to penetrate between Epirus and Macedonia. To the extreme Italian left, the Parma and Piemonte Divisions were on the defensive at Korcë.

In defense along the Albanian border, the Greeks had deployed four infantry divisions of three regiments each. These resisted the invaders while King George II of Greece appealed to Britain for assistance. His request won friendly reception from British Prime Minister Winston L. S. Churchill. Although Metaxas, not wanting to offend Hitler, requested only weapons and equipment, Churchill favored sending an expeditionary force. In any case, London immediately dispatched five Royal Air Force (RAF) squadrons and an interservice mission.

On 31 October, British forces arrived on the islands of Crete and Lemnos, placing British bombers within range of the Romanian Ploesti oil fields. In response, on 4 November, Hitler ordered his Army High Command to begin preparations for a German attack on Greece.

The same day that the Italian invasion began, on 28 October, Mussolini met with Hitler in Florence and proudly informed him of the event. Mussolini's triumph was short-lived, however, as the Greek army, commanded by General

Alexandros Papagos, offered stiff resistance. Indeed, by the end of the month, the Italian offensive had ground to a halt. The Greeks mobilized reserves for a total force of 18 divisions, with French-supplied artillery superior to that of the Italians. They were, however, inferior in air assets. By 1 November, the Greeks had launched a series of counterattacks that stopped the Italians on the Kalamas River. The Italians made no progress on the Epirus Front, whereas the Julia Division arrived at the Metsovon Pass only to be counterattacked and cut off as the Greeks advanced toward to the Korcë basin, there overrunning the Parma and Piemonte Divisions. The Italian High Command ordered the Venezia and Arezzo Infantry Divisions, deployed on the Yugoslavian border, to reinforce the front. On their arrival, though, they were obliged to retreat in chaos before a spirited Greek advance that aimed to cut the road from Korcë to Perati and envelop the invaders turned defenders. The only possible option for the Italians was to withdraw their entire line into Albania. This took place on 8 November, a bleak time for the Italian army in the campaign. The following day, Italian commander General Visconti-Prasca was replaced by deputy chief of the Italian High Command General Ubaldo Soddu, who then formed the Italian forces into the Albanian Army Group.

Although Mussolini boasted on 19 November that he would "break Greece's back," a day later he received a sharply critical letter from Hitler. It criticized Mussolini's move, which had opened a new front that allowed the British to operate in the Balkans. The Germans were already preparing Operation BARBAROSSA, an invasion of the Soviet Union, and for security reasons did not wish to disclose their plans to the Italians.

As a consequence of the Italian failure, Marshal Badoglio came under fire, and on 26 November he and other military leaders were forced to resign . On 4 December, general of the army Ugo Cavallero replaced him. Cavallero demanded more power for the chief of General Staff and directly helped to facilitate the crisis on the Albanian Front. Cavallero would shortly take over command of the Albanian Army Group from Soddu, who retired in disgrace.

In early December, the Italian retreat from Greece back into Albania continued, forcing Mussolini to seek assistance from Hitler. The Italian "parallel war" now came to an end, along with the illusion that Italy was a great power. With the help of German transport aircraft, the Italians flew in reinforcements and shipped equipment to Valona, but this caused great confusion; units that had hurried to the front quickly disintegrated under Greek pressure and the effects of the winter weather. Moreover, it was difficult for the Italians to transport supplies to the front lines, as all had to be shipped from Italy, and there were not enough pack mules. To make things worse, on 9 December British Commonwealth units under Lieutenant General Archibald Wavell launched a successful offensive in North Africa that overran the more

numerous Italian troops. By 6 January 1941, the British had seized the Libyan border town of Bardia.

The British now faced the strategic problem of having to choose between exploitation of their North African successes and stiffening Greek resistance. On 6 January 1941, Churchill told the chiefs of staff that it would be better to delay exploiting the situation in North Africa in order help Greece seize the port of Valona and avoid military defeat. Churchill therefore informed Wavell that Tobruk would be taken, but follow-up operations would depend on the situation in Greece, which would be the priority. This was also partly because intelligence revealed that German forces were concentrating for a possible offensive in the Balkans. Apparently, the Greeks did not need much outside assistance, as they attacked Klisura and forced the Italians to abandon it. At that point, the Greek drive died, meeting stiffening Italian resistance, which successfully defended Berat and therefore Valona, but at a high price.

On 19 January 1941, Mussolini met Hitler and asked him for assistance to check the British Commonwealth advance in North Africa. Mussolini did not, however, request any help in the Greek theater of operations. Meanwhile, for propaganda purposes, Mussolini demanded that senior Fascist Party leaders join Italian troops at the front. Thus Foreign Minister Ciano took command of a bomber group, and ideologue Bruno Bottai joined an Alpini battalion.

A British military mission arrived in Athens on 22 February to study the situation and propose shipment by sea of an expeditionary corps to Greece. The following day, the Greeks accepted the offer, whereon Britain dispatched some of its best North African forces to Greece: 60,000 men with 240 field artillery pieces, 32 medium artillery guns, 192 antiaircraft guns, and 142 tanks under Lieutenant General Henry Maitland Wilson. In addition, under German pressure, Bulgaria signed the Tripartite Pact on 1 March, and German army units began to flow in force into Bulgaria to deploy for the future campaign. A few days later, the first British convoy to Greece sailed from Alexandria, and by 7 March, British troops began to disembark at Piraeus.

The Italians tried to force the situation in order to avoid the impression that they had been "saved" by the Germans. In March, General Cavallero launched 27 divisions in an offensive to reach Klisura. It failed and cost 12,000 Italian casualties. On 28 March, in an effort to check the British convoys bringing military aid to Greece, the Italian navy suffered an important naval defeat at the Battle of Matapan.

Meanwhile, on 25 March under heavy pressure, Yugoslavia adhered to the Tripartite Pact. But on the night of 26–27 March, a military coup d'état forced Prince Regent Paul into exile and General Dušan Simović formed a new government. This event prompted German military intervention. On 6 April, with Italian and Hungarian assistance, German forces invaded both Yugoslavia and Greece.

During the Italo-Greek War of October 1940–April 1941, the Greek army suffered 13,408 killed and 42,485 wounded. The Italians lost 13,775 dead, 50,874 wounded, and 25,067 missing. In addition, the campaign cost Italy reinforcements to North Africa, especially in equipment, which went instead to Albania. Thus, the British successes in North Africa in large part resulted from the Italian invasion of Greece.

Alessandro Massignani

See also

Badoglio, Pietro; BARBAROSSA, Operation; Bulgaria, Role in War; Cape Matapan, Battle of; Churchill, Sir Winston L. S.; Ciano, Galeazzo; Greece, Air Force; Greece, Army; Hitler, Adolf; Italy, Air Force; Italy, Army; Italy, Navy; Mussolini, Benito; Paul, Prince Regent of Yugoslavia; Wavell, Sir Archibald Percival; Wilson, Henry Maitland; Yugoslavia

References

Bitzes, John G. *Greece in World War II to April 1941*. Manhattan, KS: Sunflower University Press, 1982.

Cervi, Mario. *The Hollow Legions: Mussolini's Blunder in Greece, 1940–1941*. Trans. Eric Mosbacher. New York: Doubleday, 1971.

Knox, MacGregor. *Mussolini Unleashed, 1939–1941*. Cambridge, England: Cambridge University Press, 1981.

Montanari, Mario. *L'Esercito Italiano nella Campagna di Grecia*. 2nd ed. Rome: Ufficio Storico, 1991.

Greece Campaign (April 1941)

Important Balkan Theater campaign pitting Greek and British Empire forces against German and Italian forces. In the spring of 1941, German leader Adolf Hitler sent forces into Greece. His decision was prompted by his desire to eject the British from the Aegean and eastern Mediterranean; to protect his southern flank—especially the Romanian oil fields at Ploesti—before launching Operation BARBAROSSA, the invasion of the Soviet Union; and to assist Italy, his faltering ally. During the winter of 1940–1941 and into March 1941, German troops were stationed first in Romania and then in Bulgaria, threatening the Greek Second Army. Greece was led by General M. Alexander Koryzis, who succeeded general and dictator Ioannis Metaxas on the latter's death in late January 1941. General Alexander Papagos commanded the Greek army.

Greece was already at war, having been invaded by Italy in October 1940. The Greeks had not only repelled that invasion, but they had launched a counterinvasion of Albania. Papagos had committed the majority of the Greek army on that front in the northwest, where Lieutenant General Georgios Tsolakoglou's First Greek Army of 16 divisions faced 28 Italian divisions of the Eleventh and Ninth Armies in Albania and had repulsed a large Italian offensive in March.

Lieutenant General K. Bacopoulus's weaker Second Greek Army held the Greek frontier with Yugoslavia and Bulgaria to the northeast. However, the army was dangerously split.

Three divisions were strung out along the Metaxas Line of defensive works east of the Struma River in Macedonia facing Bulgaria. Three other Greek divisions were with the British contingent, including the weak 19th Division, the Greek army's only motorized division. The 19th Division was equipped with a few captured Italian L3 "tankettes," some worn-out British Bren carriers, and trucks.

British Prime Minister Winston L. S. Churchill had ordered to Greece from North Africa some of the best British Empire troops there, commanded by Lieutenant General Henry Maitland Wilson. Known as Force W, they were taking up position along the Aliakmon Line, named for the Greek river just southwest of Salonika. Force W consisted of a New Zealand division, an arriving Australian division, and a British armor brigade. Royal Air Force (RAF) units had been fighting in Greece from early November 1940. Altogether, slightly more than 60,000 British Empire forces were in Greece in April 1941.

Because the Italian army was tying down the bulk of the Greek army on the Albanian front, the highly trained, much stronger, and more technologically advanced German army was able without much difficulty to slice through Greek forces to the east. In their attack, the Axis powers enjoyed overwhelming air superiority. Italian air force units operating from Albania alone were equal to the total Allied air strength in Greece, and the German air force had as many Stuka dive-bombers in the theater as the total number of Allied first-line aircraft.

The German invasion of Greece from Bulgaria began on 6 April 1941. Field Marshal Wilhelm List had command. His Twelfth Army was made up of the equivalent of six corps (a seventh was transferred to the Second Army, which invaded Yugoslavia on 12 April) and included three panzer divisions. Leading the assault were the 2nd Panzer Division (known as the "Vienna Division" for the number of Austrians in it), the 9th Panzer Division, and the 5th and 6th Mountain Divisions. List's aim was to smash through the Metaxas Line and drive on Athens.

One of the most dramatic attacks of the campaign occurred on the morning of 7 April, when German aircraft bombed the Greek port of Piraeus and hit two freighters loaded with ammunition. The resulting blasts, heard 150 miles away, destroyed 41,942 tons of shipping and demolished docks. Overwhelming Axis air superiority confined most Allied movements to nighttime and was perhaps the key factor in the Axis victory.

Within three days of the start of their offensive, German forces had seized the port city of Salonika and breached the Metaxas Line. They also had taken 60,000 Greeks prisoner. On 12 April, the Greek High Command ordered General Tsolakoglou to withdraw his First Army from Albania. Lacking mobility and with much of its equipment worn out, the First

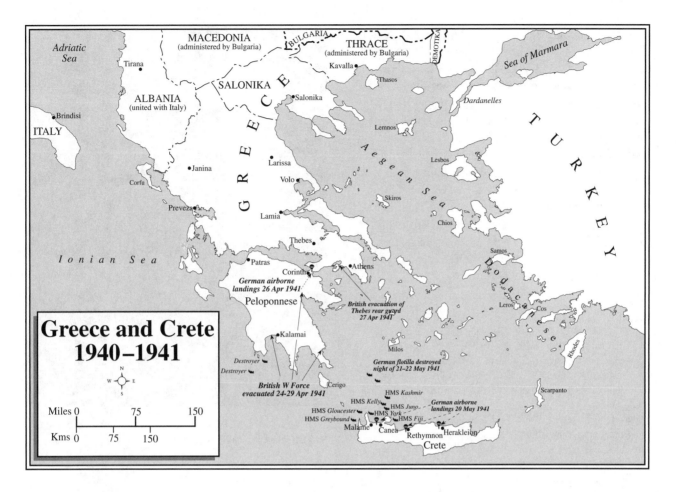

Greece and Crete 1940–1941

Miles 0 — 75 — 150

Kms 0 — 75 — 150

Army fell back slowly, only to surrender on 23 April to a joint German-Italian military commission.

The 2nd Panzer Division, meanwhile, was advancing along the Greek eastern coast toward the British forces, which were only just arriving and taking up defensive positions. The 2nd Panzer Division engaged the 2nd New Zealand Division and forced it to retreat. Additional German forces advanced through Yugoslavia and into central Greece from Bitolj, isolating eastern Greece. The Greeks fought hard with what resources they had, but they were simply overwhelmed. With defeat looming, General Papagos promised Wilson that the Greeks would do their best to protect the British forces while they evacuated.

With the defeat of his country imminent, Greek Prime Minister Alexandros Koryzis committed suicide on 18 April. His successor, Emanuel Tsouderos, pledged to assist British Empire troops in evacuating Greece. On 23 April, the same day that the Greek army was forced to surrender, Greek King George II fled his nation to Egypt and there set up a government in exile.

On 24 April, the British abandoned Thermopylae and began withdrawing into the Peloponnesus. Royal Navy ships, meanwhile, braved Luftwaffe attacks to carry out night evacuations of British forces from ports in eastern Greece. On 26 April, the Germans carried out a daring paratroop operation in an effort to cut off the British withdrawal. Using gliders, they successfully seized the only bridge over the Corinth Canal. Although the British managed to destroy part of the bridge with artillery fire, the Germans quickly rebuilt it and used the bridge to press into the Peloponnesus. Wilson managed to fight his way through, evacuating most of his troops. More than 50,000 British Empire forces were evacuated in Operation DEMON, although most of their equipment had to be abandoned. The last formal evacuation took place on 30 April; many of the troops were then sent to Crete. Some resistance continued in the Greek islands until 4 May. British naval losses were 2 destroyers and 4 merchant ships; the Greeks lost in the campaign 3 destroyers and a torpedo boat as well as 43 merchant ships of 63,975 tons.

In the entirety of the Greek Campaign, the Germans lost 2,559 killed (including 200 aircrew) and 5,820 wounded. The Greek army sustained 13,408 killed, 42,485 wounded, and 270,000 prisoners. Italian losses during April were 13,775 dead, 54,874 wounded, and 25,067 missing. The British suffered 5,100 dead, wounded, and missing and some 7,000 taken prisoner.

General Tsolakoglou then headed a collaborationist Greek government in Athens; Greece was divided into German, Italian, and Bulgarian occupation zones. In May, the Germans took Crete by airborne assault. German troops then controlled that island as well as Lemnos, Lesbos, and Chios; some smaller islands in the Aegean; the Turkish border region; Salonika; and the port of Athens and its surrounding area. Bulgarian forces occupied much of Macedonia, and Italy controlled the remainder of the Greek mainland as well as most of the Greek Mediterranean islands.

Some historians have suggested that Germany's invasion of Greece and Yugoslavia delayed Operation BARBAROSSA. However, other factors, especially the need to wait for dry weather for the panzers, were more important. Nonetheless, the panzer divisions that had seen service in Greece had to undergo refit and were thus not immediately available for BARBAROSSA. The campaign also exacted a toll in equipment and in precious stocks of fuel.

Jack Greene

See also

Albania, Role in War; Balkans Theater; Churchill, Sir Winston L. S.; Crete, Battle of; Dodecanese Islands; Greece, Air Force; Greece, Army; Greece, Navy; Greece, Role in War; Greece Campaign (28 October 1940–March 1941); List, Sigmund Wilhelm; Metaxas, Ioannis; Papagos, Alexandros; Wilson, Henry Maitland; Yugoslavia

References

Bitzes, John G. *Greece in World War II to April 1941,* Manhattan, KS: Sunflower University Press, 1982.

Rossides, Eugene T., ed. *Greece's Pivotal Role in World War II and Its Importance to the U.S. Today,* Washington, DC: American Hellenic Institute Foundation, 2001.

Schreiber, Gerhard, et al. *Germany and the Second World War: The Mediterranean, South-east Europe, and North Africa, 1939–1941.* Vol. 3. Oxford: Clarendon Press, 1995.

Thies, Klaus-Jurgen. *Der Zweite Weltkrieg im Kartenbild: Der Balkanfeldzug und die Eroberung von Kreta.* Vol. 4. Osnabruck: Zellar Verlag, 1996.

Acting U.S. Secretary of State Joseph C. Grew, 1943. (Photo by Marie Hansen/Time Life Pictures/Getty Images)

Grew, Joseph Clark (1880–1965)

U.S. diplomat and undersecretary of state. Born on 27 May 1880 in Boston, Massachusetts, into a prominent family, Joseph Grew attended Groton School and Harvard University. He then joined the United States diplomatic service, transferring from the consular to the foreign service in 1904. Throughout his life, Grew's influential contacts, including Presidents Theodore Roosevelt and Franklin D. Roosevelt, facilitated his career.

Grew initially enjoyed postings to Cairo, Mexico City, Russia, Berlin, Vienna, and Denmark. He attended the 1919 Paris Peace Conference and the 1922–1923 Lausanne Conference on Near Eastern affairs. After serving as undersecretary of state from 1923 to 1927, in which capacity he helped to implement the 1924 Rogers Act's reorganization of the Foreign Service, Grew became ambassador to Turkey. In 1932, he was appointed the first career U.S. ambassador to Japan, remain-

ing in Tokyo until Japan declared war on the United States in December 1941.

Grew's wife, Alice Vermandois Perry, was descended from Commodore Matthew Perry, who opened Japan to western influence in 1853. She had spent her youth in that country and knew many of its leading figures. Grew firmly hoped that Japan's growing antagonism toward the United States might be reversed. He urged greater American sympathy for Japan's economic problems and sought more latitude as ambassador in handling Japanese-American relations. Grew's regular swings from optimism to pessimism over each successive new Japanese government and his eagerness to conciliate successive new governments brought clashes with Stanley K. Hornbeck, head of the State Department's Division of Far Eastern Affairs.

Seeking to avoid what increasingly seemed to be an inevitable conflict, in October 1939 Grew publicly warned that, if Japan wished to avoid severe American retribution, it must alter its increasingly bellicose international stance. This precipitated harsh Japanese press attacks on him. Subsequently, he unsuccessfully urged a personal meeting between President Franklin D. Roosevelt and Japanese Premier Prince Konoe Fumimaro, which he later unconvincingly claimed might have averted war.

Interned after the Japanese attack on Pearl Harbor and repatriated to the United States in spring 1942, Grew returned to

Washington as a special assistant to Secretary of State Cordell Hull, becoming director of the Division of Far Eastern Affairs in 1944. As undersecretary of state from December 1944 to August 1945, Grew opposed further collaboration with Soviet Russia, unsuccessfully sought to prevent the use of nuclear weapons against Japan by urging American acceptance of a negotiated peace settlement rather than unconditional surrender, and helped to preserve the Japanese emperor's status as nominal head of state. Grew retired in August 1945. He died at Manchester-by-the-Sea, Massachusetts, on 25 May 1965.

Priscilla Roberts

See also

Hirohito, Emperor of Japan; Hull, Cordell; Konoe Fumimaro, Prince; MacArthur, Douglas; Pearl Harbor, Attack on; Roosevelt, Franklin D.

References

Bennett, Edward M. "Joseph C. Grew: The Diplomacy of Pacification." In Richard Dean Burns and Edward M. Bennett, eds., *Diplomats in Crisis*, 65–89. Wilmington, DE: Scholarly Resources, 1974.

Grew, Joseph C. *Ten Years in Japan.* New York: Simon and Schuster, 1944.

———. *Turbulent Era: A Diplomatic Record of Forty Years.* Walter Johnson, ed. 2 vols. Boston: Houghton Mifflin, 1952.

Heinrichs, Waldo H., Jr. *American Ambassador: Joseph C. Grew and the Development of the United States Diplomatic Tradition.* Boston: Little, Brown, 1966.

Nakamura Masanori. *Japanese Monarchy: Ambassador Joseph Grew and the Making of the "Symbol Emperor System," 1931–1991.* Armonk, NY: M. E. Sharpe, 1992.

Grizodubova, Valentina Stepanovna (1910–1993)

Russian air force colonel and sole woman commanding officer of a men's wing during World War II. Born in Kharkiv on 31 January 1910, the daughter of an aircraft designer, Valentina Grizodubova graduated from Penza Flying Club in 1929, Kharkiv Flying School, and Advanced Flying School in Tula in 1933. She mastered many types of aircraft, setting seven world records in the process. On 24–25 September 1938, Grizodubova flew nonstop from Moscow to the Pacific in an ANT-37. For this pioneer flight she, her copilot Polina Osipenko, and her navigator Marina Raskova received the award of Hero of the Soviet Union, the highest Soviet military decoration. They were the first Soviet women to be thus honored.

In May 1942, Grizodubova was appointed commanding officer of the 101st Long-Range Air Regiment (renamed 31st Krasnosel'sky Guards Bomber Regiment in 1944). She successfully demonstrated the suitability of the Li-2 (modified DC-3) for use as a night bomber. In June 1942, Grizodubova led her unit in delivering supplies to the besieged city of Leningrad. She was noted for flying more than her male colleagues and sometimes flew as copilot to monitor her pilots' performance.

In September 1942, Grizodubova's unit was placed at the disposal of Central Partisan Headquarters. Overcoming dense enemy flak and engaging enemy fighters, her aircrews flew more than 1,850 supply missions, and on their return they evacuated wounded partisans and children. In 1943, Grizodubova prevailed on her superiors not to decrease these flights.

Grizodubova flew about 200 wartime missions and was awarded many prestigious military decorations. A senior official of civil aviation after the war, Grizodubova also served on the executive board of several veterans' organizations, assisting numerous former prisoner-of-war camp inmates who were persecuted by Soviet authorities. As a member of the Soviet parliament, she courageously criticized Soviet dictator Josef Stalin's reign of terror. Grizodubova died in Moscow on 1 May 1993.

Kazimiera J. Cottam

See also

Leningrad, Siege of; Raskova, Marina Mikhailovna; Soviet Union, Air Force; Soviet Women's Combat Wings; Stalin, Josef; Women in World War II

References

Cottam, Kazimiera J. *Women in War and Resistance: Selected Biographies.* Nepean, Canada: New Military Publishing, 1998.

Verkhozin, A. M. *Samolety letiat k partizanam* (Supplying partisans). 2nd ed. Moscow: Izdatel'stvo Politicheskoi Literatury, 1966.

———. "Polkom komanduet zhenshchina" (Wing commander). In L. F. Toropov, ed., *Geroini* [Heroines], vol. 1, 2nd ed. Moscow: Politizdat, 1969.

Groves, Leslie Richard (1896–1970)

U.S. Army general who oversaw the MANHATTAN Project. Born in Albany, New York, on 17 August 1896, Leslie "Dick" Groves attended the University of Washington and the Massachusetts Institute of Technology. He secured an appointment to the U.S. Military Academy, from which he graduated in 1918. He then entered the Army Corps of Engineers.

After initial training at the Engineer School at Fort Humphreys (later Fort Belvoir), Virginia, Groves served in Hawaii, Texas, Nicaragua (where he was awarded the Nicaraguan Medal of Merit for restoring water to Managua following an earthquake), Washington, D.C., and Missouri. Assigned to the War Department in 1939, Groves became chief of the Operations Branch and in 1941 deputy head of the Construction Division. In these capacities, Groves oversaw the vast expansion of military camps and training facilities across the United States. He then supervised construction of the Pentagon, the world's largest office building.

Major General Leslie Groves, who was in charge of the MANHATTAN Engineer District and oversaw the building of facilities for testing of the first atomic weapons. (Hulton Archive)

His success in a variety of engineering projects led to Groves's promotion to brigadier general and assignment in September 1942 to head the MANHATTAN Project, charged with construction of an atomic bomb. In this capacity, Groves controlled 129,000 personnel and $2 billion in spending. He won promotion to major general in March 1944. This vast effort resulted in the explosion of the first atomic device at Alamogordo, New Mexico, on 16 July 1945. Groves advised President Harry S Truman to use the bomb and helped select Japanese target cities.

After the war, Groves sought international control over atomic energy. When this did not occur, Groves organized the Army Forces Special Weapons Project to study military uses of atomic energy. Promoted to lieutenant general in January 1948, Groves retired from the army that same month and became vice president for research of the Rand Corporation. He retired altogether in 1961. Groves died in Washington, D.C., on 13 July 1970.

Ryan E. Doltz

See also
Atomic Bomb, Decision to Employ; Hiroshima, Bombing of; MANHATTAN Project; Nagasaki, Bombing of; Truman, Harry S

References
Gosling, F. G. *The Manhattan Project: Science in the Second World War.* Washington, DC: U.S. Department of Energy, 1990.
Groves, Leslie R. *Now It Can Be Told: The Story of the Manhattan Project.* New York: Harper and Brothers, 1962.
Lawren, William. *The General and the Bomb.* New York: Dodd, Mead and Co., 1988.
Nichols, Kenneth D. *The Road to Trinity.* New York: William Morrow, 1987.
Norris, Robert S. *Racing for the Bomb: General Leslie R. Groves, The Manhattan Project's Indispensable Man.* South Royalton, VT: Steerforth Press, 2002.

Gruenther, Alfred Maximilian (1899–1983)

Born at Platte Center, Nebraska, on 3 March 1899, Alfred Gruenther graduated fourth in his class in 1919 from the U.S. Military Academy. Commissioned in the field artillery, he completed the Field Artillery School in 1920 and served there as an instructor until 1922. He then served with the 9th Field Artillery in 1922 and 1923. Gruenther served in the Philippines with the 24th Field Artillery from 1924 to 1926. He returned to the 9th Field Artillery until August 1927, when he began the first of eight years at West Point as instructor and assistant professor of chemistry and electricity.

Promoted to captain in 1935, Gruenther graduated from the Command and General Staff School in 1937 and the Army War College in 1939. From October 1941 to October 1942, Gruenther was deputy to the army chief of staff and then chief of staff of the Third Army. He was promoted to colonel in December 1940 and to brigadier general in March 1941. In August 1942, Gruenther was appointed deputy chief of staff of Lieutenant General Dwight D. Eisenhower's Allied Force Headquarters and Headquarters Command, Allied Force in London, where he helped plan the invasion of North Africa (Operation TORCH). Promoted to temporary major general in February 1943, Gruenther became chief of staff of Lieutenant General Mark W. Clark's Fifth Army and was a principal planner for the Allied invasion of Sicily and Salerno, Italy. In November 1944, when Clark took command of the 15th Army Group in Italy, Gruenther continued as his chief of staff. Following the war, Gruenther was deputy commander of U.S. occupation forces in Austria in 1945 and 1946. He next became deputy director of the new National War College and then the first director of the U.S. Joint Staff on its establishment in 1947. Promoted to lieutenant general, during 1949 and 1950 Gruenther was deputy chief of staff for plans and then chief of staff for Supreme Headquarters, Allied Powers in Europe (SHAPE) from 1950 to 1953. Promoted to general in 1951, he was Supreme Allied Commander, Europe from 1953 to 1956. He retired in July 1956 because of physical disability. Although Gruenther never commanded troops in combat, he was a superb staff officer.

Following his retirement, Gruenther was president of the American Red Cross from 1957 to 1965 and director of several corporations. He died in Washington, D.C., on 30 May 1983.

Uzal W. Ent

See also
Bradley, Omar Nelson; Cassino/Rapido River, Battles of; Clark, Mark Wayne; Eisenhower, Dwight D.; Italy Campaign; North Africa Campaign; Rome, Advance on and Capture of; Sicily, Invasion of; TORCH, Operation

U.S. Army General Alfred M. Gruenther. (Photo by Dmitri Kessel/Time Life Pictures/Getty Images)

References

Bradley, Omar N. *A General's Life.* New York: Simon and Schuster, 1983.

Fisher, Ernest F., Jr. *The United States Army in World War II: The Mediterranean Theater of Operations: Cassino to the Alps.* Washington, DC: Center of Military History, 1977.

Guadalcanal, Land Battle for (August 1942–February 1943)

Bitter contest between the Japanese and the Americans that marked a turning point in the Pacific war. The struggle on Guadalcanal was protracted, and the period from August 1942 to February 1943 saw some of the most bitter fighting of the war. In all, there were some 50 actions involving warships or aircraft, 7 major naval battles, and 10 land engagements.

Guadalcanal is an island in the Solomon chain northeast of Australia. It lies on a northwest-southeast axis and is 90 miles long and averages 25 miles wide. Guadalcanal's southern shore is protected by coral reefs, and the only suitable landing beaches are on the north-central shore. Once inland, invading troops faced dense jungle and mountainous terrain, crisscrossed by numerous streams. The Guadalcanal Campaign encompassed not only Guadalcanal, but Savo and Florida Islands as well as the small islands between Florida and Guadalcanal: Tulagi, Tanambogo, and Gavutu.

In January 1942, Japanese amphibious forces had landed in the Bismarck Archipelago between New Guinea and the Solomon Islands. They quickly wrested Kavieng on New Ireland Island and Rabaul on New Britain from the Australians. The Japanese consolidated their hold and turned Rabaul into their principal southwest Pacific base. By early March, the Japanese landed at Salamaua and Lae in Papua and on Bougainville. Their advance having gone so well, the Japanese decided to expand their defensive ring to the southeast to cut off the supply route from the United States to New Zealand and Australia. On 3 May, the Japanese landed on Tulagi and began building a seaplane base there. Between May and July, the Japanese expanded their ring farther in the central and lower Solomons. These operations were carried out by Lieutenant General Imamura Hitoshi's Eighth Army from Rabaul. The first Japanese landed on Guadalcanal on 8 June. On 6 July, their engineers began construction of an airfield near the mouth of the Lunga River.

The discovery of the Japanese effort on Guadalcanal led to the implementation of Operation WATCHTOWER. Conceived and pushed by U.S. Chief of Naval Operations Admiral Ernest J. King, it called for securing Tulagi as an additional base to protect the United States–Australia lifeline and as a starting point for a drive up the Solomons to Rabaul. On 1 April 1942, the Pacific was divided into two commands: U.S. Vice Admiral Robert L. Ghormley, commanding in the South Pacific, was to take the southern Solomons including Guadalcanal, and General Douglas MacArthur's forces were to secure the remainder of the Solomons and the northwest coast of New Guinea, the final objective being Rabaul.

If the Japanese were allowed to complete their airfield on Guadalcanal, they would be able to bomb the advanced Allied base at Espiritu Santo. U.S. plans to take the offensive were now stepped up, and a task force was hurriedly assembled. From Nouméa, Ghormley dispatched an amphibious force under Rear Admiral Richmond K. Turner, lifting Major General Alexander A. Vandegrift's 19,000-man reinforced 1st Marine Division. A three-carrier task force under Vice Admiral Frank J. Fletcher provided air support. This operation involved some 70 ships.

On 7 August 1942, the Marines went ashore at Tulagi, Florida, Tanambogo, Gavutu, and Guadalcanal, surprising the small Japanese garrisons (2,200 on Guadalcanal and 1,500 on Tulagi). On the same day, the Marines seized the harbor at Tulagi, and by the next afternoon they had also secured the airfield under construction on Guadalcanal, along with stocks of Japanese weapons, food, and equipment. Supplies for the Marines were soon coming ashore from transports in the sound between Guadalcanal and Florida Islands, but this activity came under attack by Japanese aircraft based at

A casualty from the front-line fighting at Guadalcanal being transferred from the makeshift stretcher before being taken through jungle and down river to a nearby hospital. (National Archives)

Rabaul. Vandegrift told Fletcher he would need four days to unload the transports, but Fletcher replied that he was short on fuel and in any case could not risk keeping his carriers in position off Guadalcanal for more than 48 hours.

Stakes were high for both sides. The fiercest fighting occurred for the airfield, renamed Henderson Field for a Marine aviator killed in the Battle of Midway. Vandegrift recognized its importance and immediately established a perimeter defense around it. Eating captured rations and using Japanese heavy-construction equipment, the U.S. 1st Engineer Battalion completed the airfield on 17 August. As early as 21 August, the day the Japanese mounted a major attack on the field, the first U.S. aircraft landed there. The Japanese now found it impossible to keep their ships in waters covered by the land-based American aircraft during the day, and they found it difficult to conduct an air campaign over the lower Solomons from as far away as Rabaul.

The lack of a harbor compounded U.S. supply problems, as did Japanese aircraft attacks. Allied "coast watchers" on islands provided early warning to U.S. forces of Japanese air and water movements down the so-called Slot of the Solomons. The battle on Guadalcanal became a complex campaign of attrition. The Japanese did not send their main fleet but rather vessels in driblets. American land-based air power controlled the Slot during the day, but the Japanese initially controlled it at night, as was evidenced in the 8 August Battle of Savo Island. Concern over the vulnerability of the U.S. transports led to their early removal on the afternoon of 9 August along with most of the heavy guns, vehicles, construction equipment, and food intended for the Marines ashore. The Japanese sent aircraft from Rabaul, while initially U.S. land-based aircraft flying at long range from the New Hebrides provided air cover for the Marines as fast destroyer transports finally brought in some supplies. American possession of Henderson Field tipped the balance. U.S. air strength there gradually increased to about 100 planes.

At night the so-called Tokyo Express—Japanese destroyers and light cruisers—steamed down the Slot and into the sound to shell Marine positions and to deliver supplies. The latter effort was haphazard and never sufficient; often, drums filled with supplies were pushed off the ships to drift to shore. One of the great what-ifs of the Pacific War was the failure of the Japanese to exploit the temporary departure of the U.S. carrier task force on 8 August by rushing in substantial reinforcements.

Actions ashore were marked by clashes between patrols of both sides. Colonel Ichiki Kiyonao, who had arrived with his battalion on Guadalcanal in early August, planned a large-scale attack that took little account of U.S. Marine dispositions. His unit was effectively wiped out in the 21 August 1942 Battle of the Tenaru River. Ichiki's men refused to surrender, and they and their commander were killed in the fighting. Marine losses were 44 dead and 71 wounded; the Japanese lost at least 777 killed. From 12 to 14 September, strong Japanese forces attempted to seize U.S. Marine positions on Lunga Ridge overlooking Henderson Field from the south. The Japanese left 600 dead; American casualties were 143 dead and wounded. Both sides continued building up their strength ashore as naval and air battles raged over and off Guadalcanal.

From 23 to 25 October, the Japanese launched strong land attacks against Henderson Field. Fortunately for the Marine defenders, the attacks were widely dispersed and uncoordinated. In these engagements, the Japanese suffered 2,000 dead, while U.S. casualties were fewer than 300. Immediately after halting this Japanese offensive, Vandegrift began a six-week effort to expand the defensive perimeter beyond which the Japanese could not subject Henderson to artillery fire. Meanwhile, Admiral Kondō Nobutake's repositioning of vessels and Vice Admiral William F. Halsey's instructions to Rear Admiral Thomas Kinkaid to seek out the Japanese fleet resulted in the 26 October Battle of the Santa Cruz Islands.

Fighting on land continued on Guadalcanal. On 8 December, Vandegrift turned command of the island over to U.S. Army Major General Alexander M. Patch, who organized his forces into the XIV Corps, including the 2nd Marine Division, replacing the veteran 1st Marine Division, which was withdrawn, and the 25th Infantry Division. At the beginning of January 1943, Patch commanded 58,000 men, whereas Japanese strength was then less than 20,000.

Ultimately, the Americans won the land struggle for Guadalcanal thanks to superior supply capabilities and the failure of the Japanese to throw sufficient resources into the battle. The Americans were now well fed and well supplied, but the Japanese were desperate, losing many men to sickness and simple starvation. At the end of December, Tokyo decided to abandon Guadalcanal.

Meanwhile, on 10 January, Patch began an offensive to clear the island of Japanese forces, mixing Army and Marine units as the situation dictated. In a two-week battle, the Americans drove the Japanese from a heavily fortified line west of Henderson Field. At the end of January, the Japanese were forced from Tassafaronga toward Cape Esperance, where a small American force landed to prevent them from escaping by sea. Dogged Japanese perseverance and naval support, however, enabled some defenders to escape. The Japanese invested in the struggle 24,600 men (20,800 troops and 3,800 naval personnel). In daring night operations during 1–7 February 1943, Japanese destroyers evacuated 10,630 troops (9,800 army and 830 navy).

The United States committed 60,000 men to the fight for the island; of these, the Marines lost 1,207 dead and the army 562. U.S. casualties were far greater in the naval contests for Guadalcanal; the U.S. Navy and Marines lost 4,911 and the Japanese at least 3,200. Counting land, sea, and air casualties, the struggle for Guadalcanal had claimed 7,100 U.S. dead and permanently missing. The Japanese advance had now been halted, and MacArthur could begin the long and bloody return to the Philippine Islands.

Troy D. Morgan and Spencer C. Tucker

See also

Cape Esperance, Battle of; Coral Sea, Battle of the; Fletcher, Frank Jack; Ghormley, Robert Lee; Guadalcanal Naval Campaign; Halsey, William Frederick, Jr.; Ichiki Kiyonao; Imamura Hitoshi; King, Ernest Joseph; Kinkaid, Thomas Cassin; Kondō Nobutake; MacArthur, Douglas; Patch, Alexander McCarrell, Jr.; Santa Cruz Islands, Battle of the; Savo Island, Battle of; Tassafaronga, Battle of; Turner, Richmond Kelly; Vandegrift, Alexander Archer

References

Bergerud, Eric. *Touched with Fire: The Land War in the South Pacific.* New York: Viking, 1996.

Frank, Richard B. *Guadalcanal: The Definitive Account of the Landmark Battle.* New York: Random House, 1990.

Hough, Frank O., Verle E. Ludwig, and Henry I. Shaw. *History of Marine Corps Operation in World War II: Pearl Harbor to Guadalcanal.* Washington, DC: Government Printing Office, 1963.

Miller, John, Jr. *United States Army in World War II: The War in the Pacific: Guadalcanal, the First Offensive.* Washington, DC: Government Printing Office, 1949.

Mueller, Joseph N. *Guadalcanal 1942: The Marines Strike Back.* London: Osprey, 1992.

Tregaskis, Richard. *Guadalcanal Diary.* New York: Random House, 1943.

Guadalcanal Naval Campaign (August 1942–February 1943)

Significant and prolonged South Pacific sea-land-air campaign. The campaign for Guadalcanal comprised several naval engagements and several vicious land battles fought from August 1942 to February 1943. On Guadalcanal (90 by 25 miles in size) in the Solomon Islands, U.S. Marines and army troops attacked Japanese land forces, while the U.S. Navy battled the Japanese navy offshore.

Before the battle, U.S. planners were able to build up Pacific Theater resources more quickly than anticipated and take the offensive against the Japanese. This campaign, Operation WATCHTOWER, was the brainchild of U.S. Chief of Naval Operations Admiral Ernest J. King. It had as its objective the seizure of the islands of Tulagi and Gavatu as a preliminary step in securing the Solomons and then the recapture of the Philippines and the eventual defeat of Japan. These plans soon changed when intelligence revealed that the Japanese were building an airstrip on the nearby island of Guadalcanal. Once operational, such a base would pose a serious threat to Allied operations in the South Pacific. Therefore, its seizure became the primary objective of the campaign.

Although hamstrung by a lack of adequate resources because of sealift required for Operation TORCH, the British and American invasion of North Africa, Vice Admiral Robert Ghormley pieced together forces from the United States, Australia, and New Zealand for the invasion. Resources were so meager that some of his officers nicknamed the plan Operation Shoestring. Major General Alexander A. Vandegrift commanded the 1st Marine Division landing force, and Vice Admiral Frank Jack Fletcher had charge of the naval support element.

The U.S. Navy's tasks were to sustain forces ashore and provide naval and air protection for the Marines defending the airfield, which was captured shortly after the landing and renamed Henderson Field. The lack of a harbor compounded supply problems. The Japanese operated aircraft from Rabaul and later from other closer island airfields, but Allied "coast watchers" on islands provided early warning of many Japanese naval movements.

The Marines went ashore beginning on 7 August, but the sealift was so limited that they were without much of their heavier equipment and heavy artillery. The first naval engagement with the Japanese occurred on the night of 8–9 August 1942 in the Battle of Savo Island. A Japanese cruiser squadron overwhelmed an Allied force of equal size, sinking one Australian and three U.S. cruisers and damaging several destroyers, losing none of its own ships. The battle clearly showed the superiority of Japanese night-fighting techniques. The battle was the worst defeat ever suffered by the U.S. Navy in a fair fight, but it was only a tactical success, because the Japanese failed to go after the vulnerable American troop transports off Guadalcanal and Tulagi.

Nonetheless, the Battle of Savo Island and Japanese air attacks led Fletcher and Rear Admiral Richmond K. Turner to withdraw supporting naval forces from Guadalcanal, leaving the Marines ashore isolated, bereft of naval support, and

short of critical supplies. Long-range aircraft and destroyers did bring in some resources. The Japanese made a critical mistake in not capitalizing on the U.S. vulnerability to commit their main fleet assets. For the most part, they sent only smaller units in driblets, chiefly in the form of fast destroyers. The so-called Slot was controlled by the United States during the day but the Japanese owned it at night.

The next major confrontation at sea off Guadalcanal came on the night of 24–25 August in the Battle of the Eastern Solomons. Fletcher's carrier-based aircraft intercepted and attacked the covering group for a Japanese convoy of destroyers and transports carrying 1,500 troops to Guadalcanal. The Americans sank the Japanese light carrier *Ryujo* and damaged another ship, but the U.S. fleet carrier *Enterprise* was located and attacked by Japanese aircraft and badly damaged. The Japanese destroyers and transports delivered the reinforcements and the destroyers and then shelled Henderson Field, although a U.S. Army B-17 sank one of the Japanese ships.

On 31 August, the U.S. carrier *Saratoga* was torpedoed by a Japanese submarine and put out of action for three months. That left only the carrier *Wasp* available for operations in the South Pacific. On 15 September, the *Wasp* was in turn torpedoed and sunk while it was accompanying transports lifting the 7th Marine Regiment to Guadalcanal from Espiritu Santo. A Japanese torpedo also damaged the battleship *North Carolina*, which, however, held her place in the formation. Admiral Turner continued to Guadalcanal, delivering the 7th Marine Regiment safely three days later.

Heavy fighting, meanwhile, was occurring on Guadalcanal; the Japanese were mounting unsuccessful attacks to recapture Henderson Field. The next big naval encounter off Guadalcanal was the Battle of Cape Esperance during the night of 11–12 October. The Japanese sent in their supply ships at night (the so-called Tokyo Express). U.S. ships equipped with radar detected a Japanese convoy off the northwest coast of Guadalcanal. In the ensuing fight, the Japanese lost a cruiser and a destroyer, and another cruiser was heavily damaged. The Americans lost only a destroyer and had two cruisers damaged. The first Allied success against the Japanese in a night engagement, the Battle of Cape Esperance, was a great boost to U.S. morale. A few days later, Admiral Chester W. Nimitz replaced the methodical Ghormley with the offensive-minded Vice Admiral William "Bull" Halsey.

A major engagement occurred on 26–27 October in the Battle of the Santa Cruz Islands. Rear Admiral Thomas Kinkaid and his Task Force 16 centered on the carrier *Enterprise* followed Admiral Halsey's instructions to engage Japanese forces under Admiral Kondō Nobutake. Each side conducted carrier strikes against the other. U.S. aircraft inflicted severe damage on the heavy carrier *Shokaku,* putting her out of action for nine months, and damaged the light carrier *Zuiho.* On the U.S. side, the heavy carrier *Hornet* was

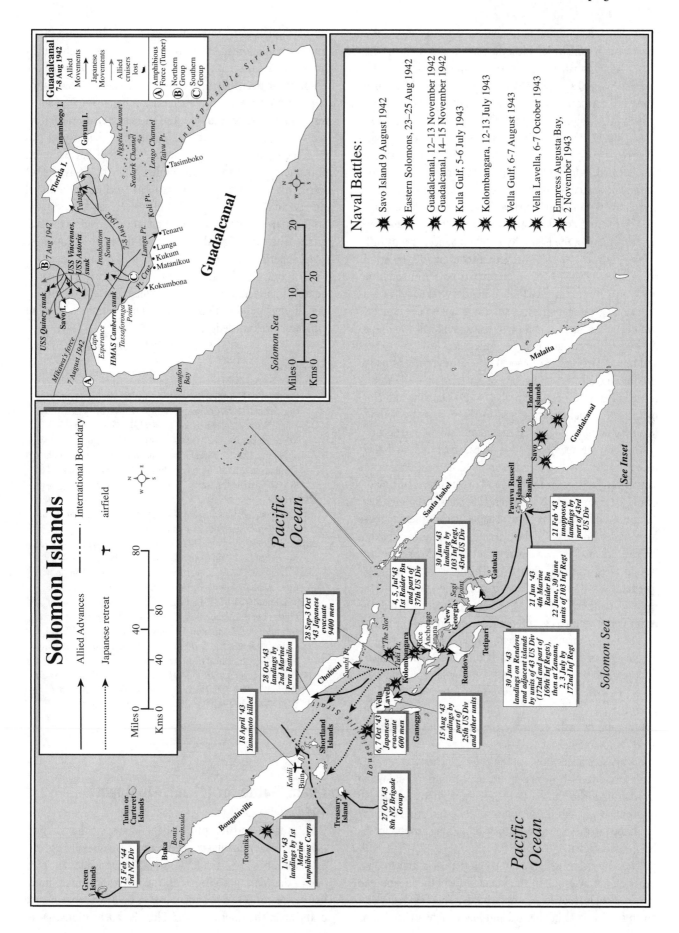

Guadalcanal
7–8 Aug 1942

Allied Movements →
Japanese Movements →
Allied cruisers lost

Ⓐ Amphibious Force (Turner)
Ⓑ Northern Group
Ⓒ Southern Group

Indespensible Strait

Florida I. Tanambogo I.
Gavutu I.

Ngella Channel
Sealark Channel
Lengo Channel
Ngella Channel

Tulagi

7 Aug 1942

Koli Pt.
Taivu Pt.

Tasimboko

USS Vincennes,
USS Astoria
sunk

Ironbottom
Sound

7–8 Aug

Tenaru
Lunga Pt.
Lunga
Kukum
Matanikou

Ⓒ

Ⓑ 7 Aug 1942

USS Quincy sunk

Savo I.

USS Vincennes,
USS Astoria
sunk

Mikawa's force

HMAS Canberra sunk

Tassafaronga
Point

Kokumbona

Guadalcanal

Cape
Esperance

7 August 1942

Ⓐ

Beaufort
Bay

Solomon Sea

Miles 0   10   20
Kms 0   10   20

Naval Battles:

✸ Savo Island 9 August 1942
✸ Eastern Solomons, 23–25 Aug 1942
✸ Guadalcanal, 12–13 November 1942
✸ Guadalcanal, 14–15 November 1942
✸ Kula Gulf, 5–6 July 1943
✸ Kolombangara, 12–13 July 1943
✸ Vella Gulf, 6–7 August 1943
✸ Vella Lavella, 6–7 October 1943
✸ Empress Augusta Bay,
   2 November 1943

Solomon Islands

→ Allied Advances
⇢ Japanese retreat
— · — International Boundary
✚ airfield

Miles 0   40   80
Kms 0   40   80

Malaita

Florida
Islands

Guadalcanal

Savo

See Inset

*Pacific
Ocean*

Santa Isabel

21 Feb '43
unopposed
landings by
part of 43rd
US Div

Pavuvu Russell
Islands

Banika

30 Jun '43
landing by
103 Inf Regt,
43rd US Div

Gatukai

"The Slot"

4, 5, Jul '43
1st Raider Bn
and part of
37th US Div

Sumbi Pt.

Viru Pt.

Segi
Point

New
Georgia

Segi

Rice
Anchorage

Zanana

21 Jun '43
4th Marine
Raider Bn

22 June, 30 June
units of 103 Inf Regt

Tetipari

Rendova

30 Jun '43
landings on Rendova
and adjacent islands
by units of 43 US Div
(172nd and part of
169th Inf Regts),
then at Zanana,
2, 3 July by
172nd Inf Regt

28 Sep–3 Oct
'43 Japanese
evacuate
9400 men

Choiseul

28 Oct '43
landings by
2nd Marine
Para Battalion

Kolombangara

Vella
Lavella

15 Aug '43
landings by
part of 25th US Div
and other units

Ganogga

Bougainville Strait

18 April '43
Yamamoto killed

Shortland
Islands

6, 7 Oct '43
Japanese
evacuate
600 men

Solomon Sea

*Pacific
Ocean*

Kahili

Buin

Bonis
Peninsula

Buka

Tulun or
Carteret
Islands

Bougainville

Toronika

27 Oct '43
8th NZ Brigade
Group

Treasury Island

1 Nov '43
landings by 1st
Marine
Amphibious Corps

Green
Islands

15 Feb '44
3rd NZ Div

badly damaged and had to be abandoned while under tow; she was soon sunk by Japanese destroyers. Kondō then withdrew. He had won a major victory over the Americans, but he had also lost 100 aircraft and experienced pilots, half again as many as the Americans. Had he continued to pursue the withdrawing U.S. ships, he might have destroyed the *Enterprise.*

During 12–15 November, a series of intense sea fights occurred in what became known as the Naval Battle of Guadalcanal. It took place near the entrance to Ironbottom Sound (so named for being the resting place of many Allied and Japanese ships) off Savo Island between Guadalcanal and Tulagi. In the first, U.S. ships and aircraft fought to block reinforcement of the island by 13,000 Japanese troops in 11 transports, escorted by destroyers, all commanded by Admiral Tanaka Raizo. At the same time, a powerful squadron under Abe Hiroaki arrived to shell Henderson Field. In a confused engagement, both sides suffered heavily. The Japanese lost the battleship *Hiei* and two cruisers sunk; all other Japanese vessels were damaged. The Americans lost two cruisers and four destroyers. A cruiser and a destroyer were close to sinking, and all other ships, save one, were damaged. Among those killed were Rear Admirals Daniel Callaghan and Norman Scott. Tanaka was obliged to retire, and the planned Japanese bombardment of Henderson Field did not occur.

On 13–14 November the Japanese returned, and their heavy cruisers shelled Henderson Field. But the Americans sank seven Japanese transports and two cruisers. During the third phase on 14–15 November, U.S. warships under Rear Admiral Willis A. Lee met and defeated yet another Japanese force under Kondō when the two sides met near Savo Island. The Americans lost two destroyers, but Kondō lost the battleship *Kirishima* and a destroyer. The net effect of the three-day battle was that Tanaka landed only some 4,000 troops (he rescued another 5,000 on his return to Rabaul), whereas the Americans regained control of the waters around the island.

The last major naval battle for Guadalcanal occurred on 30 November at Tassafaronga Point. The Japanese again attempted to land reinforcements on Guadalcanal and were surprised by a larger U.S. Navy task force. However, the Japanese once more demonstrated their superior night-fighting ability. In the exchange, the Japanese lost a destroyer, and the Americans lost a cruiser.

Japanese leaders now came to the conclusion that they could no longer absorb such losses in trying to hold on in Guadalcanal. The final battle of the campaign was a skirmish off Rennell's Island on 30 January 1943. In early February 1943, the Japanese evacuated their remaining ground forces from Guadalcanal.

The Americans won the campaign thanks largely to their superior supply capability and the failure of the Japanese to throw enough resources into the battle. The Tokyo Express down the Slot was haphazard and inadequate; often drums full of supplies were simply pushed off ships to drift to shore. The campaign for Guadalcanal proved to be as much a turning point for the United States as Midway. The Japanese advance had been halted, opening the way for the long island-hopping advance toward Japan. In combatants the Japanese lost 1 light carrier, 2 battleships, 3 heavy cruisers, 1 light cruiser, 14 destroyers, and 8 submarines. Particularly serious from the Japanese point of view was the loss of 2,076 aircraft (1,094 to combat) and many trained pilots. U.S. Navy losses were 2 heavy carriers, 6 heavy cruisers (including the Royal Australian Navy *Canberra*), 2 light cruisers, and 15 destroyers, but new U.S. naval construction more than offset the U.S. losses. The campaign also destroyed the myth of Japanese naval superiority.

U.S. control of the air had rendered the Japanese ships vulnerable to attack. It also allowed Allied forces to determine the timing and location of offensive operations without Japanese foreknowledge.

William P. McEvoy and Spencer C. Tucker

See also

Cape Esperance, Battle of; Eastern Solomons, Battle of the; Fletcher, Frank Jack; Ghormley, Robert Lee; Guadalcanal Land Campaign; Guadalcanal Naval Campaign; Halsey, William Frederick, Jr.; Japan, Navy; King, Ernest Joseph; Kinkaid, Thomas Cassin; Kondō Nobutake; Lee, Willis Augustus "Ching"; Midway, Battle of; Nimitz, Chester William; Savo Island, Battle of; Tanaka Raizo; Tassafaronga, Battle of; TORCH, Operation; Turner, Richmond Kelly; United States, Navy; Vandegrift, Alexander Archer

References

Frank, Richard B. *Guadalcanal: The Definitive Account of the Landmark Battle.* New York: Random House, 1990.

Grace, James W. *The Naval Battle of Guadalcanal: Night Action, 13 November 1942.* Annapolis, MD: Naval Institute Press, 1999.

Hamel, Eric M. *Guadalcanal: Decision at Sea: The Naval Battle of Guadalcanal, November 13–15, 1942.* New York: Crown, 1988.

Hough, Frank O., Verle E. Ludwig, and Henry I. Shaw. *History of U.S. Marine Corps Operations in World War II: From Pearl Harbor to Guadalcanal.* Washington, DC: Government Printing Office, 1966.

Lundstrom, John B. *The First Team and the Guadalcanal Campaign.* Annapolis, MD: Naval Institute Press, 1994.

Morison, Samuel Eliot. *History of United States Naval Operations in World War II.* Vol. 5, *The Struggle for Guadalcanal, August 1942–February 1943.* Boston: Little, Brown, 1948.

Guam, Battle for (21 July–10 August 1944)

U.S. invasion and recapture of the largest of the Mariana Islands. Some 100 miles south of Saipan, Guam is at its greatest extremity some 34 miles long and 7 miles wide. The only one of the Marianas group controlled by the United States before the war, it had been acquired in 1898 as a consequence of the Spanish-American War. Little had been done to pre-

The U.S. Marines salute the U.S. Coast Guard after the fury of battle had subsided and the Japanese on Guam had been defeated, ca. August 1944. (National Archives)

pare the island against attack, and its 200-man Marine garrison, supported by Guamanian police and volunteers, was overwhelmed on 10 December 1941, following three days of fighting, by a 5,500-man Japanese brigade.

U.S. Admiral Ernest King, chief of naval operations, argued as early as January 1943 for an invasion of the Mariana Islands. Although originally planned for 18 June 1944, the invasion of Guam was delayed by more than a month because operations against Saipan took longer than anticipated and the task force reserve of the 27th Division had to be ordered there. Consequently, commander of Fifth Fleet Vice Admiral Raymond A. Spruance rescheduled the operation for 21 July. Marine Corps Lieutenant General Roy S. Geiger commanded the landing force of the 3rd Marine Division, 1st Provisional Marine Brigade, and the army's 77th Infantry Division.

Its limestone terrain veiled in labyrinthine vegetation, Guam was well suited for defense. The island's numerous ridges, hills, valleys, and caves allowed Lieutenant General Takashina Takeshi's 18,500 defenders to magnify their limited artillery resources. In close proximity to one another on the western shore were the two most important military installations: the fortified air base on Chote Peninsula and the navy yard at Apra Harbor.

The invasion was preceded for two days by the longest sustained naval bombardment of the Pacific islands campaigns to that point. The invasion force came ashore on the morning of 21 July in a two-pronged assault five miles apart. The 3rd Marine Division landed on the beach north of Apra Harbor to capture the nearby navy yard; the 1st Provisional Marine Brigade joined with the foremost elements of the 77th Infantry Division below the harbor to take the large airfield on the Orote Peninsula. Poor maps and stiff Japanese resistance prevented an advance of more than a few miles beyond the two designated American beachheads for four days. Enough Japanese guns survived the preliminary naval bombardment to inflict numerous casualties on the exposed American troops.

Late in the afternoon of 25 July, the 1st Provisional Marine Brigade finally seized the road bisecting the neck of the Orote Peninsula, severing Japanese access to the island's interior. That night, the trapped Japanese troops attempted to escape in General Takashina's ill-conceived banzai attack, only to be shattered by concentrated Marine artillery fire. Surviving Japanese were gradually eliminated over the next few days.

In an attempt to splinter the American beachhead north of Apra Harbor, at about 3:00 A.M. on 26 July Takashina mounted a well planned 3,900-man counterstrike against the unsuspecting 3rd Marine Division. Exploiting an unintended gap between two Marine regiments, the attackers swiftly penetrated the American position. Wild fighting ensued, involving support personnel as well as frontline defenders.

Despite initial gains and having inflicted 800 Marine casualties, after three hours the Japanese attack ground to a complete halt. It had cost an astounding 3,500 (95 percent) of the attacking force dead. Takashina's expensive counterattack proved catastrophic to his already inadequate force. Intermittent fighting continued for several weeks across much of the island's thickly forested interior as organized Japanese resistance slowly dissolved in the face of the Americans' steady northward advance. With the bulk of the island under American control, on 10 August Geiger pronounced active combat operations on Guam at an end.

The loss of Guam and the remainder of the Marianas deprived the Japanese navy of airfields and anchorages and cut Japan's major supply artery with the South Pacific and its large air and naval base at Truk in the Caroline Islands. The United States launched devastating B-29 bombing raids against Japan itself after it gained control of Guam, Saipan, and Tinian.

William B. Rogers and Phillip M. Sozansky

See also
Geiger, Roy Stanley; King, Ernest Joseph; Mariana Islands, Naval Campaign; Spruance, Raymond Ames
References
Arthur, Robert, and Kenneth Cohimia. *The Third Marine Division.* Washington, DC: Infantry Journal Press, 1948.
Congdon, Don, ed. *Combat WWII: Pacific Theater of Operations.* New York: Arbor House, 1983.
Crowl, Philip A. *U.S. Army in World War II: The War in the Pacific: Campaign in the Marianas.* Washington, DC: Office of the Chief of Military History, Department of the Army, 1960.
Gailey, Harry. *The Liberation of Guam: 21 July–10 August 1944.* Novato, CA: Presidio Press, 1988.
Morison, Samuel Eliot. *History of United States Naval Operations in World War II.* Vol. 8, *New Guinea and the Marianas, March 1944–August 1944.* Boston: Little, Brown, 1953.

Guandong (Kwantung) Army

Elite Japanese military force in Manchuria comprising Heilongjiang (Heilungkiang), Jilin (Kirin), and Liaoning Provinces. The Guandong Army (identified at the time as the Kwantung Army) was formed in April 1919 to protect Japanese interests in the part of southern Manchuria that Japan leased from China after the 1904–1905 Russo-Japanese War. Japan stationed one division there to defend the so-called Guandong Leased Territory and the South Manchurian Railway zone. For several years, the territory had been administered by the Guandong governor general, who also commanded Japan's expeditionary forces. In April 1919, a new joint civil/military administration was instituted, and the Guandong Army was charged with maintaining security. The Guandong Army consisted of an independent garrison of six battalions along with a division rotated every two years.

Facing a rising tide of Chinese nationalism and anti-Japanese sentiment in Manchuria, a handful of activist Guandong Army staff officers undertook unauthorized initiatives, such as the assassination in June 1928 of Manchurian warlord Zhang Zuolin (Chang Tso-lin). On 18 September 1931, Lieutenant Colonel Ishihara Kanji and Colonel Itagaki Seishiro arranged to blow up a section of Japanese railway track outside Mukden (now Shenyang), Liaoning Province, which they then falsely blamed on the Chinese. The Mukden Incident was the excuse for the Guandong Army to initiate fighting with local Chinese forces. In this, the so-called Manchurian Incident, the Guandong Army (without the approval of the Tokyo government) embarked on the conquest of most of the rest of Manchuria, leading to the establishment on 1 March 1932 of Manzhouguo (Manchukuo). In 1934, the Japanese installed as ruler Aixinjueluo Puyi (Aisingioro P'u-i, known to Westerners as Henry Puyi), the last emperor of China's Qing (Ch'ing) dynasty. The new state was then known as Manzhoudiguo (Manchoutikuo, the Manzhu [Manchu] Empire). It was in fact a puppet Japanese state.

The leaders of the Guandong Army regarded the Soviet Union as Japan's chief enemy. Throughout the 1930s, the two sides increased their forces in the border area of Korea, Manchuria, and the Soviet Far East, and border clashes between Japanese and Soviet troops increased. These confrontations included some heavy fighting in the Chagkufeng Incident (July-August 1938) and the Nomonhan Incident (May-September 1939).

Following the German invasion of the Soviet Union in June 1941, the Guandong Army expected a German victory. It conducted a mobilization exercise to prepare for an attack on the Soviet Union between August and October as soon as the Soviets had transferred forces from Manchuria to the European Front. Twelve Japanese divisions in Manchuria, two in Korea, and two from Japan participated in this exercise. Much to the disappointment of Guandong Army leaders, Tokyo decided instead to move into resource-rich south Asia. Supreme Headquarters in Tokyo enjoined Guandong Army leaders to avoid all border conflicts. Following Japan's string of early victories in Southeast Asia and the Pacific, and again anticipating a German victory, Japan withdrew forces from the Pacific Theater to reinforce the Guandong Army for war against the Soviet Union.

However, in conjunction with U.S. advances in the Pacific from February to July 1944, Supreme Headquarters withdrew 10 army divisions and 2 air divisions from Manchuria to the Pacific. The Guandong Army became a hollow force and easily fell prey to Soviet forces, which invaded Manchuria at the end of the war. Within two weeks of the Soviet strike into Manchuria, commander of the Guandong Army General Yamada Otozō surrendered, and the Guandong Army was disarmed. Some 60,000 men of the Guandong Army were killed in the fighting. After the cease-fire, another 185,000 died in Manchuria. About 600,000—including Japanese troops from North Korea, Sakhalin, and the Kuril Islands—were detained in prisoner-of-war camps, where they were

forced to work through 1950. The last group of prisoners was not released until 1956. In those labor camps, more than 55,000 died of illness or malnutrition.

Asakawa Michio

See also
Ishiwara Kanji; Manchuria Campaign; Yamada Otozō
References
Harries, Meirion, and Susie Harries. *Soldiers of the Sun: The Rise and Fall of the Imperial Japanese Army.* New York: Random House, 1992.
Takashi Nakayama. *Kanto Gun [Guandong Army].* Tokyo: Kōdan Sha, 2000.

Guderian, Heinz (1888–1953)

German army general. Born to a Prussian family in Kulm, Germany, on 17 January 1888, Heinz Guderian attended cadet schools and was commissioned a lieutenant in the 10th Hannoverian Jäger Battalion in January 1908. During World War I, he became a communications specialist, serving as assistant signals officer in Fourth Army headquarters until 1918, when he was appointed to the General Staff.

Guderian was active in the Freikorps during 1919, in which he served as chief of staff of the "Iron Division." He was later selected to be retained as one of 4,000 officers in the 100,000-man Reichswehr. Guderian was assigned to the transport troops in 1922. Returning to the General Staff in 1927, he became an advocate of mechanization based on British and French theorists. He was given command of an experimental motorized battalion in 1931 with which he demonstrated armored reconnaissance techniques. He was promoted to colonel in 1933, and in October 1935 he took command of the 2nd Panzer Division, one of only three being formed. He was promoted to Generalmajor (U.S. equiv. brigadier general) in August 1936.

In 1937, Guderian published his treatise on armored warfare (*Achtung-Panzer!*), which espoused the combination of tanks, dive-bombers, and motorized infantry that is characterized as blitzkrieg (lightning war). Rapid promotion followed as Guderian helped expand Germany's armored forces. He became Generalleutant (U.S. equiv. major general) and participated with his division in the occupation of Austria. In October, Guderian was promoted to general of panzer troops and appointed chief of mobile troops with direct access to Adolf Hitler.

During the invasion of Poland, Guderian commanded the XIX Panzer Corps, demonstrating through aggressive operations the soundness of blitzkrieg. He reached the pinnacle of operational command during the invasion of France in May 1940 when he led his panzer corps across the Meuse River at Sedan and raced to the English Channel to cut Allied forces off in Belgium.

During Operation BARBAROSSA, the June 1941 invasion of the Soviet Union, Guderian, now a full general, commanded

German General Heinz Guderian. (Photo by Hulton Archive/Getty Images)

the 2nd Panzer Group in Army Group Center, where he cooperated with General Hermann Hoth's 3rd Panzer Group to encircle large Soviet forces at Minsk on 10 July. Guderian then was ordered south to assist General Paul L. E. von Kleist's 4th Panzer Group encircle more than 600,000 Russians in the Kiev pocket in September. Guderian's short temper and mercurial disposition toward superiors eventually led him to be relieved of command in December over tactical disputes.

Following a year of inactivity, Guderian was recalled to duty by Hitler as inspector general of armored troops in March 1943. Guderian made great efforts to rebuild the worn panzer forces. After the assassination attempt against Hitler in July 1944, Guderian was appointed chief of the General Staff. He stood up to Hitler on numerous occasions, leading to his dismissal on 28 March 1945. Taken prisoner by U.S. forces at the end of the war, Guderian was not prosecuted for war crimes, although he remained a prisoner until June 1948. Guderian died at Schwengen, Bavaria, on 14 May 1953. A headstrong and aggressive battlefield commander, Guderian turned mechanized theory into practice and established a legacy as the father of blitzkrieg warfare.

Steven J. Rauch

See also

Armored Warfare; BARBAROSSA, Operation; Blitzkrieg; France, Battle for; Hitler, Adolf; Hoth, Hermann; Kiev Pocket, Battle of the; Kleist, Paul Ludwig Ewald von; Poland Campaign

References

Guderian, Heinz. *Achtung-Panzer! The Development of Armoured Forces: Their Tactics and Operational Potential.* Trans. Christopher Duffy. London: Arms and Armour Press, 1993.

———. *Panzer Leader.* Trans. Constantine Fitzgibbon. London: Harborough, 1957.

Macksey, Kenneth. *Guderian: Creator of the Blitzkrieg.* New York: Stein and Day, 1976.

Guernica, Kondor Legion Attack on (26 April 1937)

The Spanish town of Guernica was bombed by German and Italian aircraft during the Spanish Civil War. When the Nationalists revolted against the Republican government of Spain in July 1936, Germany and Italy sent aid to the Nationalist side. Chancellor Adolf Hitler provided aircraft collectively known as the Kondor Legion commanded by Generalmajor (U.S. equiv. brigadier general) Hugo Sperrle.

By early 1937, the Nationalists' failure to capture Madrid shifted attention to the Basque provinces in the north. Spanish General Emilio Mola commanded the assault on the ground, promising to raze the region if it did not surrender. The air component was largely independent under German control. By late April 1937, Sperrle's chief of staff, Colonel Wolfram von Richthofen, discerned an opportunity to cut off the Republican retreat by bombing the Renteria bridge near the Basque town of Guernica. The Basques were a distinct ethnic group with their own language, customs, and tradition of representative government. Guernica was the spiritual center of the Basque people, the home of their parliament and of El Arbol, a sacred oak under which Spanish kings had traditionally promised to respect Basque rights.

On 26 April 1937, Richthofen ordered air assaults on the Renteria bridge as well as the surrounding suburbs to block the retreat of Basque troops. At approximately 4:40 P.M., the first German bomber appeared over Guernica and dropped its payload on a plaza near the bridge. Some 25 minutes later three more bombers arrived, followed by fighters that strafed the panicked population. Shortly after 6:00 P.M., waves of German and Italian bombers reached the town. Because smoke and dust blanketed the target, coupled with primitive bombsights, crews simply dropped their bombs into the city. More than 100,000 pounds of high explosives and incendiaries rained down on Guernica.

Normally Guernica numbered 5,000 inhabitants, but uncounted refugees and soldiers had swollen the population. As a result, exact casualty figures remain elusive, but the dead certainly numbered in the hundreds. Although the raid razed more than half of the town's structures, the Renteria bridge survived, as did the Basque parliament and El Arbol. Even so, Richthofen expressed pleasure with the results.

That evening press reports reached the major European capitals concerning the bombing, many depicting it as a premeditated terror attack. The Nationalist press claimed that the city was burned by the Republicans to discredit the Nationalist cause. Not until the 1970s did the Spanish government admit Nationalist involvement in Guernica's destruction.

Learning of the tragedy in Paris, Spanish artist Pablo Picasso began work on a mural depicting the anguish and devastation. Scholars often credit this work, *Guernica*, for connecting the Basque town with the indiscriminate destruction of modern war.

Rodney Madison

See also

Franco, Francisco; Germany, Air Force; Hitler, Adolf; Kondor Legion; Richthofen, Wolfram von

References

Large, David Clay. "Guernica: Death in the Afternoon." *MHQ: The Quarterly Journal of Military History* 1 (Summer 1989): 8–17.

Southworth, Herbert Rutledge. *Guernica! Guernica! A Study of Journalism, Diplomacy, Propaganda, and History.* Berkeley: University of California Press, 1977.

Thomas, Gordon, and Max Morgan Witts. *Guernica: The Crucible of World War II.* New York: Stein and Day, 1975.

Whealey, Robert H. *Hitler and Spain: The Nazi Role in the Spanish Civil War, 1936–1939.* Lexington: University Press of Kentucky, 1989.

Guerrillas

See Partisans/Guerrillas.

Gustav Gun

The Krupp 80 cm K(E), known as the *schwere Gustav* (heavy Gustav), was the largest artillery piece ever built. A railway gun that had to move over a specially laid double track, it was supported by two bogies, each with 20 axles. The gun weighed 1,344 tons and had a bore diameter of 31.5 inches. Using a 3,000-lb propellant charge, it fired two different types of projectiles. The 10,560-lb high-explosive round had a maximum range of nearly 30 mi. The 15,600-lb concrete-piercing shell had a maximum range of 23 mi.

The German army ordered three 80 cm K(E) guns in 1937 for the specific mission of demolishing the French forts on the Maginot Line. However, by the time the first gun was delivered in late 1941, France had long since fallen. In January 1942, Heavy (Railway) Artillery Unit 672 was formed to man the gun; the unit moved to the Crimea in April. The gun, nicknamed "Dora" by the crew, was not ready to fire its first round in the siege of Sevastopol until 5 June. Between then and 17 June, it fired a total of 48 rounds in combat. The rounds all landed anywhere from 197 ft to 2,400 ft from their targets. Nonetheless, the shells were

> The Gustav Gun was the largest artillery piece ever built at 1,344 tons and a range of 30 miles.

large enough that their destructive power contributed to the fall of Forts Stalin, Lenin, Siberia, and Maxim Gorki.

After the fall of Sevastopol, the Gustav gun returned to Germany to receive a new barrel. Plans to send the gun to Leningrad were preempted by the Soviets having raised the siege. Some sources report that the gun fired against the Poles during the Warsaw Rising in August 1944, but that has never been confirmed.

The second 80 cm K(E) was completed and delivered, but the crew was never raised. The third gun was still incomplete when the war ended. In April 1945, the German army destroyed both completed weapons.

The Gustav gun was a technical masterpiece, but it was a tactical white elephant. Under the best of conditions, it never fired more than seven or eight rounds per day. Once the gun reached its designated firing position, it required three to six weeks to assemble and place into battery. Its entire detachment numbered 1,420 men, commanded by a colonel with his own headquarters and planning staff. The main gun crew numbered 500, most of whom moved, prepared, and serviced the ammunition. The remainder of the unit consisted of an intelligence section, two antiaircraft artillery battalions, and two guard companies.

David T. Zabecki

See also

Artillery Doctrine; Artillery Types; Leningrad, Siege of; Maginot Line; Sevastopol, Battle for

References

Hogg, Ian V. *German Artillery of World War Two.* Mechanicsburg, PA: Stackpole Books, 1975.

———. *The Guns, 1939–45.* New York: Ballantine Books, 1970.

———. *The Illustrated Encyclopedia of Artillery.* Secaucus, NJ: Chartwell Books, 1988.

Lewis, John E. *Railway Guns.* New York: Avalon Books, 1982.

H

Haakon VII, King of Norway (1872–1957)

Born on 3 August 1872 at Charlottenlund Castle near Copenhagen, Denmark, Prince Charles was the second son of the future King Frederik VIII of Denmark. Charles was educated by private tutors and entered the Danish navy at age 14. In 1893, he became an officer, and in 1896 he married Princess Maud of Great Britain, daughter of King Edward VII. They had one son, Alexander, later renamed Olaf. Norway declared independence from Sweden in 1905 and Charles was elected its constitutional monarch, choosing the Norwegian title of Haakon VII.

Haakon worked to establish a modern monarchy. His motto was "All for Norway." He hoped Norway could remain neutral during World War II, but when the Germans invaded his country in April 1940, Haakon rejected demands that he appoint pro-Nazi Vidkun Quisling as premier and urged his people to resist. Haakon reluctantly left Norway aboard a British warship on 7 June 1940 with his son Olaf and members of the Storting (parliament) for exile in Britain. As head of the Norwegian government in exile, Haakon spoke to his people via radio, explaining that the Norwegian constitution allowed him to wage war against the Germans from abroad and refusing to abdicate. During the rest of the war, Haakon was heavily involved in the resistance movement; he became both Norway's symbol of resistance and its rallying point.

Haakon was warmly welcomed on his return to Oslo on 7 June 1945, exactly five years from his departure and the fortieth anniversary of Norway's independence. His spirited wartime activities had created a strong bond between him and his people. Haakon spent the immediate postwar years helping with reconstruction. He also dispensed with the formali-

King Haakon VII of Norway. (Library of Congress)

ties of court life, endearing himself further to the Norwegians. This well-loved "people's king" died at Oslo on 21 September 1957. He was succeeded by his son, who reigned as Olaf V.

Annette Richardson

See also
Norway, German Conquest of (1940); Norway, Role in War; Quisling, Vidkun Abraham Lauritz Jonsson; Resistance

References
Derry, Thomas K. *A Short History of Norway*. London: G. Allen and Unwin, 1957.
Greve, Tim. *Haakon VII of Norway: Founder of a New Monarchy*. Trans. Thomas Kingston Derry. London: Hurst, 1983.
Michael, Maurice Albert. *Haakon, King of Norway*. London: Allen and Unwin, 1958.

Haile Selassie, Emperor of Ethiopia (1892–1975)

Haile Selassie was emperor of Ethiopia (also known as Abyssinia). He was born at Ejersagoro on 23 July 1892 as Tafari Makonnen. His father was Ras Makonnen, a Coptic Christian and leading general and political figure. Tafari was a grandnephew of Emperor Menelik II (reigned 1889–1913).

An excellent student, Tafari attended both the Capucin school and the palace school. From age 13, he governed Harer, Selale, and Darass. On Menilek's death, his grandson Lij Iyasu succeeded to the throne, but he Islamized the government. The Christians denounced this policy, and Iyasu was deposed. Menilek's daughter, Empress Sawditu I (reigned 1916–1930) made the progressive-minded Tafari the regent and heir. From 1917 to 1928 he traveled in the west expressly to absorb the culture and ideas.

Tafari was proclaimed emperor on Sawditu's death in 1930. Declaring himself a direct descendant of King Solomon and the Queen of Sheba, Tafari adopted the name Haile Selassie, meaning "might of the trinity." His suppression of slavery was a matter of personal pride. He established the Bank of Ethiopia and promulgated a new criminal code. Selassie soon earned a worldwide reputation as a humanitarian, although he centralized power in his own person and was in fact a royal dictator.

Selassie took his country's disputes with Italy to the League of Nations. Italy's invasion in 1935 found the Ethiopians no match for the invaders, who had complete air supremacy and employed poison gas. Selassie fled to Britain in 1936, appealing for support in a masterful but unsuccessful address to the League of Nations. Following Italy's entry into World War II in June 1940 and the extension of the fighting to Africa, British forces liberated Ethiopia, and Selassie returned to his capital in triumph in 1941.

Selassie's progressive policies after the war included political reform, social reform, and a national assembly in 1955.

Haile Selassie, Emperor of Ethiopia (1930–1936 and 1941–1974). (Photo by Hulton Archive/Getty Images)

His focus in the 1960s and 1970s was pan-African. In 1960, he crushed a revolt of army officers and intellectuals who advocated further reforms. He was successfully overthrown on 12 September 1974 and placed under palace arrest. Selassie died mysteriously on 17 August 1975.

Annette Richardson

References
Lockot, Hans Wilhelm. *The Mission: The Life, Reign, and Character of Haile Selassie I*. New York: St. Martin's Press, 1989.
Marcus, Harold G. *Haile Selassie I: The Formative Years, 1892–1936*. Los Angeles: University of California Press, 1987.
Mosley, Leonard. *Haile Selassie: The Conquering Lion*. London: Weidenfeld and Nicolson, 1964.
Schwab, Peter. *Haile Selassie I: Ethiopia's Lion of Judah*. Chicago: Nelson-Hall, 1979.

Halder, Franz (1884–1972)

German army general. Born on 30 August 1884 in Würzburg, Germany, Franz Halder joined a Bavarian field artillery regiment in 1902 and attended the Bavarian Staff College in Munich before the outbreak of World War I. As a result of his training, Halder served throughout the war as a staff officer at the division through army-group levels on both the Western and Eastern Fronts. His performance during World War I secured him a position in the postwar Reichswehr (state armed forces). Serving in both command and staff positions during the interwar years, he was promoted to colonel in December 1931, to Generalmajor (U.S. equiv. brigadier general) in October 1934, to Generalleutnant (U.S. equiv. major general) in August 1936, and to General der Artillerie (U.S. equiv. lieutenant general) in February 1938. In October 1938, Halder was appointed chief of the army General Staff.

Halder played a crucial role in the planning and execution of Germany's campaigns before World War II and during its first years. By the end of the Polish Campaign in 1939, he had convinced the German army commander in chief, Generaloberst (U.S. equiv. full general) Walther von Brauchitsch, to place overall responsibility for operations in his hands. His claims to sole authorship of the 1940 campaign in France were unjustified, although Halder was at the center of the campaign's successful execution. Halder was promoted to Generaloberst in July 1940.

Anticipating future operations in the east, Halder established a planning group in the summer of 1940 to develop a campaign plan against the Soviet Union. His lack of vision and unwillingness to encourage innovation among his subordinates, however, resulted in a plan that did not fully address the Red Army's capabilities or clearly identify the campaign's objectives. Failing to defeat the Red Army in the summer of 1941, Halder maintained his belief that the German army would decide the campaign at the gates of Moscow.

Through the spring of 1942, Halder became increasingly disillusioned with Adolf Hitler's conduct of operations, particularly the 1942 offensive on the Eastern Front. By September, the Führer had had enough of the army chief of staff's intransigence and summarily relieved him on 24 September. Halder remained on the inactive list, keeping in contact with Colonel General Ludwig Beck, former chief of the General Staff and a leader of the resistance against Hitler. As a result of these exchanges, Halder was imprisoned in the Flossenbürg concentration camp in the aftermath of the 20 July 1944 attempt on Hitler's life. Halder's association with Beck was sufficient to prevent his conviction at the International Military Tribunal at Nuremberg. Halder then spent 14 years with the U.S. Army Historical Division and received the Meritorious Civilian Service Award in 1961. Halder died on 2 April 1972 in Aschau, West Germany.

David M. Toczek

See also
BARBAROSSA, Operation; Beck, Ludwig; Belgium Campaign; Brauchitsch, Heinrich Alfred Hermann Walther von; Caucasus Campaign; France, Battle for; Hitler, Adolf; Poland Campaign;

German General Franz Halder. (Photo by Hulton Archive/Getty Images)

SICHELSCHNITT, Operation; Stauffenberg, Claus Philip Schenk von; Zeitzler, Kurt von

References
Addington, Larry H. *The Blitzkrieg Era and the German General Staff, 1865–1941.* New Brunswick, NJ: Rutgers University Press, 1971.
Halder, Franz. *The Halder Diaries: The Private War Journals of Colonel General Franz Halder.* Boulder, CO: Westview Press, 1976.
Leach, Barry A. "Halder." In Correlli Barnett, ed., *Hitler's Generals*, 101–128. New York: William Morrow, 1989.

Halifax, Edward Frederick Lindley Wood, Earl of

See Wood, Edward Frederick Lindley (Earl of Halifax).

Halsey, William Frederick, Jr. (1882–1959)

U.S. Navy admiral. Born in Elizabeth, New Jersey, on 30 October 1882, William Halsey Jr. was a naval officer's son. He graduated from the U.S. Naval Academy in 1904 and was commissioned an ensign in 1906. Halsey served in the Great White Fleet that circumnavigated the globe from 1907 to 1909 and was then in torpedo boats. When the United States entered World War I in April 1917, Halsey was a lieutenant commander and captain of a destroyer. He then commanded destroyers operating from Queenstown, Ireland.

Following World War I, Halsey's service was mostly in destroyers, although he also held an assignment in naval intelligence and was a naval attaché in Berlin. Promoted to captain in 1927, he commanded the *Reina Mercedes*, the Naval Academy training ship, and became fascinated by naval aviation. Halsey attended both the Naval War College and Army War College, and in 1935, despite his age, he completed naval flight training and took command of the aircraft carrier *Saratoga*. Promoted to rear admiral in 1937, Halsey assumed command of Carrier Division 2 of the *Enterprise* and *Yorktown*. He was promoted to vice admiral in 1940.

Halsey was at sea on 7 December 1941 when Japanese aircraft attacked Pearl Harbor. In early 1942, Halsey's carriers raided Japanese central Pacific installations and launched Colonel James Doolittle's raid on Tokyo in April. Acute skin disorders requiring hospitalization removed him from the Battle of Midway in June 1942. In October 1942, Halsey replaced Admiral Robert Ghormley as commander of the South Pacific and began the most successful phase of his career. He was promoted to admiral in November. Despite severe tactical losses, Halsey retained strategic control of the waters around Guadalcanal in late 1942, and during 1943 he supported operations in the Solomon Islands and into the Bismarck Archipelago. Halsey came to be known as "Bull" for his pugnacious nature.

In March 1943, Halsey took administrative command of the Third Fleet, although he continued his command in the South Pacific until June 1944. In the Battle of Leyte Gulf, the Japanese battle plan and the flawed American command system combined with Halsey's aggressiveness to shape one of the more controversial episodes of the war. On 24–25 October, a Japanese force centered on four fleet aircraft carriers that were largely bereft of aircraft under Admiral Ozawa Jisaburo decoyed Halsey and his entire Task Force 38 away from the U.S. landing sites, leaving the sites vulnerable to a powerful Japanese surface force under Kurita Takeo. Although Halsey destroyed most of Osawa's force in the Battle of Cape Engaño, disaster for the support ships off Leyte was only narrowly averted when Kurita lost his nerve. Widely criticized for not coordinating his movements with Vice Admiral Thomas Kinkaid, who had charge of the invasion force of Seventh Fleet, Halsey never admitted responsibility. He instead blamed the system of divided command.

Halsey endured further condemnation when he took the Third Fleet into damaging typhoons in December 1944 and

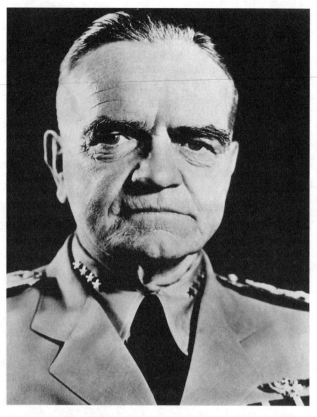

U.S. Navy Admiral William Frederick Halsey, Jr. (Library of Congress)

June 1945. Still, his flagship, the *Missouri*, hosted the formal Japanese surrender on 2 September 1945. Promoted to admiral of the fleet in December 1945, Halsey retired in April 1947. He then served on the boards of several large corporations. Halsey died at Fisher's Island, New York, on 16 August 1959.

John A. Hutcheson Jr. and Spencer C. Tucker

See also

Aircraft Carriers; Aviation, Naval; Cape Esperance, Battle of; Carrier Raids, U.S.; Central Pacific Campaign; Doolittle, James Harold "Jimmy"; Ghormley, Robert Lee; Guadalcanal Naval Campaign; Japan, Official Surrender; Kinkaid, Thomas Cassin; Kolombangara, Battle of; Kula Gulf, Battle of; Kurita Takeo; Leyte Gulf, Battle of; Leyte, Landings on and Capture of; MacArthur, Douglas; McCain, John Sidney; Mitscher, Marc Andrew; Nimitz, Chester William; Ozawa Jisaburo; Philippines, U.S. Recapture of; Santa Cruz Islands, Battle of; Solomon Islands, Naval Campaign; Southwest Pacific Theater; Spruance, Raymond Ames; Tassafaronga, Battle of; Vella Gulf, Battle of; Vella Lavella, Sea Battle of; United States, Navy

References

Cutler, Thomas J. *The Battle for Leyte Gulf, 23–26 October 1944*. New York: Harper Collins, 1994.

Halsey, William Frederick, Jr. *Admiral Halsey's Story*. New York: McGraw Hill, 1947.

Potter, E. B. *Bull Halsey*. Annapolis, MD: Naval Institute Press, 1985.

Reynolds, Clark G. *The Fast Carriers: The Forging of an Air Navy*. New York: McGraw-Hill, 1968.

———. "William F. Halsey, Jr.: The Bull." In Jack Sweetman, ed., *The Great Admirals: Command at Sea, 1587–1945*, 482–505. Annapolis, MD: Naval Institute Press, 1997.

Hamburg, Raids on (24 July–3 August 1943)

The air battle of Hamburg, Operation GOMORRAH, consisted of a series of six raids in July and August 1943 that destroyed a large portion of the city and killed more than 45,000 people. Most of them died in the horrendous firestorm of the night of 27 July, the first such conflagration induced by bombing. More than half of the residential units in the city were destroyed, and 900,000 people lost their homes. The Americans and British bombed the city many times later in the war, but none of those raids approached the results or notoriety of the July attack.

Four of the attacks were mounted at night by the Royal Air Force (RAF), and two in daylight by the U.S. Army Air Forces (USAAF) Eighth Air Force. The initial British operation, which began the night of 24 July, featured the first use of chaff, code-named WINDOW, in combat. The cloud of metallic strips blotted out large segments of enemy radar screens and provided cover for aircraft that stayed within the pattern, cloaking the bomber stream. This helped keep losses relatively low during RAF operations; only 87 British bombers were lost out of more than 3,000 sorties.

The USAAF sent 252 B-17 Flying Fortresses over Hamburg on 25 and 26 July but lost 17 aircraft. In addition, the American bombing accuracy was poor, since primary targets were often obscured by smoke from the earlier RAF raid. The Americans dropped only about 300 tons of bombs on the city, whereas RAF bombers delivered more than 8,000 tons.

The second British attack combined concentrated bombing with ideal weather conditions of high temperature and low humidity to produce an unexpected firestorm, which was further helped along because most of Hamburg's firefighters were in distant sectors of the city dealing with the results of the earlier attacks. Most of the dead had heeded the advice of local authorities to stay in basement shelters, where they were

Bombed buildings, Hamburg, Germany, July 1943. (Library of Congress)

asphyxiated by carbon monoxide or crushed by collapsing buildings. However, taking to the streets was no guarantee of safety. Those who fled the shelters sometimes met even more horrible deaths, sucked into fires by high winds or caught in molten asphalt.

German armaments minister Albert Speer feared that if the Allies could quickly follow up with six similar devastating firestorms, the German economy might collapse. However, although RAF Bomber Command tried, it could not achieve the same result until its February 1945 assault on Dresden.

Hamburg itself recovered surprisingly quickly, and the Luftwaffe changed its defensive tactics to counter the RAF night-bombing campaign. Scholarship conducted 50 years after the bombing of Dresden has considerably lowered the casualty figures from that bombing; it appears that the 27 July attack on Hamburg, not the Dresden bombing, was the deadliest air raid in the European Theater. The raids on Hamburg set a standard that RAF Bomber Command found difficult to duplicate and still provide a vivid symbol of the horrors of the bombing of cities and of total war.

> The air battle of Hamburg killed more than 45,000 people and 900,000 people lost their homes.

Conrad C. Crane

See also

Aircraft, Bombers; Dresden, Air Attack on; Radar; Strategic Bombing

References

Brunswig, Hans. *Feuersturm über Hamburg.* Stuttgart: Motorbuch Verlag, 1978.

Middlebrook, Martin. *The Battle of Hamburg.* New York: Charles Scribner's Sons, 1981.

Webster, Charles, and Noble Frankland. *The Strategic Air Offensive against Germany.* 4 vols. London: Her Majesty's Stationery Office, 1961.

Hand Grenades

Numerous types of hand grenades were used by the military forces during World War II. The U.S. military used offensive, defensive, and special-use grenades. The MkIII A1, a can-shaped grenade filled with 8 oz of flaked TNT, was used for offensive purposes because no fragmentation took place after the initial explosion. The MkII "pineapple" grenade was for defensive use and was based on the old British "Mills Bomb" design. Troops could not assault forward because of the fragmentation of its serrated shell, which created a 10-yard killing radius. The M15 WP "Willie Pete" or white-phosphorous grenade, used for smoke generation and the assaulting of caves and pillboxes, saw limited use. In tight quarters, the almost 2 lb M15 WP created severe eye, respiratory, and skin injuries.

The standard hand grenade for British forces was the revised M36 Mills Bomb. It had a serrated cast-iron body filled with TNT and was used defensively. Of note was the screw-in fuse, which was put in place prior to combat. To use the grenade, the user pulled the pin and then threw the grenade. When the grenade left the user's hand, the spring-loaded lever was released, activating the fusing sequence. A more specialized grenade was the "Gammon Bomb" (No. 82), a 20 oz cloth bag filled with plastic explosive. It had an attached screw-off metal cap that was removed to arm the device. The Gammon Bomb was effective against pillboxes and bunkers.

The French military drew on the venerable F1 defensive grenade. This grenade had a serrated body and used a 5 sec delay fuse activated by a pin-and-lever system similar to that found in the British M36.

The standard German hand grenades were the high-explosive stick grenade (*Stielhandgranate* 24) and the high-explosive hand grenade (*Eihandgranate* 39). The offensive *Stiel.* 24, universally known as the "potato masher" grenade, contained a bursting TNT charge and could be fitted with a fragmentation sleeve for defensive use. The igniter was activated by pulling the porcelain bead found in the handle behind the metal cap. A heavier *Stiel.* 43 variant existed; it contained almost twice the TNT charge and could also be fitted with a fragmentation sleeve. The offensive *Ei.* 39 is egg-shaped, and its older and newer designs differed slightly. The TNT filler was initiated by a detonator and friction igniter. More specialized German grenades were the offensive wooden and concrete improvised hand grenades (*Behelfshandgranate-Holz* and *Beton*) and numerous forms of smoke grenades (*Nebelhandgranate*) based on stick, conventional, egg, and glass body designs.

The Italian army used three main types of grenades, known as "Red Devil Grenades" from their color. All used a pull firing pin. The Breda Model 35 (introduced in 1935) weighed 7 oz and had only 2 oz of TNT; the SRCM Model 35 also weighed 7 oz but had only 1.5 oz of TNT. The OTO Model 35 weighed 7.4 oz and had 2.5 oz of TNT. Italian grenades tended to have too little explosive filler and broke into large fragments, so that often they did little damage to their targets. The Breda Model 42 with a handle (potato-masher style) was developed to attack enemy tanks and contained 1.5 lb of TNT.

Hand grenades in use by Japanese forces were the Model 91 (1931), Model 97 (1937), Model 99 (1939), and Model 23. The Model 91 had a serrated body and was for defensive use. Its fuse had to be struck against a hard object, such as a helmet, to ignite it. The Model 97 was a newer variation of the

A Marine (second from right) throws a hand grenade against a Japanese position, Saipan 1944. (Library of Congress)

Model 91. It had a shorter fuse delay time of 4–5 sec rather than 7–8 sec, could not be fired from a discharger, and was carried by all frontline troops. The lighter Model 99 Kiska had a smooth, cylindrical body and a flange at either end. It also used an impact fuse, and because it was smaller, it could be used for offensive purposes. The Model 23 looked like the Model 91 but had two lugs and rings on the side for mooring so it could also be used in booby traps. It had a pull-type friction igniter fuse and was filled with granular TNT. Other more specialized grenades included the 18 oz incendiary grenade, the incendiary stick grenade, and the high-explosive stick hand grenade.

Soviet hand grenades were based on the Type-1933, Type-1942, and F-1 models. The Type-1933 (RGD-33) was composed of a grenade head and a throwing handle. It could be used in either a defensive or an offensive mode, depending on whether the fragmentation jacket (normal and lightened types) was used over the grenade head. Detonation time was 3.2 to 3.8 sec after fuse ignition. The can-shaped Type-1942 (RG-42) was for offensive and defensive use. Although it created a lethal bursting radius, it was somewhat smaller than average because of the lighter scored squares found in its internal metallic belt. The F-1 was for defensive use. Externally, it resembled the U.S. MkII pineapple grenade, but it was based on either the standardized (UZRG) or Koveshnikov fuse. Because it expelled heavy fragments out to 656 ft, the F-1 was only thrown from trenches or other covered positions.

Robert J. Bunker

See also
Infantry Tactics
References
The Official Soviet Army Hand Grenade Manual. Trans. James Gebhardt. Boulder, CO: Paladin Press, 1998 (reprint of 1944/1974 manuals).

U.S. Department of the Army. *Hand and Rifle Grenades. FM 23–30.* Washington, DC: U.S. Government Printing Office, 1949.

U.S. War Department. *Handbook on Japanese Military Forces*. Baton Rouge: Louisiana State Press, 1995 (reprint of 1944 handbook).

———. *Handbook on German Military Forces*. Baton Rouge: Louisiana State University Press, 1995 (reprint of 1945 handbook).

Harbor, Artificial

See Mulberries.

Harriman, William Averell (1891–1986)

Key U.S. diplomat posted to Great Britain and the Soviet Union during World War II. Born on 15 November 1891 in New York City—the son of Edward Henry Harriman, owner of the Union Pacific Railroad and one of the wealthiest U.S. businessmen—W. Averell Harriman initially pursued a career as a venture capitalist and with Union Pacific. In 1920, he invested in German shipping, Soviet manganese mine concessions, and aviation. In 1931, he merged his investment firm with an established merchant bank to form Brown Brothers Harriman. From the late 1920s onward, a burgeoning interest in politics caused Harriman to support the Democrats and back President Franklin D. Roosevelt's reformist New Deal policies. Harriman held several posts in the National Recovery Administration and sought a World War II government job.

In March 1941, Roosevelt sent Harriman to London as "defense expediter" to coordinate and facilitate the anticipated flood of American wartime supplies to Britain under the newly established Lend-Lease program. Harriman quickly established a warm and confidential relationship with Britain's wartime prime minister, Winston L. S. Churchill. He often bypassed the U.S. ambassador, John G. Winant, to report directly to White House aide Harry Hopkins and serve as an unofficial liaison between Churchill and Roosevelt. In London, Harriman, although married, began a clandestine love affair with Churchill's daughter-in-law, Pamela Digby Churchill, who eventually (in 1971) became his third wife.

When Germany invaded Russia in June 1941, the United States extended Lend-Lease aid to the Soviet Union, and dealings with Moscow likewise fell within Harriman's remit. In 1943, Harriman replaced Admiral William H. Standley as U.S. ambassador to the Soviet Union, where he remained until 1946, attending the major wartime Allied conferences at Tehran, Yalta, and Potsdam. In late 1944, when Soviet troops allowed occupying German forces to suppress Polish rebels in Warsaw before themselves mopping up the remaining

Germans (a policy deliberately designed to eliminate future opponents of a Soviet-backed Polish regime), Harriman sent diplomatic dispatches to Washington sounding one of the earliest official warnings against future Soviet designs for the nations of eastern Europe.

Harriman subsequently held numerous other government positions under Democratic presidents, gaining the reputation of advocating a firm but flexible and nonalarmist stance toward the Soviets. Harriman died in Yorktown Heights, New York, on 26 July 1986.

Priscilla Roberts

See also
Churchill, Sir Winston L. S.; Hopkins, Harry Lloyd; Lend-Lease; Potsdam Conference; Roosevelt, Franklin D.; Stalin, Josef; Tehran Conference; Warsaw Rising; Yalta Conference

References
Abramson, Rudy. *Spanning the Century: The Life of W. Averell Harriman, 1891–1986*. New York: Morrow, 1991.
Bland, Larry. "W. Averell Harriman: Businessman and Diplomat, 1891–1945." Ph.D. dissertation, University of Wisconsin, 1972.
Harriman, W. Averell, and Elie Abel. *Special Envoy to Churchill and Stalin, 1941–1946*. New York: Random House, 1975.
Isaacson, Walter, and Evan Thomas. *The Wise Men: Six Friends and the World They Made*. New York: Simon and Schuster, 1986.
Mayers, David. *The Ambassadors and America's Soviet Policy*. New York: Oxford University Press, 1995.

Harris, Sir Arthur Travers (1892–1984)

Royal Air Force air chief marshal and commander of Bomber Command. Born on 13 April 1892 in Cheltenham, England, Arthur Harris joined a Rhodesian regiment at the beginning of World War I. In 1915, he transferred to the Royal Flying Corps and became a pilot, and by the end of the war he commanded the 44th Squadron. After the war, he served in India and Iraq and commanded a training school. He completed the Army Staff College (1927), again served in the Middle East, and then held posts at the Air Ministry (1933–1937).

On the outbreak of World War II, Harris commanded Number 5 Bomber Group. He then was deputy chief of the Air Staff and headed a mission to Washington. Dissatisfaction with the course of British strategic bombing led to his appointment in February 1942 as head of Bomber Command and his promotion to air chief marshal.

Harris committed himself to maintaining Bomber Command as an independent strategic arm. In May 1942, he launched the first of the 1,000-plane raids against Köln (Cologne), which did much to raise morale at home. Harris, who was nicknamed "Bomber," maintained that massive bombing would break German civilian morale and bring about an end to the war. Harris ordered Bomber Command to conduct massive night raids against German cities. Among

Neillands, Robin. *The Bomber War: The Allied Air Offensive against Nazi Germany.* New York: Peter Mayer Publishers, 2001.

Probert, Henry. *Bomber Harris: His Life and Times.* London: Greenhill Books, 2001.

Saward, Dudley. *Bomber Harris: The Story of Sir Arthur Harris.* Garden City, NY: Doubleday, 1985.

Royal Air Force Air Chief Marshall Sir Arthur Harris/Commander. (Library of Congress)

other missions, Harris directed the May 1943 raid on the Ruhr dams by 617th Squadron, the July 1943 raid against Hamburg, attacks against German rocket factories at Peenemünde in August 1943, the November 1943 attacks against Berlin, and the destruction of Dresden in February 1945.

Harris remains controversial, especially because of his seeming lack of concern over collateral bomb damage. He was at odds with his superior, chief of the Air Staff Air Marshal Charles Portal, and others who sought to target specific industries considered essential to the Nazi war effort. What appeared to be indiscriminate bombing of cities also brought harsh criticism on Harris at the end of the war. His aircrews, however, remained fiercely loyal to him.

Harris retired from the RAF in September 1945 and headed a South African shipping company. His memoir, *Bomber Offensive*, was published in 1947. Made a baronet in 1953, Harris died on 5 April 1984 at Goring-on-Thames, England.

Thomas D. Veve

See also
Berlin, Air Battle of; Dresden, Air Attack on; Hamburg; Köln; Peenemünde Raid; Portal, Sir Charles Frederick Algernon

References
Harris, Arthur T. *Bomber Offensive.* London: Collins, 1947.

Hart, Thomas Charles (1877–1971)

U.S. Navy admiral. Born in Davison, Michigan, on 12 June 1877, Thomas Hart graduated from the U.S. Naval Academy in 1897 and was commissioned an ensign in 1899. He served in Cuban waters on the battleship *Massachusetts* during the Spanish-American War and commanded a submarine force of seven boats based in Ireland during World War I.

Between the world wars, Hart commanded submarine and cruiser forces and the battleship *Mississippi.* He graduated from the Naval War College in 1923 and the Army War College in 1924. In 1929, Hart was promoted to rear admiral and took command of submarines in the Atlantic and Pacific Fleets from 1929 to 1931. He was superintendent of the Naval Academy from 1931 to 1934. He commanded a cruiser division of the Scouting Force from 1934 to 1936 and served as a member of the navy's General Board from 1936 to 1939.

In June 1939, Hart was promoted to full admiral and given command of the small U.S. Asiatic Fleet. During the next years, he accelerated fleet training and drills and made plans to defend the Philippine Islands and to cooperate with the British and Dutch if war broke out with Japan. Lacking the resources to counter the Japanese invasion of the Philippines in December 1941 and denied air support from the U.S. Army's Far East Air Force, Hart sent his surface units to the Netherlands East Indies (NEI) at the end of the month and moved his headquarters to Java.

In January 1942, Hart was appointed commander of the naval forces of the American-British-Dutch-Australian Command (ABDACOM), which was charged with defending the NEI. Hart had no chance of success, for his resources were limited and he had no prospect of reinforcements. Moreover, the British and Dutch disagreed with his plans for using his ships. At the end of January, Hart sent his cruisers and destroyers against Japanese forces in the Battle of Makassar Strait, but the Dutch wished to concentrate ABDACOM's ships for the defense of Java. As a result, in February 1942, Hart relinquished his command to Vice Admiral C. E. L. Helfrich of the Netherlands navy and returned to the United States. Later that month, most of ABDACOM's ships were lost in the Battle of the Java Sea.

Hart served with the General Board until his retirement in February 1945, when he was appointed a U.S. senator from

U.S. Admiral Thomas C. Hart. (Photo by Bernard Hoffman/Time Life Pictures/Getty Images)

Connecticut, a post he held until 1947. Hart died in Sharon, Connecticut, on 4 July 1971.

John Kennedy Ohl

See also
Java Sea, Battle of the; Makassar Strait, Battle of; Madoera Strait, Battle of; Philippines, Japanese Capture of
References
Leutze, James. *A Different Kind of Victory: A Biography of Thomas C. Hart.* Annapolis, MD: Naval Institute Press, 1981.
Morison, Samuel Eliot. *History of United States Navy Operations in World War II.* Vol. 3, *The Rising Sun in the Pacific, 1931–April 1942.* Boston: Little, Brown, 1948.
Morton, Louis. *United States Army in World War II: The War in the Pacific: The Fall of the Philippines.* Washington, DC: Office of the Chief of Military History, 1953.

Hartmann, Erich Alfred (1922–1993)

Luftwaffe fighter pilot and highest-scoring ace of all time. Born in Weissach, Germany, on 19 April 1922, Erich Hartmann grew up in an aviation-minded family. His mother learned to fly in 1929, and Hartmann was an avid glider pilot as a young man. Hartmann joined the Luftwaffe in October 1940 and began his flight training in March 1941. At the time,

the Luftwaffe was not desperate for pilots, and Hartmann was the beneficiary of nearly 19 months' training before his first posting. In October 1942, he reported to Staffel (squadron) 7, III Gruppe (group), Jagdgeschwader (fighter wing) 52 (7.III/JG52) on the Eastern Front. The veterans nicknamed the youthful Hartmann "Bubi" (lad). Hartmann would spend the next two and one-half years in various units in JG52.

On his nineteenth sortie, Hartmann scored his first victory. He continued to score steadily, although his career nearly came to a sudden end when he was shot down and captured after his ninetieth victory. He managed to escape and eventually return to German lines. Hartmann continued to run up his score, and he was awarded the Knight's Cross in October 1943 after 150 victories. By August 1944, he had doubled his total. He was awarded every order of the Knight's Cross—Oak Leaves, Swords, and eventually Diamonds, Germany's highest military award.

Known as the "Black Devil of the Ukraine" by his Soviet opponents in recognition of his skill and the paint scheme of his aircraft, Hartmann scored his 352nd and last victory on 8 May 1945. He surrendered his fighter group to a U.S. Army unit but was handed over to the Soviets. Tried and convicted as a war criminal, Hartmann was imprisoned until his repatriation in late 1955.

Hartmann joined the new Federal Republic of Germany air force in 1956 and was appointed commander of the newly formed JG71 Richthofen. He retired in 1970 as a colonel. In retirement, Hartmann remained active in German civilian aviation, operating flight schools and participating in fly-ins, sometimes with other World War II aces. Erich Hartmann died on 19 September 1993 at Weil im Schönbuch.

M. R. Pierce

See also
Barkhorn, Gerhard; Germany, Air Force; Göring, Hermann Wilhelm
References
Hartmann, Ursula. *German Fighter Ace Erich Hartmann: The Life Story of the World's Highest Scoring Ace.* West Chester, PA: Schiffer Military History, 1992.
Toliver, Raymond F., and Trevor J. Constable. *Fighter Aces of the Luftwaffe.* Fallbrook, CA: Aero Publishers, 1977.
———. *The Blond Knight of Germany.* Blue Ridge Summit, PA: Aero Books, 1985.

Hausser, Paul "Papa" (1880–1972)

German Schutzstaffel (SS) general. Born on 7 October 1880 at Brandenburg, Paul Hausser joined the army and was commissioned a lieutenant in 1899. He served during World War I as a staff officer on both the Western and Eastern Fronts and rose to the rank of major in 1918. Hausser joined the Reichswehr of the Weimar Republic but retired in 1932 as lieutenant general. Hausser joined the Nazi SS in 1934, and as an inspector for its academies he helped train the armed SS units, the nucleus of the Waffen-SS.

In October 1939, Hausser commanded one of the two new SS combat divisions (Waffen-SS) and led this division, known as Das Reich, in campaigns in France (1940) and Yugoslavia (1941) and on the Eastern Front in the invasion of the Soviet Union, where he was wounded and lost an eye. He returned to active duty, and from June 1942 to June 1944, he commanded the first SS army corps formation, I SS Panzer Corps (later II Panzer Corps). During the Battle of Kharkov in early 1943, Hausser ignored Adolf Hitler's directives and ordered a retreat. He was criticized for this decision, but he was able to save his troops from annihilation and then retake Kharkov, which contributed significantly to the stabilization of the German Front. He also participated in the Battle of Kursk.

Transferred to France in June 1944, Hausser took command of the Seventh Army, which resisted the Allied invasion of Normandy. Hausser was seriously wounded in August during the desperate escape of his army at Falaise. He was promoted to Oberstgruppenführer and full general of the Waffen-SS in January 1945, and his last command, dating from 28 January, was of Army Group G in the southern part of the German Western Front. Hausser tried to organize an effective resistance against the advancing Allies, but it was impossible to meet Hitler's expectations, and the Führer removed him from command on 4 April 1945. He spent the remainder of the war on the staff of Field Marshal Albert Kesselring, commander in chief, west. Hausser is generally regarded as the most militarily accomplished of the Waffen-SS generals.

Hausser was imprisoned in May 1945 and not released until 1948. In the postwar Federal Republic of Germany, Hausser became the leader of Waffen-SS veterans. An author, Hausser insisted in his books that his men had been "soldiers as any others." Hausser died at Ludwigsburg, Germany, on 21 December 1972.

Martin Moll

See also
Alsace Campaign; Dietrich, Josef "Sepp"; Falaise-Argentan Pocket; France Campaign; Germany, Collapse of; Hitler, Adolf; Kesselring, Albert; Kharkov, Battle of; Kursk, Battle of; Normandy Invasion and Campaign; Waffen-SS

References
Hausser, Paul. *Soldaten wie andre auch: Der Weg der Waffen-SS.* Osnabrück, Germany: Munin-Verl, 1966.

Stein, George H. *The Waffen SS: Hitler's Elite Guard at War, 1939–1945.* Ithaca, NY: Cornell University Press, 1966.

Yerger, Mark C. *SS-Oberstgruppenführer und Generaloberst der Waffen-SS Paul Hausser.* Winnipeg, Canada: M. C. Yerger, 1986.

———. *Knights of Steel: The Structure, Development and Personalities of the 2. SS-Panzer-Division "Das Reich."* Lancaster, PA: M. C. Yerger, 1994.

He Yingqin (Ho Ying-ch'in) (1890–1987)

Nationalist Chinese Army general. Born into a landowning family in Xinyi (Hsing-i), Guizhou (Kweichow) Province on 2 April 1890, He Yingqin (Ho Ying-ch'in) received a thorough military education in both Chinese and Japanese military schools. After the outbreak of the Chinese Revolution in 1911, he returned to China and joined the revolutionary forces in Shanghai, Jiangsu (Kiangsu). Following the ill-fated "Second Revolution" in 1913, he returned to his studies in Japan, which he completed in 1916. In 1924, he was appointed chief instructor at the newly founded Huangpu (Whampoa) Military Academy, and he participated in the Northern Expedition. He became a close associate of Jiang Jieshi (Chiang Kai-shek) and directed military operations against dissident Guomindang (GMD [Kuomintang, KMT], Nationalist) forces as well as the Red Army in the "Extermination Campaigns" of the 1930s.

He was ordered to appease the Japanese in the humiliating Tanggu (Tangku) Truce of 1933 and the He-Umezu

Chinese Nationalist General He Yingqin (Ho Ying-Ch'in). (Photo by Leonard Mccombe/Time Life Pictures/Getty Images)

Agreement of 1935, resulting in widespread student demonstrations against GMD policy. After the Lugougiao (Lukouch'iao) Marco Polo Bridge Incident and the onset of a full Sino-Japanese War in 1937, He was appointed chief of staff of the Chinese army. Between 1942 and 1944, he developed a prickly rivalry with U.S. Lieutenant General Joseph W. Stilwell, commander of forces in the China-Burma-India Theater and Allied chief of staff to Jiang. He also clashed with General Chen Cheng (Ch'en Ch'eng), Stilwell's choice for Chinese commander. When Stilwell was relieved of command in 1944, He was relieved of his war portfolio but not his military position.

On 9 September 1945, He formally received the Japanese surrender in Nanjing (Nanking) in Jiangsu from General Okamura Yasuji, commander of Japanese forces in China. During the Chinese Civil War period, He's political fortunes waned. In 1949, he joined the Nationalists on Taiwan. He served as chief Chinese delegate to the United Nations' Military Advisory Committee (1946–1948) and then as chairman of the Strategy Advisory Committee in Taiwan (1950–1958). He died in Taipei on 21 October 1987.

Errol M. Clauss

See also
China, Army; China, Role in War; Jiang Jieshi; Okamura Yasuji; Stilwell, Joseph Warren

References
Eastman, Lloyd. *Seeds of Destruction: Nationalist China in War and Revolution, 1937–1949.* Stanford, CA: Stanford University Press, 1984.
Chi, Hsi-sheng. *Nationalist China at War: Military Defeats and Political Collapse, 1937–45.* Ann Arbor: University of Michigan Press, 1982.
Tuchman, Barbara. *Stilwell and the American Experience in China, 1911–1945.* New York: Macmillan, 1970.

Heisenberg, Werner (1901–1976)

German nuclear physicist. Born in Würzburg, Germany, on 5 December 1901, Werner Heisenberg graduated in 1923 from the University of Munich with a doctorate in physics. Heisenberg subsequently established a reputation as a talented scientist. One of his greatest accomplishments was his theory of quantum mechanics, for which he won the Nobel Prize in physics in 1932. By the late 1930s, despite being an opponent of the Nazi regime, Heisenberg was the leader of the German project to manufacture an atomic weapon.

This endeavor, known as the *Uranverein*, occupied Heisenberg throughout the war. The project was not successful, but the cause of its failure is still a matter of debate. Heisenberg claimed after the war that he had tried to impede the project

German physicist Werner Heisenberg. (Library of Congress)

as best he could to deny the Nazis an atomic bomb, a claim that some scholars contest. A principal cause of the project's failure was a lack of resources. The dearth of material and the resulting slow progress in research led to a mid-1942 report to Adolf Hitler that projected the development of a German atomic bomb as being several years in the future. Hitler, convinced that Germany would not be able to deploy such a weapon during World War II, consequently took little interest in the project.

Following the defeat of Germany, Heisenberg was among those German physicists briefly imprisoned in Britain by the Allies. In 1946 he was allowed to return to Germany and reorganized at Göttingen the Institute for Physics, later known as the Max Planck Institute for Physics. Heisenberg remained active in the field of physics in subsequent years. He died in Munich on 1 February 1976.

Eric W. Osborne

See also
Nuclear Weapons

References
Cassidy, David Charles. *The Life and Science of Werner Heisenberg.* New York: W. H. Freeman, 1992.
Powers, Thomas. *Heisenberg's War: The Secret History of the German Bomb.* Cambridge, MA: Da Capo Press, 2000.

Helicopters

Helicopters are a type of aircraft supported through the air by the aerodynamic lift created by one or more rotors, essentially rotating wings or blades, turning about a substantially vertical axis. The interest in helicopters came about because of its highly valued ability to ascend and descend almost vertically and to land in relatively small areas without benefit of lengthy landing strips.

Probably the first helicopterlike design was by artist and inventor Leonardo da Vinci in the fifteenth century. Three hundred years later in 1783, inspired by a "flying top" toy brought from China, two Frenchmen named Launoy and Bienvenu built a working model of a vertical-flight machine. In the mid-nineteenth century, British nobleman Sir George Cayley built a full-size, unpowered heloglider that flew a few feet with his coachman aboard.

These early designs had two problems: their flight was uncontrolled, and they lacked a source of power for sustained flight. With the advent of gasoline engines and shortly after the first heavier-than-air flight of Orville and Wilbur Wright, French inventor Charles Renard built a small helicopter that flew pilotless. He was followed in 1907 by Louis Breguet and Paul Cornu, who each built a manned machine that lifted off the ground, but both suffered from control problems. In 1909, before turning his inventive powers to producing large fixed-wing aircraft for the Russian tsar, Igor Sikorsky experimented with rudimentary helicopters, but he was unable to solve control and stability problems.

Between 1916 and 1918, Austrian Lieutenant Stefan Petroczy and Theodore von Karman designed and built two prototype vertical-lift machines for the Central Powers during World War I. The second made more than 30 successful flights before it crashed. The war ended before a third could be built. The designers of these machines handled problems of control and stability by tethering the machines to cables anchored to the ground.

During the 1920s, a Frenchman named Dourheret, the American father-and-son team of Emile and Henry Berliner, and George de Bothezat, a Russian under American contract, all produced vertical-lift machines. All efforts were disappointing because of stability and control problems. But in 1923, Spanish engineer Juan de la Cierva solved one instability problem—caused because the retreating blade produced less lift than the advancing blade—by hinging the blades for more flexibility. Although Cierva's invention was a rotary-wing aircraft, it was not a true helicopter. It was an autogiro or gyroplane that depended on a propeller to provide horizontal movement while the unpowered rotating wings provided the

A canteen worker handing a cup of tea to the pilot of a Sikorsky R-4 helicopter hovering overhead at the RAF Helicopter School in Andover in January 1945. (Photo by Fox Photos/Getty Images)

lift. As working rotary-wing aircraft, autogiros held the field through the late 1920s and early 1930s.

The first true helicopters appeared in the 1930s in the United States, France, and Germany. In France, Louis Breguet and René Dorand built a twin-rotor helicopter that set the speed record in 1935 and the endurance and distance records in 1936. In 1937, Heinrich Focke's helicopter set new records for time aloft, speed, distance, and altitude. Igor Sikorsky, who had emigrated to the U.S. in 1919, made his maiden helicopter flight in a craft of his own design in 1939.

Despite these successes, more autogiros than helicopters were used during World War II. Only Japan and the Soviet Union used autogiros in a very limited role in support of their ground forces, and the Japanese used some in service with their navy for antisubmarine warfare and liaison. Britain deployed a few to France for observation and communications duties in 1939, but the defeat of France ended those activities.

The U.S. military program to develop helicopters began in the late 1930s and fell under the direction of the U.S. Army

Air Corps. While other services—primarily the navy—looked into the possibility of helicopter use, in May 1942 the Army Air Forces took delivery of the first practical helicopter put into military service, a Sikorsky R-4.

Helicopters had no real impact in World War II. The German army used a small number of them for reconnaissance, supply, transport, and casualty evacuations, and the navy used them for shipboard reconnaissance and antisubmarine patrol. By the end of the war, more than 100 Sikorsky R-4 helicopters had been delivered to the U.S. Army Air Forces, Navy, and Coast Guard and to Britain's Royal Air Force and its Fleet Air Arm. These helicopters were used in experiments, primarily antisubmarine warfare, and for search-and-rescue operations. In April 1944, one of the four U.S. Army Air Forces R-4s sent to India for experimentation was used to rescue four men from an airplane crash site in Burma behind Japanese lines.

By the end of the war, helicopters had entered limited military service, and some had seen combat. Many commanders believed the helicopter was too fragile and vulnerable for the battlefield and too difficult to maintain. Despite its tentative beginnings, in later wars the helicopter would come to revolutionize military operations by providing entrance to and exit from the battlefield by means of the air while being nearly uninhibited by terrain.

Arthur T. Frame

References
Ahnstrom, D. N. *The Complete Book of Helicopters*. New York: World Publishing, 1954.
Beard, Barrett T. *Wonderful Flying Machines: A History of U.S. Coast Guard Helicopters*. Annapolis, MD: Naval Institute Press, 1996.
Everett-Heath, John, *Helicopters in Combat: The First Fifty Years*. London: Arms and Armour Press, 1992.
Keating, Bern. *Chopper! The Illustrated Story of Helicopters in Action*. New York: Rand McNally, 1976.
Prouty, Raymond W. *Military Helicopter Design Technology*. London: Janes Defense Data, 1989.

Hershey, Lewis Blaine (1893–1977)

U.S. Army general and director of the Selective Service System. Born in Angola, Indiana, on 12 September 1893, Lewis Hershey graduated from Tri-State College in Angola in 1914. He was then principal of Flint High School in Indiana. Hershey had joined the National Guard in 1911, and he was promoted to first lieutenant in 1916. After the United States entered World War I, Hershey was activated for military service. He served on the Mexican border and then in France, but too late to see combat. Promoted to captain, he returned to the United States in September 1919 and received a regular army commission in July 1920.

Over the next decade Hershey held a variety of routine assignments. He was left permanently blind in his left eye

from a polo accident in 1927. He graduated from the Command and General Staff School in 1931 and the Army War College in 1933. Promoted to major in 1935, Hershey was assigned to Washington that September as secretary of the Joint Army and Navy Selective Service Committee of the War Department General Staff, tasked with developing a system for raising military manpower in the event of need. This undertaking led to the Selective Service Act.

Hershey became deputy director of Selective Service in 1940. In July 1941, President Franklin D. Roosevelt appointed him the director. During World War II, Hershey oversaw the mobilization of more than 10 million men for the U.S. armed forces gathered from a network of 6,400 local draft boards. He was promoted to major general in April 1942.

The original Selective Service Act expired in 1947, but with the coming of the Cold War, Congress reinstated it the next year, and President Harry S Truman reappointed Hershey the director of Selective Service. The system worked efficiently during the Korean War and again during the Vietnam War. President Richard Nixon pledged to dismiss Hershey; he favored centralized and nationalized draft classifications, which ran counter to Hershey's locally run system. Nixon relieved Hershey in 1970, promoting him to full general in compensation and reassigning him as presidential adviser on manpower. Hershey retired from the army in April 1973. He died in Angola, Indiana, on 20 May 1977.

P. Robb Metz

See also
Roosevelt, Franklin D.; Selective Service Act; Truman, Harry S
References
Flynn, George Q. *Lewis B. Hershey: Mr. Selective Service*. Chapel Hill: University of North Carolina Press, 1985.
———. *The Draft, 1940–1973*. Lawrence: University Press of Kansas, 1993.
Gerhardt, James M. *The Draft and Public Policy*. Columbus: Ohio State University Press, 1971.
Seiverling, R. E. *Lewis B. Hershey: A Pictorial and Documentary Biography*. Hershey, PA: Keystone Enterprises, 1969.

Hess, Walter Richard Rudolf (1894–1987)

German deputy Führer. Born on 26 April 1894 in Alexandria, Egypt, to a German merchant family, Rudolf Hess volunteered for the 1st Bavarian Infantry Regiment in August 1914 during World War I, but in the last weeks of the war he became an officer pilot. Following the war, Hess settled in Munich and began university studies in history, economics, and geopolitics. An early member of the National Socialist Party, he became a close associate of Adolf Hitler and participated in the Beer Hall Putsch of November 1923. Hess was sentenced to prison for 18 months, during which time he

Deputy Führer of the German Reich Rudolf Hess, 1940. (Hulton Archive)

acted as private secretary to Hitler, working with Hitler on *Mein Kampf*. On his release, Hess secured a position with the geopolitician Karl Haushofer.

In December 1932, Hess became head of the Central Political Committee of the National Socialist Party. He had the reputation of being a slavish follower of Hitler. Power mattered little to him; Hitler's approval was all. In April 1933, three months after becoming German chancellor, Hitler named Hess deputy Führer. A member of the Nazi inner circle, Hess was nonetheless not up to the tasks demanded of him. Traces of madness surfaced, and he was not well physically.

On 10 May 1941, six weeks before the German invasion of the Soviet Union (Operation BARBAROSSA), Hess, having learned to pilot the Me-110 long-range German fighter, flew solo from Germany to Scotland. In a rather extraordinary feat of navigation, he piloted the aircraft to within 10 miles of his goal, the estate of the Duke of Hamilton, where he bailed out and was taken prisoner. Much speculation remains as to the reason for Hess's flight. Most likely, Hess hoped to broker a peace agreement between Britain and Germany, but this had no authority from Hitler. The German government admitted the event but denied any official backing. In any case, Hess was immediately taken prisoner by British authorities.

Hess remained in prison in Britain for the remainder of the war. One of the major defendants before the International War Crimes Tribunal at Nuremberg, Hess was found guilty of conspiracy to wage aggressive war and crimes against peace. He was sentenced to life in prison. During his trial, Hess revealed to the world the secret agreements of the Soviet-German Non-aggression Pact of 23 August 1939 that had provided for a partition of the Baltic states and Poland between Germany and the Soviet Union. The Soviets never forgave Hess and refused repeated British requests that he be released on medical grounds, especially when he was the only inmate of Spandau Prison in Berlin. Hess served the longest time of any of the Nuremberg defendants sentenced to prison. He died at Spandau on 17 August 1987.

Eugene L. Rasor and Spencer C. Tucker

See also
BARBAROSSA, Operation; German-Soviet Non-aggression Pact; Hitler, Adolf; International Military Tribunal: The Nuremberg Trials

References
Douglas-Hamilton, James. *Motive for a Mission: The Story behind Hess's Flight to Britain.* New York: St. Martin's, 1971.
Manvell, Richard, and Heinrich Fränkel. *Hess: A Biography.* New York: Drake Publishers, 1973.
Nesbit, Conyers, and Georges Van Acker. *The Flight of Rudolf Hess: Myths and Reality.* Stroud, UK: Sutton, 1999.
Stafford, David, ed. *Flight from Reality: Rudolf Hess and His Mission to Scotland, 1941.* London: Pimlico, 2002.

Hewitt, Henry Kent (1887–1972)

U.S. Navy admiral. Born in Hackensack, New Jersey, on 11 February 1887, H. Kent Hewitt graduated from the U.S. Naval Academy in 1906. He then joined the global cruise of President Theodore Roosevelt's Great White Fleet. During World War I, Hewitt commanded destroyers in European waters. Between the wars, he alternated shore duty as an instructor at the Naval Academy, battleship tours, staff assignments, and study at the Naval War College (1929).

In 1933, Hewitt took command of Destroyer Division 12. He was promoted to captain the next year. Hewitt then commanded the cruiser *Indianapolis*. In December 1939, he took over Cruiser Division 8. He was promoted to rear admiral in December 1940 and commanded task groups on neutrality patrols in the Atlantic. Following U.S. entry into the war in December 1941, in April 1942 Hewitt assumed command of the Amphibious Force, Atlantic Fleet. As such, he was responsible for U.S. amphibious forces in the Atlantic and Europe. Hewitt was the U.S. naval officer most involved in the development of amphibious doctrine in the Mediterranean and European Theaters during the war. He had charge of every major Allied amphibious operation in the Mediterranean Theater during the war.

Hewitt was promoted to vice admiral in November 1942, and in March 1943 he assumed command of the U.S. Navy Eighth Fleet. Working within an Allied command structure in which he was subordinate to the British Admiral Sir Andrew Browne Cunningham, and forced to coordinate military and naval operations and deal with such forceful characters as Major General George S. Patton, Hewitt demonstrated considerable diplomatic ability. Hewitt's mathematical and logistical skills were equally fully exercised in planning and directing complicated large-scale landing operations, reinforced by naval gunfire support, in North Africa (November 1942), Sicily (July 1943), Salerno (September 1943), and southern France (1944). His most difficult decision was whether to proceed with Operation TORCH, the North African landings, despite adverse weather conditions. He elected to proceed, a difficult choice that led to military success.

Promoted to full admiral in April 1945, shortly afterward Hewitt assumed command of the Twelfth Fleet, U.S. naval forces in European waters. He returned to the United States in October 1946 and took a special assignment at the Naval War College in Rhode Island before becoming naval representative to the United Nations Military Staff Committee. Hewitt retired in March 1949 and died at Middlebury, Vermont, on 15 September 1972.

Priscilla Roberts

See also

Amphibious Warfare; Cunningham, Sir Andrew Browne; DRAGOON, Operation; Patton, George Smith, Jr.; Salerno Invasion; Sicily, Invasion of; TORCH, Operation

References

Belot, Raymond de. *The Struggle for the Mediterranean, 1939–1945.* Princeton, NJ: Princeton University Press, 1951.

Hewitt, H. Kent. *The Memoirs of Admiral H. Kent Hewitt.* Edited by Evelyn M. Cherpak. Newport, RI: Naval War College Press, 2002.

Jones, Matthew. *Britain, the United States, and the Mediterranean War, 1942–1944.* New York: St. Martin's Press, 1996.

Morison, Samuel Eliot. *History of United States Naval Operations in World War II.* Vol. 2, *Operations in North African Waters (October 1942–June 1943).* Boston: Little, Brown, 1947.

———. *History of United States Naval Operations in World War II.* Vol. 9, *Sicily, Salerno, Anzio (January 1943–June 1944).* Boston: Little, Brown, 1954.

———. *History of United States Naval Operations in World War II.* Vol. 11, *The Invasion of France and Germany, 1944–1945.* Boston: Little, Brown, 1957.

Heydrich, Reinhard Tristan Eugen (1904–1942)

Chief of the German security police and Sicherheitsdienst (SD, Security Service). Born in Halle, Germany, on 7 March 1904, Reinhard Heydrich believed in the stab-in-the-back legend (that the German army had not been defeated militarily in World War I, but had been undone by the collapse of the German home front) and in the myth of Aryan supremacy. He joined the Freikorps at age 16 and the German navy in 1922. Planning to make the navy his career, Heydrich was forced to resign in 1931 following an indiscretion with another officer's daughter. That same year, Heydrich joined the National Socialist Party and became active in the Sturmabteilung (SA, Storm Troops) in Hamburg. Heydrich's managerial abilities and Germanic appearance led Schutzstaffel (SS, bodyguard troops) chief Heinrich Himmler to appoint him as head of the SD. Heydrich soon built the SD into a powerful organization, and by 1933 he was an SS-Brigadeführer.

After directing the opening of Dachau, the first of many Nazi concentration camps, Heydrich helped to organize the 1934 purge of the SA (the "Night of the Long Knives"), in which the SA leadership was liquidated. Feared even within party ranks for his ruthlessness and known as the "Blond Beast," Heydrich helped create the Nazi police state. He also played a leading role in the 9 November 1938 Kristallnacht (Night of Glass), an orgy of SA violence against the German Jewish community.

Following the invasion of Poland, Heydrich assumed command of the Reichssicherheitshauptamt (RSHA, Reich Main Security Office), which was responsible for carrying out Hitler's extermination of the Jews. He established the Einsatzgruppen killing squads charged with executing Jews and members of opposition groups in German-controlled Poland and later in the Soviet Union. Heydrich was also a leading participant at the Wannsee Conference on 20 January 1942, when top Nazis planned the extermination of European Jewry.

Although he still retained his other duties, Heydrich in late 1941 became the Reich protector of Bohemia and Moravia. On 27 May 1942, British-trained Czech commandos ambushed Heydrich's car, seriously wounding him. Heydrich died on 4 June 1942. In retaliation for his death, the Germans destroyed the village of Lidice and murdered many of its inhabitants.

Cullen Monk

See also

Concentration Camps, German; Czechoslovakia; Germany, Home Front; Himmler, Heinrich; Holocaust, The; Lidice Massacre

References

MacDonald, Callum. *The Killing of Reinhard Heydrich.* New York: Free Press, 1989.

Whiting, Charles. *Heydrich: Henchman of Death.* Barnsley, UK: Leo Cooper, 1999.

Himmler, Heinrich (1900–1945)

German political figure and leader of the Schutzstaffel (SS, bodyguard units). Born on 7 October 1900 in Munich, Hein-

Heinrich Himmler (wearing glasses) inspects a prisoner of war camp in Russia, circa 1940–1941. (Heinrich Hoffman Collection, ca. 1946, National Archives)

rich Himmler attended secondary school in Landshut. During World War I, he progressed from clerk to officer cadet in the 11th Bavarian Regiment. He then studied agriculture at the Munich Technical High School from 1918 to 1922. Himmler joined the National Socialist Party and played a small role in the November 1923 Munich Beer Hall Putsch. Although he remained politically active, he also married, bought a farm, and raised poultry.

In January 1929, Adolf Hitler appointed Himmler as head of the SS. Within a few years, Himmler built the SS from a force of 200 men into an organization 50,000 men strong with its own distinctive black uniform, personal devotion to Hitler, and ethos. In 1934, Reichsführer (leader) of the SS Himmler gained control of the Gestapo. Hitler rewarded him for his active role in the 1934 Blood Purge by making the SS

an independent organization second only to his own immediate authority. In June 1936, Himmler also gained control of all the police forces of Germany.

Although he was physically far removed from the ideal Aryan type, Himmler was a fanatical adherent of Nazi racial theories. He busied himself with fantastic schemes to breed a new race of "pure Aryans"—an SS version of the medieval knights—who would rule Europe from the Atlantic to the Urals. He set up special Lebensborn homes for unmarried mothers with impeccable racial antecedents, and special schools (the SS Junkerschulen) for training the SS future elite. Hitler, despite his promise to the German army, allowed Himmler to establish armed SS formations, known as the SS Verfügungstruppen (emergency troops), from which came the divisions of the Waffen-SS during World War II. The SS also came to have considerable economic interests, including armaments factories. By 1939, Himmler's influence overshadowed the Nazi Party; many high-ranking officials, even in the military, found it prudent to hold SS ranks. Himmler was one of the most important figures in Germany, and perhaps the most dreaded.

Controlling Germany's racial policies, Himmler directed the "final solution"—the extermination of the Jews as well as the incurably ill, the disabled, gypsies, and homosexuals. The SS already ran the concentration camps. It now established and ran the death camps as well.

> Heinrich Himmler was one of the most important figures in Germany, and perhaps the most dreaded.

After the July 1944 bomb plot against Hitler, Himmler took command of the Reserve Army. In November 1944, Hitler gave Himmler command of Army Group Rhine, and during January–April 1945, he had charge of Army Group Vistula—two positions for which he was utterly unqualified. In April 1945, Himmler attempted to negotiate a surrender to the Western Allies. A furious Hitler stripped him of his posts. Himmler attempted to flee but was captured by British troops. Identified on 23 May 1945, Himmler committed suicide by means of a hidden cyanide capsule.

Annette Richardson

See also
Heydrich, Reinhard Tristan Eugen; Hitler, Adolf; Holocaust, The; Waffen-SS; Wannsee Conference

References
Breitman, Richard. *The Architect of Genocide: Himmler and the Final Solution*. New York: Knopf, 1991.
Fest, Joachim C. *The Face of the Third Reich*. New York: Pantheon Books, 1970.
Krausnick, Helmut, and Martin Broszat. *The Anatomy of the SS State*. London: Collins, 1968.
Manvell, Roger. *Heinrich Himmler*. London: Heinemann, 1965.

Hirohito, Emperor of Japan (1901–1989)

Japanese emperor. Born at the Aoyama Palace in Tokyo on 29 April 1901, the oldest son of Emperor Taisho, Japan's future emperor was named Hirohito by his grandfather the Emperor Meiji. His imperial title was Michinomiya. Hirohito was heir to the chronically ill and frail Emperor Taisho. During a six-month period in 1921, Hirohito traveled in Europe, and his visit to Britain and his meeting with King George V profoundly shaped his view of constitutional monarchy.

On 25 December 1926, Hirohito acceded to the throne on the death of his father, ushering in the Shōwa period in Japanese history. His reign spanned more than six decades. The new emperor's close advisers included political moderates who desired close relations with Britain and the United States. They also hoped that Hirohito might reverse the decline in popular reverence for the Imperial throne that had occurred in the Taisho period.

In his early years as emperor, Hirohito and his imperial entourage found Prime Minister Tanaka Giichi's hard-line China policy at best problematic. This was one reason why Hirohito harshly reprimanded the military officer turned politician over his response to the June 1928 assassination of Zhang Zuolin (Chang Tso-lin) in Manchuria. When Tanaka's successor Hamaguchi Osachi was placed in a politically untenable position over the 1930 London Naval Disarmament Treaty, Hirohito did voice unequivocal support for cooperation with Britain and the United States and threw the weight of his support behind the beleaguered civilian prime minister. Although these actions no doubt illustrated Hirohito's desire for peace, they inexorably enmeshed him in the rough-and-tumble political process and made his entourage vulnerable to attack by hard-liners.

These experiences in the early years of his reign and his observations of European governments led Hirohito to conclude that he must defer to cabinet decisions. On the basis of this particular understanding of his constitutional function, Hirohito chose, despite personal reservations, to accept policies presented to him by the cabinet at key historical junctures, such as the outbreak of the military conflict with China in 1937 and the Japanese attack on Pearl Harbor.

Hirohito rendered an independent political judgment only twice: when the cabinet was unable to act effectively on the attempted coup by army junior officers on 26 February 1936 and when Japan accepted the Potsdam Declaration and Hirohito called on the Japanese people to surrender at the end of World War II. Such studied self-restraint did not make him a hapless stooge. As head of state under the Meiji constitutional system, Hirohito often expressed his concerns and opinions to those who made policy recommendations to him, but he usually upheld the cabinet's decision. After the war, some Western historians, notably David Bergamini, alleged that Hirohito had been deeply in sympathy with Japanese expansionist policies, but the available documentation largely contradicts this. During the war, Hirohito's role as commander in chief became more pronounced, but his reprimands and exhortations to the military during the conflict should be understood in their proper historical context. As a wartime head of state, he acted to try to win the war. Although threatened with military revolt, Hirohito decided to accept the Potsdam Declaration, risking a possible coup d'état when he made the decision to surrender.

In the new postwar Japanese constitution, the emperor became the symbol of the nation. In keeping with the new

Hirohito, Emperor of Japan, wearing imperial regalia and Shinto priest headdress. (Library of Congress)

constitutional principle of popular sovereignty, the emperor carried out certain ceremonial duties with the advice and approval of the cabinet. In 1971, Hirohito traveled to Europe, and in 1975 he went to the United States. Hirohito died in Tokyo on 7 January 1989. In Japan he is commonly referred to as Emperor Shōwa.

Kurosawa Fumitaka

See also

International Military Tribunal: Far East; Japan, Home Front; Potsdam Conference; Sugiyama Hajime; Tanaka Giichi

References

Bergamini, David. *Japan's Imperial Conspiracy.* 2 vols. New York: Morrow, 1971.

Bix, Herbert P. *Hirohito and the Making of Modern Japan.* London: Duckworth, 2001.

Drea, Edward J. *In the Service of the Emperor: Essays on the Imperial Japanese Army.* Lincoln: University of Nebraska Press, 1998.

Kawahara, Toshiaki. *Hirohito and His Times: A Japanese Perspective.* New York: Kodansha, 1990.

Large, Stephen S. *Emperor Hirohito and Shōwa Japan: A Political Biography.* London and New York: Routledge, 1992.

———. *Emperors of the Rising Sun: Three Biographies.* Tokyo: Kodansha International Ltd., 1997.

Titus, David A. *Palace and Politics in Prewar Japan.* New York: Columbia University Press, 1974.

Wetzler, Peter. *Hirohito and War: Imperial Tradition and Military Decision Making in Prewar Japan.* Honolulu: University of Hawaii Press, 1998.

Hiroshima, Bombing of (6 August 1945)

The U.S. bombing of the Japanese city of Hiroshima was the first use of the atomic bomb. On 25 July 1945, commander of United States Strategic Air Forces General Carl Spaatz received orders to use the 509th Composite Group, Twenti-eth Air Force, to deliver a "special bomb" attack on selected target cities in Japan, specifically Hiroshima, Kokura, Niigata, or Nagasaki. Following rejection of conditions promulgated by the Potsdam Proclamation on 26 July, a declaration threatening Japan with total destruction if unconditional surrender was not accepted, President Harry S Truman authorized use of the special bomb.

Assembled in secrecy and loaded on the Boeing B-29 Superfortress *Enola Gay*, the bomb consisted of a core of uranium isotope 235 shielded by several hundred pounds of lead, encased in explosives designed to condense the uranium and initiate a fission reaction. Nicknamed "Little Boy," the bomb possessed a force equivalent to 12,500 tons of TNT (12.5 kilotons).

The *Enola Gay*, commanded by Colonel Paul Tibbets, departed Tinian at 2:45 A.M. on 6 August. Two B-29s assigned as scientific and photographic observers followed, and the three aircraft rendezvoused over Iwo Jima for the run over Japan. Captain William Parsons of the U.S. Navy completed the bomb's arming in the air shortly after 6:30 A.M. The flight to Japan was uneventful, and Tibbets was informed at 7:47 A.M. by weather planes over the targets that Hiroshima was clear for bombing. Japan's eighth largest city (it had about 245,000 residents in August 1945), Hiroshima was an important port on southern Honshu and headquarters of the Japanese Second Army.

The *Enola Gay* arrived over the city at an altitude of 31,600 feet and dropped the bomb at 8:15:17 A.M. local time. After a descent of some nearly 6 miles, the bomb detonated 43 seconds later some 1,890 feet over a clinic and about 800 feet from the aiming point, Aioi Bridge. The initial fireball expanded to 110 yards in diameter, generating heat in excess of 300,000 degrees Centigrade, with core temperatures over 50 million degrees Centigrade. At the clinic directly beneath the explosion, the temperature was several thousand degrees. The immediate concussion destroyed almost everything within 2 miles of ground zero. The resultant mushroom cloud rose to 50,000 feet and was observed by B-29s more than 360 miles away. After 15 minutes, the atmosphere dropped radioactive "black rain," adding to the death and destruction.

Four square miles of Hiroshima's heart disappeared in seconds, including 62,000 buildings. More than 71,000 Japanese died, another 20,000 were wounded, and 171,000 were left homeless. Some estimates place the number of killed at more than 200,000. About one-third of those killed instantly were soldiers. Most elements of the Japanese Second General Army were at physical training on the grounds of Hiroshima Castle when the bomb exploded. Barely 900 yards from the explosion's epicenter, the castle and its residents were vaporized. Also killed was one American prisoner of war in the exercise area. All died in less than a second. Radiation sickness began the next day and added to the death toll over several years.

HISTORIOGRAPHICAL CONTROVERSY
The Decision to Employ the Atomic Bomb

Of historiographical controversies associated with World War II, few, if any, have produced as much venom as that surrounding the American use of atomic bombs against the Japanese cities of Hiroshima and Nagasaki in August 1945. Although the morality of using atomic weapons against what were arguably civilian targets has been an issue of debate, the controversy has really revolved around the two major questions: what motivated the Harry S Truman administration to use the bombs in combat, and was dropping the bombs necessary to secure a Japanese surrender without an invasion of the home islands?

There was little controversy in the United States at the time the bombs were dropped, and Truman said he never lost any sleep over the decision.

Debate on the U.S. use of atomic bombs began in earnest in the spring of 1965 with the publication of Gar Alperovitz's *Atomic Diplomacy: Hiroshima and Potsdam.* Drawing evidence from previously unexploited documents, Alperovitz argued that the primary motivation for the Truman administration's decision to use the bombs was to intimidate the Soviet Union. Alperovitz asserted that the bombs were not needed to end the war in the Pacific or to obviate a U.S. invasion of Japan and that President Truman and Secretary of State James Byrnes ignored viable alternatives to the bombs because they wanted Moscow to see the new terrible weapon in U.S. possession.

In making his claims, Alperovitz offered a revision to the official explanation for the decision to use the bombs. This had been put forth most cogently by Henry L. Stimson, U.S. secretary of war from 1940 to 1945, in "The Decision to Use the Atomic Bomb" *(Harper's Magazine,* February 1947). Stimson held that the bombs had been dropped to shorten the Pacific war, to eliminate the need for an invasion of the Japanese home islands

(scheduled for 1 November 1945), and to save American lives (perhaps 1 million had the invasion taken place). Although Alperovitz was not the first to challenge the official explanation, his conclusions, unlike those found in earlier revisionist works by William Appleman Williams, D. F. Fleming, and Herbert Feis, engendered heated responses from several scholars and established the parameters for ongoing debate about the development, use, and legacy of the atomic bombs.

During the ensuing decades, new scholarship on the atomic bomb question, much of it based on new primary source material, produced a revision of Alperovitz's revisionism. The resulting synthesis combined elements of both the official and revisionist positions, while adding fresh perspectives. Fashioned by the research efforts of Barton J. Bernstein, Martin J. Sherwin, J. Samuel Walker, and others, this synthesis held that diplomatic considerations played a secondary role and that the Truman administration's primary objective in using the bombs was to shorten the Pacific war and save American lives—although not the 500,000 to 1 million commonly quoted by adherents to the official explanation. Additionally, the new scholarship emphasizes that the bomb had been developed with the assumption that, once completed, it would be used in combat, and that this contributed to its employment; that domestic political considerations influenced American policymakers; that viable alternatives to both invasion and atomic bombs existed; and that in all probability, the Pacific war would have ended before the 1 November 1945 scheduled invasion of Kyushu, even without the bombs.

Although many scholars have come to accept the synthesis interpretation in whole or in part, debate about use of the atomic bombs has not ceased. Adherents to both the official and revisionist positions continue to argue their cases while

refusing to accept any significant modifications of their interpretations. The question concerning use of the atomic bomb retains the power to inflame public passions, a fact perhaps best exemplified by the furor over the Smithsonian Institution's proposed 1995 exhibit of the *Enola Gay,* the Boeing B-29 bomber that dropped the first bomb at Hiroshima.

Bruce J. DeHart

See also
Atomic Bomb, Decision to Employ; Byrnes, James Francis; Groves, Leslie Richard; Hirohito, Emperor of Japan; Hiroshima, Bombing of; MANHATTAN Project; Nagasaki, Bombing of; Truman, Harry S

References
Alperovitz, Gar. *The Decision to Use the Bomb and the Architecture of an American Myth.* New York: Alfred Knopf, 1995.
Bernstein, Barton J. "The Atomic Bomb and American Foreign Policy, 1941–1945: An Historiographical Controversy." *Peace and Change* (Spring 1974): 1–16.
———. "Understanding the Atomic Bomb and the Japanese Surrender: Missed Opportunities, Little-Known Disasters, and Modern Memory." *Diplomatic History* (Spring 1995): 227–273.
Maddox, Robert J. *Weapons for Victory: The Hiroshima Decision Fifty Years Later.* Columbia: University of Missouri Press, 1995.
Sherwin, Martin J. *A World Destroyed: The Atomic Bomb and the Grand Alliance.* New York: Alfred Knopf, 1975.
Stimson, Henry L. "The Decision to Use the Atomic Bomb." *Harper's Magazine* (February 1947): 97–107.
Walker, J. Samuel. *Prompt and Utter Destruction: Truman and the Use of the Atomic Bombs against Japan.* Chapel Hill: University of North Carolina Press, 1997.

The ruins of Hiroshima after the dropping of the atomic bomb. (Hulton Archive)

Following three observation circuits over Hiroshima, the *Enola Gay* and its escorts turned for Tinian, touching down at 2:58 P.M. The bombing mission, 12 hours and 13 minutes long covering 2,960 miles, changed the nature of warfare but did not end the war. Truman released a statement on 7 August describing the weapon and calling on Japan to surrender, but his message was ignored by most Japanese leaders as propaganda. The United States dropped another atomic bomb on 9 August, this time on Nagasaki.

Mark E. Van Rhyn

See also
Aircraft, Bombers; Atomic Bomb, Decision to Employ; Japan, Surrender of; MANHATTAN Project; Nagasaki, Bombing of; Potsdam Conference; Spaatz, Carl Andrew "Tooey"; Strategic Bombing; Truman, Harry S

References
Maddox, Robert James. *Weapons for Victory: The Hiroshima Decision Fifty Years Later*. Columbia: University of Missouri Press, 1995.

Nobile, Philip. *Judgment at the Smithsonian: The Bombing of Hiroshima and Nagasaki*. New York: Marlowe and Company, 1995.

Pacific War Research Society. *The Day Man Lost: Hiroshima, 6 August 1945*. Tokyo: Kodansha International Ltd., 1972.

Thomas, Gordon, and Max Morgan-Witts. *Enola Gay*. New York: Stein and Day, 1977.

Hitler, Adolf (1889–1945)

Leader (Führer) of Germany. Born on 20 April 1889 in Braunau am Inn, Austria, Adolf Hitler had a troubled childhood. He was educated at primary school and Realschule in Linz, but he dropped out at age 16. Hitler aspired to become an artist, and on the death of his mother Klara in 1907 (his father Alois had died in 1903), he moved to Vienna. He attempted to enroll at the Viennese Academy of Fine Arts but was unsuccessful. Hitler lived in flophouses and made some money selling small paintings of Vienna scenes to frame shops. It was in Vienna that Hitler developed his hatred of Jews, who had assimilated into Vienna society. But he also developed an aversion to internationalism, capitalism, and socialism. He developed an intense sense of nationalism and expressed pride in being of German descent.

Probably to avoid compulsory military service, Hitler left Austria in May 1913 and settled in the south German state of Bavaria. On the outbreak of World War I, he enlisted in the Bavarian army and served in it with distinction. Here he found the sense of purpose he had always previously lacked. He saw extensive military action, was wounded, and served in the dangerous position of Meldegänger (runner). Temporarily blinded in a British gas attack, Hitler ended the war in a military hospital. He had risen to the rank of lance corporal and won the Iron Cross First Class, an unusual distinction for someone of his rank.

> While in power, sales of his book *Mein Kampf* and his images made Hitler immensely wealthy.

After the war, Hitler returned to Munich and worked for the military, reporting to it on political groups, and he then became involved in politics full time. In the summer of 1919, Hitler joined the Deutsche Arbeiterpartei (German Worker's Party), later known as the Nationalsozialistische Deutsche Arbeiterpartei (NSDAP, National Socialist Party or Nazi party). His oratorical skills soon made him one of its leaders. Disgruntled by Germany's loss in the war, Hitler became the voice of the dispossessed and angry. He blamed Germany's defeat on the "November criminals"—the communists, the Jews, and the Weimar Republic.

Taking a cue from Benito Mussolini's march on Rome the previous year, on 8 November 1923 Hitler and his followers attempted to seize power in Bavaria as a step toward controlling all of Germany. This Beer Hall Putsch was put down by the authorities with some bloodshed. Hitler was then arrested and brought to trial for attempting to overthrow the state. He used his trial to become a national political figure in Germany. Sentenced to prison, he served only nine months (1923–1924). While at the Landsberg Fortress, he dictated his stream-of-consciousness memoir, *Mein Kampf (My Struggle).* Later, when he was in power, royalties on sales of the book and his images made him immensely wealthy, a fact he deliberately concealed from the German people.

Hitler formed few female attachments during his life. He was involved with his niece, Geli Raubal, who committed sui-

Adolf Hitler at Nazi party rally, Nuremberg, Germany, circa 1928. (National Archives)

cide in 1931, and later with Eva Braun, his mistress whom he hid from the public. Deeply distrustful of people, Hitler was a vegetarian who loved animals and especially doted on his dogs. He was also a severe hypochondriac, suffering from myriad real and imagined illnesses.

Hitler restructured the NSDAP, and by 1928 the party had emerged as a political force in Germany, winning representation in the Reichstag. In April 1932, Hitler ran against Field Marshal Paul von Hindenburg for the presidency of Germany. Hitler railed against the Weimar Republic for the Versailles Treaty at the end of World War I, the catastrophic inflation of 1923, the threat posed by the communists, and the effects of the Great Depression. Hindenburg won, but Hitler received 13 million votes in a completely free election, and by June 1932 the Nazis were the largest political party in the Reichstag.

On 30 January 1933, Hindenburg appointed Hitler chancellor. Hitler quickly acted against any political adversaries. Fresh elections under Nazi auspices gave the Nazis in coalition with the Nationalists a majority in the Reichstag. An Enabling Act of March 1933 gave Hitler dictatorial powers. On the death of Hindenburg in August 1934, Hitler amalgamated the office of president and took control of the armed forces. In the "Night of the Long Knives" of July 1934, Hitler purged the party and also removed several political opponents. Hitler also reorganized Germany administratively, dissolving political parties and labor unions and making Germany a one-party state. Nazi Germany became a totalitarian state that Hitler, now known as the Führer (leader), ruled alone.

Resistance to the Nazis was crushed, and many dissidents were sent to concentration camps. The ubiquitous Gestapo kept tabs on the population, but the state was not characterized solely by repression by any means. In the first several years, Hitler was carried forward on a wave of disillusionment with the Weimar Republic, and a plebiscite showed that a solid majority of Germans approved of his actions.

Almost on assuming political power, Hitler initiated actions against the Jews. They were turned into a race of "untouchables" within their own state, unable to pursue certain careers and a public life. The Nuremberg Laws of 1935 defined as Jewish anyone with one Jewish grandparent. That a terrible fate would be their lot was clear in Hitler's remarks that war in Europe would lead to the "extinction of the Jewish race in Europe."

In 1934, Hitler took Germany out of the League of Nations and the Geneva disarmament conference. Germans were put back to work; and rearmament, albeit at first secret (it was announced openly in 1935), was begun. Hitler's most daring gamble was in March 1936, when he marched German troops into the Rhineland and remilitarized it. In November 1937, he announced plans to his top advisers and generals for an aggressive foreign policy and war, and in March 1938 he began his march of conquest with the Anschluss (annexation) of Austria. That fall, he secured the Sudetenland of Czechoslovakia, and in March 1939, he took over the remainder of Czechoslovakia. Poland was the next pressure point. To secure his eastern flank, in August 1939 Hitler concluded a nonaggression pact with the Soviet Union. On 1 September 1939, German forces invaded Poland, touching off World War II.

Applying new tactics of close cooperation between air and ground elements centered in a war of movement that came to be known as the blitzkrieg (lightning war), the German military enjoyed early success on the battlefield. Poland was taken within one month. When Britain and France, which had gone to war with Germany on the invasion of Poland, rejected peace on a forgive-and-forget basis, Hitler invaded the west. Norway and Denmark were taken beginning in April 1940. France and Benelux fell in May and June. Hitler's first rebuff came in the July-October 1940 Battle of Britain, when the Luftwaffe failed to drive the Royal Air Force from the skies, a necessary precursor to a sea invasion. After next securing his southern flank in the Balkans by invading and conquering Greece and Yugoslavia in April 1941, Hitler

invaded the Soviet Union that June. When the United States entered the war against Japan in December 1941, Hitler declared war on the United States.

Increasingly, Germany suffered the consequences of strategic overreach: German troops not only had to garrison much of Europe, but they also were sent to North Africa. Hitler's constant meddling in military matters, his changes of plans, and his divide-and-rule concept of administration all worked to the detriment of Germany's cause. On Hitler's express orders, millions of people, mainly Jews, were rounded up and systematically slaughtered.

From mid-January 1945, Hitler took up residence in Berlin. He refused negotiation to the end, preferring to see Germany destroyed. Hitler married Eva Braun on 29 April 1945, and—rather than be taken by the Russians, who were then closing in on Berlin—he committed suicide in the bunker of the Chancellery on 30 April 1945.

Wendy A. Maier

See also
BARBAROSSA, Operation; Britain, Battle of; France, Battle for; Germany, Home Front; July Bomb Plot; Mussolini, Benito; Poland Campaign
References
Bracher, Karl Dietrich. *The German Dictatorship: The Origins, Structure, and Effects of National Socialism.* New York and Washington, DC: Praeger, 1970.
Bullock, Alan. *Hitler: A Study in Tyranny.* New York: Harper, 1952.
Burleigh, Michael. *The Third Reich: A New History.* New York: Hill and Wang, 2000.
Fest, Joachim C. *Hitler.* Trans. Richard and Clara Winston. New York: Harcourt Brace Jovanovich, 1974.
Flood, Charles Bracelen. *Hitler: The Path to Power.* Boston: Houghton Mifflin, 1989.
Gordon, Sarah. *Hitler, Germans, and the Jewish Question.* Princeton, NJ: Princeton University Press, 1988.
Hitler, Adolf. *Mein Kampf.* New York: Houghton Mifflin, 1999.
Jones, J. Sydney. *Hitler in Vienna, 1907–1913: Clues to the Future.* New York: Stein and Day, 1983.
Kershaw, Ian. *Hitler.* 2 vols. New York: W. W. Norton. 1999–2000.
Shirer, William L. *Berlin Diary, 1934–1941.* London: Sphere, 1970.

Ho Chi Minh (1890–1969)

Revolutionary Vietnamese leader who aided the Allies against the Japanese in World War II. Born Nguyen Sinh Cung on 19 May 1890 in the Annam region of French Indochina, Ho Chi Minh was the son of a scholar and government official. Later he would use some 100 different aliases. After graduation from high school, Nguyen became a teacher. In 1911 he hired on as cook's assistant on a French merchant ship. He then held a variety of jobs, including gardener, waiter, photographer's assistant, and assistant pastry chef, finally settling in London.

Vietnamese nationalist leader Ho Chi Minh. (Hulton Archive/Getty Images)

When World War I began, Nguyen moved to Paris. There he changed his name to Nguyen Ai Quoc ("Nguyen the patriot") and busied himself organizing the Vietnamese community in France, which had swollen in numbers during the war. Nguyen joined the French Socialist Party and became its spokesman in colonial matters. Ignored in his efforts to secure a hearing for Vietnamese independence at the Paris Peace Conference (1919), Nguyen was one of the founders of the French Communist Party in 1920. He then participated in the Vietnamese underground independence movement and in activities of the Communist International (Comintern) in the Soviet Union and China. In 1930, he helped to fuse various Vietnamese communist groups into the Indochinese Communist Party.

In the 1940s, Nguyen took the name Ho Chi Minh ("he who enlightens"). During World War II, Ho fought against both the French and the Japanese (who had arrived in Indochina in 1940). In 1941, Ho founded the Vietminh (League for the Independence of Vietnam), a nationalist front organization to end foreign control of Vietnam. In 1942, he was arrested in China by the Nationalist government but was released in 1943 in order to organize anti-Japanese intelligence activities throughout Indochina.

Ho's Vietminh worked with the U.S. Office of Strategic Services (OSS) to supply intelligence on Japanese activities, provide tactical support to Allied operations, and rescue downed American pilots. By war's end, Ho and the Vietminh had succeeded in liberating much of northern Vietnam from Japanese control. The Japanese had arrested the French officials and military in March 1945, so when Japan surrendered in August, the Vietminh was the only effective organized force in the northern party of Vietnam. The Vietminh then seized control of Hanoi, and Ho was declared president of Vietnam on 20 September 1945.

Despite an arrangement worked out with Ho by a representative of the French government, Paris persisted in attempting to reestablish French control over all of Vietnam, and fighting broke out in November 1946. In 1954, following its military defeat in the Battle of Dien Bien Phu, the French government agreed at the Geneva Conference to recognize the independence of the Democratic Republic of Vietnam in northern Vietnam. It also agreed to a plebiscite in the southern part of the country on the issue of independence. With the failure to hold that plebiscite, fighting resumed, this time involving the United States, which supported the southern Republic of Vietnam government. Ho died in Hanoi on 3 September 1969, not living to see Vietnam reunited in 1975.

A. J. L. Waskey and Spencer C. Tucker

See also

French Indochina; Office of Strategic Services; Partisans/Guerrillas

References

Duiker, William J. *Ho Chi Minh: A Life*. New York: Hyperion, 2000.

Halberstam, David. *Ho*. New York: Vintage Books, 1971.

Lacouture, Jean. *Ho Chi Minh: A Political Biography*. New York: Vintage Books, 1968.

Marr, David G. *Vietnam, 1945: The Quest for Power*. Berkeley: University of California Press, 1995.

Ho Ying-ch'in

See He Yingquin.

Hobby, Oveta Culp (1905–1995)

U.S. officer and Women's Army Corps commanding officer. Born on 19 January 1905 at Killeen, Texas, Oveta Culp attended Mary Hardin Baylor College in Killeen, Texas, and then stud-

Colonel Oveta Culp Hobby talks with Auxiliary Margaret Peterson and Captain Elizabeth Gilbert at Mitchell Field, New York. (*World Telegram and Sun* photo by Al Aumuller, Library of Congress)

ied law at the University of Texas at Austin. From 1925 to 1931 and from 1939 to 1941, she was parliamentarian of the Texas House of Representatives. In 1931, Culp married *Houston Post* publisher and former Texas governor William P. Hobby.

During the 1930s, Oveta Hobby was an editor for the *Houston Post*. In June 1941, she was appointed head of the Women's Activities Section of the U.S. Army to coordinate matters concerning the wives and dependents of army personnel. She then became director of the subsequent Women's Interest Section, War Department Bureau of Public Relations.

Following the Japanese attack on Pearl Harbor, Hobby was asked to head a task force to determine how a possible volunteer women's corps could assist the army. Chief of staff General George C. Marshall and Secretary of War Henry Stimson supported her work, and after Hobby recommended establishment of the Women's Auxiliary Army Corps (WAAC), Marshall asked her to command it.

Hobby had to overcome numerous problems, such as lack of funds and supplies and lack of cooperation from other army organizations, such as the engineers. Hobby and staff members drew barracks plans and attempted to redesign the standard-issue WAAC uniform to be more appealing to women, but the Quartermaster Corps rejected the design as too wasteful of cloth. Hobby was successful, however, in securing equal pay for women. In July 1943, the WAAC received full army status, and "Auxiliary" was dropped from the name, making it the Women's Army Corps (WAC). Hobby also oversaw the integration of female African American officers. Hobby was the first woman colonel in the U.S. Army.

During Hobby's tenure, the number of jobs approved for WACs expanded from 54 to 239. Hobby traveled to Europe and Africa to inspect WAC units, and she traveled with Eleanor Roosevelt to England to review Great Britain's women's auxiliary forces. Hobby's WACs proved their competence doing military work that freed men for frontline service.

Hobby resigned her post in the summer of 1945 and was hospitalized for exhaustion. Among her many honors, she was presented the Distinguished Service Medal, the first woman to receive this highest noncombat award.

Hobby continued to support civil rights and humanitarian issues. A lifelong Democrat, Hobby nonetheless backed Dwight D. Eisenhower for president, and in 1953 he named her the first secretary of the Department of Health, Education and Welfare. She resigned the position in 1955 and returned to help her husband with the *Houston Post*. Hobby died in Houston, Texas, on 16 August 1995.

Elizabeth D. Schafer

See also
Eisenhower, Dwight D.; Marshall, George Catlett; Roosevelt, Eleanor; Stimson, Henry Lewis; United States, Home Front; Women in World War II

References
Allen, Ann. "The News Media and the Women's Army Auxiliary Corps: Protagonists for a Cause." *Military Affairs* 50 (April 1986): 77–83.

Clark, James A., with Weldon Hart. *The Tactful Texan: A Biography of Governor Will Hobby*. New York: Random House, 1958.

Shire, Al, compiler and ed. *Oveta Culp Hobby*. Houston, TX: W. P. Hobby, 1997.

Treadwell, Mattie. *The Women's Army Corps*. Washington, DC: Office of the Chief of Military History, Department of the Army, 1954.

Hodges, Courtney Hicks (1887–1966)

U.S. Army general and commander of the First Army. Born in Perry, Georgia, on 5 January 1887, Hodges attended the U.S. Military Academy for one year, but he dropped out for academic reasons and enlisted in the army. In 1909, Hodges earned a commission. He then served in the Philippines and in the 1916 Punitive Expedition into Mexico. During World War I, he fought in France in the Saint Mihiel and Meuse-Argonne Offensives, ending the war as a temporary lieutenant colonel.

Hodges attended the Field Artillery School in 1920 and then served as an instructor at West Point. He graduated from the Command and General Staff School in 1925, taught at the Infantry School, and then graduated from the Army War College. In 1938, he was appointed assistant commandant of the Infantry School at Fort Benning, Georgia. Promoted to major general in May 1941, Hodges was assigned as chief of infantry. He assumed command of X Corps in May 1942. In February 1943, he was promoted to lieutenant general and took over the Southern Defense Command and Third Army. In January 1944, Hodges joined the First Army in Britain,

U.S. General Courtney Hodges. (Photo by Gabriel Benzur/Time Life Pictures/Getty Images)

which was then preparing for the Normandy Invasion, as deputy commander under Lieutenant General Omar Bradley.

In August 1944, Hodges succeeded to command of the First Army when Bradley moved up to head the Twelfth Army Group. First Army then defended Mortain, reduced the Falaise-Argentan pocket, helped in the liberation of Paris, penetrated the Siegfried Line, captured Aachen, and suffered heavy casualties in the Hürtgen Forest. In December 1944, the First Army bore the brunt of the German Ardennes counteroffensive. To deal with the crisis, General Dwight D. Eisenhower temporarily reorganized his command structure and placed a portion of First Army—and Hodges—under British Field Marshal Bernard Montgomery, who thought Hodges was at his breaking point. Eisenhower refused any suggestion that Hodges be relieved, and Hodges' performance in the Battle of the Bulge vindicated Eisenhower's view. The First Army rallied to hold the northern shoulder of the Bulge and then played an important role in the successful counterattack. First Army soldiers crossed the Rhine at Remagen, joined in the closing of the Ruhr pocket, and, at the end of the war, linked up with Soviet forces on the Elbe River.

In April 1945, Hodges was promoted to general. Following V-E Day, he and the First Army were under orders for the Pacific Theater to lead the invasion of Honshu when the Japanese surrendered. After the war, Hodges remained in command of the First Army until his retirement in 1949. He died in San Antonio, Texas, on 16 January 1966.

Thomas D. Veve

See also

Ardennes Offensive; Bradley, Omar Nelson; Eisenhower, Dwight D.; Falaise-Argentan Pocket; Hürtgen Forest, Campaign; Remagen Bridge; Rhine Crossings; Ruhr Campaign

References

Cole, Hugh M. *United States Army in World War II: The European Theater of Operations: The Ardennes: Battle of the Bulge.* Washington, DC: Office of the Chief of Military History, 1965.

Weigley, Russell F. *Eisenhower's Lieutenants.* Bloomington: Indiana University Press, 1981.

Hoepner, Erich (1886–1944)

German army general. Born in Frankfurt an der Oder on 14 September 1886, Erich Hoepner was commissioned in the army in 1906. He fought in World War I as a company commander and General Staff officer. After the war, Hoepner participated in the 1920 Kapp Putsch. He remained in the German army after the war in different troop and staff commands. In 1933, Hoepner became chief of staff in the 1st Military District, continuing in the military despite his opposition to Adolf Hitler and National Socialism. Promoted to Generalmajor (U.S. equiv. brigadier general) in 1936, Hoepner was part of a plot by the German Resistance during the 1938 Czechoslovakian crisis to remove Hitler from power. His orders were to lead his 1st Light Division to prevent Schutzstaffel (SS) troops from reaching Berlin, but the plot collapsed with the Munich Agreement.

Taking command of XVI Army Corps, General Hoepner led his men in the occupation of Bohemia and Moravia in March 1939. Promoted in April to General der Kavalerie (U.S. equiv. lieutenant general), he led XVI Corps in the invasion of Poland as part of the Tenth Army, advancing 140 miles to Warsaw in only a week. In the invasion of France and Low Countries in May 1940, his corps spearheaded the advance of the Sixth Army to Liège and then on to Dunkerque, later taking Dijon. Hoepner was promoted to Generaloberst (U.S. equiv. full general) in July 1940.

Hoepner commanded 4th Panzer Group in Operation BARBAROSSA, the invasion of the Soviet Union. A leading exponent of armored warfare, Hoepner favored a bold thrust to seize Leningrad during the 1941 advance, but Hitler ordered his forces to join Army Group Center under Field Marshal Fedor von Bock with the mission of taking Moscow from the north. His panzers got to within 20 miles of the city when they were stalled by Soviet resistance and the onset of winter.

Following the Soviet counterattack in December 1941, Hoepner put his career in jeopardy when in early January he began withdrawing some of his units to save them from certain annihilation by Soviet forces. Hitler removed several of his generals on the Eastern Front, but he made a special example of Hoepner, who was court-martialed and cashiered. Publicly humiliated, Hoepner was denied the right to wear a uniform or his decorations. This treatment turned him into an active conspirator against the Nazi regime.

Hoepner was deeply involved in the 20 July 1944 plot against Hitler, and he was designated to take command of the Home Forces should General Friedrich Fromm prove unreliable. He was also considered as a possible minister of war. With the failure of the plot, Hoepner rejected an opportunity to commit suicide, preferring to go on trial. Arrested and tried by the People's Court, Hoepner, having been tortured by Gestapo interrogators, appeared uncertain during the trial before Judge Roland Freisler. He was found guilty and executed by being hanged by wire suspended from meat hooks at Plotzensee Prison in Berlin on 8 August 1944.

Joseph C. Greaney and Spencer C. Tucker

See also

Bock, Fedor von; Hitler, Adolf; Munich Conference and Preliminaries; Stauffenberg, Claus Philip Schenk von

References

Clark, Alan. *Barbarossa: The Russian-German Conflict, 1941–1945.* New York: Quill, 1965.

Gill, Anton. *An Honourable Defeat: A History of German Resistance to Hitler, 1933–1945.* New York: Henry Holt, 1994.

Holcomb, Thomas (1879–1965)

U.S. Marine Corps general and commandant. Born on 5 August 1879 in New Castle, Delaware, Thomas Holcomb joined the U.S. Marine Corps in 1900, serving with the North Atlantic Fleet, Beijing, and the Philippines in the early twentieth century. An excellent instructor, he always emphasized marksmanship training, reflecting his own skills as a world champion in long-range shooting and a member of the Marine Corps Rifle Team and contributing to his unit's success in World War I. From November 1917 to August 1918, Holcomb commanded the 2nd Battalion, 6th Regiment in France, fighting tenaciously during the spring 1918 German offensive and at Belleau Wood. As executive officer of the 6th Marine Regiment, he took part in other combat actions.

Between the wars, Holcomb spent further tours in Germany, Cuba, and Beijing. He graduated from the Fort Leavenworth Army Staff College, the Naval War College, and the Army War College and served in the Office of Naval Operations, winning promotion to brigadier general in 1935. The following year, President Franklin D. Roosevelt appointed him major general and commandant of the Marine Corps, advancing him above more senior officers.

As commandant, Holcomb undertook initiatives that would bear fruit during the Pacific war. He greatly enhanced the Marines' growing capacity for amphibious warfare, developing several new types of landing craft. He supervised the expansion of the Marine Corps from 16,000 officers and men in 1936 to 50,000 in mid-1941, 143,000 six months later, and more than 300,000 by 1945, comprising six combat divisions and four air wings. In December 1940, Roosevelt appointed Holcomb to a second term as commandant, and in February 1942, Holcomb was promoted to lieutenant general. Holcomb trained and equipped the Marines but had no operational control over their activities in the field. After disputes in 1942 at Guadalcanal between Rear Admiral Richmond Kelly Turner and Marine commander Major General Alexander Vandegrift, Holcomb insisted on the definition of clear lines of authority in joint amphibious operations. He won the decision that navy and Marine Corps commanders would enjoy equal authority and that superior officers would resolve any disputes. As commandant, he also resisted racial integration of the Marines on the grounds that it would detract from combat efficiency.

Holcomb reached mandatory retirement age in August 1943, but Roosevelt retained him in post and made him the first Marine officer ever to become full general. At the end of 1943, Holcomb insisted on making way for a younger successor and retired. He then spent four years as ambassador to South Africa, seeking modest mitigation of that nation's racial policies. Holcomb returned to the United States in 1948. He died in New Castle, Delaware, on 24 May 1965.

Priscilla Roberts

See also

Roosevelt, Franklin D.; Turner, Richmond Kelly; United States, Marines; Vandegrift, Alexander Archer

References

Gordon, John. "General Thomas Holcomb and 'The Golden Age of Amphibious Warfare.'" *Delaware History* 21 (1985): 256–270.

Heinl, Robert D., Jr. *Soldiers of the Sea: The U.S. Marine Corps, 1775–1962.* 2d ed. Baltimore, MD: Nautical and Aviation Publishing Company of America, 1991.

Hough, Frank O., et al. *History of U.S. Marine Corps Operations in World War II.* Vol. 1, *Pearl Harbor to Guadalcanal.* Washington, DC: Government Printing Office, 1958.

Millett, Allan R. *"Semper Fidelis": The History of the United States Marine Corps.* Rev. and expanded ed. New York: Free Press, 1991.

Shaw, Henry. *Opening Moves: Marines Gear Up for War.* Washington, DC: History and Museums Division, United States Marine Corps, 1991.

U.S. Army Fifth Air Force planes bomb the Japanese-held base of Hollandia in New Guinea, 1944. (Hulton-Deutsch Collection/Corbis)

Hollandia, Battle of (22–26 April 1944)

Important battle in New Guinea. In early 1944, General Douglas MacArthur's Allied forces in the Southwest Pacific Area (SWPA) were advancing along the northeastern coast of New Guinea. Following the capture of Saidor, MacArthur planned to seize Hansa Bay about 120 miles to the northwest. But after the seizure of the Admiralty Islands in early March, he decided to bypass Hansa Bay and leap nearly 600 miles northwest to Hollandia in New Guinea.

Hollandia (now Sukarnapura), a major Japanese air and supply base, held two crucial advantages for the Allies. The port of Hollandia in Humboldt Bay was the best-sheltered anchorage along a lengthy stretch of the New Guinea coast, and the surrounding area had four airstrips. Together these assets could provide a major staging base for future operations in western New Guinea and the Philippine Islands. In addition, SWPA's intelligence determined that Hollandia was garrisoned only by a small force of 11,000 Japanese troops from the 6th Air Division, most of them service personnel. By attacking Hollandia, MacArthur could avoid potentially bloody battles to the east at Hansa Bay and Wewak, both of which were more strongly defended.

MacArthur and his staff were compelled to include a simultaneous attack at Aitape, 140 miles east of Hollandia. Airstrips there would provide a permanent staging area within range of Hollandia, enabling the Allies to seize command of the air. The Hollandia and Aitape invasions together required a flotilla of more than 200 ships and 80,000 personnel.

During late March and early April 1944, Allied pilots destroyed most of the 6th Air Division's aircraft, paving the way for the landing of ground troops on 22 April. At the same time, General Adachi Hatazō, commander of the Eighteenth Army headquartered on Rabaul, regrouped his battered forces near Hollandia. U.S. forces, meanwhile, carried out a remarkable counterintelligence scheme to divert Adachi. False radio transmissions, decoy raids, patrols, and bombing convinced the Japanese that an Allied assault at Hansa Bay was imminent.

The landing, dubbed Operation RECKLESS, was entrusted to Lieutenant General Robert L. Eichelberger's I Corps. One regiment from the 24th Infantry Division went ashore at Tanahmerah Bay, and another regiment from the 24th Division and two regiments from the 41st Infantry Division landed at Hollandia about 25 miles to the east. Simultaneously, a regiment from the 41st Division and a regiment from the 32nd Infantry Division landed at Aitap, 125 miles to the southeast to secure a fighter strip. Their chief opposition came in the form of the marshy beaches themselves. Later that day, the 163rd Regimental Combat Team took Aitape against only limited resistance, demonstrating the effectiveness of the Hansa Bay ruse. With Aitape in hand, the ground forces at Hollandia trudged through trackless marsh and bog to encircle the three main Japanese airfields. Confusion, fear, and lack of weaponry prompted a large-scale Japanese retreat west.

Suppressing remaining resistance, U.S. forces secured Hollandia on 26 April 1944 only four days after the initial landings, although mop-up operations continued for several weeks. The most telling evidence of the Allied air attacks before the landings was the wreckage of more than 340 Japanese aircraft on Hollandia's runways. Allied casualties were 159 killed and 1,100 wounded. The Japanese lost 3,300 dead and 600 prisoners. At Aitape, all objectives were secured by 25 April at a cost of 3 American dead. About 600 Japanese were killed, and 27 were taken prisoner. Another 6,000 Japanese were either killed by units from the 24th Division or died from starvation and disease as they retreated from Hollandia to Wadke-Sarmi 140 miles to the west.

Operation RECKLESS was a major triumph for MacArthur. It split the Japanese forces defending New Guinea in half, leaving the Eighteenth Army isolated in eastern New Guinea. It also gave MacArthur a superb base from which to increase the tempo of operations in the SWPA, and before long U.S. engineers had turned Hollandia into a vast complex of military, naval, and air facilities occupied by 140,000 men.

John Kennedy Ohl and Bryan Joseph Rodriguez

See also
Admiralty Islands Campaign; Eichelberger, Robert Lawrence; Krueger, Walter; MacArthur, Douglas; New Guinea Campaign; Quebec Conference (14–23 August 1943); Rabaul; Signals Intelligence

References
Chwialkowski, Paul. *In Caesar's Shadow: The Life of General Robert Eichelberger.* Westport, CT: Greenwood Press, 1993.
Drea, Edward J. *MacArthur's ULTRA: Codebreaking and the War Against Japan, 1942–1945.* Lawrence: University Press of Kansas, 1992.
———. *New Guinea.* Washington DC: U.S. Army Center of Military History, 1993.
James, D. Clayton: *The Years of MacArthur.* Vol. 2, *1941–1945.* Boston: Houghton Mifflin, 1975.
Smith, Robert Ross. *The United States Army in World War II: The War in the Pacific: The Approach to the Philippines.* Washington, DC: Office of the Chief of Military History, 1953.
Taaffe, Stephen R. *MacArthur's Jungle War: The 1944 New Guinea Campaign.* Lawrence: University Press of Kansas, 1998.

Holocaust, The

Nazi effort to exterminate the Jews of Europe during World War II. Historians have developed several interpretations of the Holocaust. While some see it as the last, most horrible manifestation of historical anti-Semitism, others view it as the outcome of factors inherent in Western civilization, such as economic rationalization, technocracy, and the eugenics movement. The "intentionalists" see Adolf Hitler as the crucial factor in the Holocaust, determined on the destruction of the Jews from the beginning. A straight line supposedly runs from his earliest anti-Semitic comments through World War II and his final testament of April 1945. On the other hand, the "functionalists" see the persecution of the Jews as a slowly developing process, exhibiting no overall plan. Not until after the beginning of World War II, when the Nazis found themselves in control of well over 3,000,000 Jews, did the full implementation of the Holocaust occur. Attempts have been made to reconcile these positions, for example, emphasizing the fusion of anti-Semitism with bureaucratic techniques of extermination.

The French Revolution of 1789 saw the beginning of the process of emancipation of the European Jews and their increasing assimilation into European society. At the same time, traditional Christian anti-Judaism gave way to modern racial anti-Semitism, fostered by hyper-nationalism, Social Darwinism, and pseudo–racial "science." Anti-Semites made the Jews the scapegoat for all the supposed ills of the modern world, including capitalism, socialism, and the press.

Anti-Semitism was a pan-European movement, as is exemplified by the Dreyfus Affair in France. Indeed, eastern Europe (especially Russia) was the scene of violent pogroms and ritual murder trials into the twentieth century. In about 1900, agents of the tsarist secret police, the Okrana, wrote the *Protocols of the Elders of Zion,* a forgery proclaiming a Jewish conspiracy to dominate the world.

**Jewish Population, Europe, before and after World War II
(with inset of Jewish Population in Poland)**

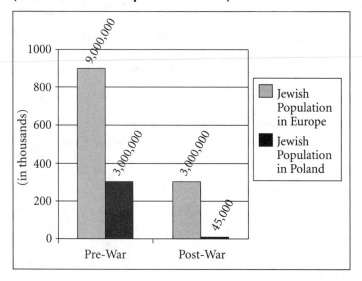

By 1900, Jews in Germany numbered about 600,000 of a population of 60 million. Jews were prominent in such areas as banking, journalism, and medicine. Some 85 percent were assimilationists and enthusiastically supported Germany during World War I. Nonetheless, Germany's defeat in World War I and the accompanying economic turmoil of the early 1920s allowed extremist right-wing groups such as the National Socialist German Workers Party, led by Adolf Hitler, to spread. These groups held Jews responsible for everything from betraying Germany on the home front during World War I to causing the evils of urban life. Whether it stemmed from his Vienna years, as portrayed in *Mein Kampf*, or developed essentially after his entry into politics at the end of World War I, Hitler's obsessive, pathological anti-Semitism, its identification with Bolshevism, and a crude social Darwinism became the core of his and Nazism's ideology.

Hitler's overall role and guilt in fostering the persecution of the Jews is clear. After 1934, however, he gradually withdrew from domestic politics, fostering power struggles among various party agencies. In this atmosphere, his lieutenants attempted to anticipate his wishes—a process that led to increasingly radical anti-Jewish measures.

The Nazis' assumption of power in 1933 led to increased random attacks on Jews. The Nazis did not appear to have a coordinated plan to deal with the "Jewish question." Indeed, the years 1933 to 1938 saw a tension between party radicals such as Joseph Goebbels and Julius Streicher and moderates such as foreign minister Konstantin von Neurath and economics minister Hjalmar Schacht, who feared that anti-Semitic actions would damage Germany's international position and economic recovery. Some level of anti-Semitism was common among many Germans, but there is little evidence that most Germans were imbued with an elimination-ist anti-Semitism, ready to murder Jews once they were given the opportunity.

The opening of the Nazi attack included a one-day unsuccessful boycott of Jewish stores on 1 April 1933 and the 7 April Law for the Restoration of the Professional Civil Service, which dismissed non-Aryans from government service. Although the boycott was unpopular with large sections of the public and the civil service law included exemptions such as World War I veterans, these actions began a gradual process that by 1939 would lead to the exclusion of Jews from German life.

On 14 July 1933, the Law for the Prevention of Genetically Diseased Offspring was promulgated, which by 1937 led to the sterilization of some 200,000 people. Although the Nazi eugenics program was not aimed specifically at Jews, and indeed was influenced by the general European and American eugenics movement, it ran on a parallel track with the anti-Jewish legislation. By World War II, the two tracks would merge in a program of euthanasia and mass murder.

In September 1935, the so-called Nuremberg Laws were passed by a special session of the Reichstag convened during the Nazi Party rally of that month. The laws were drawn up in great haste during the rally itself, indicative of the unsystematic nature of Nazi policy concerning the Jews during the 1930s. Jews became subjects, not citizens; it became illegal for Jews to marry or have extramarital relations with non-Jews. On 14 November, a supplementary law was enacted, defining a "full Jew" (having three or four Jewish grandparents) and the categories of first-degree and second-degree *Mischling* (mixed race).

In 1938 there was another major escalation of anti-Jewish persecution. In Austria after the *Anschluss* in March, a wave of humiliations, beatings, and murders occurred that were worse than anything else seen so far in Germany. The Nazis quickly set up agencies to forcibly expropriate Jewish businesses and expedite emigration, the latter effort led by Adolf Eichmann, Zionist expert of the Sicherheitsdienst (SD, Security Service). Some scholars see this sequence of violence, expropriation, and emigration as a model for how the Nazis would later attempt to handle the "Jewish question," with emigration replaced by something far worse.

During the spring and summer of 1938, violent attacks on Jews in Germany increased, culminating in the pogrom of 9–10 November. In retaliation for the murder of the third secretary of the German Embassy in Paris, Ernst von Rath, by Jewish youth Herschel Grynspan, Jews were attacked all over Germany, businesses were vandalized, and synagogues were burned. The streets were so covered with glass they appeared to be made of crystal, hence the term "crystal night" to describe the event. Party, police, and governmental offices all were complicit in the pogrom. Estimates hold that some 91 Jews died, 30,000 were arrested, and a like number were sent to concentration camps. A total of 267 synagogues were burned, and 7,500 businesses were vandalized. The Jews received no insurance payments and in fact were fined more than a billion Reichsmarks.

The period from November 1938 to the outbreak of World War II saw the removal of Jews from virtually all aspects of German society. During a Reichstag speech in January 1939, Hitler made his infamous threat that if international Jewry succeeded in starting another world war, the result would not be its victory but "the annihilation of the Jewish race in Europe."

By the time the war broke out, more than half of German and Austrian Jews had departed Germany, the official policy of which still promoted emigration. Emigrants were subject to expropriation and payment of flight taxes. Few countries were willing to increase their quota of Jewish immigrants, however. International conferences such as that held in Évian, France, in July 1938 proved fruitless.

After their conquest of Poland in the fall of 1939, the Nazis found themselves in control of some 2 million Jews. Another million were in the Soviet sphere of occupation. Nazi treatment of Poles and Jews, considered inferior races, was brutal. Western Poland was annexed to Germany, and the eastern part was turned into the General Government under Nazi lawyer Hans Frank. To facilitate the implementation of Nazi policies, head of the Schutzstaffel (SS) Heinrich Himmler on 27 September amalgamated all police and security services in the Reichssicherheitshauptamt (RSHA, Reich Security Main Office) under Reinhard Heydrich.

On 21 September, Heydrich issued instructions to Einsatzgruppen (mobile strike forces) leaders in which he distinguished between the "final aim" of Jewish policy and the steps leading to it. Jews were to be moved from the countryside and concentrated in cities near rail lines, implying the ghettoization of Polish Jews. Each ghetto was to elect a Jewish Council (Judenrat) that would be responsible for carrying out Nazi orders. In October, Jews were expelled from the annexed area of Poland, called the Warthegau, into the General Government. In addition, Frank ordered that all Jews must perform compulsory labor and wear a Star of David on the right sleeve of their clothing.

Despite the mention of the "final aim" and the brutality of these measures, most scholars do not believe the Nazis had yet adopted the idea of mass extermination. Their main goals during 1940 were either fostering emigration by Jews or deporting them to a colony in Africa or the Near East.

The first major ghetto was established in Lodz in February 1940. The Warsaw ghetto, the largest, was established in October 1940. Ghettos were in older sections of cities, with inadequate living space, housing, and food. They were surrounded by walls and barbed wire, and attempts to leave were punished by death. Disease and starvation were common. Jewish Councils had their own police forces, which were themselves brutal in enforcing Nazi orders. The Nazi film *The Eternal Jew* (1940) cynically portrayed these conditions as normal Jewish living habits.

Despite the terrible conditions, Jews secretly practiced their religion, educated their children, and maintained cultural activities. In Warsaw, the historian Emmanuel Ringelblum started the Oneg Shabbat ("in celebration of the Sabbath"), a secret organization that chronicled life in the ghetto. Its records, partly recovered after the war, are an invaluable picture of ghetto life.

In a speech to senior army officers on 30 March 1941 preceding the invasion of the Soviet Union (Operation BARBAROSSA), Hitler maintained that, in contrast to war in the west, the war against the Soviet Union would be a war of annihilation, a brutal campaign to subjugate inferior Slavs and to exterminate Jewish-Bolshevism. Hitler's BARBAROSSA Decree of 13 May 1941 and the Commissar Order of 6 June 1941, as well as orders issued by various generals, called for liquidation of the Bolshevik leadership without trial, reprisals against whole villages for partisan actions, and the freeing of military personnel from prosecution for crimes against civilians. These orders would pave the way for military complicity in war crimes against Russian soldiers and civilians and against the Jews.

After the German invasion of the Soviet Union on 22 June 1941, four Einsatzgruppen, each numbering 600–1,000 men, swept through the conquered territories in the wakes of the invading armies, shooting Communist Party functionaries and especially male Jews. The Einsatzgruppen were drawn primarily from various security and SS units. The German army provided no obstacles to their actions and in some cases actively cooperated with them. After their numbers were augmented in August, the Einsatzgruppen rapidly expanded their killing of Jews, including women and children. Between June and August the Einsatzgruppen killed approximately 50,000 Jews; in the next four months some 500,000 would perish. On 29 and 30 October at Babi Yar near Kiev, some 33,000 Jews were shot, and their bodies were dumped in a ravine. Hitler had undoubtedly given the overall approval to widen the killing in August, and he regularly received reports of Einsatzgruppen activities.

Collaborators throughout eastern Europe actively aided —and in some cases, outdid—the Nazis. For example, the German invasion of Lithuania was accompanied by horrendous butchery of Lithuanians against Lithuanians. Germany's Romanian allies actively murdered Jews. On 22 October, the Romanian military headquarters in Odessa was blown up and 60 lives were lost. In reprisal, Romanian army units massacred 19,000 Jews and locked another 20,000 in warehouses in a nearby village, which were then set on fire and machine-gunned. Babi-Yar and Odessa were perhaps the two worst massacres of the war.

Although no written order has come to light and although Hitler confined himself to murderous ranting about the Jews, there can be no doubt that the Holocaust proceeded with Hitler's express knowledge and desire. Scholars are divided,

Slave laborers in the Buchenwald concentration camp near Jena; many had died from malnutrition when U.S. troops of the 80th Division entered the camp, 16 April 1945. (National Archives)

however, about when exactly the "final solution" was put into effect. Some authorities place the decision as early as the spring of 1941 during the planning for Operation BARBAROSSA, and others argue that there was a gradual escalation of measures throughout the summer and fall of 1941. Hitler's final decision may have come on 12 December 1941, in a talk to party leaders at the Reich Chancellery, one day after his declaration of war on the United States. Hitler now saw the events he had described in his speech of 30 January 1939 as coming to pass: the Jews had started a world war, and now they would perish.

On 20 January 1942, the much-postponed Wannsee Conference held for the purpose of coordinating activities by various agencies with regard to the "final solution" took place. Chaired by Reinhard Heydrich, it included major SS and government agency representatives. Europe's Jewish population was set at an exaggerated figure of 11 million. The Jews—even those not under Nazi control—were to be "evac-

uated" to the east. This "final solution to the Jewish question" would be implemented first in the General Government. Hitler's hatred of the Jews, the realization that the war against the Soviet Union would not be over quickly, the huge number of Jews in eastern Europe augmented by deportations from the west, and killing actions initiated by local commanders all combined to replace deportation with systematic mass murder.

Since execution by shooting was too inefficient and was stressful for the shooters, the Nazis began gassing victims. The model for mass murder came from the euthanasia program, which had been ordered by Hitler on 1 September 1939 and which officially ended in August 1941 after strong protests from German churches. Known as the T-4 program (named after its headquarters at Tiergartenstrasse 4 in Berlin), it had been responsible for killing some 5,000 children and 70,000 to 80,000 adults, at first by injection and then by carbon monoxide. Several T-4 staff members were transferred to the extermination program of eastern Europe.

In December 1941, Chelmno, near Lodz in the Warthegau, was the first extermination center to begin operation. Between March and July 1942, in connection with Operation REINHARD (the plan to kill the Jews of the General Government), three more death camps were set up: Belzec, Sobibor, and Treblinka. Deportations to these camps from Polish ghettos took place throughout 1942 and into the fall of 1943.

As Jews were rounded up, they were told they were being resettled to labor camps in the east. When the Jews arrived in the camps, their belongings were confiscated and they were then forced to undress and to move down a ramp ("the tube") into gas chambers falsely labeled as showers. The Jews were then killed with gas fed into the chamber. Special units of Jewish prisoners called Sonderkommandos removed the dead from the gas chambers, collected their possessions, and then buried the corpses in mass graves. Eventually, the Sonderkommandos too were killed. Jews from all over occupied Europe, as well as Roma (gypsies), were killed in these camps. Authorities estimate the approximate death toll at 1.9 million.

Majdanek (near Lublin in the General Government) and Auschwitz (in a section of southern Poland annexed to Germany) operated as concentration, extermination, and forced-labor camps. Exterminations in gas chambers began in Majdanek in the fall of 1942 and greatly increased in November 1943, when the Nazis launched Operation HARVEST FESTIVAL to kill off the remaining Jews in the General Government. By the time Soviet forces overran Majdanek in July 1944, some 360,000 people had died.

Auschwitz I was set up as a concentration camp in May 1940. Here the Nazis brutally murdered thousands at the "Black Wall" and carried on gruesome pseudoscientific medical experiments, including sterilization, castration, and hypothermia. Auschwitz II or Auschwitz-Birkenau was essentially an extermination camp. It began operations on 3 September 1941 when 900 Soviet prisoners of war died after being gassed with Zyklon B, crystallized hydrogen cyanide. By 1943, four large gas chamber/crematoria were at work as Jews from all over Europe were brought to Auschwitz. Work to expand the facility continued essentially until the summer of 1944. During the spring and summer of 1944, more than 400,000 Hungarian Jews were deported to Auschwitz and gassed. A conservative estimate puts the overall death toll here at 1.1 million Jews, 75,000 Poles, 21,000 Roma, and 15,000 Soviet prisoners of war.

Prisoners destined for the camps were packed into unheated and unventilated cattle cars with no food and perhaps one bucket for a toilet. Many died before reaching the camp. Upon arrival, prisoners underwent "selection": those unfit for work were immediately sent to the gas chambers, which were disguised as showers. Sonderkommandos cleaned the gas chambers, cremated the corpses, and collected valuables.

In the fall of 1941, I. G. Farben decided to build a Buna (synthetic rubber) plant at Auschwitz to exploit cheap slave labor. The so-called Auschwitz III expanded into a 40-square-mile area with numerous subcamps. Periodic selections singled out weak and sick workers for extermination.

Numerous survivors, including Elie Wiesel and Primo Levi, have described the brutal Auschwitz camp regime, which was intended to dehumanize its victims. "Kapos"—usually incarcerated criminals—enforced order. Hunger was all-pervasive. Finally, on 27 January 1945, Soviet forces liberated the few remaining prisoners in Auschwitz. Some 60,000 had been forced on death marches to camps in Germany. Many died on the marches or before the German camps were liberated.

Between 1942 and early 1945, the Nazis extended the Holocaust to occupied western, central, and southern Europe. Numerous government agencies including the RSHA, the Transport Ministry, and the Foreign Office lent their assistance. Adolf Eichmann, head of RSHA Jewish Affairs and Evacuation Affairs (coded IV-B-4), coordinated the deportations. The European rail system was taken over and used to move Jews east to the killing sites.

> Although the exact numbers will never be known, it is believed that between 3.5 and 6 million people died in the Holocaust.

In many places, the Nazis were assisted by collaborationist authorities, but elsewhere, such as in Denmark and in Italian-held areas, they were actively resisted by local officials. The result was that thousands of Jews went into hiding or were assisted in escaping the Nazi dragnet. Although exact numbers will never be known, it is estimated that 3.5 million to 4 million people died in the six death camps. When victims of pogroms, the Einsatzgruppen, and those who died of overwork, starvation, and disease are added, the Holocaust claimed some 6 million lives.

Resistance was made difficult by numerous factors—the impossibility of believing the reality of what was happening, the hostility of local populations, the difficulty of obtaining weapons, the deception of the Nazis, and the decision of Jewish councils to obey Nazi demands in hopes of saving the lives of the remnant Jewish population that worked in defense industries.

Most Jews who were rounded up for execution or transport to a camp went without resistance. In some cases, however, open rebellion broke out. The most famous example is the Warsaw Rising, beginning on 19 April 1943, in which 700 to 1,000 resistance fighters in the Warsaw ghetto held off several thousand heavily armed German and Baltic auxiliaries under SS-Brigadeführer Joseph (Jürgen) Stroop for almost four weeks. Revolts in Treblinka in August 1943 and in Sobibor in October 1943 led to the closing of these camps. On 7 October 1944, the Sonderkommando at Auschwitz revolted, killing several SS men and blowing up one of the crematoria. All were killed in the ensuing escape attempt. In several cases, Jews were able to escape the ghettos and either join or form their own partisan groups that fought against the Nazis.

Allied officials were clearly aware of the Holocaust by late 1942, but like the Jews themselves, they had difficulty believing what they were hearing. In addition, anti-Semitism was still strong in many countries. American State Department official Breckinridge Long worked actively to keep Jewish refugees out of the United States. In the Allied countries, winning the war was the first priority. American Jewish organizations were hesitant to make waves or press President Franklin D. Roosevelt for fear of stirring up even more anti-Semitism. In a still-controversial decision, the Allies refused to bomb the Auschwitz camp or the rail lines leading to it. Not until early 1944 did Roosevelt create the War Refugee Board, after the Treasury Department had exposed the State Department's duplicity.

Some governments or individual diplomats resisted the Nazis. The Danish people ensured the rescue of more than 95 percent of Danish Jews. The Bulgarian government refused to give over its native Jews, although it handed over Jews in occupied territories. The Italian fascist government refused cooperation with the Nazis, and Franco's government allowed Jewish refugees to travel through Spain. Diplomats defied their orders by issuing visas to Jews. The Swede Raoul Wallenberg and other diplomats in Budapest rescued thousands of Jews in the summer and fall of 1944 by issuing false papers and setting up safe havens. Citizens from France to Poland sheltered Jews, in some cases for years, at tremendous risk to themselves. In 1940, Chiune Sugihara, a minor diplomat in the Japanese consulate in Kaunas, Lithuania, quietly defied his government's orders and issued illegal visas to more than 2,000 Jewish families.

In the case of the churches, it was more often individuals than institutions that did rescue work. Numerous Protestant, Eastern Orthodox, and Catholic clergy and laymen intervened to help Jews, whereas others remained silent or backed Nazi actions. Controversy still surrounds the role of Pope Pius XII, who never publicly condemned the Holocaust, even when the Jews of Rome were being rounded up in October 1943.

As the Nazi empire crumbled in late 1944 and early 1945, Himmler and others carried out increasingly desperate negotiations, attempting to trade Jewish lives for ransom. As the Soviet army moved westward, hasty attempts were made to dismantle camps and burn victims' bodies. Prisoners were forced on death marches back to camps within Germany. By May 1945, the last of the camps had been overrun. Some 50,000 prisoners were liberated, but many were so sick and emaciated they died soon after. In his political testament of 29 April 1945, Hitler blamed the war on the Jews and called on Germans to continue the struggle against international Jewry.

The pre–World War II Jewish population of Europe had been approximately 9 million. At the end of the war, 3 million remained. In Poland, some 45,000 survived out of a prewar population of 3 million, many of whom were Hasidic Jews. In the words of the sect's founder, Israel Ba'al Shem Tov: "In forgetfulness is the root of exile. In remembrance the seed of redemption."

Donald E. Thomas Jr.

See also

Allied Military Tribunals after the War; Babi Yar Massacre; BARBAROSSA, Operation; Catholic Church and the War; Chemical Weapons and Warfare; Collaboration; Commissar Order; Concentration Camps, German; Eichmann, Karl Adolf; Goebbels, Paul Josef; Heydrich, Reinhard Tristan Eugen; Himmler, Heinrich; Hitler, Adolf; Jewish Resistance; Pius XII, Pope; Resistance; Roosevelt, Franklin D.; Wannsee Conference; Warsaw Ghetto Uprising

References

Bartov, Omer, ed. *The Holocaust: Origins, Implementations, Aftermath.* London and New York: Routledge, 2000.

Bauer, Yehuda. *A History of the Holocaust.* New York: Franklin Watts, 1982.

Friedlaender, Saul. *Nazi Germany and the Jews.* Vol. 1, *The Years of Persecution, 1933–1939.* New York: HarperCollins, 1997.

Hilberg, Raul. *The Destruction of the European Jews.* 3d ed. New Haven, CT: Yale University Press, 2002.

Kershaw, Ian. *Hitler.* 2 vols. New York: W. W. Norton, 1998 and 2000.

Laqueur, Walter, ed. *The Holocaust Encyclopedia.* New Haven, CT: Yale University Press, 2001.

United States Holocaust Memorial Museum. *Historical Atlas of the Holocaust.* New York: MacMillan, 1996.

Hong Kong, Battle of (8–25 December 1941)

Battle for British Asian colony, the capture of which by Japan symbolized the defeat of western imperialism in Asia. The colony of Hong Kong, 400 square miles of islands and an adjacent peninsula on the coast of Guangdong, South China, was both the headquarters of the Royal Navy's China Squadron and a significant entrepôt and commercial center. From the mid-1930s onward, the British Joint Chiefs of Staff believed that, in the event of attack by Japanese forces, Hong Kong would be indefensible.

In 1935, Major General Sir John Dill, director of military operations, ranked Hong Kong's strategic significance far

British prisoners of war departing Hong Kong for a Japanese prison camp in December 1941. (Photo by Keystone/Getty Images)

below that of Singapore, Britain's other naval base. A 1939 strategic review also assigned Britain's interests in Europe much greater importance than those of Hong Kong. British leaders nonetheless feared that a failure to defend Hong Kong or even the evacuation of civilians would signal their country's intention of abandoning its Asian position and damage the morale of the embattled Chinese Guomindang (GMD [Kuomintang, KMT], Nationalist) government in its struggle to resist Japanese invasion.

By June 1940, sizable Japanese forces blocked Hong Kong's access to the Chinese mainland. That August, Dill—now chief of the Imperial General Staff—recommended the withdrawal of the British garrison. Although Prime Minister Winston L. S. Churchill accepted this recommendation, it was not implemented. Some women and children were evacuated to Manila in the Philippines, and in October 1941, Britain accepted the Canadian government's ill-considered offer to send 2 Cana-

dian battalions to reinforce the 2 Scottish and 2 Indian battalions already manning Hong Kong's defenses.

Even with this assistance, Hong Kong's defenses remained decidedly inadequate: 12,000 troops, augmented by the Hong Kong and Singapore Royal Artillery and the civilian Hong Kong Volunteer Defense Force, were too few to man the colony's main lengthy defense line (Gindrinker's Line), which ran 3 miles north of Kowloon in the New Territories. Air and naval forces comprised a pitiable 7 airplanes, 8 motor torpedo boats, and 4 small gunboats. It was generally known that many Japanese civilians in the colony were fifth columnists, agents only awaiting the opportunity to facilitate a Japanese assault. The British government had no intention of sending any further assistance but merely expected its defenders to stave off inevitable defeat as long as possible.

On 8 December 1941, as Japanese forces simultaneously attacked Pearl Harbor, a surprise raid on Kai Tak airfield by

Taiwan-based Japanese bombers destroyed all 7 British airplanes. Twelve battalions of the 38th Division of the Japanese Twenty-Third Army, commanded by Lieutenant General Sano Tadayoshi, crossed the Shenzhen River separating the New Territories and mainland China. Churchill urged Hong Kong's defenders to resist to the end, but within 24 hours Japanese forces had breached Gindrinker's Line. British commander Major General Christopher M. Maltby ordered a retreat to Hong Kong island, and by 12 December, Japanese troops held Kowloon.

Sano's artillery began heavy bombardments of British positions on Victoria, the central district, but Maltby refused a 14 December ultimatum to surrender and the following day repulsed a Japanese attempt to land troops on the island. A second attempt three nights later succeeded, and Japanese forces swiftly advanced across the island to its southern coast, splitting British forces. Despite heavy losses, British troops fought fiercely, on 20 December compelling Sano to halt temporarily to regroup his forces. The advance soon resumed, however, and by 24 December Japanese units had destroyed the water mains, leaving their opponents as short of water as they were of ammunition. On 25 December 1941, the British governor negotiated an unconditional surrender.

Immediately afterward, the Japanese victors treated their defeated foes with great brutality, massacring many of the defending forces, Chinese and western, including hospitalized wounded men. They raped and sometimes killed hospital nurses and other captured women. Surviving prisoners of war and Allied civilians were interned for the duration of the war, often in severe conditions, while the supposedly liberated Chinese population likewise experienced harsh and arbitrary rule and numerous atrocities.

Hong Kong remained under Japanese occupation until August 1945 when, despite the hopes of Chinese Nationalist leader Jiang Jieshi (Chiang Kai-shek) that it would revert to China, British forces reestablished control. Hong Kong subsequently remained a British colony until its 1997 reversion to China.

Priscilla Roberts

See also

China, Role in War; Churchill, Sir Winston L. S.; Dill, Sir John Greer; Jiang Jieshi; Pearl Harbor, Attack on

References

Barham, Tony. *Not the Slightest Chance: The Defence of Hong Kong, 1941.* Hong Kong: University of Hong Kong Press, 2003.

Birch, Alan, and Martin Cole. *Captive Christmas: The Battle of Hong Kong, December 1941.* Hong Kong: Heinemann Asia, 1979.

Carew, Tim. *Fall of Hong Kong.* London: Anthony Blond, 1960.

Ferguson, Ted. *Desperate Siege: The Battle of Hong Kong.* Toronto: Doubleday Canada, 1980.

Gandt, Robert. *Season of Storms: The Siege of Hong Kong, 1941.* Hong Kong: South China Morning Post, 1982.

Lindsay, Oliver. *The Lasting Honour: The Fall of Hong Kong, 1941.* London: Hamish Hamilton, 1978; 2d ed. London: Collins, 1997.

Hopkins, Harry Lloyd (1890–1946)

U.S. diplomat and presidential adviser to Franklin D. Roosevelt. Born on 17 August 1890 in Sioux City, Iowa, Harry Hopkins graduated from Grinnell College in 1912. He became a social worker in New York City and then joined President Roosevelt's New Deal administration first as head of the Federal Emergency Relief Administration (1933–1935) and then, from 1935 to 1938, as head of the Works Progress Administration (WPA). Roosevelt named him secretary of commerce in 1938.

Stomach cancer and ill health caused Hopkins to step down in 1940 to become an adviser to Roosevelt. In this position, he had great influence with Roosevelt, and he also served as an intermediary between Roosevelt and other Allied leaders. In January 1941, Hopkins flew to Britain as a personal envoy of Roosevelt to coordinate the Lend-Lease Act. He convinced Roosevelt to ignore U.S. Ambassador Joseph Kennedy's pessimistic reports regarding Britain's ability to remain in the war. To secure an agreement in discussions about the Atlantic Charter on 14 August 1941, Hopkins helped smooth over differences between Roosevelt and British Prime Minister Winston L. S. Churchill on the issue of colonialism. Another example of Hopkins's influence was his ability in 1944 to convince chairman of the Joint Chiefs of Staff Admiral William Leahy to continue supplying British forces in Greece, even though the United States disagreed with London's policy toward communist rebels there. Hopkins was not always successful, as in Moscow in June 1945, when he failed to secure Russian leader Josef Stalin's support for democratic reforms in Poland that had been agreed to at the Yalta Conference the previous February.

After Roosevelt's death, Hopkins assisted the new president, Harry S Truman, in arrangements for the Potsdam Conference. Hopkins also played a leading role in the formation of the United Nations. Forced by ill health to retire from public life in fall 1945, Hopkins died in New York City on 29 January 1946.

T. Jason Soderstrum

See also

Atlantic Charter; Casablanca Conference; Churchill, Sir Winston L. S.; Lend-Lease; Potsdam Conference; Roosevelt, Franklin D.; Stalin, Josef; Tehran Conference; United Nations, Formation of; Yalta Conference

References

Adams, Henry Hitch. *Harry Hopkins: A Biography.* New York: Putnam, 1977.

Hopkins, June. *Harry Hopkins: Sudden Hero, Brash Reformer.* New York: St. Martin's Press, 1999.

McJimsey, George. *Harry Hopkins: Ally of the Poor and Defender of Democracy.* Cambridge, MA: Harvard University Press, 1987.

Sherwood, Robert. *Roosevelt and Hopkins: An Intimate History.* Rev. ed. New York: Harper, 1950.

Tuttle, Dwight William. *Harry L. Hopkins and Anglo-American Soviet Relations, 1941–1945.* New York: Garland, 1983.

Horii Tomitaro (1890–1942)

Japanese army general. Born in Hyogo Prefecture on 7 November 1890, Horii Tomitaro was commissioned as a second lieutenant in the Imperial Japanese Army in December 1911. Following several staff and line postings, Horii commanded a battalion beginning in August 1932. He was promoted to colonel in August 1937, and in July 1938 he was attached to headquarters of the 8th Depot Division. Horii then took command of the 82nd Infantry Regiment. By August 1940, he was a major general commanding the 55th Regimental Group. This formation consisted mostly of the reinforced 144th Infantry Regiment and was better known as the South Seas Detachment.

At the start of World War II, Horii's force quickly captured Guam. On 4 January 1942, Imperial General Headquarters ordered Horii to prepare to take Rabaul. Escorted by the aircraft carriers *Kaga* and *Akagi*, the invasion force landed in the predawn darkness of 23 January. The Australian garrison there was quickly overwhelmed, and Horii's soldiers proceeded to torture and execute many of the prisoners.

The South Seas Detachment formed most of the Japanese invasion force intended to capture Port Moresby in May 1942. This operation triggered the Battle of the Coral Sea, the first naval battle fought only with carrier aircraft. To Horii's disappointment, the transports carrying his soldiers turned back to Rabaul on 9 May.

Horii's South Seas Detachment was then ordered to advance by land south over the Owen Stanley Mountains to Port Moresby. Japanese forces went ashore at Buna beginning on 20 July. The Japanese drove off the few defenders and soon reached Kokoda. Horii himself reached Buna by mid-August. By 21 August, he had more than 8,000 combat troops and 3,000 construction workers under his command. Soon Horii, riding his white horse, was at the head of the Japanese advance. By mid-September, the Japanese had pushed to within 30 miles of Port Moresby.

The American landing on Guadalcanal in August 1942 drew away Japanese reinforcements intended for New Guinea. Disease, malnutrition, and combat severely reduced Horii's command. The terrain also proved to be a formidable obstacle. In addition, a Japanese supporting attack on Milne Bay was defeated, allowing the Allies to pour reinforcements into Port Moresby. On 24 September 1942, Horii was ordered to withdraw toward Buna. An Allied counterattack soon turned the retreat into a rout. Horii was inspecting rear-guard positions on 12 November when his party was cut off by an Australian attack near Wairopi. That night, Horii and his aides tried to cross the Kumusi River on a raft of logs. The raft came apart in the turbulent water, and Horii, his chief of staff, and two others were drowned. His death was confirmed 10 days later.

Tim J. Watts

See also
Coral Sea, Battle of the; Milne Bay, Battle of; New Guinea Campaign; Papuan Campaign; Rabaul
References
McCarthy, Dudley. *Southwest Pacific Area: First Year: Kokoda to Wau*. Canberra: Australian War Memorial, 1959.
Milner, Samuel. *United States Army in World War II: The War in the Pacific: Victory in Papua*. Washington, DC: Office of the Chief of Military History, 1957.
Paull, Raymond. *Retreat from Kokoda: The Australian Campaign in New Guinea 1942*. London: Secker and Warburg, 1983.

Horrocks, Sir Brian Gwynne (1895–1985)

British army general. Brian Horrocks was born on 7 September 1895 in Ranikhet, India, and educated at the Royal Military Academy, Sandhurst. He was commissioned in 1914. Wounded at Ypres in October 1914, Horrocks was captured and spent the next four years as a prisoner of the Germans. He then volunteered to go to Russia on a mission to assist White forces in Siberia, and he was a prisoner of the Red forces from January to October 1920. An outstanding athlete, Horrocks competed in the 1924 Olympic Games in the pentathlon.

In the 1930s, Horrocks attended the Staff College of Camberley, and he was subsequently an instructor there. In 1939, Horrocks commanded a battalion in the 3rd Division in France, where he made an excellent impression on his commander, Bernard Montgomery. Promoted to brigadier general in June 1940 during the Dunkerque evacuation, Horrocks then commanded the 9th Armored Division. In August 1942, when Montgomery took over the Eighth Army, he named Horrocks, now a lieutenant general, to head XIII Corps. XII Corps played a key role in repelling the Afrika Korps attack at the crucial Battle of Alma Halfa, and it fought against the 21st Panzer Division at El Alamein. Horrocks then took command of X Corps and led it during the successful flanking maneuver at Mareth in March 1943. During April and May 1943, Horrocks commanded IX Corps during the final drive against Tunis.

In June 1943, while preparing for the invasion of Italy, Horrocks was badly wounded during an air raid on Bizerte. This kept him out of action for a year. In August 1944, Horrocks took command of XXX Corps, which he led until the end of the war in General Miles Dempsey's Second British Army. Accomplishments of XXX Corps included the capture of Amiens, Brussels, Antwerp, and Bremen and helping to reduce the Ardennes salient. Horrocks is best remembered for his role during Operation MARKET-GARDEN, when XXX Corps failed to relieve the British 1st Airborne Division at Arnhem. Horrocks called the failure "the blackest moment of my life."

After the war, Horrocks commanded the British Army of the Rhine before his war wounds forced his retirement in 1949. Horrocks later wrote his autobiography, *A Full Life* (1960), and became a television commentator. Horrocks died in Fishbourne, England, on 4 January 1985.

Thomas D. Veve

See also

Alam Halfa, Battle of; Ardennes Offensive; Dempsey, Miles Christopher; El Alamein, Battle of; Mareth, Battle of; MARKET-GARDEN, Operation; Montgomery, Sir Bernard Law

References

Horrocks, Brian. *A Full Life*. London: William Collin's Sons, 1960.
———. *Escape to Action*. New York: St. Martin's, 1961.
Ryan, Cornelius. *A Bridge Too Far*. London: Hamish Hamilton Limited, 1974.
Warner, Philip. *Horrocks: The General Who Led from the Front*. London: Hamish Hamilton Limited, 1984.

Horthy de Nagybánya, Miklós (1868–1957)

Hungarian navy admiral in World War I, politician, and regent of Hungary. Born in Kenderes, Hungary, to landed gentry on 18 June 1868, Miklós Horthy de Nagybánya graduated from the Naval Academy in 1886 and entered the Austro-Hungarian navy, where he served for 32 years. As a captain, Horthy commanded the successful May 1917 attack on the Otranto Barrage, during which he was wounded in both legs. Horthy became a hero in Hungary for his role in the battle, which led to his promotion to rear admiral in March 1918. That same month, following mutinies in the fleet, Emperor Karl promoted Horthy to vice admiral and named him commander of the Austro-Hungarian battle fleet.

Following the war, Horthy retired. He soon entered politics as the leader of the conservative White forces against the communist government of Béla Kun. On 1 March 1920, Horthy became regent of Hungary and head of the executive authority. At first Horthy had little power, but his power

Hermann Göring (right, hat with feather) with Admiral Horthy (center, facing Göring), regent of Hungary, at Carinhall, Göring's country estate. (Library of Congress)

increased sharply after 1937 when he refused to be bound by decisions of the Hungarian Parliament.

In domestic policy, Horthy rejected universal and secret suffrage and land reform. In foreign policy, his chief aim was revision of the Treaty of Trianon of 1920, by which Hungary had lost two-thirds of its territory and population. For this reason, although he was strongly anti-Fascist, Horthy sought the support of, and an alliance with, Germany and Italy. His diplomatic efforts were successful in that between 1938 and 1940, Hungary recovered some of the territory it had lost after World War I to Czechoslovakia, Romania, and Yugoslavia.

Horthy successfully managed to afford involvement in the war in September 1939. By April 1941, however, pressure from Adolf Hitler, coupled with promises of additional territory and access to the Adriatic, led to Hungarian military operations against Yugoslavia on the Axis side. Horthy was also forced to send troops to fight on the Eastern Front against the Soviet Union, but he resisted German efforts to have him deport Hungarian Jews.

In 1943, Horthy was already considering escaping from Hitler's grasp and negotiating with the Allied powers. Aware of this activity and determined to keep Hungary in the war on his side, Hitler sent German troops to occupy the country on 19 March 1944. Horthy remained in his post. In September, Soviet troops invaded Hungary from Romania, and on 28 September Horthy dispatched representatives to Moscow. There they signed a preliminary armistice agreement on 11 October, which Horthy announced publicly four days later. A lack of coordination with army chief of staff General János Vörös led to a continuation of the fighting. The German army then occupied Budapest and took Horthy's son hostage, forcing Horthy to appoint Ferenc Szálasi, head of the German Arrow Cross (Fascist) Party, as "Leader of the Nation."

The Germans then removed Horthy to Bavaria, where he was captured by the Americans. In 1946, Horthy appeared as a witness at the postwar International Military Tribunal at Nuremberg. The Yugoslav government requested his extradition so that he might be tried there for war crimes, but the U.S. authorities refused the request. Horthy then moved to Portugal, where he remained. The Soviet occupation and subsequent communist government of Hungary made it impossible for him to return there. Horthy wrote his memoirs in 1953, but they were not published in Hungary until 1990. He died in Estoril, Portugal, on 9 February 1957. In 1993, following the departure of the last Soviet soldiers from Hungary, Horthy's remains were reburied in Kenderes, Hungary.

Anna Boros-McGee

See also
Hungary, Army; Hungary, Role in the War; International Military Tribunal: The Nuremberg Trials; Vörös, János

References
Benesik, Gábor. *Alexander Horthy: The Governor and His Era.* Budapest: Magyar Mercuaius, 2001.
Horthy, Miklós. *Memoirs.* New York: R. Speller, 1956.
Vígh, Károly. "A kormányzó országlásának a vége. 1944. Október 15" [End to the governor's power: 15 October 1944]. *Élet és Tudomány* 49 (1994): 1262–1264.

Hoth, Hermann (1885–1971)

German army general. Born in Neuruppin near Berlin on 12 April 1885, Hermann Hoth joined the army in 1904. He graduated from the Prussian War Academy in 1913 and became an intelligence officer. A staff officer during and after World War I, he became a specialist in armored warfare.

In 1935, Hoth took command of the 18th Division and was promoted to major general. Promoted to lieutenant general, in November 1938 he commanded the XV Motorized Corps and distinguished himself in the invasion of Poland in September 1939. With his panzer group, Hoth also distinguished himself in the invasion of France and Benelux in May 1940. In this campaign, he pushed through the Ardennes Forest to the English Channel and then into Normandy and Brittany. Hoth won promotion to full general in July. His formation was redesignated 3rd Panzer Group in November. He led it in the invasion of the Soviet Union in June 1941. Hoth commanded the Seventeenth Army in Ukraine from October 1941 to June 1942, when he took command of Fourth Panzer Army. Hoth's task was to encircle Voronezh and then drive south to the lower Don River. He led this army across the Don and toward the Caucasus and lower Volga.

Although Hoth subsequently failed to break through Soviet defenses to Stalingrad, he subsequently carried out a successful counteroffensive that helped open an escape route around Rostov for Army Group A. The Fourth Army helped restore the German lines and participated in the Battle of Kursk in July 1943. That November, Adolf Hitler dismissed the capable and well-liked Hoth for his "defeatist attitude."

Tried by a U.S. military court after the war for "crimes against humanity" committed by subordinates, Hoth was found guilty and sentenced at Nuremberg in October 1948 to 15 years in prison. He was released in 1954 and then wrote on armored warfare. His memoir, *Panzer-Operationen*, was published in 1956. Hoth died at Goslar/Harz on 25 January 1971.

Spencer C. Tucker

See also
BARBAROSSA, Operation; France, Battle for; Kursk, Battle of; Poland Campaign; Stalingrad, Battle of

References
Brett-Smith, Richard. *Hitler's Generals.* San Rafael, CA: Presidio Press, 1976.

Hoth, Hermann. *Panzer-Operationen: die Panzer-gruppe 3 und der operative Gedanke der deutschen Führung Sommer 1941*. Heidelberg: K. Vowinckel, 1956.

Mellenthin, F. W. von. *Panzer Battles: A Study of the Employment of Armor in the Second World War*. Norman: University of Oklahoma Press, 1956.

Hu Tsung-nan

See Hu Zongnan.

Hu Zongnan (Hu Tsung-nan) (1896–1962)

Chinese Nationalist general, known as the "King of the Northwest." Born in Zhenhai (Chenhain), Zhejiang (Chekiang), on 16 May 1896, Hu Zongnan (Hu Tsung-nan) received a primary education in the Confucian classics and became a teacher. In 1924, he studied at the newly founded Huangpu (Whampoa) Military Academy. As a Jiang Jieshi (Chiang Kai-shek) loyalist, Hu participated in the 1926–1928 Northern Expedition and continued to fight warlords, the Kuomintang (KMT [Guomindang, GMD], Nationalist), and Communist forces through the 1930s.

On the outbreak of the Sino-Japanese War in 1937, Hu participated in the defense of Shanghai in Jiangsu (Kiangsu) Province as commander of the First Army. In 1938, he received command of the Seventeenth Army Group and was responsible for military training in northwest China, with headquarters at Xian (Sian), Shaanxi (Shensi). He was assigned the dual task of resisting the Japanese in north China and containing the Communists in northern Shaanxi, where he became the center of the powerful "Huangpu clique" in Chinese military politics. In 1939, he commanded the Thirty-Fourth Group Army. In 1943 he received command of the First War Area comprising Hebai (Hopei), Northern Shandong (Shantung), Henan (Honan), Anhui (Anhwei), and Shaanxi.

In the spring of 1944, the Japanese began their ICHI-GŌ Campaign, which was aimed at removing China from the war. Hu's forces were hit hard but were able to prevent the Japanese from entering Shaanxi Province. In 1945, at war's end, Hu traveled to Zhengzhou (Chengchow) in Henan Province to accept the surrender of the Japanese forces.

After the war and Jiang's order to go on the offensive against the Communists, Hu marched into northern Shaanxi and captured Yan'an (Yenan) in March 1947. This victory marked the high-water mark of Nationalist achievement in the Chinese Civil War. As his forces became isolated from other GMD troops and supplies, they were eventually routed and then wiped out during 1949 by the Communists. Hu and a small group of advisers escaped to Hainan Island and eventually made their way to Taiwan. He served the Nationalist government in Taiwan as commander of the guerrilla forces on Dachen (Tach'en) Island and ended his career in command of Nationalist forces in the Penghus (Pescadores). He retired in late 1959 and died in Taipei on 14 February 1962.

Errol M. Clauss

See also
China, Army; China, Civil War in; China, Role in War; ICHI-GŌ Campaign; Jiang Jieshi; Sino-Japanese War

References
Ch'i, Hsi-sheng. *Nationalist China at War: Military Defeats and Political Collapse, 1937–45*. Ann Arbor: University of Michigan Press, 1982.

Eastman, Lloyd. *Seeds of Destruction: Nationalist China in War and Revolution, 1937–1949*. Stanford, CA: Stanford University Press, 1984.

Hull, Cordell (1871–1955)

U.S. secretary of state from 1933 to 1944. Born in the community of Star Point in Pickett County, Tennessee, on 2 October 1871, Cordell Hull studied law at National Normal University in Lebanon, Ohio, and the Cumberland Law School in Lebanon, Tennessee. In 1892, he entered Tennessee state politics as a Democrat. During the 1898 Spanish-American War, Hull volunteered and spent several months in the army. He was elected to Congress in 1903, and in 1930 he became senator for Tennessee. He resigned that position in 1933 when President Franklin D. Roosevelt appointed him secretary of state.

An old-fashioned Jeffersonian Democrat and progressive, Hull admired President Woodrow Wilson; Hull had supported U.S. membership in the League of Nations following World War I. As secretary of state, he favored free trade, peace agreements, international conferences, and reliance on legal principles and institutions. During the 1930s, Hull negotiated numerous reciprocal trade agreements with other nations. He also devoted particular attention to revitalizing U.S. relations with Latin America through the "Good Neighbor" policy, whereby his country renounced the right to intervene in Latin America, and through the conclusion of related hemispheric security agreements.

President Roosevelt, who preferred to retain personal control of American foreign policy, frequently bypassed Hull. This tendency became more pronounced as World War II approached, and Hull found it both irritating and frustrating. Even so, since the two men fundamentally shared the same perspective on international affairs, Hull chose not to resign. Hull believed the European dictators posed a dangerous threat to all free nations and, believing that arms embargoes were ineffective and generally favored aggressors, he

U.S. Secretary of State Cordell Hull. (Library of Congress)

opposed the various neutrality acts passed by Congress between 1935 and 1939. He was inclined to be slightly less conciliatory than Roosevelt and was unenthusiastic toward Roosevelt's 1938–1939 peace messages to European powers.

Once war began in Europe, Hull staunchly supported Great Britain and France against Germany and Italy. However, he was virtually excluded from the Anglo-American Destroyers-Bases Deal of summer 1940 and the drafting of Lend-Lease legislation some months later. Nor did he attend the Anglo-American military staff conversations held in Washington early in 1941 or the mid-August 1941 Argentia Conference that drafted the Atlantic Charter. Roosevelt, preoccupied with European affairs from April to December 1941, delegated to Hull responsibility for protracted American negotiations with Japan. The objective of the negotiations was to reach a temporary agreement in Asia, where Japan had been at war with China since 1937. In the negotiations, Japan also sought further territorial gains from British, French, and Dutch territorial possessions. Despite the expressed concern of American military leaders that the United States was unprepared for a Pacific war, by late November 1941 Hull—who was privy to intercepted Japanese cable traffic—believed that war was inevitable, and he refused to contemplate further American concessions to Japanese demands.

After the Japanese attack on Pearl Harbor, Hull was often excluded from major meetings, including the 1942 Casablanca Conference, the 1943 Cairo and Tehran Conferences, and the 1944 Quebec Conference, a summit meeting of Allied leaders. Hull opposed Roosevelt's decision, announced at Casablanca, to demand the unconditional surrender of the Axis nations, believing this would encourage them to continue the war. Hull also opposed the 1944 Morgenthau Plan to partition a defeated Germany and eradicate its industrial capacity, and with the assistance of Secretary of War Henry L. Stimson, he succeeded in obtaining the scheme's ultimate rejection.

Hull put great effort into establishing the 1942 United Nations alliance of anti-Axis nations. Following his Wilsonian instincts, he then concentrated on planning for the postwar United Nations, an international security organization that would replace the defunct League of Nations. Under Hull's guidance, the State Department drafted the proposals for the United Nations Charter accepted at the 1944 Dumbarton Oaks Conference and adroitly won bipartisan congressional support for these. Addressing Congress in late 1943, Hull overoptimistically stated that the projected new organization would eliminate spheres of influence, the balance of power, and international alliances and rivalries. He shared Roosevelt's anticolonial outlook and his belief that the United States should treat China as a great power and thereby encourage it to become one.

Increasingly poor health led Hull to resign after the November 1944 presidential election. Consulted on the terms of the July 1945 Potsdam Declaration urging Japan to surrender, Hull insisted that it include no promise to retain the emperor. Hull was awarded the Nobel Peace Prize in 1945 and lived quietly in retirement, producing lengthy memoirs. Suffering from strokes and heart problems, he died in Bethesda, Maryland, on 23 July 1955.

Priscilla Roberts

See also

Casablanca Conference; Destroyers-Bases Deal; Dumbarton Oaks Conference; Lend-Lease; Morgenthau, Henry, Jr.; Pearl Harbor, Attack on; Quebec Conference (12–16 September 1944); Roosevelt, Franklin D.; Stimson, Henry Lewis; Tehran Conference; United Nations, Formation of

References

Gellman, Irwin F. *Secret Affairs: Franklin Roosevelt, Cordell Hull, and Sumner Welles.* Baltimore, MD: Johns Hopkins University Press, 1995.

Hull, Cordell. *Memoirs of Cordell Hull.* 2 vols. New York: Macmillan, 1948.

Pratt, Julius W. *Cordell Hull, 1933–44.* 2 vols. New York: Cooper Square, 1964.

Schlesinger, Stephen. *Act of Creation: The Founding of the United Nations.* Boulder, CO: Westview Press, 2003.

Utley, Jonathan G. *Going to War with Japan, 1937–1941.* Knoxville: University of Tennessee Press, 1985.

Hump, The

Allied air transport route supplying China from India. With Japanese forces controlling all of coastal China even before the U.S. entry into World War II, supplies to the Nationalist Chinese trickled along the Burma Road into western China. Recognizing the inadequate rate of supply, in November 1941 the Chinese National Aviation Corporation (CNAC) successfully devised a route through the Himalaya Mountains between Kunming, China, and Assam in upper India.

In 1942, the Japanese captured Burma, thereby cutting off all overland access to the Nationalist government headed by Jiang Jieshi (Chiang Kai-shek). U.S. President Franklin D. Roosevelt believed it vital to support Jiang, and military planners wanted to use China as the jumping-off point for the eventual invasion of the Japanese home islands as well as a base for strategic bombing. The U.S. Army Air Forces (USAAF) used the route pioneered by the CNAC to accomplish these tasks, although it was not ideal. A single narrow-gauge railroad connected Assam to the Indian coast.

The air route itself was more than 500 miles and very dangerous. Japanese air activity, unpredictable weather, the lack of navigational aids, unmapped territory, and peaks rising above 20,000 feet all made flying especially treacherous. Conflicting demands by Generals Claire Chennault and Joseph Stillwell—and also from Jiang—confused the supply situation. The deployment of B-29s to China in 1944 further strained the logistical chain.

The aircraft available were also inadequate. Initially, the twin-engine Douglas C-47 Skytrain was the main aircraft used, but it could only carry 2.5 tons of supplies. The twin-engine Curtiss C-46 Commando entered service before it had been fully tested. It could carry 5 tons of supplies, but early mechanical problems led to numerous accidents. Finally, late in the war the Douglas C-54 Skymaster, a four-engine transport capable of carrying 10 tons of cargo, became available.

Infrastructure also had to be created from scratch. Thousands of laborers built runways in China of crushed rock by hand. Trucks were scarce, so fuel was often transported in cans and aircraft fueled by lines of people passing these containers.

Supplies over the Hump began slowly. In July 1942 only 85 tons of supplies were delivered. Not until 1944 did transport over the Hump become rationalized. First, Major General William Tunner assumed command of the China-India Air Transport Command directly answerable to USAAF commanding general General Henry H. Arnold in Washington. The Hump operation marked the first time air transport was autonomous from the local or theater commander. Tunner regularized crew rotation, aircraft maintenance, and loading and unloading procedures. Largely through his work, during July 1945 Allied aircraft flew more than 70,000 tons of cargo over the Himalayas. The Hump route was very costly. Over 500 aircraft were lost and more than 1,300 pilots and crewmen were killed or missing in action in the course of the Allied operation, which ended in September 1945.

Rodney Madison

See also

Aircraft, Transports; Burma Road; Chennault, Claire Lee; China, Role in War; China-Burma-India Theater; Jiang Jieshi; Lend-Lease; Stilwell, Joseph Warren

References

Craven, Wesley Frank, and James Lea Cate, eds. *The Army Air Forces in World War II. The Pacific Theater.* Vol. 5. *Matterhorn to Nagasaki, June 1944 to August 1945.* Washington DC: Office of Air Force History, United States Air Force, 1983.
Ethell, Jeff, and Don Downie. *Flying the Hump: In Original World War II Color.* Osceola, WI: Motorbooks International, 1995.
Spencer, Otha C. *Flying the Hump: Memories of an Air War.* College Station: Texas A&M University Press, 1992.

Hungary, Air Force

Under the terms of the Treaty of Trianon following World War I, Hungary was forbidden a military air service. Between the two world wars, however, the Hungarian government secretly worked to establish, develop, and modernize an air force. The Hungarian air force came into being as an independent arm on 1 January 1939. For financial reasons but also because it lacked the industrial infrastructure (especially machine tools) and raw materials required, Hungary did not attempt to produce its own combat aircraft but purchased them from abroad, chiefly from Italy. In the late 1930s, however, it did begin production of an excellent short-range biplane reconnaissance aircraft, the Weiss Manfred 32 Sólyom (Hawk).

The Hungarian air force was first deployed in April 1941 during the invasion of Yugoslavia. At the time, it had on paper 302 aircraft, but only 189 of them were operational and most were obsolete. After Hungary declared war on the Soviet Union in late June 1941, the air force was deployed to the Eastern Front. In 1942, the 2nd Air Force Brigade was established with 76 aircraft to support operations of the Second Hungarian Army in the Soviet Union. Almost half of its aircraft were gone by early 1943, and those that remained were merged into German squadrons.

In 1943, under terms of an agreement with the German government, Hungary began production of the Messerschmitt Bf-109 fighter to offset production from German factories destroyed by Allied bombing. Hungary also produced the Me-210. The terms of the agreement provided that 40 percent of aircraft production was to remain in Hungary, but this pledge was not kept. Nonetheless, Hungary was able to add some 170 modern aircraft to its inventory by 1944.

The revitalized Hungarian air force suffered devastating air raids by the Allied powers beginning in 1944. Remaining aircraft were then removed to Austria. Ammunition and fuel shortages meant that no Hungarian aircraft participated in the last weeks of the war. Those that remained were either destroyed by their crews or handed over to Allied forces. During the war, Hungary produced 1,182 aircraft and 1,482 aircraft engines. Among the aircraft were 488 Bf-109s and 279 Me-210s. Of these, Hungary received only 158.

Anna Boros-McGee

See also

Aircraft, Fighters; Germany, Air Force; Yugoslavia Campaign (1941)

References

Kozlik, Viktor, György Punka, and Gyula Sárhidai. *Hungarian Eagles: The Hungarian Air Force, 1920–1945.* Aldershot, UK: Hikoui, 2000.

Szabó, Miklós. *A Magyar Királyi Honvéd Légiero, 1938–1945* [The Hungarian Royal Air Force, 1938–1945]. Budapest: Zínyi Kiadó, 1999.

———. "The Development of the Hungarian Aircraft Industry, 1938–1944." *Journal of Military History* 65, no. 1 (January 2001): 56–76.

Hungary, Army

The Treaty of Trianon between the Allied powers and Hungary following World War I limited both the quantity and quality of Hungary's armed forces. The army was restricted to a maximum of 35,000 officers and men, and it was not allowed any heavy artillery, tanks, or military aircraft. Hungary was also forbidden to organize and train reservists. The armed forces, consisting of seven mixed brigades and a river flotilla, could take up arms only for the maintenance of internal order or to oppose a foreign invasion of Hungary. Having been stripped of two-thirds of its territory and population following World War I, Hungary was also deficient in war-related industry and resources.

In 1938, an agreement between Hungary and the neighboring Little Entente states of Czechoslovakia, Romania, and Yugoslavia recognized Hungary's right to rearm. The Hungarian government increased the military budget, but in September 1939 the army numbered only 9 light divisions or brigades. In 1941, it had 27 light divisions or brigades of 2 regiments each. Each regiment numbered about 4,000 men, so the effective size of the infantry force was only 216,000 men. There were also 2 cavalry brigades and 2 motorized brigades. Most of the equipment was obsolete; its rifles were old and they frequently jammed, and the army had no antitank guns. Although Hungary produced its own tanks, it had only 190 of these, and they were too light for combat operations on the Eastern Front, where the army would do most of its fighting. Even by 1943, the army had only one-third of the motor transport required and had to use civilian vehicles.

In the spring of 1941, Hungary conducted its first military operation since World War I when it sent a mechanized army corps to support the German invasion of Yugoslavia. The army was still under-equipped when Hungary officially entered the war on 26 June 1941 with a declaration of war on the Soviet Union. For operations in the Soviet Union, the army assembled an expeditionary force designated the Mobile Corps and commanded by General Ferenc Szombathelyi. Numbering some 44,000 men, it consisted of 2 infantry brigades (a mountain brigade and a border guard brigade), a cavalry brigade, and 10 Alpine battalions, 6 of which used bicycles. Nonetheless, it contained the army's best-trained and best-equipped troops. It was assigned to the German Seventeenth Army, and partly because Soviet forces were then retreating, the Mobile Corps reached the Donets River. In the autumn of 1941, some Hungarian army light infantry divisions were assigned the task of guarding German rear areas in the central part of the front. Although poorly armed and equipped, these divisions effectively carried out their assignment and were not withdrawn until the autumn of 1944.

Under heavy German pressure, Hungary made a major military effort in 1942, deploying Gusztáv Jány's Second Hungarian Army to the Eastern Front. Consisting of three army corps, an armored division, and a mixed Air Force regiment and numbering about 200,000 men, the Second Army fought with General Maximilian von Weich's Army Group B in the Ukraine. Between June and September 1942, it helped drive back Soviet forces behind the Don River, suffering losses of nearly 22,000 men in the process.

Although the Germans provided the Second Army with some equipment, including tanks, much of this was obsolete and, in any case, inadequate in quantity. The Germans supplied only a few antitank guns, and the Hungarians did not have the heavy-caliber guns necessary to stop Soviet tanks. Opposing Soviet forces enjoyed a vast superiority in manpower, guns, tanks, artillery, and stocks of ammunition. Moreover, there had been no effective resupply since the summer campaign of 1942. Weapons and equipment would not work in the bitter cold of winter, there was no winter clothing, and even food was in short supply.

On 12 January 1943, Soviet forces—which outnumbered Hungarian forces by three to one in manpower and had a decided edge in military equipment including tanks, aircraft, and artillery—launched a massive offensive across the Don River and pushed the Hungarians back, causing heavy casualties and material losses. Perhaps 160,000 men in the Second Army died in the battle or subsequent retreat. The Don catastrophe confirmed the Hungarian government's worst

Over 50 Hungarian soldiers are shown in an effort to recover this disabled Soviet tank. It was captured by Hungarian forces who had been fighting on the Eastern Front alongside the German troops. (© Bettmann/Corbis)

fears, and the government used the excuse that its war industries were unable to manufacture new equipment and arms fast enough to equip additional troops in order to avoid dispatching the men to the Eastern Front. The light divisions in occupation duties remained, however.

In March 1944, German forces occupied Hungary and put additional pressure on Hungary to assist with the war. As Soviet forces advanced west, the government deployed the First Hungarian Army to the Ukraine. Part of the German Army Group South, it consisted of 4 infantry divisions, 1 light division, 1 armored division, and 2 mountain brigades. The First Army held its positions until the end of July 1944, when it was forced to withdraw to the Carpathian Mountains. By early autumn, it became obvious that the weak Hungarian forces would be unable to stop Soviet and Romanian troops from invading the country. Army morale plummeted, especially when the Germans took control in Budapest and the fascist Arrow Cross seized control of the government. Whole Hungarian units melted away. Planned new fascist military

units were not organized in time to see action. The leaders of the army hoped to be able to hold out until they could surrender to U.S. and British forces, but this proved impossible. For most of the Hungarian military, the war ended in February 1945, although some Hungarian formations withdrew with German units into Austria and Germany.

Anna Boros-McGee

See also

Eastern Front; Horthy de Nagybánya, Miklós; Hungary, Air Force; Hungary, Role in War; Ukraine Campaign; Yugoslavia Campaign (1941)

References

Abbott, Peter, Nigel Thomas, and Martin Windrow. *Germany's Eastern Front Allies, 1941–45*. London: Osprey, 1982.

Dombrádi, Lóránd. *A Magyar Királyi Honvédség, 1919–1945* [The Hungarian Royal Army, 1919–1945]. Budapest: Zrínyi Katonai Kiadó, 1987.

Gosztonyi, Péter. *A Magyar Honvédség a Második Világháborúban* [The Hungarian army in World War II]. Budapest: Európa, 1992.

Madej, W. Victor. *Southeastern Europe Axis Armed Forces Handbook.* Allentown, PA: Valor, 1982.

Ölvedi, Ignác. "55 éve történt: a magyar királyi elsö hadsereg támadása és védelembe vonulása Gallíciában 1944 tavaszán" [It happened 55 years ago: The attack of the First Hungarian Army in Galicia in spring 1944]. *Társadalom és Honvédelem* 3 (March-April 1999): 81–100.

Hungary, Role in War

In 1939, Hungary was a nation of some 10 million people. At least half of the population still made its living from agriculture. The government—headed by Regent Miklós Horthy de Nagybánya, who had wide powers—steadfastly rejected calls for land reform, and more than half the arable land of Hungary was owned by only some 10,000 landowners. Horthy, who remained head of the government from 1920 to 1944, also beat back proposals for universal suffrage.

The chief Hungarian foreign policy objective between the two world wars was revision of the 1920 Treaty of Trianon. Virtually all Hungarians saw the treaty as a national humiliation. It had destroyed the economy and national territorial integrity of Hungary by stripping away some two-thirds of the territory and population. It also consigned 3 million Hungarians to foreign rule. Revisionist sentiment meant the Horthy government fell easy prey to German promises of territorial aggrandizement if Hungary joined the Axis. As a result of the Munich Conference and First Vienna Decision in the autumn of 1938, the German occupation of Czechoslovakia on 15 March 1939, and the Second Vienna Decision in August 1940, Hungary received some of the territories lost after World War I without having to take part in any military operations. Hungary's new alliance with Italy and especially with Germany seemed to be working to the nation's advantage. In return, Hungary provided Germany with increasing amounts of raw materials and food. During the war, Hungary also emerged as a major source of oil for the Reich, ultimately surpassed only by Romania.

In December 1940, the Hungarian government concluded a friendship agreement with Yugoslavia. A few months later, however, Adolf Hitler decided to attack Yugoslavia, and he insisted that Hungary participate in the military operations. Rather than dishonor himself with such an act, Hungarian Prime Minister Pál Teleki committed suicide. Regent Horthy, new Prime Minister László Bárdossy, and chief of staff of the army General Henrik Werth were all committed to Hungarian participation in the invasion of Yugoslavia. They hoped in the process to gain additional territory and cement the alliance with Germany. Hungary entered the war on 11 April 1941.

When Germany invaded the Soviet Union in June 1941, it called on Hungary to participate fully in the war effort. Hungary suspended diplomatic relations with the Soviet Union, and on 27 June, after a northern Hungarian city was bombed by aircraft identified as Soviet (but which were in fact of unknown origin), Hungary declared war on the Soviet Union. Hungarian army leaders expected a rapid German victory over the USSR.

By the end of June, Hungarian troops were deployed on the Eastern Front. Hungarian forces were split: offensive units advanced with German forces into Soviet territory, and an occupying force provided security for the German rear areas. Much to its chagrin, Hungary ultimately found itself at war with Britain and the United States. The United States declared war on Hungary on 5 June 1942.

In January 1942, under heavy German pressure, Bárdossy promised to send additional troops to the Eastern Front. On 9 March 1942, largely because the Germans had failed to secure a quick victory over the Soviets, Horthy replaced Bárdossy as prime minister with Miklós Kállay. The new prime minister sought to continue his predecessor's policy of open cooperation with Germany while also conducting secret negotiations with the Anglo-Saxon powers in the hope of extricating Hungary from the war.

Meanwhile, between April and June 1942, the Second Hungarian Army of 200,000 men was sent to the Eastern Front to bolster German forces there. Hungarian forces in the Soviet Union suffered from obsolete and insufficient equipment, poor logistics, and insufficient ammunition. The tragic defeat of the Second Hungarian Army near Voronezh in the Battle of the Don River during the winter of 1943 was a catastrophe for Hungary that resulted in the deaths of some 120,000 troops.

Following this loss, Kállay was more determined than ever to extricate Hungary from the war. His secret diplomacy intensified even as Hungarian participation in military operations was being curtailed. This angered Hitler, who demanded nothing less than full Hungarian participation in the war. Hitler was also upset by secret Hungarian negotiations with the western Allies to withdraw from the war, an activity about which pro-German individuals within the Budapest government kept him well-informed.

Alarmed by the Hungarian government's attempts to leave the war, on 19 March 1944 Hitler sent in German troops to occupy the country and force its continued participation on the German side. Under German pressure, Horthy also appointed Döme Sztójay, a pro-German former Hungarian ambassador to Berlin, as the new prime minister. Anti-Nazi parties were banned, and politicians opposed to German policy were arrested. The Hungarian government was also forced to deploy additional soldiers to the Eastern Front to fight against the Soviets. One irony of the German occupation was the reduced economic value of Hungary to the Reich, thanks to the occupation costs, the mass arrest and deportation of Jews, and increased Allied bombing.

In an attempt to decrease German influence, on 29 August 1944 Horthy appointed a new prime minister, Géza Lakatos, who ordered Hungarian army units to attack southern Transylvania to halt a Soviet-Romanian invasion. Understanding that the war was lost, Horthy dispatched a delegation to Moscow to negotiate an armistice with the Soviet Union, the terms of which were agreed to on 11 October 1944.

On 15 October 1944, Horthy announced over the radio Hungary's unconditional surrender. Because of a lack of coordination with army chief of staff János Vörös, the Hungarian army continued to fight, and Horthy's attempt at surrender failed. The Germans then took over Budapest and forced Horthy to step aside in favor of Ferenc Szálasi, leader of the Arrow Cross (the Hungarian fascist party) as prime minister and head of state. Horthy was then arrested by the Gestapo and removed to Germany with his family. During Szálasi's brief tenure, a reign of terror swept Hungary. Thousands of people, including many Jews who had sought refuge in Budapest, were arrested and executed or sent to concentration camps.

Meanwhile, the Soviet army continued to advance, and by December 1944 it laid siege to Budapest. Two and a half months later, the remaining German forces in Buda surrendered. Meanwhile, Hungarian representatives signed an armistice in Moscow on 20 January 1945. Most fighting in the country ended in February 1945, and the last German troops were forced from Hungarian soil on 13 April 1945. The country then passed from German to Soviet army control.

Anna Boros-McGee

See also
Eastern Front; Hitler, Adolf; Horthy de Nagybánya, Miklós; Hungary, Air Force; Hungary, Army; Ukraine Campaign; Vörös, János; Yugoslavia Campaign (1941)

References
Abbott, Peter, Nigel Thomas, and Martin Windrow. *Germany's Eastern Front Allies, 1941–45*. London: Osprey, 1982.

Szabó, A. Ferenc. "A titokzatos bombázás" [The mysterious bombing]. *Új Honvédségi Szemle* 55 (June 2001): 88–100.

Szakály, Sándor. "Magyarország belépése a második világháború kűzdelmeibe" [Hungary's entry into World War II]. *Új Honvédségi Szemle*, 45 (October 1991): 20–24.

Zsigmondi, László. "A 2. magyar hadsereg vereségének előzményei és körülményei" [Circumstances that led to the defeat of the Second Hungarian Army]. *Új Honvédségi Szemle* 47 (February 1993): 13–20.

Hunter-Killer Groups

Specialized antisubmarine units formed to hunt and destroy submarines before they could attack and to provide roving support for convoy escort groups. In late 1942, as production and delivery of antisubmarine vessels increased, the British began forming support groups—permanently established formations charged with reinforcing hard-pressed convoy escorts. Unlike escort groups, these units trained and exercised intensively to develop and master techniques for hunting and destroying enemy submarines. Their existence and the imminent arrival of large numbers of escort carriers from U.S. shipyards spurred the deployment of specialized hunter-killer units in the navies of the British Commonwealth and the United States.

The Atlantic Convoy Conference of 1–12 March 1943 mandated the formation that year of 10 hunter-killer groups, each centered on an escort carrier. Five British and Canadian groups would support operations in the North Atlantic, and five American groups were to attend to the needs of the Middle Atlantic.

Although convoy support was a significant role, the most important mission of these groups was to locate, intercept, and destroy U-boats before they could attack the slow merchantmen. Central to implementation of this mission were significant advances in three areas: code-breaking, high-frequency direction finding (HF/DF, or "huff-duff"), and radar. By mid-1943, even though significant changes had occurred in the German naval cipher, Allied decoders were able to read 80 percent or more of the U-boat arm's traffic. Furthermore, the British and American submarine tracking rooms were able to predict submarine movements with a fair degree of accuracy on the basis of types of traffic, even if the message itself was unreadable.

High-frequency direction finding also was important in tracking and locating submarines. Shore-based installations became sufficiently sophisticated to give close "fixes," whereas advances in miniaturization produced sets suitable for installation aboard ships. From late 1942, half of all U.S. destroyer and escort production was fitted with HF/DF. The British followed suit in the spring of 1943.

Code-breaking, direction finding, and tracking ashore provided the hunter-killer groups with close approximations of the positions of U-boats at sea. Shipborne huff-duff, the new centimetric radar sets, and improved sonar equipment and procedures, together with the groups' organic aircraft, substantially enhanced their location rates. Better depth charges, ahead-throwing weapons, and aircraft-launched rockets or homing torpedoes eased the task of sinking the target. Hunter-killer groups trained together thoroughly, developed new coordinated tactics, and, above all, focused on locating and destroying U-boats rather than protecting convoys.

From the moment of their deployment, Allied hunter-killer groups played a major role in the destruction of Germany's U-boats. For example, between May and December 1943, the group formed around the American escort carrier *Bogue* sank 10 U-boats in the Atlantic; between June 1943 and January 1944, the Royal Navy's 2nd Support Group destroyed

14 submarines. The attack on *U-358* illustrates the significance of persistent attack made possible by adherence to a single mission: the British 1st Support Group maintained continuous contact for 38 hours and expended 530 depth charges before forcing the submarine to the surface and carrying out its destruction.

Paul E. Fontenoy

See also

Antisubmarine Warfare; Atlantic, Battle of the; Depth Charges; Sonar

References

Blair, Clay. *Hitler's U-Boat War*. Vol. 2, *The Hunted, 1942–1945*. New York: Random House, 1998.

Morison, Samuel Eliot. *History of United States Naval Operations in World War II*. Vol. 10, The Atlantic Battle Won, May 1943–May 1945. Boston: Little, Brown, 1956.

Roscoe, Theodore. *United States Destroyer Operations in World War II*. Annapolis, MD: Naval Institute Press, 1953.

Roskill, S. W. *The War at Sea*. Vol. 3, psarts 1 and 2. London: Her Majesty's Stationary Office, 1960.

Y'Blood, William T. *Hunter-Killer: U.S. Escort Carriers in the Battle of the Atlantic*. Annapolis, MD: Naval Institute Press, 1983.

Hürtgen Forest Campaign (12 September–16 December 1944)

Although it is little remembered today, the battle for the Hürtgen Forest was one of the worst defeats ever suffered by the U.S. Army. In three months of combat operations, the Americans sustained almost 33,000 casualties but accomplished almost nothing tactically or operationally in the process.

By late August 1944, the apparently defeated German army had been pushed out of France and back to the borders of the Reich. Many GIs began to believe that the war would be over by Christmas. But the situation changed as the Allies reached German territory and the defenses of the German West Wall (called the Siegfried Line by the Americans but never by the Germans). In the central sector of the West Wall defensive line lay the dark and almost impenetrable Hürtgen Forest.

At that point in the war, the Allied logistics system was stretched to the breaking point, and the advancing armies were on the verge of running out of ammunition and fuel. Allied military planners were faced with the two strategic options of attacking Germany—on a broad front or on a narrow front. Lieutenant General George S. Patton Jr. and Field Marshal Sir Bernard Montgomery were the two leading advocates of the narrow-front approach, but each general thought his forces should execute the "dagger thrust" into the heart of the Reich.

Pressed hard by Montgomery, Supreme Commander, Allied Expeditionary Forces General Dwight D. Eisenhower

agreed in September 1944 to support the British plan for a combined ground and airborne thrust into Holland and then across the Rhine River at Arnhem. Launched on 17 September, Operation MARKET-GARDEN soon failed. With supplies starting to dwindle to a trickle, the western Allies had no real choice other than to revert to the broad-front strategy of applying even pressure against the Germans all along the line.

Just prior to the start of MARKET-GARDEN, the U.S. First Army, commanded by Lieutenant General Courtney H. Hodges, breached the West Wall in two places and attacked the city of Aachen immediately north of the Hürtgen Forest. Hodges's 250,000-man force consisted of eight veteran divisions in the U.S. VII, V, and VIII Corps. After taking Aachen, Hodges planned to attack around the north end of the Hürtgen Forest across the flat open Rhine plain toward the city of Köln (Cologne). But Hodges also believed that he had to first secure the Hürtgen Forest to avoid dangerously exposing his southern flank.

The Hürtgen Forest is a classic piece of defender's terrain. It is an interlaced network of bald, exposed ridgelines and deeply wooded ravines, and the Roer River runs through the middle of the forest and then out across the Rhine plain. The small river itself was not a significant military obstacle, but a series of dams high in the forest had created a huge artificial lake holding millions of gallons of water. By releasing that water at the right moment, the Germans could flood the Rhine plain, which would slow, disrupt, and channelize Allied military movement for weeks. Those dams, in the vicinity of the town of Schmidt, were the one significant military operational objective in the Hürtgen Forest; but ironically, neither side appeared to recognize that significance until the battle was almost over.

Although the German army had a reputation as the master of mobile, offensive warfare, it also was tenacious and resourceful in the defense. The German army group commander in that sector, Field Marshal Walter Model, was a master defensive tactician.

The Hürtgen Forest campaign started on 12 September when the veteran 9th Infantry Division attacked the southern end of the forest in an attempt to move through a passage known as the Monschau Corridor. The 9th Infantry Division took the town of Lammersdorf in the south, but it was stopped just short of Germeter in the center of the forest. In late October, the 9th Infantry Division was withdrawn from the line after suffering 4,500 casualties. The 28th Infantry Division replaced it.

The U.S. First Army planned another attack, this time with VII Corps, commanded by Major General J. Lawton Collins. It was to move through the northern passage called the Stolberg Corridor. As a diversionary effort to draw off German forces, Major Leonard Gerow's V Corps to the south would attack with one division against Schmidt on the far side of the

U.S. tanks advance to the battle front in the Hürtgen Forest, November 1944. (Photo by U.S. Signal Corps/Time Life Pictures/Getty Images)

Kall River gorge. The supporting attack was scheduled for 2 November, and the main attack was to follow on 5 November. However, VII Corps could not get ready in time, and the main attack was postponed—first until 10 November and then until 16 November. For some reason, the timing for the supporting attack never changed.

The 28th Infantry Division launched the attack toward Schmidt with all three of its infantry regiments attacking in diverging directions, which dissipated rather than concentrated its combat power. The most notable feature of that battle was the near-epic struggle to get a handful of M-4 tanks and M-10 tank destroyers down the steep and narrow forest trail into the Kall River gorge and back up the other side to the open ground near the towns of Kommerscheidt and Schmidt. The 112th Infantry Regiment took Schmidt on 3 November. The Germans counterattacked immediately, supported by PzKpfw-V Panther tanks.

Despite the gallant fight against superior odds, in which antitank platoon leader Lieutenant Turney Leonard earned a posthumous Medal of Honor, all American armor east of the Kall River was destroyed. By 8 November, the 28th Infantry Division was pushed back almost to its starting positions, having sustained 6,184 casualties in only 7 days of fighting. Major General Norman Cota, the 28th Infantry Division commander, was widely criticized for the tactically stupid offensive scheme, a plan that actually had been imposed on him by V Corps. Cota had tried to protest it.

The 28th Infantry Division was relieved in the line by the 8th Infantry Division on 13 November. Three days later, the Americans launched the postponed main assault, with VII Corps' 104th, 1st, and 4th Infantry Divisions attacking through the north of the forest. South of VII Corps and just to the north of where the 28th Infantry Division had been mauled, V Corps' 8th Infantry Division launched a supporting attack. Once again, the Americans ran into a determined and skillful German defense. The attackers suffered heavy casualties in exchange for mere yards of ground. The GIs fought under terrible conditions of snow, rain, mud, cold, and almost impenetrable woods in fierce infantry combat reminiscent of World War I.

The Americans were still trying to punch their way through the Hürtgen Forest and making almost no progress when, on 16 December, the Germans launched their Ardennes Offensive to the south. The almost complete tactical and operational surprise the Germans achieved brought the Hürtgen Forest campaign to a halt, as all Allied forces focused on containing the Germans in the Battle of the Bulge. Even after the major German offensive was turned back, the Americans did not take Schmidt and the Roer River dams until early February 1945. Just before the Germans withdrew, they managed to blow up the valves controlling the spillway of the Schwammenauel Dam, the major dam in the system.

The Hürtgen Forest campaign was a brilliantly executed economy-of-force operation by the Germans. Most of the German records from that period did not survive, but Germany probably suffered more casualties than did the United States. Nonetheless, the Germans held the vastly better supplied and better equipped attackers to a dead standstill for three months, while just a few miles to the south, three German field armies assembled in almost complete secrecy for the Ardennes Offensive.

The Hürtgen Forest area today is little different than it was in late 1944 before the battle started. The forest has returned, and the tree lines are much as they were. The towns and villages have been reestablished and are today only slightly more built up than they were at the time of the battle. Very few markers or memorials exist to indicate the prolonged and savage fighting. Yet, almost 60 years after the battle hardly a year goes by without another discovery of human remains in the forest known as the "dark and bloody ground."

David T. Zabecki

See also

Collins, Joseph Lawton; Eisenhower, Dwight D.; Gerow, Leonard Townsend; Hodges, Courtney Hicks; MARKET-GARDEN, Operation; Model, Walter; Montgomery, Sir Bernard Law; Patton, George Smith, Jr.

References

MacDonald, Charles B. *United States Army in World War II: Special Studies: Three Battles: Arnaville, Altuzzo, and Schmidt.* Washington, DC: Department of the Army, U.S. Center of Military History, 1952.

———. *United States Army in World War II: The European Theater of Operations: The Siegfried Line Campaign.* Washington, DC: Department of the Army, U.S. Center of Military History, 1963.

———. *The Battle of the Huertgen Forest.* New York: Jove, 1983.

Miller, Edward G. *A Dark and Bloody Ground: The Hürtgen Forest and the Roer River Dams, 1944–1945.* College Station: Texas A&M University Press, 1995.

HUSKY, Operation

See Sicily, Invasion of.

I

Iba Field, Attack on (8 December 1941)

Japanese air attack in the Philippines Islands, simultaneous with the raid on Clark Field. The Japanese planned to fly at night from Formosa (Taiwan) to avoid interception, arriving at first light to strike Nichols and Clark Fields, the main U.S. fighter and bomber bases in the Philippines. However, early-morning fog on Formosa grounded the aircraft of the Japanese navy's Eleventh Air Fleet. With no prospect of surprise, planners decided to ignore Nichols Field in favor of Iba, a pursuit-aircraft base northwest of Manila on Luzon's west coast. An attack on Iba would cover the flank of the Japanese force attacking Clark. When the fog lifted on the morning of 8 December, 54 twin-engine navy Mitsubishi G4M1 Type medium bombers (known to the Allied side by the code name BETTY) of the Takao and Kanoya Air Groups and 50 Mitsubishi A6M Reisen (Zero) fighters of the 3rd Air Group took off from Formosa and flew toward the Philippines.

At Iba, the U.S. 3rd Pursuit Squadron flew 16 P-40Es off the grass strip about 11:45 A.M. to intercept the Japanese planes, reportedly heading for Manila. This action was the Americans' second scramble of the morning. They failed to detect any Japanese, and the planes raced back when they heard Iba Field's radio warn of a hostile force approaching from the sea. The 3rd Pursuit Squadron reached Iba low on fuel and, in any case, failed to locate the Japanese aircraft. The squadron entered the landing pattern at 12:45 P.M. Six aircraft landed just as the Japanese bombers and fighters struck. Japanese bombs tore into barracks, service buildings, and maintenance equipment. A bomb also destroyed Iba's radar, a fatal blow to subsequent U.S. air-defense efforts.

A few American pilots turned their aircraft against the Zeros, despite near empty fuel tanks. The nimble Japanese shot down five P-40s, and swirling dogfights ran three more Americans out of gas. These desperate American attacks prevented the Zeros from strafing Iba. Ultimately, however, the 3rd Pursuit lost 16 P-40s in the air and on the ground—nearly the entire squadron—as well as 45 trained pilots and mechanics. Damage to the field and equipment was significant.

The unexpected success of the Japanese raids on Clark and Iba stunned both the Japanese and the Americans. The attacks crippled General Douglas MacArthur's air force and made possible the safe approach of the Japanese invasion convoys.

John W. Whitman

See also
Brereton, Lewis Hyde; Japanese Raid on; MacArthur, Douglas; Philippines, Japanese Capture of

References
Bartsch, William H. *Doomed at the Start: American Pursuit Pilots in the Philippines, 1941–1942.* College Station: Texas A&M University Press, 1992.
———. *December 8, 1941: MacArthur's Pearl Harbor.* College Station: Texas A&M University Press, 2003.
Craven, Wesley F., and James E. Cate, eds. *The Army Air Forces in World War II.* Vol. 1, *Plans and Early Operations, January 1939 to August 1942.* Chicago: Office of Air Force History, University of Chicago Press, 1948.
Edmonds, Walter D. *They Fought with What They Had.* Boston: Little, Brown, 1951.
Sakai, Saburo. *Samurai!* New York: E. P. Dutton, 1957.

ICEBERG, Operation

See Okinawa, Invasion of.

ICHI-GŌ Campaign (April–December 1944)

Last major Japanese offensive in China during the war. In spring 1944, the war was going badly for the Japanese. With Lieutenant General Joseph W. Stilwell's forces progressing in northern Burma, the Japanese launched their last offensive in China. Known as the ICHI-GŌ Campaign (Operation NUMBER ONE), it was aimed primarily at the Nationalist forces; the Japanese strategic objectives were to destroy these forces, capture air bases in southeast China, consolidate control over eastern China, and secure control of the Beijing (Beiping)-Hankow-Canton railroad line. The Japanese also hoped to relieve some of the pressure on their forces in Burma and establish a stronger base in China from which to resist any potential Allied invasion of the Japanese home islands.

The first phase began in March and lasted until July 1944, with the offensive being mounted on a broad front across central and south China. Japanese aims were to press toward the Nationalist capital of Chongqing (Chungking), open up direct communications with French Indochina, and capture airfields in southeast China being used by U.S. aircraft to attack Japanese ground forces and shipping. The early phase of the operation went well for the Japanese, with Nationalist forces quickly collapsing. This situation ended whatever hope remained among Western leaders that China might play a major role in the defeat of Japan.

In northern China during April and May, the Japanese cleared the Beijing-Hankow railway and took Henan Province, even though they had to move at night to avoid constant attacks from Major General Claire Chennault's Fourteenth Air Force. Despite their air superiority, the Chinese Nationalist forces lost almost every time they met the Japanese. Some Chinese soldiers were even attacked by their own people, enraged by earlier mistreatment, and on occasion, starving peasants actually killed retreating Chinese troops and welcomed the Japanese.

Nationalist military failures exacerbated the already rocky relationship between Nationalist Chinese leader Jiang Jieshi (Chiang Kai-shek) and Stilwell, as well as that between Chennault and Stilwell. Stilwell was convinced that the key to restoring China lay in reopening a land supply to Chongqing through Burma, whereas Chennault feared for the preservation of his airfields in eastern China. Jiang, realizing that the Americans were going to defeat the Japanese in due course, seemed more concerned with the threat posed to his regime by the Chinese Communists. In fall 1944, the rift led to Stilwell's dismissal.

Phase two of the ICHI-GŌ Campaign began in July with a pincer movement by two Japanese armies, one from Wuhan and one from Canton, attempting to take Guilin and open a land route between central China and Southeast Asia. By November, all of Guangxi and eastern Hunan had been overrun, and the Japanese were threatening Guiyang, capital of Guizhou Province. In the process, the Japanese captured all but three of the U.S. airfields in south China. The Allies feared that if Guiyang fell, the Japanese might capture Kunming and Chongqing. But the Japanese were not able to advance farther, and in December, they attacked Guiyang but were repulsed. ICHI-GŌ was over.

In early 1945, the Japanese began limited offensives to consolidate the gains of 1944, but these failed to accomplish much, since the threat of war with the Soviet Union forced them to transfer several divisions to defend Manchuria and the Japanese mainland. Between May and July, the Nationalist Chinese used this situation to recover Guangxi and western Guangdong, but most Chinese lands captured by the Japanese during the ICHI-GŌ Campaign remained in their hands until the end of the war. The ICHI-GŌ offensive also greatly benefited Communist forces in China, who took advantage of the Nationalist defeats to occupy more territory and greatly expand their army.

William Head

See also
Chennault, Claire Lee; Jiang Jieshi; Stilwell, Joseph Warren
References
Byrd, Martha. *Chennault: Giving Wings to the Tiger.* Tuscaloosa: University of Alabama Press, 1987.
Ch'i Hsi-sheng. *Nationalist China at War: Military Defeats and Political Collapse, 1937–45.* Ann Arbor: University of Michigan Press, 1982.
———. "The Military Dimension, 1942–1945." In James C. Hsiung and Steven I. Levine, eds., *China's Bitter Victory: The War with Japan, 1937–1945,* 157–184. Armonk, NY: M. E. Sharpe, 1992.
Romanus, Charles F., and Riley Sunderland. *United States Army in World War II: China-Burma-India Theater—Stilwell's Command Problems.* Washington, DC: Office of the Chief of Military History, Department of the Army, 1956.
Tuchman, Barbara. *Stilwell and the American Experience in China, 1911–1945.* New York: Macmillan, 1971.
Wilson, Dick. *When Tigers Fight: The Story of the Sino-Japanese War, 1937–1945.* New York: Viking, 1982.

Iida Shōjirō (1888–1975)

Japanese army general and conqueror of Burma in 1942. Born in Yamaguichi Prefecture, Japan, in 1888, Iida Shōjirō joined the army in 1908. He graduated from the War College in

December 1915 and was promoted to captain in December 1918. Iida participated in Japan's Siberian Intervention and served two terms as an instructor at the Infantry School between postings to infantry regiments. By August 1934, he commanded 4th Infantry Regiment, Guards Division. Promoted to lieutenant general in August 1939, he then commanded the Guards Division. In July 1941, Iida's Twenty-Fifth Army occupied French Indochina. He established his headquarters in Saigon and prepared for an invasion of Thailand.

In December 1941, Iida took command of the newly formed Fifteenth Army, consisting of the 33rd and 55th Infantry Divisions, charged with occupying Thailand. Beginning on 8 December, his superior forces easily overcame light Thai resistance. The Thai government then accepted occupation and signed a mutual defense pact with Japan.

On 20 January 1942, Iida's divisions crossed into Burma. Iida had only 35,000 men and limited supplies. The terrain sharply circumscribed Japanese operations, forcing the troops to abandon most of their heavy weapons and vehicles and utilize animals to carry their provisions. Although Japanese air attacks on Rangoon failed to close that port, Iida quickly outmaneuvered British forces. The Japanese force-marched along jungle trails, often outdistancing the motorized British. On 8 March, his men took Rangoon, and Iida immediately used that port to receive reinforcements and supplies. The fall of Rangoon also cut the Burma Road and isolated China from Western aid. By May, British and Chinese forces in Burma had been driven back to India and China, respectively. The Japanese had inflicted some 30,000 casualties, with their own ground force losses numbering only 7,000.

In April 1943, Iida was assigned to the General Defense Command. He retired in December 1944 but was recalled to command the Thirtieth Army in Manchuria in July 1945. He had barely taken up his post before it was overrun by the Red Army in August. Iida was taken prisoner and only released in 1950. He died in Tokyo on 23 January 1975.

Tim J. Watts

See also

Burma Theater; Manchuria Campaign

References

Carew, Tim. *The Longest Retreat: The Burma Campaign, 1942.* London: Hamilton, 1969.

Grant, Ian L., and Kazno Tamayama. *Burma 1942: The Japanese Invasion.* Chicester, UK: Zampi Press, 1999.

Lunt, James D. *A Hell of a Licking: The Retreat from Burma, 1941–2.* London: Collins, 1986.

Imamura Hitoshi (1886–1968)

Japanese army general and commander of the Eighth Area Army at Rabaul. Born in Miyagi Prefecture, Japan, on 4 October 1886, Imamura Hitoshi was commissioned into the Imperial Japanese Army in December 1907. He graduated from the War College in 1915 and then was an observer in Britain and India. In April 1932, Imamura took command of the 57th Infantry Regiment, followed in March 1935 by command of the 40th Infantry Regiment. He then served as deputy chief of staff of the Guandong (Kwantung) Army in Manchuria and then assumed the post of commandant of the Army Infantry School. Imamura commanded the 5th Infantry Division in China from November 1938 to March 1940. He returned to China as commander of the Twenty-Third Army in June 1941.

In December 1941, Imamura took command of the Sixteenth Army, which was intended to conquer the Netherlands East Indies. During the invasion of Java on 1 March 1942, the transport that was carrying him, the *Rujo Maru*, was sunk in the Battle of Sunda Strait. Clinging to a piece of wood, Imamura managed to reach shore. His force soon after overran the Dutch defenders on Java, and on 9 March, Imamura accepted the surrender of all remaining Allied forces in the Netherlands East Indies. As military governor of the former Dutch colony, he established a liberal occupation policy and freed Indonesian dissidents from prison.

In November 1942, Imamura took command of the new Eighth Area Army at Rabaul. Imperial General Headquarters had realized that General Hyakutake Haruyashi could not adequately direct operations on both Guadalcanal and New Guinea. Hyakutake took direct control of the Seventeenth Army on Guadalcanal, and General Adachi Hatazo took over the units on New Guinea, now designated the Eighteenth Army. Imamura was unable to deliver two new divisions to Hyakutake when the Japanese navy failed to control the sea around Guadalcanal. Instead, he had to order Hyakutake to evacuate Guadalcanal.

Imamura's efforts to reinforce New Guinea were also hampered by growing Allied airpower. The complete destruction of a convoy in the Battle of the Bismarck Sea in March 1943 convinced Imamura that New Guinea would also be lost. Within weeks, operations on New Guinea were transferred to the Second Area Army, and Imamura was left with only the Seventeenth Army.

Hyakutake and his Seventeenth Army were cut off on Bougainville by an American invasion in November 1943. On 25 March 1944, Imamura ordered the aggressive Hyakutake to cease offensive operations and adopt a purely defensive stance. Imamura himself was isolated at Rabaul with 70,000 troops when Australian forces captured the rest of New Britain. He hoped his presence would provide a strategic benefit to Japan, and he surrendered in 1945 only after Emperor Hirohito ordered him to do so. Tried and convicted of war crimes after the war, Imamura was imprisoned until 1954. He died in Tokyo on 4 October 1968.

Tim J. Watts

See also

Bismarck Sea, Battle of; Bougainville Campaign; Guadalcanal, Land Battle for; Hirohito, Emperor of Japan; International Military Tribunal: Far East; New Guinea Campaign; Rabaul

References

Frank, Richard B. *Guadalcanal.* New York: Random House, 1990.

Hayashi, Saburo. *Kogun: The Japanese Army in the Pacific War.* Westport, CT: Greenwood Press, 1959.

Morison, Samuel Eliot. *History of United States Naval Operations in World War II.* Vol. 5, *The Struggle for Guadalcanal, August 1942–February 1943.* Boston: Little, Brown, 1949.

Imphal and Kohima, Sieges of (March–July 1944)

Crucial battles that marked the turning point in the defense of India. In February 1944, Lieutenant General Mutaguchi Renya, commander of the Japanese Fifteenth Army in Burma, undertook an invasion of eastern India, partly in response to raids by the British. Mutaguchi hoped to forestall a British offensive and perhaps spark a revolt against British rule in India. He mustered about 220,000 men for his campaign, but his effort was hampered by a lack of heavy artillery and a tenuous supply line. The campaign was made more difficult by the mountainous terrain of eastern India, where the towns and villages were usually situated on saddles connecting high, rugged ridges. Mutaguchi's plan was to cut the road running south to Imphal from the supply depot at Dimapur. Then, after his troops had infiltrated the British-Indian positions, he planned to seize the high ground, force his opponents to retreat, and utilize captured supplies to march farther west.

The Japanese offensive opened in earnest on 11–12 March 1944, after Mutaguchi feinted south of Imphal and then surrounded it with his 33rd and 15th Divisions, cutting off supplies and laying siege to 150,000 British-Indian defenders. British Lieutenant General William Slim, commander of the defending Fourteenth Army, had expected an attack but was surprised by the speed of the Japanese advance. He countered by flying ammunition, provisions, fuel, and the 5th Indian Division into Imphal to reinforce the defenders. The British also benefited from having the 254th Tank Brigade at Imphal, the only armor in the battle. The British tanks played a decisive part in reopening the road and placing the Japanese infantry around Imphal on the defensive by the beginning of the monsoon season in May.

Meanwhile, Japanese Lieutenant General Satō Kōtoku's 31st Division had surrounded the key village of Kohima,

On Imphal front, Sikh signaler (left) operates walkie-talkie for British officers, listening to patrols reporting Japanese positions. (Library of Congress)

north of Imphal. If Kohima fell, all British units to the south would have been forced to retreat. But the 161st Indian Brigade at Kohima held, and once again, Slim turned to his air transports, flying the 2nd Infantry Division into Dimapur; that unit then pushed down the road to relieve Kohima. When the troops broke the circle about the village on 18 April, Slim went over to the attack.

General Satō held his ground, forcing the British-Indian troops to evict the Japanese from their positions yard by yard. Finally, on 2 June, ignoring orders from Mutaguchi to stand to the last man, Satō withdrew his battered division. Mutaguchi ordered the remainder of his army to retreat a month later.

British-Indian casualties in the campaign were about 15,000 men, but Japanese losses exceeded 90,000. The latter included several thousand troops of Subhas Chandra Bose's Indian National Army. The Japanese defeat at Imphal and Kohima paved the way for the British and Chinese offensives into Burma the next year.

Terry Shoptaugh

See also

India; Slim, Sir William Joseph

References

Allen, Louis. *Burma: The Longest War, 1941–45*. New York: St. Martin's Press, 1984.

Ienaga, Saburo. *The Pacific War*. New York: Pantheon, 1978.

Kirby, Stanley Woodburn. *The War against Japan*. Vol. 3, *The Decisive Battles*. London: Her Majesty's Stationery Office, 1961.

Swinson, Arthur. *Kohima*. London: Cassell, 1966.

Incendiary Bombs and Bombing

Air-delivered ordnance used to damage or destroy physical structures by means of fire; a form of strategic bombing intended to cause widespread damage to industrial and population centers, that is, firebombing.

During the early days of World War II, proponents of strategic bombing advocated large-scale air attacks against vital enemy military and industrial targets. These air raids were to be carried out during the day to facilitate precision bombing and maximize damage. However, both the German Luftwaffe during the Battle of Britain and the Royal Air Force (RAF) Bomber Command during raids over Germany suffered such great losses of men and material that both turned to nighttime area attacks. To compensate for the inherent loss of accuracy, they also turned to the use of incendiary bombs (IBs). In addition to the physical destruction these bombs caused, the use of incendiaries was calculated to have a devastating effect on the morale of the civilian populations in enemy cities.

The Luftwaffe employed chiefly the 2.2 lb B1 El, containing a mixture of magnesium and thermite, in raids against Great Britain. One of the most infamous Luftwaffe firebombing raids was conducted against the city of Coventry on 14–15 November 1941. In that one raid, the Germans dropped more than 56 tons of incendiaries, causing extensive damage and casualties.

The RAF's Bomber Command began experimenting with incendiary bombing in the early months of 1942, and on 2 May 1942, the head of Bomber Command, Air Chief Marshal Sir Arthur Harris, ordered the first thousand-plane raid against the German city of Köln (Cologne). Using a mixture of high-explosive and incendiary bombs, the attack on 30–31 May destroyed over 8 square miles of the city. Assessment of these early attacks convinced Harris that widespread devastation could be achieved with the right combination of ordnance in strikes conducted over several successive days and nights. The RAF would launch the night attacks with high explosives creating the fuel for the incendiaries that followed. The British 4 lb magnesium IB and the 30 lb phosphorous IB would then begin the fires. More high explosives would follow to disrupt fire-fighting and rescue units, concluding with another round of incendiaries. The U.S. Army Air Forces (USAAF) Eighth Air Force would also participate with "precision" (actually, area) daylight bombing on areas missed by the previous night's raid. The most famous of these perfected raids were against the cities of Hamburg and Dresden.

> On the night of 9–10 March 1945, 334 B-9 bombers dropped more than 2,000 tons of incendiaries on central Tokyo.

Beginning on the night of 24 July 1943 and lasting until 2 August, the attack on Hamburg, code-named Operation GOMORRAH, created a firestorm that destroyed over 6,000 acres of the city and killed at least 40,000 Germans. Then, on 13–14 February 1945, 1,400 RAF bombers attacked the city of Dresden at night, with 1,350 U.S. bombers following the next day. The resulting firestorm destroyed much of the city and killed tens of thousands of people. Following the Dresden raid, firebombing came under close scrutiny by the British and American governments and was suspended for the remainder of the European conflict.

In the Pacific Theater, the USAAF began experimenting with incendiary bombing in early 1945. Major General Curtis LeMay, who took over command of the Marianas-based bombing campaign against the Japanese home islands in January 1945, was under pressure from Washington to reduce the loss rates for the B-29 bombers in missions over Japan and increase the effectiveness of the high-altitude, daylight, precision-bombing attacks against major Japanese cities.

LeMay decided on low-level nighttime bombing runs with aircraft stripped of much of their protective armament in order to maximize bomb loads.

On the night of 9–10 March 1945, 334 B-29 bombers dropped more than 2,000 tons of incendiaries on central Tokyo. Unlike the magnesium-thermite and phosphorous bombs commonly used in Europe, the B-29s carried 100 lb, oil-gel M47 bombs and 6 lb, gelled-gasoline M69 bombs, calculated to be most effective against the wood and paper building materials so common in Japanese cities. The resulting firestorm destroyed 16 square miles of the city and killed an estimated 100,000 Japanese. Over the next weeks, B-29s fire-bombed the major Japanese cities, save the shrine city of Kyoto. The damage to Japan's major industrial cities was so extensive that LeMay was convinced he had found the means to end the war in the Pacific without an invasion of Japan itself.

The tactical potential of incendiary bombing was only beginning to be realized. Allied aircraft employed napalm—jellied gasoline ignited by thermite—against Japanese positions throughout the island-hopping campaigns. Incendiary bombing continued to be used on a wide scale in the Korean and Vietnam conflicts.

Stephen L. Gibbs

See also

Aircraft, Bombers; Britain, Battle of; Dresden, Air Attack on; Harris, Sir Arthur Travers; LeMay, Curtis Emerson; Strategic Bombing; Tokyo, Bombing of (1945)

References

Boyne, Walter J. *Clash of Wings: World War II in the Air.* New York: Simon and Schuster, 1994.

Freeman, Roger A. *The Mighty Eighth War Manual.* Osceola, WI: Motorbooks International, 1991.

Neillands, Robin. *The Bomber War: The Allied Air Offensive against Nazi Germany.* New York: Overlook Press, 2001.

Wood, Tony, and Bill Gunston. *Hitler's Luftwaffe.* New York: Crescent Books, 1978.

India

India, with a population of 319 million in 1941, played an important role in World War II. Its location, population, vast extent, and resources all made it vital to the Allied war effort. India became the base for British operations against Burma and for resupply efforts to China. It was also a key source of manpower, important raw materials, and finished goods.

In September 1939, Lord Linlithgow (Victor Alexander John Hope, 2nd Marquess of Linlithgow), the viceroy of India from 1936 to 1943, declared war on Germany and Italy on behalf of India and suspended the Government of India Act of 1935. Although this move was constitutionally correct, Linlithgow's failure to consult with the Indian legislature proved politically disastrous, as the British government had been endeavoring to encourage representative government by Indian elites. In response to Linlithgow's action, a large number of Congress Party members resigned their government posts. This outcome was ironic, as most Indians, including many princes and Congress Party leader Jawaharlal Nehru, opposed the Axis. A small number of Indian politicians, most notably Mohandas K. Gandhi, opposed all wars as a matter of principle.

In March 1942, Sir Richard Stafford Cripps arrived in India with a proposal for granting immediate self-rule after the war ended. The Congress Party rejected this offer and answered with the Quit India movement, announced on 8 August 1942. The movement called for an immediate end to British rule in India and involved mass struggle by nonviolent means. The British responded by arresting 60,000 leaders of the Congress Party, including both Nehru and Gandhi. Although the Muslim League also rejected the Cripps Plan, it benefited from its more moderate stance, and the influence of its leader, Mohammed Ali Jinnah, grew.

As noted, India was an important source of manpower for the Allied war effort. In 1938, British War Secretary Leslie Hore-Belisha recommended that the Indian army be reorganized, since too many British soldiers were deployed in India. But in June 1939, the Chatfield Commission held that a wholly Indian military was not feasible. The commission members believed British troops were necessary to keep peace between Muslims and Hindus—and, not incidentally, to maintain British control. In consequence, no major reorganization or modernization of the Indian army occurred. In 1939, the army numbered 189,000 men, of whom 65,000 were in administrative or communication positions. Much of the army's equipment was obsolete. Moreover, the army had no antitank units and only eight antiaircraft guns; there was also a serious shortage of artillery, let alone modern types.

The British government in India believed that the country would not be heavily involved with the war, particularly not overseas. Consequently, in the first eight months of the conflict, the government accepted only 53,000 volunteers to supplement existing forces. Even so, two brigades of the Indian army were deployed to Egypt in October 1939. And in 1940, Indian troops were dispatched to the Afghan border, Iraq, Malaya, Burma, and East Africa.

The Indian military grew considerably during the war. Defense spending increased from 49.5 million rupees in 1939–1940 to 395.3 million in 1945–1946. The army also expanded apace. A total of 2,644,323 men served in the Indian army during the war, of whom approximately 2 million were combatants. Indian forces fought in Syria, North Africa, East Africa, the Middle East, Malaya, Greece, Sicily, and Italy. A total of 179,935 became casualties, including prisoners of war (POWs). Indians formed the bulk of Allied fighting troops in

A worker in one of India's fast-expanding munitions plants in the early 1940s. During the war, India produced more than 50 different kinds of arms and ammunition. (Library of Congress)

Southeast Asia; of 1 million British troops in the region, more than 700,000 were Indian. Although Muslims were only 27 percent of the total Indian population, they formed two-thirds of the Indian troops in North Africa, Italy, Malaya, and Burma.

In April 1942, in order to counter a possible Japanese invasion of India from Burma, the British commander in chief, General Archibald P. Wavell, reorganized the Indian army structure of independent commands and formed it into Central Command and three armies: Northwestern, Central, and Eastern. In December 1942, the Eastern Army attacked into the Arakan, and the next year, it became General Sir William J. Slim's Fourteenth Army. In 1943, the British command placed more emphasis on jungle training, which stood Indian forces in good stead when they engaged the Japanese.

In the Japanese capture of Singapore in February 1942, 60,000 Indian troops became POWs. Radical Indian nationalist politician Subhas Chandra Bose and the Japanese convinced some 25,000 of them to join the Indian National Army (INA, also known as the Azad Hind Fanj) and fight to end

British rule in India. The Japanese viewed this force as an effective tool against British power, whereas its members saw themselves as an army of national liberation. Ultimately, some 7,000 INA troops were attached to Japanese units and fought in the Imphal Offensive into India. The remainder were used as auxiliaries. Most of the poorly trained and poorly equipped INA forces were either taken prisoner or deserted.

The rapid acceleration of the Indian war effort, especially following the Japanese attack on Pearl Harbor, spurred tremendous economic growth and led to a major expansion of India's industrial base. India contributed vast amounts of material to the British Empire's war effort, including raw materials, steel, locomotives and rolling stock, assault craft, and electrical components. Batteries produced in India were a vital component of air-to-ground communications, and India took the lead in manufacturing parachutes and uniforms and in assembling tens of thousands of armored vehicles from Canadian and U.S. components. India also supplied more than 50,000 stretchers, in excess of 1 million blankets,

250,000 mosquito nets, 1.5 million water-testing tablets, and 160 tons of mosquito-repellent cream. Further, to cope with the Allied rubber shortage, India established rubber plantations, experimented with reclaimed rubber, and produced considerable quantities of tires and hoses. It also produced alloy steels for guns and small arms, bayonets, shells, primers, and explosives, as well as steel for the manufacture of antiaircraft guns, antitank shells, and light machine guns.

In addition, Indian princes contributed on an individual basis to the war effort, donating material goods such as blankets, woolen cloth, silk for parachutes, and rubber products. The nawab of Bhopal liquidated his investments in the United States and used the money to purchase a squadron of Spitfire aircraft.

The war brought restrictions on movement, civil rights, and food supplies. As the threat of a Japanese attack increased, the viceroy ordered a "scorched-earth" policy that mandated the confiscation of all bicycles and boats in major coastal cities such as Calcutta. These seizures threatened the livelihood of many Indians and made food distribution more difficult. Between 1940 and 1942, prices of basic consumer goods increased an average of 250 percent, and the government began rationing grain, sugar, and cloth. Bengal was especially hard hit, for a famine there in 1943 claimed between 700,000 and 1.5 million lives; it was brought on, in part, by Japanese attacks against shipping along India's east coast. In addition to the high prices for food, India was unable to secure food imports from Burma after it was controlled by the Japanese.

> India supplied more than 50,000 stretchers, 1 million blankets, 250,000 mosquito nets, and 160 tons of mosquito-repellent cream.

Once the war had ended, it was apparent that the British could not long retain their control of India: the war had strengthened indigenous nationalist movements. Consequently, on 20 February 1947, the Labour government in London announced that it would transfer power to India no later than June 1948. However, despite Gandhi's pleas, religious animosity led to the partition of India. The Muslim eastern and western portions became Pakistan on 14 August 1947; a day later, the remainder of India became independent.

Laura J. Hilton

See also
China-Burma-India Theater; Gandhi, Mohandas Karamchand; Imphal and Kohima, Sieges of; Slim, Sir William Joseph; Wavell, Sir Archibald Percival

References
Ahmad, Manzoor. *The Indian Response to the Second World War.* New Delhi: Intellectual Publishing House, 1987.

Bhatia, H. S., ed. *Military History of British India, 1607–1947.* New Delhi: Deep and Deep, 1977.

Dodwell, H. H. *Cambridge History of India.* Vol. 6, *1858–1969.* New Delhi: S. Chand, 1972.

Farwell, Byron. *Armies of the Raj: From the Mutiny to Independence, 1858–1947.* New York: W. W. Norton, 1989.

Fay, Peter Ward. *The Forgotten Army: India's Armed Struggle for Independence, 1942–1945.* Ann Arbor: University of Michigan Press, 1993.

Hauner, Milan. *India in Axis Strategy: Germany, Japan, and Indian Nationalists in the Second World War.* Stuttgart, Germany: Klein-Cotta, 1981.

Vohra, Ranbir. *The Making of India.* Armonk, NY: M. E. Sharpe, 1997.

Indian Ocean, Japanese Naval Operations in (March–May 1942)

By late March 1942, the Japanese placed primary importance on the elimination of British naval forces in the Indian Ocean that might threaten the oil-rich East Indies. Imperial Headquarters therefore decided to attack Colombo and Trincomalee on Ceylon (Sri Lanka), off India. The Japanese hoped this move would force the British westward; spread panic in India and cause the British to divert resources there from Burma; and open the way to the conquest of Madagascar, which would enable them to cut Allied supply lines to the Pacific, Egypt, and the Soviet Union.

British Vice Admiral James Somerville commanded the Eastern Fleet, with 29 ships. He split his ships into Force A and Force B. The main body, Force A, consisted of his fastest ships: 2 fleet aircraft carriers, 1 battleship, 2 heavy cruisers, 2 light cruisers, and 6 destroyers. Force B consisted of 1 light carrier, 4 old R-class battleships, and a hodgepodge of 11 old cruisers and destroyers. Somerville faced a superior Japanese force under Vice Admiral Nagumo Chūichi. His First Air Fleet consisted of 5 large aircraft carriers (the *Kaga* remained in Japan), 4 battleships, 2 heavy cruisers, 1 light cruiser, and 11 destroyers.

En route to Ceylon, the Japanese attacked Port Darwin in Australia and, on 27 February, sank the U.S. seaplane tender *Langley*, bound for Java with aircraft. On 23 March, the Japanese took the Andaman Islands, securing the sea route to Rangoon from Singapore. Two days later, Nagumo's ships entered the Indian Ocean.

Earlier, on 7 March, the battleships *Haruna* and *Kongo* had shelled Christmas Island, located 190 miles southwest of Java and considered important for its phosphate resources. A Japanese task force, commanded by Rear Admiral Kyuji Kubo and consisting of 3 cruisers, 2 destroyers, and transports, then arrived. Japanese troops forced the island's surrender on 31 March. The U.S. submarine *Seawolf* scored a hit on Kubo's flagship, the light cruiser *Naka*, which had to be towed to Singapore for repairs. Several months later, the

Japanese withdrew from Christmas Island because it was unsuitable for any military facilities.

The attack on Ceylon, code-named Operation C, consisted of a strike against Colombo on 5 April and another on Trincomalee on 9 April. The British believed the Japanese planned to attack Ceylon beginning on 1 April, and Somerville stationed his ships south of Ceylon on 31 March.

Late on 2 April, however, Somerville, who feared a Japanese submarine attack and a daylight air attack on his ships, split his fleet. He sent the majority to Addu Atoll, a small refueling base in the Maldives some 600 miles southwest of Ceylon. He also dispatched the cruisers *Dorsetshire* and *Cornwall* to Colombo and the light carrier *Hermes* and the destroyer *Vampire* to Trincomalee. Immediately after the British ships reached Addu Atoll on 4 April, the Japanese were sighted 360 miles south of Ceylon. The main British force was now too far away to attack the Japanese, but bases on Ceylon were put on high alert. Somerville realized that he had blundered and recalled the two cruisers to Addu Atoll. The *Hermes* and *Vampire* were to rendezvous once they were finished fueling.

At 8:00 A.M. on Easter, 5 April, Japanese aircraft struck Colombo. Forty-two British fighters met the attackers, which were protected by escorting fighters. The Japanese planes destroyed shipping and paid particular attention to shore installations: railroad yards, repair shops, and the airfield. High-altitude Japanese bombers sank an immobilized armed merchant cruiser and a destroyer, and they severely damaged a submarine tender. The raid, completed by 8:35, cost the Japanese only 7 aircraft, whereas the British lost 25. Once the Japanese had recovered their planes, a floatplane spotted the *Dorsetshire* and *Cornwall* at sea, and Nagumo launched 88 aircraft against them. The Japanese sank both British heavy cruisers in short order. Somerville had set out from Addu Atoll to engage the Japanese but failed to locate them. When Force B joined him the next day, he regarded it as a liability and promptly dispatched it to Kenya.

Nagumo, meanwhile, moved his ships toward Trincomalee. Believing the Japanese were next going to attack Addu Atoll, Somerville positioned his ships off the atoll, 1,000 miles from the Japanese fleet. With the threat to India's coast and the sinking of merchant ships, the British decided to cede the eastern Indian Ocean to the Japanese and sent Force A to the western coast of India. The *Hermes* and *Vampire* were ordered to hug the coast and join Force A.

The Japanese raid on Trincomalee, beginning at 7:25 A.M. on 9 April and conducted by 91 bombers and 38 fighters, was met by 23 British aircraft. The Japanese planes found no warships in the harbor, but they did sink a merchant ship there. They concentrated on the shore installations and airfield and shot down 9 British Hurricane fighters, as well as 5 Blenheim bombers sent against the Japanese carrier *Akagi* as she retired (the British bombers scored no hits). That afternoon,

Japanese aircraft spotted the *Hermes* and *Vampire* at sea. Nagumo sent 90 aircraft against them, and the *Hermes*, with no planes aboard, and her escorting destroyer were promptly sent to the bottom.

As part of this same operation, the Japanese convoyed their 18th Infantry Division to Rangoon without incident. It arrived there on 7 April. Also, a Japanese raiding force attacked the sea-lanes off India's east coast. This Malaya Force, commanded by Vice Admiral Ozawa Jisaburo, consisted of the light carrier *Ryujo*, 5 heavy cruisers, 1 light cruiser, and 4 destroyers. Between 5 and 6 April, it sank 19 merchant ships (92,000 tons) and damaged 3 others. Air strikes by Japanese aircraft flying from Burma brought this total up to some 185,000 tons of shipping sunk, and Japanese submarines operating off India's west coast sank an additional 32,000 tons.

By 10 April, the Japanese had pushed the British navy out of most of the Indian Ocean, created a buffer against British naval raids on the East Indies and other Japanese possessions, and destroyed significant British military assets. Nagumo concluded that he had achieved his objectives and ordered the First Air Fleet to return to Japan. His fleet had been at sea for many months, and its ships badly needed refitting.

Ultimately, their Indian Ocean victory fueled a belief in their own invincibility among the Japanese and led to the overexpansion of their empire. The extended Japanese Indian Ocean operation also meant that many of the ships were unavailable for the next big sea fight, the Battle of the Coral Sea in May.

Benjamin E. Nehrke

See also
Aircraft Carriers; Coral Sea, Battle of the; Nagumo Chūichi

References
Andrieu d'Albas, and Emmanuel Marie Auguste. *Death of a Navy: Japanese Naval Action in World War II*. Trans. Anthony Rippon. New York: Devin-Adair, 1957.
Dull, Paul S. *The Battle History of the Imperial Japanese Navy*. Annapolis, MD: Naval Institute Press, 1978.
Roskill, Stephen W. *The War at Sea*. Vol. 2, *The Period of Balance*. London: Her Majesty's Stationery Office, 1956.
Thomas, David A. *Japan's War at Sea: Pearl Harbor to the Coral Sea*. London: A. Deutsch, 1978.

Indianapolis, Sinking of (July–August 1945)

The sinking of the U.S. heavy cruiser *Indianapolis* by a Japanese submarine in the Philippine Sea two weeks before the end of the war remains controversial to this day. Built in Camden, New Jersey, and commissioned in 1932 at the Philadelphia Navy Yard, the *Indianapolis* (CA-35) displaced 9,800 tons and was 610' in length. The engines drove her at a maximum speed of 32.5 knots, and she mounted 9 × 8-inch and 8 × 5-inch guns. She had carried President Franklin D. Roosevelt as a passenger during three cruises in the 1930s, and she served with distinction in the Pacific Theater throughout the war.

While shelling Okinawa prior to the invasion of the island, the *Indianapolis* was severely damaged by a Japanese bomber in late March 1945, necessitating a voyage to Mare Island, California, for repairs. After the work was completed, the ship, under the command of Captain Charles B. McVay III, was ordered to carry to the island of Tinian the internal components of the two atomic bombs to be dropped on Hiroshima and Nagasaki. The *Indianapolis* subsequently departed on a high-speed voyage from San Francisco, arriving at Tinian 10 days later, on 26 July. She next stopped at the island of Guam and departed on 28 July with orders to proceed to Leyte. While traveling without escort—under radio silence at 17 knots in moderate seas with good visibility—she was torpedoed twice by the Japanese submarine *I-58* in the early morning hours of 30 July; she sank in only 12 minutes. Survivors were spotted by a U.S. Navy aircraft on 2 August. Of some 800 members of her 1,199-man crew who initially survived the sinking, only 316 were eventually rescued. The vast majority of those who died fell victim to sharks and exposure. The incident remains the worst case of shark attacks in history.

Following a court of inquiry into the loss of the *Indianapolis*, Admiral Chester Nimitz proposed reprimanding McVay. Instead, however, Secretary of the Navy James Forrestal followed the advice of the chief of naval operations, Fleet Admiral Ernest King, and ordered McVay to stand trial by court-martial. McVay was subsequently found guilty of an error of professional judgment in unreasonably placing the *Indianapolis* at risk by failing to steer a zigzag course; he was acquitted of inefficiency in ordering his crew to abandon ship. The court unanimously recommended clemency, and Forrestal remitted the sentence of the court-martial. McVay retired as a rear admiral in 1949; he committed suicide in 1968.

In recent years, crew members of the *Indianapolis* have endeavored to clear McVay's name. They have pointed out the poor visibility at the time the ship was sunk, the ship's engine problems, and the fact that McVay had not been informed of Japanese submarine activity. Also, McVay's request for escorts had been refused, even though the *Indianapolis* lacked antisubmarine detection devices. In 2001, the U.S. Congress passed a resolution exonerating McVay of any wrongdoing.

Glenn E. Helm

See also
Battle Cruisers; Forrestal, James Vincent; King, Ernest Joseph; Nuclear Weapons; Submarines

References
Boyd, Carl. "Attacking the *Indianapolis*." *Warship International* 13, no. 2 (1976): 15–25.

Kurzman, Dan. *Fatal Voyage: The Sinking of the USS "Indianapolis."* New York: Atheneum, 1990.

Lech, Raymond B. *All the Drowned Sailors.* New York: Stein and Day, 1982.

Newcomb, Richard F. *Abandon Ship: The Saga of the U.S.S. "Indianapolis," the Navy's Greatest Sea Disaster.* New York: Harper Collins, 2001.

Infantry Tactics

Firepower and maneuver are the two primary elements of applied combat power. Firepower delivers the destructive force necessary to defeat an enemy's ability and will to fight. Maneuver is the movement of combat forces to gain positional advantage, usually in order to deliver or to threaten to deliver fire by direct or indirect means. Artillery and aircraft deliver fire on the modern battlefield. The tank, though considered a maneuver weapon, really combines both elements, firepower and maneuver. The infantry is primarily a maneuver force.

Infantry is defined traditionally as the branch of an army made up of units trained to fight on foot. Despite the appearance of large-scale mechanization in World War II, infantry dominated the battlefield in that war as it has since the dawn of human history—and as it is likely to do so well into the high-tech future. Early in the nineteenth century, the Prussian military theorist Carl von Clausewitz wrote, "The end for which a soldier is recruited, clothed, armed, and trained, the whole object of his sleeping, eating, drinking, and marching is simply that he should fight at the right place and the right time." Clausewitz was talking primarily about the infantryman.

The World War II infantryman had much in common with his counterpart in the Roman legions 2,000 years earlier. In both eras, the individual infantryman lived and fought on the ground, day or night, in all weather, on all types of terrain. In both eras, he carried almost everything he needed on his back, he fought with handheld weapons, and his primary mission was to close with and destroy an enemy. The World War II infantryman, however, had far greater destructive power, reach, and staying power than his ancient counterpart. A World War II infantry company was more lethal than an entire infantry regiment of Napoleon's era. This advance resulted not only from the reach and rate of fire of modern weapons but also from communications technology that allowed an infantry company commander or even a platoon leader to call in the fire of an entire divisional artillery or air force fighter-bombers.

American infantrymen were the best equipped of World War II. The German infantrymen arguably were the best trained and best led. Soviet infantrymen were probably the toughest and most inured to physical hardship. The question of which army fielded the best infantrymen overall is open to debate, but the

U.S. infantrymen charge a German position during the Normandy campaign. Prone soldier in foreground is preparing to fire a rifle grenade. (Hulton Archive)

battlefield performance of the Australians, the New Zealanders, and the Gurkhas was consistently outstanding.

As with the tactics of the other arms, infantry tactics have always been a function of the technology and culture of the times. Most armies entered World War I with tactical doctrines that assumed mobile operations would be the norm. But infantrymen on both sides of the front lines in 1914 encountered previously unimaginable levels of firepower delivered by the new technologies of quick-firing artillery, the magazine-fed rifle, and especially the machine gun. Unable to survive the withering fire on the surface of the earth, the troops dug in. With the onset of trench warfare, the military planners on all sides spent the rest of the war searching for the tactical methods that would break the deadlock and restore mobility to the battlefield. They were close to achieving the solution by the time the war ended in 1918.

Contrary to popular belief, most armies did not spend the period between the two world wars training and organizing for a repetition of trench warfare. The majority of professional soldiers concluded soon after World War I that positional warfare had been an anomaly. But during the 1920s and the early part of the 1930s, an almost universal revulsion to all things military combined with the social, political, and economic factors of the era to retard advancements in military technology and doctrine. France, which had suffered more than any other of the Western Allies, especially adopted a defensive attitude to warfare and entrenched itself behind the Maginot Line.

The Allied armies ended World War I with massive stockpiles of weapons and equipment, which also tended to retard advancements in military technology. For economic reasons, political leaders insisted that the existing stocks be consumed before new weapons were developed and fielded. Germany, however, was in a different situation. The draconian provisions of the Versailles Treaty ironically worked to Germany's longer-term military advantage. Deprived of virtually all its armaments in 1919, the German military was forced to make a fresh start, both technologically and doctrinally.

Many of the technologies that had their primitive origins in World War I matured in the interwar years and radically altered the face of ground combat in World War II. Doctrinally, the modern concept of combined-arms operations also emerged in World War I. Combined-arms operations are those in which the effects of infantry, artillery, armor, air support, engineers, communications, and the like are all brought to bear on an objective in a coordinated and synchronized manner that produces a multiplier effect greater than the sum of its parts. Each of the combat arms has particular strengths and weaknesses. In a combined-arms effort, the strength of one arm compensates for the weakness of another. Tanks, for example, are vulnerable to light infantry armed with antitank weapons such as the bazooka or the Panzerfaust. By combining infantry with tanks, the infantry protects the tanks from enemy infantry while the tanks provide their own infantry with increased firepower and mobility.

Motorization was one of the major technological differences between World War I and World War II. During the earlier conflict, the primary source of battlefield motive power was human and horse muscle, as it had been for thousands of years. By the start of World War II, however, the American and British armies were completely motorized. The Soviet and German armies were partially motorized, but they and the Japanese and Italian forces continued to use horses and mules on a large scale. Despite the popular image of Germany's fast-moving mechanized armies, the Germans' field artillery and much of their infantry supply trains were horse-drawn right up to the end of the war.

The requirement for infantry to keep up with armored vehicles in fast-paced combat led to the development of motorized infantry and then mechanized infantry, also called armored infantry. Motorized infantry units, which first appeared near the end of World War I, were transported in trucks to assembly areas, where they dismounted and then deployed for combat. Mechanized infantry troops moved in various types of armored personnel carriers that usually were tracked or half-tracked. The armored personnel carriers mounted machine guns and heavier weapons that provided additional firepower. Mechanized infantry units usually dismounted from their vehicles to fight but sometimes fought from them. German mechanized infantry troops, known as panzergrenadiers, were an integral element of their panzer divisions.

German commanders always tried to avoided launching set-piece frontal attacks, the most costly form of combat. They preferred, wherever possible, to attack around an enemy's flanks, using the operational principles articulated by Count Helmut von Moltke in the late nineteenth century: *Umfassen, Einschliessen, Vernichten*—fix, encircle, destroy. When a deliberate attack was unavoidable, the Germans usually opted for a penetration with conventional infantry, supported closely by engineers, artillery, and tactical air support.

Once a penetration or flanking movement succeeded, the German panzers exploited by encircling the enemy, from two directions in a pincer if possible. After the jaws of the pincer closed, the attacking force formed two concentric rings, one facing inward to hold and destroy the trapped enemy force and the other facing outward to prevent any relief efforts. The Germans called this tactic a *Kesselschlacht*—a cauldron battle—and used it very successfully and on a large scale in many of the early battles in the Soviet Union in the summer of 1941. Later on the Western Front, the Germans themselves fell victim to the Kesselschlacht at Falaise and the Ruhr pocket.

A key element of German tactics was the concept of *Auftragstaktik*, which loosely translates into English as "mission tactics." Despite the popular stereotypes, reinforced by countless Hollywood movies and television programs, the common German soldier of World War II was anything but stupid and unimaginative, and his officers and noncommissioned officers (NCOs) were neither machinelike nor inflexible autocrats. German leaders, down to the most junior officers and NCOs, were encouraged to be flexible and innovative in their approach to accomplishing their assigned missions. German operations orders generally described what subordinate units had to accomplish and the time in which it needed to be done. The question of how to carry out the task was left to the subordinate leaders, who were supposed to understand the overall intentions of their commanders at least two levels up. The result was that German units, even large units such as divisions, could react quickly to changes in the tactical situation, often acting on only verbal, fragmentary orders.

The primary document for German operations and tactics was a manual called *Truppenführung* (Unit Command), which was issued in 1934 and remained in force until the end of the war. It remains, to this day one, of history's most influential milestones in the development of tactical doctrine. Yet for all its tactical sophistication, the German army became overextended and ground down by the demands of waging a two-front war. To maintain their massive armies in the field, the Germans were forced to decrease training times progressively and even to commit training units to combat during emergencies. The decline in infantry quality meant that infantry units survived for shorter periods in combat and thus had to be replaced at a faster rate. It was a vicious cycle. In response, German commanders tried to rely more heavily on firepower as the conflict wore on, but the German army was chronically short of artillery throughout the war.

The fighting in the Soviet Union was more infantry-intensive than that in North Africa or in western Europe. After the initial successes of 1941, the Germans' so-called blitzkrieg began to fail because the panzer forces and even more so the Luftwaffe became more and more thinly spread over the vast spaces in the east. As that happened, the advantage slowly shifted to the Soviets, with their vast numbers of infantry divisions and their overwhelming superiority in artillery tubes. Although some battles, such as Kursk, were classic clashes of armor, the foot soldier dominated the set-piece urban fight for Stalingrad.

Early in the war, Soviet attacks had great difficulty breaking through German defenses. The Soviet solution was to put the bulk of a unit's combat power as far forward as possible, with as many as 19 of a division's 27 infantry companies in the front line for a typical divisional deliberate attack. Later in the war, the German defenses developed much greater depth as they were being pushed back from Soviet territory. In response, the Soviets developed echeloned attack tactics.

Infantrymen do not fight as individuals. They fight as part of a carefully synchronized team, and each member of that team performs a specialized function. The basic infantry tactical unit is a squad—or section—of 8 to 15 soldiers commanded by a junior-ranking NCO. The squad is the largest unit that a leader can command by direct personal influence on the individual soldier. As the building blocks of larger combat units, the squads' organization and structure were a direct reflection of the tactical doctrine of the larger army.

At the start of World War II, the German infantry squad consisted of 10 men organized into two groups. The 4-man machine-gun group (gunner, assistant gunner, and 2 ammunition bearers) was armed with the excellent MG-34 light machine gun. The 5-man rifle group supported the machine-gun group. The two groups advanced by mutually supporting fire and movement, coordinated and synchronized by the squad leader. The Germans placed particular emphasis on selecting and training squad leaders. But by 1943, manpower shortages forced the Germans to reduce the infantry section to 9 men.

The organization of the French infantry squad was superficially similar to that of the Germans, but its method of maneuvering reflected the overwhelming defensive mentality of the French army. The Germans believed that fire and movement complemented each other, but the French believed that movement was only possible once fire superiority was established. The French squad had 12 men, organized into a 6-man light-machine-gun or automatic-rifle team, and a 5-man rifle team. Rather than maneuvering individually and providing mutual support to each other, the two teams were linked rigidly to the machine gun. The function of each member of the squad was defined in terms of the gun—fire it, move it, feed it, and protect it.

The Soviets and the British had the smallest infantry squads. The Soviet squad had 9 men and a light machine gun. The British infantry squad consisted of a corporal, 7 men, and the Czech-designed Bren gun as the automatic weapon. The Bren, which was much lighter than the Lewis gun it replaced, facilitated an increased emphasis on fire and movement within the British infantry.

The U.S. Army did not become involved in ground combat operations until late 1942. The American infantryman, armed with the outstanding semiautomatic M1 rifle, could produce a far greater rate of fire than either his Axis enemies or his Canadian and British allies, all of whom generally were armed with bolt-action rifles. The 12-man American infantry squad was organized into three teams. The squad leader (a sergeant) usually moved with the 2-man scout (Able) team. Once an enemy objective was located, the squad leader ordered the 4-man fire (Baker) team, which was based on a Browning automatic rifle (BAR), to lay down a base of fire. The 5-man maneuver (Charlie) team then attacked the objective in short rushes. In practice, the unbalanced teams and especially the low rate of fire of the BAR made the American infantry squad particularly vulnerable to casualties. After World War II, American infantry squads were reconfigured into two evenly balanced teams.

Many popular beliefs about the infantry and infantrymen are false. Infantrymen, for example, are not the intellectual underclass of an army. Modern infantry combat has become so technical, so fast-paced, and so lethal that only the quick-witted, physically fit, and highly trained can survive it. Nor did the infantry suffer the highest casualty rates in World War II. Combat aircrews and, above all, submarine crews had higher rates. Few would argue, however, that the "poor bloody infantry"—as the British called them—led the hardest lives in the war. Regardless of the overall scheme of maneuver of the larger unit, every attack is a frontal attack at the level of the individual infantry soldier.

David T. Zabecki

See also

Antitank Guns and Warfare; Armored Warfare; Falaise-Argentan Pocket; Kursk, Battle of; Maginot Line; Mines, Land; Ruhr Campaign; Stalingrad, Battle of

References

Bidwell, Shelford, and Dominick Graham. *Fire-Power: British Army Weapons and Theories of War, 1904–1945.* Boston: Allen and Unwin, 1982.

Citino, Robert M. *The Path to Blitzkrieg: Doctrine and Training in the German Army, 1920–1939.* Boulder, CO: Lynne Rienner, 1999.

Clausewitz, Carl von. *On War.* Ed. and trans. Michael Howard and Peter Paret. Princeton, NJ: Princeton University Press, 1976.

Corum, James. *The Roots of Blitzkrieg: Hans von Seeckt and German Military Reform.* Lawrence: University Press of Kansas, 1992.

English, John A., and Bruce I. Gudmundsson. *On Infantry.* Westport, CT: Praeger, 1994.

Marshall, S. L. A. *Men against Fire: The Problem of Battle Command in Future War.* New York: William Morrow, 1947.

Zabecki, David T., and Bruce Condell, eds. *On the German Art of War: "Truppenführung."* Boulder, CO: Lynne Rienner, 2001.

Ingersoll, Royal Eason (1883–1976)

U.S. Navy admiral whose logistical skills contributed to the success of the Normandy Invasion. Born in Washington, D.C., on 20 June 1883, Royal Ingersoll was the son of a

U.S. Navy Admiral Royal E. Ingersoll. (Bettmann/Corbis)

distinguished admiral. Graduating from the U.S. Naval Academy in 1905, he participated in the final portion of the Great White Fleet's voyage around the world. Quietly intellectual, unobtrusive, a superb administrator and skilled seaman, Ingersoll filled assorted staff, teaching, and sea-going assignments. Heading the Navy Department Communications Office during World War I, he ably directed its enormous wartime expansion and subsequently directed U.S. communications at the Paris Peace Conference in 1919.

Following tours as the executive officer of two battleships, Ingersoll headed the branch of naval intelligence responsible for code-breaking efforts against the Japanese. In 1927, he graduated from the Naval War College and was promoted to captain. He then held staff assignments and commanded cruisers. For three years, from 1935 to 1938, Ingersoll headed

the War Plans Division, where he helped revise Plan Orange against Japan. In 1937, he launched informal discussions with Great Britain on potential Anglo-American cooperation in any future conflict with Japan.

Promoted to rear admiral in 1938, Ingersoll commanded Cruiser Division 76. He was recalled from sea duty in 1940 and became assistant to Chief of Naval Operations Admiral Harold R. Stark. Ingersoll played a crucial role in helping prepare the U.S. Navy for war. In January 1942, as a vice admiral, he took command of the Atlantic Fleet, based at Norfolk, Virginia; his mission was to counter the German U-boat campaign, thereby safeguarding Atlantic lines of communication and protecting convoys bound for Europe, and to secure the Western Hemisphere. In June 1942, his only son and namesake, a naval lieutenant, died in action at the Battle of Midway. Ingersoll was promoted to full admiral the following month. That November, his vessels transported the U.S. Western Task Force to Morocco in Operation TORCH, thenceforth supporting Allied operations in the Mediterranean.

From May 1943, Ingersoll worked closely with the new Tenth Fleet, established under the direct command of Chief of Naval Operations Admiral Ernest J. King. Ingersoll's logistical and managerial skills proved particularly valuable in deploying American forces to maximum effect, and, by substantially neutralizing German submarine forces, greatly facilitated the June 1944 Normandy landings.

In November 1944, Ingersoll became commander, Western Sea Frontier, to implement the complex transfer of American naval forces from the Atlantic to the Pacific for the projected invasion of Japan, a task effectively obviated by the sudden end of the war in August 1945. He retired one year later. Ingersoll died in Washington, D.C., on 20 May 1976.

Priscilla Roberts

See also
King, Ernest Joseph; Midway, Battle of; Stark, Harold Raynesford "Betty"; TORCH, Operation
References
Hughes, Terry, and John Costello. *The Battle of the Atlantic.* New York: Dial, 1977.
Macintyre, Donald. *The Naval War against Hitler.* New York: Scribner's, 1961.
Morison, Samuel Eliot. *History of the United States Naval Operations in World War II.* Vol. 1, *The Battle of the Atlantic, 1939–1943.* Boston: Little, Brown, 1947.

Ingram, Jonas Howard (1886–1952)

U.S. Navy admiral who was given command of the Atlantic Fleet in 1944. Born in Jeffersonville, Indiana, on 15 October 1886, Jonas Ingram graduated from the U.S. Naval Academy. A gunnery specialist, he served at sea in the Atlantic during World War I on Admiral Hugh Rodman's staff. Between the wars, Ingram held seagoing commands, taught football and athletics at the Naval Academy, directed naval public relations in Washington, learned to fly as a naval aviator, and took staff courses.

In 1940, Rear Admiral Ingram assumed command of Cruiser Division 2, subsequently rechristened Task Force 23 and then the Fourth Fleet, stationed in Brazilian waters to secure the South Atlantic against Nazi ships and submarines. Promoted to vice admiral in 1942, he worked closely with Brazilian officials, winning their consent to the construction of American air, naval, and military facilities on Brazilian territory, while helping to upgrade Brazilian naval and air capabilities. Under Ingram's supervision, Ascension Island, 1,000 miles from Brazil's coast, became one of the largest existing air bases, enabling him to launch both aerial and naval attacks

on German U-boats. In late 1943, Ingram declared the Atlantic secure from Brazil to West Africa. In November 1944, he was promoted to full admiral and took command of the Atlantic Fleet, protecting shipping routes between North America and the European Theater—and especially troop convoys—against the final German submarine sorties.

Ingram retired from the navy in 1947 to become commissioner of the All-American Football Conference and a vice president of Reynolds Metal Company. He died in San Diego, California, on 10 September 1952.

Priscilla Roberts

See also
Antisubmarine Warfare; Atlantic, Battle of the
References
Conn, Stetson, and Byron Fairchild. *The Western Hemisphere: The Framework of Hemispheric Defense.* Washington, DC: U.S. Government Printing Office, 1960.
Hughes, Terry, and John Costello. *The Battle of the Atlantic.* New York: Dial, 1977.
Macintyre, Donald. *The Naval War against Hitler.* New York: Scribner's, 1961.
Reynolds, Clark G. *Famous American Admirals.* New York: Van Nostrand Reinhold, 1978.

Inoue Shigeyoshi

See Inouye Shigeyoshi.

Inouye (Inoue) Shigeyoshi (1889–1975)

Japanese navy admiral who advocated a negotiated end to the war. Born in Miyagi Prefecture, Japan, on 9 December 1889, Inouye (Inoue) Shigeyoshi graduated from the Naval Academy in 1909. His early career included both sea duty and staff assignments. Inouye attained flag rank in 1935. Two years later, he was appointed chief of the Naval Affairs Bureau. He shared Navy Minister Admiral Yonai Mitsumasa's belief that radical elements in the officer corps posed a threat to Japan's future. In 1939, Inouye was promoted to vice admiral and appointed chief of staff of the China Area Fleet.

Convinced that naval aviation would play a vital role in any future conflict, he successfully lobbied for appointment as chief of the Naval Aeronautics Bureau in 1940 in order to gain practical experience. In that position, he drafted a memorandum entitled "Modern Weapons Procurement Planning," in which he attacked the construction of battleships and called for greater emphasis on aircraft carriers and naval aircraft.

Inouye's views caused him to fall from favor. In August 1941, he was transferred to command the Fourth Fleet on

Truk, a backwater assignment. When World War II began, he led the forces that captured Guam and Wake Islands from the Americans. As other islands fell to the advancing Japanese, Inouye's area of responsibility expanded to include Rabaul and the Gilbert Islands.

In April 1942, Inouye was charged with planning and executing the invasion of Port Moresby. He remained in Rabaul while seven naval task forces, as well as land-based naval aircraft, moved against Tulagi, Guadalcanal, and Port Moresby in early May. The resulting Battle of the Coral Sea was a Japanese tactical victory, but the unavailability of close-air support due to the loss of an aircraft carrier in the battle led Inouye, on 8 May, to postpone the landing at Port Moresby. The commander of the Combined Fleet, Admiral Yamamoto Isoroku, was furious at this decision but unable to reverse Inouye's orders.

Inouye's Fourth Fleet was then largely relegated to logistical duties, and operations in the South Pacific were turned over to the Eighth Fleet. Inouye was relieved in October 1942 and took command of the Japanese Naval Academy. He was recognized as an advocate of peace, and when Admiral Yonai was recalled as navy minister after Tōjō Hideki's fall in August 1944, Inouye became vice minister. In May 1945, he was promoted to full admiral and became a member of the Supreme War Council. He spent the next months working for an end to the war. Inouye died in Miyagi on 15 December 1975.

Tim J. Watts

See also
Coral Sea, Battle of the; Rabaul; Southwest Pacific Theater; Tōjō Hideki; Yamamoto Isoroku

References
Dull, Paul S. *A Battle History of the Imperial Japanese Navy (1941–1945)*. Annapolis, MD: Naval Institute Press, 1978.

Thomas, David Arthur. *Japan's War at Sea: Pearl Harbor to the Coral Sea*. London: A. Deutsch, 1978.

Van der Vat, Dan. *The Pacific Campaign: World War II—The U.S.-Japanese Naval War, 1941–1945*. New York: Simon and Schuster, 1991.

International Military Tribunal: Far East (Tokyo War Crimes Trials) (1946–1948)

Trials of senior Japanese leaders after World War II. General of the Army Douglas MacArthur, heading the military occupation of Japan, established the International Military Tribunal for the Far East, popularly known as the Tokyo War Crimes Trials. The body held sessions in Tokyo from 3 May 1946 to 12 November 1948. Trials conducted by the tribunal were similar to those held at Nuremberg, Germany. The defendants were 28 senior Japanese military and civilian leaders, chosen from among 250 Japanese officials originally accused

Sentences imposed by Far East Military Tribunal

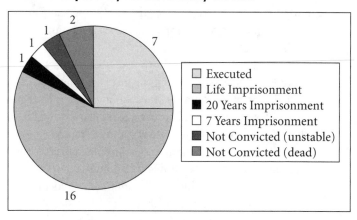

of war crimes. General Tōjō Hideki, who held various posts including prime minister and chief of the General Staff, was the best-known defendant among the 18 military officers and 10 civilians charged. General MacArthur, with President Harry S Truman's support, exempted Emperor Hirohito from trial because of concerns over potential Japanese resistance to military occupation. More than 2,200 similar trials, including some held in Tokyo that preceded the tribunal, were conducted in areas formerly occupied by Japan, ranging from China to Pacific islands including Guam. The trials generated strong emotions, and they remain controversial to this day.

The Toyko tribunal consisted of 11 judges, 1 each from Australia, Canada, China, Great Britain, the Netherlands, New Zealand, the Soviet Union, the United States, France, India, and the Philippines. The Philippine justice was a survivor of the Bataan Death March. The tribunal's chief prosecutor, Joseph B. Keenan, was appointed by President Truman. Keenan's credentials included service as a former director of the U.S. Justice Department's Criminal Division as well as assistant to the U.S. attorney general. His staff included 25 lawyers. The tribunal was not bound by technical rules of evidence normally observed in a democracy and could admit any evidence that it chose, including purported admissions or statements of the accused.

The tribunal sought to establish clearly the principle that aggressive war was a crime and to prevent or deter future crimes against peace. Those who planned and initiated aggressive war in contravention of treaties, assurances, and international agreements were to be considered common felons. The tribunal also claimed jurisdiction over conventional war crimes and crimes against humanity, such as murder, mass murder, enslavement, deportation of civilian populations, and persecutions based on political or racial grounds in connection with other crimes under tribunal jurisdiction.

Some defendants were accused of being responsible for the actions of personnel under their command who had committed crimes against prisoners of war and civilian internees.

These offenses included murder; beatings; torture; ill-treatment, including inadequate provision of food and clothing and poor sanitation; rape of female nurses and other women; and the imposition of excessive and dangerous labor. Charges of murder were also leveled in cases involving the killing of military personnel who had surrendered, laid down arms, or no longer had means of defense, including survivors of ships sunk by naval action and crews of captured ships.

Seeking to conduct a fair trial, the tribunal gave each of those accused a copy of his or her indictment in Japanese, and trial proceedings were conducted in both English and Japanese. Defendants had a right to counsel, and the defense could question witnesses. Subject to court approval, the defense could also request the appearance of witnesses and the provision of documents. The mental and physical capacity of the accused to stand trial was also considered. After a conviction, the tribunal had the power to impose a death sentence or other punishment on a defendant. Of the 28 original defendants, 25 were convicted. Seven (including Tōjō) were sentenced to death by hanging, 16 to life imprisonment, 1 to 20 years of incarceration, and another to 7 years in prison. The remaining 3 were not convicted, 1 being declared mentally unstable and 2 dying before their trials ended.

As with the Nuremberg trials, the tribunal has been accused of promulgating "victors' justice," and some have called the proceedings racist. But fueled by horror at continuing military atrocities in places such as Bosnia and Cambodia, a legacy of the Tokyo and Nuremberg trials has been the widespread international support for a permanent war crimes tribunal. The U.S. government, however, has resisted the formation of such a body, fearing that it could be politically influenced to harass American military forces operating overseas.

Glenn E. Helm

See also

Bataan Death March; Burma Road; Hirohito, Emperor of Japan; International Military Tribunal: The Nuremberg Trials; Japan, Air Forces; Japan, Army; Japan, Navy; Japanese Surrendered Personnel; MacArthur, Douglas; Nanjing Massacre; Tōjō Hideki; Truman, Harry S

References

Kei, Ushimura. *Beyond the "Judgment of Civilization": The Intellectual Legacy of the Japanese War Crimes Trials, 1946–1949*. Trans. Steven J. Ericson. Tokyo: International House of Japan, 2003.

Maga, Timothy P. *Judgment at Tokyo: The Japanese War Crimes Trials*. Lexington: University Press of Kentucky, 2001.

Minear, Richard H. *Victors' Justice: The Tokyo War Crimes Trial*. Princeton, NJ: Princeton University Press, 1971.

Piccigallo, Philip R. *The Japanese on Trial: Allied War Crimes Operations in the East, 1945–1951*. Austin: University of Texas Press, 1979.

U.S Department of State. *Trial of Japanese War Criminals: Documents 1. Opening Statement by Joseph B. Keenan, Chief of Counsel, 2. Charter of the International Military Tribunal for the Far East, 3. Indictment*. Washington, DC: U.S. Department of State, 1946.

International Military Tribunal: The Nuremberg Trials (16 October 1945– 20 November 1946)

The Allies were determined to hold German leaders, both civilian and military, accountable for the war and the mass killings that had taken place in German-occupied Europe. British Prime Minister Winston L. S. Churchill and Soviet leader Josef Stalin agreed in 1941 to try those guilty of war crimes. The logistics and framework needed to carry out this policy were discussed throughout the war. At Moscow in October 1943, a declaration signed by British, Soviet, and U.S. representatives stated that war criminals would be brought to trial. Such a procedure was further discussed at important meetings at Tehran (November–December 1943), Yalta (February 1945), and Potsdam (July 1945). Finally, the London Agreement of 8 August 1945 set forth the method—a court trial—and identified jurisdiction. Although the Soviets proposed that the trials be held within their zone of occupation, in Berlin, the Western Allies insisted on Nuremberg.

The city of Nuremberg was selected because the palace of justice there had received only minimal damage during the war. The large stone structure had 80 courtrooms and over 500 offices and thus offered sufficient space for a major international legal proceeding. Furthermore, an undestroyed prison was part of the justice building complex, so all prospective defendants could be housed on site. Moreover, the proclamation of the Third Reich's racial laws against the Jews had been made at Nuremberg. U.S. Army personnel prepared the palace of justice for the trial, repairing damage and laying thousands of feet of electrical wire.

Broadly speaking, the Nuremberg proceedings fell into two categories. The first set—and the subject of this essay—took place between November 1945 and October 1946 and involved the trial of 22 defendants before an international military tribunal (IMT) established by Britain, France, the Soviet Union, and the United States. Subsequently, a series of

Sentences imposed by Nuremberg Military Tribunal

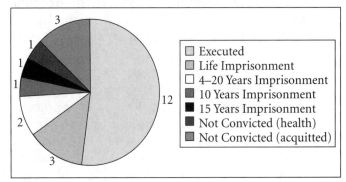

The 21 defendants at the Nuremberg War Crimes Trial sitting in the dock awaiting sentencing, Nuremberg, Germany. Among the defendants are (front row; left to right): Hermann Göring, who received the death penalty; Rudolf Hess, life imprisonment; and Joachim von Ribbentrop, who also received the death penalty. (Hulton Archive)

other trials were held at Nuremberg until the spring of 1949 before U.S. tribunals in the American zone of occupation, involving nearly 200 other defendants.

The Nuremberg IMT opened on 8 October 1945. Judges from France, Great Britain, the Soviet Union, and the United States presided. The Western judges dressed in traditional robes, whereas the Soviet judge wore a military uniform. Judge Iola T. Nikitschenko, a Soviet, presided during the first session.

The prosecution presented indictments against 24 major criminals and 6 organizations. The individuals were Martin Bormann, deputy Führer after 1941 (tried in absentia); Karl Dönitz, admiral and commander of the navy from 1943 to 1945; Hans Frank, governor-general of Poland; Wilhelm Frick, minister for internal affairs; Hans Fritzsche, head of the Radio Division of the Ministry of Propaganda; Walther Funk, minister of Economic Affairs; Hermann Göring, Reichsmarschall (Reich Marshal) and commander of the Luftwaffe; Rudolf Hess, deputy Führer until May 1941; Alfred Jodl, army general and head of Operations, Oberkommando der Wehrmacht (OKW); Ernst Kaltenbrunner, head of the Sicher-

heitsdienst (SD, Security Service); Wilhelm Keitel, army field marshal and chief of OKW; Gustav Krupp von Bohlen und Halbach, industrialist and head of Krupp armaments; Robert Ley, head of the Labor Front (he committed suicide on 26 October 1945); Konstantin Neurath, protector of Bohemia and Moravia from 1939 to 1943; Franz von Papen, former vice chancellor and ambassador to Turkey; Erich Raeder, grand admiral and commander of the navy until 1943; Joachim von Ribbentrop, foreign minister; Alfred Rosenberg, minister for the Occupied Territories in the East until 1941; Fritz Saukel, plenipotentiary for the mobilization of labor; Hjalmar Schacht, president of the Reichsbank, from 1933 to 1939 and minister of economics from 1934 to 1937; Baldur von Shirach, leader of the Hitler Youth and Gauleiter (area commander) of Vienna; Arthur Seyss-Inquart, commissioner for the Netherlands from 1940 to 1945; Albert Speer, minister of armaments from 1942 to 1945; and Julius Streicher, publisher of the newspaper *Der Sturmer*. The indicted organizations were the Nazi Party (NSDAP), the Schutzstaffel (SS), the SD, the Gestapo, the General Staff, and Hitler's cabinet.

The charter governing the proceedings declared that the IMT's decisions would be made by majority vote. British Lord Justice Geoffrey Lawrence, president of the court, would cast the deciding vote in the event of a tie among the four sitting judges. The charter identified four categories of crimes: (1) crimes against peace: planning and/or preparing a war of aggression and violating international agreements; (2) crimes against peace: participating in a conspiracy to plan a war of aggression; (3) war crimes: a violation of custom and laws of war, use of slave labor, killing of hostages; and (4) crimes against humanity.

The trial itself lasted 218 days, and some 360 witnesses gave either written or verbal testimony. A new simultaneous translation system allowed the trial to proceed efficiently and swiftly in four languages. Although the defense was given the right to call its own witnesses, it was not allowed to bring forth any evidence against the Allies.

The proceedings at Nuremberg laid bare before the world the horrific crimes committed by the Third Reich. Most revealing were testimonies regarding the brutalities of the death camps. When shown German films of concentration camps, some of the defendants wept or became noticeably upset.

One aspect of the trial that caused debate at the time was the legality of trying military officers. Some suggested it was the role of military officers to carry out orders, but this defense was disallowed at Nuremberg. The prevailing view held that German military leaders had knowingly approved and planned aggressive war and had sanctioned war crimes.

On 1 October 1946, U.S. Army Colonel Burton Andrus led 21 defendants into the somber courtroom. (Martin Bormann was tried in absentia, Robert Ley had committed suicide, and Gustav Krupp von Bohlen und Halbach was too weak to be present.) Sir Geoffrey Lawrence announced that the verdicts would be delivered first, followed by the sentencing. Twelve defendants were sentenced to death by hanging (the counts on which they were found guilty are in parentheses): Hans Frank (3 and 4), Wilhelm Frick (2, 3, and 4), Hermann Göring (all four), Alfred Jodl (all four), Ernst Kaltenbrunner (3 and 4), Wilhelm Keitel (all four), Robert Ley (all four), Joachim von Ribbentrop (all four), Alfred Rosenberg (all four), Fritz Saukel (3 and 4), Arthur Seyss-Inquart (2, 3, and 4), and Julius Streicher (1 and 4).

Göring escaped the hangman's noose by committing suicide with poison smuggled into the prison. Franz von Papen, Hans Fritzsche, and Hjalmar Schacht were the only defendants to be acquitted. Charges against Gustav Krupp von Bohlen und Halbach were dropped on the grounds that he was physically unable to stand trial. The remaining defendants received various terms, ranging up to life in prison: Karl Dönitz, 10 years (2 and 3); Walter Funk, life imprisonment (2, 3, and 4); Rudolf Hess, life imprisonment (1 and 2); Konstantin Neurath, 15 years (all 4); Erich Raeder, life imprison-

ment (1, 2 and 3); Baldur von Schirach, 4 to 20 years (1 and 4); and Albert Speer, 4 to 20 years (3 and 4). Of those imprisoned, Rudolf Hess lived the longest. He died in Spandau Prison in 1987 at age 93.

Even before the trial ended in 1946, debate began on the validity of the tribunal. Although some have argued that the IMT was merely a case of the victor trying the vanquished, it nonetheless exposed the horrors of the Third Reich, most especially the Holocaust, the use of slave labor, and the heinous war crimes.

Gene Mueller

See also

Bormann, Martin Ludwig; Churchill, Sir Winston L. S.; Dönitz, Karl; Frick, Wilhelm; Göring, Hermann Wilhelm; Hess, Walter Richard Rudolf; Hitler, Adolf; Holocaust, The; Jodl, Alfred; Keitel, Wilhelm; Moscow Conference; Potsdam Conference; Raeder, Erich; Ribbentrop, Ulrich Friedrich Willy Joachim von; Rosenberg, Alfred; Saukel, Fritz; Speer, Albert; Stalin, Josef; Tehran Conference; Yalta Conference

References

Andrus, Burton C. *I Was the Nuremberg Jailer*. New York: Coward-McCann, 1969.
Conot, Robert W. *Justice at Nuremberg*. New York: Harper and Row, 1983.
Davidson, Eugene. *The Trial of the Germans*. London: Macmillan, 1966.
International Military Tribunal. *Trial of the Major War Criminals*. 41 vols. Washington DC: U.S. Government Printing Office, 1949.
Persico, Joseph. *Nuremberg: Infamy on Trial*. New York: Penguin, 1994.
Smith, Bradley F. *Reaching Judgment at Nuremberg*. New York: Basic Books, 1977.
———. *The Road to Nuremberg*. New York: Basic Books, 1981.
Sprecher, David A. *Inside the Nuremberg Trials: A Prosecutor's Comprehensive Account*. 2 vols. Lanham, MD: University Press of America, 1999.
Taylor, Telford. *Final Report of the Secretary of the Army on the Nuremberg War Crime Trials under Control Council Law No. 10*. Washington, DC: U.S. Government Printing Office, 1949.
———. *The Anatomy of the Nuremberg Trials: A Personal Memoir*. New York: Alfred A. Knopf, 1992.

Iran

During World War II, Iran was occupied by British and Soviet troops, with the United States becoming an important new factor in Iranian politics. Germany had a significant economic influence and presence in Iran prior to the outbreak of the war, for in the 1930s, Reza Shah Pahlavi (r. 1925–1941), founder of the new dynasty, had turned to Germany for economic assistance. The shah's sympathy toward Germany, which had no tradition of imperial intervention in Iran or the Middle East, was well known, along with his distrust of Britain and the Soviet Union, both of which had dominated Iran in the nineteenth and early twentieth centuries.

U.S. Lend-Lease fighters and bombers intended for the Soviet Union at a delivery depot in Iran. (Hulton-Deutsch Collection/Corbis)

When the war began in Europe in September 1939, Reza Shah declared Iran's neutrality. However, after the Germans attacked the Soviet Union in June 1941, Iranian involvement in the war became inevitable. The USSR and Great Britain, Iran's perennial enemies, once again formed an alliance. As German troops pushed eastward and threatened the Caucasus, the strategic significance of Iran for the Allies grew. The Allied objectives in Iran were to protect the British-controlled oil fields in Khuzistan; to employ Iran and, in particular, its newly built Trans-Iranian Railroad to channel military supplies to the Soviet Union; and to curb the activities of German agents in Iran.

The British and Soviet representatives in Iran demanded that the government expel German nationals and let the Allies use the railroad to transport war materials. When Reza Shah refused to comply on the grounds of Iran's neutrality, the Allies invaded and occupied the country. On 25 August 1941, Soviet forces entered Iran from the northwest and the British entered from Iraq. The Allied forces suppressed Iranian military and naval resistance in just three days. Left with no choice, Reza Shah abdicated on September 1941, and his 22-

year-old son, Muhammad Reza, succeeded him. Reza Shah was sent into exile and died in 1944 in South Africa.

The fate of Iran in World War II resembled that which had prevailed in World War I: once more, Iran was occupied and dominated by foreign powers. The Soviet and British zones of occupation were consistent with the spheres of influence into which Iran had been divided by the humiliating Anglo-Russia Convention of 1907. The Soviets occupied the north, the British took control in the south, and Tehran and other central areas were put under joint Anglo-Soviet protection. In January 1942, Iran, the Soviet Union, and Great Britain signed the Tripartite Treaty of Alliance, whereby the great powers promised to respect the territorial integrity, sovereignty, and political independence of Iran; to safeguard the Iranian economy from the effects of the war; and to withdraw from Iranian territory within six months of the cessation of hostilities.

By the spring of 1942, Iran had severed diplomatic relations with Germany, Italy, and Japan and expelled their nationals. On 9 September 1943, Iran declared war on Germany. Two months later, one of the most important Allied meetings of the war, the Tehran Conference, was held, with the participation of U.S. President Franklin D. Roosevelt, British Prime Minister Winston L. S. Churchill, and Soviet leader Josef Stalin. Recognizing the help provided by Iran to their war effort, the three Allied leaders promised during the meeting to provide economic assistance to Iran and address its problems after the war.

The war had a devastating impact on Iran. It lost effective sovereignty to the domination of the occupying powers, and the central government that had been strengthened by Reza Shah became ineffective. Political instability and social disintegration grew, and economic hardship developed. Further, the use of major roads and the Trans-Iranian Railroad for the transportation of supplies to the Soviet Union disrupted Iranian trade; the demands of Allied troops aggravated inflation; and a poor harvest in 1942 led to widespread famine. Short-lived cabinets were unable to deal with the emergency situation, resulting in social unrest and the rise of separatist movements. All of these factors and the new political freedom resulting from the paralysis of a dysfunctional government led to a surge in political activity by various groups and parties. Political conflict among them was encouraged by the occupying powers.

During the course of their involvement, the Soviet Union and Britain revived and intensified their rivalry in Iran, a contest that was an integral part of what had been known as the "Great Game" in the late nineteenth and early twentieth centuries. Each side tried to expand its own influence and to limit the other's influence. The Soviets closed their zone of occupation to free entry. They supported left-wing trade unions in the north and the Communist Party, which had been banned in 1937 but was revived in 1941 under the new name of Tudeh (Masses). The Soviets also patronized the separatist leftist movements in Iranian Kurdistan and Azerbaijan. One result of these Soviet activities was the establishment of an autonomous state of Azerbaijan in December 1945. Meanwhile, the British in the south supported conservative elements, including the tribes, Muslim clerics, and the proponents of monarchy. They also sponsored the right-wing, pro-Western, and anticommunist National Will Party.

During the war, Washington became aware of the economic importance of Iran, stemming from its oil and its strategic location. After the United States entered the war, American troops arrived in Iran. The Persian Gulf Command, which eventually numbered 30,000 men, helped orchestrate the movement of supplies from the gulf to northern Iran, where they were handed over to the Soviets. American financial and military advisers were also sent to Iran at the request of the Iranian government. Between 1942 and 1943, a financial mission headed by Arthur Millspaugh worked on reorganizing Iran's finances. A mission headed by Colonel H. Norman Schwarzkopf took charge of the reorganization of the Gendarmerie (rural police).

In the first half of 1944, two American oil companies and then the Soviet government attempted to receive oil concessions from the Iranian government in order to undermine the monopoly of the Anglo-Iranian Oil Company. The Majles (Parliament), however, passed a bill, authored mainly by Mohammad Mossadeq, that prohibited oil-concession agreements with any foreign company until after the end of the war.

British and American troops withdrew from Iran in January 1946, whereas the Soviet occupation of the northern provinces of Azerbaijan and Kurdistan lasted until May 1946 when, under pressure from the United Nations, the Soviets withdrew.

Elena Andreeva

See also

Caucasus Campaign; Churchill, Sir Winston L. S.; Roosevelt, Franklin D.; Stalin, Josef; Tehran Conference

References

Lenczowski, George. *Russia and the West in Iran, 1918–1948: A Study in Big-Power Rivalry.* Ithaca, NY: Cornell University Press, 1949.

Ramazani, Rouhollah K. *Iran's Foreign Policy, 1941–1973: A Study of Foreign Policy in Modernizing Nations.* Charlottesville: University Press of Virginia, 1975.

Saikal, Amin. *The Rise and Fall of the Shah.* Princeton, NJ: Princeton University Press, 1980.

Wilber, Donald N. *Iran: Past and Present.* Princeton, NJ: Princeton University Press, 1955.

Iraq

The Middle Eastern nation of Iraq was the object of a peripheral but critical struggle between Great Britain and the Axis powers in 1941. Iraq was a major oil producer (2.5 million tons in 1940), and were that nation to side with Hitler, its location on the Persian Gulf would have enabled Germany to threaten British trade, supplies, and troop movements to and from India. Granted nominal independence by Britain in 1930, Iraq was a Hashemite monarchy. The 1930 treaty that established Iraq's *de jure* independence also protected British oil interests there and granted Britain military bases at Habbaniya, about 25 miles west of Baghdad, and near Basra.

Iraq was unstable, and there were numerous coups and coup attempts. In December 1938, pro-British General Nuri al-Said came to power. Instability in Iraq increased, however, when King Ghazi I died in an automobile accident in April 1939. As the new king, Faisal II, was only four, his uncle Abdul Illah acted as regent. Meanwhile, Nuri put down an attempted coup by a group of army officers in March 1939 and another in February 1940. Nuri wanted to declare war on Germany but encountered opposition from Iraqi nationalists who sought concessions from Britain first. In consequence, Nuri followed Egypt's lead and declared Iraq's neutrality. Relations with Germany were severed, although those with Italy were not.

The Camel Corps of the Arab Legion practices firing from camelback in Transjordan. (Corbis)

Axis successes in the Mediterranean beginning in the fall of 1940 encouraged Iraqi nationalists, who believed that the circumstances were right for Iraq to end remaining British control. Another issue involved the long-standing Iraqi opposition to British policies in Palestine.

In March 1940, Rashid Ali replaced Nuri as prime minister, although Nuri remained in the government as foreign minister. Rashid Ali now came under the influence of four nationalist, pro-Axis Iraqi army generals who called themselves the "Golden Square." In March 1941, however, the regent secured Rashid Ali's resignation because of the latter's pro-Axis connections and reluctance to break relations with Italy. Taha al-Hashimi became prime minister. Axis military successes and hints of Axis aid emboldened the Golden Square, which staged a coup on 2 April that reinstated Rashid Ali in power. He immediately formed a cabinet that contained a number of individuals known to have Axis connections. The regent and Nuri fled.

Encouraged by hints of Axis aid, Rashid Ali refused to honor British demands to enforce provisions of the 1930 treaty that allowed the transportation of British troops from Basra across Iraq. The Iraqi government also positioned troops and artillery around the British bases in Iraq. Fighting broke out at the British air base at Habbaniya on 2 May when Iraqi troops opened fire. The British air force immediately went into action, and Britain also dispatched some 5,800 troops, including the 1,500-man Arab Legion from Transjordan under the command of Major John B. Glubb. It was soon obvious that the British would triumph over the five poorly trained and inadequately equipped divisions of the Iraqi army unless the Axis powers immediately dispatched assistance.

The German government now brought pressure to bear on the Vichy government of France, which then ordered French High Commissioner of the Levant General Henri Dentz to allowed the transit of Axis aid to Iraq through Syria. Axis arms and equipment then began to be transported via Aleppo to Mosul to assist Rashid Ali, albeit it in insufficient quantities to affect the outcome of the fighting. Meanwhile, British forces broke the siege at Habbaniya. The British occupied Falluja on 20 May and surrounded Baghdad by the end of the month. Rashid Ali, some supporters, and the German and Italian ministers fled to Iran. In deference to Nuri and Regent Abdul Illah, the British did not enter Baghdad. This decision allowed the remnants of the Golden Square to attack Baghdad's Jewish community and kill some 150 Jews there.

Nuri again became prime minister, with a pro-British administration. Following its return to the British side, Iraq became an important supply center for Allied assistance to the Soviet Union until the end of the war. The government broke diplomatic relations with Vichy France on 18 November 1941, and it declared war on Germany, Italy, and Japan on 16 January 1943, the same day on which it announced its adherence to the UN Declaration.

Jack Vahram Kalpakian and Spencer C. Tucker

See also

Auchinleck, Sir Claude John Eyre; Dentz, Henry Ferdinand; Egypt; France, Vichy; India; Iran; Nuri al-Said; Syria

References

Butt, Gerald. *The Lion in the Sand: The British in the Middle East.* London: Bloomsbury, 1995.

Hamdi, Walid M. *Rashid al-Gailani and the Nationalist Movement in Iraq, 1939–1941: A Political and Military Study of the British Campaign in Iraq and the National Revolution of May 1941.* London: Darf, 1987.

Hopwood, Derek, Habib Ishow, and Thomas Koszinowski, eds. *Iraq: Power and Society.* Reading, UK: Ithaca Press, 1993.

Kedourie, Elie. "Operation Babylon: The Story of the Rescue of the Jews of Iraq." *New Republic* 199, no. 1 (17 October 1988): 48–50.

Marr, Phebe. *The Modern History of Iraq.* Boulder, CO: Westview Press, 2004.

Simons, Geoff. *Iraq: From Sumer to Saddam.* London: Macmillan, 1994.

Warner, Geoffrey. *Iraq and Syria, 1941.* Newark: University of Delaware Press, 1974.

Ireland

Irish nationalists had long demanded independence from Great Britain. Following bloodshed and the passage of home rule legislation in Britain, the Irish Free State came into being in December 1921. In 1937, with the promulgation of a new constitution, the new state became known as Eire (Ireland in Gaelic). Not included in this sovereign nation were the six largely Protestant counties in the north; these were known as Northern Ireland or Ulster and remained part of the United Kingdom.

Parliamentary elections in 1932 had brought the Fianna Fail Party to power, and Eamon de Valera became president of the executive council. In April 1938, de Valera negotiated agreements with London that removed British naval installations and troops from the republic, making Eire responsible for its own defense. Other agreements provided for Ireland to pay a final settlement of the land annuities, as well

as annual payments to compensate Britain for losses sustained in the violence of the 1920s. Each nation was also accorded favored-nation status in trade with the other. All causes of difference between Great Britain and Eire were thus removed, except for the vexing question of partition. Benefiting from popular support for the diplomatic agreements, de Valera won the elections of June 1938, giving the Fianna Fail a decisive majority.

The outbreak of World War II provided de Valera another opportunity to show that Eire was independent of Great Britain. In contrast to other members of the British Commonwealth, Eire at once declared its neutrality, a stance supported by the majority of its 2.9 million people. In any case, the country was in no position to make a major military contribution in troops. In September 1939, its army numbered about 7,500 men, its navy consisted of two patrol boats, and its air service had only four effective fighter aircraft. However, the inability of the Royal Navy to use the ports returned to the Irish in 1938 was a serious handicap for the Allies in the Battle of the Atlantic. During the war, de Valera steadfastly rejected British government offers, tendered even by Prime Minister Winston L. S. Churchill, to resolve partition in return for an end to Irish neutrality.

There was also some pro-German sentiment among the Irish. Anti-Semitic bills were brought before the Dail (the Irish Parliament), and de Valera refused to expel Axis diplomats; further, on Adolf Hitler's death, he went in person to the German Embassy to express his condolences. However, Eire did allow British overflights of its territory, and it returned downed Allied pilots to Northern Ireland instead of interning them; it also allowed British patrol craft in its waters. Thousands of Irish also volunteered for service in the Allied armies. During the war, more than 180,000 people left Eire for Northern Ireland or the United Kingdom, 38,544 of whom volunteered for service with the British armed forces, including some 7,000 deserters from the Irish army and several thousand Irish citizens living in the United Kingdom.

Acts of violence by the illegal Irish Republican Army (IRA) were a problem for the Eire government, which feared the British might use these incidents as an excuse to intervene. During the war, de Valera sharply increased the size of the Irish army and auxiliary forces to some 250,000 men (albeit poorly armed and trained) in order to forestall this possibility. Ireland suffered economically during the war, but de Valera doggedly pursued his policies. In 1948, Eire became the Republic of Ireland.

Northern Ireland was an important base for Allied operations during the war. Soon after the Japanese attack on Pearl Harbor, U.S. President Franklin D. Roosevelt and Churchill agreed that Northern Ireland and Scotland would provide bases for the Allied troop buildup for the invasion of France. The Americans agreed to take over the defense of Northern

The arrival of U.S. troops in Northern Ireland, 24 January 1942. (Photo by PNA Roto/Getty Images)

Ireland, thus allowing British soldiers to be deployed elsewhere. Ireland officially protested this agreement.

The first of hundreds of thousands of American soldiers arrived in Northern Ireland in late January 1942. During the course of the war, the United States constructed new bases and airfields and improved the naval facilities at Derry. Early troop deployments to Northern Ireland trained and took part in Operation TORCH and the North Africa Campaigns. Northern Ireland also played a major role in the massive buildup for the Normandy Campaign. U.S. troops at bases in Armagh, Cookstown, Lurgan, Newcastle, Newry, and Omagh trained for the D day landings, and units of the Eighth Air Force of the U.S. Army Air Forces operated out of the air base at Greencastle. Aircraft assembly, testing, service, and repair stations were built in Langford and Lodge. Airfields and ports were also used to protect the convoys ferrying troops and materials across the Atlantic Ocean.

Recognizing the importance of Northern Ireland to Allied plans, the German Luftwaffe bombed targets in Belfast as well as the Greencastle airfield. Throughout the war, however, the people of Northern Ireland accommodated American soldiers by building cinemas and clubs. As in Britain, local groups arranged entertainment and hospitality events. Unfortunately for the people of Ireland, sectarian violence continued on the island after the war, as the IRA sought to bring about the union of Northern Ireland with the Republic of Ireland.

Robert W. Duvall and Spencer C. Tucker

See also
Atlantic, Battle of the; Churchill, Sir Winston L. S.; OVERLORD, Operation; Roosevelt, Franklin D; TORCH, Operation

References
Carroll, Joseph T. *Ireland in the War Years, 1939–1945*. Lanham, MD: International Scholars Publications, 1997.

Doherty, Richard. *Irish Men and Women in the Second World War.* Dublin: Four Courts Press, 1999.

Fisk, R. *In Time of War: Ireland, Ulster, and the Price of Neutrality, 1939–45*. Philadelphia: University of Pennsylvania Press, 1983.

Foster, R. F. *Modern Ireland, 1600–1972*. New York: Penguin, 1990.

Ironside, Sir William Edmund (First Baron Ironside) (1880–1959)

British army general and chief of the Imperial General Staff from 1939 to 1940. Born 6 May 1880 in Edinburgh, William Ironside graduated from the Royal Military Academy, Woolwich and was commissioned into the Royal Artillery in 1899. He served in the Boer War and on the Western Front in World War I, rising to command a brigade by 1918. Ironside commanded British forces in Archangel, Russia, during the 1918–1919 expedition that attempted to overturn the Bolshevik regime and was knighted. A large man, he was (naturally) widely known as "Tiny."

Ironside's service between the wars was, like that of many officers in those thin years for the British military, a difficult period of marking time while awaiting the retirement or death of those senior to him. He served in India and was named to command the Eastern District of Britain in 1936. But as he noted in a diary that was later published, there were few men and even less equipment in the British military at the time. Early in 1938, Ironside became governor of Gibraltar, but he was called home as inspector general of Overseas Forces in May 1939.

On 3 September 1939, Ironside was named chief of the Imperial General Staff (CIGS) by Leslie Hore-Belisha, Prime Minister Neville Chamberlain's war secretary, despite the fact that he had never held any staff position in the War Office. Although convinced the Middle East would be the critical theater of war, Ironside understood the need to bolster French defenses. However, his impatient and brusque manner limited his effectiveness during the trying period of the "Phony War." In early 1940, he worked closely with First Lord of the Admiralty Winston L. S. Churchill to promote a Scandinavian strategy to outflank the Germans. The relationship between the two men cooled when the Norwegian Campaign descended into disaster in April.

On 27 May 1940, as the Germans swept through northern France, Ironside was replaced as CIGS and shifted to command the Home Forces. He readily admitted he had been ill suited for the CIGS post and welcomed a return to a real command. Less than two months later, however, Alan Brooke replaced him, and Ironside retired. He was promoted to field marshal and created Baron (Lord) Ironside of Archangel in 1941. He died on 22 September 1959 in London.

Christopher H. Sterling

See also
Brooke, Sir Alan Francis; Churchill, Sir Winston L. S.
References
Bond, Brian. "Ironside." In John Keegan, ed., *Churchill's Generals*, 17–33. New York: Grove Weidenfeld, 1991.

British General William Edmund Ironside, 1940. (Corbis)

Ironside, Lord. *Archangel: 1918–1919*. London: Constable, 1953.
Ironside, Lord, ed. *High Road to Command: The Diaries of Maj.-Gen Sir Edmund Ironside, 1920–22*. London: Leo Cooper, 1972.
Macleod, Col. Roderick, and Denis Kelly, eds. *Time Unguarded: The Ironside Diaries, 1937–1940*. New York: McKay, 1962.

Ishiwara Kanji (1889–1949)

Japanese army general and head of the East Asian League. Born in Akita Prefecture, Japan, on 18 January 1889, Ishiwara Kanji graduated from the Military Academy in 1909. Following routine service in Korea, he entered the Army Staff College and graduated second in his class in November 1918. He spent the years from 1922 to 1924 in independent study in Germany, which exposed him to European military thought and gave him an opportunity to observe the results of World War I.

Ishiwara's experience in Europe, as well as his adherence to the Nichiren sect of Buddhism, led him to theorize that in the future, Japan would engage in an apocalyptic war with the United States. This struggle, which he dubbed "the Final War," would be a protracted total war in which airpower would play a decisive role. Ishiwara believed, however, that Japan could overcome its material inferiority by harnessing the economic resources of the Asian mainland, especially Manchuria and Mongolia. He published his theories in a book entitled *Thoughts on the Final Global War.*

In 1928, Ishiwara was posted to Manchuria, where he served as chief of operations for the Japanese Guandong (Kwantung) Army. Impelled by his sense of the urgency of preparing for the Final War, Ishiwara played a major role in planning and carrying out the Japanese army's seizure of Manchuria beginning in 1931. Shortly before the establishment of the puppet state of Manzhouguo (Manchukuo) in 1932, he returned to Japan. Promoted to colonel, he headed the Operations Section of the army General Staff. After becoming a major general, he was in charge of General Staff's Operations Division. Nonetheless, Ishiwara's considerable earlier influence as a military theorist waned during the 1930s. Marginalized for his tacit support of a failed officers' rebellion in February 1936, as well as for his increasingly outspoken criticism of Japan's war with China (he was chief of staff of the Guandong Army in 1937 and 1938), he was promoted to lieutenant general but was forced into retirement in 1941.

Ishiwara headed the Toa Remmei (East Asian League), which opposed Premier Tōjō Hideki's policies during the war. He briefly returned as an adviser to the "Surrender Cabinet" and urged that Japan conclude a peace.

Following the war, Ishiwara was investigated by the Allied occupation authorities, who briefly considered trying him as a war criminal. Instead, he testified as a prosecution witness at the Tokyo War Crimes Trials in 1947. Ishiwara died in Akita Prefecture on 15 August 1949.

John M. Jennings

See also

Guandong Army; Manzhouguo ; Tōjō Hideki

References

Barnhart, Michael A. *Japan Prepares for Total War: The Search for Economic Security, 1919–1941.* Ithaca, NY: Cornell University Press, 1987.

Peattie, Mark R. *Ishiwara Kanji and Japan's Confrontation with the West.* Princeton, NJ: Princeton University Press, 1975.

Ismay, Hastings Lionel (First Baron Ismay of Wormington) (1887–1965)

British army general and chief of staff to the British War Cabinet. Born 21 June 1887 in Naini Tal, India, Hastings Ismay graduated from Sandhurst and was commissioned in the Royal Army in 1905, posted to the cavalry in India. During World War I, he served in British Somaliland. He returned to India between 1922 and 1925 and again as military secretary

Lord Hastings Lionel Ismay, secretary-general of NATO (1952–1957), with the newly adopted NATO emblem behind him. (Photo by Keystone/Getty Images)

to the viceroy, from 1931 to 1933. Early in his life, he was affectionately dubbed "Pug" for his amiable expression.

Ismay served in the War Office in Britain as assistant secretary (1925–1930), deputy secretary (1936–1938), and secretary (1938–1939) of the Committee of Imperial Defense. He was then named deputy military secretary to the War Cabinet (1939–1940) under Neville Chamberlain. When Winston L. S. Churchill became prime minister on 10 May 1940, Ismay served as his military chief of staff. He was promoted to lieutenant general in 1942 and general in 1944. All with whom he worked during the war, from Churchill down, attested to his invaluable and essential efforts, keeping paper moving and all channels of communication open. Ismay attended virtually all the summit conferences and acted as the primary channel between the service chiefs of staff and the cabinet. Both patient and informed, he was also not afraid to express the truth and could be critical when necessary and supportive at other times. Ismay admired Churchill greatly, but he could disagree with him; similarly, he was evenhanded with the chiefs of staff, sometimes adopting their viewpoints and at other times disagreeing or suggesting alternatives. With his two assistants, Ian Jacob and Leslie Hollis (both of whom became generals and were knighted), Ismay was the essential oil in the British High Command.

After retiring from the army in 1946, Ismay served as chief of staff to the viceroy of India, Lord Louis Mountbatten, from March to November 1947 and was then made a peer (becoming First Baron Ismay of Wormington). In Churchill's second government, he served as secretary of state for Commonwealth relations (1951–1952). He became the first secretary-general of the North Atlantic Treaty Organization (NATO) in 1952, retiring five years later. Ismay died in Broadway, England, on 17 December 1965.

Christopher H. Sterling

See also
Churchill, Sir Winston L. S.; Great Britain, Army
References
Ismay, General Lord. *Memoirs*. New York: Viking, 1960.
Leasor, James. *The Clock with Four Hands*. New York: Reynal, 1959. (Published in England as *War at the Top*.)
Richardson, Charles. *From Churchill's Secret Circle to the BBC: The Biography of Lt. General Sir Ian Jacob*. London: Brassey's, 1991.
Wingate, Sir Ronald. *Lord Ismay: A Biography*. London: Hutchinson, 1970.

Italy, Air Force

In the period between World Wars I and II, the Royal Italian Air Force (Regia Aeronautica) was regarded as one of the most advanced in the world, winning 96 international aviation awards. In 1939, Italy also had the third-largest European commercial air fleet, behind only Germany and the United Kingdom. Moreover, with the possible exception of Japan, Italy had more interwar combat experience than any other nation, from the suppression of the Senussi in Libya to the Italo-Ethiopian War and culminating in the Spanish Civil War, where the Italians contributed more aircraft than did Germany. Between 1935 and 1939, Italy expended 1,500 aircraft in combat, and an additional 925 planes were exported. The Royal Italian Air Force was also the most Fascist of the three services and the favorite of Italian dictator Benito Mussolini and the Fascist Party.

Yet in World War II, the Italian air force was found wanting. When Italy entered the war in June 1940, its air force had almost 1,000 front-line aircraft, backed by about 2,000 second- and third-line aircraft. But these figures were deceptive. Italy had a few high-performance planes—those that had set a number of aviation records—but most of the aircraft were, in fact, obsolete.

The chief of staff and undersecretary of the Regia Aeronautica, General Giuseppe Valle, commanded the air force. Italy was organized into three air zones, with several regional commands and army-air cooperation units and land- and sea-based naval reconnaissance units. The air force retained control of all pilots, and coordination between the three military branches was poor at best. The lack of a coherent air philosophy and an effective building program compounded the problem.

General Valle was relieved of his command on 31 October 1939, charged with responsibility for the poor state of the air force when it was mobilized at the beginning of the war. He was placed on trial, and although he was later freed, the public mistakenly held him responsible for the state of unpreparedness. General Francesco Pricolo commanded the air force from 31 October 1939 to 14 November 1941, when he was, in turn, replaced by General Rino Corso Fougier until 26 July 1943.

Italy joined the war in June 1940 and only fought in the Battle for France for several weeks, after which it received some French aircraft. Later, Mussolini insisted on sending aircraft to Belgium to assist in the Battle of Britain. The Germans thought the planes would be far more useful in North Africa. They proved hopelessly inadequate in the skies over Britain and had to be withdrawn. In 1941, Italy sent a more effective air contingent to fight in the Soviet Union.

In the Mediterranean Theater, the Italian air force was invoked in air strikes against Malta, targeted on British merchant ships and naval units operating near Italy. It also conducted raids against Gibraltar and Palestine and even as far afield as the Persian Gulf. However, the Italians soon learned that aircraft that had been successful against stationary merchant ships docked in harbors during the Spanish Civil War were ineffective in high-altitude bombing attacks against warships. Indeed, early in the war, the aircraft occasionally attacked Italian warships by mistake, although recognition improved as the war unfolded. But not until March 1941 did the air force place liaison officers on board warships at sea.

> On any given day, operational efficiency in the Italian Air Force was rarely higher than 70%.

The Italian air force was more successful in fighting in the Balkans, against Greece and Yugoslavia. It also fought in the Western Desert from 1940 to 1943, as well as in Ethiopia. When fielding modern machines—the later models with German engines—the air force was effective. But despite the fact that the Italian air force had operated in Libya since 1911, its aircraft still lacked dust filters on the eve of war, and its tactics were reminiscent of World War I acrobatics.

With the exception of three fighters embarked on two battleships late in the war, the only sea-based air effort (apart from ship-launched reconnaissance aircraft) involved the crash conversion of two passenger ships into aircraft carriers. Neither was completed by the armistice. The failure to develop aircraft carriers seriously affected Italian naval operations in the war, largely because of the short range of Italy's land-based fighters.

On the whole, Italy's aviation industry was badly organized and inefficient, producing a wide variety of aircraft types in small numbers. The various companies involved resisted manufacturing each other's more successful designs, and the almost artisan production methods resulted in production times that were more than 50 percent longer than for comparable German aircraft. The Italian air force largely depended on radial engines, but these low-powered machines seldom exceeded 1,000 hp. Adoption of the bulkier but much more powerful German-designed Daimler-Benz in-line engine helped solve that problem.

The fact that the CR-42, a wood-and-canvas biplane fighter with nonretractable landing gear, was still in production in 1944 (and a serious candidate for the Daimler-Benz engine) reveals the sad state of Italian aircraft production. Italian fighters were almost all underarmed, due to financial considerations and poorly designed, weak wings. Radios were not installed in all aircraft until 1942; fuel was stored in thinly lined, leaking tanks; most airfields were dirt runways; and pilots were slow to adapt to closed canopies. On any given day, operational efficiency was rarely higher than 70 percent. Ground-support aircraft, based on precepts developed by General Amadeo Mecozzi, were so poorly designed that early in the war, Italy simply retired its ground-attack planes and purchased 159 Ju-87 Stuka dive-bombers from Germany.

One area in which the Italian air force excelled was the torpedo-bomber. Although use of this plane was hindered by interservice rivalry before the war, the torpedo-bomber was deployed to units by late 1940. German air units later successfully emulated Italian torpedo-bombing tactics and purchased torpedoes from Italy. Yet the Italians chose simply to adapt a three-engine SM-79 level bomber for torpedo bombing rather than design a true torpedo-bomber.

Although Italy formally embraced the concept of strategic bombing developed by General Giulio Douhet, it did not practice it. Ironically, Douhet had more influence on British and U.S. air policies then at home. Italy did produce a partially successful four-engine bomber, the P-108, but only in small numbers. With the armistice in September 1943, there were two Italian air forces: one for the Fascist state in the north and another, utilizing many different Allied aircraft, that fought for the Allied government in the south.

Jack Greene

See also

Aircraft, Bombers; Aircraft, Fighter; Balbo, Italo; Britain, Battle of; Malta, Air Battles of; Mussolini, Benito

References

Arena, Nino. *La Regia Aeronautica, 1939–1943.* 4 vols. Rome: Uffico Storico, 1982–1986.

Dunning, Chris. *Courage Alone: The Italian Air Force, 1940–1943.* Aldershot, UK: Hikoki Publications, 1998.

Greene, Jack, and Alessandro Massignani. *The Naval War in the Mediterranean, 1940–1943.* London: Chatham Publishing, 1998.

Rastelli, Achille. *La portaerei italiana.* Milan, Italy: Mursia, 2001.

Shores, Christopher. *Regia Aeronautica.* 2 vols. Carrolton, TX: Squadron/Signal Publications, 1976.

Italy, Army

When Italy entered World War II on 10 June 1940, the Regio Esercito (Royal Army) had 1,630,000 men under arms. This figure would rise during the war to 2,563,000. King Victor Emmanuel III was nominal commander in chief, with the title of *comandante supremo delle Forse Armato dello Stato* (supreme commander of the Royal Army of the Kingdom of Italy), but Italian dictator Benito Mussolini exercised actual command.

Contrary to popular misconceptions, some units of the army fought well in World War II, but the army itself was basically a light infantry force lacking in equipment and poorly prepared for a modern European war. In 1940, it numbered 73 divisions—43 infantry; 5 Alpine; 3 light; 2 motorized; 3 armored; 12 "self-transportable," with a regiment of truck-drawn artillery; 3 militia, and 2 Libyan. Many military formations were understrength, and much of the army's equipment was obsolete at best. Morale was not always optimal, for many Italians thought their nation was on the wrong side in the war. The men were often indifferently led, as many officer appointments were made on the basis of party loyalty rather than ability.

An Italian infantry division was composed of two infantry regiments, an artillery regiment, an engineer company, and occasionally an attached Blackshirt (Voluntary Militia for National Security, or MVSN) legion. The "binary" division had only about 10,000 men at full strength. The royal infantry regiments pledged allegiance to the king, but the highly motivated Blackshirt legions, which numbered about 1,300 men each, swore loyalty to Mussolini. Many regular army officers deeply resented the inclusion of Blackshirt regiments in the army. In 1940, the equivalent of four MSVN divisions were destroyed in fighting in North Africa. Eventually, "M battalions" made of Blackshirts fought in the Soviet Union and in Yugoslavia. They also manned antiaircraft artillery batteries throughout the Italian Empire.

In 1940, the Italian army had more than 8,000 artillery pieces, which were classified as divisional (field), corps (medium), and army (heavy). Much of the artillery was left over from World War I, and some guns were modernized World War I prizes, such as pieces manufactured at Skoda. In 1940, Italy had more than 1,200 tanks, but most were only two-man light "tankettes." Many of the larger models were too thinly armored to stop armor-piercing bullets, let alone stand up to northern European armor.

On 20 June 1940, Mussolini entered the war by attacking France in the western Alps with 32 divisions. The Italians did poorly, being largely held at bay by 5 French divisions. When the leaders in Paris surrendered on 24 June, the Italians took a small portion of southeastern France. The French admitted to having 37 soldiers killed in the campaign; Italian losses were 631.

On 28 October 1940, on short notice, Mussolini sent Italian troops into Greece from Albania. The invasion involved fewer than 100,000 Italian troops, and by late November, the

Italian Carro Armato MII/39 medium tanks in northern Egypt. (Hulton Archive)

Greek army had driven the Italian army back into Albania, where both forces suffered heavily in a bloody stalemate during the winter. Hitler came to the rescue of his ally on 6 April 1941, when German forces invaded Greece and conquered it in a few short weeks. Italian forces, chiefly the Second Army, also participated in the invasion and conquest of Yugoslavia that same month.

Italy's subsequent occupation of portions of Yugoslavia, France, Corsica, and Greece tied down numerous divisions. Resistance efforts created an ever growing list of casualties. During their occupation of Yugoslavia, the Italians raised a number of units usually organized on religious lines—Catholic, Orthodox Christian, and Muslim—from men seeking to fight the Partisans.

After Hitler invaded the Soviet Union in June 1941, Mussolini eagerly offered Italian forces. Eventually, Italy sent more than 250,000 men to the Soviet Front. Most of the Italian Eighth Army was lost in the Battle of Stalingrad. Included in Italian forces operating mainly in the Ukraine was a Croatian legion raised in Croatia. The Italians also helped organize a small Cossack anticommunist volunteer group. If the units sent to the Soviet Union had been added to forces in North Africa, they might well have affected the outcome of the struggle there.

Italy made a major military effort in North Africa in order to fulfill Mussolini's dream of establishing a great Italian empire. Before the war, Italy had colonized Libya, Eritrea,

Somalia, and Ethiopia (Abyssinia). Italian forces there were, however, underequipped and undergunned compared with the British forces they had to fight.

Amedeo Umberto di Savoia, the duke of Aosta, commanded forces in Italian East Africa (Somalia, Ethiopia, and Eritrea). Of his 256,000 men, 182,000 were "indigenous" levies. European colonists, including some Blackshirt troops, formed part of the units under the duke's command. Fighting there began in early July 1940 when the Italians captured a number of small British posts, but they halted their offensive in the Sudan when intelligence estimates magnified the actual British forces arrayed against them.

On 4 August, the Italians invaded British Somaliland from Ethiopia. They were able to overwhelm the small British forces defending that colony. The British withdrew to Aden, and their losses were only one-tenth those of the Italians. During the 1940–1941 winter, the British built up their resources, and beginning on 19 January 1941, they went on the offensive. By the end of 1941, the British had secured control of Italian East Africa.

In North Africa, Field Marshal Rodolfo Graziani commanded some 236,000 Italian troops. After the defeat of France, Italian forces were shifted to eastern Libya to face the British in Egypt. Major General Richard O'Connor, the British commander in Egypt, had only 31,000 men—largely from the 4th Indian Division and the 7th Armoured Division, later reinforced by the 6th Australian Division. Graziani appeared to be in position to overwhelm the outnumbered British; however, his troops were short of heavy artillery, tanks, and antitank and antiaircraft weapons, as well as transport and logistical support. A shortage of radios often reduced communications to relaying information by messenger.

On 13 September 1940, Graziani, pressed to act prematurely by Mussolini, launched an offensive against the British. The Italians fared badly, and by December, the British had penetrated the Italian chain of forts that were protecting the Libyan border but set too far apart to be mutually supporting. Many Italian units fought effectively but to no avail. By January 1941, the British had taken some 100,000 Italian prisoners.

In February 1941, General Erwin Rommel arrived in Libya with his Afrika Korps (Africa Corps). Although smaller in number than the Italian force and officially under Italian control, the Afrika Korps quickly became the dominant partner. The Germans were far better equipped and more effectively organized and led. By contrast, the Italians lacked mobility, adequate staffing, and an effective system of command and control.

The Italians fought back and forth across northern Africa until they were finally defeated at Tunis in May 1943. A major factor in the Axis defeat was Britain's control of Malta, which enhanced the British ability to intercept by sea and air supplies destined for Axis troops in North Africa. British communications intelligence, notably ULTRA intercepts, also played a role in the Allied victory.

In July 1943, the British and Americans invaded Sicily, held by 190,000 Italians and 40,000 Germans. The performance of Italian units varied widely. The newly formed and indifferently equipped coastal divisions, composed of middle-aged home guards, often surrendered without a fight. Certain defeat in Sicily led the Fascist Grand Council to strip Mussolini of power in July. Marshal Pietro Badoglio then formed a new government, and on 3 September, he signed a secret armistice with the Allies, to go into effect five days later. The Germans, well aware of Italian efforts to switch sides, immediately implemented plans to take control of Italy. When the Germans occupied Rome on 10 September, King Victor Emmanuel III and Badoglio fled south and made Brindisi the new seat of government. Meanwhile, German troops arrested and disarmed Italian army units. More than 600,000 Italians were deported to labor camps in Germany.

German commando units rescued Mussolini on 12 September 1943 and set up the Italian Social Republic (RSI), with its capital at Salo in the north. Many Fascists joined the new RSI army. New units and those from the former Italian army that remained loyal to fascism were formed into various bodies. The first of these was the Esercito Nazionale Repubblicano (ENR, National Republican Army), arranged into four divisions composed of formations newly raised by officers still loyal to Mussolini and mixed with some autonomous older units. Many thousands were recruited into the ENR divisions from among Italian soldiers interned by the Germans. These formations were usually trained in Germany and then deployed to Italy. Most of their fighting was against partisans.

The Guardia Nazionale Repubblicano (GNR, National Republican Guard) replaced the old Blackshirts. Basically a policing unit, it ultimately numbered 80,000 men. It was assigned to local security duties and fighting the partisans. Some GNR units in occupied France and Yugoslavia continued occupation duties in cooperation with the Germans.

As the struggle with the partisans intensified, all ablebodied Fascists were organized into a new militia, the Brigate Nere (Black Brigades). Formed in June 1944 as an armed branch of the RSI's new Fascist Party, this militia eventually numbered some 30,000 men. Composed of fanatical Fascists, it engaged in a no-holds-barred struggle with the partisans. The members of the Black Brigades were motivated by the belief that they would be killed in the event of a Fascist defeat.

The "X" MAS (Decima Mas) unit was an autonomous force organized by Prince Julio Valerio Borghese. Composed of 25,000 volunteers, it gained a reputation for effective and hard fighting against the partisans, primarily Tito's Yugoslav Partisans in Istria. It also included a women's unit. In addition, the Germans recruited Italian volunteers into the Waffen-SS. These units had both Italian and German names and usually were commanded by German officers. They performed well on the Anzio Front and against partisans.

In the south of Italy, the newly reorganized government led by King Emmanuel and Badoglio established an "army of the south," with the status of a cobelligerent force. It was organized as the Corpo Italiano di Liberazione (CIL, Italian Liberation Corps). Composed of old Italian Royal Army men and units, to which new recruits were added, the CIL was formed into six weak divisions, known as "combat groups." With the transfer of some Allied units to participate in the Riviera landings in France, four of these divisions were brought into the line and saw combat. They fought well and sustained casualties of 1,868 dead and 5,187 wounded. Many Italians also served with the Allied forces in support units, handling transportation and ammunition and other supplies. Some of these units were muleteers working in the rugged mountain tracks. Partisan forces also fought in the north, behind German lines. As the war drew to a close, thousands joined partisan groups in order to sanitize their pasts or ensure their futures.

The Italian army suffered substantial casualties in the war. The total of those in the army who died fighting the Allies, in German reprisals following the armistice with the Allies, and in fighting the Germans probably exceeded 300,000 men. In addition, an unknown but large number were wounded, and some 600,000 were taken as prisoners.

A. J. L. Waskey

See also

Afrika Korps; Albania, Role in the War; Artillery Doctrine; Badoglio, Pietro; Balkans Theater; BARBAROSSA, Operation; Cephalonia Island; De Bono, Emilio; El Alamein, Battle of; France, Battle for; Graziani, Rodolfo; Greece, Italy Campaign; Mussolini, Benito; North Africa Campaign; O'Connor, Richard Nugent; Rommel, Erwin Johannes Eugen; Somalia; Stalingrad, Battle of; Tanks, All Powers; Tripartite Pact; Tunis, Battle of; Tunisia Campaign; Victor Emmanuel III, King of Italy; Western European Theater of Operations; Yugoslavia

References

Jowett, Philip S. *The Italian Army, 1940–1945: Africa, 1940–1943.* Oxford: Osprey Publishing, 2000.

———. *The Italian Army, 1940–1945: Europe, 1940–1943.* Oxford: Osprey Publishing, 2000.

———. *The Italian Army, 1940–1945: Italy, 1943–1945.* Oxford: Osprey Publishing, 2001.

Keefer, Louis E. *Italian Prisoners of War in America, 1942–1946: Captives or Allies?* Westport, CT: Greenwood Press, 1992.

Lamb, Richard. *War in Italy, 1943–1945.* New York: St. Martin's Press, 1993.

Madeja, W. Victor. *Italian Army Order of Battle, 1940–1944.* Allentown, PA: Game Marketing, 1990.

Nafziger, George F. *The Italian Order of Battle in WW II: An Organizational History of the Divisions and Independent Brigades of the Italian Army.* 3 vols. West Chester, OH: Nafziger Collections, 1996.

Tyre, Rex. *Mussolini's Soldiers.* Osceola, WI: Motorbooks International, 1995.

———. *Mussolini's Afrika Korps: The Italian Army in North Africa, 1940–1943.* Bayside, NY: Axis Europa Magazine, 1996.

Italy, Home Front (1940–1945)

There was little enthusiasm among Italy's 42 million people when Italian dictator Benito Mussolini took his nation into World War II in June 1940. The timing was conditioned by Mussolini's desire to profit from German military successes and also by the illusion that Italy might compete with its ally for the spoils. During the nearly two decades that Mussolini had held power, his Fascist secret police and judicial system of special courts had silenced the internal opposition. The minority of Italians who totally opposed the war were mostly abroad.

Initial Italian military failures in 1940 were offset in the public eye by the overall Axis successes that extended into the fall of 1941. Weekly propaganda newsreels trumpeted Axis battlefield victories. Such claims were tempered in October 1942, however, when the Western Allies began bombing northern Italian cities. At the same time, the tide clearly was turning against the Axis powers in North Africa. The war at last became a grim reality in urban Italy, with many people forced to abandon the cities. The destruction of the Italian Eighth Army in the Soviet offensives in the Stalingrad area during the 1942–1943 winter only strengthened the public mood. Despite the Fascist regime's eavesdropping and censorship, opposition to Mussolini's policies grew. Strikes in the northern industrial cities in March 1943 surprised the authorities.

For political reasons, Mussolini sought to maintain, insofar as possible, the appearance of normalcy on the domestic front. Morale plummeted, however, with the introduction of rationing in 1941. Coffee, sugar, and soap had already been rationed since 1939. But with the war, the Italian average daily caloric intake progressively declined because Italy was not self-sufficient in food, especially wheat. Per capita daily calorie intake went from 2,100 in 1943 to 1,800 in 1944–1945, although some Italians were able to supplement this with black-market purchases. Only those who worked in heavy labor might have more. This further depressed morale, especially because rations for nonworking Italians, primarily the elderly or disabled, were well below the national average and totally inadequate. The overall situation deteriorated thanks to an inefficient distribution system and increased Allied bombing of railroad lines.

Times were hard for most Italians. By 1942, newspapers were reduced to four pages (and later, to two). Essentials were in short supply. Rationing meant that one might purchase one pair of new shoes or a few articles of clothing per year. Repeated increases in wages were more than offset by inflation, which, although rampant, was not so severe as to wreck the economy. Government deficits ballooned, and the government printed more paper money; circulation of paper money quadrupled between 1940 and 1943, and a lively black market flourished, thanks to the fact that farmers refused to bring their food products to the government collection points. Following the Allied invasion and German occupation, the food situation worsened for most Italians, especially in the more populous, urbanized northern part of the country, where the standard of living fell back to the levels of 1861.

Labor was in short supply, given the country's needs for military manpower. Agricultural requirements compelled Mussolini to recall 600,000 soldiers from the front on the eve of the Greek Campaign to assist with the harvest, with obvious military consequences. In three years of war, Italy mobilized some 5 million men for military service, and an additional 3,850,000 workers of military age were employed in war production at the end of 1941. In 1943, this figure was reduced to 3,638,000, but it was still high.

Italy was handicapped by having few natural resources; its industry lacked even the most basic raw materials. The nation consumed 12 million tons of coal per year, but only 1 million tons came from domestic production. Iron ore was scarce, and Italy had no oil of its own, being forced to rely on Germany, where supplies were also short. Civilian automobile travel was almost completely forbidden, and Italy had to make do with a limited quantity of natural gas from the Po River valley.

U.S. soldier shares his food rations with hungry villagers in the Cassino area in Italy, 1944. (Hulton-Deutsch Collection/Corbis)

Despite problems, Italian industry managed to produce 7,000 artillery pieces, although half these were of 47 mm or smaller caliber; 10,545 aircraft; and some 60,000 trucks of rather high quality. This last figure may be compared with a total of 71,000 private and commercial vehicles produced in 1939. Much of this military equipment, however, was obsolescent. Industry emphasized quantity and older designs rather than switching to newer designs with potential dips in production. Thus, in 1943, Italy continued to produce biplanes at the expense of modern aircraft designs. The same approach was followed in Italy's rather small production run of some 2,500 tanks. The country never attempted to produce under license the far better German models. In sum, Italy's war industry was less effective than it had been in World War I.

Homeland defense was organized in fifteen corps areas and was centered on coastal batteries manned by the Milizia Artiglieria Maritima (MILMART, naval artillery militia) and

Guardia alla Frontiera (GAF, border guards). Along its Alpine border, Italy already maintained an old fortified line. Between 1938 and 1943, it added a new one, which could only have been directed against its German ally. Protection against amphibious assault was difficult, given the country's long coastline. When Italy entered the war, it had only 200 modern antiaircraft batteries (all lacking fire-direction systems) with which to defend the cities and industrial areas, as well as strategic targets such as bridges, rail lines, and the like.

For defense against invasion, Italy also fielded some 400 battalions of territorial units of various types, but they were poorly armed; some were equipped with nineteenth-century Wetterli rifles. During the war, a few mobile units were added. Regular army units resting or training in Italy were also available. The government sought to counter the threat of paratroopers and saboteurs by the formation of some 350 platoon-level army units, often motorized or equipped with bicycles. These were, for instance, reasonably successful in tracking down British paratroops dropped in Calabria on 10 February 1941. To these forces should be added the three main police corps—the police, the military police (the Carabinieri) and the Financial Guard.

Mussolini's disastrous policies and the Allied invasion of Sicily brought about the dictator's fall, engineered not by outside pressures but within his own party from the Fascist Grand Council, which deposed him on 25 July 1943. The new government, headed by Marshal Pietro Badoglio, signed an armistice with the Allies, which was announced on 8 September, after Allied forces invaded Italy itself. The Germans then occupied much of the country and disarmed many Italian military units that were left without orders. Italy became the battleground for outside powers, with bitter fighting persisting until 2 May 1945.

After the armistice, there were several different administrations: the Allied military government in the south (which printed its own occupation money); the Italian government under King Victor Emanuel III, which became a cobelligerent from October 1943 on and took over many liberated areas from the military; and German-occupied Italy to the north. The Germans rescued Mussolini from imprisonment and installed him in the north as head of the puppet Italian Social Republic (RSI). Some provinces of northern Italy, however, were directly controlled by the Third Reich. The German Armaments Ministry took control of northern industries, which produced surprisingly well, given the difficult conditions.

As the Allies struggled with the Germans in Italy, Italian Resistance fighters also fought the Germans and other Italians. The Resistance in the north liberated some mountainous territories and proclaimed them to be independent. The north suffered from the civil war, hunger, and Allied bombing. The south was far better off. Although it had little in the way of industry, it could at least rely on Allied help in the form of food and goods.

Italy entered the war hoping to expand its overseas empire and win military glory. Instead, the nation lost its existing empire, was invaded, and became a battlefield and the scene of a civil war. The prolonged fighting and slow Allied advance up the length of the Italian peninsula severely damaged Italy. The war destroyed some 8 percent of the nation's industrial plant, demolished a considerable amount of housing (mostly in the cities), and severely dislocated the railroads (60 percent of the locomotives were lost, along with half of the rolling stock). Some 5,000 bridges were destroyed, and agricultural production fell by 60 percent. Nonetheless, by 1948, the nation was able to regain the economic levels of 1938, and it experienced considerable growth in the 1950s and 1960s.

Alessandro Massignani

See also
Badoglio, Pietro; Italy, Air Force; Italy, Army; Italy, Navy; Italy Campaign; Mussolini, Benito; Stalingrad, Battle of; Victor Emanuel III, King of Italy

References
Della Volpe, Nicola. *Difesa del territorio e protezione antiaerea*. Rome: Ufficio Storico SME, 1986.
Ferrari, Paolo. *L'industria bellica italiana dopo 18 settembre in L'Italia in guerra: Il quarto anno 1943*. Rome: Ussmm, 1994, pp. 331–349.
Harrison, Mark. *The Economics of World War II*. Cambridge: Cambridge University Press, 1998.
Knox, McGregor. *Mussolini Unleashed, 1939–1941*. Cambridge: Cambridge University Press, 1981.
Mack Smith, Denis. *Mussolini's Roman Empire*. New York: Viking, 1976.
———. *Mussolini: A Biography*. New York: Alfred A. Knopf, 1982.
———. *Modern Italy: A Political History*. Ann Arbor: University of Michigan Press, 1997.
Rochat, Giorgio. *L'esercito italiano in pace e in guerra*. Milan, Italy: RARA, 1991.
Tosi, Francesca Ferratini, Gaetano Grassi, and Massimo Legnani. *L'Italia nella Seconda Guerra Mondiale e nella resistenza*. Milan, Italy: Franco Angeli, 1988.

Italy, Navy

In the interwar period, the Royal Italian Navy (Regia Marina) had been designed to fight the French navy in surface naval battles reminiscent of the 1916 Battle of Jutland. On the eve of World War II, the navy began transforming itself, albeit unsuccessfully, into an "oceanic" navy that would not be confined by the British-controlled Mediterranean choke points of Gibraltar and the Suez. In the unlikely event that funding and resources were made available, the Italian navy by 1942 would include 9 battleships, 3 aircraft carriers, 36 cruisers (including 12 small Capitani Romani–class, of which 3 were completed before the armistice), and 84 oceangoing submarines. The navy had 5.4 officers for every 100 sailors (France had 7.5 and Britain 9.2 officers per 100 sailors), and many of the sailors were volunteers.

On the eve of Italy's 10 June 1940 entry into the war, the navy was consuming about 33 percent of the annual military budget, placing it well behind the army but ahead of the air force. The core of the navy was built around the new 30-knot, massive, Littorio-class battleships armed with 9 × 15-inch guns. Two were being completed when war was declared, and a third was added during the war. Italy also had two small, older, and completely rebuilt and speedy World War I–era battleships ready for sea and two others that were almost ready. Although they were the weakest Axis battleships of the war, they were more powerful than any cruiser.

Italy also had 7 heavy cruisers, 12 light cruisers (adding 3 during the war), 59 destroyers (adding 10), 62 large torpedo boats (adding 17), and 113 submarines (adding 32). Various escorts, raiders, MAS-style patrol torpedo (PT) boats, and successful war-built corvettes—the 700 ton Gabbiano-class, of which 28 were completed before the armistice—rounded out the major fleet units.

Although it was a substantial force on paper, the Italian navy suffered from fundamental problems. Italy lagged in several key areas of naval technology. One area was sonar, which was just beginning to be introduced at the start of the war. Also, in the disastrous March 1941 Battle of Matapan, the Italians discovered to their dismay that the Allies had deployed radar on their warships. The Italians did not deploy their first warship radar until a year later, in March 1942. Ironically, Italy's scientific community had been working on radar in the mid-1930s, but the Italian government did not fully support its efforts. Of ULTRA intercepts, the Italians knew nothing, although they assumed the Germans were letting the Allies know about Italian operations, and the Germans assumed the Italians were doing the same.

Italian ship armor plate was inferior as judged by Allied standards. Italian heavy ships relied on long-range gunnery, but guns in cruiser and destroyer turrets were mounted too close to each other, thus interfering in the flight of shells, a problem compounded by an immoderate 1 percent weight tolerance for shells. This resulted in excessive salvo spreads, as opposed to the much tighter British salvos.

The Italians sought to avoid night fighting by their heavy ships, and the navy lacked flashless night charges for ships with 8-inch or larger guns, an error not rectified until 1942. The navy dropped night-fighting training for large ships in the 1930s, precisely when the British navy was adopting such tactics for its heavy ships, including battleships. Italian losses in night surface actions during the war would be heavy and almost completely one-sided.

Italy also experienced problems with its submarines. There were three classes of subs. The large oceangoing submarines were part of the new oceanic navy. Many were based out of Bordeaux, France. In 189 patrols, they sank over 500,000 tons of Allied ships, with another 200,000 tons damaged. They also conducted mostly ineffective runs to Japan for key war supplies, and they operated in the Indian Ocean and Red Sea. Medium and small submarines hunted closer to home. In the Mediterranean Sea, these classes conducted 1,553 patrols with dismal results when contrasted to the successes tallied by far fewer German submarines dispatched to that theater. This outcome was, in part, due to the Italian doctrine that called for submarines to submerge during daytime and wait for a target to come within range. The Italians eschewed attacks on the surface in wolf packs at night. Their torpedoes were reliable but had smaller warheads than those of most other nations, thus causing less damage. Despite its long coastline and its colonies, Italy had only 25,000 mines in 1939, and most dated of these from World War I.

In the 1920s, the Italians experimented with the snorkel, a tube to the surface that allowed submarines to secure air while submerged, but they ultimately dropped its development as a dead end. Their submarines also suffered from slow submerging speeds—they were two or three times slower than German boats. Italy also had to rebuild many of its submarines during the war because their large sails (the superstructure where the surface bridge and periscope were located) were easily picked up by radar. Italian periscopes were too short, and the Mediterranean itself was a much clearer sea then the Atlantic, which made it easier for Allied pilots to locate submerged submarines.

Italy also failed to develop the aircraft carrier. Italian dictator Benito Mussolini and the navy High Command believed that the country's long coastline and the many Italian islands and bases in the central Mediterranean rendered aircraft carriers unnecessary. But the slow communication and response between the Italian navy and air force, fueled by interservice rivalries, meant that too few planes arrived too late too often: early in the war, Italian planes actually attacked Italian ships several times. High-level bombing of warships under way also proved to be ineffective. Mussolini changed his mind about the aircraft carrier, and during the war, he twice intervened personally to secure the conversion of two passenger ships to carriers, although neither was completed before the end of the war.

Italy also failed to develop torpedo-bombers before the war, in large part because of interservice jealousy. The air force, with only limited funds, opposed development of torpedo-bombers, preferring to use the money for high-altitude bombers. So although the Italian navy developed a torpedo for air launch, it was not until the war was several months old that the air force carried out its first torpedo attack. In the course of the war, the Italians achieved several successes with these airplanes.

The most innovative naval arm was the "X" MAS (Decima Mas). This unit was made up of (1) midget submarines; (2) underwater swimmers trained in sabotage; (3) surface speedboats filled with explosives and piloted by crewmen who jumped off shortly before the vessels hit their targets; and (4) the slow-moving torpedo, or SLC, which was ridden by two men under water into enemy harbors. The most successful of these weapons was the SLC, directly developed from a World War I weapon that was employed against Austria-Hungary with good results; it was usually launched from a submarine. The most spectacular success for the SLCs occurred on 18 December 1941, when three of them entered Alexandria harbor and crippled the British battleships *Queen Elizabeth* and *Valiant*. With the exception of the midget submarines, the naval High Command ignored these weapons until 1935 and then only grudgingly supported junior officers involved in innovative development. A more forceful development program begun after World War I might well have made an important difference in World War II.

In spite of these limitations, the fuel-strapped Italian navy fought bravely during the war and transported to Africa 85 percent of the supplies and 92 percent of the troops that left port. In numerous battles above, on, and below the seas, the navy sank many Allied warships and forced the British to maintain a powerful naval force at both ends of the Mediterranean. In September 1943 when Italy switched sides in the war, the bulk of the Italian fleet joined the Allies.

Italian naval losses before the armistice consisted of 1 battleship, 11 cruisers, 44 destroyers, 41 large torpedo boats, 33 MAS-style PT boats, 86 submarines, and 178 other vessels. After the armistice, Italy lost 1 battleship, 4 destroyers, 5 large torpedo boats, 25 MAS boats, 3 submarines, and 23 other vessels. Mussolini's Italian Social Republic, organized in north Italy, seized some Italian warships, and most of these were subsequently sunk; the most important was the heavy cruiser *Bolzano*. Total wartime personnel losses for the Italian navy came to 28,837, with 4,177 of this number occurring after the armistice. Up to the armistice, Italy also lost 2,018,616 tons of merchant shipping.

Jack Greene

See also

Battleships; Calabria, Battle of; Cape Matapan, Battle of; Cunningham, Sir Andrew Browne; Great Britain, Navy; Mussolini, Benito; Signals Intelligence; Sirte, First Battle of; Sirte, Second Battle of; Somerville, Sir James Fownes; Vian, Sir Philip Louis

References

Bragadin, Marc' Antonio. *The Italian Navy in World War II*. Annapolis, MD: Naval Institute Press, 1957.

Cernuschi, Enrico. *Le navi da guerra italiane, 1940–1945*. Parma, Italy: Ermanno Albertelli Editore, 2003.

Giorgerini, Giorgio. *La guerra italiana sul mare: La marina tra vittoria e sconfitta, 1940–1943*. Milan, Italy: Mondadori, 2001.

Greene, Jack, and Alessando Massignani. *The Naval War in the Mediterranean, 1940–1943*. London: Chatham Publishing, 1998.

Knox, MacGregor. *Hitler's Italian Allies: Royal Armed Forces, Fascist Regime, and the War of 1940–1943*. Cambridge: Cambridge University Press, 2000.

Sadkovich, James J. *The Italian Navy in World War II*. Westport, CT: Greenwood Press, 1994.

Italy Campaign (1943–1945)

At the American-British Casablanca Conference in January 1943, with a cross-Channel invasion of France no longer an option for that year, British Prime Minister Winston L. S. Churchill and U.S. President Franklin D. Roosevelt and their military staffs agreed to follow the Axis defeat in North Africa with an invasion of Sicily. Several weeks later, the Americans also agreed to a subsequent invasion of the Italian Peninsula. This campaign would allow the Allies to retain the strategic initiative, expand their control in the Mediterranean, open a second front on the mainland of Europe to relieve pressure on the Soviets, and provide air bases closer to strategic bombing targets in Austria, Romania, and parts of Germany.

In a month-long campaign commencing on 10 July 1943, in their largest amphibious assault in the war to date, Allied troops defeated Axis forces in Sicily. The Allied conquest of Sicily had a profound effect in Italy, where, faced with growing unrest and the reluctance of Italian forces to oppose the Allies, the Fascist Grand Council launched a coup d'état that overthrew Italian dictator Benito Mussolini and installed a new government led by Marshal Pietro Badoglio. Secret negotiations between the Allies and the new Italian government for an armistice began immediately but soon became bogged down by the Allied insistence on unconditional surrender. A "short military armistice" was eventually signed, on 3 September. Meanwhile, however, Adolf Hitler used the interlude to move another 16 German divisions to Italy, including the crack 1st SS Panzer Division from the Soviet Union.

The Germans then occupied the entire country and took control of most of the Italian army. Much of the Italian fleet escaped to Malta. On 12 September 1943, German commandos led by Schutzstaffel (SS) Standartenführer Otto Skorzeny rescued Mussolini from captivity in the mountains at Grand Sasso in a daring airborne raid. Hitler then installed Mussolini as head of the Italian Social Republic (RSI) in northern Italy.

The strategic logic for continuing the Allied campaign in the Mediterranean appeared obvious to the British Chiefs of Staff, who saw an invasion of Italy as an opportunity to accomplish several goals: to continue the ground war against Germany utilizing experienced troops who would otherwise remain idle for a year; to draw Axis troops away from France and the Soviet Union; and possibly to create opportunities elsewhere in the eastern Mediterranean. The U.S. Joint Chiefs of Staff, however, were far less convinced and believed that Allied efforts should be directed to the cross-Channel invasion of France, now sanctioned for the spring of 1944. They were also skeptical of British motives, fearing that the postwar preservation of colonial interests was a high priority for Britain—a goal they vehemently opposed. A final decision to invade the Italian mainland was not made until the Trident Conference in Washington in May 1943, but there was no strategic plan other than to continue the existing operations. The Americans were reluctant to commit to a new Italian campaign, and there was no new, large-scale amphibious landing in northern Italy. Any such operation would have been beyond the range of Allied fighter aircraft, and it is an open question whether that type of operation and an airborne raid to capture Rome would have brought the campaign to a rapid conclusion.

The Allied invasion plan envisaged a pincer movement across the Straits of Messina by General Sir Harold Alexander's 15th Army Group, with the first objective being the vital southern Italian port of Naples. In Operation BAYTOWN, Lieutenant General Bernard Montgomery's Eighth Army crossed from Sicily to Reggio di Calabria on 3 September, followed by the British 1st Airborne Division, which landed by sea at Taranto six days later. The main assault, by 165,000 troops of the Anglo-U.S. Fifth Army under Lieutenant General Mark W. Clark, went ashore at Salerno in Operation AVALANCHE, 35 miles south of Naples, on 9 September. Salerno was chosen chiefly because it was the farthest point in the north for which air support could be provided from Sicily. The Allies hoped that, once ashore, their invading forces would somehow find a way to open the road to Rome before the end of the year.

German Field Marshal Albert Kesselring had convinced Hitler that Italy could be easily defended because of its ideal terrain. The central mountainous spine of the Apennines rises above 10,000 feet and has lateral spurs that run east and west toward the coast, between which are deep valleys containing wide rivers flowing rapidly to the sea. The north-south roads were confined to 20-mile-wide strips adjacent to the Adriatic and Tyrrhenian coasts, where the bridges that carried them were dominated by natural strong points.

Kesselring formed the six divisions in the south of Italy into the Tenth Army under General Heinrich von Vietinghoff, but he had anticipated a landing at Salerno and stationed the 16th Panzer Division in the area. At Salerno, Fifth Army attacked with two corps abreast: the U.S. VI Corps and the British X Corps. Initial resistance was light, but the Germans reinforced by 11 September and, despite their weakness, launched a counteroffensive that almost split Fifth Army between the two invading corps. By 15 September, the beachhead was secure, in large part because of an overwhelming weight of firepower in the form of accurate naval gunfire and massive air support and because more reserves were landed. Fifth Army then began an advance on Naples, 30 miles away. Montgomery, disappointed that he had only been assigned a secondary role, was needlessly cautious in his advance—so much so that a group of dismayed war correspondents drove themselves through German-occupied territory to contact Fifth Army more than a day before Montgomery's advanced units managed to do so on 16 September.

Two days later, Kesselring ordered a fighting withdrawal to the first of the series of mountainous, fortified defensive lines, from which the Germans planned to defend the approaches to Rome. On 1 October, Fifth Army captured Naples while Eighth Army advanced up the Adriatic coast and captured the airfields at Foggia; there, the Allies installed the U.S. Fifteenth Air Force to launch strategic bombing raids against the Reich. By early October, the two Allied armies had formed a continuous, 120-mile line across the peninsula running along the Volturno and Biferno Rivers. But in the previous three weeks, Fifth Army alone had taken 12,000 casualties.

Henceforth, the campaign in Italy became a slow, remorseless, and grinding battle of attrition, and as the rain and snow turned the battlefield into a muddy quagmire, the appalling struggles resembled World War I battles. Kesselring had fortified a series of defensive lines, known collectively as the Winter Line, between Gaeta and Pescara. The western end based on the Garigliano and Rapido Rivers, known as the Gustav Line, was particularly strong and hinged on the great fortress of the Benedictine abbey at Monte Cassino.

On 12 October, the Allies began the Volturno River Campaign, with the objective of seizing the approaches to Rome. Their plan was too ambitious, given the Germans' skill at defending the mountainous terrain. Between the Volturno and Rome lay 120 miles of rugged country. Fifth Army's VI Corps successfully attacked across the line of the Volturno River, and X Corps seized two crossings. To exploit the success, General Clark ordered an advance across the entire Fifth Army front. Particularly in the VI Corps area, poor roads, demolished bridges, and the difficulties of bringing supplies forward combined with German resistance to slow the advance. Meanwhile, in a series of bitterly contested actions, Eighth Army crossed the Trigno River and advanced to the Sangro River. By 15 November, however, the Germans had stopped the advance along the Winter Line, a position that extended along the Garigliano River to Mount Camino, the Mignano gap, the mountains to the northeast, and the Sangro River to the Adriatic Sea.

The Winter Line Campaign, lasting from 15 November 1943 to 15 January 1944, marked the failure of the Allied plan for a major winter offensive. Eighth Army was to break through on the Adriatic coast and then swing left behind the Germans, at which time Fifth Army would advance. When the two came within supporting distance, Fifth Army would launch an amphibious operation south of Rome. Although its efforts to break into the German position were initially successful, Eighth Army fell victim as much to weather as to the German defense. In early December, the Sangro River, vital to Eighth Army communications, rose 8 feet, and bridges were under water or washed away.

By mid-December, it was clear that the efforts to break through the German defenses were futile. Meanwhile, Fifth Army successfully cleared the heights dominating the Mignano gap after much hard fighting, but it was stopped at the Rapido River. Allied forces had reached the defensive position of the Gustav Line, which generally ran along the Garigliano, Rapido, and Sangro Rivers. One of the key points was the town of Cassino on the Rapido. However, four successive attacks by Fifth Army failed to make any significant

SWITZ-
ERLAND

*Line reached by Allied
forces in Western
Europe, 7 May 1945*

AUSTRIA

*Line reached by
Soviet forces,
7 May 1945*

HUNGARY

Bolzano

7 May

Sondrio
Aosta
Varese
Como
Trento
Belluno
Udine
Pordeno
Gorizia
Trieste

Milan
Brescia
Vicenza
Treviso
Vercelli
Verona
Padova
Venice
Turin
Pavia
Cremonia
Rovigo
Asti
Piacenza
23 Apr
Parma
Ferrara

*Line reached by
Yugoslav partisans,
7 May 1945*

30 Apr
Cuneo
Genoa
Modena
Bologna
Ravenna
Rimini

YUGOSLAVIA

16 Jan - 8 Apr 1945

Savona
La Spezia
Massa
Imperia
Lucca
Pesaro
Pisa
Leghorn
Florence
Arezzo

GOTHIC LINE
(26 Aug 44-15 Jan 45)

Anacon

Ligurian Sea

Siena
17 Jun

Grosseto
Ascoli Piceno
Teramo
9 Jun
Pescara

Corsica
(FRANCE)

*Corsica evacuated by
German forces,
18 Sep–4 Oct 1943*

Viterbo
5 Jun

THE WINTER LINE
(15 Nov 43 - 11 May 44)

Adriatic Sea

*Allies enter Rome
4 Jun 1944*

Rome
Cassino
Isernia
Anzio
Gaeta
Capua
8 Oct
28 Sept
Foggia
25 Sep
Bari
14 Sep
Brindisi

**SHINGLE
22 Jan 1944**

Sassari
Nuoro

Naples
Salerno
Potenza
Matera
Taranto
Lecce

Oristano

**SLAPSTICK
9 Sep 1943**

Sardinia
Tyrrhenian Sea

**AVALANCHE
9 Sep 1943**

Cagliari

Cosenza

*Sardinia evacuated by
German forces,
18 Sep 1943*

9 Sep

**BAYTOWN
3 Sep 1943**

*3 Sep 1943
Italy surrenders*

Palermo
Messina
Trapani
Reggio di Calabria

Caltanissetta
Enna
Catania
Agrigento
Ragusa
Syracuse

Operations in Italy

1943-1945

**HUSKY
10 Jul 1943**

Mediterranean Sea

MALTA

0   Miles   100

headway. The winter campaign had degenerated into a situation in which two separate armies were attempting to penetrate the Gustav Line.

In four months, the Allies had slogged just 70 miles from Salerno and were still 80 miles from Rome. Fifth Army alone had incurred 40,000 casualties, far exceeding German losses, and a further 50,000 men were sick; meanwhile, six experienced divisions were withdrawn for the cross-Channel invasion of France, Operation OVERLORD. The supreme Allied commander of the European Theater of Operations and U.S. forces in Europe, General Dwight D. Eisenhower, and Montgomery also departed to lead the cross-Channel invasion. In recognition of British predominance in Italy, General Maitland "Jumbo" Wilson was appointed to head the Mediterranean Command, and Lieutenant General Oliver Leese became commander of Eighth Army.

Kesselring, who was appointed commander of Army Group C on 21 November, now had 15 (albeit weakened) divisions in Tenth Army vigorously holding the Gustav Line. On 22 January 1944, in an attempt to unhinge this force, the Allies launched another amphibious landing, Operation SHINGLE, at Anzio, 30 miles south of Rome. The U.S. VI Corps, under Major General John Lucas, achieved complete surprise and safely landed 70,000 troops within a week, but it failed to exploit the advantage. Churchill later wrote, "I had hoped that we were hurling a wild cat on to the shore, but all we got was a stranded whale."

Kesselring hastily improvised eight divisions into Fourteenth Army, commanded by General Eberhard von Mackensen. This force resolutely counterattacked at Anzio, employing "Goliath" remote-controlled, explosive-filled miniature tanks for the first time in the war. The beachhead was saved only by the excellent tactical use of intelligence in one of ULTRA's most important triumphs. Major General Lucian K. Truscott replaced Lucas, but for three months, he could do no more than hold the defensive ring. Meanwhile, Allied forces to the south were unable to break through the Gustav Line. Losses were heavy on both sides as the Allies battered against the line. VI Corps held on at Anzio but was unable to break out of the beachhead. A stalemate persisted until spring.

On 17 January, V Corps launched an attack on the Gustav Line but was forced to call it off within a month, after the badly exhausted troops had advanced just 7 miles, at a cost of 17,000 casualties. The New Zealand Corps then attempted a direct assault on Monte Cassino, preceded by the questionable bombing by 145 B-17 Flying Fortresses that destroyed the famous monastery. The 1st Parachute Division troops defending the heights were some of the German army's finest, and they did not flinch. They now took up positions in the ruined monastery. A third attack by New Zealand and Indian infantry, using even heavier air and artillery bombardments, also failed to break through, not least because the rubble created an impregnable defensive position.

On 11 May, the Allies launched a fourth attack, Operation DIADEM, in which General Alexander coordinated Fifth and Eighth Armies as an army group for the first time. The aim was to destroy the German armies. In an astonishing feat of arms, Polish and Free French troops seized Monte Cassino, and XIII Corps broke the Gustav Line in a set-piece battle. Moreover, Kesselring, who had been duped into expecting another amphibious landing farther north, was slow to send reinforcements southward.

Alexander was alerted to the German movements through ULTRA intelligence, and when victory seemed complete, he ordered the Anzio breakout on 23 May. He planned for the U.S. VI Corps to strike directly inland to encircle the German Tenth Army. Rome would thus be ripe for the taking, but more important, the Germans would be unable to form any organized defenses in the rest of Italy, enabling the rapid occupation of the country right up to the Alps. However, Clark, perhaps the most egocentric Allied commander in the war, was enticed by the glory of capturing Rome and altered the direction of his thrust toward the city. Fifth Army linked up with VI Corps on 25 May and made the triumphant march into Rome on 4 June, but the spectacle of the first capture of an Axis capital was eclipsed by the Allied invasion of France two days later.

Clark's change of objective from Alexander's intent enabled Kesselring to withdraw to the Pisa-Rimini Line, 150 miles north of Rome. This line was the first of the next series of defense lines across the peninsula that were known collectively as the Gothic Line, which he reached in August. Alexander still hoped to make for Vienna, but the Italian Campaign had assumed a definite secondary status to the invasion of France. Six divisions were withdrawn in the summer, and when the autumn rains and mud forced operations to be suspended at the end of the year, another seven divisions were withdrawn.

A prolonged Allied tactical air-interdiction program during the autumn and winter of 1944 effectively closed the Brenner Pass and created an acute German fuel shortage that drastically reduced the mobility of Army Group C in northern Italy (commanded by Vietinghoff after Kesselring was severely injured in a road accident in October). Although the Germans still had over half a million men in the field, the Allies had been invigorated in both spirit and outlook by substantial reinforcements, including the Brazilian Expedition Force, and an abundant array of new weapons.

On 9 April, after the ground had dried, Alexander launched his spring offensive, with Eighth Army attacking through the Argenta gap. Fifth Army struck on 15 April, and just 10 days later, both Allied armies met at Finale nell'Emilia, after having surrounded and eliminated the last German forces. The

Allies then advanced rapidly northward, the Americans entering Milan on 29 April and the British reaching Trieste on 2 May. Fifth Army continued to advance into Austria, linking with the U.S. Seventh Army in the Brenner Pass on 6 May.

The isolated and hopeless position of German and RSI forces led Schutzstaffel (SS) General Karl Wolff, military governor and head of the SS in northern Italy, to initiate background negotiations for a separate surrender as early as February 1945. The talks, facilitated by Allen Dulles, head of the U.S. Office of Strategic Services in Switzerland, held much promise, although they were complicated and took place in an atmosphere of mutual suspicion and mistrust. Wolff wished to avoid senseless destruction and loss of life and to repel the spread of communism; he also hoped to ingratiate himself with the West in case war crimes trials were held in the future. From the Allied perspective, Wolff offered the prospect of preventing the creation of a Nazi redoubt in the Alps. The head of the SS, Heinrich Himmler, halted the talks in April, forestalling their conclusion before the Allied spring offensive, but by 23 April, Wolff and Vietinghoff decided to disregard orders from Berlin. Wolff ordered the SS not to resist the Italian partisans on 25 April, and an unconditional surrender was signed four days later, to be effective on 2 May, six days before the German surrender in the West.

The Italian Campaign gave the Allies useful victories in the interval between the reconquest of the Mediterranean and the reconquest of northwest Europe. In a theater of increasingly secondary importance, Kesselring's position was merely a defensive one, and the best the Allies could claim was that they kept 22 enemy divisions from fighting in another theater. Allied casualties came to 188,746 for Fifth Army and 123,254 for Eighth Army, whereas German casualties were about 434,646 men. The Italian Campaign did, however, afford the Allies experience in amphibious operations and the stresses of coalition warfare, all of which proved invaluable during the invasion of France.

Philip L. Bolté and Paul H. Collier

See also
Alexander, Sir Harold Rupert Leofric George; Amphibious Warfare; Anzio, Battle of; Badoglio, Pietro; Cairo Conference; Carpet Bombing; Casablanca Conference; Cassino/Rapido River, Battles of; Churchill, Sir Winston L. S.; Clark, Mark Wayne; Eisenhower, Dwight D.; Freyberg, Bernard Cyril; Germany, Collapse of; Himmler, Heinrich; Hitler, Adolf; Italy, Home Front; Joint Chiefs of Staff; Juin, Alphonse Pierre; Kesselring, Albert; Leese, Sir Oliver William Hargreaves; Lucas, John Porter; Montgomery, Sir Bernard Law; Mussolini, Benito; Office of Strategic Services; Rome, Advance on and Capture of; Roosevelt, Franklin D.; Salerno Invasion; Sicily, Invasion of; Skorzeny, Otto; Trident Conference; Truscott, Lucian King, Jr.; Unconditional Surrender; Vietinghoff gennant Scheel, Heinrich Gottfried von; Wilson, Henry Maitland

References
Carver, Michael. *The War in Italy, 1939–1945*. London: Macmillan, 2001.
D'Este, Carlo. *World War II in the Mediterranean, 1942–1945*. Chapel Hill, NC: Algonquin Press, 1990.
Gooch, John. *Italy and the Second World War*. London: Cass, 2001.
Graham, Dominick, and Shefford Bidwell. *Tug of War: The Battle for Italy, 1943–45*. London: Hodder and Stoughton, 1986.
Higgins, Trumbull. *Soft Underbelly: The Anglo-American Controversy over the Italian Campaign, 1939–1945*. New York: Macmillan, 1968.
Howard, Michael. *The Mediterranean Strategy in the Second World War*. London: Greenhill, 1968.
Lamb, Richard. *War in Italy, 1943–1945: A Brutal Story*. New York: St. Martin's Press, 1993.
Starr, Chester G., ed. *From Salerno to the Alps*. Nashville, TN: Battery Press, 1986.
Strawson, John. *Italian Campaign*. London: Secker and Warburg, 1987.

Itō Seiichi (1890–1945)

Japanese navy admiral who ordered the attack on Pearl Harbor and later commanded Japan's Second Fleet. Born in Fukuoka, Japan, on 26 July 1890, Itō Seiichi graduated from the Naval Academy in 1911 and the Naval War College in 1923. He studied at Yale University in the United States in 1928 and was promoted to captain in 1930. He held cruiser commands before assuming command of the battleship *Haruna* in 1936. Promoted to rear admiral in 1937, he became chief of staff of Second Fleet. Itō then served in the Navy Ministry between 1938 and 1940. In November 1940, he took command of Cruiser Division 8.

In April 1941, Itō became chief of staff of the Combined Fleet, and in September, he was appointed vice chief of the navy General Staff under Admiral Nagano Osami. He was promoted to vice admiral that October and played a key role in the development of Japanese naval strategy in the Pacific war. Reluctant to see Japan go to war against the United States, he opposed the Pearl Harbor attack, but Admiral Yamamoto Isoroku, commander of the Combined Fleet, urged Nagano to authorize the plan. On 1 December 1941, with the fleet already at sea, Itō ordered the attack on Pearl Harbor. He held his staff post for more than three years, but he desired a naval command.

In December 1944, he was appointed to command the Second Fleet. The Japanese navy had already been crushed in the Battle of Leyte Gulf the previous October, and Itō's fleet was the only operative Japanese navy force. On 5 April 1945, Admiral Toyoda Soemu ordered Operation TEN-GO, whereby Second Fleet would join the battle for Okinawa, which had recently been invaded by U.S. forces. This operation was so reckless that Itō refused the order. His fleet lacked both aircraft carriers and aircraft, which were essential to protect its ships from air attack. Moreover, the fleet would be provided only enough fuel for a one-way trip from Kyushu to Okinawa.

It was obvious to Itō and others that Toyoda intended to send the 7,000 men of the fleet on a suicide mission.

Ultimately, Vice Admiral Kusaka Ryunōsuke prevailed on him to obey the order, and on 6 April, Itō set out with the battleship *Yamato* and eight destroyers. The plan called for the *Yamato* to fight its way to the U.S. invasion site, destroy as many American ships as possible, and then beach itself to act as a stationary battery. On 7 April 1945, the Second Fleet ships were attacked by U.S. Vice Admiral Marc A. Mitscher's Fast Carrier Task Force 58 in the East China Sea, and the *Yamato* was sunk, along with Itō and 3,700 of her crew.

Kotani Ken

See also
Kamikaze; Leyte Gulf, Battle of; Mitscher, Marc Andrew; Nagano Osami; Okinawa, Invasion of; Toyoda Soemu; Yamamoto Isoroku; *Yamato*, Suicide Sortie of

References
Morison, Samuel Eliot. *History of United States Naval Operations in World War II.* Vol. 14, *Victory in the Pacific, 1945.* Boston: Little, Brown, 1961.

Yoshida Mitsuru. *Requiem for Battleship "Yamato."* Trans. Richard Minear. Seattle: University of Washington Press, 1985.

———. *Teitoku Itō Seiichi no Syogai* ([The life of Admiral Itō Seiichi). Tokyo: Bungeishunjyu, 1986.

Iwabuchi Sanji (1893–1945)

Japanese navy admiral who vigorously defended Manila in the waning months of the war. Born in Niigata Prefecture, Japan, on 2 March 1893, Iwabuchi Sanji graduated from the Naval Academy in 1915. Trained as a pilot, he then become a gunnery specialist and entered the Gunnery School in 1923. Between 1930 and 1933, he served as a gunnery officer on cruisers and battleships. Promoted to captain in 1937, Iwabuchi was assigned to command the training cruiser *Kashii* in 1941, then the battleship *Kirishima* in April 1942. His battleship took part in the Battle of Midway and the campaign for the Solomon Islands during 1942. On 15 November 1942, in the naval Battle of Guadalcanal, the *Kirishima* was fatally damaged by gunfire from the U.S. battleship *Washington* and had to be scuttled.

Promoted to rear admiral in May 1943, Iwabuchi was appointed commander of the 31st Naval Special Base Force in Manila. In November 1944, he was also assigned 4,000 army personnel and named commander of the Manila Naval Defense Force. General Yamashita Tomoyuki, commander of Japanese forces in the Philippines, ordered Iwabuchi's forces to evacuate Manila and conduct a protracted struggle in the mountainous regions of northern and central Luzon as well as east of Manila, but Iwabuchi refused to carry out the order. Commanding 15,000 navy and 4,000 army personnel, he was determined to defend Manila to the last. During three weeks

in February 1945, there was fierce house-to-house fighting in Manila, and most Japanese forces chose to fight to the death rather than surrender. Iwabuchi died near the end of the battle on 26 February at Intramuros; he received a brevet promotion to vice admiral after his death.

Iwabuchi's decision to defend Manila to the last resulted in the deaths of some 16,000 Japanese troops, 1,000 American forces, and perhaps 100,000 civilians. Some of the latter were deliberately massacred by Japanese troops, but most were killed by U.S. artillery fire. Iwabuchi's actions also resulted in the trial and execution of General Yamashita as a war criminal.

Kita Yoshito

See also
Manila, Battle for; Philippines, U.S. Recapture of; Yamashita Tomoyuki

References
Lear, Elmer Norton. *The Japanese Occupation of the Philippines: Leyte, 1941–1945.* Ithaca, NY: Cornell University Southeast Asia Program, 1961.

Smith, Robert Ross. *The United States Army in World War II: The War in the Pacific—Triumph in the Philippines.* Washington, DC: U.S. Government Printing Office, 1963.

Iwo Jima, Battle for (19 February– 26 March 1945)

The penultimate test of U.S. Marine Corps amphibious doctrine and practice. By the end of 1944, American forces had secured from Japan control of the Mariana Islands to provide air bases for B-29 strategic bombers that could strike Japan. En route to Japan, these bombers flew over Iwo Jima (Sulphur Island). Located in the Japanese Bonin Islands, halfway between the Marianas and Japan, the pork-chop-shaped volcanic island of Iwo Jima is from 800 yards to 2.5 miles wide and 5 miles long, with a total area of some 8 square miles.

Iwo Jima housed a large radar facility that gave Tokyo advance notice of impending air attacks, as well as three airstrips for fighter aircraft used to harass the U.S. bombers. As a consequence, U.S. commanders formulated Operation DETACHMENT to seize Iwo Jima. In American hands, the island's airstrips would provide emergency landing facilities for bombers returning from Japan and also allow U.S. fighters stationed there to escort bombers the entire length of their missions.

Japanese leaders realized the strategic importance of Iwo Jima and began reinforcing it a year prior to the American invasion. Lieutenant General Kuribayashi Tadamichi, the island's commander, disregarded the traditional Japanese defensive doctrine of meeting the enemy at the shoreline and implemented a new strategy that relied on 1,500 interlocking strong points inland, designed for a battle of attrition. His

Flag raising on Iwo Jima, 23 February 1945. (National Archives)

force of 21,000 men dug out thousands of yards of tunnels in the soft volcanic rock to connect natural caves, underground bunkers, and man-made "spider-traps" from which concealed defenders could infiltrate and attack any enemy positions. These extensive subterranean complexes would also shield the defenders from extensive preliminary air and naval bombardment by U.S. forces. Japanese artillerymen also preregistered the beachheads to maximize the effectiveness of their own shelling. Kuribayashi ordered the defenders to die in place and to kill at least 10 Americans before dying themselves. He was, however, handicapped by a lack of fresh water. The absence of a natural harbor limited Japanese reinforcement of the island, and U.S. submarines also sank a number of Japanese supply ships, including one transport with a regiment of Japanese tanks.

Beginning in August 1944, U.S. Army aircraft in the Marianas subjected Iwo Jima to air strikes, and from 8 December, the island came under daily attack. Three heavy cruisers bombarded Iwo Jima three times in December and twice in January. Then, for two weeks beginning in late January, Seventh Air Force bombed Iwo Jima day and night, and B-29s struck it twice. In all, U.S. forces dropped 6,800 tons of bombs and fired 22,000 rounds of 5-inch to 16-inch shells prior to the invasion, the heaviest bombardment of the Pacific war. Still, the naval bombardment of the island, begun on 16 February 1945, lasted only three days, a far shorter period than V Marine Amphibious Corps commander Lieutenant General Holland M. "Howlin' Mad" Smith had requested. Smith led a force of 80,000 men, supported by Admiral Raymond A. Spruance's Fifth Fleet. Vice Admiral Richmond Kelly Turner had overall charge of the invasion.

On 19 February 1945, 30,000 U.S. Marines from the 3rd, 4th, and 5th Marine Divisions stormed ashore, only to encounter Iwo Jima's coarse, black volcanic sand. Heavy surf smashed the landing craft against the island's shelf, and the deep sand immobilized many vehicles on the beach. The

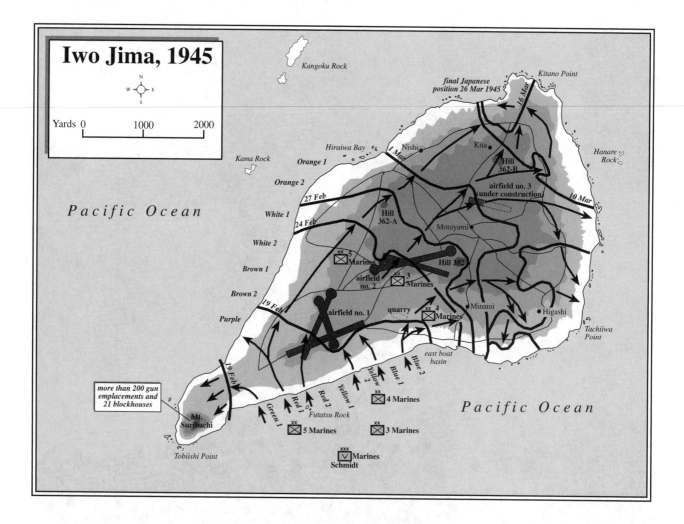

resulting logjam of men and equipment on the beachhead provided prime targets for highly accurate Japanese artillery fire. With little or no cover, the Marines had no choice but to fight their way inland. One group wheeled south, toward the island's most prominent terrain feature, the 556-foot Mount Suribachi, while the majority of the Marines attacked northward toward the first airfield. On D+4 (the fourth day after the initial landing), Marines reached the crest of Mount Suribachi, and although still under fire, they raised a small American flag. A few hours later, another group raised a second, larger flag as Associated Press reporter Joe Rosenthal impulsively snapped a photo. Rosenthal's picture of these five Marines and one navy corpsman planting the second flag became a Marine Corps icon and the symbol for American victory in the Pacific. The photograph remains one of the most widely reproduced images of all time.

Marines assaulting the main line of resistance to the north waded through rain-soaked sand into a maze of Japanese pillboxes, bunkers, and caves. Assisted by flamethrowers, demolition charges, bazookas, tanks, and air support, they pushed their way through Kuribayashi's defenses for 36 days, sometimes advancing only a few feet per day. By 26 March

1945, nearly 70,000 Marines had conquered most of the island, at a cost of approximately 6,500 dead and 20,000 wounded. More than 95 percent of the Japanese defenders died during the same period, and pockets of Japanese resistance continued to emerge from concealed cave complexes throughout April and May, resulting in 1,600 additional Japanese deaths. Fewer than 300 Japanese were taken prisoner.

Was the capture of Iwo Jima worth the high cost? With the island firmly in U.S. possession, U.S. bombers pounded the Japanese homeland unabated. In the midst of the heaviest fighting on 4 March, the first of 2,500 U.S. bombers made emergency landings on the island, and some 2,000 B-29s force-landed there from March to August. Given that these planes carried 10-man crews, this represented up to 20,000 airmen. The U.S. Army Air Forces (USAAF) VII Fighter Command moved to Iwo Jima and began to send its long-range P-47 Thunderbolts and P-51 Mustangs as escorts with the B-29s to Japan. The bombers now mixed medium-level daytime raids with the low-level night attacks. With the USAAF fighters along, losses of Japanese planes mounted rapidly, while those of the B-29s continued to decline.

The struggle for Iwo Jima epitomized the courage and esprit of the Marine Corps during the war. Twenty-two Marines, four navy corpsmen, and one navy officer on Iwo Jima earned the Medal of Honor (almost half of them posthumously), accounting for one-third of all such medals won by Marines during the entire war. Fleet Admiral Chester Nimitz testified to the level of courage and bravery among the Americans fighting on Iwo Jima in stating, "Among the Americans who served on Iwo Jima, uncommon valor was a common virtue."

Derek W. Frisby

See also

Central Pacific Campaign; Flamethrowers; Kuribayashi Tadamichi; Mariana Islands, Naval Campaign; Nimitz, Chester William; Smith, Holland McTyeire; Spruance, Raymond Ames; Strategic Bombing; Turner, Richmond Kelly; Vandegrift, Alexander Archer

References

Alexander, Joseph. *Closing In: Marines in the Seizure of Iwo Jima.* Washington, DC: History and Museums Division, Headquarters, U.S. Marine Corps, 1994.

Bradley, James. *Flags of Our Fathers.* New York: Bantam Books, 2000.

Wright, Derrick. *The Battle for Iwo Jima, 1945.* Phoenix Mill, UK: Sutton Publishing, 1999.

J

Japan, Air Forces

Japan did not possess an independent air force during World War II. Instead, the army and navy each had their own air service. Each had different hypothetical enemies in the interwar period: the army planned to fight against the Soviet Union, and the navy expected to fight the United States and Britain in the western Pacific Ocean. As a consequence, each service developed its own air arm tailored to meet its particular needs.

Unfortunately for the Japanese war effort, neither service cooperated with the other. Army and navy aircraft employed different electrical systems; when the Japanese developed an Identification, Friend or Foe (IFF) capability, army operators on Iwo Jima in 1944 could not identify Japanese navy aircraft as friendly. Further, aircraft factories were divided between those areas that made army planes and those producing naval aircraft, and each kept design developments secret from the other. There was no exchange of data. The navy's Zero fighter was superior to the army's Hayabusa, but the navy did not want to share the Zero with the army. If the army had adopted the Zero, the number of Japanese fighter aircraft produced during the war would have been greatly increased. There was little standardization between the Zero and Hayabusa, even in small screw parts.

Japan also failed to develop heavy bombers comparable to those of Britain and the United States. Not until January 1944 did the army and navy agree to develop a joint, 6-engine heavy bomber, dubbed the "Fugaku," but this project came too late and had to be abandoned. Finally, each service also concealed its weaknesses from the other; thus, it was 1945 before army leaders discovered how catastrophic the 1942 Battle of Midway had been for the Japanese naval air arm.

At the beginning of the Pacific war in December 1941, the Japanese army possessed 4,800 aircraft. Most army fighters were of the obsolescent Nakajima Ki-27 Type 97 ("Abdul" in the Allied recognition system). The army had only 50 first-class fighters—the Nakajima Ki-43 Hayabusa ("Oscar"), which made its debut over Malaya in December 1941. The Ki-43 gradually became the army's most numerous fighter; 5,751 were built during the war. Later, the army introduced new fighters: the Nakajima Ki-44 Shoki ("Tojo"), with initial deliveries in September 1942; the Kawasaki Ki-61 Hien ("Tony"), in August 1942; and the Nakajima Ki-84 Hayate ("Frank"), in April 1944. The best of Japan's wartime army fighters to reach mass production, the Ki-84 was superior to the North American P-51 Mustang and Republic P-47 Thunderbolt in certain respects. The Japanese army had no heavy bombers or dive-bombers and only three medium types: the Mitsubishi Ki-21 Type 97 ("Gwen"), the Nakajima Ki-49 Donryu ("Helen"), and the Mitsubishi Ki-67 Hiryu ("Peggy").

As of December 1941, the Imperial Japanese Navy air arm, which played a major role in the early battles in the Pacific, possessed 3,000 airplanes, 1,300 of which were with the fleet in 1941. Most numerous of its aircraft was the excellent, highly maneuverable Mitsubishi A6M Zero fighter ("Zeke"). Others included the Nakajima B5N Type 97 torpedo-bomber and light bomber ("Kate"); the Aichi D3A Type 99 carrier dive-bomber ("Val"); and two twin-engine, land-based medium bombers, the Mitsubishi G3M ("Nell") and the G4M Type 1 ("Betty"). Zero fighters took part in every major Japanese operation of the war. In the first six months of the war, the Zero was superior to any Allied fighter aircraft. Japan produced a total of 10,370 Zeros during World War II. As new

Allied aircraft were introduced, the Japanese navy developed new aircraft, such as the Kawanishi NIK2-J Shiden ("George") and the Nakajima B6N Tenzan ("Jill").

In the Sino-Japanese War and the first stage of the Pacific war, the Japanese air forces met with considerable success. They dominated the skies over China and instituted strategic bombing of Chinese cities in 1938. The Japanese naval air arm was undoubtedly the best in the world, and Japanese pilots were among the best trained. In 1941, first-line Japanese pilots had 500 to 800 flying hours, and 50 percent of army pilots and 10 percent of navy pilots had combat experience against China and/or the Soviet Union.

On 7 December 1941, the naval air arm executed the attack on Pearl Harbor, conclusively demonstrating the supremacy of airpower in modern naval warfare and establishing the effective combination of carriers and aircraft. A few days later, navy land-based aircraft sank the British battleship *Prince of Wales* and the battle cruiser *Repulse* off Malaya. For the first time, a self-defending battleship under way had been sunk by aircraft, which showed that in the future, ships would require air protection. However, in 1942, Japanese air forces suffered heavy losses in the Battles of Midway and Guadalcanal. These battles spelled the ruin of the fine Japanese naval air arm and revealed the serious flaw of an inadequate pilot-replacement system; much of the trained naval air arm was lost in the battle and could not be replaced. The army also sustained heavy aircraft and pilot losses over New Guinea in 1943, and navy air squadrons were badly hurt at Truk and the Caroline Islands from February to April 1944.

The Battle of the Philippine Sea ("the great Marianas turkey shoot") in June 1944 and the Battle of Leyte Gulf in October 1944 finished off the Japanese naval air arm as an effective fighting force. The army and navy delivered new planes, such as the Hayate and Tenzan, but shortages of adequately trained pilots and fuel negated any advantage. By 1944, Japan was so short of aviation fuel that it could scarcely train its pilots; Japanese aviators had only about 120 hours of flying time before combat.

Japan produced some excellent, highly maneuverable aircraft during the war, but they tended to be lightly armored and caught fire easily. The Zero fighter was essentially unarmored, and Allied pilots dubbed the G4M Type 1 ("Betty") bomber "the flying cigarette lighter" because it so readily caught fire. Japanese aircraft simply could not sustain heavy damage. The

> In the period between 1940 and 1945, the U.S. built 297,199 aircraft; during the same period, the Japanese built 74,656.

planes also tended to be more lightly armed than their U.S. counterparts. When the Boeing B-29s began the strategic bombing of Japan, Japanese fighters had difficulty shooting them down. The Japanese planes also lacked airborne radar.

As Japan faced overwhelming Allied forces by late 1944, the military instituted kamikaze suicide attacks. Such strikes were ordered by Vice Admiral Ōnishi Takijirō during the Battle of Leyte Gulf, and they reached culmination in the Battle of Okinawa between April and June 1945. The kamikaze strike proved highly effective: the U.S. Navy sustained greater personnel losses from these attacks during the Battle of Okinawa than in all its previous wars combined. Yet even this new tactic could not turn the tide for Japan.

In the period between 1940 and 1945, the United States produced 297,199 aircraft; during the same period, Japan produced 74,656. In the Pacific war, the Japanese army lost 15,920 planes and the Japanese navy 27,190.

Kotani Ken

See also
Aircraft, Bombers; Aircraft, Fighters; Genda Minoru; Guadalcanal, Land Battle for; Japan, Army; Japan, Navy; Kamikaze; Kato Takeo; Leyte Gulf, Battle of; Midway, Battle of; Ōnishi Takijirō; Pearl Harbor, Attack on; Philippine Sea, Battle of the; *Prince of Wales* and *Repulse*; Yamamoto Isoroku

References
Mainichi Series: Nihon Koukushi (History of Japanese aircraft). Tokyo: Mainichi Shinbunsya, 1979.
Marder, A. J. *Old Friends, New Enemies.* Oxford: Clarendon Press, 1981.
Roberts, J. B. *Japanese Aircraft of the Pacific War.* London: G. P. Putnam, 1979.

Japan, Army

The Imperial Japanese Army (Dai Nippon Teikoku Rikugun) defies easy or simple recounting, in no small measure because Japanese official histories of World War II begin in September 1931 with the start of the Manchurian Campaign. Thus, any account of the Japanese army and the war really has to cover a 14-year period and to be divided into two very separate parts. One of these parts concerns its campaigns both on the ground and in the air because the Rikugun, as with the navy, had its own air force. Also, the Rikugun was involved in two wars, one in East Asia and the other in the Pacific and Southeast Asia, that were largely separate from one another, and both contained a number of campaigns that again were very largely separate from one another. Thus, the war in East Asia divides into the campaign in Manchuria, 1931–1932; the Sino-Japanese War, 1937–1944; and the final phase of the war, after December 1944, which saw major Japanese withdrawals throughout southern China and then defeat at Soviet hands in August 1945 in northern China and Manchuria. This accounting leaves unlisted the period of Japanese encroachment in northern China and Inner Mongolia between 1932 and 1936, in which time the power of the Chinese Nationalist Party—the Guomindang, or GMD (Kuomintang, or KMT)—was neutralized in these areas, as well as the four-phase China war of 1927 to 1945.

The other part concerns the process by which the Rikugun came to dominate the political process in Japan and, in effect, to control the Japanese state. This was the most important single dimension of Rikugun activity because of its results and implications, but the process by which the army came to dominate the Japanese state was, in turn, the product of developments that reached back into the 1920s and beyond, at least to the Russian and Chinese Civil Wars. In the course of the these two conflicts, Japanese military formations found themselves undertaking operations without direct control and guidance from superior authority in Tokyo. This situation bred a habit of independent action, which over time came to be identified with the belief that action could and would not be repudiated by Tokyo. The first real example of this came in 1928, when Japanese military personnel from the Guandong (Kwantung) Army, the garrison force in Manchuria, murdered the local warlord, but the Army Ministry blocked all moves to have those responsible tried by courts-martial, on the grounds that such proceedings would be damaging to the army's prestige. The cabinet gave way, and having surrendered on such a crucial matter, it had no real basis on which to oppose deliberate insubordination when events revealed powerful support within Japan for the Guandong Army's action in 1931 and 1932 in overrunning Manchuria.

The Manchurian episode was crucial to the process whereby the Imperial Army in effect came to control the state. Officers of the Guandong Army staged the Mukden (Shenyang) Incident in Liaoning on 18 September 1931, and what followed amounted to a coup inside Mukden by the Guandong Army. After an emergency cabinet meeting in Tokyo, the Japanese government announced that it was committed to a policy of nonaggression within Manchuria, but the Army Ministry declared that it would not consult the cabinet about future policy but would be bound by the Guandong Army's decisions. The cabinet immediately denied the Guandong Army's request for three divisions and ordered the Korean command not to provide reinforcements for that army, whereon the Korean command did just that on 21 September. The government found itself confronted by a fait accompli and outmaneuvered at every turn by a military that played the card of public opinion against any attempt to halt proceedings inside Manchuria. The government fell in December; then, on 15 May 1932, the new premier, Inukai Tsuyoshi, was assassinated by a group of naval officers and army cadets.

This event marked the beginning of the military's domination of the political process within Japan because in its aftermath, the Rikugun would only nominate an army minister if a party leader did not head the government. After the 15 May incident, governments could only be formed with the assent of the military and only if they were prepared to accede to the military's demands. When Hirota Kōki became prime minister in July 1936 in the wake of the army mutiny on 26 February 1936, he found that the army minister had effective veto power over all appointments. In practice, the army could refuse to appoint an army minister or use the threat of resignation in order to ensure compliance with its will. There was to be no basic change in such arrangements until Japan was overwhelmed by national defeat.

In terms of the major military commitments in this 14-year period, the Manchurian Campaign was of minor importance. There was no serious, sustained, or coherent resistance within Manchuria, set up by the Japanese as a puppet state known as Manzhouguo (Manchukuo, and after 1934 Manzhoudiguo [Manchoutikuo], the Manzhou [Manchu] Empire). The Sino-Japanese War, which began in 1937, was another matter. The ease with which Japanese forces overran northern China after July 1937 was testimony to the extent of Japanese success over the previous five years, but the real point was that the Rikugun found itself involved in a protracted war it had not sought and that tied down its resources. As in 1932, the Japanese navy instigated fighting in Shanghai in Jiangsu (Kiangsu) Province, and again, the army had to be deployed there to rescue its sister service: it could only do so by extensive mobilization and escalation of a crisis it would have preferred to have resolved through threat, intimidation, and a series of piecemeal Chinese surrenders, rather than war. The war and the Japanese military effort quickly widened.

There were some defeats along the way, the most notable being in front of Tai'erzhuang (Tai'erh-Chuang) on 6–7 April 1938. The next day, Imperial General Headquarters formally sanctioned an escalation of the war by ordering the capture of Xuzhou (Hsuchow), Jiangsu Province. This move enabled the Japanese military to link what had been two very separate efforts, in northern and central China, and then to develop the offensive that would result in the capture of the Wuhan cities of Hubei (Hupeh) Province in October.

The period after 1938 was notable for two developments, namely, the rice raids that began in Hubei Province in late 1940 and then the opening of the "Three All"—"Kill All, Burn All, Destroy All"—campaigns in Communist-held/infected areas in northern China. In the course of this and subsequent Japanese operations, the population of Communist base areas was reduced from an estimated 44 million to 25 million by a policy of mass deportations, murder, and deliberate starvation. The Communists were neutralized as a threat, with no major guerrilla activity in northern China for the remainder of the war, but as in all matters Japanese in this war, success was an illusion. By 1938, if not before, the Japanese army, with

Japanese army tanks approaching the Singapore Causeway, February 1942. (Hulton Archive)

a million troops in China, found itself learning again the truth of the Clausewitzian dictum that it is easy to conquer but hard to occupy. The reason for this was the adoption by the GMD regime in China of a policy of protracted resistance that precluded negotiations. The Japanese countered with a strategic bombing offensive, but this did not bring the GMD leadership to surrender. Perhaps the only point of real interest in these campaigns was the first attempt by any armed force to use airpower to kill a head of state. On 30 August 1941, army bombers attacked a villa in Chongqing (Chungking) in Sichuan (Szechwan), where Jiang Jieshi (Chiang Kai-shek) was known to be taking part in staff talks.

These efforts ran concurrently with defeats at Soviet hands. Japanese commitments in China dictated a cautious policy in Manchuria and Inner Mongolia, but in 1938 and 1939, several small and two major clashes occurred between Japanese and Soviet forces. The first major clash took place between 11 July and 10 August 1938 in the area around Zhanggufeng (Chang-ku-feng) where Manchuria, Korea, and the Maritime Provinces met; the second occurred between May and September 1939 in the area between the River Halha and Nomonhan. In both cases, single Japanese divisions attempted to clear Soviet forces from their territorial holdings, but in the first action, the Japanese were checked, and in the second, they were subjected to attack by an enemy possessing overwhelming numerical superiority in aircraft, tanks, and artillery. Beginning on 20 August, the Soviets undertook an offensive that literally shredded the Komatsubara Force and then totally destroyed one infantry regiment on the banks of the Halha. By mid-September, the Japanese had brought three fresh divisions to Nomonhan, but by this stage, both sides had very little interest in continuing the battle, and a local truce was arranged: the Zhanggufeng and Nomonhan disputes were resolved in June 1940.

The defeat at Nomonhan coincided with the 1939 German-Soviet Non-aggression Pact, and Germany's act, together with the Anglo-French declaration of war on Germany, caused Japan to adopt a cautious policy and wait on events. The German victory in northwest Europe in spring 1940 was immediately followed by a change of government. On 21 July, Prince Konoe Fumimaro replaced the more circumspect Yonai Mitsumasa as prime minister. The two services' precondition for allowing Konoe to form a government was his prior acceptance of their demands for a treaty with Germany and Italy, additional credits for the army, a nonaggression treaty with the Soviet Union, and the adoption of a forward strategy in southeast Asia.

In the China theater, however, the international situation offered the army the means to isolate the Chinese Nationalist regime by intimidating the British and French colonial authorities in Southeast Asia. The German attack on the Soviet Union in June 1941 and the U.S. embargo of various goods, which was drastically extended that July, placed Japan in a situation in which a choice had to be made. At the navy's insistence, Japan's leaders decided to move into Southeast Asia to ensure access to raw materials. Without these assets, Japanese leaders believed their nation could not survive as a great power, even if this move meant war with the United States.

The army's role in such a war would be to provide garrisons in the islands that were to mark the defensive perimeter on which the Americans would be fought to a standstill. The navy's belief was that the fleet and land-based aircraft would be able to meet the Americans more or less on the basis of equality and thereafter fight them to exhaustion. A stalemate would then force the United States to reach some kind of negotiated settlement. Although this has been overlooked, the role of the army in the Pacific war was therefore very limited in one sense, and even in the initial phase, during which Southeast Asia was overrun, the commitment of the Imperial Army remained modest. The campaigns in Burma, Malaya, the Netherlands East Indies, and the Philippines involved only 11 Japanese divisions, the equivalent of a single army, and after these conquests were completed, no single campaign, whether in the southwest, central or north Pacific, involved a corps equivalent or more in the field until that in the Philippines in 1944 and 1945. Admittedly, the defeats Japan incurred in eastern New Guinea (March 1942 to December 1943) and thereafter along the northern coast of the island (December 1943 to May 1944) and in the central and upper Solomons (February to November 1943) did involve more than a corps equivalent, but these were a series of local defeats largely separated from one another. Probably no single reverse, even that on Guadalcanal (August 1942 to February 1943) at the very beginning of second-phase operations, involved more than two divisions.

The only defeat of corps-sized proportions incurred by the Rikugun prior to the Philippines Campaign was in Burma at Imphal and Kohima in the 1943–1944 campaigning season, the so-called March on Delhi that went disastrously wrong. The origins of this defeat lay in the ease with which the Japanese, with just one division, had frustrated a corps-sized British offensive in the Arakan in 1943, a campaign in which the Japanese outthought and outfought British forces with ease and one that bears comparison with the original campaigns of Japanese conquest in Southeast Asia.

In these 1941–1942 campaigns, the Japanese had no military margin of superiority, but they outfought individual enemies that were defensively dispersed and subjected to successive amphibious assaults by Japanese forces enjoying local air and naval superiority. The campaigns, conducted across a frontage of more than 3,000 miles, were characterized by economy of effort and even an almost aesthetic quality, as successive landings penetrated to the depth of Allied defenses.

Thereafter, the problem for Japan and the Rikugun was threefold. First, once they were no longer taking the initiative in the Pacific, Japanese garrisons were subjected to an overwhelming attack by massively superior Allied assets. No force could sustain itself against such an attack, and no resistance, however protracted and effective in terms of tying down U.S. military assets, could alter a pattern of defeat that brought American forces astride Japanese lines of communication to the south and took the war to the home islands. Second, the Rikugun deployed formations to the Pacific primarily at the expense of garrison forces in Manchuria and China, where these formations were not easily replaced. By 1944, ammunition shortages precluded Rikugun live-fire training. By August 1945, the class of 1945 was basically untrained, and the 1944 class was little better. The army, which had numbered some 24 divisions in the mid-1920s and 51 divisions in December 1941, raised 3 armored and 107 infantry divisions for service overseas: 1 tank and 55 infantry divisions remained in the home islands.

Despite these numbers, the quality of the army was declining because Japan quite simply lacked adequate industrial capacity to meet the requirements of total war. Japanese output in 1944 was equivalent to 4 percent of the American production of mortars, 4.7 percent of tanks, 8 percent of antiaircraft ammunition, perhaps 10 percent of all ordnance, and 6.5 percent of small-arms ammunition. With minimum capability, the divisions in the home islands in 1945 were singularly ill prepared to resist assault landings.

The Japanese army never, as it happened, experienced defeat in the home islands, but it faced defeat repeatedly on the continental mainland. The year 1945 saw Japanese forces defeated throughout Burma (with the exception of Tenasserim) and, in August, also throughout Manchuria, northern China, and Korea, as well as on Sakhalin and in the Kuriles, when Soviet forces put together a masterly short campaign. The Japanese forces numbered some 750,000 troops, but of these, some 300,000 were Manchurians suited only to garrison duties. The Japanese troops were mustered in 17 infantry divisions, equipped with 1,155 tanks, 5,360 artillery pieces, and 1,800 aircraft, but these were utterly routed by an enemy force consisting of 1 tank and 11 infantry armies. Seeking to consolidate what they held and to allow removal of formations to more important theaters, the Japanese had already begun major withdrawals within China, ending the period of Japanese successes that had begun in spring 1944 when Japan undertook a series of offensives throughout southern China. The Japanese conduct of these operations resembled their previous efforts in terms of brutality.

In July 1945, the Japanese army had 26 infantry divisions in China and another 7 in Korea, but even so, its position was hopeless. The extent of failure can be gauged by the fact that

Japan managed to conjure into existence an alliance that included the world's most populous country; the greatest empire; the greatest industrial, naval, and air power; and the greatest military power. However unintentional, this was a formidable achievement, but it went in tandem with fundamental failure by the army leadership to comprehend the nature of the war in which it was involved. Drawing on its own highly selective interpretation of Japanese history and hobbled by the fact that, never having been defeated, it could not understand defeat, the army was dominated by an ethos that stressed a castelike reverence for rank and was strictly hierarchical. A very formal organization, it had no real capacity for flexibility and initiative at the lower levels. Its broad distaste for political and economic liberalism coexisted with its belief in what it deemed traditional Japanese martial values—specifically, its willingness to die in order to fight. The war was to prove, however, that sacrifice could not confound superior enemy matériel.

H. P. Willmott

See also
Arakan, First Campaign; China, Army; China, Role in War; Guadalcanal, Land Battle for; Guandong Army; Imphal and Kohima, Sieges of; Jiang Jieshi; Konoe Fumimaro, Prince of Japan; Manchuria Campaign; Manzhouguo; New Guinea Campaign; Philippines, U.S. Recapture of; Sino-Japanese War; Zhanggufeng/Khasan, Battle of

References
Boyle, John. *China and Japan at War: The Politics of Collaboration.* Stanford, CA: Stanford University Press, 1972.
Cook, Haruko Taya, and Theodore F. Cook. *Japan at War: An Oral History.* New York: New Press, 1992.
Coox, Alvin. *Kogun: The Japanese Army in the Pacific War.* Quantico, VA: Marine Corps Association, 1959.
Crowley, James. *Japan's Quest for Autonomy: National Security and Foreign Policy, 1930–1938.* Princeton, NJ: Princeton University Press, 1966.
Dower, John. *Japan in Peace and War.* New York: New Press, 1993.
Drea, Edward J. *In the Service of the Emperor: Essays on the Imperial Japanese Army.* Lincoln: University of Nebraska Press, 1998.
Harries, Meirion, and Susie Harries. *Soldiers of the Sun: The Rise and Fall of the Imperial Japanese Army.* New York: Random House, 1991.

Japan, Home Front during the War

Japan experienced the demands of total war as intensely as any other principal combatant in World War II. In 1931, the Japanese Guandong (Kwantung) Army had conquered all Manchuria, and in 1937, the Sino-Japanese War began. It has indeed become customary among Japanese to associate the era of total war for their country with the decade preceding World War II.

Young school girls pressed into service in factories to help with the Japanese war effort, 1945. (Photo by Keystone/Getty Images)

Although Japan was a major industrial power with a population of 73 million people in 1939, it was decidedly deficient in natural resources and not even self-sufficient in food. Virtually everything Japan needed had to come by sea, a vulnerability the United States was quick to exploit. Japan's leaders discounted these economic difficulties and believed that the territories conquered in war, especially the Dutch East Indies, would bring them the resources they required.

Japan lacked the industrial base of its Western enemies. In 1941, for example, it produced 6.7 million tons of steel, whereas the United States produced 73.9 million tons. To some extent, too, Japan was already exhausted by years of fighting in China when its government undertook yet another war with an even more formidable opponent in the United States.

The period of warfare from at least 1937 to 1945 is customarily referred to by the Japanese as a "dark valley" of unrelieved misery and pain. The Great Depression brought widespread hardship to Japan, which was exacerbated by sharp increases in military expenditures prior to 1937 that created a serious balance-of-payments problem and an inflationary crisis. Between 1937 and 1940, real wages fell by 17 percent. By 1939, Japan was spending about 36 percent of its gross national product (GNP) on the military, as opposed to only 23 percent in Germany and 8 percent in Britain.

The Japanese government took early action to control and allocate its dwindling resources effectively. In preparation for total war, it instituted full-scale mobilization measures, whereby it directed systematic programs to put more people to work in agriculture and in ammunition plants. One way to facilitate this was by using women in these sectors. Initially, the government rejected this move as a sign of national weakness, but essentially, it had no other choice. By 1945, women constituted nearly 42 percent of the labor force, a figure higher than that in the United States. By the 1940s, girls as young as 12 were deemed eligible for the workforce.

Japan did have some success in its efforts to increase industrial production. During the period from 1940 to 1944, production increased 25 percent, although much of this rise occurred because the government consolidated production in larger firms. Even so, Japanese efforts in this regard paled beside the achievements of the United States.

The demands of total war went beyond economics to include a variety of efforts designed to strengthen the national will. The nation underwent political restructuring that brought both the dissolution of political parties and the establishment of the Imperial Rule Assistance Association (IRAA) in October 1940. Although the IRAA failed to achieve its goal of restructuring Japanese society along the lines of the Fascist states in Europe, its establishment symbolized increasing domestic repression. Simultaneously, governmental monitoring of dissidents increased. The Special Higher Police and the Military Police carefully monitored religious sects, Koreans, and suspected leftists and pacifists.

The Japanese people fully supported war with the United States, which they believed had been forced on their nation by American economic policies designed to cripple Japan. Nonetheless, the government instituted rigid censorship and used propaganda and the state-controlled education system to strengthen national spiritual mobilization. As the diarist Kiyoshi Kiyosawa noted, the Japanese were bombarded with appeals to remember their "spiritual" superiority over their enemies. Ultranationalist societies, all to some extent proclaiming Japan's destiny to expand its territory on the Asian continent, also proliferated. In addition, the government established several women's patriotic societies designed to improve civil defense, welcome soldiers home from the battlefront, visit hospitals to comfort the sick and wounded, and raise money for the relief of bereaved families. Small communities were also organized, so that everyday life was systematized to impose a shared social unity in which people might monitor their neighbors, and privacy became a thing of the past. Perhaps the saddest manifestation of Japan's response to total war was the decision late in the war to utilize suicide missions. The so-called kamikaze played on the courage and fatalism of young men who believed their country faced destruction and hoped their deaths would serve family and country.

Early in the Pacific war, food shortages became apparent. In December 1940, the government began food rationing on a ticket system. Often, basic necessities, such as cotton and soy sauce, were also strictly rationed. The scarcity of food caused black markets and serious malnutrition.

Even while Japanese society was reorganizing in response to the demands of total war, actions by Japan's military enemies forced increasing disruptions of the emerging total war system. One particular concern was the vulnerability of Japan's major cities to aerial attack, as the strategic bombing of civilian centers became part of the new era of total war. The April 1942 Doolittle raid first demonstrated this vulnerability to the Japanese people. Although the raid inflicted little physical damage, it had a pronounced psychological effect.

From June 1944, the United States began a strategic bombing campaign directed against Japanese industry, the bulk of which was located in the cities. Constructed largely of wooden buildings, the cities were appallingly vulnerable to firebomb attack, as shown in the great 9–10 March 1945 raid on Tokyo, probably the most destructive in the history of air warfare; it claimed some 120,000 lives and was followed by other attacks. One by one, the Japanese cities became burned-out shells. Americans justified these attacks as essential to reach and destroy the largely dispersed Japanese industrial base, but civilians paid a horrific price. By the time Japan surrendered in August 1945, every major city except the shrine city of Kyoto had been torched, and some 10 million Japanese had fled the cities to escape the raids.

The government began this resettlement in August 1944 by moving 350,000 urban schoolchildren between the ages of 8 and 12 into village temples, shrines, and inns. In 1945, a further 450,000 elementary school students were evacuated. Although Germany's surrender in May 1945 seemingly offered Japan a chance to extricate itself from a clearly worsening situation, the government refused to take the initiative, and U.S. forces stepped up their firebombing of what was left of Japan's major cities. In some cases, this bombing merely rearranged the rubble. Meanwhile, submarine attacks on Japanese shipping and aerial mining of Japanese harbors and coastline destroyed the already marginal Japanese shipping capacity, cutting off the flow of vital imports of food and oil and further damaging the economy.

Finally, in August 1945, the United States dropped atomic bombs on Hiroshima and Nagasaki. At the same time, the Soviet Union honored its pledge at Potsdam and declared war on Japan. Hundreds of thousands of lives were lost as a result of this "twin shock," and Japan finally surrendered. The nation was devastated both physically and psychologically.

Majima Ayu

See also

B-29 Raids against Japan; Hiroshima, Bombing of; Japan, Occupation of; Japan, Official Surrender; Japan, Surrender of; Kamikaze; Nagasaki, Bombing of; Potsdam Conference; Tokyo, Bombing of (18 April 1942); Tokyo, Bombing of (9–10 March 1945); Women in World War II

References

Cook, Haruko Taya, and Theodore Cook. *Japan at War: An Oral History*. New York: New Press, 1992.

Dower, John W. *Japan in War and Peace: Selected Essays*. New York: Free Press, 1993.

Gibney, Frank, ed. Senso: *The Japanese Remember the Pacific War—Letters to the Editor of the* Aashi Shimbun. Trans. Beth Cary. Armonk, NY: M. E. Sharpe, 1995.

Harvens, Thomas. *Valley of Darkness: The Japanese People and World War Two*. New York: Norton, 1978.

Japan, Navy

By the 1920s, the Nippon Teikoku Kaigun (Imperial Japanese Navy, or IJN), which dated only from the late 1860s, ranked as the third-largest navy in the world. By then, it had fought three wars, and at the Battle of Tsushima in May 1905, it won one of the most comprehensive and annihilating victories ever recorded in naval warfare. The IJN was to fight two more wars, one in the western Pacific, directed against China, and the other throughout the Pacific, eastern and southeast Asia, and the Indian Ocean. The latter resulted in utter and total national defeat and the destruction of the Kaigun as a service.

From 1907 onward, IJN leaders identified the United States as the enemy against which preparations had to be made. Yet the Kaigun faced a basic and insoluble problem, namely, Japan's acceptance of the limitation of its navy to three-fifths those of the United States and Great Britain, as agreed at the 1921–1922 Washington Naval Conference. This stance resulted from the conviction of Minister of the Navy Admiral Kato Tomosaburo that the only thing worse for Japan than an unrestricted naval construction race with the United States would be war against that country. Kato believed an unrestricted naval race could only bring the remorseless and irreversible erosion of Japan's position relative to the United States, and Japan therefore had to seek security through peaceful cooperation and diplomatic arrangements rather than through international rivalry and conquest. Kato and others viewed the navy as a deterrent and, in the event of war, a defense; however, they also believed Japan's best interests would be served not by confrontation and conflict with the United States but by arrangements that limited American naval construction relative to Japan and so provided the basis of future American recognition and acceptance of Japan's regional position. The problem was that events unfolded in a manner that forced the IJN into planning for a war that, by its own calculations, it was certain to lose.

The basis of this position was twofold. First, the Kaigun found itself obliged to fight not one but two wars. It would have to confront an American enemy that would seek battle and undertake major amphibious undertakings across the western Pacific to bring the war to Japanese home waters. It would also be obliged to fight a maritime war to defend Japanese shipping and seaborne trade. Losing either would result in Japan's full-scale defeat, no matter whether its navy lost a naval war that left the merchant fleet intact and undiminished or whether Japan was defeated in a maritime war that left its fleet's naval forces unreduced. In the event, Japan and the Kaigun suffered a double defeat, both naval and mercantile.

In a very obvious sense, the maritime defeat was one that could have been predicted. Four Shimushu- or Type A-class escort warships were ordered under the 1937 naval estimates, but none was begun before November 1938, to be completed between June 1940 and March 1941. In December 1941, these four ships were the only purpose-built escorts in service with the IJN, and they all lacked underwater detection gear (sonar).

Quite simply, Japanese industry did not have the capacity to build and service both warships and merchantmen, nor to build both fleet units and escorts (see Table 1). Japan's limited industrial capacity forced it to choose between warships and merchantmen, between building and refitting. Moreover, the Kaigun had no real understanding of trade defense and the principles of convoy. Not until November 1943 did the navy institute general convoy, and lacking sufficient escorts and integrated air defense, this practice merely concentrated targets rather than protecting shipping.

Herein, too, lay the basis of Japan's naval defeat in the Pacific. In order to fight and defeat the American attempt to carry the war across the Pacific, the Kaigun developed the *zengen sakusen* (all-out battle strategy), a concept that envisaged the conduct of the decisive battle in five phases. Submarines gathered off the Hawaiian Islands would provide timely reports of U.S. fleet movements, and with top surface speeds of 24 knots, they were to inflict a series of nighttime attacks on U.S. formations. It was anticipated they would suffer accumulated losses of one-tenth of strength in this phase and the same in the next, when Japanese shore-based aircraft, especially built for superior range and strike capability, would engage American formations. The enemy would then be subjected to night attack by massed destroyer formations, Japanese battle cruisers and cruisers being used to blast aside escorts: the Japanese anticipated massed scissors attacks using as many as 120 Long Lance torpedoes in a single effort. Thereafter, with U.S. formations losing their cohesion and organization, Japanese carriers would join the battle, employed in separate divisions rather than concentrated, in order to neutralize their opposite numbers. Finally, Japanese battleships would engage the American battle line, in what Japanese planners expected to be the decisive battle. In the 1930s, when these ideas were formulated, the Japanese expected the main battle would take place around the Marianas.

The Kaigun organized its formations and building and refitting programs accordingly. Destroyers featured torpedo armaments, and battleships and cruisers emphasized armament, speed, and armor rather than range. The Yamato-class battleships, at their full displacement of 71,659 tons, carried a main armament of 9 × 18.1-inch guns, an armored belt of 16 inches, and turrets with a maximum of 25.6 inches of armor; they had a top speed of 27.7 knots and a range of 8,600 nautical miles at 19 knots or 4,100 nautical miles at 27 knots. These ships were deliberately conceived as bigger and more formidably armed and protected than any American battleship able to use the Panama Canal. The Japanese quest for qualitative superiority extended through the other classes of

Table 1
Wartime Commissioning/Completion of Major Units by the Japanese and U.S. Navies

	CV	CVL	CVE	BB	CB	CA	CL	DD	Esc/ DE	CD/PF	SS
December 1941											
Imperial Japanese Navy	—	—	—	—	—	—	—	—	—	—	—
U.S. Navy	—	—	—	—	—	—	1	2	—	—	2
1942											
Imperial Japanese Navy	2	2	2	2	—	—	1	10	—	—	20
U.S. Navy	1	—	11	4	—	—	8	84	—	—	34
1943											
Imperial Japanese Navy	—	1	2	—	—	—	3	12	18	—	36
U.S. Navy	6	9	24	2	—	4	7	126	234	65	56
1944											
Imperial Japanese Navy	5	1	—	—	—	—	3	7	20	72	35
U.S. Navy	7	—	33	2	2	1	11	78	181	8	80
January–September 1945											
Imperial Japanese Navy	—	—	—	—	—	—	—	3	20	39	20
U.S. Navy	4	—	9	—	—	8	6	61	5	—	31
Wartime totals											
Imperial Japanese Navy	7	4	4	2	—	—	7	32	58	111	116
U.S. Navy	18	9	77	8	2	13	33	349	420	73	203

Note: The drawing of direct comparisons between different types of warships, specifically escorts, is somewhat difficult. Counted under the heading "Esc" in the Japanese listings are named escorts and patrol boats; under the heading "CD" are the *kaiboken*, or coastal defense ships. These types were not the direct equivalents of U.S. destroyer escorts and frigates, respectively, but diversity precludes these types of American and Japanese ships being compared with anything but one another. U.S. figures exclude Lend-Lease vessels.

Dashes = zero	CL = light cruiser
CV = fleet carrier	DD = destroyer
CVL = light carrier	Esc = escort
CVE = escort carrier	DE = destroyer escort
BB = batttleship	CD = coastal defense ship
CB = battle cruiser	PF = frigate
CA = heavy cruiser	SS = submarine

warships. As part of this process, the Kaigun developed the famous Long Lance torpedo; land-based and carrier-based aircraft such as the A6M Zero-sen and long-range Betty bomber; and long-range submarines, one type equipped with seaplanes in order to extend scouting range: individually and collectively, these were qualitatively unequaled in 1941 and 1942, and in terms of night-fighting capability in 1941, the Kaigun undoubtedly had no peer.

Despite these apparent advantages, the Japanese naval battle plan represented an inversion of the reality of what was required. By December 1941, the Kaigun had basically secured parity in the Pacific with the United States, with warships, carrier air groups and aircraft, and a pool of trained manpower that were qualitatively probably the best in the world. The problem, however, was that Japan and its armed services lacked the means to fortify the islands of the central and western Pacific. The perimeter along which the Japanese planned to fight the Americans to a standstill largely consisted of gaps. Japan had neither the shipping nor the base organizations needed to transform the island groups into the air bases that were essential to the fleet. The latter, moreover, could not be guaranteed to be permanently ready to meet any American move, which would, by definition, be made in a

strength and at a time that all but ensured American victory. Individual Japanese bases or even several bases within a group or neighboring groups could be overwhelmed by an enemy free to take the initiative and choose when to mount offensive operations, a second flaw within the zengen sakusen concept. By 1942, the Kaigun was only prepared to fight the battle it intended to win, and it could only win the battle it intended to fight. Instead, of course, the battle it was called on to fight was not the one for which it had prepared.

The IJN, moreover, faced not one enemy but two. It opened hostilities with a total strength of 10 battleships; 6 fleet and 3 light fleet carriers and 1 escort carrier; 18 heavy and 20 light cruisers; 111 destroyers; and 71 submarines. A token of its future problems lay in the fact that only 1 fleet unit, a destroyer, was not in service on 6 December 1941. But even when it went to war, the Kaigun faced a prewar U.S. Navy that, between May 1942 and November 1943, fought it to a standstill. After that date, the Kaigun faced a wartime U.S. Navy, virtually every ship of which had entered service after Pearl Harbor. The Japanese shipbuilding effort from 1942 to 1944, though substantial, was simply overwhelmed by a truly remarkable American industrial achievement: 18 U.S. fleet carriers to 7 for Japan, 9 light fleet carriers to 4, 77 escort car-

Table 2
The State of Japanese Shipping, 1941–1945 (in tons)

Year	Built	Captured and Salvaged	Total Acquisitions	Lost	Net Loss in Year	Shipping Available on		Tonnage Afloat	Laid up	Percent Laid up
1942	266,000	566,000	832,000	1,065,000	-233,000	31 March 1942	6,150,000	5,375,000	775,000	12.61
						31 December 1942	5,942,000			
1943	769,000	109,000	878,000	1,821,000	-943,000	31 March 1943	5,733,000	4,833,000	900,000	15.70
						31 December 1943	4,999,000			
1944	1,699,000	36,000	1,735,000	3,892,000	-2,157,000	31 March 1944	4,352,000	3,527,000	825,000	18.96
						31 December 1944	2,842,000			
1945	559,000	6,000	565,000	1,782,000	-1,217,000	31 March 1945	2,465,000	1,659,000	806,000	32.70
						15 August 1945	1,625,000	948,000	677,000	41.66

Note: The figures and calculations within this table have been developed by the contributor and through his research. The information has been compiled from various sources to give a possible window into the subject of the table.

riers to 4, 8 battleships to 2, 13 heavy and 33 light cruisers to 4 light cruisers, 349 destroyers and 420 destroyer escorts to 90, and 203 submarines to 116. U.S. superiority was not simply numerical: radio, radar, and diversity of weaponry were all areas in which the Kaigun could not match its U.S. enemy but was systematically outclassed as the war entered its second and third years.

During 1943 and 1944, the Americans acquired such overwhelming numerical superiority that the Kaigun was denied not merely any chance of victory but even any means of effective response. Between 26 December 1943 and 24 October 1944, Japanese warships and aircraft destroyed no American fleet units, if U.S. submarines are excluded. The simple truth was not just that the Japanese were prepared to die in order to fight but also that the only way the Japanese could fight was to die.

Events in 1945 conspired to demonstrate the singular ineffectiveness of such a course of action, as Japanese losses between July 1944 and August 1945 reflected both this dilemma and the wider national defeat. In the war overall, the Kaigun lost 1,028 warships of 2,310,704 tons, of which 631 warships of 1,348,492 tons were destroyed in the last 13 months of the war (see Table 2). The wartime losses incurred by the merchant fleet—not the service auxiliaries—told the same story, totaling 1,181.5 merchantmen (there were navy, army, and civilian ships and, occasionally, shared ships, which are here calculated as one half a ship) of 3,389,202 tons, of which 811 vessels of 2,077,249 tons were lost in this same final period, after the Battle of the Philippine Sea. Losses of this order were both the cause and the result of defeat, in practice reducing the Kaigun to no more than an ever less effective coastal defense force.

By August 1945, Japan had been pushed to the edge of final, total, and comprehensive defeat, losing all semblance

of strategic mobility. Its industry was in end-run production; its people would have died by the millions from disease and starvation had the war lasted into spring 1946. To all intents and purposes, the Kaigun had by then ceased to exist, as American carrier air groups flew combat air patrol over Japanese airfields. A remarkable American achievement, unparalleled in 400 years, had reduced the Kaigun to impotent irrelevance. States, especially great powers, are rarely defeated by naval power, but in this case, the Kaigun had been entirely powerless to prevent such an outcome.

H. P. Willmott

See also

Aviation, Naval; Battle Cruisers; Battleships; Destroyers; Naval Warfare; Submarines; Torpedoes; United States, Submarine Campaign against Japanese Shipping; *Yamato*

References

Dull, Paul S. *A Battle History of the Imperial Japanese Navy, 1941–45.* Annapolis, MD: Naval Institute Press, 1978.

Evans, David C., and Mark R. Peattie. Kaigun: *Strategy, Tactics & Technology in the Imperial Japanese Navy, 1887–1941.* Annapolis, MD: Naval Institute Press, 1997.

Ike Nobutaka, ed. and trans. *Japan's Decision for War: Records of the 1941 Policy Conferences.* Stanford, CA: Stanford University Press, 1967.

Kurono Taeru. *Nihon wo horoboshita kokubohoshin* (The Imperial defense policy that ruined Japan). Tokyo: Bungeishunju, 2002.

Nomura Minoru. *Tenno, Fushiminomiya to Nihonkaigun* (Emperor Hirohito, Prince Fushimi and the Imperial Japanese Navy). Tokyo: Bungeishunju, 1988.

Peattie, Mark R. *Sunburst: The Rise of Japanese Naval Air Power, 1909–1941.* Annapolis MD: Naval Institute Press, 2001.

Pelz, Stephen E. *Race to Pearl Harbor: The Failure of the Second London Naval Conference and the Onset of World War II.* Cambridge, MA: Harvard University Press, 1974.

Japan, Official Surrender (2 September 1945)

On 10 August 1945, the Japanese government issued a statement accepting the terms of the Potsdam Declaration of July that had outlined "unconditional surrender." The following day, U.S. Secretary of State James Byrnes accepted Japan's offer to end hostilities. Emperor Hirohito announced Japan's surrender to the Japanese people on 15 August.

The official Japanese surrender ceremony took place at 9:00 A.M. on 2 September aboard the U.S. battleship *Missouri* in Tokyo Bay. The supreme commander for the Allied powers, General Douglas MacArthur, formally accepted the Japanese capitulation by signing the instrument of surrender. Foreign Minister Shigemitsu Mamoru and General Umezu Yoshijiro signed for Japan. Admiral Chester W. Nimitz represented the United States, followed by General Hsu Yung-ch'ang for China, Admiral Sir Bruce Fraser for the United Kingdom, Lieutenant General Kuzma Derevyanko for the Soviet Union, General Sir Thomas Blamey for Australia, Colonel L. Moore Cosgrave for Canada, General Jacques Le Clerc for France, Admiral C. E. L. Helfrich for the Netherlands, and Air Vice Marshal Leonard Isitt for New Zealand.

Scott T. Maciejewski

See also

Byrnes, James Francis; Hirohito, Emperor of Japan; Japan, Surrender of; MacArthur, Douglas

References

Butow, Robert J. C. *Japan's Decision to Surrender*. Stanford, CA: Stanford University Press, 1954.

Frank, Richard B. *Downfall: The End of the Imperial Japanese Empire*. New York: Random House, 1999.

"The End of the War in the Pacific: Surrender Documents in Facsimile." National Publication no. 46–6. Washington, DC: U.S. Government Printing Office, 1945.

Japan, Role in the War

The efforts of Japan, one of the three major Axis powers of World War II, to enhance its own position in East and Southeast Asia were responsible for making the conflict a truly global one and the Pacific region one of the two major fulcrums of a worldwide war. From the late nineteenth century onward, a modernizing Japan sought to become the dominant power in Asia, replacing the European empires and subjecting China and Southeast Asia to its own effective hegemony. In 1895, Japan annexed the Chinese island of Taiwan (Formosa), which it retained until 1945. After its victory in the 1904–1905 Russo-Japanese War, Japan sought to replace Japanese influence in the northeastern Chinese provinces of Manchuria. In 1910, it annexed the neighboring state of Korea.

Japanese leaders, who quickly joined World War I in 1914 on the side of the Allied powers of Great Britain and France, saw that conflict primarily as an opportunity to secure further gains in Asia. By the end of 1914, they had taken over the German concession in Shandong (Shantung) Province, China, and driven Germany from various Pacific possessions—the Marshall, Caroline, and Marianas Islands—that Japan annexed. In early 1915, Japan also demanded substantial political, economic, and territorial concessions from China, which would have given it a special status in that country. Under pressure, the Chinese government initially accepted most of the Twenty-One Demands, but it later repudiated them. From 1918 to 1920, Japanese troops also intervened in northeast Russia in the Vladivostok area, as did British and American forces. Their mission was supposedly to protect rail communications links and safeguard Allied supplies in the region after the Bolshevik government that took power in November 1917 negotiated the peace of Brest-Litovsk with Germany and abandoned the war. Japan's allies, however, feared that Japan sought permanent territorial gains at Russian expense, something they hoped their own forces might manage to prevent.

At the 1919 Paris Peace Conference, Japan sought to replace Germany in the Shandong concession. Student protests in China, which began on 4 May 1919 in Beijing, forced Japan to renounce its privileges formally, but in practice, the area remained under effective Japanese control. Under the 1921–1922 Washington conference treaties, Japan agreed to accept a fleet only three-fifths the size of those of Great Britain and the United States and to respect both the territorial integrity of China and the interests of other nations, including the Western colonial powers, in the Pacific region. Throughout the 1920s, Japanese troops from the Guandong (Kwantung) Army remained stationed in north China, supposedly to safeguard Japan's special economic interests in China. The chaotic state of much of China, divided between rival warlord armies and the Republican governments of the Nationalist Party—the Guomindang, or GMD (Kuomintang, or KMT)—of Sun Yixian (Sun Yat-sen) and his successor, the military leader Jiang Jieshi (Chiang Kai-shek), was an additional pretext for the Japanese military presence.

In 1931, units from the Guandong Army deliberately staged the Mukden Incident, an episode in which Japanese officials alleged Chinese troops had sabotaged Japanese-controlled railway lines near Mukden (Shenyang) in Manchuria. This event became the pretext for Japanese forces, without authorization from the civilian government in Tokyo, to take over all of northeast China; there, in March 1932, they established the puppet state of Manzhouguo

(Manchukuo, later Manzhoudiguo [Manchoutikuo]), a nominally independent nation under the rule of the last emperor of China, Aixinjueluo Puyi (Aisingioro P'u-i, known to Westerners as Henry Puyi). In response to protests from the League of Nations—most of whose member nations, together with the United States and the Soviet Union, refused to recognize the new state and imposed rather weak economic sanctions on both Japan and Manzhouguo—Japan withdrew from the league in 1933.

Japanese forces were also based throughout much of north China, their presence a perennial irritant to the Chinese government, with the potential to provoke military clashes. For much of the 1930s, the Chinese Nationalist government, now firmly under the control of President Jiang Jieshi (who had consolidated his military position in the late 1920s), effectively acquiesced in Japanese demands. Although Jiang believed that war with Japan was probably inevitable in time, he sought to defer this until, with the benefit of German military advisers, he had successfully modernized China's armed forces. In the early 1930s, his first priority was to eliminate the GMD's major political rival, the Chinese Communist Party (CCP). The CCP was led by the charismatic and innovative Mao Zedong (Mao Tse-tung), against whose forces Jiang mounted annual campaigns every year from 1930 to 1935. Only after December 1936, when another leading Chinese politician, the Manchurian warlord Zhang Xueliang (Chang Hsüen-liang) captured him and made his release conditional on joining with the Communists to form a united Chinese front against the Japanese, did Jiang reluctantly and temporarily renounce his deeply rooted anti-Communist hostility. The two camps never trusted each other, and political factionalism within the GMD also persisted throughout the war, hampering Jiang's freedom of action and his ability to wage effective warfare against Japanese forces.

Full-scale war between Japan and China began in July 1937, when long-standing tensions with Japan—provoked by Japan's effective annexation of Manchuria in 1931 and a continuing series of territorial, economic, and political incursions in other areas—caused the escalation of a small skirmish near the Lugouqiao (Lukouch ao) Marco Polo Bridge, close to Beijing (Peking) in Hebei (Hopeh). The Chinese invariably referred to the conflict as the "War of Resistance against Japanese Aggression." Until December 1941, when China formally declared war on Japan and thus aligned itself with the Western Allies after the Japanese attack on Pearl Harbor, Japan dismissively referred to the conflict as the "China Incident"; after that date, it became part of the "Greater East Asia War."

In its early stages, the war was one of rapid movement and military victory for Japan. In late July 1937, Japanese troops took over the entire Beijing-Tianjin (Tientsin) area of north China. They inflicted a series of major defeats upon Jiang's military, wiping out most of his modernized units and, over the following 18 months, successively taking Shanghai and Nanjing (Nanking), Guangzhou (Canton), and Wuhan, China's provisional capital after Nanjing fell. Although Chinese troops had occasional triumphs, notably the April 1938 Battle of Taierzhuang (Hsieh Chan T'ai-Erh-Chuang), these were rarely followed up. Japanese leaders assumed Jiang would sue for peace before the end of 1938, but to their frustration, he refused to do so. Instead, he adopted a strategy of trading space for time, based on the assumption that by retreating, the Chinese could force the Japanese to overextend themselves, making them vulnerable to a lengthy war of attrition. This prediction proved substantially correct, as by 1940, Japanese forces were bogged down in an inconclusive war in mainland China, occupying vast tracts of territory without fully controlling them. Even so, despite the scorched-earth policy Jiang followed, the regions he ceded to Japanese rule from March 1940, exercised through the puppet regime of renegade Chinese politician Wang Jingwei (Wang Ching-wei), included most of China's leading cities, its major industrial areas, and most of the fertile and densely populated agricultural regions.

Much as they did between 1914 and 1918, Japanese leaders in the 1930s believed the deteriorating European situation offered them further opportunities to enhance their influence in Asia. From May 1932, when military cadets assassinated Japanese premier Inukai Tsuyoshi, Japan's military largely dominated the government. In November 1936, Japan and Nazi Germany, whose National Socialist dictator Adolf Hitler had pursued increasingly aggressive policies in Europe since 1933, signed the Anti-Comintern Pact, an agreement directed at all Communist states and individuals, whom both these authoritarian and Fascist regimes perceived as their chief ideological opponents. The prime target was the Soviet Union, whose territory both Germany and Japan ultimately coveted. In 1937, Fascist Italy also joined the pact, effectively aligning all the dissatisfied have-not states of the post–World War I era together. In 1938 and 1939, Japanese forces in Manchuria and Mongolia clashed repeatedly with Soviet units, encounters that culminated in August 1939 in a major Soviet victory at the Battle of Nomonhan on the Manchurian border, the world largest tank battle to that date.

In October 1938, the Japanese government announced its intention of creating a New East Asian Order, which would end western colonialism in the region and replace it with Japanese leadership and dominance. One year later, in September 1939, Germany invaded Poland, whereon Britain and France declared war on Germany. The spring 1940 German blitzkrieg quickly brought the defeat of Belgium and the Netherlands as well as French and German domination of virtually all of western Europe, leaving Britain embattled against Hitler and British, Dutch, and French colonial possessions vulnerable to

Japan. In September 1940, Japan, Germany, and Italy signed the Tripartite Pact, obliging each nation to assist the others should another country attack them, though not to assist in a war in which one of three was itself the aggressive party. Japanese officials hoped this agreement would persuade Great Britain and the United States to make concessions to Japanese interests in East Asia, including pressuring the recalcitrant Chinese government into a peace settlement that would end the war in China and grant Japan easy control of much of that country. They also sought Western acquiescence in the establishment of Japanese bases in French Indochina, which would be particularly useful in interdicting the flow of military and other supplies to southwest China.

For some months, Japanese military and political leaders debated whether they should follow a northern strategy and attack the Soviet Union or a southern strategy designed to enhance their position in Southeast Asia at the expense of Britain, France, the Netherlands, and the United States. After bitter debate, Japan picked the second option in April 1941 and signed a neutrality pact with the Soviet Union, while opening protracted negotiations with the United States in the hope of persuading the American government to accept Japanese dominance in both China and French Indochina. In late July 1941, Japanese troops moved into French Indochina, allowing the Vichy-affiliated colonial authorities to continue as the nominal government but establishing bases and effectively controlling the colony. The American government responded by freezing Japanese assets in the United States and imposing a complete embargo on trade with Japan. Japan purchased virtually all its oil from the United States and only had sufficient stockpiles to supply its military for two years. The two countries continued intensive diplomatic negotiations for several more months, but until early December 1941, most Japanese leaders, unwilling to relinquish, moderate, or compromise their ambitions in China and Southeast Asia, believed war with the United States and other Western states was inevitable. Japan was under some pressure from Germany to take military action against its enemies; Hitler would have preferred that Japan move against the Soviet Union, which his forces had invaded in June 1941, but he settled for Japanese action against Britain and the United States, even though he was not yet formally at war with the latter.

Negotiations between Japan and the United States finally broke down at the end of November. On 7 December 1941, carrier-based Japanese warplanes attacked the U.S. Pacific Fleet at its base at Pearl Harbor, Hawaii, only declaring war after this assault had taken place. Japanese forces quickly swept through and conquered much of Southeast Asia, and by mid-1942, they controlled the former American colony of the Philippines; Dutch Indochina (Indonesia); and the British colonies of Malaya, Singapore, Burma, and Hong Kong. They also threatened Australia and India. Japan now controlled most of the valuable economic resources it had coveted, including the oil wells of Dutch Indochina, Malaya's tin and rubber, and Southeast Asia's rice fields. Defeating Japan took second place in Allied strategy to victory over Germany and Italy, which both declared war on the United States immediately after Pearl Harbor. Even so, in the long run, Japan could not match the United States in industrial capacity or population, and it found itself unable to continue the war indefinitely. Although Japan proclaimed the establishment of the Greater East Asia Co-prosperity Sphere, to which all those areas under its hegemony could belong, and although it established quasi-independent collaborationist governments in China, the Philippines, and Burma, Japanese rule was far from popular with its new subjects. Japanese military successes undoubtedly played a crucial role in the dissolution of Western imperialism in Asia once World War II was over, but brutal atrocities committed against the local populations and the blatant exploitation of all available resources for the Japanese war effort undercut Japan's claims to gratitude as the power that had liberated most of Asia from Western colonial dominance.

Japan's strategy rested on the hope of a quick victory in Asia, after which its leaders trusted they would be able to persuade the Western allies, especially the United States, to accept a negotiated peace. In June 1942, the U.S. victory in the Battle of Midway, in which the American fleet destroyed three of Japan's four fleet carriers, effectively restricted the Japanese navy to defensive operations in the future. The rapid drives by Japanese troops through much of Southeast Asia ended about the same time, and Japanese military power reached its furthest extent in summer 1942. Throughout the war, the China theater continued to tie down over a million Japanese troops. In late 1942, Allied forces under the command of General Douglas MacArthur began the selective island-hopping campaigns in the Pacific that would gradually isolate Japan, interdicting the shipment of vital supplies and slowly threatening the Japanese homeland. Although Japanese forces often fought bitterly, exhibiting the bravery of desperation, they found themselves increasingly outnumbered and outequipped, with little hope of reinforcements. On the home front, the Japanese civilian population—like those of the areas occupied by Japan and, indeed, Japanese soldiers as well—experienced increasing privations from 1943 on, with food and other staples rationed and in ever shorter supply. From summer 1944, American airplanes sub-

Over 1.5 million Japanese soldiers and civilians died in World War II, and ten times that many were displaced.

jected all major Japanese cities except the shrine city of Kyoto to ferocious bombing raids, and after three months of heavy fighting, U.S. troops took the island of Okinawa in late June 1945, opening the route for the invasion of Japan itself.

By the summer of 1945, facing what seemed inevitable defeat, some Japanese politicians sought to explore the possibility of a negotiated peace, using the still officially neutral Soviet Union as an intermediary, but these talks proved inconclusive. Military leaders in Japan were still determined to fight on and defend the homeland islands to the last. At the July 1945 Potsdam Conference of Allied leaders, Soviet president Josef Stalin agreed to enter the war against Japan. Receiving word that the first atomic bomb test had been successful, U.S. President Harry S Truman called on Japan to surrender forthwith or face horrific attacks from new weapons of unparalleled destructiveness. The Potsdam Declaration proved unavailing, and on 6 August 1945, an American B-2 bomber exploded a nuclear device over the Japanese city of Hiroshima. Two days later, the Soviet Union declared war on Japan, and on 9 August, a second bomb was dropped on the city of Nagasaki. By this time, Soviet troops had already begun a highly effective campaign in Manchuria. Faced with the prospect of additional casualties in a homeland invasion and uncertain whether Japan might have to endure yet further nuclear attacks, the Emperor Hirohito exerted his authority over the still recalcitrant Japanese military on 14 August and made a radio broadcast accepting the terms of the Potsdam Declaration. Three days later, he instructed Japanese forces to lay down their arms.

Japan ended the war devastated—its cities in ruins, its population starving, its shipping and trade largely destroyed, and its colonial empire gone. Over 1.5 million Japanese soldiers and civilians died during the war, and until 1952, the country was under American occupation. Ironically, Cold War pressures soon meant that Japan became a crucial ally of its former enemies, especially of the United States, and the linchpin of American strategy in Asia. China, by contrast, where the Sino-Japanese War helped to weaken the Nationalist government and enhance the position of the Chinese Communist Party (which took power in October 1949), was for several decades after that event a sworn enemy of its former ally, the United States. Other Asian powers undoubtedly had long memories of Japanese wartime atrocities against their countries, and they particularly resented efforts by the Japanese government and nationalist organizations to minimize these or even deny that they ever occurred. Yet by encouraging the Japanese economic recovery, the United States helped to make Japan Asia's strongest economic power, thereby enabling it to achieve the dominant position in the Asia-Pacific region for which Japanese leaders had strived since the late nineteenth century.

Priscilla Roberts and Saito Naoki

See also

Aixinjueluo Puyi; Atomic Bomb, Decision to Employ; Burma Theater; China, Role in War; China-Burma-India Theater; French Indochina; Guandong Army; Hirohito, Emperor of Japan; Hong Kong, Battle of; Japan, Army; Japan, Home Front during the War; Japan, Navy; Japan, Surrender of; Jiang Jeshi; Malaya Campaign; Manchuria Campaign; Manzhouguo; Mao Zedong; Netherlands East Indies; Pearl Harbor, Attack on; Philippines, Japanese Capture of; Shanghai, Battle of; Singapore, Battle for

References

Cook, Haruko Taya, and Theodore F. Cook. *Japan at War: An Oral History*. New York: New Press, 1992.

Dower, John. *War without Mercy: Race and Power in the Pacific War*. New York: Pantheon, 1986.

Hanneman, Mary. *Japan Faces the World, 1925–1952*. New York: Longman, 2001.

Haslam, Jonathan. *The Soviet Union and the Threat from the East, 1933–41: Moscow, Tokyo, and the Prelude to the Pacific War*. Pittsburgh, PA: University of Pittsburgh Press, 1992.

Ienaga Saburo. *The Pacific War, 1931–1945*. New York: Random House, 1978.

Iriye Akira. *Power and Culture: The Japanese-American War*. Cambridge, MA: Harvard University Press, 1981.

———. *The Origins of the Second World War in Asia and the Pacific*. New York: Longman, 1987.

Lamb, Margaret, and Nicholas Tarling. *From Versailles to Pearl Harbor: The Origins of the Second World War in Europe and Asia*. New York: Palgrave, 2001.

Li, Narangoa, and Robert Cribb. *Imperial Japan and National Identities in Asia, 1895–1945*. New York: Routledge, 2003.

Marshall, Jonathan. *To Have and Have Not: Southeast Asian Raw Materials and the Origins of the Pacific War*. Berkeley: University of California Press, 1995.

Spector, Ronald H. *Eagle against the Sun: The American War with Japan*. New York: Free Press/Macmillan, 1985.

Japan, Surrender of (15 August 1945)

By early 1945, it was clear to most observers that Japan could not hope to win the war. The U.S. captured Iwo Jima in February. Okinawa, secured in June, could be used as a staging area for a U.S. invasion of the Japanese home islands. Germany, Japan's only remaining ally, had been defeated in May. Meanwhile, B-29 Superfortresses flying from the Marianas were destroying Japan's cities, while submarines cut off Japanese seaborne trade and B-29 aerial mining eliminated much of the important coastal trade, raising the specter of starvation for the Japanese people. Still, Japan fought on.

Revisionist historians have held that since the Japanese government was, by this time, seeking desperately to leave the war, employing the atomic bomb against Japan was unnecessary. Intercepts of diplomatic messages, however, indicate that Japan had still not reached the decision to surrender when the first bomb was dropped. Although Emperor Hirohito and his principal advisers had concluded that Japan could not win the

U.S. Fleet Admiral Chester W. Nimitz signs surrender documents recognizing the defeat of Japan as officials and soldiers look on, USS Missouri, Tokyo Bay, Japan. General Douglas MacArthur (left), Admiral William F. Halsey (center), and Rear Admiral Forrest P. Sherman (right) stand behind Nimitz. (Hulton Archive)

war, they hoped for a negotiated settlement after a last "decisive battle" that would force the Allies to grant more favorable peace terms. On 28 July, the Japanese government formally rejected acceptance of the Potsdam Declaration, as demanded by U.S. President Harry S Truman two days before—a refusal that led Truman to decide to employ the atomic bomb.

On 6 August 1945, the United States dropped an atomic bomb on the Japanese city of Hiroshima. About 100,000 people perished outright or died later from radiation effects; another 40,000 were injured, and most of the remaining population suffered some long-term radiation damage. Even so, this carnage was less than that inflicted in the firebombing of Tokyo in March 1945. Meeting with the emperor, the army leadership still strongly opposed accepting the Potsdam Declaration.

On 8 August, the Soviet Union declared war on Japan, with Josef Stalin honoring his pledge at Yalta to enter the war

against Japan "two or three months after the defeat of Germany." One day later, Soviet troops invaded Manchuria in force. That same day, a B-19 bomber dropped a second atomic bomb, on Nagaski. The blast there claimed about 70,000 dead, either killed outright or dying later from radiation, and it injured as many more.

After prolonged meetings with his top advisers, Emperor Hirohito made the decision for peace on 14 August. He stated that as onerous as it would be to order the surrender, have the Japanese homeland occupied, and see loyal servants face possible trial as war criminals, these considerations had to be weighed against the devastation facing the Japanese people in a continuation of the war.

Braving possible assassination by high-level fanatics determined to stage a coup d'état and fight to the end, Hirohito communicated this decision over the radio on 15 August at noon

Tokyo time, the first occasion on which the Japanese people had heard his voice. In the course of his remarks, Hirohito said, "We have resolved to pave the way for a general peace for all generations to come by enduring the unendurable and suffering what is unsufferable." He referred specifically to the atomic bombs when he said, "Moreover, the enemy has begun to employ a new and more cruel bomb, the power of which to do damage is indeed incalculable, taking the toll of many innocent lives." On 2 September, the final terms of surrender were signed aboard the battleship *Missouri* in Tokyo Bay, and the Japanese islands came under the rule of a U.S. army of occupation.

Spencer C. Tucker

See also

Atomic Bomb, Decision to Employ; Hirohito, Emperor of Japan; Hiroshima, Bombing of; Iwo Jima, Battle for; Japan, Official Surrender; Manchuria Campaign; Nagasaki, Bombing of; Okinawa, Invasion of; Potsdam Conference; Truman, Harry S; United States, Submarine Campaign against Japanese Shipping

References

Butow, Robert J. C. *Japan's Decision to Surrender.* Stanford, CA: Stanford University Press, 1954.

Craig, William. *The Fall of Japan.* New York: Dial Press, 1967.

Frank, Richard B. *Downfall: The End of the Imperial Japanese Empire.* New York: Random House, 1999.

Japanese Americans

After the Japanese attack on Pearl Harbor, there was tremendous paranoia in the United States regarding Japanese Americans and a general belief among the U.S. counterintelligence community, including the Federal Bureau of Investigation (FBI), that Japanese Americans were engaged in widespread spying for Japan. Certainly, racism, especially on the West Coast of the United States, played a role. During the conflict, the U.S. government treated Japanese Americans very differently from German Americans and Italian Americans.

On 11 December 1941, the FBI ordered the detention of 1,370 Japanese classified as "dangerous enemy aliens." By early January 1942, many notable American politicians were calling for the complete removal of Japanese immigrants and many Japanese American citizens from the entire West Coast. Later that year, the California State Personnel Board voted to remove all "descendants of natives with whom the United States is at war" from civil service positions. Although this act clearly included German and Italian Americans, it was only enforced on Japanese. Almost simultaneously, the U.S. Army created 12 West Coast "restricted zones," in which enemy aliens were confined to a 5-mile radius around their homes and subjected to a curfew; again, this measure pertained almost exclusively to the Japanese.

School children, Manzanar Relocation Center, California. (Photograph by Ansel Adams/Library of Congress)

Then, on 19 February 1942, President Franklin D. Roosevelt signed Executive Order (EO) 9066, authorizing the secretary of war to define military areas "from which any or all persons may be excluded as deemed necessary or desirable." Secretary of War Henry Stimson ordered Lieutenant General John DeWitt, commander of Fourth Army and the Western Defense Command, to enforce EO 9066. On 2 March, DeWitt issued Public Proclamation No. 1, creating military areas in Washington, Oregon, California, and parts of Arizona and declaring the right to remove German, Italian, and Japanese aliens and anyone of "Japanese ancestry" living in specified military areas should the need arise. In March, the government opened its first concentration camp, Manzanar, in Owens Valley, California. That same month, the government began the forced removal of Japanese Americans from the military zones. By 7 August, eight months after Pearl Harbor, General DeWitt announced the complete evacuation of 111,000 Japanese (64 percent of whom were U.S. citizens) from two of the major military zones to army concentration camps. Included in the removal were West Coast Japanese and those having at least one grandparent who had emigrated from Japan. Forced to settle their personal affairs immediately, the Japanese were removed to 10 camps located in California, Arizona, Colorado, Idaho, and Utah.

Ultimately, the government did allow 35,000 Japanese to leave the camps in return for loyalty oaths and pledges not to settle on the West Coast. Japanese living in the Hawaiian Islands were untouched. That U.S. territory contained the nation's largest concentration of Japanese Americans: 150,000 people, representing 37 percent of the islands' population. Deporting them would have destroyed the islands' economy.

Despite its actions in forcibly relocating Japanese Americans, the U.S. government began recruiting American-born Nisei (second-generation) Japanese for the armed forces in 1943. The Nisei 442nd Regimental Combat Team, recruited from Japanese American volunteers from the mainland concentration camps and from Hawaii, fought with distinction in the European Theater of Operations and became one of the most highly decorated units in U.S. military history. The 442nd also proved to be an invaluable asset in the Pacific Theater, decoding communications, interrogating prisoners, and broadcasting propaganda. In June 1943, while the Nisei were fighting and dying in the Pacific and European Theaters, California Governor Earl Warren signed a proclamation forbidding Japanese Americans from filing for fishing licenses.

By 1945, the U.S. government began authorizing the return of Japanese Americans to their homes. Racism continued, however, for in that same year, Hood River, Oregon, removed the names of 17 Nisei soldiers from its community roll of honor because they were Japanese. During the four years the United States was at war, even as thousands of Japanese were detained in military camps, only 10 people were convicted of spying for Japan; all were Caucasian. Not until a half century later did the U.S. government admit its mistake regarding the Japanese Americans and make partial restitution.

John Noonan

See also
Roosevelt, Franklin D.; Stimson, Henry Lewis
References
Houston, James D. *Farewell to Manzanar: A True Story of Japanese American Experience during and after the World War II Internment.* New York: Bantam Books, 1983.
Lowman, David D. MAGIC: *The Untold Story of U.S. Intelligence and the Evacuation of Japanese Residents from the West Coast during WW II.* Provo, UT: Athena Press, 2001.
Ng, Wendy. *Japanese American Internment during World War II: A History and Reference Guide.* Westport, CT: Greenwood Press, 2002.

Japanese-Soviet Neutrality Pact (13 April 1941)

Important diplomatic treaty between the Soviet Union and Japan. The failure to coordinate policy and exchange information was typical of the Axis powers in World War II. When the Soviet Union and Germany concluded their nonaggression pact on 23 August 1939, the Japanese were caught by surprise, and when Japanese Foreign Minister Matsuoka Yōsuke visited Berlin in March 1941, Adolf Hitler ordered that he not be informed about Operation BARBAROSSA, Germany's plan to invade the Soviet Union.

On the way back to Tokyo, Matsuoka stopped in Moscow, where he concluded the Japanese-Soviet Neutrality Pact on 13 April 1941. This agreement guaranteed territorial inviolability as well as neutrality in case either power became involved in hostilities with a third nation. The agreement had far-reaching consequences, as it provided for Japanese neutrality when Germany invaded the Soviet Union in June 1941. The treaty was to be valid for five years, with an automatic extension for an additional five years unless one side declared otherwise.

Since 1939, Tokyo had sought an agreement with the Soviet Union to remove a threat from that direction as it attempted to conquer China. The Japanese side first raised the idea of a nonaggression pact in May and June 1940 when the fall of France allowed Tokyo to contemplate a move against the European colonies in Southeast Asia, in which Soviet neutrality would be essential.

Negotiations between Japan and the USSR began in August 1940. During the ensuing negotiations, the Soviets pursued a cautious approach, suggesting a neutrality agreement instead of a nonaggression pact in order not to strain its relationship with the Western powers, whereas the Japanese urged a more binding treaty modeled after the German-Soviet pact of 1939, with the undisguised goal of Japanese expansion southward. The Japanese memorandum resembled the content of the secret protocol of the German-Soviet pact, calling on the Soviet Union to recognize the traditional interests of Japan in Outer Mongolia and the three provinces of northern China (i.e., Manchuria) and to agree that French Indochina and the Netherlands East Indies lay within the Japanese sphere of influence. In return, Japan agreed to look favorably on a Soviet advance into Afghanistan and Persia (Iran).

The Japanese-Soviet Neutrality Pact of April 1941 greatly facilitated Japanese expansion in the southeastern Pacific and its attack on the United States. Josef Stalin's policy toward Japan in the summer and fall of 1941 resembled his attitude toward Germany before June 1941. He ordered his generals in the Soviet Far East to avoid any hostilities with Japan along their common border in Manchuria and Mongolia. Even if Japanese forces should attack, the Soviet Pacific Fleet was to withdraw northward.

Despite this treaty, Japan contemplated attacking the Soviet Union in the fall of 1941. Leaders of the Guandong (Kwantung) Army in Manchuria especially supported such a move, but Tokyo decided in favor of a move south into the vacuum created by the temporary weakness of the European powers in Southeast Asia. Tokyo reached its decision on the basis of the outcome of earlier fighting with the Soviets, the difficult weather in Siberia, and the absence from that region of oil and rubber, the two natural resources Japan needed most critically at that time.

The Soviet-Japanese Neutrality Pact of 1941 was of immense assistance to the Soviet Union in its war with Germany. Had Germany and Japan cooperated militarily against the Soviet Union, that country would probably have been defeated, and the Axis powers might have won World War II. Thanks to Japan's neutrality, the Soviet Far East provided the Soviet Western Front with 250,000 men between 1941 and 1944. The pact also allowed the Soviet Union to benefit from substantial and vital U.S. Lend-Lease aid. Simultaneously, Japan gained immensely from the pact. During its war with the United States, it received from the Soviet Union 40 million tons of coal, 140 million tons of wood, 50 million tons of iron, 10 million tons of fish, and substantial quantities of gold from Siberia and the Soviet Far East. Soviet trade helped make possible Japan's war with the United States.

The Soviet Union ultimately broke the nonaggression pact with Japan in 1945. At the February 1945 Yalta Conference, Stalin promised his Western allies that his country would enter the war against Japan "two or three months" after the end of the war in Europe, in return for territorial concessions in the Far East. Three months to the day, on 8 August 1945, the Soviet Union declared war on Japan.

Eva-Maria Stolberg

See also

BARBAROSSA, Operation; German-Soviet Non-aggression Pact; Hitler, Adolf; Stalin, Josef; Yalta Conference

References

Haslam, Jonathan. *The Soviet Union and the Threat from the East, 1933–1941*. London: Macmillan, 1992.

Lensen, George A. *The Strange Neutrality: Soviet-Japanese Relations during the Second World War, 1941–1945*. Tallahassee, FL: Diplomatic Press, 1972.

Slavinskij, Boris N. *Pakt o neitralitete mezhdu SSSR i Iaponiei: Diplomaticheskaia istoriia, 1941–1945gg*. Moscow: Novina, 1995.

Sugimori Kōji, and Fujimoto Wakio. *Nichi-Ro Ni-So kankei 200 nen shi* (200 years of Russo-Japanese and Soviet-Japanese Relations). Tokyo: Shinjidaisha, 1983.

Java Sea, Battle of the (27 February 1942)

Naval battle marking the end of organized Allied resistance at sea in the Netherlands East Indies. By January 1942, the Allied defense of the southwest Pacific was collectively organized in the American-British-Dutch-Australian (ABDA) Command.

On 24 February, two Japanese invasion forces set sail for Java. A Dutch patrol plane discovered the eastern force some 50 miles north of Surabaya on 27 February. Rear Admiral Takagi Takeo commanded a force of 2 heavy cruisers, 2 light cruisers, and 14 destroyers covering 41 transports. Dutch Admiral Karel Doorman commanded the ABDA striking force of 2 heavy cruisers, 3 light cruisers, and 9 destroyers, representing all four ABDA nations. In the ensuing engagement, the lack of coordination was a major factor limiting Allied effectiveness. There was no plan of attack, and each nationality used different radio frequencies, signals, and tactics. Furthermore, the Allied crews were exhausted, and many ships were in need of either maintenance or repair. At 4:16 P.M., the Japanese opened the battle. Soon thereafter, the heavy cruisers USS *Houston*—her aft turret inoperable from earlier battle damage—and HMS *Exeter* returned fire. The Japanese scored the first hit when a dud shell struck Doorman's flagship, the Dutch cruiser *De Ruyter*. At 4:35 P.M., the Japanese launched a mass torpedo attack, without success. Shortly after 5:00 P.M., Japanese ships made another torpedo attack, this time sinking the Netherlands destroyer *Kortenaer*. Concurrently, a Japanese shell knocked out most of *Exeter*'s boilers, which disrupted Doorman's formation. Further adding to the disarray, HMAS *Perth* made smoke to protect the disabled British cruiser. The Allies were now in confusion. Two British destroyers covering *Exeter*'s withdrawal engaged the Japanese ships, and during this engagement, shells from HMS *Electra* hit the Japanese light cruiser *Jintsu*, flagship of Rear Admiral Tanaka Raizo's destroyer squadron. Several Japanese destroyers pounded *Electra* in return until she sank at 6:00 P.M. American destroyers made a torpedo and gun attack shortly thereafter, holing but not sinking the Japanese destroyer *Asagumo*.

Under cover of darkness, Doorman futilely attempted to reach the Japanese transports. He tried a run along the Java coast, during which HMS *Jupiter* struck a Dutch mine and eventually sank. HMS *Encounter* lingered to pick up survivors. Being low on fuel and having no remaining torpedoes, the American destroyers also withdrew. That left Doorman with only four cruisers, which the Japanese detected just after 11:00 P.M. A Japanese torpedo struck *De Ruyter* aft, and the

British heavy cruiser HMS *Exeter* sinking during the Battle of the Java Sea. (Corbis)

ship sank. Doorman perished with his flagship. A torpedo hit also doomed *Java*. Before losing contact, Doorman had ordered *Houston* and *Perth* to withdraw to Batavia. In the Battle of the Java Sea, the Allies lost two light cruisers and three destroyers. Three cruisers and six destroyers (four American) survived. The Japanese lost no ships, although one destroyer suffered moderate damage and other units light damage. The battle was the last major naval engagement preceding the Japanese conquest of the Netherlands East Indies.

Rodney Madison

See also

Netherlands East Indies; Southwest Pacific Theater; Sunda Strait, Battle of; Tanaka Raizo

References

Dull, Paul S. *A Battle History of the Imperial Japanese Navy, 1941–1945.* Annapolis, MD: Naval Institute Press, 1978.

Morison, Samuel Eliot. *History of United States Naval Operations in World War II.* Vol. 3, *The Rising Sun in the Pacific, 1931–April 1942.* Boston: Little, Brown, 1948.

Schultz, Duane P. *The Last Battle Station: The Story of the U.S.S. Houston.* New York: St. Martin's Press, 1985.

Van Oosten, F. C. *The Battle of the Java Sea.* Annapolis, MD: Naval Institute Press, 1976.

Jeep

U.S. World War II military vehicle. The jeep was developed in answer to the army's need for a rugged, fast, small motor vehicle designed for reconnaissance and utility uses and capable of operating cross-country.

At Fort Benning, Georgia, in the late 1930s, Captain Robert G. Howie and Master Sergeant Melvin C. Wiley built a machine-gun carrier made of parts from junked automobiles, but it was not sufficiently rugged. In 1940, Howie was detailed to the American Bantam Car Company in Baltimore to help produce a more robust design. The president of Bantam, Harry Payne, had previously developed a small truck for logging camps and construction sites, and he set about, with Howie's assistance, to modify this vehicle for sale to the army.

Shortly thereafter, the U.S. Army Ordnance Department sent invitations to 135 companies to bid on a quarter-ton 4-by-4 truck. Only Bantam and Willys Overland submitted bids. In short order, Bantam produced 70 small trucks. Although enthusiastically received, these vehicles suffered from numerous mechanical problems. Willys, meanwhile, developed two prototype test vehicles at its own expense and independent of the contract. The company ignored some of the army specifications, which had stressed lightness, and concentrated instead on performance and ruggedness.

Meanwhile, the secretary of the General Staff, Major General Walter Bedell Smith, interceded, touting the Bantam version to the army chief of staff, General George C. Marshall. In November 1940, Bantam received a contract for 1,500 trucks. Doubts persisted that the company could fulfill its contract, so the government also ordered 1,500 of the Willys version, and the Ford Motor Company was talked into building 1,500 of its own design. In addition, the vehicle weight was increased to 2,160 lb. Tests of the three vehicles were conducted. Both the Ford and Bantam versions contained smaller engines, and the Bantam proved unreliable mechanically. The Willys was over the weight limit, but engineers managed to pare it down to meet the 2,160 lb limit—but only if the vehicle was clean.

The new vehicle had a 60 hp engine and was capable of a speed of 55 mph. It could climb steep grades and ford streams up to 18 inches deep. Willys engineers called it the "jeep" after a popular cartoon character, although almost until the end of the war, soldiers generally referred to it as a "peep." "Jeep" was the term used by Willys, civilians, and the newspapers, and it stuck.

The jeep was remarkably successful. It could easily transport four men and 800 lb of equipment and even trail a 37 mm antitank gun. Wartime production amounted to some 650,000

Four Japanese-American U.S. Army servicemen ride in a jeep, towing a supply trailer on a rural road in France. (Hulton Archive)

units. The jeep, with some modifications, remained in the army inventory until the mid-1980s.

Keith L. Holman

See also
Logistics, Allied; Marshall, George Catlett; Photographic Reconnaissance; Red Ball Express; Smith, Walter Bedell

References
Colby, C. B. *Military Vehicles: Gun Carriers, Mechanical Mules, Ducks and Super Ducks.* New York: Coward McCann, 1956.
Perret, Geoffrey. *There's a War to Be Won: The United States Army in World War II.* New York: Random House, 1991.

Jeschonnek, Hans (1899–1943)

German air force general and early architect of the Luftwaffe. Born in Hohensala, Prussia, on 9 April 1899, Hans Jeschonnek volunteered for military service at age 15 during World

War I. Accepted as a cadet to the Military School at Berlin-Lichterfeld, he was commissioned a second lieutenant in 1915. Two years later, he completed flight training and was posted to the Western Front. By the end of the war, he had two victories, or kills, to his credit.

After the war, Jeschonnek continued in the Reichswehr, serving in the Ordnance Department from 1923 to 1928. He graduated at the top of his class from the General Staff College in 1928. In September 1933, he became adjunct to Aviation Minister Erhard Milch and played an important role in the secret building of the Luftwaffe. He was next assigned as Luftwaffe chief of operations in 1937, and a year later, he was promoted to colonel. Appointed chief of staff of the Luftwaffe in February 1939, he was made a brigadier general that August and a full general in 1942.

An ambitious and hard-working officer, Jeschonnek was totally dedicated to Adolf Hitler and National Socialism. He never questioned policies and took Hitler at his word. Informed by the Führer that he intended to wage a short war, Jeschonnek never prepared the Luftwaffe for a protracted campaign, nor did he mobilize the production assets to ensure an adequate number of replacement aircraft. Devoted to tactical aviation, he insisted that all bombers be able to dive-bomb, which increased the weight of aircraft and reduced bomb loads.

As the war progressed and Germany's fortunes turned, the head of the Luftwaffe, Hermann Göring, shifted more and more blame on his young chief of staff. Eventually, the burdens of the war and the bickering and backstabbing at the higher levels of command overcame Jeschonnek. Made a scapegoat by Göring for the Luftwaffe's failure to stop the Allied bombing of Germany and to supply Sixth Army at Stalingrad, Jeschonnek committed suicide on 18 August 1943 at Hitler's headquarters at Rastenburg, Germany.

M. R. Pierce

See also
Germany, Air Force; Göring, Hermann Wilhelm; Milch, Erhard
References
Bekker, Cajus. *The Luftwaffe War Diaries*. New York: Da Capo Press, 1994.
Faber, Harold. *Luftwaffe: A History*. New York: New York Times Books, 1977.
Mitcham, Samuel W. *Eagles of the Third Reich: The Men Who Made the Luftwaffe*. Novato, CA: Presidio, 1997.

Jet and Rocket Aircraft

Aircraft propelled by gas turbines or rocket engines. Compared to the piston engine, the gas turbine (or jet engine) (see Table 1) promised to offer unrivaled power-to-weight ratios, provided that the metallurgical, mechanical, and aerodynamic design problems could be solved. While still a Royal Air Force (RAF) cadet in 1928, Frank Whittle argued that the gas turbine was a practical power unit. He continued to work on the idea and formed his own company, Power Jets, in 1935. In Germany, Hans-Joachim Pabst von Ohain developed a jet engine that first ran in 1937, flying it in a Heinkel 178 test aircraft in August 1939. Whittle's prototype engine flew in the Gloster E28/39 in May 1941.

The Germans also experimented with rocket fighters, with the Messerschmitt Me-163 entering service in June 1944 against U.S. bombers. The Me-163 had an incredible climb but used a highly corrosive fuel that was inclined toward instability, and many pilots

> The first mass-produced U.S. jet fighter was the P-80 Shooting Star, with a top speed of over 500 mph.

were lost in landing accidents. Less than 50 Me-163s were operational at any one time; they had limited success, but their effect was mainly psychological.

The first operational jet fighter was the British Gloster Meteor, which entered service in July 1944. The Meteor I was distinctly underpowered and had serious limitations as a fighter, being difficult to control at speeds over Mach 0.67. It was armed with four 20 mm cannons. All World War II jet and rocket aircraft had compressibility problems at high speeds and were generally slow to accelerate at low speeds, but they were much better than propeller-driven rivals at high speed, easily outclassing them in acceleration and zoom climb.

The German Messerschmitt Me-262 first flew on jet power in July 1942 and also entered operational service in July 1944, but it was a much better fighter than the Meteor. In common with most jets, it was vulnerable during the landing and take-off phases. It was armed with four 30 mm cannons. A total of 1,200 were built, but only about 200 entered squadron service. The Heinkel He-162 jet fighter utilized nonstrategic materials and required an experienced pilot during the takeoff and landing phases. Armed with two 20 mm cannons, the He-162 was prone to catastrophic structural failure if carelessly handled. A handful of He-162s became operational in April 1945.

The German Arado 234 "Blitz" was the world's first jet bomber. A prototype flew for the first time in June 1943, but delays in securing its engines meant that it did not enter service—and then, in only very limited numbers as a reconnaissance variant—until August 1944. The first bomber version was operational in December 1944. A total of 210 were built.

The Japanese also built such aircraft. Their Yokosuka Ohka MXY 7 Oka ("Cherry Blossom"), built at the Yokosuka Naval Arsenal, was essentially a rocket-propelled, man-guided missile, carried to the target area under a specially converted Mitsubishi G4M Betty bomber. Once the pilot was in position, the canopy was sealed shut. Employed in combat from March 1945, most of these planes were shot down by Allied navy fighters, although one did sink the U.S. destroyer *Monnert L. Abele* in April.

The Bell P-59 Airacomet was the only jet aircraft of the U.S. Army Air Forces (USAAF) to see combat in the war. The twin-engine, straight-wing P-59 flew for the first time in October 1942. It had a top speed of only 400 mph and offered few advantages over the piston-powered U.S. aircraft then in service. Fifty production models were initially deployed with the 412th Fighter Group in 1945. Although the P-59 proved a valuable testing platform, the first mass-produced U.S. jet fighter was the Lockheed P-80 Shooting Star. Utilizing the British H-1 turbojet engine, it first flew in January 1944 and exceeded 500 mph on its first flight. The U.S. Army ordered 5,000 P-80s, but with the end of the war, production was scaled back to 917 aircraft. Ultimately, 1,714 were built.

Andy Blackburn

Table 1
Jet and Rocket Aircraft Specifications

Plane	In Service	Engine	Span	Length	Wing Area	Normal Takeoff Weight	Maximum Speed	Combat Ceiling (500 ft/min)	Range*	Armament/ Payload
Messerschmitt Me-163B-1 (mid-1944)	Mid-1944	1 × 3,748 lb thrust Walter Liquid rocket	30 ft, 7.5 in.	19 ft, 2.5 in.	199.0 sq ft	9,502 lb	597 mph at 29,500 ft	37,500 ft (estimated)	80 miles (estimated)	2 × 30 mm MK 108 cannon
Gloster Meteor Mk I (mid-1944)	Mid-1944	2 × 1,700 lb thrust Rolls-Royce Welland turbojet	43 ft, 0 in.	41 ft, 3 in.	374.0 sq ft	11,800 lb	410 mph at 30,000 ft	37,500 ft	750 miles (estimated)	4 × 20 mm Hispano cannon
Messerschmitt Me-262A-1a (mid-1944)	Mid-1944	2 × 1,984 lb thrust Junkers Jumo turbojet	40 ft, 11.5 in.	34 ft, 9.5 in.	233.6 sq ft	14,101 lb	541 mph at 19,685 ft	35,000 ft	652 miles	4 × 30 mm MK 108 cannon
Arado Ar-234B (late 1944)	Mid-1944	2 × 1,984 lb thrust Junkers Jumo turbojet	46 ft, 3.5 in.	41 ft, 5.5 in.	284.0 sq ft	20,870 lb	461 mph at 19,500 ft	30,000 ft (estimated)	1,012 miles	Typically, 1 × 1,102 lb or 2 × 551 lb bombs
Yokosuka Ohka (early 1945)	Early 1945	3 × 588 lb thrust Type 4 solid rocket	16 ft, 9.75 in.	19 ft, 10.75 in.	64.6 sq ft	4,720 lb	534 mph at sea level	not applicable	37 miles maximum	Nose-mounted warhead of 2,646 lb
Heinkel He-162A-2 (early 1945)	Early 1945	1 × 1,764 lb thrust BMW 003 turbojet	23 ft, 7.5 in.	29 ft, 8.5 in.	120.6 sq ft	6,184 lb	562 mph at 19,690 ft	34,500 ft (estimated)	385 miles	2 × 20 mm MG 151 cannon

*Range is maximum flyable distance on internal fuel, including reserves. Combat radius for jet aircraft would typically be 30 to 35 percent of this value at high altitude, 15 to 18 percent if at sea level.

Source: Brown, Eric M., *Wings of the Luftwaffe* (Shrewsbury, UK: Airlife, 1993); Ethell, Jeffrey, and Alfred Price, *World War II Fighting Jets* (Shrewsbury, UK: Airlife, 1994); and Jarrett, Philip, ed., *Aircraft of the Second World War* (London: G. P. Putnam, 1997).

See also

Aircraft, Bombers; Aircraft, Fighters; Aircraft, Reconnaissance and Auxiliary; Kamikaze; Whittle, Sir Frank

References

Brown, Eric M. *Wings of the Luftwaffe*. Shrewsbury, UK: Airlife, 1993.

Ethell, Jeffrey, and Alfred Price. *World War II Fighting Jets*. Shrewsbury, UK: Airlife, 1994.

Jarrett, Philip, ed. *Aircraft of the Second World War*. London: G. P. Putnam, 1997.

Jewish Resistance

The Nazis exterminated 6 million Jews during World War II. Those who claim that Jews went as meekly as sheep to the slaughter ignore the many instances of remarkable courage in the face of this staggering crime against humanity. In reality, Jewish resistance took many forms. That it often proved futile reflects the poignant vulnerability of Jews rather than any lack of bravery or courage.

Resistance may be divided into the two general categories of passive and active. Passive resistance took the form of cultural and spiritual endurance and assertiveness. Jews confined to ghettos such as Warsaw continued to practice their culture and religion despite prohibitions. They organized symphonies, drama clubs, schools, and other voluntary and educational associations. They also risked their lives by trading across ghetto walls, despite threats of torture and execution.

Passive resistance drew on a long and esteemed Jewish tradition of outlasting the persecutor. Initially believing that the Nazis and their various European sympathizers wanted to put Jews in their place, not in their graves, Jewish leaders sought to endure discriminatory laws, pogroms, and deportations, hoping for an eventual relaxation of anti-Semitic policies or perhaps even a defeat on the battlefield.

Thus, Jewish resistance remained largely nonviolent until 1943, in part because the Germans succeeded in deceiving the Jews. They were helped in this by the fact that the German soldiers of World War I had generally behaved decently, treating Jewish noncombatants humanely. Jews in Poland and the east initially expected similar behavior from the Nazi invaders. Even after it became apparent that Nazi soldiers and especially police were intent on human butchery on a scale previously unimaginable, Jewish cultures that embraced the sanctity and sheer joy of life found it difficult to comprehend a culture built on hate and murderous brutality, especially one that continued to worship civilized icons such as Goethe and Beethoven. Many Jews put their faith in God—hoping for the best, preparing for the worst, yet not daring at first to think the unthinkable.

When Jewish communities and individuals recognized the unthinkable—that the Nazis and their various European allies wanted to exterminate systematically all Jews in Europe—active and armed resistance increased. Active resistance included acts of industrial sabotage in munitions factories or isolated bombings of known Nazi gathering spots. One must recognize, however, the near utter futility of such efforts, given the impossibility of Jews "winning" pitched battles against their killers. The Nazis had machine guns, dogs, and usually superior numbers, and they could call on tanks, artillery, and similar weapons of industrialized modern warfare. The Jewish resisters were often unarmed; at best, some might have pistols or rifles with limited ammunition, perhaps supplemented by a few hand grenades. Such unequal odds often made the final result tragically predictable, yet many Jews decided it was better to die fighting than to face extermination in a death camp.

When it became apparent that they were being deported to Treblinka to be gassed, the Jews of Warsaw at first refused to assemble and then led a ghetto uprising in April 1943, the ferocity of which surprised the Germans. More than 2,000 German soldiers, supported by armored cars, machine guns, flamethrowers, and unlimited ammunition, faced approximately 750 Jews with little or no military training. The Schutzstaffel (SS) general in command, Jürgen Stroop, estimated he would need two days to suppress the uprising. In fact, he needed a full month, as Jews, armed mainly with pistols, homemade grenades, and Molotov cocktails, fought frantically and ferociously from street to street and bunker to bunker. The Warsaw uprising was only the most famous example of nearly 60 other armed uprisings in Jewish ghettos.

Resistance was less common in death camps such as Chelmno, Sobibor, and Treblinka, mainly because there was not sufficient time for resistance networks to form. Resistance requires leaders, organization, and weapons. These elements cannot be improvised and employed in a few hours or even days: months of planning and training are required. Despite nearly insurmountable difficulties, however, Jews did revolt at all three of these death camps, as well as at Auschwitz-Birkenau and 18 forced-labor camps.

One of the most extraordinary acts of Jewish resistance took place at Treblinka. On 2 August 1943, one year after the inauguration of the camp, a group of Jewish prisoners rose up, killed their guards, burned the camp, and escaped. Of 600 prisoners who got away, only about 40 survived the war.

Jews also participated actively in resistance networks in Poland, the Soviet Union, France, and other countries. Their plight was difficult in the extreme, since anti-Semitism within these networks often required Jews to hide their ethnicity. In some cells of the Polish Resistance, Jews were killed outright. Many Soviet partisans distrusted and exploited Jews; nevertheless, between 20,000 and 30,000 Jews fought as partisans in the USSR against Nazi invaders. In France, Jews made up less than 1 percent of the population yet 15 to 20 percent of the French underground. In 1944, nearly 2,000 Jewish resisters in France united to form the Organisation Juive de

Combat (Jewish Fighting Organization), which supported Allied military operations by attacking railway lines and German military installations and factories.

Impressive as it was, Jewish resistance was always hamstrung for several reasons. In general, Jews lacked combat experience, since many countries forbade Jewish citizens from serving in the military. As with Soviet prisoners-of-war (POWs) taken by the Germans, many Jews, especially those confined in ghettos, were weakened by disease and deliberate starvation. Under these conditions, trained Soviet soldiers died with hardly a murmur of protest, so it is not surprising that Jewish families who had never been exposed to the hardships of war would likewise succumb.

The Nazis succeeded in creating a Hobbesian state of nature in which people were so focused on surviving from hour to hour that their struggles consumed virtually all their energy and attention. Dissension within Jewish communities also inhibited resistance, with older Jews and members of the Judenräte (Jewish councils) tending to support a policy of limited cooperation with the Nazis, hoping that by contributing to the German war effort, they might thereby preserve the so-called productive elements of Jewish communities.

More controversially, Jewish resistance was hampered by weak and irresolute international support. Although Western leaders often condemned Nazi actions, they took little action. Official Catholic and Protestant statements were equally tentative. Irresolute and sporadic support unintentionally played into the hands of the Nazis as they planned for Jewish extermination.

Observant Jews were people of God's law, the Torah, who put their faith in God, with Jewish culture in general tending to disavow militant actions. Confronted by murderous killing squads possessing all the tools of industrialized mass warfare, some Jews nevertheless resisted courageously, both passively and actively. That their resistance often ended tragically does not mean that it failed. Indeed, Jewish resistance was the acorn from which the modern oak of the Israeli Defense Forces sprang.

William J. Astore

See also
Babi Yar Massacre; Concentration Camps, German; Holocaust, The; Partisans/Guerrillas; Prisoners of War; Resistance; Warsaw Ghetto Uprising

References
Ainsztein, Reuben. *Jewish Resistance in Nazi-Occupied Eastern Europe.* New York: Barnes and Noble, 1974.
Druks, Herbert. *Jewish Resistance during the Holocaust.* New York: Irvington, 1983.
Gutman, Israel. *Resistance: The Warsaw Ghetto Uprising.* Boston: Houghton Mifflin, 1994.
Langbein, Hermann. *Against All Hope: Resistance in the Nazi Concentration Camps, 1938–1945.* Trans. Harry Zohn. New York: Paragon, 1994.
Rohrlich, Ruby, ed. *Resisting the Holocaust.* New York: Berg, 1998.
Steiner, Jean-François. *Treblinka.* Trans. Helen Weaver. New York: Simon and Schuster, 1967.
Suhl, Yuri, ed. *They Fought Back: The Story of Jewish Resistance in Nazi Europe.* New York: Schocken Books, 1975.

Jiang Jieshi (Chiang Kai-shek) (1887–1975)

Chinese general and Guomindang (Nationalist) politician, president of China from 1928 to 1949 and of the Republic of China on Taiwan from 1949 to 1975. Born on 30 October 1887 in Zhejiang Province, China, Jiang Jieshi entered the Chinese military as a career officer in 1908. After joining a revolutionary organization that sought to overthrow the Qing government, Jiang welcomed the successful 1911–1912 Chinese Revolution. In 1920, he allied himself with Sun Yixian (Sun Yat-sen), the head of the Guomindang, or Nationalist, Party and president of China from 1920 until his death in 1925. In Guangzhou (Canton), where he became commandant of the Guomindang Huangpu (Whampoa) Military Academy in 1924, Jiang rapidly developed his own power base. After Sun's death, Jiang undertook the 1926–1927 Northern Expedition, suppressing the Communist movement and subjugating warlords to Nationalist rule. In December 1927, he consolidated his power by marrying Song Meiling (Soong May-ling), daughter of a politically and financially influential Shanghai Christian family.

In 1928, Jiang became head of the Nanjing-based Guomindang government, continuing his ferocious anti-Communist campaigns. Antiforeign and authoritarian in outlook, he promoted a revival of Confucian social and political values. When Japanese forces seized China's northeastern province of Manchuria in 1931 and established the puppet state of Manzhouguo (Manchukuo), he protested to the League of Nations but received little concrete assistance from that organization, and in 1933 and 1935, Jiang signed agreements with Japan whereby he acquiesced, at least temporarily, to Japan's domination of northern China. Although he began building up and modernizing Chinese military forces, his continuing drive to eliminate the Chinese Communist Party aroused serious discontent. In 1935, his northern warlord ally Zhang Xueliang and his troops broke off an anti-Communist military campaign. In the subsequent December 1936 Xi'an Incident, Zhang kidnapped Jiang and forced him to agree to join an anti-Japanese united front with the Communists.

In July 1937, Japanese and Chinese forces clashed at the Marco Polo railway bridge near Beijing, an incident that quickly—probably against the original intentions of both sides—escalated into full-scale war between Japan and

Generalissimo Jiang Jieshi (Chiang Kai-shek) inspecting high-ranking officers of Officers Training Corps at Lushan, Kinkiang, Jiangxi Sheng. (Library of Congress)

China. From August to November, Jiang staunchly resisted Japanese assaults on Shanghai, but he eventually abandoned that city and in quick succession also lost Nanjing (Nanking), his capital, and Wuhan (Hangzhou or Hankow). Fighting steadily at Changsha and other cities, Jiang nonetheless gradually fell back westward. In late 1938, he established his capital in Chongqing (Chungking) in the southwestern Province of Sichuan. Jiang's overall strategy was to wage a protracted war of attrition, forcing Japanese troops to overextend their lines and occupy territory they could never fully control.

Jiang repeatedly sought assistance from Western powers (especially the United States and Britain), but until 1940, he only received modest American financial and military aid and the imposition of limited economic sanctions on Japan. Japan's formal September 1940 alignment with Germany and Italy in the Axis Tripartite Alliance brought increased aid from the United States, including some airplanes. In response to Japanese demands on the Vichy government for air bases in Indochina and other concessions, American policy toward Japan hardened, and sanctions were tightened beginning in the summer of 1940. In autumn 1941, President Franklin D. Roosevelt repeatedly demanded that Japanese forces withdraw from Chinese territory. He also permitted volunteer American aviators to fight under Colonel Claire Lee Chennault, Jiang's American air adviser.

After the sudden Japanese attack on the United States at Pearl Harbor, China formally declared war on Japan, and the Allies appointed Jiang supreme commander in the China theater. When dealing with his Allied partners, he uncompromisingly defended China's interests, demanding, for instance, the end of Western colonialism and special privileges in China, together with additional wartime assistance to China. At the 1943 Cairo Conference, the Allies also accepted Jiang's demand that China regain all territories ceded to Japan since the 1890s.

Chennault and Jiang enjoyed good relations, sharing the ill-founded faith that airpower alone could win the war against Japan. Jiang sought to conserve his best forces for the postwar struggle he anticipated with the Communists, who consolidated their own power around their wartime base at Yan'an (Yenan) in Shaanxi (Shensi) Province. His attitude provoked acerbic disputes with General Joseph W. Stilwell, the American commander of the China-Burma-India Theater, who sought to build up a strong Chinese army, preferably under his own command, to mount a large anti-Japanese ground campaign. Stilwell's plans implied major reforms to upgrade the Chinese army. Although Jiang was not personally corrupt, many of his military and civilian associates were. As a consequence, such measures would have jeopardized his tenuous hold on the loyalties of a large number of his semi-independent military field commanders, at least some of whom deliberately embezzled part of the funding intended to support their troops and thereby fielded poorly equipped and understrength units. In 1944, Roosevelt withdrew Stilwell from China. Jiang enjoyed better relations with his successor, General Albert Wedemeyer. The China theater stalemated, and neither Jiang nor the Japanese ever won a decisive victory over the other, though Chinese opposition tied down more than a million Japanese troops.

As the war ended, Jiang faced renewed threats from his Communist opponents, who, with Soviet assistance, quickly took control of much of northern China. In late 1945 and 1946, lengthy American mediation efforts headed by the wartime chief of staff, General George C. Marshall, failed to avert civil war between Guomindang and Communist forces. In 1949, Jiang fled to the island of Taiwan; he served as president of the Republic of China until his death in Taibei (Taipei) on 5 April 1975. On numerous occasions, he fruitlessly attempted to persuade the United States to restore his rule over the Chinese mainland, whose legitimate government he still claimed to head. Tough and authoritarian but limited in vision, Jiang skillfully and shrewdly balanced and maneuvered among the various Chinese factions, but he lacked the broader ability to unify his countrymen around the Guomindang.

Priscilla Roberts

See also

Cairo Conference; Chennault, Claire Lee; China, Civil War in; China, Role in War; China-Burma-India Theater; Flying Tigers; Mao Zedong; Marshall, George Catlett; Nanjing Massacre; Roosevelt, Franklin D.; Shanghai, Battle of; Stilwell, Joseph Warren; Wedemeyer, Albert Coady; Zhou Enlai

References

Ch'i, Hsi-heng. *Nationalist China at War: Military Defeats and Political Collapse, 1937–1945*. Ann Arbor: University of Michigan Press, 1982.

Chiang Kai-shek. *Soviet Russia in China: A Summing Up at Seventy*. New York: Farrar, Straus and Cudahy, 1957.

Crozier, Brian. *The Man Who Lost China: The First Full Biography of Chiang Kai-shek*. New York: Scribner's, 1976.

Fairbank, John K., and Albert Feuerwerker, eds. *The Cambridge History of China*. Vol. 13, *Republican China, 1912–1939, Part 2*. Cambridge: Cambridge University Press, 1986.

Fenby, Jonathan. *Generalissimo: Chiang Kai-shek and the China He Lost*. New York: Free Press, 2003.

Furuya, Keiji. *Chiang Kai-shek: His Life and Times*. New York: St. John's University Press, 1981.

Lattimore, Owen. *China Memoirs: Chiang Kai-shek and the War against Japan*. Tokyo: Tokyo University Press, 1990.

Payne, Robert. *Chiang Kai-shek*. New York: Weybright and Talley, 1969.

Jodl, Alfred (1890–1946)

German army general who was chief of operations for Adolf Hitler's regime. Born on 10 May 1890 in Würzburg, Germany, Alfred Jodl joined a Bavarian field artillery regiment in 1910 and served on the Western Front for the first two years of World War I. After recuperating from wounds he received there, he was transferred to the Eastern Front and served with a Hungarian artillery regiment before moving back to the west and finishing the war as a general staff officer. His superior performance secured him a position in the postwar Reichswehr (State Armed Forces). Serving primarily in staff positions during the interwar years, Jodl was assigned in 1939 as a Generalmajor (U.S. equiv. brigadier general) to the Oberkommando der Wehrmacht (OKW, or Armed Forces High Command) as chief of the Wehrmachtführungsamt (Armed Forces Operations Office, renamed in 1940 to Wehrmachtführungsstab, or Armed Forces Operations Staff). Promoted to General der Artillerie (U.S. equiv. lieutenant general) in 1940, he held this position until the German surrender in May 1945.

Despite his position as Adolf Hitler's chief of operations, Jodl had little direct influence on the planning and execution of Germany's military campaigns, a result of Hitler's unwillingness to delegate authority to OKW. He was an admirer of the Führer's successes in 1939 and 1940, but Jodl was not slavish in his devotion to Hitler. After investigating Army Group A's lack of progress during the Caucasus Campaign of 1942, he returned to endorse the commander's actions, thus contradicting Hitler. In the inevitable tirade that followed, he stood his ground against Hitler, reportedly giving as good as he got. Yet, even though he was disillusioned with his commander in chief and with the conduct of the war, Jodl held true to his belief in obedience and duty and remained at his post for the remainder of the war. He was promoted to Generaloberst (U.S. equiv. full general) in January 1944.

Brought before the International Military Tribunal at Nuremberg after the war, Jodl was tried as a war criminal for crimes against peace, war crimes, and crimes against humanity. Found guilty on all counts, he was condemned to death and hanged on 16 October 1946.

David M. Toczek

See also

Caucasus Campaign; Denmark Campaign; Germany, Surrender of; Hitler, Adolf; Keitel, Wilhelm; Norway, German Conquest of

References

Görlitz, Walter. "Keitel, Jodl, and Warlimont." In Correlli Barnett, ed., *Hitler's Generals,* 139–169. New York: William Morrow, 1989.

Warlimont, Walter. *Inside Hitler's Headquarters.* Trans. R. H. Barry. New York: Praeger, 1964.

Joint Chiefs of Staff

Ad hoc organization composed of the chiefs of the U.S. military services, formed to coordinate strategic planning with the British Chiefs of Staff during World War II. The Joint Chiefs of Staff was originally formed in January 1942, soon after the United States entered World War II, when the British chiefs went to Washington to reaffirm earlier informal agreements. One proposal that the Anglo-American chiefs agreed on was the establishment of a permanent organization for collaboration—the Combined Chiefs of Staff, defined as the British Chiefs of Staff and their opposite numbers from the United States. It was primarily to provide these opposite numbers to the British membership in the Combined Chiefs that the U.S. Joint Chiefs of Staff was created.

Initially, the Joint Chiefs of Staff consisted of the army chief of staff, General George C. Marshall; the commanding general of the army air forces and deputy chief of staff for air, Lieutenant General Henry H. Arnold; the chief of naval operations, Admiral Harold R. Stark; and the commander in chief of the U.S. Fleet, Admiral Ernest J. King. In March 1942, the positions held by Stark and King were combined under King, and Stark was sent to London to command U.S. Naval Forces in Europe. In July, President Franklin D. Roosevelt brought the former chief of naval operations, Admiral William D. Leahy, out of retirement and appointed him chief of staff to the president. This position was the forerunner of today's chairman of the Joint Chiefs of Staff.

Throughout the war, the U.S. Joint Chiefs followed the British lead and established their primary subordinate organization, the Joint Planning Staff, along the British pattern. In early 1942, most U.S. planning was done by the War and Navy Departments, which focused primarily on Europe and the Pacific, respectively. By 1943, however, the practice of joint and combined planning was carried out by joint committees and coordinated by the Joint Planning Staff and then submitted to the Joint Chiefs for approval. The National Security Act of 1947 finally codified the establishment of the Joint Chiefs of Staff.

Arthur T. Frame

See also

Arnold, Henry Harley "Hap"; Combined Chiefs of Staff; King, Ernest Joseph; Leahy, William Daniel; Marshall, George Catlett; Stark, Harold Raynsford "Betty"

References

Harrison, Gordon A. *United States Army in World War II: European Theater of Operations—Cross-Channel Attack.* Washington, DC: Center of Military History, 1951.

Korb, Lawrence. *The Joint Chiefs of Staff.* Bloomington: Indiana University Press, 1976.

Journalism and the War

Recognizing that mass popular support was fundamental to the prosecution of a total war by their entire societies, both the Western democracies and the totalitarian regimes involved in the war co-opted their various media resources to support their war efforts. Manipulation of the press as an organ for wartime state propaganda first became prevalent during World War I, when the governments of the United Kingdom, Germany, tsarist Russia, and France, followed by that of the United States, employed a combination of comprehensive censorship, coercion, and legislation to ensure that the mass media printed only officially sanctioned versions of events relating to the war. During the interwar period, however, these tactics produced a severe backlash, which was particularly pronounced in the United States.

In the totalitarian states, including all three Axis nations and also the Soviet Union and China, state control of the media was already well established when the war began. These countries had no long-standing tradition of a free press as a voice against government encroachments on the rights of the people, and throughout the war, their mass media functioned primarily as outlets through which governments could present their preferred version of reality. Until August 1945, for example, press and radio told the Japanese people that their armies were still winning glorious victories overseas. In those territories occupied by Axis armies, the press was quickly reduced to a similar condition. In both Axis and occupied states, however, some clandestine publications circulated—at great danger to their authors and distributors, who ran the risk of arrest and imprisonment or execution, fates that frequently befell them.

The United Kingdom and the United States each had a strong free press tradition, and in these states, the government control over the press in wartime was more restrained. With the onset of World War II, Great Britain and France again placed restrictions on their media, which applied to both radio and print journalism. Some of these constraints affected not only their own citizens but also foreign journalists reporting from Allied countries, who could be denied access to sensitive areas and also to the facilities they needed to transmit their stories. In practice, many leading American correspondents were staunchly pro-Allies in sympathy, and the Allied censors therefore granted them considerable latitude. Edward R. Mur-

Press censors at work in the British Ministry of Information, 1940. (Hulton-Deutsch Collection/Corbis)

row of Columbia Broadcasting Service, for example, transmitted radio broadcasts from the London Blitz that gave the American people a sense of the war's immediacy and helped to generate popular support for Britain's battle against Adolf Hitler's forces. The United States, a neutral during the first two years of the war, retained its tradition of independent journalism based on the foundation of the First Amendment to the U.S. Constitution. This ended when that country entered the war after Japan's surprise attack on Pearl Harbor on 7 December 1941.

In part because the very nature of the Japanese attack struck almost all Americans as the epitome of duplicitous and dishonorable behavior, U.S. media representatives immediately acceded to their government's requests that they submit to censorship, engage in self-censorship, and submit any questionable materials to the government and the military for vetting prior to their release. Even movies were expected to showcase the official view of the war—that all American soldiers were patriotic and honorable and their enemies evil,

untrustworthy, and despicable. The media also presented a sanitized, even glamorized view of war, playing down its horrific aspects and ensuring that only enemy soldiers, not the home team, were seen to encounter gruesome deaths. Before the advent of television, straight battlefield reporting was highly restrained, emphasizing the heroism of commanders and troops on one's own side and omitting the filth, foul language, and other unsavory aspects that also formed part of the combat experience. As in other nations at war, such censorship in the United States created a public perception that all its fighting men and women were brave and patriotic, that the home front was united behind the war effort, and that government decisions were wise and just. If reported at all, military disasters were presented as merely minor reverses. One exception was that the press was encouraged to pillory fraudulent activities or overly opportunistic "war profiteering." Even so, in both Britain and the United States, newspaper criticism of governmental incompetence, especially instances in which officials had allegedly been inefficient in prosecuting the war effort, continued to appear, often as part of the normal political process, which was by no means suspended during the war.

Military commanders expected war correspondents accredited to their forces to function primarily as adjuncts to their own efforts, disseminating only those messages and images acceptable to the government. Only occasionally, as when Lieutenant General George S. Patton Jr. slapped a hospitalized soldier who had suffered a nervous breakdown, did correspondents report news that was unflattering or discreditable to the military. These policies brought a near total suspension of in-depth investigative journalism over a wide range of topics. The complete censorship of communications coming from military units (extending even to the personal correspondence of soldiers) made reporters doubly dependent on the goodwill of the armed forces. One by-product of this was to preclude the publication of critiques of military operations or strategy in the open forum of the press.

As a result, in almost all combatant nations, the bulk of World War II military journalism consisted of variations on the "personal interest" or "feature" story. Generally, these stories eschewed hard facts (who, what, when, where) for profiles emphasizing human interest stories. In the United States, the recognized master of this format was the military journalist Ernie Pyle, whose affinity for the common infantryman won him the label "friend of the dogface." Pyle produced classic pieces that became more realistic over time and, as he moved to the Pacific Theater, grew increasingly honest and made less effort to minimize the misery and deprivation the fighting troops experienced. Even today, his famed dispatch entitled "The Death of Captain Wasko" remains a staple for American soldiers. Like a number of other war correspondents, Pyle paid the ultimate price for his efforts to accompany soldiers to the front when a Japanese sniper killed him on the island of Ie Shima off Okinawa in the closing days of the war.

Together with many other well-known American journalists, among them the young Walter Cronkite, Pyle often wrote for the *Stars and Stripes*, a four-page (later, eight-page) daily newspaper produced by the armed forces and widely circulated among the troops. This journal first appeared during the American Civil War and reappeared in World War I; in 1942, the U.S. military resumed its publication in London, with the first issue carrying an article by Army Chief of Staff General George C. Marshall lauding its contributions to morale in World War I. The paper's editors and correspondents accompanied the U.S. forces through their various campaigns and had to locate suitable publication facilities as they moved through the different theaters of war. In 1945, the *Stars and Stripes* also began to issue a Pacific edition, and from World War II onward, it continued to appear without a break. Unlike publications designed for a civilian audience,

the *Stars and Stripes* could afford to be somewhat more frank about the rigors and dangers of combat. Both Marshall and General Dwight D. Eisenhower, supreme commander of the Allied Expeditionary Forces, took pride in the fact that this newspaper belonged to the "free press" and instituted a hands-off policy forbidding military censorship of its contents. Although its articles were far more honest than those in similar Axis publications designed for the troops, contributors to the *Stars and Stripes* were usually, in practice, military employees who firmly supported the overriding wartime objective of victory. On those occasions the newspaper criticized military practices it considered unfair or inefficient, it did so from the perspective of the insider who sought to improve an institution he fundamentally supported and on which, indeed, he depended.

Throughout World War II, the media in all belligerent countries were expected to support their own nation's war effort. Although press controls were far more stringent in totalitarian countries, even democracies with a traditionally strong free press exercised a substantial degree of censorship over the media and demanded that print and broadcast outlets alike publish nothing potentially detrimental to the war effort. Bulky equipment often made live newsreel coverage from the front impracticable, and except when the intention was to stir up popular feeling against the enemy, newspapers were forbidden to disturb the public by featuring overly graphic photographs of bodies of soldiers or civilians who had suffered particularly horrific deaths. In practice, even where censorship was relatively restrained, the home front media usually presented a simplistic and sanitized view of the experience of combat troops in fighting that deliberately minimized brutality, dirt, and bodily discomforts; omitted the mention of savage fighting tactics or atrocities unless these were committed by the enemy; and tended to present all soldiers from their own country as invariably brave, heroic, steadfast, and patriotic. Although there were other reasons for such sentiments, practices of this type undoubtedly contributed to the continuing popular view of World War II as a "good war." In the 1960s, when war reporting became far more graphic and immediate, with vivid images of actual combat and civilian deaths in Vietnam televised within hours throughout the United States and the rest of the world, public attitudes toward the Vietnam conflict quickly became far more ambivalent than they had been toward World War II.

Robert Bateman and Priscilla Roberts

See also

Censorship; Literature of World War II; Pyle, Ernest Taylor "Ernie"

References

Collier, Richard. *The Warcos: The War Correspondents of World War II*. London: Weidenfeld and Nicolson, 1989.

Cornebise, Alfred E. *Ranks and Columns: Armed Forces Newspapers in American Wars*. Westport, CT: Greenwood Press, 1993.

Desmond, Robert W. *Tides of War: World News Reporting, 1931–1945.* Iowa City: University of Iowa Press, 1984.

Emery, Michael C. *On the Front Lines: Following America's War Correspondents across the Twentieth Century.* Washington, DC: American University Press, 1995.

Hutton, Oram C., and Andrew A. Rooney. *The Story of the "Stars and Stripes."* New York: Farrar and Rinehart, 1946.

Knightley, Phillip. *The First Casualty: The War Correspondent as Hero and Myth-Maker from the Crimea to Kosovo.* Baltimore, MD: Johns Hopkins University Press, 2002.

Short, K. R. M., ed. *Film and Radio Propaganda in World War II.* Knoxville: University of Tennessee Press, 1983.

Sorel, Nancy Caldwell. *The Women Who Wrote the War.* New York: Time Warner, 1999.

Zumwalt, Ken. *The "Stars and Stripes": World War II and the Early Years.* Austin, TX: Eakin Press, 1989.

Juin, Alphonse Pierre (1888–1967)

French army marshal who participated in the Italian Campaign later in the war. Born at Cape Rosa near Bône, Algeria, on 16 December 1888, Alphonse Juin joined the French army and completed two years of obligatory enlisted service. He then entered the French Military Academy of St. Cyr in 1910 and was commissioned two years later, graduating first in his class. His classmate Charles de Gaulle became a close friend. Juin immediately served in Morocco with the 1st Regiment of Algerian Tirailleurs, undertaking large-scale pacification operations under General Louis Hubert Lyautey, who would become his long-term patron. During World War I and in North Africa, where he served both before and after the war, the highly decorated Juin demonstrated almost foolhardy courage, together with unconventional tactical military brilliance.

Juin studied and taught at the École Supérieure de la Guerre (1919–1921, 1933–1935). He also attended the Higher Command Course in Paris (1938–1939), but he spent most of the interwar period with the French North African Army in staff assignments, participating in pacification campaigns. By 1935, he had risen to colonel and commanded a regiment in Algeria.

In December 1939, Juin took command of the 15th Motorized Infantry Division in France. From 10 to 29 May 1940, in the Battle for France, he and his troops performed well in Belgium and northern France, covering the Allied retreat to Dunkerque and helping to make possible the evacuation there. On 30 May, German troops captured Juin; at the insistence of General Maxime Weygand, he was repatriated in June 1941. Sent by the Vichy government as a major general to North Africa, he commanded French troops in Morocco and, from November as lieutenant general and then general, French troops in Algeria and Tunisia as well. Juin worked to build up his forces so that they could defend North Africa

General Alphonse Juin, chief of staff of the French Committee of National Defense, in England to meet the chiefs of staff of the three British services. (Hulton Archive)

against any invader. He had no advance knowledge of the Anglo-American North African landings (Operation TORCH) in November 1942, but later that month, he was instrumental in persuading Admiral Jean Darlan to order a cease-fire.

Briefly heading the French army detachment on the Tunisia Front (1942–1943), Juin was soon occupied with the preparation of the French Expeditionary Corps (CEF), which deployed to Italy in November 1943. To command this corps, he accepted a voluntary reduction in rank to lieutenant general. In Italy, he established a good working relationship with the U.S. Fifth Army's temperamentally difficult commander, Lieutenant General Mark W. Clark. Juin convinced Clark and his superior, British General Sir Harold Alexander, to take advantage of his colonial North African troops' expertise in mountain warfare. The CEF displayed its mettle from January 1944 and played a decisive role in the Allied breakthrough of the German Gustav Line to Rome in May. Outflanking the

Germans in the Apennines, the CEF enabled the Allied capture of Monte Cassino in May 1944 and Siena and Florence that July. Juin was arguably the ablest Allied commander in the 1943–1945 Italian Campaign.

In 1944, Juin favored reinforcing Allied troops in Italy, but General Charles de Gaulle, head of the Fighting French government-in-exile, insisted on French participation in the scheduled Allied landings in southern France and ordered Juin to relinquish his troops to General Jean de Lattre de Tassigny for that purpose. De Gaulle later wrote that de Lattre was better suited than the colonial Juin to lead soldiers in metropolitan France, but there has been speculation that he preferred that no single general except himself emerge from the war as France's principal military hero.

Juin served as chief of the French defense staff (1944–1947), resident general in Morocco (1947–1951), inspector general of the armed forces (1951), and commander of the North Atlantic Treaty Organization (NATO) land forces in Central Europe (1951–1956). Made a marshal of France in 1952, Juin outspokenly opposed Algerian nationalism and was embittered by de Gaulle's decision to grant Algerian independence in 1962. He died in Paris on 27 January 1967.

Priscilla Roberts and Richard G. Stone

See also

Alexander, Sir Harold Rupert Leofric George; Cassino/Rapido River, Battles of; Clark, Mark Wayne; Darlan, Jean Louis Xavier François; de Gaulle, Charles; Dunkerque, Evacuation of; France, Battle for; Italy Campaign; Lattre de Tassigny, Jean Joseph Marie Gabriel de; TORCH, Operation; Weygand, Maxime

References

Clayton, Anthony. *Three Marshals of France: Leadership after Trauma.* London: Brassey's, 1992.

Crémieux-Brilhac, Jean-Louis. *Les Français de l'an 40.* 2 vols. Paris: Gallimard, 1990.

de Gaulle, Charles. *The Complete War Memoirs of Charles de Gaulle.* 1955–1959. New York: Carroll and Graf, 1998.

Goutard, Adolphe. "Marshal Alphonse Juin." In Michael Carver, ed., *The War Lords: Military Commanders of the Twentieth Century,* 596–611. Boston: Little, Brown, 1976.

Horne, Alistair. *To Lose a Battle: France, 1940.* Boston: Little, Brown, 1969.

Ordioni, Pierre. *Tout commence à Alger, 1940–1945.* Paris: Éditions Albatros, 1985.

July Bomb Plot (20 July 1944)

Assassination attempt on Adolf Hitler's life. The effort to kill Hitler on 20 July 1944 was, however, only the most visible sign of resistance to the Führer and the last in a string of assassination plots. Many prominent Germans were involved in this activity. The plot included Foreign Ministry officials Adam von Trott zu Solt, Ulrich von Hassell, and Count Friedrich von Schulenberg. Carl Goerdeler, the former mayor of Leipzig, was perhaps the most prominent civilian involved. Military leaders included Field Marshal Erwin von Witzleben, Generals Ludwig Beck and Friedrich Olbricht, and Admiral Wilhelm Canaris, head of the Abwehr. Opposition to Hitler within the military crystallized after Operation BARBAROSSA, the German invasion of the Soviet Union in June 1941. Disillusioned by the brutal actions carried out by Germany in the USSR, a group of young officers made several attempts to kill Hitler. They planted bombs on his airplane and in the pockets of his overcoat and carried them into meetings with the Führer. Incredibly, fate always intervened to foil each attempt.

Killing Hitler would exempt members of the Wehrmacht from their oath of allegiance and make a coup d'état possible. And even if this move would not secure better terms from the Allies, at least there would be a moral victory. In early 1944, a new leader instilled the movement with renewed hope. Count Claus Schenk von Stauffenberg became disillusioned with Nazi occupation policies on the Eastern Front. He had been badly wounded in Tunisia that year, losing his left eye, right hand, and two fingers on his left hand. While recovering in Germany, he dedicated himself to the task of killing Hitler. Appointed chief of staff of the Reserve Army in July, Stauffenberg developed a daring scheme to assassinate the Führer.

Stauffenberg openly developed a plan, under the code name VALKYRIE, for the Berlin garrison to impose military control on the city in case of a rebellion by the millions of foreign workers employed there. This plan provided cover for the plot to suppress the Schutzstaffel (SS) after Hitler had been removed. The police chief and commandant of Berlin supported the plan, and Stauffenberg carefully coordinated with sympathetic military officials in Paris and Vienna. He hoped to carry off the coup before any Allied invasion could occur and then negotiate an end to the war.

D day occurred before an attempt could be made, however, and many conspirators argued that the invasion rendered the question of assassination moot. Stauffenberg remained determined. Twice he carried explosives to meetings where Hitler was to appear; twice circumstances stayed the event. Then, on 20 July 1944 at a meeting of Hitler and the General Staff near Rastenburg, East Prussia (Ketrzyn, Poland), Stauffenberg armed the bomb concealed in his briefcase and set it down 6 feet from the Führer, and slipped from the meeting to signal the start of the coup d'état.

Through an accident, the bomb was moved, and it only wounded Hitler. Meanwhile, while waiting for confirmation that the Führer was dead, Stauffenberg's coconspirators hesitated and then divided. When news came that Hitler was still alive, the plot collapsed as SS leader Heinrich Himmler and the head of the Armed Forces High Command (OKW), Field Marshal Wilhelm Keitel, moved quickly to crush it. Troops loyal to Hitler arrested the leading conspirators. Beck was permitted to commit suicide, whereas Stauffenberg and Olbricht were shot out of hand. Further investigation by the Gestapo revealed the breadth of the activity, which came as a surprise to the regime. Ultimately, some 7,000 people were arrested. The leaders were tortured and subjected to farcical "trials" before the People's Court and then executed in the most hideous fashion, with the event filmed for the amusement of Hitler and other Nazi leaders. In all, perhaps 5,000 opponents of the regime, no matter what the level of their involvement in the plot, were executed.

As the best-known act of resistance in Nazi Germany, the unsuccessful attempt of military leaders to kill Hitler remains controversial. Some scholars hail it as an act of conscience that laid the foundations for a new Germany, but others note that the attempt did not come until Germany was on the brink of defeat. They interpret it, moreover, simply as a repudia-tion of Hitler himself and not of Nazi principles in general. Whether an act of conscience or a simple coup attempt, the only serious, internal attempt to end Nazi power in Germany resulted in failure.

Timothy C. Dowling

See also

BARBAROSSA, Operation; Beck, Ludwig; Canaris, Wilhelm Franz; Himmler, Heinrich; Hitler, Adolf; Keitel, Wilhelm; Stauffenberg, Claus Philip Schenk von; Witzleben, Erwin von

References

Gallante, Pierre, with Eugène Silanoff. *Operation VALKYRIE: The German Generals' Plot against Hitler*. New York: Harper and Row, 1981.

Kershaw, Ian. *Hitler, 1936–1945: Nemesis*. New York: W. W. Norton, 2000.

Mason, Herbert Molloy, Jr. *To Kill the Devil: The Attempts on the Life of Adolf Hitler*. New York: W. W. Norton, 1978.

Toland, John. *Adolf Hitler*. New York: Anchor Books, 1992.

K

Kaiten

Japanese suicide submarines. By late 1944, the situation for Japan in the Pacific had deteriorated to the point that its leaders turned to extraordinary measures in an attempt to stem the tide of Allied victories. Already employing kamikaze suicide pilots, the Japanese also focused on developing and building the *kaiten* ("turning the heavens") suicide submarine, which was really nothing more than a Type 93 Japanese torpedo with a small compartment for a pilot.

The individual kaiten torpedo was to be lashed to the deck of a submarine and transported under water to the approximate location of a U.S. ship or naval anchorage. Following the appropriate ceremony, the pilot would leave the submarine and enter the kaiten while it was submerged. The kaiten would then be released and propelled at high speed by its oxygen-fueled engine to smash into the enemy ship. Capable of sustaining a speed of 40 knots for one hour, the kaiten could outrun any American warship. There was no provision for the kaiten to be recovered by the launching submarine. Although the Japanese Naval General Staff had insisted that a means be provided for the pilot to be ejected from the kaiten about 150 feet from impact, no pilot is known to have attempted to escape from his speeding torpedo as it approached the target. The first group of kaiten pilots began training in August 1944, and several submarines were modified to carry the submersibles. All kaiten pilots were volunteers.

The first kaiten mission occurred in November 1944 when three submarines, each carrying four kaiten, departed Japan to attack U.S. fleet anchorages in the Caroline Islands. The kaiten were launched on the morning of 20 November. Although three could not get under way because of mechanical difficulties, five others set off for anchored U.S. warships in Ulithi Lagoon. Explosions followed, with the Japanese later claiming three aircraft carriers and two battleships were sunk. In reality, one U.S. tanker, the *Mississinewa*, was sunk. One submarine, still carrying her four kaiten, was detected by U.S. warships and sunk.

More kaiten missions followed. A kaiten unit composed of three submarines sailed for Iwo Jima on 22 February 1945. One was sunk by the U.S. destroyer escort *Finnegan*, which was escorting a convoy from Iwo Jima to Saipan when it happened on the Japanese submarine. The surviving submarines inflicted no damage on the U.S. anchorage at Iwo Jima.

The last kaiten operation saw six submarines sortie between 14 July and 8 August 1945, each carrying five or six kaiten. Again, mechanical problems plagued the operation, and three submarines had to turn back to Japan. The kaiten from the others attacked U.S. ships off Okinawa in the most successful of the suicide missions. On 24 July, a kaiten from *I-53* sank the destroyer escort *Underhill*, with a loss of 114 officers and men.

The kaiten effort had failed. Only two U.S. ships had been sunk, one each on the first and the last kaiten missions, but eight of the carrying submarines were sunk, with almost 900 crewmen lost. The kaiten, as with the kamikaze pilots, were an indication that the Japanese had run out of alternatives to counter the rapidly advancing Allied forces on their march toward Japan.

James H. Willbanks

683

See also
Japan, Navy; Kamikaze; Okinawa, Invasion of
References
Boyd, Carl, and Akihiko Yoshida. *The Japanese Submarine Force and World War II*. Annapolis, MD: Naval Institute Press, 1995.
Jentschura, Hansgeorg, Dieter Jung, and Peter Mickel. *Warships of the Imperial Japanese Navy, 1869–1945*. Annapolis, MD: Naval Institute Press, 1986.
Kemp, Paul. *Underwater Warriors*. Annapolis, MD: Naval Institute Press, 1996.

Kalinin, Recapture of (15 December 1941)

Major battle during the Soviet counteroffensive to throw back the German army in its drive to Moscow. Kalinin (now Tver), situated some 100 miles northwest of Moscow, served as the northern linchpin in the defense of the Soviet capital. Retreating to within 40 miles of Moscow, the Soviets brought up 100 fresh divisions, including 34 from Siberia that were specially trained for winter warfare. From mid-November to 4 December, German casualties had reached some 85,000 in the Moscow area alone. The unusually early and harsh winter, with temperatures as low as -31°F (-37°C), had brought most motorized transport to a halt. The German army, unlike its Soviet counterpart, was ill prepared to fight in such conditions.

To complicate the situation further, German leader Adolf Hitler had issued orders on 1 December that threw the German High Command into disarray. On that date, Hitler relieved Field Marshal Karl Gerd von Rundtstedt as commander of Fifth Panzer Army and personally took command of this crucial sector of the front before Moscow. That same day, Field Marshal Fedor von Bock, commanding Army Group Center (Heeresgruppe Mitte), relayed the message that German troops were completely exhausted. The German drive against Moscow had ground to a halt.

On 30 November, Soviet leader Josef Stalin had agreed to plans drawn up by the chief of the Soviet General Staff, Marshal Boris M. Shaposhnikov, and the next day, the General Staff made final preparations for the offensive. On 5 December, the Soviet commander on the Moscow front, General Georgii K. Zhukov, started the first great Soviet counteroffensive in the Kalinin sector. Siberian troops, who were extremely effective in cold-weather operations, were used for these actions. The next day, Zhukov ordered a general offensive against German forces west of Moscow—Army Group Center. Some 88 Soviet divisions with 1,700 tanks and 1,500 aircraft attacked 67 German divisions (many of them understrength) on a 500-mile-long front between Kalinin and Jelez.

They pushed back the completely exhausted Germans, encircling them where possible and forcing a general retreat.

Hitler, however, forbade anything but the shortest withdrawals. On 8 December, with the Red Army achieving many breakthroughs, he ordered his troops to go over to purely defensive operations and hold their positions at all costs. This decision, though helping to ensure that the retreat did not turn into a general rout, condemned thousands of Germans to death. On 13 December, Soviet forces moved to relieve Leningrad, extending the counteroffensive to the northwest. On 14 December, German troops departed Kalinin, which the Soviets entered the next day. Hitler assumed command of the German army on 19 December, and German forces managed to establish a stable front line some 55 miles west of Moscow one day later. The Red Army's winter counteroffensive continued into February 1942, although its greatest gains were registered at its beginning.

Thomas J. Weiler

See also
BARBAROSSA, Operation; Bock, Fedor von; Hitler, Adolf; Kaluga, Battle of; Moscow, Battle of; Rundstedt, Karl Rudolf Gerd von; Shaposhnikov, Boris Mikhailovich; Zhukov, Georgii Konstantinovich
References
Dupuy, Trevor N. *Great Battles on the Eastern Front*. Indianapolis, IN: Bobbs-Merrill, 1982.
Fugate, Bryan I. *Operation Barbarossa: Strategy and Tactics on the Eastern Front, 1941*. New York: Presidio, 1985.
Glantz, David M. *Barbarossa: Hitler's Invasion of Russia, 1941*. Stroud, UK: Tempus Publishing, 2001.

Kaluga, Battle of (26–30 December 1941)

The culmination of the Soviet winter offensive in December 1941 that threw back advancing German forces and halted their drive on Moscow. Kaluga is situated some 90 miles southwest of Moscow; the Germans had taken it on 12 October 1941.

Reinforced by 100 fresh divisions, the Soviets launched a massive counteroffensive to save Moscow on 5–6 December 1941. The action took place in subzero temperatures and with German forces completely spent and strung out along a front of 560 miles, from Kalinin in the north to Yelets in the south. During the first days of their offensive, the Soviets registered significant progress. Where possible, they avoided frontal assaults, endeavoring to flank and get behind the German positions and cut them off, creating maximum confusion and panic. Partisans also struck the overextended German communication and supply lines.

Fearful of encirclement, German troops destroyed what they could and then withdrew. On 13 December, the Soviet government issued a communiqué announcing that the German effort to take Moscow had failed. On 14 December, Soviet General Ivan Zakharin's Forty-Ninth Army went on the offensive north of Tula against Army Group Center (Heeresgruppe Mitte). Despite German leader Adolf Hitler's order of 16 December calling for "fanatical resistance," the right wing of the German Fourth Army on the east bank of the Oka collapsed, and on 17 December, Aleksin fell. The offensive continued in the direction of Tarusa, which was taken the next day.

A special mobile group under Lieutenant General V. S. Popov, including cavalry, infantry, and tank units, then moved in deep snow through the woodlands on the southern bank of the Oka. The offensive to recapture Kaluga began on 17 December. In three days, Popov's troops covered nearly 60 miles, and by the evening of 20 December, they had Kaluga in sight. The Germans there were taken completely by surprise. During the morning of the next day, the 154th Rifle Division, supported by the 31st Cavalry Division and tanks, attacked the railway station.

On 26 December, German resistance in the Nara-Fominsk area broke and the city was retaken. Borovsk and Maloyaroslavets soon fell. On 28 December, Hitler issued a new order calling for every hamlet and farm to be turned into defensive positions and held at all costs. Counterattacks ordered could not be realized, however. German tanks were no longer capable of offensive operations but could only cover retreating infantry units.

Much more adept at fighting in winter conditions, the Soviets threw back every German attempt to stop their advance. Unable to cover and plug the ever increasing number of holes appearing in their front line, the Germans had to withdraw even farther west. On 30 December, Soviet forces completely secured Kaluga. The Soviet offensive ended on 5 January 1942. The Soviet army had established a line between Uhnov, Kirov, and Ludinovo and completed the encirclement of Army Group Center. The German army had lost 25 percent of its original strength in the east and been handed its first strategic defeat.

Thomas J. Weiler

See also
BARBAROSSA, Operation; Kalinin, Recapture of; Keitel, Wilhelm; Moscow, Battle of; Rundstedt, Karl Rudolf Gerd von; Zhukov, Georgii Konstantinovich

References
Dupuy, Trevor N. *Great Battles on the Eastern Front*. Indianapolis, IN: Bobbs-Merrill, 1982.

Fugate, Bryan I. *Operation Barbarossa: Strategy and Tactics on the Eastern Front, 1941*. New York: Presidio, 1985.

Glantz, David M. *Barbarossa: Hitler's Invasion of Russia, 1941*. Stroud, UK: Tempus Publishing, 2001.

Werth, Alexander. *Russia at War, 1941–1945*. New York: E. P. Dutton, 1964.

Kamikaze

Japanese suicide pilot. The special corps of suicide aviators was organized by Rear Admiral Arima Masafumi in 1944 to compensate for the critical shortage of skilled Japanese pilots and the increasingly desperate situation of the Japanese forces after the Battle of the Philippine Sea. The term *kamikaze* means "divine wind" and derives from two legendary Japanese victories over invading Mongol forces in the thirteenth century. At that time, a typhoon or kamikaze wind destroyed the Mongol fleet as it lay off Japan in preparation for an invasion. The Japanese had long believed that this kamikaze wind was a divine intervention, and over many centuries, they had come to accept the proposition that Japan was shielded from calamity by a supernatural force much greater than any man might assemble. Japanese leaders hoped that the kamikaze pilots, like the wind that had saved their land from Mongol conquest seven centuries earlier, would spare Japan an Allied victory and occupation in the twentieth century.

Admiral Arima had little trouble in recruiting pilots for his suicide missions. Thousands of young Japanese volunteered. A last-ditch defensive measure, the kamikaze missions succeeded in wreaking havoc on Allied warships without sapping Japan's other resources. The first kamikaze missions were flown during the Battle of Leyte Gulf in October 1944 when 24 volunteer pilots of the Japanese navy's 201st Air Group on Leyte attacked a force of U.S. escort carriers. During this action, one carrier, the *St. Lô*, was sunk, and two others were heavily damaged.

The kamikaze plane operated as a kind of guided missile with human control. Kamikaze pilots tried to crash their planes into enemy ships. Most kamikaze aircraft were ordinary fighters or light bombers, often loaded with bombs and extra gasoline tanks. Many of the aircraft were old (some were biplanes with nonretractable gear), but later, the Japanese also used a new aircraft, which was a piloted rocket. Specifically developed for suicide missions, this aircraft, called "Baka" by the Allies for the Japanese word for fool, was carried to the target area by a medium bomber. Dropped from an altitude of over 25,000 feet, the rocket would glide to about 3 miles from its target before the

> At least 1,450 kamikaze pilots gave their lives at Okinawa, sinking or damaging 263 Allied ships, resulting in the deaths of 5,000 men.

A Japanese kamikaze pilot tries to crash his plane onto the deck of a U.S. Pacific Fleet warship, 1 January 1945. (Hulton Archive)

pilot turned on the three rocket engines, accelerating the craft to more than 600 miles per hour in its final dive.

After Leyte was nearly secured, the Allies prepared to land on Luzon. With the loss of Leyte, there was little the Japanese could do to stop the American advance, but they decided to make the Luzon Campaign a costly one for their adversaries. Having lost the bulk of their fleet in the various encounters with Allied forces in the Battle of Leyte Gulf, the Japanese had to turn in force to kamikazes to combat the Allied fleet. During the landing of American forces on Luzon, kamikaze pilots constantly harassed the U.S. ships. One estimate holds that 1 out of every 4 kamikazes hit its target and that 1 out of every 33 sank a ship.

During the Battle for Iwo Jima, the kamikaze threat was lessened because of the distance between the island and the nearest Japanese air bases. However, there were still kamikaze attacks. On 21 February 1945, kamikazes sank the escort carrier *Bismarck Sea* and damaged the fleet carrier *Saratoga* (with the loss of some four dozen of her aircraft), as well as the escort carrier *Lunga Point*, a cargo ship, and two LSTs (landing ships, tank).

The kamikaze effort reached its zenith during the Battle of Okinawa, when the Allied task force was repeatedly attacked by waves of suicide planes. This tactic was new. Previously, kamikazes had operated in separate and individual attacks. During this battle, however, the fleet was subjected to massed kamikaze raids. These *kikusui* (floating chrysanthemum) raids, as the Japanese called them, were far more devastating than single kamikaze attacks and took a heavy toll of Allied ships. In several of the raids, more than 350 planes were sent against the fleet. Often, these suicide missions were supported by conventional air attacks conducted simultaneously. By the end of the campaign for Okinawa, at least 1,450 kamikaze pilots had given their lives for their emperor; in the process, they sank or damaged 263 Allied ships, resulting in the deaths of 5,000 men—the greatest losses ever suffered by the U.S. Navy in a single battle and more than it had lost in all the wars of U.S. history to that point.

The effect of the kamikaze attacks, particularly during the Battle of Okinawa, had a major impact on Allied strategic planners as they contemplated an invasion of the Japanese home islands. If several thousand of these suicide pilots could wreak havoc on Allied forces in Leyte, Iwo Jima, and Okinawa, what might one expect when Japan was invaded? No doubt, this consideration played a role in the decision to employ the atomic bomb.

James H. Willbanks

See also

Iwo Jima, Battle for; Kaiten; Leyte Gulf, Battle of; Okinawa, Invasion of

References

Axell, Albert. *The Eternal Kamikaze: Japanese Suicide Gods.* New York: Longman, 2002.

Belote, James H., and William M. Belote. *Typhoon of Steel: The Battle for Okinawa.* New York: Harper and Row, 1970.

Gow, Ian. *Okinawa: Gateway to Japan.* Garden City, NY: Doubleday, 1985.

Hoyt, Edwin Palmer. *The Kamikazes.* New York: Arbor House, 1983.

Inoguchi Rikihei and Nakajima Tadashi, with Roger Pineau. *The Divine Wind: Japan's Kamikaze Force in World War II.* New York: Bantam Books, 1978.

Kan'in Kotohito, Imperial Prince of Japan (1864–1945)

Japanese general and member of the Imperial family. Born on 22 September 1864 in Kyoto, Japan, Prince Kan'in Kotohito received the title of Imperial Prince Kan'in in 1872. Educated at the Army Cadet School, he studied in the French Army Cadet School and the Cavalry School from 1878 to 1882. Following his return to Japan, he served in almost all major cavalry posts in the army. During the 1904–1905 Russo-Japanese War, Major General Prince Kan'in served in the headquarters of Manchuria Expeditionary Army. Promoted to lieutenant general, he commanded both the 1st Division and the Imperial Guards Division. Kan'in was promoted to field marshal in 1919.

As a "grand old man" of the Imperial Army, Kan'in occupied the post of chief of staff of the army between December 1931 and October 1940. His age made him a mere figurehead, providing the opportunity for radical midrank officers to increase their influence in army decision making. Prince Kan'in died in Tokyo on 20 May 1945.

Tohmatsu Haruo

See also

Japan, Army; Japan, Role in War

References

Large, Stephen S. *Emperor Hirohito and Shōwa Japan: A Political Biography.* London and New York: Routledge, 1992.

Morley, James W. *Japan Erupts: The London Naval Conference and the Manchurian Incident, 1928–1932.* New York: Columbia University Press, 1984.

Shillony, Ben-Ami. *Politics and Culture in Wartime Japan.* Oxford: Clarendon Press, 1981.

Kasserine Pass, Battle of (14–22 February 1943)

Axis counteroffensive in Tunisia and a tactical defeat for the Allies. By late 1942, U.S. and British forces invaded Vichy-held French North Africa (Operation TORCH) while the British Eighth Army pushed Italian and German forces from Egypt into Libya. Italy and Germany then rushed reinforcements to Tunisia, but Axis forces there soon found themselves sandwiched between two Allied armies. Victory for the Allies seemed only a matter of weeks away, until the friction of logistics, poor weather, and overconfidence provided the Axis an opportunity to seize the initiative and launch a counterstroke.

Hindering any Axis operation was the issue of who controlled the two armies in Tunisia. German Field Marshal Albert Kesselring in Italy had overall tactical command of Axis forces in the Mediterranean. Under him, Field Marshal Erwin Rommel commanded Panzerarmee Afrika (Panzer [or Tank] Army Africa) in southern Tunisia, and Colonel General Hans Dieter Jürgen von Arnim commanded the Fifth Panzerarmee in the north. The Axis plan called for von Arnim's 10th and 21st Panzer Divisions to move through Faid Pass and destroy American forces at Sidi bou Zid. Rommel was to seize Gafsa on the Allied right flank and then move north to link up with von Arnim. Although the Axis forces enjoyed combat experience, effective air support, and better equipment, the murky command arrangement mitigated against decisive success on the battlefield.

For the Allies in Tunisia, the embryonic nature of coalition operations began to manifest itself at all levels, to include integrating the French into the operational structure. The major U.S. element was Lieutenant General Lloyd Fredendall's II Corps, which held the southern flank between Faid and Maknassy Passes. Fredendall, both overconfident and overly cautious, deployed his inexperienced troops in unsupportable positions and unnecessarily complicated the command-and-control structure. His main battle element, the 1st Armored Division, was scattered into small detachments and could not fight as a complete unit. Fredendall directed operations from an elaborate underground command post some 70 miles from the front in Tebessa, which caused both superiors and subordinates to question his competence.

During a raging sandstorm on 14 February 1943, over 200 of von Arnim's tanks, supported by aircraft, began an attack reminiscent of the early blitzkriegs. The Americans' inexperience and poor leadership proved no match for the veteran panzer divisions, which quickly bypassed and isolated over 2,500 Americans near Sidi bou Zid. In two days, the Allies lost six battalions of infantry, armor, and artillery, leaving the 1st Armored Division in shambles. As Axis forces attacked

American soldiers examine a captured Italian Carro Armato M15/42 medium tank taken during a successful Allied counteattack at Kasserine Pass in southeastern Tunisia, February 1943.   (Hulton-Deutsch Collection/Corbis)

toward Sbeitla, the demoralized Americans began a general retreat, during which they destroyed supplies to prevent their capture by the Axis forces.

As the Allies rushed reinforcements forward to stabilize their defense, the German command debated the objective. Rommel wanted complete operational control in order to cut Allied lines of communications and capture the logistics base at Tebessa. But Kesselring refused to grant Rommel's request and subsequently ordered the attack toward Le Kef and Allied reserves. This disagreement diluted the Axis attack and provided the Allies valuable time to recover and rest their disorganized forces.

On 19 February, Rommel struck at Kasserine Pass, a constricted defile 800 yards wide between 4,000-foot hill masses. The pass was guarded by a mixed force of more than 2,000 U.S. infantrymen and engineers, as well as French artillery, including a battalion of tank destroyers, all commanded by Colonel Robert Stark. Fredendall ordered Stark to "pull a

Stonewall Jackson." Stark's command held until the next day, when an Axis attack supported by Nebelwerfer rockets broke through his defense. Deterred from gaining Tebessa by a strong Allied defense, Rommel ordered his forces toward Thala, where they swept through a British armor rear guard. An apparent Axis victory was blunted by a dramatic reinforcement of U.S. artillery on 21 February. Frustrated by stiffening Allied resistance and an inability to gain firm control of all the Axis forces, Rommel withdrew on 22 February to face General Bernard Montgomery's Eighth Army along the Mareth Line to the east.

Aided by Axis indecision, the Allies had held just long enough, but the cost was high. Records on both sides are fragmentary, but the Allies sustained nearly 4,000 casualties, with 60 artillery pieces and 64 armored vehicles captured. II Corps probably lost 20 percent of its engaged forces, as well as up to 400 armored vehicles and more than 200 artillery pieces. Kasserine Pass was a serious defeat for the inexperienced proving the involvement of personnel from the Narodnyy Kommissariat Vnutrenniakh Del (NKVD, or People's Commissariat for Internal Affairs) in the deaths of some 15,000 Polish officers in the Katyń Forest of eastern Poland in 1940. The general secretary of the Communist Party of the Soviet Union and president of the USSR, Mikhail Gorbachev, handed over a list of the victims to Polish President Wojciech Jaruzelski. In October 1992, Russian President Boris Yeltsin produced more archival documents, helping to determine the burial sites of missing officers not found near Katyń. Even in the light of Gorbachev's glasnost and perestroika policies, this admission of Soviet responsibility for the massacre was still a bombshell.

The USSR had consistently denied murdering captured Polish army officers after its occupation of eastern Poland ever since Radio Berlin announced, on 13 April 1943, that German troops, tipped off by local inhabitants, had discovered mass graves near Smolensk. That June, the German Field Police reported that 4,143 bodies had been found in the Katyń Forest, all fully dressed in Polish army uniforms. Some 2,815 corpses were later identified by personal documents in their pockets. Without exception, all the officers, ranking from general to noncommissioned officer, had been killed by shots in the back of the head. Medical examination later showed that a few bodies had jaws smashed by blows or bayonet wounds in their backs or stomachs, probably sustained when the individuals tried to resist execution.

The Germans predictably tried to exploit the Katyń murders for propaganda purposes, pointing out to their wartime enemies that any alliance with the "Bolshevik" perpetrators of this atrocity was too dangerous to continue. By then, General Władysław Sikorski's London-based Polish government-in-exile and General Władysław Anders, then commander of the Polish forces in the USSR and the Middle East, had been worrying for a considerable time over the fate of the missing Polish officers. Following the Soviet-Polish agreement in the summer of 1941, a small but steady trickle of Poles arrived at the reopened Polish Embassy in Kuibyshev. These individuals, from prison camps scattered over the western parts of the USSR, agreed that their fellow servicemen had been transferred to unknown destinations when the NKVD liquidated these camps in April 1940. The arrivals at Kuibyshev turned out to be the few survivors of the Katyń Forest Massacre. The massacre was apparently a Soviet effort to deprive the Poles of their natural leaders, who would undoubtedly protest a Soviet takeover.

After numerous fruitless discussions on the subject with Soviet authorities, including dictator Josef Stalin himself, the Polish government-in-exile came to believe the German announcement of April 1943 and demanded an independent investigation by the International Committee of the Red Cross (ICRC). This move caused the Kremlin to accuse the Polish

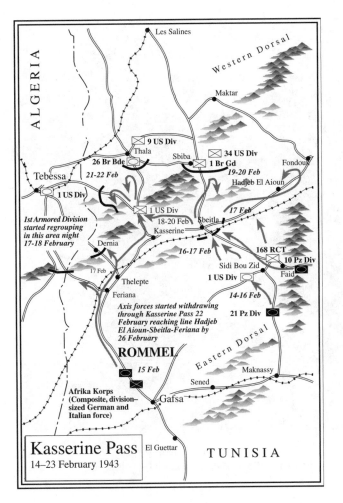

Americans. The U.S. commander in North Africa, General Dwight D. Eisenhower, quickly took steps to reshuffle his command including the replacement of Fredendall as commander of II Corps by Major General George S. Patton Jr.

Steven J. Rauch

See also
Arnim, Hans Jürgen Dieter von; Eisenhower, Dwight D.; Fredendall, Lloyd Ralston; Kesselring, Albert; Montgomery, Sir Bernard Law; Patton, George Smith, Jr.; Rommel, Erwin Johannes Eugen; TORCH, Operation; Tunisia Campaign

References
Blumenson, Martin. *Kasserine Pass*. Boston: Houghton Mifflin, 1967.
Howe, George F. *Northwest Africa: Seizing the Initiative in the West*. Washington, DC: Center of Military History, 1957.
Morris, Roy. "American Baptism of Fire at Kasserine Pass." *WWII History* 1, no. 2 (March 2002): 34–43, 82.

Katyń Forest Massacre (1940)

World War II Soviet atrocity in Poland. On 13 April 1990, the Soviet news agency Tass announced that a joint commission of Polish and Soviet historians had found documents

A German doctor performing an autopsy on a dead Polish soldier selected at random from a mass grave at Katyń Forest. This photo, which was used at the congressional hearings probing the Russian massacre of Polish officers believed to have taken place in 1940, was taken in 1943 when American and British soldiers held prisoner by the Germans were taken to view the massacre site. (Bettmann/Corbis)

government-in-exile of siding with the "fascist aggressors" and to break off diplomatic relations. The ICRC, pursuing its policy of neutrality, could take no action without Soviet consent. London, although embarrassed by this development, made it plain that it was unwilling to risk the breakup of the alliance with the Soviet Union against Nazi Germany over such an investigation. The United States took a similar stance.

When the Red Army finally drove the German armies westward, Moscow determined it needed to present its own investigation results in 1944. A Soviet "special commission," pointing out that the bullets found on the crime scene were manufactured in Germany, concluded that the Germans had killed the Polish officers in 1941. British and American protests notwithstanding, the Soviet prosecution raised the Katyń affair at the International Military Tribunal in Nuremberg, but since the Soviets were unable to prove the Germans guilty, the tribunal simply dropped the case. Throughout the Cold War, the issue of the Katyń Forest Massacre resurfaced time and again, partly due to the efforts of the Polish émigré community. However, it remained unresolved until the demise of the USSR.

Pascal Trees

See also

Anders, Władysław; Poland, Role in War; Sikorski, Władysław Eugeniusz; Stalin, Josef

References

The Crime of Katyń: Facts and Documents, with a Foreword by General Władysław Anders. 3rd ed. London: Polish Cultural Foundation, 1965.

Katyń, Mart 1940 g.–Sentjabr' 2000 g.: Rasstrel, Sud'by Živych—Echo Katyni, Dokumenty. Moscow: Ves' Mir, 2001.

Lauck, John. *Katyń Killings: In the Record.* Clifton, NJ: Kingston Press, 1988.

Paul, Allen. *Katyń: The Untold Story of Stalin's Massacre.* New York: Scribner's, 1991.

Szymczak, Robert. *The Unquiet Dead: The Katyn Forest Massacre as an Issue in American Diplomacy and Politics.* Ann Arbor, MI: University Microfilms International, 1985.

Zawodny, Janusz. *Death in the Forest: The Story of the Katyn Forest Massacre.* 4th ed. Notre Dame, IN: University of Notre Dame Press, 1980.

Keitel, Wilhelm (1882–1946)

German army field marshal and chief of the Oberkommando der Wehrmacht (OKW) throughout the war. Born on 22 September 1882 in Helmscherode, Germany, Wilhelm Keitel joined a Prussian field artillery regiment in 1901 and served as the regiment's staff captain during the early months of World War I. Seen to have potential, he was posted to the German General Staff, an unusual appointment for a non-Prussian and field artillery officer. His demonstrated abilities while serving during the latter part of the war secured him a position in the postwar Reichswehr. Chosen to head the Wehrmachtamt (Armed Forces Office) in 1935, Keitel became chief of staff to the commander in chief of the Wehrmacht. When Adolf Hitler assumed command of the Wehrmacht in 1938, Keitel remained as chief of staff, although with the new title of OKW chief, and he maintained that position until Germany's surrender in 1945. He was promoted to Generalmajor (U.S. equiv. brigadier general) in April 1934, Generalleutnant (U.S. equiv. major general) in January 1936, and Generaloberst (U.S. equiv. full general) in November 1938. He became a field marshal in 1940.

Although competent as a staff officer, Keitel maintained his position as a direct result of his personal loyalty to Hitler and not because of his abilities. With his headquarters responsible for only one operation during World War II, the 1940 Denmark-Norway Campaign, German commanders and staffs consistently bypassed him and OKW and went directly to Hitler. Privately, they referred to Keitel as *Lakeitel* (lackey), a reference to his relationship to Hitler and his limited influence on Germany's military operations. More than any other act, his work in the promulgation of the Commissar Order of 1941, a decree that mandated the immediate execution of all captured political officers on the Eastern Front, led to his classification as a war criminal. Brought before the International Military Tribunal at Nuremberg after the war, he pleaded not guilty to all charges, citing his responsibility to carry out superiors' orders as his defense. Convicted and condemned to death, Keitel was hanged on 16 October 1946.

David M. Toczek

See also

Commissar Order; Denmark Campaign; Germany, Surrender of; Hitler, Adolf; Jodl, Alfred; Norway, German Conquest of

Field Marshal Wilhelm Keitel, signing the ratified surrender terms for the German army at Soviet army headquarters in Berlin, Germany, 7 May 1945. (National Archives)

References

Görlitz, Walter. "Keitel, Jodl, and Warlimont." In Correlli Barnett, ed., *Hitler's Generals*, 139–169. New York: Grove Weidenfeld, 1989.

Keitel, Wilhelm. *Generalfeldmarschall Keitel: Verbrecher oder Offizier?* Ed. Walter Görlitz. Berlin: Musterschmidt-Verlag, 1961.

Warlimont, Walter. *Inside Hitler's Headquarters.* Trans. R. H. Barry. New York: Praeger, 1964.

Field Marshal Albert Kesselring. (Library of Congress)

Kesselring, Albert (1885–1960)

German air force field marshal whose air fleets participated in many of the key engagements of the war, including the invasions of Poland, France, the Low Countries, and the Soviet Union. Born in Marksheft, Bavaria, Germany, on 20 November 1885, Albert Kesselring joined the Bavarian army as an officer candidate in the 2nd Regiment of Foot Artillery in 1904 and was commissioned in 1906. A trained balloon observer, he served with his battery on the Western Front during World War I. Soon, he was on the staff of a regiment and then a division and finally with the 2nd Bavarian Army Corps until the armistice.

He continued in the postwar Reichswehr and secured his reputation as a superb administrator. Colonel Kesselring transferred to the still-secret air force in 1933 as chief of administration and military assistant to Luftwaffe State Secretary Erhard Milch; there, he helped direct the secret expansion of the air force, for which he deserves considerable credit. In June 1936, he became the Luftwaffe chief of staff as a Generalleutnant (U.S. equiv. major general).

Unable to work with Milch, Kesselring applied for retirement. Instead, the Luftwaffe chief, Reichsmarschall (Reich Marshal) Hermann Göring, gave him command of the Third Air Region and a promotion to General der Fliegers (U.S. equiv. lieutenant general). Later, he commanded 1st Air Group, which was upgraded to Luftflotte 2 (Second Air Fleet), composed of 20 bomber and fighter groups; he led this fleet in the invasion of Poland in September 1939. He commanded Luftflotte 2 in the invasion of France and the Low Countries in May 1940, his aircraft striking both Rotterdam and Dunkerque. Raised to field marshal in July 1940, Kesselring continued to command Luftflotte 2 in the Battle of Britain in 1940, when he advised Adolf Hitler to concentrate on London in order to bring up the Royal Air Force (RAF) so that it might be destroyed. He also commanded Luftflotte 2 in the invasion of the Soviet Union in June 1941. With some 1,000 aircraft, this force was the largest German air fleet in the invasion.

In December 1941, Kesselring went to Italy as commander in chief, South, a post he held until March 1945. His command encompassed the Mediterranean Basin, and there, he won the nickname "Smiling Albert" for his ability to get along with Ital-

ian leaders. Kesselring believed that the key to the supply situation in North Africa was control of Malta, and he ardently urged Hitler to take the island by airborne assault. Hitler promised to do so but never acted. Kesselring won admiration for the skillful Axis evacuations of Tunis in May 1943 and Sicily in August 1943, as well as the defense of Italy. Badly injured in a car accident in October 1944, he underwent successful brain surgery and returned to his command the following January. On 8 March 1945, he succeeded Field Marshal Karl R. Gerd von Rundstedt as commander in chief, West. On 15 April, Hitler divided the remaining Reich into two defensive zones. Admiral Karl Dönitz took command of the north, and Kesselring received command of the south. Kesselring surrendered his forces to the Western Allies on 7 May 1945.

Tried after the war for his role in the Ardeatine Caves Massacre, Kesselring was sentenced to death in 1947, but his sentence was remitted to life in prison. He was released in October 1952 as "an act of clemency" when he developed cancer of the throat. Kesselring then wrote his memoirs (published in English as *A Soldier's Record*), which criticized Hitler only for some military decisions. Kesselring also headed the

Stahlhelm, a right-wing German veterans' organization. He died in Bad Nauheim on 20 July 1960.

Spencer C. Tucker and John P. Vanzo

See also

Ardeatine Massacre; Britain, Battle of; Dönitz, Karl; Göring, Hermann Wilhelm; Hitler, Adolf; Italy Campaign; Malta; Milch, Erhard; Rundstedt, Karl Rudolf Gerd von; Sicily, Invasion of; Tunis, Battle of

References

Bidwell, Shelford. "Field-Marshal Alfred Kesselring." In Correlli Barnett, ed., *Hitler's Generals*, 265–289. New York: Grove Weidenfeld, 1989.

Kesselring, Albert. *A Soldier's Record*. Trans. Lynton Hudson. New York: William Morrow, 1954.

Macksey, Kenneth. *The Making of the Luftwaffe*. New York: D. McKay, 1978.

———. Kesselring: *German Master Strategist of the Second World War*. Mechanicsburg, PA: Stackpole Books, 1996.

Mason, Herbert. *The Rise of the Luftwaffe: Forging the Secret Air Weapon, 1918–1940*. New York: Dial Press, 1973.

German soldiers dislodged from a house on the outskirts of Kharkov taking cover outside a building that has been set on fire, 23 February 1943. (Photo by Keystone/Getty Images)

Kharkov, Battle for (1–14 March 1943)

Important Eastern Front battle. The Soviets claimed to have inflicted 1 million German casualties in the period between November 1942 and March 1943, and despite some replacements, the Germans estimated a shortfall of 470,000 men on the Eastern Front. Following their victory at Stalingrad, the Soviets drove to the Donets River in February 1943 and recaptured Kursk, Rostov, and Kharkov, leading Adolf Hitler to order a counterattack during his visit to the front between 17 and 19 February 1943. In the resulting offensive action on 20 February, Field Marshal Fritz Eric von Manstein's Southern Army Command struck the Soviet flank with a panzer attack from the south in a running battle from Krasnoarmeiskaia to the northern Donets River; Fourth Panzer Army's XL Corps encircled and destroyed what was left of Group Popov, consisting of four understrength Soviet tank corps.

The German thrust, assisted by First Panzer Army after 23 February, continued to the northeast. On 22 February, SS Panzer Corps and LVIII Panzer Corps attacked the flank of Colonel General Nikolai Vatutin's Southwest Front, the lead elements of which (XXV Tank Corps) were within 12 miles of Zaporozhye. Having run out of fuel, the latter units abandoned their equipment and made desperate efforts to escape to the north; for the most part, these attempts were successful, as the Germans took only 9,000 prisoners of war. But Manstein claimed to have killed 23,000 Soviet soldiers and destroyed or captured 615 tanks, 354 artillery pieces, and 69 antiaircraft guns.

On 1 March, Manstein began an advance on Kharkov, attempting to get behind the Soviets west of that city who were

pushing against Army Detachment Kempf, commanded by General der Panzertruppen (U.S. equiv. lieutenant general) Werner Kempf. A five-day battle for the city raged with Fourth Panzer Army getting the better of Lieutenant General Pavel S. Rybalko's Third Tank Army, which had been sent to aid the hard-pressed Southwestern Front but had gone on to Kharkov only to be cut off with the advent of the rainy season. By 5 March, the Germans had mauled units of Third Tank Army on the Berestovaya River southwest of the city, capturing 61 tanks, 225 guns, and 600 motor vehicles in a small pocket at Krasnograd.

Manstein wanted to proceed west to attack the rear of the Soviet Voronezh Front, forcing it to fight simultaneously in two directions near Poltava, but because of the rain and mud, the Germans tried to strike the Soviet flank. They attacked north on 7 March and made steady progress, driving a wedge between the Third Tank and Sixty-Ninth Soviet Armies, with pressure eventually coming from the west as Army Detachment Kempf was freed for action. The Soviets brought up II Guards Tank Corps from the east. The SS Panzer Corps, apparently desiring to present the trophy city of Kharkov to Hitler, had to be restrained to ensure that it did not launch a frontal assault on the city, which Manstein feared could produce another Stalingrad.

Hitler's visit to Manstein's headquarters on 10 March probably inspired the SS Panzer Corps commander, Lieutenant General Paul Hauser, to disobey orders and involve the Das Reich and Leibstandarte Divisions in three days of house-to-house battles. Thus, the Germans recovered Kharkov on 14 March 1943. At the same time, to the north of Army Detachment Kempf, the Gross Deutschland Division moved rapidly on Belgorod. At Gaivoron, the Germans wiped out Soviet armored forces that sought to defend Belgorod. The capture of Kharkov and Belgorod marked the end of the German counterblow, which had reestablished the Donets-Mius Line.

Claude R. Sasso

See also

Haußer, Paul "Papa"; Hitler, Adolf; Manstein, Fritz Eric von; Stalingrad, Battle of

References

Erickson, John. *The Road to Berlin.* Boulder, CO: Westview Press, 1983.

Glantz David M., and Jonathan House. *When Titans Clashed: How the Red Army Stopped Hitler.* Lawrence: University Press of Kansas, 1995.

Manstein, Erich. *Lost Victories.* Ed. and trans. Anthony G. Powell. Novato, CA: Presidio, 1982.

Kiev Pocket, Battle of the (21 August–26 September 1941)

Significant German encirclement of Soviet forces on the Eastern Front in 1941. A month into Operation BARBAROSSA, the German invasion of the Soviet Union, sharp disagreements developed between Adolf Hitler and his senior generals as to strategy. The generals—led by the army chief of staff, Colonel General Franz Halder, and the army commander, Colonel General Walther von Brauchitsch—pointed out that not all German army groups would be able to accomplish their assigned tasks. Field Marshal Fedor von Bock's Army Group Center was advancing faster than the weaker Army Groups North and South. At the same time, Hitler was preoccupied with securing the industrial and agricultural heartland of Ukraine and the Crimea and linking up with the Finns at Leningrad.

In consequence, Hitler decided on 19 July, in Führer Directive 33, to divert substantial panzer units from Army Group Center, thereby postponing the drive on Moscow. He sent Colonel General Hermann Hoth's 3rd Panzer Group north to assist in the drive to Leningrad and Colonel General Heinz Guderian's 2nd Panzer Group south to deal with the bulge created by Soviet Colonel General M. P. Kirponis's Southwestern Front with its mechanized corps. The German generals argued against this decision, pointing out that Moscow was the more important objective. Not only the political capital of the Soviet Union, it was also a major industrial area and transportation nexus. Attempts to convince Hitler that the advance on Moscow was more important failed, and he issued a final directive on 21 August that ordered a major encirclement operation, with the goal of destroying Soviet forces in northern Ukraine.

On July 10, Soviet leader Josef Stalin had appointed the barely competent Marshal S. M. Budenny to command the Southern and Southwestern Groups. German forces advanced under the capable leadership of Field Marshal Karl Gerd von Rundstedt, commander of Army Group South. Stalin poured troops into the new command, amounting ultimately to almost 1 million men, insisting that the Dnieper River Line be held at all costs.

Budenny's forces in Uman—the Sixth, Twelfth, and Eighteenth Armies—were encircled, and he remained stationary as Colonel General Ewald von Kleist's 1st Panzer Group drove around his flank to the southeast. Kleist's panzers advanced north even as Guderian's 2nd Panzer Group attacked south through the weakly held northern flank of the Southwestern Front, aiming for a linkup east of Kiev. When the Soviet army chief of staff, General Georgii Zhukov, tried to point out the dangers of encirclement to Stalin on 5 August, the latter sent him to Leningrad's defense and appointed Marshal B. M. Shaposhnikov in his stead.

By early September, Kiev was a salient endangered by advancing German troops to the north and the south. An attempt by Lieutenant General A. I. Yeremenko's newly formed Bryansk Front to halt Guderian's push south failed on 2 September, and by 11 September, the German pincers were closing on Kiev. Budenny requested authority to retreat, but Stalin preferred to replace him with Marshal S. K. Timoshenko. On 12 September, Kleist's panzers broke through the Soviet Thirty-Eighth Army, attacking north from bridgeheads at Cherkassy and Kremenchug.

Despite the onset of the rainy season, the 1st and 2nd Panzer Groups linked up at Lokhvitsa, 125 miles east of Kiev, on 16 September. Timoshenko and Nikita Khrushchev, representing the War Council of the Southwestern Direction, authorized a Soviet withdrawal, but General Kirponis feared Stalin's reaction and refused to move until Moscow confirmed the orders near midnight the next day.

The encirclement was still sufficiently porous to allow some Soviet forces to escape, including Timoshenko, Khrushchev, and Thirty-Seventh Army commander Andrei Vlasov (whose forces had defended Kiev skillfully), but Kirponis was among the dead. The Soviet Fifth and Twenty-First Armies were destroyed, along with major portions of the Thirty-Seventh and Fortieth Armies. Army Group South also claimed 665,000 Soviet prisoners taken, along with 3,500 guns and 900 tanks. For all practical purposes, the Soviet Southwestern Front ceased to exist. It had to be entirely reconstructed from the nucleus of the 15,000 men who escaped the disaster.

Ironically, this major German success, one of the greatest tactical victories of the war—despite opening a 200-mile gap in Soviet defenses and permitting the investment of the eastern Ukraine—had long-range strategic consequences. Senior German commanders, including Halder and Guderian, concluded that this diversion from the drive on Moscow had been a major blunder, ultimately dooming the German attempt to take the Soviet capital in 1941.

Claude R. Sasso and Spencer C. Tucker

See also

BARBAROSSA, Operation; Brauchitsch, Heinrich Alfred Hermann Walther von; Budenny, Semen Mikhailovich; Guderian, Heinz; Halder, Franz; Hitler, Adolf; Hoth, Hermann; Kleist, Paul Ludwig Ewald von; Leningrad, Siege of; Rundstedt, Karl Rudolf Gerd von; Stalin, Josef; Timoshenko, Semen Konstantinovich; Vlasov, Andrei Andreyevich; Zhukov, Georgii Konstantinovich

References

Clark, Alan. *Barbarossa: The Russian-German Conflict, 1941–1945.* New York: William Morrow, 1965.

Erickson, John. *The Road to Stalingrad.* Boulder, CO: Westview Press, 1983.

Glantz, David M., and Jonathan House. *When Titans Clashed: How the Red Army Stopped Hitler.* Lawrence: University Press of Kansas, 1995.

Mellenthin, F. W. von. *Panzer Battles: A Study of the Employment of Armor in the Second World War.* Trans. H. Betzler. Norman: University of Oklahoma Press, 1956.

U.S. Navy Admiral Husband E. Kimmel. (Bettmann/Corbis)

Kimmel, Husband Edward (1882–1968)

U.S. Navy admiral and commander of the Pacific Fleet at the time of the Japanese attack against Pearl Harbor, Hawaii. Born in Henderson, Kentucky, on 26 February 1882, Husband Kimmel graduated from the U.S. Naval Academy in 1904 and was commissioned an ensign in 1906. Over the next years, Kimmel served on battleships; participated in the 1914 intervention at Veracruz, Mexico; served as a naval aide to Assistant Secretary of the Navy Franklin D. Roosevelt; and was staff gunnery officer for the American battleship squadron attached to the Royal Navy's Grand Fleet during World War I.

Kimmel, a highly regarded gunnery expert, rose to the rank of rear admiral in 1937 and served at the Naval Gun Factory; he also commanded a destroyer squadron, attended the Naval War College, commanded the battleship *New York*, and served as chief of staff of the battleships in the Battle Force. From 1937 to 1939, he was budget officer of the navy, and following command of a cruiser division and of cruisers in the Battle Force, Pacific Fleet, he was named commander of the U.S. Pacific Fleet in February 1941 as a full admiral. During the next months, Kimmel put the Pacific Fleet through a vigorous training program in preparation for a possible war with Japan and refined plans for offensive operations in the western Pacific if

war came. Following the Japanese attack against Pearl Harbor on 7 December 1941, which put all of the Pacific Fleet's battleships out of commission, he was relieved of his command.

Kimmel has been the subject of considerable controversy for his actions preceding the Japanese attack. Several investigations and historians determined that he was too lax in his command and not sufficiently prepared for the possibility of war. Defenders—and Kimmel himself—believed he was made a scapegoat for the failures of Washington authorities, arguing that he was denied both crucial intelligence about deteriorating Japanese-American relations and adequate numbers of long-range reconnaissance aircraft.

On 1 March 1942, Kimmel retired in disgrace from the navy. Thereafter, he was employed by an engineering consulting firm until 1947. He died in Groton, Connecticut, on 14 May 1968.

John Kennedy Ohl

See also

Pearl Harbor, Attack on; Roosevelt, Franklin D.; Theobald, Robert Alfred

References

Gannon, Michael. *Pearl Harbor Betrayed: The True Story of a Man and a Nation under Attack.* New York: Henry Holt, 2001.

Kimmel, Husband E. *Admiral Kimmel's Story.* Chicago: Henry Regnery, 1955.

Prange, Gordon W. *At Dawn We Slept: The Untold Story of Pearl Harbor.* New York: McGraw-Hill, 1981.

Kimura Heitaro (1888–1948)

Japanese army general who assumed command of the Burma Area Army in 1944. Born in Tokyo on 28 September 1888, Kimura Heitaro joined the army in December 1908. Although trained in the artillery, he held a number of unusual positions, including that of resident officer in Germany from 1922 to 1925. In 1930, he was a member of the Japanese delegation to the London Disarmament Conference, where his naval counterpart was Captain Yamamoto Isokoru. By 1938, Kimura had advanced to the rank of lieutenant general. After commanding the 32nd Division, he served as chief of staff of the Guandong (Kwantung) Army in Manchuria.

Kimura sided with those who favored Japanese expansion, and from April 1941, he was vice minister of war and a close adviser to General Tōjō Hideki, helping to develop the Japanese military strategy for war with the United States. When Japanese efforts to secure Guadalcanal failed, he became the scapegoat, and he was removed from his post in March 1943.

Kimura returned to active military duty in August 1944, succeeding Kawabe Masakazu as commanding general of the Burma Area Army; Kawabe had been sacked as a result of the disastrous Imphal Campaign. Kimura commanded three armies of 250,000 men in 10 divisions. Expecting an attack by the British Fourteenth Army during the dry season, along the lines of earlier attacks, he planned to withdraw behind the Irrawaddy River and counterattack when British supply lines were overextended. But British commander Lieutenant General William Slim learned of Kimura's intention and revised his own plan. Employing aerial resupply, Slim was able to move forces through difficult terrain to Meiktila and Mandalay. Kimura was surprised and outmaneuvered. In fighting between 21 February and 31 March 1945, the British effectively destroyed the Fifteenth Army. Kimura then precipitously abandoned Rangoon, leaving behind much equipment and many troops. Occupying the city on 2 May, the British improved their supply lines and were in a position to continue their advance when weather permitted.

Kimura was promoted to full general in May 1945. Following the war, he was arrested and tried for war crimes. Convicted of mistreating prisoners of war during the construction of the Burma-Thailand railroad, he was executed in Tokyo on 23 December 1948.

Tim J. Watts

See also
Burma Theater; Guadalcanal, Land Battle for; Imphal and Kohima, Sieges of; Meiktila, Battle of; Tōjō Hideki; Yamamoto Isokoru
References
Allen, Lewis. *Burma, the Longest War, 1941–45.* New York: St. Martin's Press, 1984.

Japanese Army General Kimura Heitaro. (Corbis)

Brooks, Lester. *Behind Japan's Surrender: The Secret Struggle That Ended an Empire.* New York: McGraw-Hill, 1967.
Hayashi, Saburo. *Kogun: The Japanese Army in the Pacific War.* Westport, CT: Greenwood Press, 1959.
Slim, William. *Defeat into Victory.* New York: D. McKay, 1961.

King, Edward Postell, Jr. (1884–1958)

U.S. Army general and commander of the Luzon Force on the Bataan Peninsula. Born in Atlanta, Georgia, on 4 July 1884, Edward King received a law degree from the University of Georgia in 1903. He began his military career with the Georgia National Guard. In 1908, he was commissioned a second lieutenant in the U.S. Army and assigned to the 6th Field Artillery Regiment. In the following years, King served in the

Philippines, did three tours in the Office of the Chief of Field Artillery, and was both a student and an instructor at the Command and General Staff School and the Army War College. He also graduated from the Naval War College.

In September 1940, Brigadier General King returned to the Philippines to command Fort Stotsenberg. Later, he supervised artillery training for the Philippine army. During the first months of World War II, King, now a major general, was artillery officer for General Douglas MacArthur, commander of U.S. forces in the Far East. On 21 March 1942, Lieutenant General Jonathan Wainwright, commander of all U.S. forces in the Philippines, appointed King to head the Luzon Force, which was responsible for defending the Bataan Peninsula, the last major piece of territory on Luzon still in American hands. King had more than 80,000 men under his command, but their situation was hopeless. Short of food, racked by disease, exhausted from months of fighting, and cut off from any reinforcement, they were unable to stop an offensive the Japanese launched on 5 April to complete the conquest of the peninsula. King had orders from Wainwright and MacArthur to counterattack the Japanese; however, he was fearful his men would be massacred by the advancing Japanese and on his own initiative surrendered his force on 9 April, the greatest capitulation in U.S. military history. King spent the remainder of the war in Japanese prison camps in the Philippines, Formosa, and Manchuria. After the war, King served with the secretary of war's Personnel Board until his retirement in November 1946. He died in Brunswick, Georgia, on 31 August 1958.

John Kennedy Ohl

See also

Bataan, Battle of; MacArthur, Douglas; Philippines, Japanese Capture of; Wainwright, Jonathan Mayhew

References

Holt, Thaddeus. "King of Bataan." In Robert Cowley, ed., *Perspectives on World War II,* 155–171. New York: Berkeley Books, 2001.

Morton, Louis. *United States Army in World War II: The War in the Pacific—The Fall of the Philippines.* Washington, DC: Office of the Chief of Military History, Department of the Army, 1953.

Schultz, Duane P. *Hero of Bataan: The Story of General Jonathan M. Wainwright.* New York: St. Martin's Press, 1981.

Young, Donald J. *The Battle of Bataan: A History of the 90-Day Siege and Eventual Surrender of 75,000 Filipino and United States Troops to the Japanese in World War II.* Jefferson, NC: McFarland, 1992.

King, Ernest Joseph (1878–1956)

U.S. Navy Fleet Admiral and chief of Naval Operations. Born in Lorain, Ohio, on 23 November 1878, Ernest King graduated from the U.S. Naval Academy in 1901. He subsequently held a variety of appointments on cruisers, battleships, and

U.S. Admiral of the Fleet and Chief of Naval Operations Ernest Joseph King. (Library of Congress)

at the Naval Academy, where he was an instructor of ordnance and gunnery from 1906 to 1908. King commanded a destroyer in 1914. Between 1916 and 1919, he served on the staff of the commander of the Atlantic Fleet.

In 1919, Captain King headed the Naval Academy's postgraduate school. During the next seven years, the ambitious, hard-driving, and forceful King specialized in submarines. In 1926, he took command of an aircraft tender and was senior aide to the commander of Air Squadrons, Atlantic Fleet. In 1927, King underwent flight training, and the next year, he became assistant chief of the Bureau of Aeronautics. In 1929, he commanded the Norfolk Naval Air Station, and from 1930 to 1932, he commanded the aircraft carrier *Lexington.*

King then graduated from the Naval War College and, promoted to rear admiral, served as chief of the Bureau of Aeronautics from 1933 to 1936. He spent the next five years in senior naval aviation assignments, including a tour as commander of the Aircraft Base Force. In 1938, he was promoted to vice admiral. Appointed to the Navy General Board in 1939, King criticized the lack of war preparations, recommending that should the United States go to war with Japan, it had to follow an offensive Pacific naval strategy. He also proposed measures for the better integration of aircraft, submarines, and small fast ships with battleships and aircraft carriers.

In February 1941, King won promotion to admiral and was appointed commander of the Atlantic Fleet. On 30 December 1941, following the Japanese attack on Pearl Harbor, he became commander in chief of the U.S. Fleet. The following March, President Franklin D. Roosevelt appointed King as chief of naval operations, making him the only U.S. Navy officer ever to hold both positions concurrently.

As a member of the Joint Chiefs of Staff, King was a major architect of wartime strategy. He vigorously prosecuted a two-front war in both the Atlantic and the Pacific but consistently gave higher priority to operations utilizing naval forces. He was therefore more committed to extensive Pacific operations, which relied heavily on naval power, than was his colleague General George C. Marshall, the army chief of staff, who generally followed a Europe-first strategy. King forcefully implemented a strategy of aggressive advance against Japan through the Central Pacific, later modified to include a second, southwestern offensive by way of the Philippines and Taiwan. Despite feuds over authority with Secretary of the Navy Frank Knox and his successor, James Vincent Forrestal, King successfully built up American naval forces, introduced tactical and technological innovations, and contributed heavily to the Allied victory in the Pacific.

In October 1945, King abolished the position of commander in chief of naval forces, and in December, he retired, succeeded as chief of naval operations by Admiral Chester W. Nimitz. Over the next decade, he served as a special adviser to the secretary of the navy and also headed the Naval Historical Foundation. King died in Portsmouth, New Hampshire, on 25 June 1956.

Priscilla Roberts and Spencer C. Tucker

See also

Forrestal, James Vincent; Joint Chiefs of Staff; Marshall, George Catlett; Roosevelt, Franklin D.; United States, Navy

References

Buell, Thomas. *Master of Seapower: A Biography of Fleet Admiral Ernest J. King.* Boston: Little, Brown, 1980.

Hayes, Grace Person. *The History of the Joint Chiefs of Staff in World War II: The War against Japan.* Annapolis, MD: Naval Institute Press, 1982.

Love, Robert William, Jr. "Ernest Joseph King, 26 March 1942–15 December 1947." In Robert William Love Jr., ed., *The Chiefs of Naval Operations,* 137–179. Annapolis, MD: Naval Institute Press, 1980.

———. "Fleet Admiral Ernest J. King." In Stephen Howarth, ed., *Men of War: Great Naval Leaders of World War II,* 75–107. London: Weidenfeld and Nicolson, 1992.

Stoler, Mark A. *Allies and Adversaries: The Joint Chiefs of Staff, the Grand Alliance, and U.S. Strategy in World War II.* Chapel Hill: University of North Carolina Press, 2000.

King, William Lyon Mackenzie (1874–1950)

Wartime prime minister of Canada. Born on 17 December 1874, at Berlin (now Kitchener), Ontario, Canada, Mackenzie King graduated from the University of Toronto and did graduate work at the University of Chicago. He was appointed Canada's first deputy minister of labor and then briefly served as minister of labor (1908–1911). He spent the war years in the United States as the chief labor mediator for the Rockefellers, but in 1919, he returned to Canada to seek the leadership of the Liberal Party, which had been shattered by the 1917 conscription crisis. King revived the Liberals, becoming the Canadian prime minister in 1921 and winning subsequent elections in 1925, 1926, and 1935. During the 1920s, he played the central role in Canada's transition to an autonomous dominion.

A skillful administrator and consensus builder and an astute politician, King deserves much of the credit for Canada's remarkable economic and military mobilization during World War II. In September 1939, French Canadian support for the war was lukewarm at best, and a great many among the English Canadian majority questioned their fellow citizens' loyalty. King forged a precarious unity by promising his Liberal government would emphasize war production rather than expeditionary forces. This policy of "limited liabilities" did not, however, survive the defeat of France in June 1940. King also promised not to impose conscription for overseas service. Luck—the Canadian army saw little combat until mid-1943—combined with a sincere political effort not to isolate the people of Quebec and simultaneously to reach out to "moderate" English Canadians almost got the country through unscathed. With the Allies facing a desperate shortage of infantry reinforcements in the autumn of 1944 and with his own leadership at stake, King reluctantly implemented limited overseas conscription that November. In retrospect, his handling of the explosive conscription issue was a singular political achievement.

Although Canada's international stature and national pride grew dramatically during the war years, the ever cautious King was content for the country to continue playing the role of a loyal subordinate. His relationship with British Prime Minister Winston L. S. Churchill was often strained, but his government still provided enormous military, economic, and financial assistance to the "mother country," most of it ultimately at no cost. In contrast, his relationship with U.S. President Franklin D. Roosevelt was warm. Common sense, of course, dictated that King encourage closer ties with the United States. The wartime advantages of this policy were immeasurable for Canada. Few Canadians warmed to King, but in the June 1945 election, running on a platform of

Canadian Prime Minister Mackenzie King (left) and U.S. President Franklin D. Roosevelt (right) in Quebec, 19 August 1943. (Franklin D. Roosevelt Library (NLFDR)/National Archives)

progressive social and economic measures for the postwar era, his government won a majority (albeit a slender one). Worn out by his wartime exertions, King retired in October 1948. He died in Ottawa on 22 July 1950.

Patrick H. Brennan

See also

Canada, Role in the War; Churchill, Sir Winston L. S.; McNaughton, Andrew George Latta; Roosevelt, Franklin D.

References

Dawson, Robert MacGregor. *William Lyon Mackenzie King: A Political Biography.* Toronto, Canada: University of Toronto Press, 1958.

Granatstein, J. L. *Canada's War: The Politics of the Mackenzie King Government, 1939–1945.* Toronto, Canada: University of Toronto Press, 1975.

———. *How Britain's Weakness Forced Canada into the Arms of the United States.* Toronto, Canada: University of Toronto Press, 1989.

Pickersgill, J. W. *The Mackenzie King Record.* 4 vols. Toronto, Canada: University of Toronto Press, 1960–1970.

Kinkaid, Thomas Cassin (1888–1972)

U.S. Navy admiral whose forces were involved in many of the key engagements in the Pacific Theater. Born in Hanover, New Hampshire, on 3 April 1888, the son of Rear Admiral Thomas W. Kinkaid, he graduated from the U.S. Naval Academy in 1908, then served in the Great White Fleet in its circumnavigation of the globe. Kinkaid began his naval career in ordnance and aboard battleships. During World War I, he was assigned as a naval envoy at the British Admiralty. From 1929 to 1930, he attended the Naval War College. Promoted to captain in 1937, he commanded a cruiser, and two years later, he was assigned as naval attaché to Italy and Yugoslavia.

In late 1941, Kinkaid was promoted to rear admiral and took command of Cruiser Division 6. In March 1942, he led his ships in raids on Rabaul and New Guinea, then participated in the May Battle of the Coral Sea and the June Battle of

Midway. In August 1942, Kinkaid assumed command of Task Force 16, centered on the carrier *Enterprise,* and took part in the invasion of Guadalcanal and the Battles of the Eastern Solomons and the Santa Cruz Islands. In January 1943, Kinkaid took command of the North Pacific Force in Alaskan waters, his ships participating in the recapture from the Japanese of the Aleutian islands of Attu and Kiska.

Promoted to vice admiral, Kinkaid was put in charge of the Seventh Fleet, "MacArthur's Navy," in November 1943, with the mission of providing amphibious lift and protection to General Douglas MacArthur's Southwest Pacific Area forces on their approach to the Philippines. Seventh Fleet then participated in the defense of landings at Leyte by destroying attacking Japanese forces in Surigao Strait. In January 1945, Kinkaid led Seventh Fleet in the invasion of Luzon at Lingayen Gulf. Promoted to admiral in April, he took the surrender of Japanese forces in Korea in September.

Following World War II, Kinkaid briefly commanded the Eastern Sea Frontier and then the Sixteenth (Reserve) Fleet. He retired in May 1950 and died in Bethesda, Maryland, on 17 November 1972.

Landon Winkelvoss

See also

Aleutian Islands Campaign; Aviation, Naval; Coral Sea, Battle of the; Guadalcanal Naval Campaign; Japan, Navy; King, Earnest Joseph; Leyte Gulf, Battle of; MacArthur, Douglas; Midway, Battle of; Pearl Harbor, Attack on; Philippines, U.S. Recapture of; Solomon Islands, Naval Campaign; United States, Navy

References

Belote, James H., and William M. Belote. *Titans of the Seas: The Development and Operations of Japanese and American Carrier Task Forces during World War II.* New York: Harper and Row, 1975.

Wheeler, Gerald. "Admiral Thomas C. Kinkaid." In Stephen Howarth, ed., *Men of War: Great Naval Leaders of World War II,* 331–348. New York: St. Martin's Press, 1992.

———. *Kinkaid of the Seventh Fleet: A Biography of Admiral Thomas C. Kinkaid, U.S. Navy.* Washington, DC: Naval Historical Center, U.S. Navy, 1995.

Kirk, Alan Goodrich (1888–1963)

U.S. Navy admiral in charge of the American naval forces involved in the Normandy Invasion. Born in Philadelphia, Pennsylvania, on 30 October 1888, Alan Kirk graduated from the U.S. Naval Academy in 1909. He specialized in gunnery and served in the Asiatic Fleet. During the period of U.S. involvement in World War I, Kirk was stationed at the Naval Proving Ground, Dahlgren, Virginia.

In the 1920s, Kirk was executive officer of the presidential yacht and served as presidential naval aide. He next served as the gunnery officer on the battleship *Maryland.* Kirk gradu-

ated from the Naval War College in 1929 and then was an instructor there for two years. In 1931, he received his first command, a destroyer, and from 1933 to 1936, he was in the Office of the Chief of Naval Operations. He was the executive officer of the battleship *West Virginia* before taking command of the light cruiser *Milwaukee* and serving as operations officer to the commander of the U.S. Fleet. In 1939, Kirk became the American naval attaché in London, where he familiarized himself thoroughly with Royal Navy practices—practices he strongly admired, even though British condescension occasionally irked him. His forceful advocacy of greater Anglo-American cooperation and his urgent warnings in 1940 of the extreme danger Britain faced helped persuade President Franklin D. Roosevelt and his administration to assist Britain with measures potentially liable to precipitate conflict with Germany.

In March 1941, Kirk became director of Naval Intelligence, but partially because of fierce bureaucratic infighting with the War Plans Division, his office failed to produce any specific warnings of Japan's intentions vis-à-vis the United States, despite clues that an attack on American forces was being planned. In October 1941, he returned to sea duty as commander of a division of destroyer escorts in the Atlantic Fleet, fortuitously escaping responsibility for the failure to predict the Pearl Harbor raid.

Promoted to rear admiral in November 1941, Kirk became chief of staff to Admiral Harold Stark, commander of American naval forces in Europe, in March 1942. In London, he contributed substantially to Allied strategic planning. In February 1943, Kirk took command of Amphibious Force, Atlantic Fleet, and that July, he led an amphibious naval task force in the Sicily landings. His outstanding success in the face of unexpectedly difficult conditions brought him command of all U.S. naval forces for the June 1944 Normandy landings. Later that year, he commanded all U.S. naval forces in France. He was promoted to vice admiral in May 1945.

Kirk retired with the rank of admiral in March 1946. He then served as ambassador to Belgium and minister to Luxembourg until 1949 and spent a further two years as ambassador to the Soviet Union (April 1949 to October 1951) and the Republic of China (May 1962 to April 1963). Kirk died in New York City on 15 October 1963.

Priscilla Roberts

See also

Amphibious Warfare; Normandy Invasion and Campaign; Sicily, Invasion of; Stark, Harold Raynsford "Betty"

References

Belot, Raymond de. *The Struggle for the Mediterranean, 1939–1945.* Princeton, NJ: Princeton University Press, 1951.

Dorwart, Jeffery. *Conflict of Duty: The U.S. Navy's Intelligence Dilemma, 1919–1945.* Annapolis, MD: Naval Institute Press, 1983.

Jones, Matthew. *Britain, the United States, and the Mediterranean War, 1942–1944.* New York: St. Martin's Press, 1996.

Leutze, James R. *Bargaining for Supremacy: Anglo-American Naval Collaboration, 1937–1941*. Chapel Hill: University of North Carolina Press, 1977.

Morison, Samuel Eliot. *History of United States Naval Operations in World War II*. Vol. 9, *Sicily, Salerno, Anzio: January 1943–June 1944*. Boston: Little, Brown, 1954.

———. *History of United States Naval Operations in World War II*. Vol. 11, *The Invasion of France and Germany, 1944–1945*. Boston: Little, Brown, 1957.

Kleist, Paul Ludwig Ewald von (1881–1954)

German field marshal and commander of Army Group A. Born at Braunfels an der Lahn, Germany, on 8 August 1881, Paul von Kleist entered the army in 1900 and rose to the rank of captain by 1914. During World War I, he fought on both the Eastern and Western Fronts. Following the war, he served in artillery and cavalry posts. Though he was promoted to lieutenant general in August 1936, he retired in February 1938 during Adolf Hitler's purge of the army.

Recalled to active service in August 1939, Kleist commanded XXII Panzer Corps in Fourteenth Army during the invasion of Poland. He then assumed command of the army-sized Panzer Group Kleist in the May 1940 invasion of France and the Low Countries, spearheading Army Group A's advance. Promoted to full general in July 1940, Kleist commanded 1st Panzer Group in the April 1941 invasion of Yugoslavia, then First Panzer Army in Army Group South in Operation BARBAROSSA, the invasion of the Soviet Union. His forces pushed into Ukraine and devastated nearly 20 Soviet divisions, assisting in the encirclement of Kiev and establishing a bridgehead west of Rostov before being forced to retreat that winter.

Kleist's 1st Panzer Group carried out a decisive counterstroke in the First Battle of Kharkov (May 1942). Ordered to take the Caucasus oil fields, Kleist saw his forces drained away for the cauldron of Stalingrad. He commanded Army Group A in November 1942 and proved adept at defensive operations. Promoted to field marshal in February 1943, he carried out an orderly withdrawal of German forces from the Crimea that October. He then withdrew his force, redesignated Army Group South Ukraine, into Romania. Hitler lost confidence in Kleist and relieved him of command in March 1944, whereon Kleist retired.

Kleist was taken prisoner by the U.S. 26th Infantry Division on 25 April 1945. He was then turned over to Yugoslavia, where he was tried for war crimes, found guilty, and sentenced in 1948 to 15 years in prison. Extradited to the Soviet Union, he was sentenced there to an additional term of imprisonment. He died at Vladimir Prison Camp in the Soviet Union on 15 October 1954.

Roy B. Perry III

German Field Marshal Paul Ludwig von Kleist. (photo by Hulton Archive/Getty Images)

See also

BARBAROSSA, Operation; Eastern Front; Hitler, Adolf; Kiev Pocket, Battle of the; Rostov, Battle for; Stalingrad, Battle of; Yugoslavia Campaign (1941)

References

Chant, Christopher. *Hitler's Generals and Their Battles*. New York: Chartwell Books, 1976.

Erickson, John. *The Road to Stalingrad*. New York: Harper and Row, 1975.

Mitcham, Samuel W., Jr. "Field Marshal Ewald von Kleist." In Correlli Barnett, ed., *Hitler's Generals*, 249–263. New York: Grove Weidenfeld, 1989.

Kluge, Günther Adolf Ferdinand von (1882–1944)

German army field marshal and one of Adolf Hitler's most able commanders. Born at Posen, Prussia (now Poznan, Poland), into an old, aristocratic family on 30 October 1882, Günther Adolf Ferdinand von Kluge joined the army as an artillery officer in 1901. He served on the General Staff in

World War I between 1916 and 1918 and was wounded in fighting at Verdun in 1918. Kluge was selected to continue in the Reichswehr after the war. Promoted to brigadier general in February 1933, he was named inspector of Signal Troops. He became a major general in April 1934 and commanded the 6th Division in Münster. After Hitler began to expand the German army, Kluge commanded VI Corps in 1936. In 1938, Hitler purged Kluge, along with other German generals, for supporting General Werner von Fritsch, who was retired on trumped-up charges of homosexuality for his opposition to Hitler in February 1938.

With war looming, Hitler needed experienced commanders, and he recalled Kluge from retirement in October 1938 and gave him command of the newly created 6th Army Group, headquartered at Hanover. Later, the unit was redesignated as the Fourth Army. Kluge led Fourth Army during the invasion of Poland in September 1939. Proving himself an innovative commander in that campaign, he won Hitler's admiration and promotion to colonel general. Kluge led Fourth Army against France and the Low Countries in May 1940. Raised to field marshal in July, he went on to command Fourth Army in the invasion of the Soviet Union in June 1941 and Army Group Center from December 1941 to October 1943, again proving himself an effective commander.

Injured in a car accident in October 1943, Kluge went on prolonged leave during his recuperation. In July 1944, he replaced Field Marshal Karl Gerd von Rundstedt as commander in chief, West, and commander of Army Group B in Normandy. Kluge disliked the Nazis but was pleased with the territorial acquisitions made under Hitler. He was aware of the plot to assassinate the Führer, but he wavered in his support and finally declined to participate. He also failed to report it. Following the bomb attempt on Hitler's life on 20 July 1944, he came under increased Gestapo suspicion.

Kluge led the German counterattack at Avranches in August, but on its failure, he was relieved of command, on 17 August 1944, by Field Marshal Walther Model. He wrote to Hitler, urging him to make peace and end the suffering for the German people. Aware that he would be implicated in the conspiracy against Hitler and depressed by the military situation, Kluge committed suicide at Valmy, France, on 19 August 1944.

Spencer C. Tucker

See also
Hitler, Adolf; Model, Walther; Rundstedt, Karl Rudolf Gerd von
References
Lamb, Richard. "Field-Marshal Günther von Kluge." In Correlli Barnett, ed., *Hitler's Generals,* 395–409. New York: Grove Weidenfeld, 1989.
Mitcham, Samuel W., Jr. *Hitler's Field Marshals and Their Battles.* Chelsea, MI: Scarborough House, 1988, pp. 195–314.

Knox, William Franklin "Frank" (1874–1944)

U.S. secretary of the navy during the war years. Born on 1 January 1874 in Boston, Massachusetts, Frank Knox followed his political idol and role model, Theodore Roosevelt, and joined the 1st Volunteer U.S. Cavalry (the Rough Riders) in 1898 to fight in Cuba during the Spanish-American War. After mustering out, he became a highly successful newspaper editor and publisher, acquiring papers in Michigan and New Hampshire. A strong supporter of U.S. intervention in World War I, Knox served in the artillery in France in 1917 and 1918, rising from private to major. Between the wars, he returned to the newspaper business and was active in Republican politics, running unsuccessfully as the Republican vice presidential candidate in 1936.

In the late 1930s, Knox firmly believed that the United States could not remain aloof from the increasingly critical situation in Europe. Consequently, though he was unsympathetic toward President Franklin D. Roosevelt's domestic policies, he strongly endorsed the president's interventionist and pro-Allied international outlook. In 1940, Roosevelt persuaded Knox, together with former Republican Secretary of State Henry L. Stimson, to join his cabinet, with Knox serving as secretary of the navy—a step designed to win support from nonisolationist Republicans. Knox quickly recruited as assistants various able young businessmen and lawyers, such as James V. Forrestal (whom he appointed undersecretary), Ferdinand Eberstadt, and Adlai E. Stevenson. Knox utilized their industrial and organizational skills to implement expeditiously a massive naval expansion, as the U.S. Navy prepared for war in both the Atlantic and the Pacific. He also introduced modern business and management methods to the Navy Department's administration.

Knox helped to devise and lobby for the Destroyers-for-Bases deal of 1940, whereby Britain acquired American warships in exchange for leases to Caribbean naval bases, and the 1941 Lend-Lease program to aid the Allies. Like other Roosevelt administration officials, he did not predict the surprise Japanese attack on Pearl Harbor of 7 December 1941, and he rather ascribed responsibility for this U.S. defeat almost solely to the unpreparedness of the base's naval and military commanders.

Knox, who had previously found Roosevelt's pro-Allied policies insufficiently bold, welcomed American intervention in World War II. During its course, he traveled extensively to the various theaters of war. As a former newspaperman, he strongly emphasized the importance of good public relations, holding frequent press conferences. He stalwartly supported the abortive National Service Act of 1944, which would have

Secretary of the Navy W. Franklin Knox. (UPI-Bettmann/Corbis)

imposed the obligation of national service on all Americans, military and civilian alike. He died suddenly of heart failure in Washington, D.C., on 28 April 1944.

Priscilla Roberts

See also
Destroyers-for-Bases Deal; Forrestal, James Vincent; Lend-Lease; Pearl Harbor, Attack on; Roosevelt, Franklin D.; Stimson, Henry Lewis; United States, Navy

References
Albion, Robert. *Makers of Naval Policy, 1798–1947*. Annapolis, MD: Naval Institute Press, 1980.

Furer, Julius Augustus. *Administration of the Navy Department in World War II*. Washington, DC: U.S. Government Printing Office, 1959.

Lobdell, George H., Jr. "A Biography of Frank Knox." Ph.D. diss., University of Illinois, 1954.

———. "Frank Knox, 11 July 1940–28 April 1944." In Paolo E. Coletta, ed., *American Secretaries of the Navy*, vol. 2, 677–727. Annapolis, MD: Naval Institute Press, 1982.

Koenig, Marie Pierre Joseph François (1898–1970)

French army general who commanded the Free French Forces of the Interior (FFI). Born in Caen, Normandy, France, on 10 October 1898, Pierre Koenig volunteered for service in the army during World War I after obtaining his baccalaureate in 1917. He ended the war as a temporary second lieutenant with the Médaille Militaire.

After World War I, Koenig served with the French army of occupation in Germany. Promoted to lieutenant in 1920, he participated in the French occupation of the Ruhr in 1923 and then served with occupation forces in the Rhineland between 1923 and 1929. From 1931, Koenig served with the French Foreign Legion in Morocco. Promoted to captain in 1932, he participated in pacification campaigns.

With the start of World War II, Koenig departed Morocco in February 1940 and, as a major in the legion's demibrigade, fought in the Norway Campaign at Narvik. In June 1940, Koenig joined the Free French Forces of General Charles de Gaulle and commanded a battalion, fighting Vichy French forces in Africa and the Middle East in 1940 and 1941. Koenig's advance was rapid. He made colonel in June 1941 and became chief of staff of the 1st Free French Division in the Sudan, taking part in the Syria and Lebanon Campaign. Promoted to temporary major general that August, he commanded the 1st Free French Brigade in Egypt.

Koenig won renown for leading this unit in the Battle of Bir Hacheim, a critical point in the British Eighth Army's defensive line against the Afrika Korps (Africa Corps). Koenig's men held Bir Hacheim from 27 May 1942, refusing to withdraw until ordered to do so on the night of 10–11 June. Their epic stand restored French military honor following the

French General Marie Pierre Koenig, commander in chief of French forces of the interior and governor of Paris, after placing a wreath at the cenotaph in London. (Photo by Hulton Archive/Getty Images)

debacle of May–June 1940 and established the Free French as an effective fighting force.

Koenig then went to Algiers, where he was promoted to lieutenant general in May 1943. That July, he became deputy chief of staff of the French army. In April 1944, he was named commander of Free French Forces in Britain. On 25 June, he was promoted to full general, and as a member of General Dwight D. Eisenhower's staff, he took command of Free French Forces of the Interior following the Normandy Invasion. The FFI made a substantial contribution to Allied success by disrupting German lines of communication and tying down German military assets in Brittany and elsewhere.

In August 1944, Koenig became military governor of Paris. Between 1945 and 1949, he commanded the French zone of occupation in Germany, and he was promoted to General of the Army in 1946. He retired from the army in 1951 and was elected as a Gaullist deputy to the National Assembly. He served as minister of defense in 1954 and 1955 but resigned in opposition to the government's policy toward Morocco. Retiring from politics in 1958, Koenig died in Neuilly, a suburb of Paris, on 2 September 1970. He was posthumously promoted to marshal in 1984.

Spencer C. Tucker

See also

de Gaulle, Charles; Eisenhower, Dwight D.; France, Free French; Gazala, Battle of; Narvik, Operations in and Evacuation of; Norway, German Conquest of; Syria and Lebanon, Campaign in

References

de Gaulle, Charles. *The Complete War Memoirs of Charles de Gaulle.* 3 vols. Trans. Jonathan Griffin and Richard Howard. New York: Simon and Schuster, 1968.

Horne, Alistair. *The French Army and Politics, 1870–1970.* London: Macmillan, 1984.

Koga Mineichi (1885–1944)

Japanese navy admiral and commander of the Combined Fleet. Born in Saga Prefecture, Kyushu, Japan, on 25 April 1885, Koga Mineichi graduated from the Naval Academy in 1906. A specialist in naval gunnery, he also graduated from the Naval War College four years later. He served on the staff of the Second Fleet and took part in the Japanese capture of Qingdao (Tsingtao) at the beginning of World War I.

From 1916 to 1922, Koga held a number of administrative assignments ashore, including that of resident officer in France. Promoted to commander in 1922 and to captain in 1926, he was naval attaché to France between 1926 and 1928 and attended the 1927 Geneva Arms Limitation Conference. Returning to Japan in 1928, he was then secretary to the minister of the navy and a member of the Japanese delegation to the London Naval Conference of 1930. From 1930 to 1932, he commanded first the heavy cruiser *Aoba* and then the battle-

Japanese Navy Admiral Koga Mineichi. (Corbis)

ship *Ise*. Promoted to rear admiral in 1932, Koga next held a number of staff positions, including head of the Intelligence Division (1933) and vice chief of the Naval General Staff (1937). He was promoted to vice admiral in 1936.

Koga commanded Second Fleet from 1939 to 1941. He strongly opposed the conclusion of the Tripartite Pact with Germany and Italy in September 1940. In 1941, he assumed command of the China Area Fleet, supporting naval operations against Hong Kong at the beginning of the Pacific war. Promoted to full admiral in May 1942, Koga then commanded the Yokosuka Naval Station (1942–1943).

In May 1943, Koga succeeded Yamamoto Isoroku as commander in chief of the Combined Fleet following the latter's death in the Solomon Islands on 18 April 1943. By mid-1943, Japan had lost Guadalcanal as well as Attu and Kiska in the Aleutians to Allied counteroffensives. Koga worked to rebuild Japanese naval air strength and at the same time sought to retrieve the situation before it became irreversible by a decisive naval action employing the Combined Fleet. In October 1943, Koga ordered Vice Admiral Ozawa Jisaburo to launch the RO-GŌ Operation to attack U.S. naval forces in the Solomons, but Ozawa suffered a major reversal in the operation, losing 120 of 170 aircraft in November.

Koga then planned the O-GŌ Operation to smash U.S. naval forces in the Marshall Islands in February 1944. In the process of relocating his headquarters from Palau to Davao in the southern Philippines for this operation, Koga's plane was lost in a heavy storm on 31 March 1944. He was posthumously promoted to Admiral of the Fleet. Admiral Toyoda Soemu succeeded Koga as commander of the Combined Fleet.

Kotani Ken

See also
Aleutian Islands Campaign; Guadalcanal Naval Campaign; Hong Kong, Battle of; Japan, Navy; Ozawa Jisaburo; Toyoda Soemu; Yamamoto Isoroku

References
Evans, David C., and Mark R. Peattie. Kaigun: *Strategy, Tactics and Technology in the Imperial Japanese Navy, 1936–1941.* Annapolis, MD: Naval Institute Press, 1997.

Howarth, Stephen. *Morning Glory: The Story of the Imperial Japanese Navy.* London: Hamish Hamilton, 1983.

Kohima

See Imphal and Kohima, Sieges of.

Japanese Army General Kuniaki Koiso. (Photo by Keystone/Getty Images)

Koiso Kuniaki (1880–1950)

Japanese army general who became prime minister in 1944. Born in Yamagata Prefecture, Japan, on 22 March 1880, Koiso Kuniaki graduated from the Military Academy in 1900 and saw combat during the 1904–1905 Russo-Japanese War. Graduating from the General Staff College in 1910, he was posted to the General Staff in 1913. While still a junior officer, Koiso associated himself with elements in the Japanese military seeking to pursue expansion on the Asian continent. In 1916, he played a role in the Japanese army's unsuccessful attempt to foster an independence movement in Manchuria and Mongolia in order to detach those areas from China.

As he advanced in rank, Koiso continued to support not only the expansionistic aims of the Japanese military but also its attempts to dominate the government. He joined the Kokuhonsha, a right-wing political organization formed in 1924, and in March 1931, he lent his support to a military coup attempt staged by a group of junior officers. Despite his involvement in the affair, Koiso's career continued to advance. In 1937, he was appointed governor-general of Korea and promoted to full general. Koiso returned to Japan in 1939 to serve as minister of colonies.

From 1942 to 1944, Koiso again served as governor-general of Korea, where his second term was characterized by a brutal attempt to eradicate the cultural identity of the Korean people. He was recalled to Japan in July 1944 to succeed prime minister Tōjō Hideki, who had been forced to resign. Although Koiso believed that the war was lost, he attempted to bolster Japan's deteriorating war effort. He lowered the draft age, established the Supreme War Leadership Council as a liaison between the military and the cabinet, and attempted to coordinate munitions production. He could not, however, supply victories, and he was forced to resign in April 1945.

Following the war, Koiso was tried and convicted of war crimes by the International Military Tribunal for the Far East. Sentenced to life imprisonment, he died in the Sugamo Prison in Tokyo on 3 November 1950.

John M. Jennings

See also
Korea; Tōjō Hideki

References
Butow, Robert. *Japan's Decision to Surrender.* Stanford, CA: Stanford University Press, 1954.

Cumings, Bruce. *Korea's Place in the Sun: A Modern History.* New York: W. W. Norton, 1997.

Feis, Herbert. *Japan Subdued: The Atomic Bomb and the End of the War in the Pacific.* Princeton, NJ: Princeton University Press, 1961.

Frank, Richard B. *Downfall: The End of the Imperial Japanese Empire.* New York: Random House, 1999.

Kokoda Trail Campaign (July 1942–January 1943)

Important land battle fought on New Guinea. The Battles of the Coral Sea in May 1942 and Midway in June placed the Japanese navy on the defensive in the Central and South Pacific and altered Japanese plans to take the key Allied base at Port Moresby, from which they could strike Queensland, Australia, by air. The upcoming battles for Guadalcanal in the Solomon Islands and Port Moresby in New Guinea were critical to the Allies in gaining and maintaining the offensive in the Pacific Theater. The Americans struck first in the Solomons, but the Japanese took the initiative in New Guinea. While U.S. Navy and Marine elements prepared for operations in the Solomons, the supreme Allied commander in the South Pacific, General Douglas MacArthur, and his Allied Land Force commander, Australian General Sir Thomas Blamey, began a series of actions to strengthen Allied defensive positions in New Guinea, including the August 1942 deployment of two brigades of the Australian 7th Division to Port Moresby and one to Milne Bay. These moves were the prelude for a bloody, six-month-long campaign in some of the world's most difficult terrain, with far-reaching strategic consequences.

In early July 1942, the 39th Infantry Battalion of the Australian militia was sent to reinforce local Papuan infantry at Kokoda Pass in the Owen Stanley Mountains. The area was a critical terrain feature the Japanese would have to secure in order to assault Port Moresby from the north. Denied an invasion of Port Moresby by sea as a consequence of the Battle of the Coral Sea, the Japanese now endeavored to take it by land, working southwest along the treacherous Kokoda Trail that crossed the east-west Owen Stanley Mountains. The trail was as high as 8,000 feet in places and as low as 1,000 feet, with valleys that sloped 60 degrees. On 21 July, the Japanese Yokohama Force of engineer, infantry, and marine units landed at Buna on the north side of New Guinea to prepare the way for the follow-on South Sea Detachment commanded by Major General Horii Tomitaro, who arrived himself in mid-August. Horii now pushed a force inland from Gona, drove back local Allied troops, and moved up the rugged and treacherous track of the Kokoda Trail that ran south to Port Moresby. By mid-August, the Japanese had seized the passes over the Owen Stanley Mountains that ran across the island.

During the march, Japanese forces quickly fixed and bypassed the detachments of Australian and Papuan forces guarding several key areas, including Kokoda. The 21st Brigade of the Australian 7th Division was then sent to relieve the elements that had borne the brunt of the fighting. The Japanese, however, outflanked the 21st Brigade and forced it to withdraw, a maneuver repeated several times over the next few weeks. In early September, the 25th Brigade arrived to reinforce the 21st, and in mid-September, it joined in the unsuccessful defense at Ioribaiwa, some 30 miles from Port Moresby. The Japanese entered that village on 16 September in what was their last land victory of the Pacific war. There, Australian and U.S. forces under Major General Edmond F. Hering, benefiting from Allied air superiority, helped contain the Japanese advance.

On 25 August, the Japanese landed 1,900 men at Milne Bay at the eastern tip of Papua. This force planned to make its way west and support Horii's drive on Port Moresby. Australian forces, not greatly superior to the Japanese in size but with the advantage of air support, contained the landing and then mounted a counterattack. On the nights of 5 and 6 September, the Japanese evacuated 1,300 survivors, half of them wounded. The Australian victory in the Battle of Milne Bay was extremely important: both a humiliation for the Japanese and a lift for the Allies, it proved the Allies could defeat the Japanese in jungle warfare. And its outcome isolated the Japanese coming off the Kokoda Trail.

The Japanese engineers at Buna had hoped to construct a small road along the Kokoda Trail. When this proved impossible, the engineers fortified an area about 10 miles long and several miles deep between Gona and Buna on the Solomon Sea. There, 7,000 Japanese, half of them survivors of the Kokoda Trail march, awaited an Allied attack.

Fighting on Guadalcanal deprived the Japanese of resources for Papua, and during October, Allied pressure and orders from General Imamura Hitoshi on Rabaul to withdraw caused Horii to fall back over the Owen Stanley Mountains. The Australian 7th Division followed. But instead of withdrawing to the coast at Buna, Horii decided to make a stand near the Kokoda Trail between the settlements of Oivi and Gorari, a few miles east of Kokoda. He was confident of victory, but by early November, the Allies had learned much about jungle warfare, and in the Battle of Oivi-Gorari, the Australians flanked the Japanese position, driving Horii's men off the trail and into a river. Taking advantage of the dense jungle, many Japanese managed to reach the coast. Horii was not among them; he drowned a week later while crossing the Kumusi River.

In late November 1942, the Australians approached Buna from the Kokoda Trail. Meanwhile, the U.S. 32nd Division advanced up the Papuan coast in a strange collection of fishing boats and coastal vessels. Because the coast was poorly charted and also because there were numerous reefs as well as concerns over Japanese aircraft, the U.S. Navy did not support the operation with transports or warships, which adversely affected its progress. The Kokoda Trail was far too rugged to move artillery and significant quantities of supplies by that route; nor could artillery be brought in on the small U.S. Army vessels. Thus, the 32nd Division, unprepared for the jungle conditions in any case, had to go into battle without artillery support against Japanese machine-gun nests that were well dug in and concealed in the dense jungle.

The Australian-U.S. advance against the Buna-Gona fortified zone began on 18 November. Progress in the jungle and swamps was slow, and many of the troops were incapacitated by disease. Fortunately for the Allies, fighting on Guadalcanal meant that the Japanese on Papua received few supplies. The Japanese had to deal not only with disease but also with malnutrition.

Displeased with the situation, MacArthur brought in U.S. Army Lieutenant General Robert L. Eichelberger to command I Corps, ordering him to take Buna or not come back alive. Eichelberger flew to Dobodura on 1 December 1942 to take command of the American sector. An effective commander, he soon restored Allied morale. In early December, U.S. engineers were able to open an airfield near Buna, significantly improving the Allied supply situation. On 9 December, the Australians took Gona. The more heavily fortified Buna resisted U.S. pressure, but on 23 January 1943, a concerted attack by Australian and U.S. forces secured it as well.

J. G. D. Babb and Spencer C. Tucker

See also

Blamey, Sir Thomas Albert; Buna, Battle of; Coral Sea, Battle of the; Eichelberger, Robert Lawrence; Guadalcanal, Land Battles for; Guadalcanal Naval Campaign; Horii Tomitaro; Imamura Hitoshi; MacArthur, Douglas; Midway, Battle of; Milne Bay, Battle of

References

Bergerud, Eric. *Touched with Fire: The Land War in the South Pacific.* New York: Viking, 1996.

Harries, Meirion, and Susie Harries. *Soldiers of the Sun: The Rise and Fall of the Imperial Japanese Army.* New York: Random House, 1991.

Mayo, Lida. *Bloody Buna.* New York: Doubleday, 1974.

Köln (Cologne), Raid on (30–31 May 1942)

City targeted for the first thousand-plane air raid in World War II. Although the British had first bombed German industry in 1940, their successes until 1942 had been minimal. The British strategic bombing campaign suffered from a lack of bombers (prior to 1942, the Royal Air Force [RAF] Bomber Command never possessed more than 400 bombers) and an inability to hit targets with any accuracy at night. In the spring of 1942, the war was going badly for the Allies, and the Soviet Union was pressing for a second front. As the only alternative for direct offensive action against Germany, the British changed their policies on strategic bombing.

With the accession of Air Chief Marshal Sir Arthur Harris as commander of Bomber Command in February 1942, the British began a deliberate program of targeting built-up areas instead of industries. In a desperate need to boost morale at home and to demonstrate the increasing capabilities of Bomber Command, Harris proposed to Prime Minister Winston L. S. Churchill the idea of a thousand-plane raid. The plan immediately received Churchill's approval. By temporarily stripping Training Command of aircraft and securing other planes from Coastal Command, Harris assembled 1,086 aircraft, more than enough planes to cover any aborted takeoffs. The Admiralty then withdrew the 250 Coastal Command aircraft, but Harris was determined to reach the thousand-plane figure, even though it meant sending some crews who were not yet fully trained.

Köln (Cologne) and Hamburg were the two possible targets. They were selected over the more valuable Essen because each was located on a large body of water and could be readily identified by *Gee* (for G or grid), a new navigational aid. On the day of the raid, bad weather ruled out Hamburg, but Köln was clear. Known as Operation MILLENNIUM, the raid occurred on the night of 30–31 May 1942. As it worked out, Harris got 1,046 bombers aloft, 600 of them Wellingtons. His goal was to pass all aircraft over Köln in only 90 minutes.

The air raid on Köln, Germany's fifth-largest city, lasted approximately 100 minutes, with the British bombers passing over the city at an average of 11 per minute. A total of 890 bombers reached Köln and dropped more than 1,455 tons of bombs on the city, two-thirds of them incendiaries. The bombing resulted in the destruction of an estimated 13,000 homes and the razing of almost 600 acres of the city. Casualties amounted to 469 dead and over 5,000 wounded on the German side, with another 45,000 left homeless. The British lost over 300 crewmen in the 41 bombers that failed to return, a loss of just 3.8 percent. The large number of bombers overwhelmed the German fighter defenses. The considerable destruction of this raid captured the imagination of the British public amid a series of Allied defeats in North Africa and East Asia.

Following the Köln raid, the British also launched thousand-plane raids against Essen and Bremen in June 1942. The Köln raid confirmed to Harris and Bomber Command the viability and effectiveness of night area bombing. The raid also shattered German illusions about who was winning the war and caused Adolf Hitler to lose confidence in the Luftwaffe. But instead of accepting the need to strengthen Germany's air defenses, Hitler ordered retaliatory German air attacks.

C. J. Horn

See also

Aircraft, Bombers; Harris, Sir Arthur Travers; Strategic Bombing

References

Harris, Arthur. *Bomber Offensive.* New York: Macmillan, 1947.

Neillands, Robin. *The Bomber War: The Allied Air Offensive against Nazi Germany.* Woodstock and New York: Overlook Press, 2001.

Verrier, Anthony. *The Bomber Offensive.* New York: Macmillan, 1968.

Webster, Charles, and Noble Frankland. *The Strategic Air Offensive against Germany, 1939–1945.* London: Her Majesty's Stationery Office, 1961.

Kolombangara, Battle of (13 July 1943)

Naval engagement between Allied and Japanese forces off the coast of Kolombangara, a small island north of New Georgia in the Solomon Islands. Rear Admiral Walden Ainsworth commanded an Allied force of three cruisers, reinforced by five destroyers under Captain Francis McInerney and another five under Captain Thomas Ryan. Rear Admiral Izaki Shunji led the Japanese squadron of one cruiser and five destroyers. Izaki's squadron was protecting transports carrying 1,200 soldiers to Vila.

At about 12:36 A.M. on 13 July, a "Black Cat" PBY reconnaissance aircraft spotted Izaki's ships heading southeast toward Kolombangara. At 1:00 A.M., the U.S. destroyer *Nicholas* made radar contact, followed by visual contact 3 minutes later. Ainsworth ordered his squadron into a single column and headed west on a closing course. He assumed he would achieve complete surprise, since the Japanese ships lacked radar. However, the Japanese were using a new device that sensed radar impulses. In the first operational test of the device, Izaki had learned of Ainsworth's presence 2 hours earlier.

At 1:08, Izaki's squadron came within 10,000 yards of Ainsworth's forces and launched torpedoes. The American destroyer vans launched their own torpedoes 2 minutes later. Izaki then turned his column directly north, and the Japanese cruiser *Jintsu* turned her searchlights on the destroyer *Nicholas*. While the *Jintsu* fired both guns and torpedoes, Ainsworth waited until all three of his cruisers had closed the range before opening up fire. By 1:17, the *Jintsu* was dead in the water. Ainsworth then ordered his whole squadron to turn away, but the New Zealand cruiser *Leander* caught a torpedo. Severely damaged, she was nonetheless able to retire.

Black Cat aircraft then reported that two Japanese ships were escaping to the north, leaving the impression that four ships had been crippled. In reality, only the *Jintsu* had been damaged; the rest of Izaki's squadron had retired north in order to reload their torpedo tubes. In just 18 minutes, they reversed course again to reengage.

Meanwhile, Ainsworth decided to head northeast to chase what he thought were the fleeing Japanese ships. As he pursued, he was unable to locate his destroyers by radio and ordered his two cruisers to illuminate unidentified targets on radar with star shells to see if they were McInerney's destroyers. Rather than U.S. destroyers, the unidentified vessels turned out to be Japanese warships that had just fired 31 reloaded torpedoes. Their radar detectors had alerted the Japanese by 1:57 A.M. of the presence of the U.S. ships. At 2:08 Ainsworth ordered fire opened, but before this order could be followed, the cruisers *St. Louis* and *Honolulu* took torpedoes in their bows and the destroyer *Gwin* was hit amidships.

The *Gwin* was scuttled the next morning. The Allies thus had three cruisers badly damaged in exchange for the *Jintsu*, which went down with her entire crew. Personnel losses numbered 482 Japanese, 61 Americans, and 28 New Zealanders. The Japanese were able to land all 1,200 reinforcements at Vila. The Battle of Kolombangara was thus a clear Japanese victory.

Landon Winkelvoss

See also
Ainsworth, Walden Lee "Pug"; Kula Gulf, Battle of
References
Cant, Gilbert. *The Great Pacific Victory.* New York: John Day, 1946.
Gailey, Harry A. *The War in the Pacific: From Pearl Harbor to Tokyo Bay.* Novato, CA: Presidio, 1997.
Morison, Samuel E. *United States Naval Operations in World War II.* Vol. 6, *Breaking the Bismarcks Barrier.* Boston: Little, Brown, 1950.

Komandorski Islands, Battle of the (26 March 1943)

Concluding naval battle of the Aleutian Campaign in the northern Pacific and the last major daylight naval action in which aircraft played no role. The Aleutian Campaign began in June 1942 with the Japanese occupation of the islands of Attu and Kiska. To protect their northern flank, the Japanese held these islands into 1943, while U.S. bombers and submarines from Dutch Harbor, enduring terrible weather conditions, slowly cut off Japanese supplies.

To break this tightening noose and reinforce Attu, Japanese Vice Admiral Hosogaya Boshiro led a task force of the heavy cruisers *Nachi* and *Maya*, the light cruisers *Tama* and *Abukuma*, and four destroyers escorting the heavily armed, 7,000-ton converted merchant cruisers *Asaka Maru* and *Sakito Maru*, which were acting as transports. Informed that the Japanese were en route, Rear Admiral Charles McMorris set out to intercept them with a much smaller force of the heavy cruiser *Salt Lake City*, the light cruiser *Richmond* (flagship), and four destroyers. The Americans encountered the Japanese force near the Komandorski Islands.

Before dawn on 26 March 1943, U.S. radar picked up the approaching Japanese ships. McMorris, expecting only lightly escorted supply ships, made for the Japanese and closed to gun range, only to discover that he was both outnumbered and outgunned. He then attempted to maneuver, hoping to draw the Japanese eastward toward American air support and perhaps slip past their warships to attack the supply vessels.

The two task forces engaged in a running duel for four hours. With more ships, more guns, and superior torpedoes, Hosogaya could have closed on the Americans and won a decisive victory. But his ships lacked effective radar, and he hesitated to press his advantage. Late in the battle, the *Salt*

U.S. Navy antiaircraft gun on station near Attu in the Aleutian Islands. (Horace Bristol/Corbis)

Lake City was struck by shells fired by either the *Maya* or *Nachi* and lost steam. McMorris then ordered his destroyers to carry out a torpedo attack while he moved the *Richmond* in to cover the stricken *Salt Lake City*. Although the U.S. destroyers scored no hits and the destroyer *Bailey* was damaged by return fire, the attack gave the *Salt Lake City* time to again get under way. At that point, Hosogaya broke off the action and withdrew, without delivering the vital supplies to Attu. He later explained his decision on the grounds that he was low on ammunition and fuel and worried about U.S. air attacks. His superiors were not impressed by this explanation, however, and Hosogaya was relieved of his command.

Although his ships had sustained damage, McMorris had lost none of them, and he had won a strategic victory. The American 7th Infantry Division landed on Attu in May, securing that island after a hard fight against the isolated Japanese defenders. The Japanese evacuated Kiska a month later, ending the Aleutian Campaign.

Terry Shoptaugh

See also
Aleutian Islands Campaign; McMorris, Charles Horatio "Soc"
References
Garfield, Brian. *The Thousand-Mile War: World War II in Alaska and the Aleutians.* Garden City, NY: Doubleday, 1969.

Morison, Samuel Eliot. *History of United States Naval Operations in World War II.* Vol. 7, *Aleutians, Gilberts and Marshalls.* Boston: Little, Brown, 1951.

U.S. Navy, Office of Naval Intelligence. *The Aleutians Campaign, June 1942–August 1943.* Washington, DC: Naval Historical Center, 1993 (reprint of 1945 original).

Kondō Nobutake (1886–1953)

Japanese navy admiral who commanded the China Sea Fleet. Born in Osaka Prefecture, Japan, on 25 September 1886, Kondō Nobutake graduated from the Naval Academy in 1907 and became a gunnery officer. He graduated from the Naval War College in 1919 and was promoted to lieutenant commander. A resident officer in Russia in 1919 and 1920 and in Germany from 1921 to 1923, he was appointed aide to the Imperial prince in 1924. He was then assigned as a staff officer in the Grand Fleet. Promoted to captain in 1927, he was an instructor at the Naval War College. He next commanded the cruiser *Kako* and then the battle cruiser *Kongo.*

Made a rear admiral in 1933, Kondō became vice president of the Naval War College, and in 1935, he was chief of staff of the Grand Fleet. One year after being promoted to vice admiral in 1937, he took command of the Fifth Fleet. In 1939, he became vice chief of the Naval General Staff.

In September 1941, Kondō took command of the Second Fleet, and at the outbreak of the Pacific war, he provided support for the Japanese force invading Malaya. On 10 December 1941, Kondō's aircraft sank the British battleship *Prince of Wales* and the battle cruiser *Repulse.* His fleet then provided cover for Japanese forces occupying the Philippines and Java in the Netherlands East Indies.

At the Battle of Midway, Kondō commanded the Main Support Force, which did not see action. He then took a leading role in the long-running naval struggle for control of the island of Guadalcanal. He was unsuccessful in luring the U.S. naval forces into a trap in the Eastern Solomons in late August 1942, and in the Battle of the Santa Cruz Islands on 16 to 27 October, his units provided gunfire support for the Japanese land effort to retake Henderson Field. This action also led to the crippling of the U.S. carrier *Hornet* and her eventual loss. In naval actions off Guadalcanal from 12 to 15 November, his forces were defeated, losing the battleship *Kirishima.* Their withdrawal sealed the fate of Guadalcanal. Kondō then supervised the successful evacuation from the island of Japanese ground-force survivors.

In April 1943, Kondō was promoted to admiral, and he was appointed commander in chief of the China Sea Fleet the following December. In May 1945, he became military adviser to Emperor Hirohito. Kondō died in Tokyo on 19 February 1953.

Kita Yoshito

See also
Guadalcanal Naval Campaign; Hirohito, Emperor of Japan; Malaya Campaign; Nagumo Chūichi; Netherlands East Indies, Japanese Conquest of; *Prince of Wales* and *Repulse*; Santa Cruz Islands, Battle of

References
Hammel, Eric. *Guadalcanal: The Carrier Battles—The Pivotal Aircraft Carrier Battles of the Eastern Solomons and Santa Cruz.* New York: Crown Publishers, 1987.

Morison, Samuel Eliot. *History of United States Naval Operations in World War II.* Vol. 5, *The Struggle for Guadalcanal, August 1941–February 1943.* Boston: Little, Brown, 1948.

Kondor Legion

German Luftwaffe unit that served on the Nationalist side in the Spanish Civil War of 1936 to 1939. The Kondor (Condor) Legion was instrumental in the eventual Nationalist victory over the Republicans. At the same time, it provided a laboratory for the tactics, technology, and organization that the Luftwaffe would employ in World War II.

The beginning of the Spanish Civil War in July 1936 caught the Nationalist side unprepared, with many of its troops stationed in Spanish Morocco and the Republican side controlling the sea through the Spanish navy. The Nationalists sought Adolf Hitler's support, and on 26 July 1936, Hitler began to provide clandestine military aid to them by airlifting troops to Spain from North Africa. Initial support included 10 Ju-52 transports, a handful of obsolete biplane fighter aircraft, some 88 mm antiaircraft artillery, and crews.

The Ju-52s soon began the first major military airlift in history, and together with Italian aircraft, they transported more than 13,000 troops of General Francisco Franco's Army of Africa from Spanish Morocco to Spain between July and October 1936. The German biplane fighters, however, proved no match for the Republican side's Soviet fighter aircraft. In October, Hitler decided to increase the Luftwaffe presence in Spain, resulting in the official formation of the Kondor Legion in October 1936. Eventually, the legion numbered more than 5,000 "volunteers" and fielded more than 100 aircraft of various types. But a total of 19,000 men and 300 to 400 planes served in the legion over the course of the war, and the Kondor Legion was made up of regular German military units, not volunteers.

The relatively poor performance of the legion's biplanes against the Republican fighters led the Germans to employ them in a ground-support role, essentially as flying artillery. This move was instrumental in the development of Luftwaffe doctrines of close-air support for ground operations. Kondor Legion aircraft hammered Republican troop lines just before Nationalist troops assaulted, while the Germans simultaneously struck enemy rear areas to prevent reinforcement.

Members of the German Kondor Legion arriving in Gijo Harbor, Spain, 1939. (Bettman/Corbis)

These tactics proved key in a number of Nationalist ground victories.

The legion employed the most advanced German aircraft as they became available, including the Heinkel He-111 bomber and the Messerschmitt Bf-109 fighter. The legion also field-tested new aircraft, such as the first Junkers Ju-87 Stuka dive-bomber, and it experimented with new combat techniques. The legion became notorious in 1937 for its "carpet bombing" of the Basque city of Guernica.

By 1938, the Nationalists secured air superiority. The Legion quickly appeared on any front required, with its support relocated via train and air transport. Its 88 mm flak guns, originally sent to provide air defense, eventually became the backbone of Nationalist artillery batteries, serving as highly mobile field artillery. Certainly, the Kondor Legion was an important factor in the Nationalist victory. Success, however, did not come without cost: some 330 members of the Kondor Legion died in Spain, and approximately 1,000 were wounded.

Some of the Luftwaffe's leading fighter aces, such as Adolf Galland, received their baptism of fire with the legion. The Luftwaffe adopted much of the legion's organization and tactics for World War II, particularly in ground-support and psychological operations.

Jeffrey W. Stamp

See also
Franco, Francisco; Germany, Air Force; Guernica, Kondor Legion Attack on; Hitler, Adolf
References
Drum, Karl. *The German Air Force in the Spanish Civil War (Kondor Legion)*. Manhattan, KS: Sunflower University Press, 1983.
Elstoh, Peter. *Kondor Legion*. New York: Ballantine Books, 1973.
Proctor, Raymond L. *Hitler's Luftwaffe in the Spanish Civil War*. Westport, CT: Greenwood Press, 1983.
Ries, Karl, and Hans Ring. *The Legion Kondor*. Trans. David Johnston. West Chester, PA: Schiffer Publishing, 1992.

Konev, Ivan Stepanovich (1897–1973)

Marshal of the Soviet Union who would command Soviet occupation forces in Germany at war's end. Born in the vil-

Marshal of the Soviet Union Ivan Konev. (Hulton Archive/Getty Images)

lage of Lladeino, near Kirov, Russia, on 28 December 1897 and schooled to age 12, Ivan Konev initially became a lumberjack. After being conscripted into the Russian army in 1916, he served in the artillery on the Galician Front, achieved officer rank, and was demobilized in November 1917. Konev joined the Red Army and the Communist Party in 1918, serving as military commissar on an armored train on the Eastern Front. He rose to divisional commissar by 1920.

Konev played a notable role in crushing the Kronstadt Rebellion of March 1921. He graduated from the Frunze Military Academy six years later and then switched to the command side. He was given divisional command and attended special courses at the Frunze in 1934 and 1935. He went on to serve as commander of the Special Red Banner Army in the Far East and then as head of the Transbaikal Military District (1938–1941). His presence in the Far East and his political acumen helped him survive the late 1930s' great purge of the Soviet army officer corps. In the course of fighting against the Japanese in 1939, he developed a bitter rivalry with Georgii Zhukov.

Promoted to lieutenant general, Konev assumed command of the North Caucasus Military District in January 1941. In June, when the Germans invaded the Soviet Union, he received command of the Nineteenth Army. That September, he was promoted to colonel general and succeeded

Semen Timoshenko as commander of the Western Front. Terrible Soviet defeats followed, with five Soviet armies encircled and a half million men taken prisoner. Responsibility for the defeat lay with Konev and Josef Stalin, as the large encirclement could have been prevented. Zhukov then replaced Konev. However, in an appeal to Stalin, Zhukov saved Konev and made him his deputy—a favor that Konev would not repay.

When the Kalinin Front was formed in October, it was commanded by Konev as colonel general. In that post, he successfully defended the northern approaches to Moscow, and in mid-December, he drove the German army from Kalinin.

In August 1942, Konev again secured command of the Western Front when Zhukov returned to duty with the Stavka. He halted the last German drive toward Moscow and was shifted to command the Northwestern Front (February to June 1943). During the critical July 1943 Battle of Kursk, Konev commanded the strategic reserve Steppe Front, the powerful armor forces of which blunted the German panzers at Prokhorovka.

Konev secured promotion to General of the Army in August 1943. In October, his front, now known as the 2nd Ukrainian Front, played a key role in the encirclement of German forces at Korsun-Shevchenko, earning him promotion to marshal of the Soviet Union in February 1944. Taking command of the 1st Ukrainian Front that May, Konev swept through southern Poland and captured the Silesian industrial region. Zhukov was initially assigned the honor of taking Berlin, while Konev moved south of the German capital to the Elbe. But heavy German resistance allowed Konev to propose that his armor be diverted north to the city, and Stalin agreed. Thus, on 25 April 1945, Konev's tanks linked up with those of Zhukov, isolating Berlin. That same day, Konev's patrols made contact with the U.S. First Army on the Elbe at Torgau, in effect splitting Germany. Konev then commanded Soviet occupation forces in Austria.

By July 1946, Konev had succeeded Zhukov as commander of occupation and ground forces in Germany, having provided "evidence" against Zhukov during Stalin's inquiry of the latter's "improper behavior." He would go on to serve as chief inspector of Soviet Forces (1950–1952), commander of the Transcarpathian Military District (1952–1955), and commander in chief of Soviet Ground Forces (1955–1956).

On the formation of the Warsaw Pact, Soviet leader Nikita Khrushchev named Konev commander of its forces (1956–1960) in time to crush the Hungarian uprising of 1956. Konev again turned on Zhukov when Khrushchev removed him in 1957. Ironically, Konev's Zhukov-like objections to the move from conventional forces to missiles resulted in his "voluntary" retirement to the Inspectorate. During the Berlin crisis of 1961, he was called on to head Soviet Forces in Germany again, through April 1962. Konev went into "active retirement" in 1963 as a Ministry of Defense inspector. He died in Moscow ten years later, on 21 May 1973.

Claude R. Sasso

See also

Berlin, Land Battle for; Kalinin, Recapture of; Korsun Pocket, Battle of; Kursk, Battle of; Smolensk, Battle of; Stalin, Josef; Timoshenko, Semen Konstantinovich; Zhukov, Georgii Konstantinovich

References

Erickson, John. *The Road to Berlin*. Boulder, CO: Westview Press, 1983.

———. *The Road to Stalingrad*. Boulder, CO: Westview Press, 1984.

Konev, Ivan. *Year of Victory*. Moscow: Progress Publishers, 1969.

Rzheshevsky, Oleg. "Ivan Stepanovich Konev." In Harold Shukman, ed., *Stalin's Generals*, 91–107. New York: Grove Press, 1993.

Shtemenko, Sergei M. *The Soviet General Staff at War, 1941–1945*. 2 vols. Moscow: Progress Publishers, 1970.

Konoe Fumimaro, Prince of Japan (1891–1946)

Japanese politician during the war years. Born in Tokyo on 12 October 1891, Konoe Fumimaro was a member of one of the five highest-ranked aristocratic families in Imperial Japan. His father, Prince Atsumaro, was a renowned pan-Asiatic movement leader who founded Tōadōbun-shoin University in Shanghai.

A graduate of the Department of Law of Kyoto Imperial University, the young Konoe pursued a career in diplomacy and attended the Paris Peace Conference in 1919 as a junior member of the Japanese delegation. There, he observed the reality of international power politics, in which the defeated became prey to victors. Japan's failure to secure a statement on racial equality in the League of Nations Covenant disillusioned the young diplomat. Highly critical of the Anglo-American domination of the peace conference, Konoe published an article in 1920 attacking the hypocrisy of the postwar settlement.

Having served some years as a member of the House of Peers in the Japanese government, Konoe was appointed prime minister in 1937. His popularity was immense, and he enjoyed widespread support from both the military and the general public. Following the Marco Polo Bridge Incident of 7 July 1937, Konoe permitted the hard-liners in his cabinet to pursue an all-out war against China, thus making a fateful choice for Japan. In January 1938, he made the statement "*Shōkaiseki wo aiteni sezu*" (We do not negotiate with Jiang Jieshi [Ching kai-shek]), which severely hampered peace negotiations with China. With the military stalemate in China, Konoe resigned in January 1939.

Konoe was once again called to the premiership in July 1940. In his second cabinet, a drastic political restructuring was carried out in the dissolution of existing political parties and establishing the Taisei Yokusankai (Imperial Rule Assistance Association). Konoe became the first president of this organization, which was modeled on the one-party systems of Nazi Germany and the Soviet Union. While preparing for a total war at home, he agreed to the army's strategy of sending troops into northern French Indochina in September 1940. That same month, under the initiative of Foreign Minister Matsuoka Yōsuke, Japan concluded the Tripartite Pact with Germany and Italy. These actions further worsened already declining U.S.-Japanese relations. Faced with a diplomatic stalemate with the United States, Konoe resigned in July 1941 and was succeeded by General Tōjō Hideki.

After the tides of war turned, Konoe maneuvered carefully to rally anti-Tōjō elements in Japan in order to secure a negotiated peace with the Allies. In early 1945, he was designated as a special envoy to the Soviet Union to seek peace through a Soviet intermediary, which did not materialize. These actions did not, however, save Konoe from prosecution by the International War Crimes Tribunal in Tokyo after the war. Rather than face trial, he committed suicide before his arrest, on 16 December 1946 in Tokyo. His only son, Fumitaka, a junior army officer, was interned in Siberia and allegedly killed there by the Soviets.

Tohmatsu Haruo

See also

International Military Tribunal: Far East; Japan, Role in War; Jiang Jieshi; Matsuoka Yōsuke; Sino-Japanese War; Tripartite Pact

References

Morley, James William, ed. *Deterrent Diplomacy: Japan, Germany, and the USSR, 1935–1940*. New York: Columbia University Press, 1976.

———. *The Fateful Choice: Japan's Advance into Southeast Asia, 1939–1941*. New York: Columbia University Press, 1980.

———. *The China Quagmire: Japan's Expansion on the Asian Continent, 1933–1941*. New York: Columbia University Press, 1983.

———. *The Final Confrontation: Japan's Negotiations with the United States, 1941*. New York: Columbia University Press, 1994.

Skillony, Ben-Ami. *Politics and Culture in Wartime Japan*. Oxford: Clarendon Press, 1981.

Konoye Fumimaro, Prince of Japan

See Konoe Fumimaro, Prince of Japan.

Korea

Caught between three powerful neighbors—China, Russia, and Japan—Korea experienced a stormy history. The nation was long dominated or controlled by China, but Japanese leaders saw Korea as a "dagger" pointed at their country and believed that control of the peninsula was a necessary step to dominating Manchuria and China. After defeating China between 1894 and 1895, Japan went to war against Russia in 1904 and 1905. In the resulting Treaty of Portsmouth of 1905, Japan gained control of Korea. Five years later, Japan forced the Korean king to abdicate, and it formally annexed Korea.

Korean nationalists were buoyed by U.S. President Woodrow Wilson's World War I call for the "self-determination of peoples," but demonstrations in March 1919 were met with severe Japanese repression. Some Korean nationalist leaders fled abroad and established a Korean provisional government at Shanghai. In 1925, a Communist movement was formally organized within Korea. It had ties to the Communist International (Comintern).

Japanese rule in Korea was both oppressive and exploitive, a poor advertisement for the Greater East Asia Co-prosperity Sphere the Japanese government proclaimed in the late 1930s in the hope of winning support from Asian nationalist movements. Japan built highways and railroads, but they were designed for military use and to consolidate the Japanese position. It also industrialized Korea, but the economy was completely integrated with that of Japan. In 1937, the Japanese in Korea under Governor-General Koiso Kuniaki, an army general, began a process of cultural assimilation for the 24 million Koreans, banning the Korean language and literature and insisting that all education (fewer than 20 percent of Koreans were literate) be conducted in Japanese. In 1939, the Japanese began employing Korean labor in other parts of their empire, and in 1942, they introduced conscription in Korea for the Japanese army. Meanwhile, Korean nationalists and communists organized military formations in China to fight the Japanese. In 1941, these were integrated into a single military force under Yi Pon-sok, and troops of this force fought the Japanese in Burma. Communist units also formed in Siberia under the young communist leader Kim Il-sung.

During World War II, the Koreans suffered extensively. Japan ruined many of the country's industrial plants by overworking the machinery without providing adequate maintenance. It also expropriated most chemical products, especially nitrogen, causing near total soil depletion in Korea. Japan also stripped the country of much of its rice production and cattle. Unrest in Korea increased, forcing Japan to increase its military presence; by 1945, 300,000 Japanese troops were in Korea. By the end of the war, Japan had also sent 723,000 Koreans as laborers to other parts of its empire, including Japan itself. Tens of thousands of Korean women were also forced into prostitution as "comfort women" for Japanese troops.

Korea became a focus of Allied attention only as World War II was ending in Europe. The December 1943 Cairo Conference resulted in a joint statement, involving leaders of the United States, Great Britain, and China, that called for a "free and independent" Korea in "due course." But as one of many countries being freed from German or Japanese control, Korea became a focal point for clashing U.S.-Soviet interests. At the February 1945 Yalta Conference, President Franklin D. Roosevelt and Premier Josef Stalin touched on the postwar status of Korea. Roosevelt advocated a 20- to 30-year trusteeship to be administered by the United States, the Soviet Union, and China. Stalin suggested that Great Britain should also be a trustee. Following Roosevelt's death in April 1945, Stalin informed President Harry S Truman's special envoy, Harry Hopkins, that the Soviet Union was committed to a four-power trusteeship for Korea.

Agreement regarding the extent of advancement into Korea of Soviet and American military forces was not reached until the July 1945 Potsdam Conference of the great powers, following the end of fighting in Europe and before the August declaration of war against Japan by the Soviets. There, the United States proposed—and the Soviets accepted—a demarcation line along the thirty-eighth parallel to separate the different Allied forces. Soviet troops were to occupy the northern part of the country and U.S. forces the southern part. The Soviet Twenty-First Army invaded Korea at the end of the war, and U.S. Lieutenant General John Hodge's XXIV Corps occupied southern Korea beginning in early September 1945.

This occupation was supposed to be temporary, but as in the case of Germany, efforts to create a unified country foundered on the rock of the Cold War. Occupation lines became permanent, and two states appeared, the northern one under Communist control and bound to the Soviet Union and the southern state supported by the United States. In 1950, North Korean leader Kim Il-sung, with the support of the Soviet Union and China, invaded the South in an effort to unify all Korea under Communist rule. The 1950–1953 Korean War prevented him from realizing this goal, but unlike Germany, which did reunify at the end of the Cold War, Korea remains divided and is a world flash point today.

Spencer C. Tucker

See also

Cairo Conference; Cold War, Origins and Early Course of; Hopkins, Harry Lloyd; Japan, Role in War; Koiso Kuniaki; Potsdam Conference; Roosevelt, Franklin D.; Stalin, Josef; Truman, Harry S; Yalta Conference

References

Cumings, Bruce. *The Origins of the Korean War.* 2 vols. Princeton, NJ: Princeton University Press, 1981, 1990.

———. *Child of Conflict: The Korean-American Relationship, 1943–1953.* Seattle: University of Washington Press, 1983.

———. *Korea's Place in the Sun: A Modern History.* New York: W. W. Norton, 1997.

Matray, James Irving. *The Unwanted Symbol: American Foreign Policy in Korea, 1941–1950.* Honolulu: University of Hawaii Press, 1985.

McCune, George M. *Korea Today*. Cambridge, MA: Harvard University Press, 1950.

U.S. Department of State. *Background Notes, South Korea*. Washington, DC: U.S. Department of State, Bureau of Public Affairs, 1991.

Korsun Pocket, Battle of the (25 January–17 February 1944)

Important Eastern Front battle. The Battle of the Korsun Pocket, known to the Soviets as the Korsun Shevchenkovsky Operation and to the Germans as the Cherkassy pocket engagement, pitted Marshal Georgii K. Zhukov against Field Marshal Fritz Eric von Manstein. Zhukov was supervising elements of General of the Army Nikolai F. Vatutin's 1st Ukrainian Front and General of the Army Ivan S. Konev's 2nd Ukrainian Front; Manstein was leading Army Group South. The Battle of the Korsun Pocket was the first successful large-scale Soviet encirclement combat since Operation URANUS in the Battle of Stalingrad 14 months before. The battle became known as "little Stalingrad on the Dnieper."

Unlike previous major Soviet offensives, Korsun Shevchenkovsky did not result from weeks or months of careful planning and force buildup. Rather, the Soviet Stavka and the two Ukrainian fronts organized it opportunistically. The battle demonstrated a Soviet operational adaptability comparable to that shown by the Germans between 1941 and 1943.

On 28 January 1944, converging attacks by the Fifth Guards Tank Army and Sixth Tank Army cut off and isolated the bulge in the Germans' lines that was their last toehold on the Dnieper River. The Soviets trapped at least 60,000 German soldiers, including the 5th SS (Viking) Division. In response, employing the Eighth Army's XLVII Panzer Corps and the III Panzer Corps of First Panzer Army, Manstein sought to punch through the Soviet siege ring, relieve the trapped German troops, and in turn encircle the surrounding Soviet armies.

On the Soviet side, the Battle of the Korsun Pocket included six tank corps, a mechanized corps equipped with Sherman tanks, and a cavalry corps. They opposed eight German panzer divisions, a heavy tank regiment equipped with Tiger and Panther tanks, and a reinforced Schutzstaffel (SS) motorized division. Substantial amounts of infantry, artillery, and air units on both sides were also involved. The Soviets halted two German armored relief attempts and simultaneously endeavored to crush the German pocket.

When it became obvious that the German counterattacks had failed, troops in the pocket were told that they would have to save themselves. An initially successful breakout on the night of 16–17 February, obscured by a blizzard, turned into a massacre as day broke. The desperate German columns were beset by everything from air attacks to saber-swinging Soviet cavalrymen. The battle ended on 17 February.

Soviet and German claims about the numbers of troops lost in the pocket are contradictory, but at least half of the German forces trapped there were killed, wounded, or captured, and even the survivors were in no shape to fight again for weeks or months. Six German divisions were destroyed. When the battle ended, Soviet forces were poised to complete the liberation of the western Ukraine.

Dana Lombardy

See also

Konev, Ivan Stepanovich; Manstein, Fritz Eric von; Stalingrad, Battle of; Ukraine Campaign; Zhukov, Georgii Konstantinovich

References

Glantz, David M., ed. and trans. *The Korsun-Shevchenkovsky Operation (The Cherkassy Pocket), January–February 1944: The Soviet General Staff Study*. Carlisle, PA: Glantz and Orenstein, 1997.

Loza, Dmitri. *Commanding the Red Army's Sherman Tanks*. Lincoln: University of Nebraska Press, 1996.

Nash, Douglas E. *Hell's Gate: The Battle of the Cherkassy Pocket, January–February 1944*. Barnsley, UK: Pen and Sword, 2002.

Kretschmer, Otto August Wilhelm (1912–1998)

German submarine commander, the most successful of World War II. Born at Heidau, Liegnitz, Germany, on 1 May 1912, Otto Kretschmer joined the German navy in April 1930 and entered the officer training program. He subsequently served on the light cruisers *Emden* and *Köln*. In January 1936, he volunteered for submarine service and took up his first command, the *U–35*, in July 1937, in which he conducted a patrol in Spanish waters during the Spanish Civil War. In September 1937, Kretschmer assumed command of the *U–23*, a Type II coastal U-boat.

During the first eight months of World War II, Kretschmer conducted eight patrols in *U–23* in the North Sea near the coast of Great Britain but achieved little success due to the limited capabilities of his submarine. His most notable achievements were sinking a tanker in January 1940 and the destroyer HMS *Daring* in February 1940. In April 1940, Kretschmer took command of *U–99*, a much larger and more capable Type VII submarine. After two months of intensive training with his crew, he began the first of eight patrols into the Atlantic in June 1940.

During these patrols, Kretschmer refined his tactics of slipping into the middle of convoys at night and torpedoing ships from the surface, often at very close range. The success of these attacks spawned his motto "One torpedo, one ship." He also earned recognition for sinking three British armed merchant cruisers in November 1940, including two on the

Former German U-boat Commander Otto Kretschmer was chosen to be the military attaché of the Federal Republic of Germany in London after the war. (Photo by Keystone/Getty Images)

Kretschmer spent the remainder of the war as a prisoner of war in Canada, returning to Germany in December 1947. In 1955, he joined the postwar navy of the Federal Republic of Germany, the Bundesmarine, and in 1965, he became chief of staff of the North Atlantic Treaty Organization (NATO) Baltic Command, a position he held for four years. He retired in 1970 with the rank of Flotillenadmiral (U.S. equiv. rear admiral). Kretschmer died at Straubing, Germany, on 5 August 1998.

C. J. Horn

See also
Atlantic, Battle of the; Convoys, Allied; Dönitz, Karl; Submarines
References
Bekker, Cajus. *Hitler's Naval War*. New York: Zebra Books, 1974.
Blair, Clay. *Hitler's U-Boat War*. Vol. 1, *The Hunters, 1939–1942*. New York: Random House, 1996.
Doenitz, Karl. *Memoirs: Ten Years and Twenty Days*. Trans. R. H. Stevens. New York: Da Capo Press, 1997.

Krueger, Walter (1881–1967)

U.S. Army general who commanded Sixth Army in the Pacific Theater. Born in Flatow, West Prussia, on 26 January 1881, Walter Krueger emigrated to the United States in 1889. He enlisted in the army during the 1898 Spanish-American War and saw action in Cuba and in the Philippine Insurrection, earning a commission in 1901. He graduated from the Infantry and Cavalry School in 1906 and the Command and General Staff School in 1907. He was a faculty member at the army's School of the Line and Staff College between 1909 and 1912. Captain Krueger participated in the 1916–1917 Punitive Expedition into Mexico. Sent to France during World War I, he rose to be chief of staff of the Tank Corps of the American Expeditionary Forces as a temporary colonel. He was then chief of staff for VI Corps in France and IV Corps in Germany.

Krueger graduated from the Army War College in 1921 and the Naval War College in 1926 and later taught at both schools before serving with the War Plans Division for three years. He was promoted to colonel in 1932 and brigadier general in 1936 and then headed the War Plans Division from 1936 to 1938. He next commanded a brigade and was promoted to major general in February 1939, thereafter taking command of the 2nd Division at Fort Sam Houston, Texas. He went on to command VIII Corps, and in May 1941, he took command of Third Army as a temporary lieutenant general. Krueger's Third Army "won" the 1941 Louisiana training maneuvers.

When the United States entered World War II, there seemed little chance that Krueger would receive a battlefield command because of his advanced age and his skill as a trainer of soldiers. In January 1943, however, General Douglas MacArthur personally requested Krueger and Third

night of 3–4 November in a running surface engagement in which he utilized his 88 mm deck gun. This action helped to convince the British Admiralty to discontinue the use of such ships. Kretschmer was the first German submarine commander to sink 250,000 tons of Allied shipping.

The most successful U-boat commander of the war, Kretschmer was known as "the tonnage king" because of his exploits. From September 1939 to March 1941, he sank 47 merchant ships totaling 273,503 tons and earned Germany's highest award for bravery, the Knight's Cross with Oak Leaves and Swords to the Iron Cross. Kretschmer, however, eschewed efforts to propagandize his accomplishments, earning another nickname, "Silent Otto." On 17 March 1941, he successfully attacked the 10-ship HX.112 convoy south of Iceland. After expending his torpedoes, he was returning to base in France when two British destroyers attacked and sank his boat. He and 40 of his 43-man crew were rescued.

U.S. Army Lieutenant General Walter Krueger (left) and Navy Vice Admiral Thomas Kinkaid peer at the shores of Leyte in the Philippines during the opening stages of the landings in October, 1944. (Corbis)

Army for deployment to the southwest Pacific. Instead, the War Department transferred Krueger and some of his staff to Australia to activate Sixth Army. Krueger commanded Sixth Army in a series of widespread combat operations across the southwest Pacific until the end of the Pacific war, beginning with the occupation of Kiriwina and Woodlark Islands in June 1943. He headed operations against New Britain, the Admiralty Islands, New Guinea, Biak, and Morotai. By midsummer 1944, New Guinea was in Allied hands, and MacArthur was ready to return to the Philippines. Krueger led the landings at Leyte and the Lingayen Gulf. In the ensuing campaign, Sixth Army captured Manila and cleared most of Luzon Island. Promoted to general in March 1945, Krueger was scheduled to lead the invasion of Kyushu Island when Japan surrendered.

Critics thought Krueger too slow and methodical, but very few have complained about his low casualty rates relative to his successes. Although MacArthur may have been displeased at Krueger's slowness on Luzon, he still selected him to lead the planned invasion of Japan. Rarely seeking the limelight, Krueger enjoyed MacArthur's full confidence.

After the war, Krueger remained with Sixth Army during the occupation of Japan. He retired in July 1946 and died on 20 August 1967 at Valley Forge, Pennsylvania.

Thomas D. Veve

See also

Admiralty Islands Campaign; Hollandia, Battle of; Leyte, Landings on and Capture of; MacArthur, Douglas; Manila, Battle for; Philippines, U.S. Recapture of; Southwest Pacific Theater

References

Brown, John T. "Steady Ascension: A Biography of General Walter Krueger." Master's thesis, Georgia Southern University, 2002.

Krueger, Walter. *From Down Under to Nippon: The Story of Sixth Army in World War II.* Washington, DC: Combat Forces Press, 1953.

Leary, William M. "Walter Krueger: MacArthur's Fighting General." In William M. Leary, ed., *We Shall Return! MacArthur's Commanders and the Defeat of Japan, 1942–1945,* 60–87. Lexington: University Press of Kentucky, 1988.

Küchler, Georg von (1881–1968)

Germany army field marshal who took command of Army Group North in 1942. Born near Hanau, Germany, on 30 May 1881, Georg von Küchler entered the German army in 1900 and was commissioned a lieutenant the next year. Promoted to captain, he took command of an artillery battery on the outbreak of World War I, distinguishing himself in combat on the Western Front and in General Staff service.

Küchler continued in the German army after the war, and his service was marked by steady advancement. He was promoted to major in 1924, to lieutenant colonel in 1929, and to full colonel in 1932. By 1934, he was a Generalmajor (U.S. equiv. brigadier general), commanding the 1st Infantry Division in East Prussia. Promoted in 1935 to Generalleutnant (U.S. equiv. major general), Küchler was appointed to the post of inspector general of the service academies.

In April 1937, Küchler was made General der Artillerie (U.S. equiv. lieutenant general), commanding I Army Corps at Königsberg. In March 1939, his forces participated in the incorporation of Memel into the Reich. In the German invasion of Poland, Küchler commanded Third Army, which struck south from East Prussia as part of Colonel General Fedor von Bock's Army Group North. During the Polish Campaign, Küchler directed the northern portion of the envelopment of Warsaw. Although seen as a favorite of Adolf Hitler, Küchler defied Schutzstaffel (SS) leader Heinrich Himmler and ordered the courts-martial of German soldiers guilty of committing atrocities against Poles.

During the invasion of France and the Low Countries in May 1940, Küchler commanded Eighteenth Army, consisting of 11 divisions in Bock's Army Group B. He had responsibility for the invasion of the Netherlands and the linkup with highly vulnerable German airborne forces holding key bridges, cities, and installations. Following the surrender of the Netherlands on 15 May, Küchler's forces occupied Antwerp, then forced the Scheldt and drove on Ghent in Belgium. His forces then mopped up the remaining resistance following the British evacuation at Dunkerque before driving south toward Amiens and taking Paris on 14 June.

Promoted to full general in July 1940, Küchler then led his Eighteenth Army as part of Field Marshal Wilhelm von Leeb's Army Group North in Operation BARBAROSSA, the invasion of the Soviet Union. Eighteenth Army held the north flank in the advance toward Leningrad. In addition to forcing prisoners of war to clear mines, Küchler also enforced Hitler's Commissar Order, and he ordered the execution of both partisans and Gypsies.

In January 1942, Küchler took over command of Army Group North from Leeb. He was promoted to field marshal in June 1942. When the Soviets launched their great counteroffensive at Leningrad on 28 January 1944, Küchler was forced to withdraw to the Luga River. Hitler made him the scapegoat for the reverse, and on 29 January, he temporarily replaced him with Field Marshal Walther Model. On 31 January, Hitler retired him altogether.

Arrested after the war, Küchler was tried and convicted of war crimes at Nuremberg in October 1948 and sentenced to 20 years of imprisonment. Freed in February 1955, he died in Garmisch-Partenkirchen, Germany, on 25 May 1968.

Spencer C. Tucker

See also

BARBAROSSA, Operation; Commissar Order; France Campaign; Himmler, Heinrich; Hitler, Adolf; Leeb, Wilhelm Franz Josef Ritter von; Leningrad, Siege of; Model, Walther; Netherlands Campaign; Poland Campaign

References

Glantz, David M. *The Battle for Leningrad, 1941–1944.* Lawrence: University Press of Kansas, 2002.

Mitcham, Samuel W., Jr. *Hitler's Field Marshals and Their Battles.* Chelsea, MI: Scarborough House, 1990.

Kula Gulf, Battle of (6 July 1943)

Pacific Theater naval battle, the first of two night surface actions fought for control of the major deepwater entrance to New Georgia Island. Rear Admiral Walden L. Ainsworth, with a light cruiser task group, had been in the gulf on the night of 5 July 1943 on a bombardment mission and was southeast of Guadalcanal when he received orders to return and intercept a Japanese transport group believed to be making for Vila.

Joined by two destroyers from Tulagi, Ainsworth headed back, arriving off the entrance an hour after midnight. The sky was overcast, there were passing showers, and visibility was 2,000 yards or less. Radar contact was made at 1:36 A.M. on 6 July with three warships some 22,000 yards distant, standing out of the gulf 5,000 yards off the Kolombangara shore. Ainsworth immediately assumed battle formation: two destroyers in column ahead; the light cruisers *Honolulu*, *Helena*, and *St. Louis* behind them; and two destroyers astern. At the same time, Ainsworth turned left to close with the Japanese, and then, at 1:49, he came back right to unmask all guns. Radar then picked up a second Japanese group astern the first, and Ainsworth delayed opening fire as he pondered this new situation.

The Japanese were, in fact, in three groups. The first, with which Ainsworth had made contact, was Rear Admiral Akiyama Teruo's covering force of the destroyers *Niizuki* (flag), *Suzukaze*, and *Tanikaze*. The second group was made up of four destroyer-transports that Akiyama had first ordered to make for Vila; when contact was made with Ainsworth, he directed them to reverse course and join in the battle. The third group of three destroyer-transports was already unloading at Vila.

Ainsworth opened fire on the Akiyama's group at 1:57 A.M., and the rapid-firing, radar-directed 6-inch guns in which the Americans put their faith quickly hammered the *Niizuki* into a wreck. But the gunfire lit up the American battle line, and almost immediately, the *Suzukaze* and *Tanikaze* launched 16 torpedoes and escaped to the northwest. Believing that he had accounted for all three ships of Akiyama's group, Ainsworth countermarched at 2:03 A.M. to deal with the transport group. Seconds later, three Japanese Long Lance torpedoes struck the *Helena*. She sank about 2:25. At 2:18 A.M., Ainsworth took the transport group under fire, scoring some hits, but the four destroyers scattered and headed for Vila, the only casualty resulting when the *Nagatsuki* ran hard aground on Kolombangara.

Finding no targets to the west and convinced that he had accounted for many more Japanese ships than the *Niizuki*, Ainsworth, whose own ships were low on both fuel and ammunition, ordered his force to head for Tulagi, leaving the *Nicholas* and *Radford* to pick up the *Helena*'s survivors. Three times during the early morning hours, the two destroyers interrupted their work to engage Japanese ships. Although gunfire and torpedoes were exchanged, there was no major damage to either side, and by daylight, Kula Gulf was clear of the Japanese vessels.

Ronnie Day

See also

Ainsworth, Walden Lee "Pug"; Kolombangara, Battle of; New Georgia, Battle of; Vella Gulf, Battle of; Vella Lavella, Naval Battle of

References

Dull, Paul S. *A Battle History of the Imperial Japanese Navy (1941–1945).* Annapolis, MD: Naval Institute Press, 1978.

Morison, Samuel Eliot. *History of United States Naval Operations in World War II*. Vol. 6, *Breaking the Bismarcks Barrier, 22 July 1942–1 May 1944.* Boston: Little, Brown, 1960.

Garand, George W., and Truman R. Strobridge. *History of U.S. Marine Corps Operations in World War II*. Vol. 4, *Western Pacific Operations*. Washington, DC: Historical Division, U.S. Marine Corps, 1971.

Ross, Bill D. *Iwo Jima: Legacy of Valor*. New York: Random House, 1985.

Wheeler, Richard. *Iwo*. New York: Lippincott and Crowell, 1980.

Kuribayashi Tadamichi (1891–1945)

Japanese army general charged with defending Iwo Jima. Born in Nagasaki Prefecture, Japan, on 7 July 1891 to a family of samurai descent, Kuribayashi Tadamichi graduated from the Military Academy in 1914. After serving in the cavalry, he was admitted to the General Staff Academy, from which he graduated in 1923, second in his class. In 1928, he was posted to the United States as a deputy military attaché, and between 1931 and 1933, he served as military attaché to Canada. Promoted to lieutenant colonel in 1933, Kuribayashi commanded a cavalry regiment in 1936 and 1937, followed by promotion to major general in 1940 and a series of brigade commands and promotion to chief of staff of the Twenty-First Army in China in 1941. In 1943, he returned to Japan, where he commanded the 1st Imperial Guards Division until 1944.

In May 1944, Kuribayashi took command of the 109th Infantry Division and was assigned the defense of Iwo Jima, part of the Volcano Island chain located approximately 700 miles from Tokyo. Kuribayashi arrived on Iwo Jima in June and began preparing the island to meet an anticipated U.S. amphibious assault. Disregarding the advice of his subordinates and ignoring the protests of the commander of Iwo Jima's contingent of naval troops, he decided not to attempt to hold the island's beaches. Instead, he ordered his troops to construct deep and heavily fortified positions inland, centered on the 556-foot-high Mount Suribachi. Kuribayashi's aim was to exact as heavy a toll as possible on the invaders after they landed.

Iwo Jima's defenders dug in accordingly, which allowed them to withstand over two months of U.S. air strikes and naval bombardment before the American landing on 19 February 1945. Although Kuribayashi's plan succeeded in inflicting heavy casualties on the attacking Americans, he and his men were inexorably ground down. On 17 March, Kuribayashi, who had been promoted to full general, made a farewell radio broadcast to Japan. He died in action during the last few days of organized resistance, sometime in the period between 21 and 24 March, but his body was never recovered.

John M. Jennings

See also
Iwo Jima, Battle for
References
Bartley, Whitman S. *Iwo Jima: Amphibious Epic*. Washington, DC: Historical Division, U.S. Marine Corps, 1954.

Kurita Takeo (1889–1977)

Japanese navy admiral involved in the 1944 Battle of Leyte Gulf. Born in Ibaragi, Japan, on 28 April 1889, Kurita Takeo graduated from the Naval Academy in 1910. In the 1920s, he held a number of destroyer commands. Promoted to commander, Kurita was an instructor at the Torpedo School between 1928 and 1934 and again between 1935 and 1937. He was promoted to captain in 1932. He commanded the cruiser *Abukuma* in 1934 and 1935 and then the battleship *Kongo* in 1937 and 1938. Promoted to rear admiral in 1938, he commanded destroyer squadrons over the next two years.

Made a vice admiral in May 1942, Kurita commanded the Close Support Group in the Battle of Midway. Then, in August 1943, he took command of Second Fleet. In the October 1944 Battle of Leyte Gulf, Kurita commanded the 1st Strike Force (the central force) in executing Operation SHŌ-GŌ (VICTORY ONE). Kurita's force was the most powerful of those that were to converge on the U.S. landing site on Leyte Gulf; it was to proceed through San Bernardino Strait and then join up with the 3rd Force under Vice Admiral Nishimura Shoji, which would pass through Surigao Strait to the south. Kurita's force had five battleships, including the *Yamato* and *Musashi*. The two forces were to come together at the U.S. landing site and destroy the support ships there, while the U.S. covering force was drawn off by a decoy Japanese carrier force under Vice Admiral Ozawa Jisaburo.

As it worked out, Nishimura's force was destroyed, and Kurita's force was discovered by U.S. aircraft; the *Musashi* was sunk. Kurita then reversed course, but unknown to the Americans, he turned around again. Meanwhile, Admiral William F. Halsey took his entire covering Third Fleet to engage Ozawa's decoy force, as Kurita's force issued from San Bernardino Strait to engage Vice Admiral Thomas C. Kinkaid's Seventh Fleet in Leyte Gulf.

In the early morning of 25 October, Kurita's ships approached the unprotected U.S. transports and their weak support force off Leyte, and they were on the verge of being able to annihilate them when Kurita decided to withdraw. He never explained his decision publicly, but apparently, he mistakenly believed that the aircraft attacking his ships were from Halsey's force. Several days of near incessant air attacks on his ships may also have impacted the exhausted Kurita, but the reasons for his decision are still debated. Not censured for the "mysterious u-turn," as his action is known in Japan, Kurita subsequently returned to Japan. He commanded the Naval Academy from January 1945 until the end of the war. He died in Hyogo, Japan, on 19 December 1977.

Kotani Ken

See also

Halsey, William Frederick, Jr.; Kinkaid, Thomas Cassin; Leyte Gulf, Battle of; Midway, Battle of; Ozawa Jisaburo; *Yamato*

References

Cutler, Thomas J. *The Battle of Leyte Gulf, 23–26 October 1944.* New York: Harper Collins, 1994.

Morison, Samuel Eliot. *History of United States Naval Operations in World War II.* Vol. 12, *Leyte, June 1944–January 1945.* Boston: Little, Brown, 1958.

Wooldridge, E. T., ed. *Carrier Warfare in the Pacific.* Washington, DC: Smithsonian Institution Press, 1993.

Kursk, Battle of (5–13 July 1943)

Major Eastern Front battle and the largest tank engagement in history. The Battle of Kursk demonstrated the end of German dominance on the Eastern Front. The 1942–1943 winter campaign had left a 120-mile-wide bulge around Kursk, an important rail junction north of Belgorod and Kharkov, protruding 75 miles deep into German-held territory.

Adolf Hitler saw the salient as an opportunity. By reducing it, his army could regain prestige lost by previous setbacks. By April, plans to blast the Soviets from Kursk were under discussion, and they were solidified into Operation ZITADELLE (CITADEL) by early May. The plan was to reduce the salient with two armor-led pincer attacks at the northern and southern shoulders that would meet in the middle, surrounding all of the forces in the pocket. From the north near Orel, Field Marshal Günther von Kluge's Army Group Center would launch General Walther Model's Ninth Army, led by two panzer corps. The main thrust, however, would come in the south from Field Marshal Fritz Eric von Manstein's Army Group South, with Colonel General Hermann Hoth's Fourth Panzer Army moving north from near Belgorod.

Hitler left the start date for the operation open to sometime after 1 May. He then delayed it to June and again to July in order to build up the panzer forces with newly developed heavy Tiger and Panther tanks and Ferdinand 88 mm self-propelled assault guns, although they had been rushed into production and suffered from design flaws.

Katyusha multiple rocket launchers during the battle of Kursk. The Katyusha was a powerful Soviet weapon during World War II. (Photo by Slava Katamidze Collection/Getty Images)

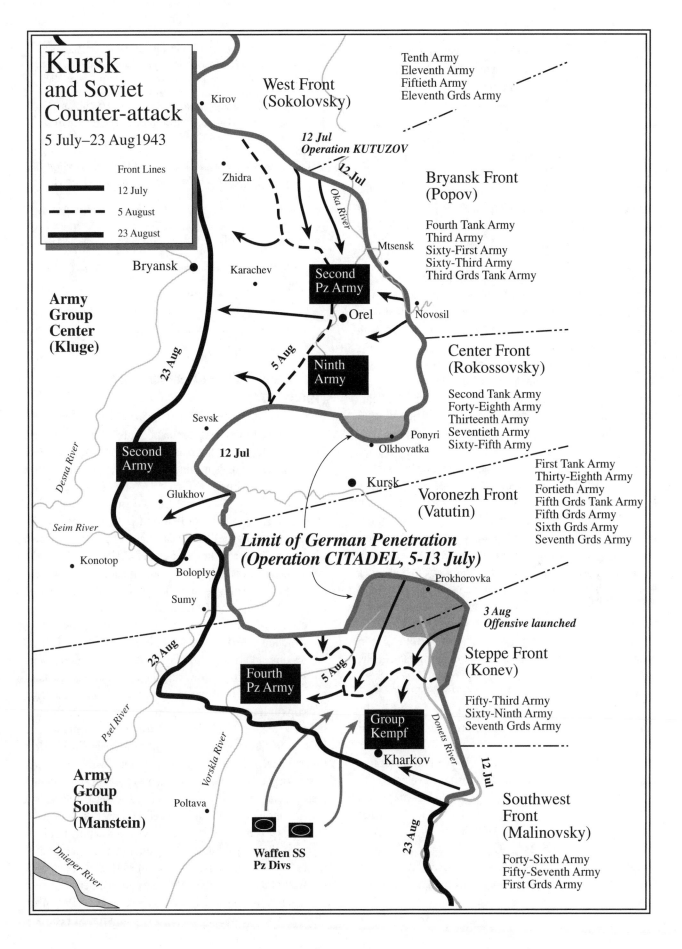

Kursk
and Soviet
Counter-attack
5 July–23 Aug 1943

Front Lines

———— 12 July

- - - - 5 August

———— 23 August

Kirov

West Front
(Sokolovsky)

12 Jul
Operation KUTUZOV

Tenth Army
Eleventh Army
Fiftieth Army
Eleventh Grds Army

Zhidra

12 Jul

Oka River

Bryansk Front
(Popov)

Bryansk

Karachev

**Second
Pz Army**

Mtsensk

Fourth Tank Army
Third Army
Sixty-First Army
Sixty-Third Army
Third Grds Tank Army

**Army
Group
Center
(Kluge)**

Orel

Novosil

23 Aug

5 Aug

**Ninth
Army**

Center Front
(Rokossovsky)

Second Tank Army
Forty-Eighth Army
Thirteenth Army
Seventieth Army
Sixty-Fifth Army

Sevsk

**Second
Army**

12 Jul

Ponyri
Olkhovatka

Desna River

Glukhov

Kursk

Voronezh Front
(Vatutin)

First Tank Army
Thirty-Eighth Army
Fortieth Army
Fifth Grds Tank Army
Fifth Grds Army
Sixth Grds Army
Seventh Grds Army

Seim River

Konotop

Boloplye

Sumy

***Limit of German Penetration
(Operation CITADEL, 5-13 July)***

Prokhorovka

3 Aug
Offensive launched

23 Aug

5 Aug

Steppe Front
(Konev)

**Fourth
Pz Army**

**Group
Kempf**

Fifty-Third Army
Sixty-Ninth Army
Seventh Grds Army

Psel River

Vorskla River

Donets River

23 Aug

12 Jul

**Army
Group
South
(Manstein)**

Poltava

Kharkov

Southwest
Front
(Malinovsky)

**Waffen SS
Pz Divs**

Forty-Sixth Army
Fifty-Seventh Army
First Grds Army

Dnieper River

The Soviets knew of the plans for the impending German offensive through reconnaissance and intelligence agents. Soviet leader Josef Stalin wanted a preemptive spoiling attack, but Stavka representative Marshal Georgii Zhukov convinced him that within the Kursk salient, the Central Front, under General Konstantin Rokossovsky, and General Nikolai Vatutin's Voronezh Front would be able to absorb the initial German blows with the defenses they had established, and to the rear, General I. S. Konev's Steppe Front could then counterattack.

Both sides built up armor and troop concentrations for the coming battle. The Germans amassed 900,000 men in 50 divisions, of which 19 were panzer and motorized, with 2,700 tanks and assault guns, 10,000 artillery pieces, and 2,000 aircraft. The delay, however, allowed the Soviets to assemble 1.3 million men, 3,600 tanks, 20,000 artillery pieces, and 2,400 aircraft. Some 300,000 local civilians joined the Red Army in laying a massive array of tank traps, minefields, and dug-in antitank guns designed to channel the German armor into kill zones for Soviet artillery.

The German attack commenced on 5 July. In the north, the Ninth Army assaulted on a narrow, 30-mile front but managed to penetrate only 6 or 7 miles in seven days of fierce fighting. The fighting resembled some of the fierce attrition battles of World War I. Fourth Panzer Army in the south did slightly better, pushing to the third Soviet defensive belt about 20 miles deep. The critical stage of the battle came between 11 and 12 July when General Hoth turned his panzer spearhead northwest to envelope the Soviet 1st Tank Army, and with about 400 tanks, his forces reached Prokhorovka Station. Zhukov responded with a counterattack of five tank armies, two coming from the Steppe Front. This engagement was a cauldron embroiling more than 1,200 tanks from both sides (three-quarters of them Soviet) in the largest tank battle of the war. By the end of 12 July, Prokhorovka lay littered with the burned-out hulks of German and Soviet tanks.

At that point, on 13 July, Hitler called off the offensive in order to withdraw panzer forces to reinforce units in Sicily, where the Allies had landed three days earlier. The German commanders had no choice but to conduct a fighting retreat in the face of a Soviet counteroffensive that began on 12 July. By 5 August, the Soviets had retaken Orel and Belgorod, and they retook Kharkov by 23 August, an action that the Soviets consider to be part of the Battle of Kursk. By that reckoning, Kursk involved 4 million men, 13,000 armored vehicles, and 12,000 aircraft, making it one of the largest battles of the war.

In the Battle of Kursk, the Germans lost an estimated 70,000 men killed, 2,900 tanks, 195 self-propelled guns, 844 artillery pieces, and 1,392 planes. More important, the battle cost the German army the strategic initiative. The Germans now began an almost continuous retreat that would end in Berlin.

Arthur T. Frame

See also

Armored Warfare; Belorussia Offensive; Eastern Front; Guderian, Heinz; Hitler, Adolf; Hoth, Hermann; Kharkov, Battle of; Kluge, Günther Adolf Ferdinand von; Konev, Ivan Stepanovich; Malinovsky, Rodion Yakovlevich; Manstein, Fritz Eric von; Rokossovsky, Konstantin Konstantinovich; Sicily, Invasion of; Stalin, Josef; Stalingrad, Battle of; Tanks, All Powers; Zhukov, Georgii Konstantinovich

References

Glantz, David M., and Jonathan M. House. *When Titans Clashed: How the Red Army Stopped Hitler.* Lawrence: University Press of Kansas, 1995.

Jukes, Geoffrey. *Kursk: The Clash of Armour.* New York: Ballantine Books, 1968.

Salisbury, Harrison E. *The Unknown War.* New York: Bantam Books, 1978.

Werth, Alexander. *Russia at War, 1941–1945.* New York: E. P. Dutton, 1964.

Kuznetsov, Nikolai Gerasimovich (1904–1974)

Soviet navy admiral, minister of the navy, deputy minister of Soviet armed forces, and commander of Soviet naval forces. Born in the Arkhangelsk Oblast of northern Russia on 24 July 1904, Nikolai Kuznetsov joined the Red Navy in 1919. After service in the Russian Civil War, he graduated from Leningrad Naval College in 1926 and from the Voroshilov Naval Academy in 1932. In 1936 and 1937, he served as the Soviet adviser to the Republican navy during the Spanish Civil War. The Great Purges exacted a frightful toll on the Soviet navy leadership, and as a consequence, Kuznetsov was named people's commissar of the navy (minister of the navy) in 1939 at just 37 years of age.

In August 1939, Kuznetsov submitted an ambitious naval construction plan designed to produce 2 aircraft carriers, 18 battleships, 48 cruisers, 198 flotilla leaders and destroyers, and 433 submarines. However, the demands and costs of overseeing widely dispersed Soviet naval actions during World War II prevented any meaningful result from this initiative. Promoted to admiral in 1940 and Admiral of the Fleet in May 1944, Kuznetsov commanded the Soviet Pacific Fleet that supported the Red Army's operations against the Japanese at the end of the war. Kuznetsov's postwar shipbuilding plan was far beyond the means of the Soviet Union's war-ravaged industries and did not reflect Soviet dictator Josef Stalin's expectations. Kuznetsov was named deputy minister of the USSR's armed forces and commander in chief of naval forces in 1946, minister of the navy in 1951, and first deputy minister of defense of the USSR and commander in chief of naval forces in 1953. Stripped of these titles in December 1955, Kuznetsov was demoted to vice admiral in February

1956 and forcibly retired, apparently because of the October 1955 explosion and sinking of the battleship *Novorossiisk* (formerly the Italian *Giulio Cesare*) while it was moored at Sevastopol. His immediate subordinate, the more progressive Admiral Sergei Georgievich Gorshkov, assumed his post and led the Soviet navy to unprecedented prominence over the next three decades. Kuznetsov was posthumously restored to his rank of Admiral of the Fleet by the Supreme Soviet in 1988, nearly 14 years after his death in Moscow on 6 December 1974.

Gordon E. Hogg

See also
Soviet Union, Navy; Stalin, Josef
References
Bialer, Seweryn. *Stalin and His Generals: Soviet Military Memoirs of World War II.* New York: Pegasus, 1969.

Kuznetsov, Nikolai Gerasimovich. *Memoirs of a Wartime Minister of the Navy.* Moscow: Progress, 1990.

Kuznetsova, R. V., A. A. Kilichenkov, and L. A. Neretina. *Admiral Kuznetsov: Moskva v Zhizni i Sudbe Flotovodtsa.* Moscow: Izd-vo "Mosgoarkhiv," 2000.

Kwajalein, Battle for (19 January–6 February 1944)

Battle for a strategic Japanese logistics base in the Marshall Islands. Kwajalein, the world's largest atoll and one of 32 separate atolls that comprise the Marshall Islands, was a primary target of the U.S. Navy's Central Pacific Campaign. As a consequence of its participation in World War I, Japan had secured the Marshalls, located approximately halfway between Pearl Harbor and the Mariana Islands. Control of the Marshalls allowed the Japanese to extend their power southeast to the Gilbert Islands. These island bases also protected their fleet anchorage to the west at Truk and the airfields to the northwest on the Marianas, which lay close enough to Japan to be within the range of U.S. strategic bombers.

Following their bloody initiation in the opposed amphibious landing on Tarawa, American military planners devised Operation FLINTLOCK to bypass the heavily defended eastern

"Paradise Lost" by the Japanese at Kwajalein. American troops arrive in a Coast Guard–manned landing craft at palm-studded Carlos Island, in the Marshall Islands, February 1944. (National Archives)

atolls and strike directly at the administrative and communication complexes centrally located on Kwajalein. A secondary assault on Eniwetok (Operation CATCHPOLE) to the west would follow. FLINTLOCK incorporated lessons learned from the Tarawa experience. The Marshalls landings benefited from a sharp increase in the quality and quantity of naval gunfire support, large-scale air bombardments of the target prior to D day, and land-based artillery prepositioned on adjacent atolls to provide additional fire support. "Frogmen" of the newly created navy underwater demolition teams scouted the beaches for potential obstacles and marked the lanes for the landing craft. Requirements and procedures for landing assault troops were revamped to increase speed and efficiency in getting ashore, and the assaulting troops would have greatly increased firepower, including more automatic weapons, flamethrowers, and demolition charges.

An unprecedented two-day aerial and naval barrage preceded troop landings by the 4th Marine Division and the army's 7th Infantry Division on 1 February 1944. The Marines stormed Roi-Namur, two islands linked by a causeway on the atoll's northern tip, while the army took responsibility for seizing the main island of Kwajalein at the southern end. Although confusion plagued the Marines' initial ship-to-shore movement, the assault on Roi met with light resistance and secured the island's airfield in a single day.

The attack on Namur's supply facilities encountered heavier opposition, and only a portion of the island had been taken by nightfall. At least 120 American casualties occurred on Namur when engineers unknowingly detonated a bunker containing torpedo warheads. Just before daybreak on 2 February, the Marines repelled a counterattack by the remaining Japanese defenders and secured the island. The more orderly landings on Kwajalein met with substantial opposition, and it required four days of intense fighting to clear the island. Nearly the entire garrison of 8,675 Japanese soldiers on Roi-Namur

and Kwajalein perished in these battles, with half of these casualties resulting from the preliminary bombardment. U.S. forces took only 265 prisoners, including 165 Korean laborers. U.S. losses were 372 dead and 1,582 wounded.

Operations FLINTLOCK and CATCHPOLE validated the American revised doctrine of amphibious warfare employing massive fire support and speed to achieve victory with minimum casualties. The success in the Marshall Islands actions also confirmed the wisdom of the Central Pacific "island-hopping" campaign, which called for bypassing and isolating Japanese strong points to move within striking distance of the Japanese home islands.

Derek W. Frisby

See also

Amphibious Warfare; Central Pacific Campaign; Eniwetok, Capture of; Gilbert Islands Campaign; Mariana Islands, Naval Campaign; Marshall Islands, Naval Campaign; Nimitz, Chester William; Smith, Holland McTyeire; Tarawa, Battle of; Truk; Turner, Richmond Kelly

References

Chapin, John C. *Breaking the Outer Ring: Marine Landings in the Marshall Islands.* Washington, DC: History and Museums Division, Headquarters, U.S. Marine Corps, 1994.

Lorelli, John A. *To Foreign Shores: U.S. Amphibious Operations in World War II.* Annapolis, MD: Naval Institute Press, 1995.

Millett, Allen R. *Semper Fidelis: A History of the United States Marine Corps.* Rev. ed. New York: Free Press, 1991.

Morison, Samuel E. *History of United States Naval Operations in World War II.* Vol. 7, *Aleutians, Gilberts and Marshalls, June 1942–April 1944.* Boston: Little, Brown, 1951.

Moskin, J. Robert. *The U.S. Marine Corps Story.* Rev. ed. New York: McGraw-Hill, 1987.

Kwantung Army

See Guandong Army.